THE ROUTLEDGE RESEARCH COMPANION TO LAW AND HUMANITIES IN NINETEENTH-CENTURY AMERICA

Nineteenth-century America witnessed some of the most important and fruitful areas of intersection between the law and humanities, as people began to realize that the law, formerly confined to courts and lawyers, might also find expression in a variety of ostensibly nonlegal areas such as painting, poetry, fiction, and sculpture. Bringing together leading researchers from law schools and humanities departments, this *Companion* touches on regulatory, statutory, and common law in nineteenth-century America and encompasses judges, lawyers, legislators, litigants, and the institutions they inhabited (courts, firms, prisons). It will serve as a reference for specific information on a variety of law- and humanities-related topics, as well as a guide to understanding how the two disciplines developed in tandem in the long nineteenth century.

Nan Goodman is Professor of English at the University of Colorado at Boulder, USA.

Simon Stern is Associate Professor of Law and English and Co-Director of the Centre for Innovation Law & Policy at the University of Toronto, Canada.

THE ROUTLEDGE RESEARCH COMPANION TO LAW AND HUMANITIES IN NINETEENTH-CENTURY AMERICA

Edited by Nan Goodman and Simon Stern

Routledge
Taylor & Francis Group
LONDON AND NEW YORK

First published 2017
by Routledge
2 Park Square, Milton Park, Abingdon, Oxon OX14 4RN

and by Routledge
605 Third Avenue, New York, NY 10017

First issued in paperback 2021

Routledge is an imprint of the Taylor & Francis Group, an informa business

Publisher's Note
The publisher has gone to great lengths to ensure the quality of this reprint but points out that some imperfections in the original copies may be apparent.

Library of Congress Cataloging-in-Publication Data
A catalog record for this title has been requested

ISBN 13: 978-1-03-209690-2 (pbk)
ISBN 13: 978-1-4724-4100-3 (hbk)

Typeset in Bembo
by Apex CoVantage, LLC

CONTENTS

Figures *viii*
Contributors *x*
Preface *xiii*

PART I
Human kinds **1**

Introduction 3
Nan Goodman and Simon Stern

1 Women: politics, culture, and the law 5
Joyce W. Warren

2 "The very idea of a slave is a human being in bondage" 20
Jeannine Marie DeLombard

3 The corporation and the transformation of American culture 35
Aaron Ritzenberg

4 Deviance in nineteenth-century American law and culture 56
Tal Kastner

5 Comparative racialization and American Indian identity in nineteenth-century America 73
Cheryl Suzack

6 The legal person: tracing the history of a forensic fiction 96
Susanna L. Blumenthal

PART II
A new archive **115**

Introduction 117
Nan Goodman and Simon Stern

7 Law in nineteenth-century American periodicals 119
Michael H. Hoeflich

8 Spectacular judgments: law and disorder in the nineteenth-century visual imagination 131
Jon Blandford

9 Legal language: expansion, consolidation, resistance 150
Robert L. Tsai

10 The impersonation of justice: lynching, dueling, and wildcat strikes in nineteenth-century America 163
Norman W. Spaulding

11 The *Somers* mutiny and the American ship of state 188
Robert A. Ferguson

PART III
Managing the human **207**

Introduction 209
Nan Goodman and Simon Stern

12 The emergence of a right to privacy 211
Milette Shamir

13 The science of identity 225
Simon A. Cole

14 The American prison, 1786–1860 242
John Cyril Barton

15 How meetings won the West 257
Andrea McDowell

16 A gatekeeping nation: Asian invasion and the rise of xenophobic immigration law 274
Edlie Wong

17 Fictions of race and personality: nineteenth-century law and Mark Twain's *Pudd'nhead Wilson* 290
Trinyan Mariano

PART IV
Affective relations **307**

Introduction 309
Nan Goodman and Simon Stern

18 Civic capacity and participatory citizenship in nineteenth-century United States 311
Yvonne Pitts

19 "Vital tissues of the spirit": constitutional emotions in the antebellum United States 323
Doni Gewirtzman

20 Beyond belief: religion, law, and popular culture in the "forgotten century" 340
Deborah Whitehead

21 Gothic stories, *mens rea*, and American criminal law 356
Laura I Appleman

Index *369*

FIGURES

3.1 Dan Beard, "The Slave Driver," from *A Connecticut Yankee in King Arthur's Court* (New York: Webster, 1889), 465 49
5.1 George A. Crofutt, "American Progress" (1873) 74
8.1 "God's Judgment upon Murder" (Boston: N. Coverly, 1812) 134
8.2 *The Hangman*, 1:20 (Boston: Charles Spear, 1845) 136
8.3 *The Prisoner's Friend*, 1:14 (Boston: Charles Spear, 1846) 137
8.4 "A Very Bad Man" (New York: Henry Robinson & Company, 1833) 140
8.5 Allegheny Court House, stereograph (Pittsburgh: S. V. Albee, 1882) 141
8.6 South view of Allegheny County Courthouse and Jail, photocopy of lithograph (Pittsburgh: photographer unknown, 1890) 142
8.7 "Maryland – Scene in the Court-House at Annapolis – Trial of Mrs. Wharton on the Charge of Murdering General Ketchum by Poison – From a Sketch by Jas. E. Taylor" (*Frank Leslie's Illustrated Newspaper*, December 23, 1871, 236) 143
8.8 "Lynching of McManus" (H.R. Farr, 1882) 145
8.9 "After Him: A Mob Seeking to Lynch a Negro at Montgomery for Assaulting a White Lady" (*Durham Daily Globe*, February 15, 1892) 146
10.1 "The Tournament of Today – A Set-to Between Labor and Monopoly" (*Puck*, August 1, 1883) 177
10.2 Frank Bellew, "The American Frankenstein" (*New York Daily Graphic*, March 18, 1873) 179
10.3 Frank Bellew, "The American Frankenstein" (*New York Daily Graphic*, April 14, 1874) 180
10.4 W. A. Rogers, "King Debs" (*Harper's Magazine*, July 14, 1894) 181
16.1 Solly H. Walter, "Now Shut the Back Gate" (*San Francisco Wasp* 21, October 27, 1888) 275
16.2 George Frederick Keller, "Immigration, East and West" (*San Francisco Wasp* 7, August 26, 1881) 279
16.3 Solly H. Walter, "There's Millions in It" (*San Francisco Wasp* 21, July 21, 1888) 286
18.1 W. A. Ford, "American Woman and Her Political Peers" (1893): a postcard depicting suffragist and temperance advocate Frances Willard among other disfranchised groups – an "idiot," a convict, a "savage," and a "lunatic" 313

20.1 Thomas Nast, drawing, "Religious liberty is guaranteed: but can we allow foreign reptiles to crawl all over us?" (1880) 344
20.2 Frontispiece to Alfreda Eva Bell, *Baodicea, the Mormon Wife: Life-Scenes in Utah* (New York: Arthur Orton, 1855) 346
20.3 The medium Eva C. with a materialization on her head and a luminous apparition between her hands (May 17, 1912) 351

CONTRIBUTORS

Laura I Appleman is Associate Dean for Faculty Research and Professor of Law at Willamette University, teaching and writing in the areas of criminal law and procedure, the jury, and nineteenth-century law and literature.

John Cyril Barton is Associate Professor of English at the University of Missouri–Kansas City. He is coauthor of *Transatlantic Sensations* (Ashgate, 2012) and author of *Literary Executions: Capital Punishment and American Culture, 1820–1925* (Johns Hopkins University Press, 2014), chapter 5 of which won the Hennig Cohen Prize for best scholarship on Melville. Barton has also published numerous essays in journals such as *Nineteenth-Century Literature*, *Arizona Quarterly*, *Law and Literature*, *Studies in American Fiction*, *Critical Horizons*, and *REAL*.

Jon Blandford is Associate Professor of English at Bellarmine University, has written book chapters on eighteenth-century confidence man Stephen Burroughs (Palgrave Macmillan, 2015) and on nineteenth-century American women's detective fiction (forthcoming from Cambridge University Press, 2017).

Susanna L. Blumenthal is the Julius E. Davis Professor of Law, Associate Professor of History, and Co-Director of the Program in Law and History Program at the University of Minnesota, is the author of *Law and the Modern Mind: Consciousness and Responsibility in American Legal Culture* (Harvard University Press, 2016).

Simon A. Cole is Professor of Criminology, Law and Society at the University of California, Irvine, and author of *Suspect Identities: A History of Fingerprinting and Criminal Identification* (Harvard University Press, 2001).

Jeannine Marie DeLombard is Associate Professor of English at the University of California, Santa Barbara, and author of *Slavery on Trial: Law, Print, and Abolitionism* (University of North Carolina Press, 2007) and *In the Shadow of the Gallows: Race, Crime, and American Civic Identity* (University of Pennsylvania Press, 2012).

Robert A. Ferguson is George Edward Woodberry Professor of Law, Literature, and Criticism at Columbia University. His latest book, in process, is *Metamorphosis: How to Transform Punishment in America.*

Doni Gewirtzman is Professor of Law at New York Law School, where he teaches constitutional law.

Nan Goodman is Professor of English and Director of the Program in Jewish Studies at the University of Colorado Boulder. She is the author of *The Puritan Cosmopolis: The Law of Nations and the Early American Imagination* (forthcoming, Oxford University Press), *Banished: Common Law and the Rhetoric of Social Exclusion in Early New England* (University of Pennsylvania Press, 2012), and *Shifting the Blame: Literature, Law, and the Theory of Accidents in Nineteenth-Century America* (Princeton University Press, 1998), as well as numerous articles. She also coedited *The Turn Around Religion in America* (Routledge, 2011).

Michael H. Hoeflich is the John H. & John M. Kane Distinguished Professor of Law at the University of Kansas School of Law. He holds degrees from Haverford, Cambridge, and the Yale Law School. He has served on the faculties of the University of Illinois College of Law, as well as at Syracuse University and the University of Kansas, where he served both as Dean of the Law School and as a faculty member.

Tal Kastner is Acting Assistant Professor at New York University Law School (JD, Yale; PhD English, Princeton), has published in legal and interdisciplinary journals and is completing a book, *The Age of Boilerplate: Agreement and Agency in American Law and Literature.*

Trinyan Mariano is Assistant Professor at Florida State University, holds a PhD in literature and a JD. Her work focuses on nineteenth- and early twentieth-century American literature, especially as it relates to legal history and jurisprudence.

Andrea McDowell is a historian and Law Professor at Seton Hall. She is writing a book, forthcoming from Harvard University Press, on self-government in the California gold rush, including miners' meetings, mining claims, dispute resolution, and criminal trials.

Yvonne Pitts is Associate Professor in the History Department at Purdue University. Her book, *Family, Law, and Inheritance: A Social and Legal History of Nineteenth-Century Kentucky* (Cambridge University Press, 2013) won the 2014 Cromwell Book Prize, awarded by the American Society for Legal History.

Aaron Ritzenberg is Senior Lecturer in the Department of English and Comparative Literature at Columbia University. He is the author of *The Sentimental Touch: The Language of Feeling in the Age of Managerialism* (Fordham University Press, 2013).

Milette Shamir is Associate Professor of English and American Studies at Tel Aviv University. Among her books and articles is *Inexpressible Privacy: The Interior Life of Antebellum American Literature* (University of Pennsylvania Press, 2006).

Norman W. Spaulding is Sweitzer Professor of Law at Stanford Law School. His research concentrates on nineteenth-century American legal history, particularly the history of the American legal profession.

Simon Stern teaches English and Law at the University of Toronto. He has published extensively on relations between legal and literary history in the eighteenth and nineteenth centuries and is editor of Book II of *Blackstone's Commentaries on the Laws of England*, for the *Oxford Edition of Blackstone* (2016). His current research examines the history and theory of legal fictions.

Cheryl Suzack is Associate Professor of English and Indigenous Studies at the University of Toronto. She is the author of *Indigenous Women's Writing and the Cultural Study of Law* (University of Toronto Press, 2016).

Robert L. Tsai is Professor of Law at American University. He is the author of *America's Forgotten Constitutions: Defiant Visions of Power and Community* (Harvard University Press, 2014) and *Eloquence and Reason: Creating a First Amendment Culture* (Yale University Press, 2008). Tsai's work spans constitutional law, theory, and history, with an emphasis on the organization and spread of political culture.

Joyce W. Warren is Professor of English and Director of Women and Gender Studies at Queens College. She is the author of *Women, Money, and the Law* (University of Iowa Press, 2005), *Fanny Fern: An Independent Woman* (Rutgers University Press, 1992), and *The American Narcissus: Individualism and Women* (Rutgers University Press, 1984).

Deborah Whitehead is Associate Professor of Religious Studies at the University of Colorado Boulder, specializing in U.S. religious and cultural history. She is author of *William James, Pragmatism, and American Culture* (Indiana University Press, 2016).

Edlie Wong is Associate Professor of English at the University of Maryland and author of *Racial Reconstruction* (NYU Press, 2015) and *Neither Fugitive nor Free* (NYU Press, 2009) and is coeditor of George Lippard's *The Killers* (University of Pennsylvania Press, 2014).

PREFACE

Nan Goodman and Simon Stern

The interdisciplinary study of law and humanities is a vital and continually evolving field. This volume is designed to capture and advance some of the most interesting current research in the field by focusing on the long nineteenth century in America, from about 1789, the year the U.S. Constitution was ratified, to 1914, the year World War I began, arguably the most fascinating period for law and humanities scholarship. Two aspects of the nineteenth century stand out in this regard: the first was the spread of the law into humanities-related fields of inquiry. It was in the nineteenth century that some of the most important and fruitful areas of intersection between the law and humanities first came to light, as people began to realize that the law was not confined to courts and lawyers but also played a part in a variety of visual and performing arts, such as painting, poetry, fiction, sculpture, photography, music, and theater. This period also saw a growing recognition of law's significance for the many humanities-related research disciplines, such as philosophy, religion, linguistics, anthropology, history, and geography, which came to define the nineteenth-century American college, where the line between the social sciences and the humanities was not as clear as it is today. The second aspect pertains to the definition of what it meant to be human in the first place. The question of who was human and how humans behaved (or were supposed to behave) was once again under construction. If we understand the humanities in the broadest sense as the study of how humans respond to and shape human experience, we can begin to appreciate how deeply intertwined the law and humanities were in nineteenth-century America, for not only was the law seen as influencing an increasing number of humanities-oriented areas of inquiry and expression, but Americans were wondering whether black people and American Indians were human in the same way white Europeans were, whether immigrants were human in the same way citizens were, whether women were as human as men, and finally whether the law could include new phenomena, such as corporations, within the category of humankind. These artistic practices and philosophical questions are a large part of what we mean when we talk about the humanities. But in this volume we use an even more capacious understanding in which the interpretation and representation of all human experience plays a part. In short, during this era, the humanities intersected with the law in establishing a critical apparatus and a vocabulary for bringing people into a broader discussion about the world, the nation, and democracy.

Although versions of this story have been told many times, its motives and manifestations have not been fully appreciated. The first implication of the expansion of law into the humanities involved the thematization of law in great works of art and literature, giving law a majesty and banality all its own. Large-scale paintings of momentous legal events, such as John Trumbull's "Declaration of Independence," which like so many nineteenth-century paintings looked back to the founding moments of the country, and more popular works, such as T. H. Matheson's "The First Prayer in Congress," William Josiah Brickey's "Missouri Courtroom," and George Cooke's "Patrick Henry Argues the Parsons's Cause," contributed to the wide dissemination of the law as a source of aesthetic reflection and representation. Literature, too, became a home for legal themes, as writers increasingly looked to the law for plot lines and characterizations. In this category, Herman Melville's *Billy Budd, Sailor (An Inside Narrative)* and Mark Twain's *The Tragedy of Pudd'nhead Wilson* figure prominently, as do the best-selling dime novels about crime and detectives by Alan Pinkerton. One effect of translating legal history and practice into artistic and literary form was to blur the lines between the two, suggesting that the law could benefit from an artistic eye and that art could itself embody a legal message, sometimes more effectively than a statute or judicial decision.

The widespread appearance of legal themes in art and literature, however, was only the most visible feature of the increasingly ramified relationship between American culture and the law in the nineteenth century. The law, by which we mean not simply the rules or norms governing human behavior but also a legal mindset that governed human thought generally, grew in concert with many other disciplines and social phenomena in this period, drawing from various fields in the humanities and contributing to them. As the law developed alongside other areas of social inquiry such as sociology and psychology, it became more interested in and responsive to human actions and beliefs than it had been before. Lawyers, judges, and legal scholars looked to studies about human behavior when drafting, applying, and writing laws.

The more intertwined the law and humanities became, the more the law took on properties we associate with social practices, especially those involving the formation of societies and associations. In much the same way that many of the founding eighteenth-century laws of America took their cue from the laws devised by the Freemasons, so too many nineteenth-century laws followed from practices that had governed extralegal associations, including those formed around the possession of livestock, mining, or land claims that Western emigrants instituted. In this vein, we might also consider the inextricable connections between law and the humanities in the form of the hypothetical legalities contemplated in much nineteenth-century imaginative writing and proposed in various efforts to revise the U.S. Constitution by such figures as the federalist lawyer James Hillhouse and the antifederalist Edmund Pendleton.[1]

In order to represent the wide variety of these law and humanities intersections, our volume defines "law" broadly, touching on regulatory, statutory, and common law in nineteenth-century America and encompassing judges, lawyers, legislators, litigants, and the institutions they inhabited, including courts, firms, and prisons. Indeed the very concept of what a lawyer did and how a lawyer came to practice was changing as the nineteenth century witnessed profound changes in the professionalization of American lawyers through the creation of Bar societies, the birth of the modern law school (which in turn fostered new kinds of legal scholarship and law journals), the development of the modern configuration of federal district and circuit courts, the first glimmerings of "large" national law firms, the establishment of the U.S. Department of Justice, an array of new reporting services, the advent of new methods for tracking citations to precedent ("Shepardization"), and, complementarily, the emergence of new styles of legal writing and argument.[2] In the course of the century, the United States incubated a brand of law and developed a legal culture that would eventually figure among the country's most significant exports. Faced at the beginning of the nineteenth century with populist hostility toward the common law and legal elites, American lawyers responded by defending the intellectual reputation of the common law and by emphasizing their own civic importance, and their efforts were so successful as to quell a widespread codification movement.[3] Even as the country's sprawling array of laws, jurisdictions, and legal discourses persisted in seemingly irreconcilable spheres, the United States was beginning to fashion a distinctively American conception of law that blended an appetite for experimenting and a concern with formality and precision.

Legal language also began to pervade many areas of American life, giving people an unprecedented stake as voters, consumers, and property owners. In the course of the century, the Supreme Court also pioneered a doctrine of judicial review which, even if rarely used to strike down legislation, enhanced the Court's own authority and served to draw an array of cases and to produce a series of decisions in which the constitutional text was of paramount concern; as a result, those judgments modeled an interpretive approach that served to focus attention more generally on the language of statutes and of the courts' previous decisions. This linguistic turn also had the effect of focusing precedent more on the precise form of words used in earlier decisions, with the result that a concern with verbal expression in both statutes and legal decisions became one of the distinctive features of American legal culture.[4] Conversely, the language of the humanities, with its proclivity toward metaphor and symbol, began to pervade the writing of lawyers and judges in briefs, judgments, statutes, and treatises – to such an extent that these texts can scarcely be distinguished from the forms of writing usually associated with the humanities.

Taking these deep connections between the human and the law seriously, we have aimed to produce a volume that can be used to open up new areas of thought for students and scholars of the period. To that end, we have divided the book up into four human-oriented sections – "Human Kinds," "A New Archive," "Managing the Human," and "Affective Relations" – each of which is intended to target how what was considered human was bound up with what was considered law.

In the first section, "Human Kinds," the chapters explore legal personae and personifications that characterized American law in the nineteenth century. These chapters give us a sense of the law as a discipline that revolved around certain characters. Women and corporations were among these characters, as were slaves, Indians, and deviants (as they were known). Examining the legal developments of the era through its primary characters, the chapters in this section give us a sense of how the law began to write itself through the prism of human variety.

In her chapter on woman as a "kind" of human, for example, Joyce Warren charts a gradual trajectory from subservience to greater equality. One of the most important features of Warren's chapter, from a law and humanities point of view, is the way in which women managed to acquire more of a voice in the legal sphere by writing about their own legal lives. As women gained access to education, for example, they had more tools for describing their own experiences; as a result, they were able to contribute to the intersection of the law and the humanities. As Warren suggests, the law began to recognize some of these changes by shifting from a system that made laws about women in the context of their marriages – as wards of their fathers and husbands – to a system that made laws about them as rights-bearing citizens, who through their own agency had legal histories and capacities of their own. Similarly, Warren reveals the strong effect women had on the law through their more literary endeavors, with Lydia Maria Child and Harriet Beecher Stowe leading the attack on slavery in novel form.

So closely connected were legal- and humanities-driven endeavors in the nineteenth century that Jeannine DeLombard calls them "interanimate." In her chapter on the slave, DeLombard sees the law coming face-to-face with the question of whether the categories of human kinds and the categories of property could be reconciled. In her discussion of the slave, DeLombard makes it plain that the laws of slavery were of existential proportions and, as she puts it, only "make sense when read in the context of the culture in which they were produced and circulated." The laws as stated in the context of legal opinions or statutes about what slaves could and could not do were only the tip of the iceberg. Slavery laws asked monumental questions, such as what constituted personhood and whether all humans fit within this category. Earlier laws had established that all persons were human, but did the law, nineteenth-century American lawyers often asked, pertain to humans who were not persons as the law defined the term? As with the subject of women, slaves and former slaves started to write about their own experiences, opening up the cultural and legal worlds to their voices and, in the process, transforming both fields of inquiry. To acknowledge that Harriet Jacobs, for instance, could write her own narrative and could model it after a genre familiar to white women readers was to recognize her literary abilities and legal personhood at the same time.

Aaron Ritzenberg considers the ways in which corporate forms modeled and facilitated attitudes and practices that became routine in American life. As Ritzenberg shows, the corporate form flourished in America far more vigorously than in Britain, especially around the middle of the nineteenth century. An important consequence of these developments was the creation of new careers, especially the career manager – a new kind of bureaucratic and economic being who had no equity in the firm but was dedicated to its administration and a figure who in turn helped to create new social relations by taking the firm's management beyond the family circle by conspiring in the separation of ownership from management. The human kinds that proliferated in the wake of these developments were pluriform, as Ritzenberg shows in the course of a discussion that includes William Dean Howells' *The Rise of Silas Lapham* (1894), Fuller's *The Cliff Dwellers* (1893), Orison Swett Marden's *Pushing to the Front, Or, Success under Difficulties* (1894), Frank Norris's muck-raking novel *The Pit* (1903), and Robert Herrick's *Memoirs of an American Citizen* (1905). Ritzenberg concludes the discussion by turning to Mark Twain's "superintendents," whose ability to "out-superintend" their rivals again suggests that a new kind of human has arrived – one endowed with extraordinary means of forming intentions and carrying them out.

In exploring the deviant as a legal figure, Tal Kastner examines the developing relationship "between norm or law and deviance or crime," focusing on the "peculiarity" of the institution of slavery and "the normative social models and counter-models precipitated by slavery, such as the penitentiary, the ideal of contract, and marriage." Kastner's discussion of legal deviants includes Hester Prynne and Melville's Bartleby as well as the prostitute, the homosexual, the suffragette, and the polygamist, all of whom point again to the dynamic interaction between legal and social norms in the post–Civil War era, as hierarchies of race and ethnicity were deployed as variously savage or overrefined and in any case magnets for illicit racial intermixing. This combination of anxieties, as Kastner shows, helps to make sense of the decision in *Plessy v. Ferguson* (1896), in which the plaintiff's indiscernible "mixture of colored blood" trumps his claim to "the reputation of belonging to . . . the white race," making him at once indelibly and invisibly non-normative.

Cheryl Suzack's chapter explores the interplay between federal courts' practices of racialization, as they functioned in settling individual claims by Native Americans who sought to be treated as naturalized citizens, and the unpredictable ways in which the claimants themselves challenged legal institutions. In particular, Suzack focuses on the difficulties that the courts faced in attempting to resolve the Indian's "peculiar status under Federal law," a status that uneasily negotiated the contrast between membership in a "domestic dependent nation" and identity as a "subject of the United States" but one who lacked full citizenship rights under U.S. law. As Suzack shows, through readings of the Supreme Court decisions in *Cherokee Nation v. Georgia* (1831), *Worcester v. Georgia* (1832), and a series of federal district court decisions in the 1870s and 1880s, the courts responded by adopting an implicit distinction between tribal communities that deserved to be regarded as having a sovereign status and others that were treated as merely the "remnants" of formerly sovereign nations, which had lost their "original character" and were now merely legal artifacts. As Suzack shows, this distinction produced a series of contradictions by which the "distinctly" sovereign communities were nonetheless subject to U.S. jurisdiction, while those made up "mere remnants" were nevertheless endowed with sufficient authority to override their members' claims to certain constitutional rights.

Examining the forms and preconditions of legal personhood, Susanna Blumenthal traces the development of the legal person, understood as the kind of agent whose qualities and competencies are sufficient that a court will give legal effect to the agent's words and acts. As Blumenthal shows, courts drew on a hierarchically organized family of legal persons, measured by reference to a benchmark that reflected "Enlightenment ideals of rationality and autonomy," combined with the assumptions of "Protestant moralism." While this description might seem to suggest that "the free, self-owning, rights-bearing, sovereign individual" of republican ideology perfectly exemplified the independence and responsibility that would characterize the legal person, Blumenthal shows how "the self . . . obtruded in . . . troubling ways" in early nineteenth-century legal culture, as federalists worried that the love of liberty had so captured the imaginations of some Americans that it led them into a wild frenzy of trade and speculation as they pursued "airy and impracticable schemes of wealth and grandeur." Ultimately, as Blumenthal shows, the law's artificial conception of personhood was best exemplified not by any clearly specified set of conditions relating to autonomy or responsibility but by the entirely notional standard of competence represented by Oliver Wendell Holmes's figure of the reasonable man, conceived as "an objective norm rather than a psychological condition."

The next section, "A New Archive," explores various media through which nineteenth-century Americans would have been exposed to legal ideas and events. This section also focuses on the ways in which new media interacted with the law to produce new genres of legal writing, new forms of dissemination and consumption of the law, and even new forms of legal regulation.

The professionalization of legal writing over the course of the nineteenth century is the main subject of Michael Hoeflich's discussion, which focuses particularly on the development of the law journal. Noting that a number of general-interest journals in the eighteenth and nineteenth centuries, such as the *American Monthly* and the *Southern Literary Messenger*, included legally trained figures among their editors, Hoeflich indicates how these journals participated in the broader literary and cultural developments that Robert Ferguson has traced in *Law and Letters in American Culture* and that Richard Squibbs has examined more recently in his work on republicanism and the periodical essay.[5] Hoeflich then turns to specialist law journals, which contributed to a national legal culture by including decisions by courts throughout the United States and helped to foster a national legal culture by exposing readers to broader perspectives on doctrinal developments and by examining trends in the practice and business of law. At the same time, Hoeflich shows, popular magazines such as *Godey's Ladies Book*, the *North American Review*, *Scientific American*, and *Harper's* continued to carry legal content. Finally, the nineteenth century also marks the advent of the student-edited law review, beginning with the *Harvard Law Review* in 1887, which offered a conception of legal scholars as participants in the national legal culture and gave law professors a new role in a discussion that had formerly centered around practicing lawyers. The new law journal was thus an emblem of the increasingly professionalizing legal culture, which now began to include scholarly perspectives in its archive.

Jon Blandford's treatment of legal spectacles focuses in particular on the various scenes involving criminal law figures, from fictional treatments of crimes and their detection to the trial and the prison. Blandford shows how, as executions began to disappear from public spaces, the spectacle of crime and punishment did not vanish but moved to other venues that facilitated different modes of mass witnessing. The penny press, exemplified by New York papers such as the *Sun*, the *Transcript*, the *Herald*, and the *Ladies Morning Star* boosted circulation by prominently featuring coverage of crimes (particularly murders), cultivating an appetite for crime reporting that prompted changes even at the more respectable papers that had formerly considered this material to be too sensational. The growing interest in crime and the psychology of the criminal is also apparent from the rise of detective fiction and a new genre of fiction that used the trial form to structure much of the action; James Fenimore Cooper's last work, *The Ways of the Hour* (1850), was one of the first in this genre, and it anticipated many of the conventions that would become standard, such as the surprise witness who later would frequently appear in Perry Mason's courtroom. Periodicals were also an abundant source of criminal imagery, as Blandford shows in his analysis of *The Prisoner's Friend* (also discussed in John Barton's chapter). Finally, Blandford also explores the extralegal spectacle of lynching, promoted and popularized through numerous venues of mass media (newspapers, postcards, photographs), which incited mass violence against African Americans.

The rhythms and idioms of legal language were constantly being adapted in a complex process of popularization and fragmentation, as Robert Tsai shows in a discussion that illustrates how legal concepts and terms leached into the vernacular and were taken up by writers who resisted the efforts of elites to control legal development. The spread of legal language was facilitated by a number of developments, including technological innovations such as the typewriter and the rotary printing press, the emergence of partisan newspapers and editorial writing, and the growing volume of official law reports. As Tsai demonstrates, the increasing visibility of the legal lexicon in the print marketplace encouraged both democratization and diversification, turning the language of property rights, self-governance, and individual liberty into a form of popular speech, at once complementing and competing with a more formal legal register that sought to define terms of property, torts, and contract law more technically. At a time of increasing professionalization, when lawyers were using legal terminology to demonstrate their sophistication and to emphasize the need for specialization, their efforts to monopolize the language of the law were repeatedly challenged by others who variously borrowed, revised, and parodied this terminology to foster an oppositional democratic culture.

For Norman Spaulding, the new archive is the law itself, which began, through codification, professionalization, and the building of grand courthouses, to swallow up what had been previously been extralegal forms of behavior and venues. Contrary to popular and scholarly opinion, Spaulding argues, forms of mediation and dispute resolution such as lynching and vigilante justice, which have always been portrayed as outside the bounds of formal law, in fact often operated with the sanction of law. For Spaulding, the law's enclosure – its perceived ability to fence itself in through adjudication and formal processes – was challenged during the nineteenth century when the very idea of acting extralegally (through striking or dueling, to name just two examples) was never as clearly outside the purview of the law as one might have thought. Spaulding's article, in short, asks us to think about the law as a capacious archive that extended in both substance and content far beyond its formal borders.

Robert Ferguson's contribution to the New Archive operates on two levels; it provides a case study of an infamous mutiny on the high seas (the *Somers* mutiny) as well as a meta-critique of how that story moved into the popular consciousness through its dissemination in popular media and in fiction of the highest order, namely, Herman Melville's *Billy Budd.* Ferguson traces the archival transformation of Melville's story from a series of facts known only to the men on board the ship in question, to a legal case in which jurisdiction could be civil or military, to a tabloid spectacle, to a literary fiction. In tracing these migrations, Ferguson provides a deep anatomy of the case, arguing that the necessity of producing a story where the facts had to be assembled prematurely was at the heart of the problem with the case from the start. "The necessity of an early coming together in the Somers case is where controversy flourished," Ferguson writes. For Ferguson, the *Somers* mutiny became an archival conundrum in part because the law demands an answer – and insists for the most part that there can be only one answer – but it cannot always control the excesses of that answer, which inevitably seep into diverse fields of thought and narrative.

The third section, "Managing the Human," considers the means by which nineteenth-century American law sought to cope with the complications and perversities of human identity and behavior.

Milette Shamir's contribution on the development of privacy law provides a perfect starting point for exploring the intersections of the law and human management in our terms. What was privacy, Shamir asks? The law in nineteenth-century America became a site for thinking about possible answers to this question. As Shamir demonstrates, with the law's first entry into this area, new notions of private life emerged, including the right to think private thoughts, to be free of the public gaze or public intrusion, and to remain out of the news or yellow press. These areas intersected with a humanities-based emphasis on previously unexplored areas of the human personality and combined to produce new expressions of liberalism, romanticism, and sentimentalism – bastions of humanistic thought – for which the nineteenth century was known.

New legal technologies for documenting and fixing human identity were only beginning to emerge at the end of the nineteenth century, as Simon Cole shows. He considers the developing treatise literature in conjunction with the writings of advocates of new forensic scientific methods and the fiction of Mark Twain. Cole shows that it was only at the end of the nineteenth century that legal treatises began to treat the law of identification as a distinct topic and that the issue was not yet at that time regarded as a science that embraced general principles, independent of other realms of knowledge and capable of making accurate assessments. Rather, as the example of George E. Harris's *Treatise on the Law of Identification* (1892) reveals, the law of identity was seen as an agglomeration of the various specific instances in which the law used whatever means were available to match shreds of evidence to the person who left them. Harris's treatise collects a wide range of cases involving forgery, imposture, fraud, and mistaken identification, arising not only in the U.S. but also in Europe and Australia. After examining the halting and tentative efforts to find a grounding for a law of identity in the late nineteenth century, Cole turns to Twain's meditations on the paradoxes of identity and duplicity in *The American Claimant* and *Pudd'nhead Wilson.* Cole focuses particularly on the latter, showing how the novel reflects the aspirations and anxieties of a society that was beginning to develop a science of identity, exhibiting at once a certain faith in the stability of identity (if measured properly) and a kind of resignation about the impossibility of matching social and legal identity.

John Barton discusses the various ways in which the prison was reconceived in the nineteenth century, an era that witnessed the advent of long-term incarceration (as against the use of prisons as temporary holding facilities in the eighteenth century), which in turn produced a new kind of figure who emerged from the extended prison sentence: the "discharged convict." Barton brings together a range of sources, including treatises on prison reform, novelistic portrayals of prisons and convicts, newspaper editorials on prison discipline and capital punishment, and periodicals devoted entirely to prison reform, such as *The Prisoner's Friend: A Monthly Magazine Devoted to Criminal Reform, Philosophy, Literature, Science and Art.* Debates over prison discipline in the 1830s and 1840s not only played out in the press but also sparked the imaginations of numerous writers, including Charles Brockden Brown, Edgar Allan Poe, George Lippard, Ned Buntline, George Thompson, William Gilmore Simms, Lydia Maria Child, E.D.E.N. Southworth, and Elizabeth Oakes Smith. As Barton shows, this wide array of sources made the prisoner a newly visible figure – one whose need for rehabilitation took on a new public prominence when considered not only as an inmate but also as a neighbor.

Western immigrants' efforts to manage their own interactions through the adoption of legal codes is the subject of Andrea McDowell's chapter. As she shows, in the early nineteenth century it was common for associations, clubs, societies, and organizations of all sorts in the Eastern United States to adopt codes and record minutes of their meetings, and this model was enthusiastically embraced by parties traveling west. Indeed, it was the appetite for formal procedures among Western immigrants that provided the motive for Henry Robert's classic *Robert's Rules of Order.* These codes covered financial arrangements and numerous other aspects of the participants' interactions, including crimes. In some instances, the commitments entailed by these written provisions served as a means of preventing the abuse of racial and ethnic minorities; in other instances, they were the very means of such abuse. The overall effect of these codes, McDowell suggests, was to create an alternative to vigilantism and feuding by providing a communal means of resolving disputes.

Edlie Wong's chapter on immigration, with its focus on the exclusionary policies of the U.S. government from the last quarter of the nineteenth century in particular, represents these exclusionary policies as a repeal of the language of inclusion that had emerged with the birth of the country. With immigration policies that distinguished between immigrants according to whether they were "desirable or "undesirable," the United States put into place harsh measures that kept entire groups of people, such as the Chinese, either out of the country or inside the country but living under severe constraints. These policies toward immigrants, Wong argues, reflected and fostered a climate in which the United States was vacillating between sympathy and revulsion for immigrants, and they exhibited the strangely passive-aggressive dance the law often did with social policy. The humanities were once again engaged in this discourse of immigration as Americans confronted the limitations of legal categories through the work of photojournalists like Jacob Riis. It soon became clear that managing these people as the law was supposed to do by either excluding or including them was far more complex than such a binary would suggest.

The difficulty, even impossibility, of managing humans according to the categories laid out by immigration law and slave law receives another hearing in Trinyan Mariano's contribution to this section on race law and Mark Twain's *Pudd'nhead Wilson.* A high point in the literary history of the nineteenth century, Twain's novel is often taught in college classes on race and literature to which Mariano's piece is a perfect complement. For Mariano, the emphasis is once again on the inadequacy of legal definitions to capture the people targeted by them. If race was becoming an index of how someone was to be treated in nineteenth-century America, what then, Twain asks, could the small town of Dawson's Landing, Missouri, make of the mystery underlying the surface of race? What could the law ultimately do with a place in which a white person could live as a black person and vice versa? When Pudd'nhead Wilson turns to the modern nineteenth-century science of fingerprinting, as Mariano demonstrates (like Simon Cole in an earlier chapter), the law moves beyond its own discipline and is forced to recognize the pieces of human existence it cannot capture with words.

The fourth and final section, "Affective Relations," looks at the ways in which nineteenth-century American law was bound up with human passions and sensations. In an era in which sentimentalism reigned supreme, the law was often thought to be a thing apart – a realm where rationality prevailed. The chapters in this section, however, reveal how central the world of affect and feelings was to nineteenth-century American law, from the tears of the victims to the shock of community spectators to the inevitable prejudice of the judge.

Yvonne Pitts's chapter on citizenship engages the subject of affect and the law by interrogating the category of capacity, which is often overlooked in favor of the other categories of race and gender. Capacity, Pitts argues, was a catchall category in which the law sought to exclude people from citizenship through determinations of their ability to reason rationally, among other things (a question that also figures in Susanna Blumenthal's discussion of legal personhood in the section "Human Kinds"). Characterizations based on insanity, moral perversion, or excessive sentiment were often deployed by lawyers to dismiss the testimony of witnesses in court or to undermine the potential of certain groups to participate fully in the public sphere. For Pitts, who surveys the exclusionary uses of capacity, one of the central points is that capacity, originally grounded in a biological notion of inferiority – through which inferior traits were attributed to certain individuals – was in fact a social construction, which relied on corresponding humanities-based patterns of thought and feeling for which the nineteenth century was famous.

In examining the affective life of the U.S. Constitution in the first half of the nineteenth century, Doni Gewirtzman looks at various arenas – legal, political, religious, literary – in which Americans mustered the contradictory resources of passion and reason, morality and formalism. Under the principle of popular sovereignty, "the People" are the ultimate arbiters of a constitutional meaning that is bound up with their collective social practices and the performative and expressive practices that accompany them. Under written constitutionalism, however, the emphasis is on long-term commitments, carefully articulated, spelled out in advance, and elaborated through processes of rational deliberation. Gewirtzman's discussion thus offers an historical lens for examining the dual-process theory of reasoning that distinguishes fast, intuitive, and relatively unreflective kinds of thinking from the slow, deliberate, and more effortful kinds of thinking that law is usually taken to require. This entails an understanding of cognitive processes and affect that is often used in contemporary scholarship to account for discrepancies between law on the books and law on the ground and to propose ways of designing legal systems so as to overcome heuristic biases. In exploring these issues, the chapter brings together U.S. Supreme Court decisions and the treatises of James Kent and Joseph Story, the manifestos of social and political groups, and the imaginative writings of James Fenimore Cooper, Harriet Beecher Stowe, and Walt Whitman, showing how widely constitutionalism's affective register resonated in the legal, intellectual, and imaginative lives of nineteenth-century Americans.

In her chapter on religion in America, Deborah Whitehead explains how a concept no less fundamental to the social order than religion emerged during the course of the nineteenth century as a kind of affect, a sensibility designated as such under the pressure of a dominant Protestant legacy. According to the First Amendment, church and state were separated in America, but in the early 1800s, as Whitehead explains, the First Amendment did not yet apply to the states, and their religiously diverse populations were vulnerable. Because Protestants understood religion as a matter of individual belief and affect rather than as a public practice to begin with, forms of religious diversity were severely limited. Not only were domestic religious movements like Mormonism susceptible to attack, but so too were those of the increasing numbers of immigrants to the country who were not used to keeping their expression of faith largely to themselves. Whitehead's chapter examines the powerful and strange intersection of the law and religion as affect to probe one of the most contested areas of American law and legal rights.

Applying Whitehead's ideas about religion as a form of affect and Mariano's notion of capacity as affect, Laura Appleman discusses the development of nineteenth-century American criminal law. With the expansion of real crime on the streets of America's major cities came a heightened emphasis on why people committed crimes or were drawn to criminal lifestyles. What mental or moral aberrations could lead to such a perverse attraction, and what parts of the criminal mind – defined in legal terms as the *mens rea* – did a criminal need to display in order to be considered guilty of criminal behavior? For Appleman, the legal answer was more often than not embedded in the gothic fiction of the period, where a wider range of the human behaviors that might lead to crime could be explored. As Appleman explains, in the nineteenth century the definition of *mens rea* went from connoting a general sense of wickedness to a more specific sense of intent required for each crime as laid out by statute. What brought about this change? Appleman argues that it was in part due to the explosion of gothic fiction and a general sense that evil was mysterious, varied, and inextricably linked to psychological instabilities.

As the contents of this volume show, the range and quantity of imaginative works and humanistic thought contributing to nineteenth-century American legal culture has, if anything, been underestimated. We have tried to present a sample here, and we acknowledge that this volume is far from exhaustive. Rather, we have taken diversity – of methodology and of subject matter – as our guide. The chapters in this volume represent some of the most interesting trajectories of scholarship in this area, but the field itself is always changing. The nineteenth century came to a close quite some time ago, but our understanding of its pivotal place in the making of a law-and-humanities–based scholarship is in some ways just getting off the ground.

Notes

1 Bradford R. Clark, "Federal Common Law: A Structural Reinterpretation," *University of Pennsylvania Law Review* 144 (1996): 1245–376; Hendrik Hartog, "Pigs and Positivism," *Wisconsin Law Review* (1985): 899–935; John Vile, *Re-Framers: 170 Eccentric, Visionary, and Patriotic Proposals to Rewrite the U.S. Constitution* (Santa Barbara, Cal.: ABC-CLIO, 2014).

2 Patti Ogden, "Mastering the Lawless Science of Our Law: A Story of Legal Citation Indexes," *Law Library Journal* 85 (1993): 1–48.

3 Robert W. Gordon, "The American Codification Movement: A Study of Antebellum Legal Reform" (book review), *Vanderbilt Law Review* 36 (1983): 431–58; on the movement's relation to contemporaneous literature, see Peter Schneck, *Rhetoric and Evidence: Legal Conflict and Literary Representation in American Culture* (Berlin: de Gruyter, 2011), 120–73; Elmer L. Widmer, *Young America: The Flowering of Democracy in New York City* (New York: Oxford University Press, 1999), 170–200.

4 Peter Tiersma, "The Textualization of Precedent," *Notre Dame Law Review* 82 (2007): 1187–278.

5 Robert A. Ferguson, *Law and Letters in American Culture* (Cambridge, Mass.: Harvard University Press, 1984); Richard Squibbs, *Urban Enlightenment and the Eighteenth-Century Periodical Essay* (New York: Palgrave Macmillan, 2014).

PART I

Human kinds

INTRODUCTION

Nan Goodman and Simon Stern

Law's power as a maker and unmaker of persons has been the subject of numerous studies, ranging from John Noonan's *Persons and Masks of the Law* (1975) to Colin Dayan's *The Law Is a White Dog* (2011). These powers range across legal domains, including business law, criminal law, and antidiscrimination law, and extend to procedural areas such as the law of standing and of group litigation. Those domains are social and geographic as well as doctrinal: in the nineteenth century, literary conceptions of deviance, social conventions regulating gender, the ability of corporations to project themselves through space by means of the railroads, and the inconsistent treatment of slave status from one jurisdiction to another all served to complicate the formal legal mechanisms for categorizing and regulating human kinds.

The chapters in this section take up these complex and often messy forms of legally fashioned personhood, showing how the courts' and legislatures' efforts to frame human identity were alternatively abetted and undermined by other symbolic forms and media. One thread that runs through these discussions involves legal means of categorizing persons by assessing or simply pronouncing on their capacities. This question arises most directly in Susannah Blumenthal's treatment of the grounds for determining whose acts and decisions would be given legal effect and in Jeannine DeLombard's examination of the complex relations between "property," "human," "person," and "man" that arose from the law's treatment of slavery. In one guise or another, however, the question reappears in nearly every chapter. Cheryl Suzack, for example, exposes the paradoxical logic that cast Native Americans as both sovereign and dependent, often rendering futile their efforts to exercise civil rights, while Tal Kastner shows how Bartleby's negative "preferences" evoke the legal situations of the prisoner and the chattel slave. Another recurrent issue involves the templates that law uses to understand and explain types of persons. Joyce Warren looks at ideological sources for legal distinctions that separated men and women according to their proper "spheres" and the ways in which those distinctions crumbled. Here again, DeLombard's observations about how religious and scientific discourses influenced ideas about slavery are also salient. The law's creativity in fashioning new persons and new forms of personhood appears most prominently in Aaron Ritzenberg's discussion of the corporation, which in turn changed Americans' ideas about character and made them reconsider the nature of personal identity. Indeed, all the chapters in this section suggest the enabling potential of these creative powers, as well as their dangers.

1

WOMEN

Politics, culture, and the law

Joyce W. Warren

In this chapter, I discuss how women's responses to the legal system helped to shape the law and legal culture in the nineteenth century. For most of the nineteenth century, women in the United States, particularly married women, functioned under legal disabilities imposed by law. In a section on the "Law," I discuss the most important laws that affected women, while in a section titled "Women's Sphere," I explain some of the ways that women were circumscribed by law and tradition. A section on "Education" provides a look at one of the major factors that led to a loosening of restrictions on women and describes the laws that aided in the change. A final section, "Women Writing about the Law," chronicles what contemporary nineteenth-century women wrote about the law and what laws they focused on, providing insight into how the law affected individual women's lives.

I. Law

The legal status of free nineteenth-century American women (white or African American) for the most part followed English common law. Although there were variations within the states, in general an unmarried woman, or *feme sole*, could not vote, hold political office, or serve on juries, but she could buy and sell property, sign contracts, and initiate a lawsuit. Once she married, however, she lost whatever legal rights she had. A married woman, or *feme covert*, was "covered" by her husband; she did not have a separate legal identity. As William Blackstone wrote in his influential *Commentaries on the Laws of England* in 1765, "The very being or legal existence of the woman is suspended during the marriage, or at least is incorporated and consolidated into that of the husband; under whose wing, protection, and *cover* she performs everything."[1] In the courts, a married woman held the status of a minor. She could not sue or be sued unless her husband was party to the lawsuit. If her husband refused to be part of the lawsuit (or was the defendant or plaintiff in a divorce case), she had to have another man appointed by the court to represent her, in addition to her lawyer. The other man could be a friend or relative; legally, he was called her "next friend" and performed the same function as a guardian who represented a minor in court.

A major consequence of the common law for a married woman was economic: her status as a *feme covert* left her with no money of her own. When a woman married, any personal property or money that she brought into the marriage or that she acquired during marriage (through inheritance, gift, or from her own earnings) legally and permanently belonged to her husband.

He could use it for any purpose that suited him and without consulting her. Ideally, he would use it to maintain the household, but he could also use it to make investments (wise or unwise) and for his own pleasure, including spending it on alcohol, gaming, or other women. If a woman owned any real estate (through inheritance or through purchase prior to her marriage), she could own the property, but she could not sell it without her husband's permission, and any profit that derived from it (rents, for example) belonged to her husband. The same was true for stock holdings.[2]

When a man died, his wife, through her "right of dower," obtained a life interest in one-third of his real estate and was entitled to one-third of his personal property after his debts were paid; however, when a woman died, her husband inherited everything, even if the money and/or personal property had been hers before marriage. If a woman's husband was heavily in debt when he died, it was possible for her to be left penniless – even if she came from a wealthy family and had brought a large amount of money into the marriage. A wealthy family could protect a daughter from this fate by establishing an equity trust in her name; this would give her access to money of her own that was not accessible to her husband or his creditors. Whereas the equity trust had long been used in England to provide a separate marriage settlement for a daughter through equity or chancery courts, American families did not often use it. Many Americans did not believe that a married woman should have independent control of her money.[3] Not all states provided the trust option (for example, New York did, but the New England states did not), and in addition, it was an expensive process not available to or practical for middle- or working-class families who would not have had the money to spare to put in trust for their daughters.

With respect to real estate, the purpose of a woman's right of dower was to provide some protection for her.[4] Her husband could not mortgage or sell real property he owned unless she signed the papers. The idea was that this would prevent her from being left homeless should her husband die. However, a woman could be coerced into signing or could sign simply because she did not understand what she was signing. After all, women were trained to believe that they should leave business and money matters to men. In England, the law required that the woman meet privately with the judge before she signed away her dower right; this was done to make certain that she understood what was at stake and to ascertain that she acted of her own free will.[5] But this safety precaution was not required in the American states. Moreover, since legally her children or husband's relatives would inherit the other two-thirds of the real estate, they could force a sale of the property if they wished, and, if the property consisted of only the house she lived in, she could legally be dispossessed of her home. One particularly egregious example of this was the 1859 case of *Horatio Judah v. Rebecca Judah*, in which Horatio brought suit against his mother after his father died, forcing the sale of the family home at 241 W. 17th Street in New York City. Not only was Rebecca by law entitled to one-third of the property, but her husband had specified in his will that she should have the right to remain in their home for her lifetime. If Uriah took this extra step because he was suspicious of his son's mercenary motives, he was proved correct because immediately after his father died, Horatio brought suit. Unfortunately for Rebecca, he won the case, and Rebecca and her daughter, Anna, a minor, were evicted from their home.[6]

Some of the inequities relating to women's property were addressed by married women's property laws, which were enacted gradually, state by state. Initially, the principal impetus for the laws was the economic Panic of 1837, during which many men lost a great deal of money, including property that their wives had brought into the marriage. The first state to pass a law protecting a married woman's property was Mississippi in 1839. The Mississippi law focused primarily on allowing a woman slave owner to continue to own her slaves ("property") after she married rather than allowing them to become the property of her husband, who under common law could sell them without his wife's permission or lose them to his creditors. One reason for the development of married women's property laws was not to protect women but to protect their wealthy fathers' hard-earned money from an irresponsible or impractical son-in-law. In New York, after the chancery courts were eliminated in 1847 and the equity trust was no longer available, some men supported the new law as an alternative means of protecting their property. Another important impetus for the new laws, particularly in the Northeastern states, was the increasing pressure from women's rights advocates, who appealed to the principle of individual rights. In the 1840s, a number of states passed laws giving married women ownership of the property they inherited or received as a gift. The substance of the laws varied by state, from the Alabama law that gave a woman separate ownership of her property but required that her husband have control over it, to the laws in the Northeastern states that enabled a woman to retain separate ownership and control. Like the trusts, these laws helped a woman from a wealthy family to keep her property, but they did nothing for middle- or working-class women, whose families had no money to gift or bequeath to them or for the married woman whose money came from her own earnings. Then in 1860, four states (Massachusetts, Maine, New York, Pennsylvania) passed Earnings Acts, which protected a woman's earnings (these included wages she received for her labor) and were particularly helpful to a woman whose husband would not or could not support his family. Other states did not begin to address the question of a wife's earnings until long after the Civil War.[7] Despite these changes, as Kathleen Sullivan points out, although the common law was modified with respect to married women's property, other aspects of *coverture* remained intact.[8]

An important aspect of a married woman's legal status that did not change throughout most of the nineteenth century was her vulnerability to domestic abuse. Legally, a man had the right to "correct" his wife by "domestic chastisement," just as he was "allowed to correct his apprentices or children."[9] For most of the century, physical abuse was expected and legal, as long as a man did not cause a "permanent injury" to his wife. As James Kent wrote (somewhat unrealistically) in *Commentaries on American Law* (1873), if a man was prone to violence, "the wife must disarm" him "by the weapons of kindness."[10] Acceptable abuse included a man's right to beat his wife "with a stick, to pull her hair, choke her, spit in her face, or kick her about the floor."[11] Since such abuse was legal, it was not considered grounds for divorce. In terms of divorce, the law differed by state, but most states did not permit absolute divorce unless the spouse could prove adultery. A legal separation could be obtained on grounds of abandonment and in some states on other grounds as well. One problem for women, however, was that if a couple separated, in most cases the children went to the father, although in individual cases a judge might find in favor of the mother if the father was proved "grossly" unfit morally or "wholly unable to provide for the safety and wants of the child."[12] In general, the father remained the preferred guardian well into the twentieth century.[13]

II. Women's sphere

The traditional role for nineteenth-century American women was domestic. All aspects of society told women that their place was in the home, subservient to their husbands. Advice books for women made that clear. Samuel Jennings, in *The Married Lady's Companion* (1808), told women that they must submit to their husbands as to God, and William Alcott wrote in *The Young Wife* (1837) that woman was created to be "man's assistant" and that marriage required "submission" to her husband.[14] Ralph Waldo Emerson told a women's rights convention in 1855 that woman was the "Angel in the parlor," whose role, he said, was to "embellish trifles"; she must not act for herself but should rely on a "good man" as her guardian.[15] That Emerson would address these words to women who had gathered to discuss the rights of women is an indication of the extent to which general opinion disregarded those rights. Moreover, this kind of "advice" was woefully unrealistic, since not all women were married and, of those who were married, not every husband was a "good man." In addition, the advice was aimed only at middle- and upper-class women whose economic situation afforded them the luxury of being an "Angel in the parlor." However, the ideology was so widespread that working-class women aspired to it as well; they regarded work before marriage as only temporary and expected to stay home after they were married. As Barbara Harris notes in *Beyond Her Sphere* (1978), in nineteenth-century white working-class families there was a "conscious effort to imitate the bourgeois style of life, and wives tended to stay at home as soon as it was economically feasible."[16] This was true also in free African American families. Liberal black leader Martin Delany declared in 1852 that black women should not work outside the home unless it was absolutely necessary for economic reasons; black women who did so for any other reason, he said, contributed to the "deep degradation of our race."[17] Delany's motivation in espousing this doctrine was in part a desire to overturn images of the black woman-as-worker that were associated with slavery. But as Oliver Horton points out, free blacks often sought to become "full participants in American life," and this involved "an obligation to live out the gender ideals of American patriarchal society."[18] That most women did not work outside the home is clear from the figures that Alice Kessler-Harris posits in *Women Have Always Worked* (1981): "Up until 1900 less than 20 percent of all women over fourteen were in the paid labor force."[19] In many instances, laws prevented married women from working outside the home. For example, school boards across the country enacted restrictions against hiring married women. It was not until the male labor shortage during World War II that public schools no longer objected to hiring married women. And it was not until the Civil Rights Act of 1964 that this discrimination against married women was officially ended. Married women during the nineteenth century were similarly banned from factory work, not by law but by management regulations. Melville's short story "A Tartarus of Maids" (1855) testifies to the practice.

Religion was a strong prohibitive factor in keeping women dependent and in the home. Christian theologians supported the idea with references to the Bible, especially to St. Paul: "Wives, submit yourselves unto your husbands as unto the Lord."[20] Religion was also influential in laws affecting women. The marriage laws, in fact, derive from biblical scripture. Throughout the Bible, a married couple is described as "one flesh" and the husband is the "head" of the wife, who is the "weaker vessel." These concepts are reflected in the common-law concept of the wife being "incorporated" into the husband, to be represented by and under "cover" of him. Religion also affected legal decisions regarding women. In an 1845 legal treatise, Edward Deering Mansfield maintained that woman was subject to her husband, which, he said, "derived from the Scripture rule."[21] At a New York constitutional convention the following year, lawyer Charles O'Conor, in opposition to proponents of a law regarding married women's property rights, asserted that marriage was a "sacred ordinance . . . based upon the gospel precept that 'they twain shall be one flesh.' "[22] Even Supreme Court decisions referenced religion. In 1873's *Bradwell v. Illinois*, in which Myra Bradwell was denied admission to the bar, Justice Joseph P. Bradley, in support of the court's decision that she could not practice law, stated that "divine ordinance" decreed that "the paramount destiny and mission of women is to fulfill the noble and benign offices of wife and mother. This is the law of the Creator."[23]

Theologians and members of the clergy issued statements condemning women who worked outside the home. In 1837, Protestant ministers in Boston published a pamphlet censuring the abolitionist Grimké sisters for giving lectures, writing that a woman should stay home "as becomes the modesty of her sex"; public speaking, they said, led to "degeneracy and ruin."[24] Theologians Horace Bushnell and John Todd asserted that women were "unsexing themselves in pursuing masculine" activities,[25] while other clergymen declared that it was "monstrous" of a woman not to subordinate herself to the "headship of man" and maintained that woman's role was wholly domestic.[26] These restrictions were not confined only to Christian women. The ideal of the Jewish woman was "The Mother in Israel," who was devoted to her family, and, as Diane Lichtenstein points out, American Jewish families "assimilated the mores, attitudes, and ideological patterns of the rising American middle class."[27]

III. Education

As Frederick Douglass comments in his *Narrative* (1845), education is "incompatible" with keeping a person in subjection.[28] For nineteenth-century women, education was a crucial factor in their century-long struggle to free themselves from restrictive laws. In colonial times, only girls from wealthy families received some education. The early town schools were for boys only; in the late eighteenth century, some schools permitted girls to come to school when the boys were not there – very early in the morning or late in the day. Education was not made widely available until the establishment of free public school systems. In the early nineteenth century, an elementary public school education was available in the Northeast, spread to the West, and then to the South after the Civil War, although the Southern states were very slow to establish public schools. Most of the common (primary) schools were coeducational, although boys and girls might be assigned to sit on separate sides of the room. In 1824, a public high school for girls was opened in Worcester, Massachusetts, and in 1826 a public high school for boys and girls opened in Bridgeport, Connecticut, although in Bridgeport, as in other early high schools, the curriculum was different for male and female students. At the opening of a public high school for girls in New York City in 1826, for example, one of the speakers noted that the girls would not be taught "abstruse science" since "such knowledge is not necessary for them." The course of study, he said, will train girls for "domestic happiness"; it will be "suited to their sex, and will prepare them for presiding with skill and prudence in those domestic stations, for which Providence has designed them."[29] When other public high schools for girls opened, they followed a similar pattern. In 1840, the first coeducational public high school in the nation opened in Lowell, Massachusetts,[30] and the first compulsory education law in the country was passed in Massachusetts in 1852, making school attendance mandatory for all children between the ages of eight and fourteen years.[31] One of the principal reasons for compulsory schooling at the time was the hope that it would "civilize" the children of immigrants so that they would be reliable and obedient workers, but it also benefited girls; before education was made mandatory, many families were reluctant to send their daughters to school. The number of public high schools nationwide multiplied after the Civil War, and by 1882 ninety percent of urban schools were coeducational institutions. A principal reason why public schools were for the most part coeducational was economic: many communities could not afford to build and support two separate schools.

The private academy or seminary for male or female students at first provided a higher level of education than the public high school, although later public high schools increased the formal offerings. Town academies usually required a small tuition fee and were endowed or supported by subscription. Few were state supported.[32] In some cases there was resistance to the establishment of free public academies for girls on the basis that women needed only a basic education. Walt Whitman, for example, opposed the establishment of a free academy for girls in New York (such as already existed for boys). In 1857, he wrote in the *Brooklyn Daily Times* that women need only "sufficient education" to become good "wives and mothers"; "no further education is necessary."[33] Although Whitman is thought of as a free rights advocate, his writings on women indicate that, except for his recognition of woman as a physical being, the freedom he advocates is clearly addressed to men alone. Viewing woman primarily as a breeder, he declares, "there is nothing greater than the mother of men," and in "Democratic Vistas" he writes of woman's "divine maternity" and says the ideal woman is the "perfect human mother."[34] In this respect, he was very much in tune with conventional attitudes toward women.

After the Civil War, the need for teachers due to the rapidly expanding number of primary schools provided the principal impetus for women's secondary education. Women teachers were preferred because they were cheaper; at most, they were paid one-third of what male teachers earned. An indication of how women's employment in education was devalued is apparent in this comment by a Massachusetts committee on the hiring of a county school superintendent in the 1870s: "As there is neither honor nor profit connected with this position, we see no reason why it should not be filled by a woman."[35] Still, teaching provided a profession for women at a time when they had few career options. As Harriet Martineau wrote in *Society in America* (1836), when she visited America, she saw only seven jobs for women: needlework, teaching, typesetting, keeping boarders, factory work, book binding, and domestic service.[36] She left out prostitution, which, if not socially acceptable, did provide a living for women whose only other option was starvation. As Fanny Fern commented in 1853, considering the dearth of job options and poor wages for women, it was not surprising that some women turned to prostitution. "Where's the marvel?" she asked.[37] A woman who had a degree in secondary education from a high school or academy was qualified to teach and thus could earn a respectable living. Catharine Beecher was an advocate of secondary education to train women to be teachers, which, she said, provided an alternative to factory work, and in the 1840s she founded several normal schools in the West. The first state-funded normal school for women appeared in 1839 in Massachusetts, and by 1892 there were 178 normal schools nationwide.[38]

Pioneering women educators who had a vision that women's education could be equal to that of men led the academy movement. Emma Willard founded the Troy Female Seminary in 1814; Catharine Beecher founded the Hartford Female Seminary in 1821; Zilpah Polly Grant founded the Ipswich Academy in 1828; and Mary Lyon, who had taught at Ipswich, founded Mount Holyoke Seminary in 1837. All of these institutions provided evidence that women could handle a challenging curriculum and led to the recognition that women could enter college. In terms of higher education, most Eastern colleges remained all male, but in the West, where the schools were not as financially secure, women were accepted as students. The first college to open its doors to women was Oberlin in Ohio, which opened in 1833 admitting women and black students into its preparatory or high school program and in 1837 into the degree program. Even here, however, traditional interpretations of "woman's role" prevailed. All students were expected to perform labor, and the tasks were divided by sex: women students washed the men's clothes, cleaned their rooms, and waited on them at table. Moreover, a woman student was not allowed to read her own essay at graduation; a man had to read it for her. Because of this, Lucy Stone refused to write an essay.[39] The state universities in Wisconsin, Michigan, and Chicago became coeducational in the 1870s, as did Cornell and Boston University, and they provided an example to other institutions. Opponents of coeducational education in institutions of higher learning were met on the one hand with arguments regarding equality, but, in the case of the Midwestern state institutions, the argument was also economic. When a new president at Wisconsin attempted to create a separate college for women, the regents noted in 1871 that coeducation saved the "time and strength of the professors," and when the regents advocated keeping separate recitation classes for women, the State Superintendent asserted in 1870 that having classes in common "greatly lessened" the expense.[40] The older, more financially secure universities in New England and most universities in the South firmly resisted the trend toward coeducational education. Instead, women's colleges were founded that strove to provide the quality of education provided at men's colleges. Elmira Female College opened in

1855, Vassar College in 1865, and Wellesley and Smith in 1875. Mount Holyoke was chartered as a college in 1888.

Opponents of women's colleges echoed the conventional assertions about women: that they were not intelligent enough for college work; that they were too "delicate" for an intellectual course of study; and that they would destroy their marriage chances. Women were also under social pressure not to pursue higher education. Marion Talbot wrote in later years that when she entered Boston University in the late 1870s, she was "completely ostracized" by her friends.[41] The most devastating opposition to women's education, however, came from the medical profession. Medical books held that women's sexual organs were responsible for all of their ills. Once women began to attain rights, particularly when some colleges began to admit women, the medical profession issued dire warnings that "masculine" pursuits, particularly intellectual work, would injure a woman's reproductive organs and thus jeopardize the future of the species. Dr. E. A. Clarke wrote in *Sex in Education* in 1873 that education not only damaged a woman's reproductive organs but caused other problems as well, including insanity, sterility, and the inability to breastfeed, and (again falling back on religion) was "a crime before God."[42] Dr. Thomas Emmet's *Principles and Practices of Gynaecology* (1879) warned that intellectual effort during the onset of puberty would impair a woman's ability to have children.[43] Clarke's book was very popular, and the "scientific" authority behind it gave young women pause in considering higher education. Martha Carey Thomas wrote later that when she had read warnings like Clarke's, she and other young women were afraid that their health would be impaired by college: "We were haunted in those days by the clanging chains of that gloomy specter, Dr. Edward Clarke's *Sex in Education*."[44] Colleges also took the warnings seriously. The University of Wisconsin issued a disclaimer, advising that an education could be hazardous to a woman's health: "It is better that the future matrons of the state should be without university training than that it should be produced at the fearful expense of ruined health."[45] It is significant that medical men did not seem to be concerned about the health of women factory workers or seamstresses – women whose work really was hazardous to their health but whose exploited labor did not represent a threat to the status quo in the way that college-educated women did. In addition to the warnings of doctors like Clarke, S. Weir Mitchell, a well-known neurologist, believed that mental activity would make a woman "sickly and weak" and unfit her "for her duties as a woman"; his famous rest cure for women required "absolute rest of the intellect."[46] Charlotte Perkins Gilman's story, "The Yellow Wallpaper," responds directly to Mitchell's theories with a nightmarish vision of what could happen to a woman subjected to his rest cure, as she had been. She implies that if she had not left the treatment, it would have driven her insane. Despite all of the warnings, women continued to pursue higher education, and before the end of the century, some went on to earn professional degrees. Some medical schools began to admit women in the 1870s, and in 1881 the University of Pennsylvania was the first law school to open its doors to women.[47]

IV. Women writing about the law

In the years following the 1848 Women's Rights Convention in Seneca Falls, women's rights activists wrote essays and gave lectures on numerous issues, but the one that stands out is the demand that women have the vote. In 1881, the first two volumes of a mammoth six-volume work were published: *A History of Woman Suffrage* by Elizabeth Cady Stanton, Susan B. Anthony, and Matilda Joslyn Gage. Consisting of historical essays, biographies, and a compilation of original documents, the work chronicled the struggle for suffrage up to the passage of the Nineteenth Amendment in 1920, beginning with the pivotal Anti-Slavery Convention in 1840 when women were denied the right to speak or even to sit in the audience. A compromise was reached where the women could be seated but they had to be curtained off so that no one could see them. It was this humiliating experience that provided the catalyst for the women's rights movement. One notable section of the *History* is the discussion of the bitter Kansas campaign of 1867, in which women who had worked to gain suffrage for black men and all women discovered that some of their former allies among the abolitionists would support only black male suffrage. This resulted in a split in the women's movement between those who were willing to take a backseat to black male suffrage and those who continued to push for universal suffrage. Feeling betrayed and "utterly deserted," the latter group, including Anthony and Stanton, accepted help from Democrats, who had previously been their opponents in the fight for abolition.[48] The 1868 passage of the Fifteenth Amendment to the Constitution enfranchising black men but not women of any race ended that particular struggle but not the animosity that had been engendered by the betrayals, anger, and racism it involved. It would be almost fifty years before the Nineteenth Amendment was passed and women finally got the vote.

In addition to writing on suffrage, women also wrote on slavery. Lydia Maria Child took an early stand, publishing her book *An Appeal in Favor of That Class of Americans Called Africans* in 1833. Child was punished for writing boldly on issues that at the time were considered unseemly for a woman to write about; her successful children's periodical failed, her other books lost sales, and publishers were loath to publish new works by her. Child, however, proceeded to publish antislavery pieces, including editorials in the *National Anti-Slavery Standard* and compelling short stories portraying the evils of slavery: "The Quadroons" (1842) and "Slavery's Pleasant Homes" (1843). The most well-known antislavery work of fiction in the nineteenth century was Harriet Beecher Stowe's *Uncle Tom's Cabin*, first serialized in the *National Era* in 1851 and appearing in book form in 1852. Translated into many languages, *Uncle Tom's Cabin* sold more copies than any other book except the Bible.[49] Stowe attacked the Fugitive Slave Act of 1850, which required law enforcers everywhere in the country to arrest escaping slaves (and even provided a bounty payment for each slave returned to slavery) and imposed a fine and imprisonment on any person who aided an escaping slave. The law led to an outburst of "slave catching" in the North, as well as to illegal kidnappings of free blacks. Northerners were outraged at what they considered an infringement on their rights, and many, like the Birds in Stowe's novel, defiantly put individual conscience above the new law. At the end of her powerful novel, Stowe assumes the persona of a preacher, warning that if the United States does not end slavery, the country will feel the effects of "that stronger law by which injustice and cruelty shall bring on nations the wrath of Almighty God!"[50]

African American women who wrote against slavery included Harriet Jacobs, whose autobiographical *Incidents in the Life of a Slave Girl* was published in 1861, with an introduction by Child. Jacobs told of her experiences as a slave, her seven years in hiding, and her escape to the North, where she was pursued by her "owners" until her New York employer bought her and set her free. Other memoirs by African American women portrayed their own experiences under slavery. The most well-known African American woman writer in the nineteenth century, Frances Harper, began lecturing against slavery in 1854 and portrayed the evils of slavery in her many published works of poetry and fiction. Her later novel *Iola Leroy* (1892) covers the period from slavery, through Reconstruction, to the experience of former slaves in the North, addressing the legal questions relating not only to slavery but also to temperance and women's rights. White Southern women also wrote novels in defense of slavery. Responding in part to *Uncle Tom's Cabin*, such works include Mary Henderson Eastman's best-selling novel, *Aunt Phillis's Cabin; or, Southern Life as It Is* (1852), which draws a picture of kind slave owners and happy slaves, comparing their lot favorably to the miserable existence of free blacks and white wage earners in the North. One of the best known of the so-called anti-Tom novels by women was Caroline Lee Hentz's *The*

Planter's Northern Bride (1854), which attempts to demonstrate that slavery is necessary because Africans are unable to function on their own and thus are better off under the "protection" of white owners. Not all Southern women defended slavery. The Grimké sisters, who grew up in slavery, lectured against it throughout the North. And E.D.E.N. Southworth, a staunch abolitionist and a Southerner, portrays the evils of slavery in numerous novels, but she also portrays the complications of antislavery opinions in the South. In *Retribution* (1849) and *India* (1853), for example, when the protagonists free all of their slaves, their friends abandon them, their fiancés break engagements, and, in both cases, they have become such pariahs in their communities that they leave the state and settle in the West.

More than male writers, women writing against slavery called attention to the impact of slavery on women, primarily with respect to the sexual abuse of slave women and girls. Stowe, in *Uncle Tom's Cabin*, portrays the tragic background of Cassy (based on Child's story "The Quadroons") and the sexual appropriation of fifteen-year-old Emmeline by Simon Legree. As Stowe says, an innocent young slave girl can be bought by "any man, however vile and brutal, however godless and merciless, if he only has money to pay for her" (359). Jacobs describes her own experience with a lecherous owner and tells the stories of other women slaves, declaring in her Preface that she wants to give women in the North "a realizing sense of the condition of two millions of women at the South, still in bondage, suffering what I suffered."[51] Women writers also addressed the negative impact of slavery on white women, particularly the wives of slave owners. Stowe portrays the frustration and helplessness of Mrs. Shelby when the slaves are sold, along with the selfishness of the pampered Marie St. Clare. Jacobs shows the cruelty of Mrs. Flint, who suffers from the humiliation of living with a man whose many sexual partners and children were residents of her own household. Jacobs comments regarding the despicable Mrs. Flint: "Slaveholders' wives feel as other women would under similar circumstances" (34), and when she sees a happy plantation bride, she remarks, "It made me sad for I knew how soon clouds would come over her sunshine" (92). Under slavery, the law that left a woman with no legal or economic power was coupled with a husband's absolute power to command other women to his bed. It was not surprising that so many Southern wives lived in a state of helpless despair or anger. As the wife of one plantation owner, Mary Boykin Chesnut, wrote, under the "*monstrous* system" of slavery, many Southern wives used opium to enable them to keep their sanity: "our men live all in one house with their wives and their concubines, and the mulattoes one sees in every family exactly resemble the white children." The wife, she said, can do nothing but "pretend" that she doesn't see what she knows is true.[52] And it was all perfectly legal.

Women writers also addressed gender-specific laws that restricted women. In 1845, three years before the Women's Rights Convention at Seneca Falls, Margaret Fuller published her seminal book on women's rights in the United States, *Woman in the Nineteenth Century*. She addressed specific laws, noting that women did not

> own property on equal terms with men; so that, if a husband dies without making a will, the wife, instead of taking at once his place as head of the family, inherits only a part of his fortune, often brought him by herself, as if she were a child, or ward only, not an equal partner.[53]

She pointed to the unjust property laws for women and women's inability to vote and run for public office. Maintaining that all opportunities – political, educational, and occupational – should be open equally to men and women, she declared that she would have "every arbitrary barrier thrown down" (260). In her newspaper articles, Fuller addressed additional legal issues. In 1845, for example, she published several antislavery newspaper articles, most notably her June 10,

1845, review of *The Narrative of Frederick Douglass.* She also wrote about prison reform and the poor (March 19, 1845) and asserted that Americans had betrayed the promise of America, citing the mistreatment of native people, the persecution of the Mormons, and the War with Mexico.[54]

A few years later, Fanny Fern began her meteoric career, publishing her first newspaper column in 1851 and within two years rising from "rags to riches" through the sales of her satirical newspaper articles and best-selling books. Critiquing the injustice of male-oriented laws, she urged women to become law-savvy so that they could protect themselves. In her novel *Rose Clark* (1856) she introduced the question of married women's property laws. When Gertrude's ex-husband, John Stahle, attempts to extract money from her after she becomes wealthy, he is confident that he will get it from her because, as he tells his friend, "All women are fools about law matters."[55] Although many women were ignorant of their legal rights, Gertrude is not the "fool" Stahle takes her to be. If they had still been married, he would have owned all of her earnings, but since they are divorced, he no longer has any claim to her money. Similarly, Fern's second husband, Samuel Farrington, had gotten a divorce in Chicago shortly before her first book was published. She sent her lawyer to Chicago to inquire into the conditions of the divorce; he found that the divorce was absolute and that Farrington had no claim to "her person or property."[56] She must have been relieved at this news, although Farrington probably would not have been so happy; when he obtained the divorce, he would have had no idea that the woman he had been married to had become the person behind the Fanny Fern pseudonym and was on her way to becoming rich.

In her autobiographical novel *Ruth Hall,* Fern addressed questions of child custody,[57] inheritance laws (76–7), and the facility with which women could be incarcerated in insane asylums (109, 112). Although the laws varied from state to state, in most states all that was needed to commit a person to an asylum was the signature of one doctor. Other literary works that portray sane women being incarcerated at the will of a male relative include Southworth's *The Hidden Hand* (1859) and Alcott's "A Whisper in the Dark." In her newspaper articles, Fern criticized laws regarding divorce, suffrage, women's inability to run for political office, spousal abuse, prison reform, prostitution, and laws that made it illegal for women to wear trousers (see, e.g., 282–3, 292–4, 299–304, 306–9, 314–19, 327–8). Fern and Fuller were both criticized for "going out of their sphere." Critics castigated Fern as "unfeminine" and "unwomanly" and attacked her for being "egotistical."[58] Critics also attacked Fuller for having a large ego, and even Emerson, an erstwhile friend, referred derisively to her "mountainous Me."[59] In fact, people regarded Fuller as so "unwomanly" that rumors of her marriage abroad were greeted with disbelief. Citing her "masculine" demeanor, Emerson expressed "surprise" that anyone would want to marry her.[60]

Although Fanny Fern was knowledgeable about the law, most nineteenth-century women were not. Women were conditioned to believe that the law and money were a man's business. In Susan Warner's 1850 best-selling novel *The Wide, Wide World,* Mrs. Montgomery is thrust into poverty and must be parted from her child because of a lawsuit that her husband has lost, yet she knows nothing about the suit or about her husband's business. She says to her daughter as they tearfully contemplate the enforced parting, "I am not apt to concern myself overmuch about the gain or the loss of money. I believe my Heavenly Father will give me what is good for me."[61] Fern came to her position through her own hard experience: her first husband's death after the loss of a lawsuit left her penniless; her second husband used his legal and economic power to force her to his will; and her father-in-law cruelly rewrote his will, disinheriting her and her two young children unless she agreed to give them up to him and never see them again. Radicalized by her experience, she resolved that she would not be a victim of ignorance and made it her business to find out her rights under the law. In her introduction to *A New Story Book for Children,* she warned women never to sign a legal document unless they had read it carefully and were certain that it would not have dire consequences for them.[62] She, as a trusting wife, had signed away her dower rights to their home and other real estate, and consequently her husband mortgaged the property. When he died in debt, she was left homeless and penniless.[63] In her own life, Fern had learned how important it was for a woman to understand the law, and in 1856 when she married for a third time (to a man eleven years her junior), she insisted that they sign a prenuptial agreement before the wedding in order to make certain that after her marriage, all of her earnings would belong to her.

Martha Tyler's novel *A Book without a Title: or, Thrilling Events in the Life of Mira Dana* (1855) is autobiographical. The book describes how Tyler's husband had taken her three children and all of her money and property from her, including her clothes, and how the police and the courts took his side all the way. He viciously sets out to "humble" her and "break her," having her arrested on false charges and maligning her reputation on the advice of his lawyer, who says, "It is an easy matter to throw dirt."[64] And, like other men at the time, he put his money in a friend's name so that he would not have to pay her alimony. A former factory worker who had been a leader in a strike in the Lowell mills, she fights back as best she can, but in the end she is left with nothing but a pittance, the court debating "whether a woman could live on two dollars per week" and deciding that she could (283). The whole experience leaves Tyler bitterly angry. She gives the lawyers Dickensian names that indicate her disgust with the law: Squire Foolsome, S. W. Cheetman, and Lawyer Renown. At the end of the novel, the main character addresses the court: "Is this the boasted justice which you stand here to dispense?" (284–5). Tyler's novel is a call for changes in the laws that, as she says, make woman a "cipher" (285).

In addition to writing about suffrage, slavery, or women's vulnerability under the law, women writers also pursued issues of class. Rebecca Harding Davis's 1861 novella *Life in the Iron Mills*, was one of the first works in American fiction to portray life from the perspective of working-class characters. She humanizes the characters in the same way that Stowe humanizes slave characters in *Uncle Tom's Cabin*. We see the dead-end lives and lack of opportunity for these hardworking people, the long hours on the job, and the miserable living and working conditions, while at the same time we see the hopelessness of their very human aspirations and yearning. Then at the end of the piece, Davis illustrates how the law functions differently for those who are at the bottom of the class hierarchy. When Hugh Wolfe is wrongly convicted of stealing the wallet of a man from a superior class, he is sentenced to nineteen years in prison. The jailer comments, " 'Twas a hard sentence, – all the law allows; but it was for 'xample's sake. These mill-hands are gettin' onbearable."[65]

Elizabeth Stuart Phelps (Ward) also portrays working-class characters in her novel *The Silent Partner* (1871). She mentions the law in two instances. The upper-class protagonist, Perley Kelso, is shocked to find that an eight-year-old boy, Bob Mell, is working in the mills. Massachusetts law at the time specified that no children under the age of ten could work in a factory.[66] The other reference to the law concerns the length of the workday. The Massachusetts mill hands work a thirteen-hour day, and when Bob Mell's father, who is English, attempts to lead a strike for a ten-hour day, citing a law that had been passed in England, he is fired. When another man testifies in favor of a ten-hour day, he is blacklisted in all of the mills in Massachusetts. Although Phelps cites these two instances where the law could help the workers, she does not seem to see that legal measures could be taken to alleviate some of the other conditions that she finds so horrifying. She cites the miserable working conditions: working with deafening noise in temperatures of 110 to 116 degrees Fahrenheit with no ventilation and the threat of being fired for opening a window; handling wool that can cause blindness; inhaling cotton fibers that cause a chronic cough; and receiving no worker compensation for injury or pension for old age. The unsafe working conditions are brought front and center when Bob Mell is sucked into a machine and killed. The workers' living conditions are equally horrendous. The Mells live in a tenement where the stairs are broken, and the building is flooded by the river every year, leaving behind offal from the mills and a stench that never goes away. Here and in her short story "The Tenth of January" (1868), in which she portrays an actual event – a fire in the mill in Lawrence, Massachusetts, and the collapse of the building due to faulty structure – Phelps calls attention to the terrible conditions and trusts to the "good will" of the factory owners and landlords to remedy the situation. Davis's solution in *Life in the Iron Mills* also does not involve the law. Despite her graphic description of miserable working and living conditions, the story concludes only with a spiritual image, pointing to the sky where "God has set the promise of the Dawn" (65). Most of the conditions that Phelps and Davis describe have since been subjected to legal correction, but whether it was because they were women unused to thinking in legal terms, neither author calls for legal solutions. However, such remedies were perhaps too new during this period. The idea of government intervention to legislate working conditions and safety became more acceptable with the Progressive movement at the turn of the century. In any case, these works provide us with an important example of how far women were removed from legal thinking at the time. Nevertheless, the authors' empathetic portrayals of social injustice, like those of Dickens, served to raise the public awareness and indignation that eventually led to government legislation.

Although writers like Phelps and Davis did not necessarily think in terms of legal solutions, women writing in relation to issues of ethnicity did look to the law, just as anti-slavery writers did. Of particular importance were writers from two ethnic groups seeking justice: Mexicans and Native Americans. After the War with Mexico ended, the United States signed the Treaty of Guadalupe Hidalgo in 1848, guaranteeing that any Mexicans who lived in the territory that had been appropriated from Mexico would retain the right to their property and would become American citizens. But after American settlers moved onto the Mexican land, the government passed laws rescinding the land guarantees in the treaty. Mexican landowners found themselves in long court battles with squatters, which either resulted in the squatters' winning title to the land or the bankruptcy of the Mexican owner – or both. Maria Amparo Ruiz de Burton describes, in her novel *The Squatter and the Don* (1885), the injustices to which the Mexican landowners were subjected. She shows how, during the long years of litigation, the squatters took over sections of the land, shooting the landowner's cattle with impunity, building houses, and planting crops. Meanwhile, the landowner had to pay higher taxes on the land that was being "improved" by the squatters. Ruis de Burton had spent ten years in litigation over her family's land, and not only did she lose the land, but she lost her money. In this novel she makes a case for reexamining the laws, which, she maintains, were passed to win the votes of the squatters: "to win their votes . . . our representatives in Congress helped to pass laws declaring all lands in California open to preemption."[67]

In her book *Life among the Piutes* (1883), Sarah Winnemucca Hopkins makes a compelling case for government action to protect Native American tribes. She tells about her childhood living with her family on tribal lands in Nevada before any contact had been made with whites and about the forcible removal of the Piutes to the Yakima reservation in Washington territory in the middle of winter, which caused many deaths. She describes how she and her brother traveled to Washington, D.C., where she met with President Rutherford B. Hayes and the Secretary of the Interior. Hopkins tells of the injustices the Piutes suffered at Yakima, and the corruption of the Indian agent who took the money the government provided for the Piutes and left them to starve. The book contains a petition to be presented to Congress, maintaining that the Piutes' land had been illegally taken from them, a letter from Mary Peabody Mann urging people to sign the petition, and documents from supporters in the Army testifying to Hopkins' character and work as an interpreter. Nothing was done. Although there was sympathy for her cause, the principal responses to her book and lectures were personal attacks on her virtue and denials from the Bureau of Indian Affairs.

In Fanny Fern's *Ruth Hall*, when Ruth visits the insane asylum and asks about a woman who is screaming for her child, the matron tells her that the woman's husband took the child from her to spite her: "She went to the law about the child, and the law, you see, as it generally is, was on the man's side."[68] One might say that this comment succinctly summarizes the general situation for nineteenth-century American women in relation to the law. Certainly it was true with respect to laws regarding women's rights in general – married women's property rights, suffrage, child custody. In criminal cases, courts sometimes found for the woman, particularly if her lawyer employed skillful rhetoric to shape the argument in her behalf, using a sympathetic narrative from popular culture.[69] Some laws varied by location, and most laws were constantly evolving. Laws and regulations affecting education gradually provided women with educational opportunities that opened the way for professional opportunities. There were many different women in nineteenth-century United States, representing different races, classes, ethnicities, and geographic locations. Looking at the concerns of women who wrote on legal issues identifies what some of those issues were and helps to illuminate their impact on individual women. The law is more meaningful when it is not abstracted from the reality of people's lives.

Notes

1 William Blackstone, *Commentaries on the Laws of England*, 4 vols., ed. Wilfrid Prest (1765–69; Oxford: Oxford University Press, 2016), 1: 284–5.

2 For discussions of these and other aspects of nineteenth-century American women's legal status, see, e.g., Joyce W. Warren, *Women, Money, and the Law: Nineteenth-Century Fiction, Gender, and the Courts* (Iowa City: University of Iowa Press, 2005); Elizabeth B. Warbasse, *The Changing Legal Rights of Married Women, 1800–1861* (New York: Garland, 1987); Lawrence M. Friedman, *A History of American Law* (New York: Simon & Schuster, 1973), 202–10; and Leo Kanowitz, *Women and the Law: The Unfinished Revolution* (Albuquerque: University of New Mexico Press, 1969), 35–41.

3 As James Fenimore Cooper wrote in *The Ways of the Hour* (1850), according to the laws of God and nature, a woman should be dependent on man and, if she had any money of her own, she should "reverently pour it into her husband's lap." *Complete Works*, Leatherstocking edition, 32 vols. (New York: Putnam, 1893), 24: 179–83, 436–8.

4 Tapping Reeve's influential American work, *Baron and Femme* (1816; New York: New York Source Book Press, 1970) portrays this as a positive feature of the common law for women, establishing husband and wife with respect to real property as "two distinct persons" (171).

5 Blackstone, *Commentaries*, 2: 87–92.

6 Cited in Warren, *Women, Money*, 203.

7 For a fuller discussion of the changing laws, see Warbasse, *Changing*; with respect to New York's laws, see Norma Basch, *In the Eyes of the Law: Women, Marriage, and Property in Nineteenth-Century New York* (Ithaca, N.Y.: Cornell University Press, 1982).

8 Kathleen S. Sullivan, *Constitutional Context: Women and Rights Discourse in Nineteenth-Century America* (Baltimore: Johns Hopkins University Press, 2007), 4.

9 Blackstone, *Commentaries*, 1: 292, 377.

10 James Kent, *Commentaries on American Law*, 4 vols., ed. Oliver W. Holmes, Jr. (Boston: Little, Brown, 1873), 2: 127.

11 Laws passed in Massachusetts and Alabama in 1871 specified these actions among those that would no longer be legal under the new laws. Terry Davidson, *Conjugal Crime: Understanding and Changing the Wifebeating Pattern* (New York: Hawthorn, 1978), 102.

12 Jamil S. Zainaldin, "The Emergence of a Modern American Family Law: Child Custody, Adoption, and the Courts, 1796–1851," *Northwestern University Law Review* 73 (1979): 1039–89.

13 For a listing of child custody laws into the 1930s, see Chester G. Vernier, *American Family Laws: A Comparative Study of the Family Law of the Forty-Eight American States, Alaska, the District of Columbia, and Hawaii (to Jan. 1, 1931)*, 5 vols. (Stanford: Stanford University Press, 1931–38), 4: 18–19.

14 Samuel K. Jennings, *The Married Lady's Companion* (New York: Dow, 1808); William A. Alcott, *The Young Wife* (Boston: Light, 1839), 27–9.
15 Ralph Waldo Emerson, "Woman," in *Complete Works*, 12 vols., ed. Edward W. Emerson (Boston: Houghton Mifflin, 1903–4), 11: 403–26.
16 Barbara Harris, *Beyond Her Sphere: Women and the Professions in American History* (Westport, Conn.: Greenwood Press, 1978), 61–2.
17 Martin Delany, *The Condition, Elevation, Emigration and Destiny of Colored People of the United States* (Philadelphia: Martin Delany, 1852), 43.
18 James O. Horton, "Freedom's Yoke: Gender Conventions among Ante-Bellum Blacks," *Feminist Studies* 12 (1980): 51–76.
19 Alice Kessler-Harris, *Women Have Always Worked* (Old Westbury, N.Y.: Feminist Press, 1981), 17–18.
20 The Epistle of Paul to the Ephesians, 5:22.
21 Edward D. Mansfield, *The Legal Rights, Disabilities and Duties of Women* (Salem, Mass.: Jewett, 1845), 307.
22 *Debates and Proceedings in the New-York Convention, for the Revision of the Constitution*, ed. Sherman Croswell and Richard K. Sutton (Albany, N.Y.: Albany Argus, 1846), 907; reprinted in *The Convention of 1846*, ed. Milo M. Quaife (Madison, Wis.: State Historical Society, 1929), 631.
23 *Bradwell v. Illinois*, 83 U.S. 130 (1873). For information on Bradwell's struggle, see, e.g., Jill Norgren, *Rebels at the Bar: The Fascinating, Forgotten Stories of America's First Women Lawyers* (New York: New York University Press, 2013), 26–43.
24 "A Pastoral Letter of the General Association of Congregational Ministers," in *History of Woman Suffrage*, 6 vols., ed. Elizabeth C. Stanton, Susan B. Anthony, and Matilda J. Gage (1881–1922; New York: Source Book Press, 1970), 1: 81–2.
25 See the reply to Bushnell and Todd by Fanny Fern in the *New York Ledger*, November 6, 1869, 4.
26 John W. Nevin, "Woman's Rights," *American Review* 2 (1848): 367–81; Jesse T. Peck, "The True Woman," *Ladies' Repository* 13 (1853): 337–41.
27 See Diane Lichtenstein, "The Tradition of American Jewish Women Writers," in *The (Other) American Traditions: Nineteenth-Century Women Writers*, ed. Joyce Warren (New Brunswick, N.J.: Rutgers University Press, 1993), 247.
28 Frederick Douglass, *Narrative of the Life of Frederick Douglass, An American Slave* (1845; New York: Barnes & Noble, 2003), 44.
29 Cited in Thomas Woody, *A History of Women's Education in the United States*, 2 vols. (New York: Science Press, 1929), 1: 526–7.
30 See, e.g., Cornelius Riordan, *Girls and Boys in School Together or Separate?* (New York: Teachers College, Columbia University, 1990), 29.
31 1852 Massachusetts Acts, chap. 240, §1.
32 Elene W. Farello, *A History of the Education of Women in the United States* (New York: Vantage, 1970), 118.
33 Walt Whitman, "Free Academies at Public Cost," *Brooklyn Daily Times*, July 9, 1857, 2.
34 Walt Whitman, *Leaves of Grass* (New York: Columbia University Press, Facsimile Text Society, 1939), 48; *Collected Writings: Prose Works, 1892*, 2 vols., ed. Floyd Stovall (New York: New York University Press, 1963–64), 2: 364, 394.
35 Cited in Woody, *A History*, 1: 516.
36 Cited in Phyllis Stock, *Better Than Rubies: A History of Women's Education* (New York: Capricorn, 1978), 185.
37 Fanny Fern, *Ruth Hall and Other Writings*, ed. Joyce W. Warren (New Brunswick, N.J.: Rutgers University Press, 1986), 248. Hereafter cited parenthetically.
38 Woody, *A History*, 1: 482.
39 Cited in Patricia Sexton, *Women in Education* (Bloomington, Ind.: Phi Delta Kappa, 1976), 47–8.
40 Woody, *A History*, 2: 241–2.
41 Cited in ibid., 2: 153.
42 Edward A Clarke, *Sex in Education, or, A Fair Chance for Girls* (1873; Boston: Houghton Mifflin, 1892), 38–60, 90–109, 127.
43 Thomas A. Emmet, *Principles and Practices of Gynaecology* (Philadelphia: Lea, 1879), 21.
44 Martha C. Thomas, "Present Tendencies in Women's College and University Education," *Educational Review* 35 (January 1908): 69. 64–85.
45 Cited in Rosalind Rosenberg, *Domestic Individualism: Imagining Self in Nineteenth-Century America* (New Haven, Conn.: Yale University Press, 1982), 12.

46 Silas W. Mitchell, *Wear and Tear; Or, Hints for the Overworked* (1887; New York: Arno, 1975), 30, 46–7, 56–7.
47 Stock, *Better Than Rubies*, 204–5.
48 *History of Woman Suffrage*, 2: 264–8.
49 Abraham Lincoln is reputed to have said to Stowe when he met her in 1862, "So you're the little woman who wrote the book that started this great war!" See Joan D. Hedrick, *Harriet Beecher Stowe: A Life* (New York: Oxford, 1994), vii.
50 Harriet Beecher Stowe, *Uncle Tom's Cabin* (1852; New York: Signet, 1998), 485.
51 Harriet Jacobs, *Incidents in the Life of a Slave Girl*, ed. Jean Fagan Yellin (1861; Cambridge, Mass.: Harvard University Press, 1987), 1. Hereafter cited parenthetically.
52 Mary B. Chesnut, *Mary Chesnut's Civil War*, ed. Comer V. Woodward (New Haven, Conn.: Yale University Press, 1981), 29.
53 Margaret Fuller, *Woman in the Nineteenth Century: The Essential Margaret Fuller*, ed. Jeffrey Steele (1845; New Brunswick, N.J.: Rutgers University Press, 1992), 257. Hereafter cited parenthetically.
54 Margaret Fuller, *At Home and Abroad*, ed. Arthur B. Fuller (1856; Boston: Roberts Brothers, 1874), e.g., 254–5, 306, 326–7.
55 Fanny Fern, *Rose Clark* (New York: Mason Brothers, 1856), 345–6.
56 The letters and a copy of the divorce decree are in the Sophia Smith Collection at Smith College; see also Joyce Warren, *Fanny Fern: An Independent Woman* (New Brunswick, N.J.: Rutgers University Press, 1992), 118.
57 See Fern, *Ruth Hall and Other Writings*, 111.
58 See, e.g., Warren, *Fanny Fern*, 124–5.
59 Margaret Fuller, *Memoirs of Margaret Fuller Ossoli*, 2 vols., ed. Ralph W. Emerson, William H. Channing, and James F. Clarke (1884; New York: Burt Franklin, 1972), 1: 236.
60 Fuller, *Memoirs*, 1: 280–1.
61 Susan Warner, *The Wide, Wide World*, 2 vols. (New York: Putnam, 1852), 1: 11.
62 Fanny Fern, *A New Story Book for Children* (New York: Mason Brothers, 1864), 17–18.
63 For a discussion of this issue, see Warren, *Fanny Fern*, 67–70.
64 Martha W. Tyler, *A Book without a Title: or, Thrilling Events in the Life of Mira Dana* (Boston: Printed for the Author, 1856), 251, 224, 189. Hereafter cited parenthetically.
65 Rebecca Harding Davis, *Life in the Iron Mills and Other Stories*, ed. Tillie Olsen (New York: Feminist Press, 1985), 50–1. Hereafter cited parenthetically.
66 Elizabeth S. Phelps, *The Silent Partner* (Boston: James R. Osgood, 1871), 111.
67 Maria A. Ruis de Burton, *The Squatter and the Don*, ed. Rosaura Sánchez and Beatrice Pita (1885; Houston: Arte Público Press, 1992), 66.
68 Fern, *Ruth Hall*, 111.
69 A. Cheree Carlson, *Crimes of Womanhood: Defining Femininity in a Court of Law* (Urbana: University of Illinois Press, 2009), e.g., 8–10.

2
"THE VERY IDEA OF A SLAVE IS A HUMAN BEING IN BONDAGE"

Jeannine Marie DeLombard

For many of us today, the idea of being bought, sold, or held as property seems irreconcilable with being recognized as a human being. Accordingly, there is an assumption that because enslaved African Americans were advertised, auctioned, mortgaged, and deeded alongside tables and chairs, cows and horses, wagons and saddles, they were therefore considered subhuman. Yet, for the most part, such was not the case. Whether they lived with enslaved African Americans in the most intimate domestic relations or merely encountered them at a distance, most Americans understood slaves to be their fellow human beings – politically, socially, or intellectually inferior, perhaps, but unquestionably members of a shared human community. As proslavery lawyer John Howard put it "the very idea of a slave is a human being in bondage."[1]

Our tendency to think of "property" and "human" as mutually exclusive statuses reveals the ongoing impact that the nineteenth-century slavery debate continues to have on legal thought in American culture. One of the most significant strategies – and enduring accomplishments – of a largely evangelical Protestant abolitionist movement was to convince the public that the enslavement of one's fellow human being amounted to a denial that the slave was, in the motto emblazoned on everything from handkerchiefs to stationery, "a man and a brother" or "a woman and a sister."[2] Prior to that transformation in consciousness, slaveholding had been widely seen as saying less about the subhuman status of captives than the inhumanity of their captors.[3] As often unwitting inheritors of this intellectual legacy, we tend to talk about slavery, humanity, and law in much the same terms as our predecessors, unaware of how much the ideas denoted by this shared vocabulary have shifted over time. One way to uncover the meanings obscured by this semantic erosion is to familiarize ourselves more thoroughly with the way earlier Americans spoke about slavery – in legislation and litigation but also in religious tracts, political propaganda, print journalism, and popular literature. This is a cumulative process, requiring us to consider more than memorable extracts from landmark documents like the U.S. Constitution or the *Dred Scott* decision. For these legal texts make sense only when read in the context of the culture in which they were produced and circulated. And seemingly nonlegal works – from the sermons of the Puritan Cotton Mather, to polemics by black activists Frederick Douglass, James McCune Smith, and Ida B. Wells, to popular novels by Harriet Beecher Stowe and Thomas Dixon – articulated even as they shaped popular legal consciousness, which in turn affected municipal, state, and federal law. Through this spectrum of cultural texts, we can see how a diverse American public understood the complicated relationship between the categories of "slave" and "human." Confusing and contradictory as their logic may have been, nineteenth-century Americans were seldom content simply to define one term against the other.

I. Human, person, man

To understand what was at stake in the practice of treating enslaved African Americans as at once property *and* human, it is important to distinguish the word "human" from a word that is too often considered synonymous: "person." Now, as then, it is grammatically correct to use the word "person" to refer to an individual human being, with "persons" and "people" indicating groups of human beings in more or less formal contexts. (Additionally, over the long nineteenth century, "man" often stood in for both the singular and the plural.) Our habit of using "human" and "people" interchangeably with "person" or "persons" in everyday speech explains why today controversy erupts when corporations are credited with personhood or fetuses are denied it. Unacquainted with the specifically legal register in which such assertions are made, many misapprehend such statements as tantamount to claims that fetuses aren't human or that corporations somehow are.

But now, as then, "person," like "property," carries a particular set of legal meanings.[4] "Human," by contrast, was largely irrelevant to nineteenth-century law; it was a term more appropriate to philosophical and scientific discourse.[5] Even the phrase "human rights," which can be traced to the seventeenth century, was originally more of a philosophical and political concept than a legal one – better known, in the wake of the American and French revolutions, as "natural rights" or "the rights of man." As John Bouvier explained in the revised 1852 edition of the nation's first law dictionary, "[i]n law, man and person are not exactly synonymous terms."[6] Whereas "[a]ny human being is a man, whether he be a member of society or not, whatever may be the rank he holds, or whatever may be his age, sex, &c.," legally, "a person is a man considered according to the rank he holds in society, with all the rights to which the place he holds entitles him, and the duties which it imposes." In other words, if a human being is a bundle of blood, bones, and flesh, a person is a bundle of rights and duties. Thus, as Sir William Blackstone had noted in the first volume of his influential *Commentaries on the Laws of England* (1765), "PERSONS . . . are divided by the law into either natural persons, or artificial," explaining that "natural persons are such as the God of nature formed us: artificial are such as created and devised by human laws for the purposes of society and government; which are called corporations or bodies politic."[7] Legally speaking, not all humans are persons, nor are all persons human.

When, in the early twentieth century, the development of international treaties and instruments guaranteeing "human rights" endowed the term "human" with fresh legal significance, its currency was due in no small part to the antebellum slavery debate. (Hence the revisionist title for John Hume's 1905 movement memoir, *Abolitionists, together with Personal Memories of the Struggle for Human Rights, 1830–1864*.[8]) Throughout the twentieth and into the twenty-first centuries, animal rights activism and biotechnology have placed additional legal pressure on the category of the "human," resulting in the term's more frequent appearance in legislation and litigation. Even today, however, "person" continues to bear a legal meaning quite distinct from "human."[9]

To clarify further the different meanings attached to "human" and "person," it may be instructive to contrast the Declaration of Independence, essentially a work of political philosophy, with the U.S. Constitution, the nation's founding legal document. Consider the stirring opening lines of the former: "When in the course of human events. . . ." By beginning the Declaration with these words, future American Philosophical Society president Thomas Jefferson sought to insert the modern world's first human-made republic into a secular, progressive history rather than a divinely ordered one. In a similarly Enlightened bid for legitimation, the Constitution's preamble identifies the source of its political authority as "We the People." But, although the Declaration goes on to make an additional nine references to "people," the Constitution all but abandons the word in favor of "person" or "persons," which together appear more than twenty times. (As we shall see, the Constitution's only other reference to "people" is in passing, as the source of electors for the House of Representatives.) Quite appropriately, the word "human" is entirely absent from the national charter.

If Blackstone was particularly well-known among the Founders and framers, legal forms and usages were by no means out of reach of everyday Americans over the long nineteenth century. As French cultural critic Alexis de Tocqueville observed after his exhaustive 1831 tour of the United States:

> The influence of the legal habits which are common in America extends beyond . . . [formal] limits. . . . Scarcely any question arises in the United States which does not become, sooner or later, a subject of judicial debate; hence all parties are obliged to borrow the ideas, and even the language, usual in judicial proceedings in their daily controversies. . . . The language of the law thus becomes, in some measure, a vulgar tongue; the spirit of the law, which is produced in the schools and courts of justice, gradually penetrates beyond their walls into the bosom of society, where it descends to the lowest classes, so that the whole people contracts the habits and the tastes of the magistrate.[10]

Even as they referred colloquially to human beings as "people" or "persons," antebellum Americans were nevertheless keenly aware of the seismic semantic shifts law could introduce. Most would have appreciated, on some level, that although the slave, as property, was routinely denied the bundle of rights and responsibilities that made one a legal "person," he or she was nevertheless a fellow human being.

Former Maryland slave-turned-orator, author, and editor Frederick Douglass presumed his audience's capacity for appreciating such legal nuances when, in December 1850, he lectured his fellow citizens of Rochester, New York, on "The Nature of Slavery." Delivering on the promise of his address's title, he found slavery's essence to lie in "the legal and social relation of master and slave" and elaborated:

> A master is one . . . who claims and exercises a right of property in the person of a fellow-man. This he does with the force of the law. . . . The law gives the master absolute power over the slave. He may work him, flog him, hire him out, sell him, and, in certain contingencies, *kill* him, with perfect impunity. The slave is a human being, divested of all rights – reduced to the level of a brute – a mere "chattel" in the eye of the law – placed beyond the circle of human brotherhood – cut off from his kind – . . . impiously inserted in a *master's ledger*, with horses, sheep, and swine. In law, the slave has no wife, no children, no country, and no home. He can own nothing, possess nothing, acquire nothing, but what must belong to another.[11]

Particularly noteworthy here is Douglass's identification of law's centrality to the process by which, as his 1845 *Narrative* put it, "a man was made a slave."[12] It is "the force of the law" that transforms a "human being" into a "slave" through the divestiture of his natural rights, which effectively reduces him to the status of a personal possession to be inventoried alongside livestock.[13] The masculine pronoun achieves the rhetorical effect of contrasting the enslaved man, denied any legitimate familial, social, civil, or political status, with the elevated but normative position of his free, white counterpart – the husband, father, citizen, and householder. For

Douglass and his contemporaries, the "Nature of the Slavery" clearly lay in "the legal and social relation of master and slave." For that very reason, the slave, like the legal person, was no natural phenomenon but an artificial construct.

II. Only 3/5 human?

One of the most persistently – and incorrectly – cited proofs that Americans thought of slaves as somehow less than human is Article 1, Section 2 of the U.S. Constitution, also known as the "3/5 Clause," which reads, in part:

> Representatives and direct Taxes shall be apportioned among the several States which may be included within this Union, according to their respective Numbers, which shall be determined by adding to the whole Number of free Persons, including those bound to Service for a Term of Years, and excluding Indians not taxed, three fifths of all other Persons.[14]

With its purpose of establishing the House of Representatives, Article 1, Section 2 provides a calculus for determining each state's representation, which, like direct federal taxes, was to be apportioned to its population. The formula derives the sum for taxation and representation by counting the number of persons deemed "free" (which here specifically includes indentured servants and "Indians" subject to taxation) and adding to that figure three-fifths of the remaining population, which implicitly refers to enslaved African Americans ("Indians not taxed" having already been excluded).

Contrary to popular belief, there is nothing here or elsewhere in the Constitution to say that the framers considered slaves to be "only three-fifths human." For one thing, the fraction refers *not* to the composition of the "persons" under discussion (with slaves ascribed only three-fifths the humanity granted to "free persons") but to the portion of the unfree population eligible to contribute to a given state's "Numbers" (with only three out of every five slaves counted for purposes of taxation and representation). The clause is often referred to as the "3/5 Compromise" because it helped assuage Northern concerns that large slaveholders, increasingly concentrated in the South, would wield disproportionate political influence by having their bound laborers (who could not, of course, vote or hold office) swell the Congressional representation of what would soon be called the "Slave States." The compromise, such as it was, lay in counting slaves at a fraction of the free population and linking that figure to the taxation imposed on the state. The Southern delegates at the Constitutional Convention would have preferred for those "other persons," slaves, to be counted on par with "free persons" for purposes of representation, if not taxation. It would have been a dubious form of equality for enslaved African Americans further to have augmented their captors' formal political power in this way.

Rather than being outraged that slaves were counted at only a 3/5 ratio to "free persons," we might better ask why these unfree "other Persons" should have been counted as such at all. For, as we have seen, persons, whether natural or artificial, are defined as having legal "rights" as well as "duties." Looking at Article 1, Section 2, we can see why tallying the number of "free persons" in the state could be relevant for calculating its correct proportion of congressional representation and taxation. But what does it mean to designate as "persons" some "other," implicitly non-"free," members of the population – that is, slaves? Compromise or no, how could a legal document like the Constitution possibly construe slaves as "persons," given that, as Frederick Douglass reminded his Rochester audience, "the slave is a human being, divested of all rights – reduced to the level of a brute – a mere 'chattel' in the eye of the law"?

To answer these questions, we turn to the clarifications offered by three of the framers, Alexander Hamilton, James Madison, and John Jay, in their essay series, *The Federalist Papers* (1787–88). As the product of an uneasy compromise at the Constitutional Convention, the 3/5 Clause was already controversial when James Madison discussed it in *Federalist* 54. Madison, writing as "Publius," offered a rebuttal to the "objection" that, "considered as property, not as persons," slaves ought to count only toward taxation, not representation.[15] The Virginian Madison, coyly adopting the perspective of "one of our Southern brethren," insisted, "we must deny the fact, that slaves are considered merely as property, and in no respect whatever as persons. The true state of the case is, that they partake of both these qualities" (332). In "being compelled to labor, not for himself, but for a master; in being vendible by one master to another master; and in being subject at all times to be restrained in his liberty and chastised in his body, by the capricious will of another," Publius admitted, "the slave may appear to be degraded from the human rank, and classed with those irrational animals which fall under the legal denomination of property" (332). But, he continued:

> in being protected . . . against the violence of all others, even the master of his labor and his liberty; and in being punishable himself for all violence committed against others – the slave is no less evidently regarded by the law as a member of the society, not as a part of the irrational creation; as a moral person, not as a mere article of property" (332).

Clearly, then, "the federal Constitution . . . decides with great propriety on the case of our slaves, when it views them in the mixed character of persons and of property (332). After all, Publius concluded, "this is in fact their true character. It is the character bestowed on them by the laws under which they live; and it will not be denied, that these are the proper criterion" (332).

As Douglass would do half a century later, Madison emphasized law's central role in the process in which the slave "appear[s] to be degraded from the human rank" by being classified as property alongside "irrational animals." Given law's power to bestow a particular "character" upon a group of people, the slave viewed as property in the eye of the law, "may appear" reduced to the level of a brute. Madison, too, traces the slave's property status to the deprivation of his most basic rights ("being compelled to labor; . . . being vendible . . . ; and . . . being subject to be . . . restrained in his liberty and chastised in his body"). Legally recognized to have, in Douglass's words, "no wife, no children, no country, and no home. . . . [and to] own nothing, possess nothing, acquire nothing," the slave was considered civilly dead in law. It was by this logic, John Bouvier explained in the first edition of his *Law Dictionary*, that enslaved natural persons – that is, human beings – "are sometimes ranked not with persons but with things."[16]

Crucially, however, the slaveholding Virginia politician differed from the former Maryland slave in his determination to resuscitate the personhood of the civilly dead slave. Madison did so by focusing on a definitively *un*civil area of law: that pertaining to crime. For it was in slaves' capacity as the victims and especially as the perpetrators of unlawful "violence" that Madison found a residual legal personhood. Regarding the slave as victim, Madison was careful to distinguish between the disciplinary, albeit potentially lethal, "chastisement" to which enslaved African Americans were routinely subject and the criminal "violence" from which they were occasionally, formally "protected." In fact, courts in slaveholding jurisdictions were periodically called upon to make such distinctions in criminal cases involving enslaved victims. It is in the figure of the enslaved offender, however, that Madison so dramatically reanimates the slave's languishing personhood. Reincarnated as a criminally culpable defendant, the civilly dead slave is no longer to be seen "as a part of the irrational creation" or as "a mere article of property" but "as a member of the society" and "as a moral person." ("Moral" should be read in its archaic sense as "social.") Recall that legal personhood comprises duties as well as rights: accordingly, the officially administered punishment of enslaved offenders offered punitive recognition of their responsibility to the society of which they, in the breach, were retroactively acknowledged to be members.

Committed to advocating immediate abolition and full African American citizenship, Frederick Douglass had excellent rhetorical reasons for ignoring how the criminous slave could disrupt the conventional "legal and social relation of master and slave" as owner and property. For his part, Madison in *Federalist* 54 offered a rationale for the Constitution's seemingly inapt reference to slaves as "persons." Technical as Madison's elaboration of the legal fiction of the slave's "mixed character" was, it highlights criminality's importance in enabling the slave to be "regarded" as something other than property – not merely "by the law" but in the eyes of the American public.[17]

If the federal Constitution followed state and colonial laws in discerning in the slave a uniquely uncivil capacity for personhood, public executions had for well over a century offered the occasion for Americans to display their belief in slaves' humanity. On May 25, 1721, the hanging of emancipated bondman Joseph Hanno, convicted of murdering his wife, prompted prolific Puritan divine Cotton Mather to preach (and later publish) a sermon on behalf of the "Miserable African."[18] Fifteen years earlier, Mather had published *The Negro Christianized: An Essay to Excite and Assist That Good Work, the Instruction of Negro-Servants in Christianity*. In his tract, noting that "it has been cavilled by some . . . Whether the *Negroes* have *Rational Souls*, or no," the minister urged his provincial readers to keep up with the Enlightened times.[19] Turning the insult back upon blacks' detractors, he exhorted his audience to "let that *Bruitish* insinuation never be Whispered any more" (23). Instead, he challenged his fellow colonists, "*Show your selves Men* and let *Rational Arguments* have their Force upon you, to make you treat not as *Bruits*, but as Men, those *Rational Creatures* whom God has made your *Servants*" (4). After all, Mather insisted, "they are *Men*, and not *Beasts* that you have bought, and they must be used accordingly" (23). "'Tis true; They are *Barbarous*," he conceded, before reminding his audience: "But so were our own *Ancestors* . . . if there be any Credit" in the portrait of the "Britons" offered "in *Caesar*[']*s Commentaries*" (23–24). Ultimately, the degree of civilization, like physical appearance, was merely a matter of surface distinction. Here in America, English masters' domestic intimacy with their "negro-servants" ensured that "they are more nearly *Related* unto us, than many others are" (6). With bound Africans living in even closer proximity than Puritan neighbors, Mather enjoined his slaveholding readership to "*Love* thy *Negro*" (6).

Nowhere did Mather and his countrymen more dramatically seek "to do what we can, for the *Souls* of our *Negroes*" than when they offered up prayers and sermons for condemned black criminals, many of whom had been enslaved (6).[20] In his Execution Day oration for Joseph Hanno, Mather followed the Puritan sermon's conventional three-part structure, opening with the relevant biblical text, providing an "Explication" of the "Doctrine" contained therein, and concluding with an "Application" to present circumstances. Hanno had been fourteen years out of slavery when he bludgeoned his wife Nanny with an axe and then, seeking to make her death look like a suicide, slit her throat with a razor.[21] However well established Hanno may have become as a freeman in their Boston community, his hanging provided Mather the ideal occasion to chastise the captive laborers in his audience. Applying his sermon to "the *Ethiopian*, and Other *Slaves* among us," the minister cautioned against a disturbing "*Fondness* for *Freedom*" in their willful neglect of the divinely ordained "Duty" of "*Servitude*."[22] Nor did he hesitate to play on his culture's association of blackness with evil to ask "all Base, and Bitter, and Froward *Husbands*" in his audience whether "the *Black Thing* that you have in Irons here before you, [was] the only One that may be charged with *Murdering his Wife* among us?" (26). Yet the "Wretched *Ethiopian*" stood primarily for

Mather as a man among men (23): Hanno's public punishment provided the minister a welcome opportunity to admonish "those that are in the *Conjugal Relation*" (24) not to "follow Courses which Grieve, and even Kill their *Wives*" – if only by speaking in such a way as to make their "*Words . . . drawn Swords* upon their *Wives*" (26). Observing that the "Glorious CHRIST is a SAVIOUR, whom *Negro's* [*sic*] themselves, yea, the *worst of Sinners* among those poor *Black Outcasts*, may be welcome to," Mather endeavored to affirm the biblical prophecy "*He shall Sprinkle many Nations*" (31). Hanno, the "Miserable African," was clearly of another, indeed, "barbarous," nation, but above all, he was a fellow man whose all-too-human failings could be instructive not merely to "Ethiopians" and "Other Slaves" but to the sharp-tongued Puritan husbands who could trace their ancestry back to the Roman invasions of Britain.

Over the course of the nineteenth century, as incarceration supplanted corporal punishment and the comparatively few remaining executions disappeared behind prison walls, Americans began to see not only enslaved but all criminals as increasingly alien figures.[23] Newly influential scientific theories of mental and racial deviance joined with the burgeoning asylum movement to set the mad, the delinquent, and the criminal apart – often, quite literally – from the rest of society.[24] Not all scientists went as far as polygenists Samuel George Morton, George Gliddon, Josiah Nott, and Louis Agassiz in finding distinct species where others saw only racial difference. Nevertheless, many in the United States drew on a combination of medical and legal rationales to demonstrate blacks' innate inferiority as fellow human beings. To appreciate the pervasiveness of such thinking, we might look to Mather's secular successor, Thomas R. Grey, author of *The Confessions of Nat Turner, the Leader of the Late Insurrection in Southampton, Va.* (1831), an allegedly first-person account of the largest slave uprising in American history. Writing up his cellblock interview with the condemned Turner, the Virginia planter and lawyer conceded that "for natural intelligence and quickness of apprehension, [he] is surpassed by few men I have ever seen."[25] Nevertheless, Grey drew on the emergent scientific discourse of deviance to characterize the slave insurgent's determined strike for freedom as "an awful, and it is hoped, a useful lesson, as to the operations of a mind like his, endeavoring to grapple with things beyond its reach."[26] Two decades later, the American public's enduring fascination with such notions of black deviance led prominent African American physician, pharmacist, and abolitionist James McCune Smith to castigate his white scientific colleagues for creating a "hideous monster of the mind," a "constructive negro . . . that haunts with grim presence the precincts of this republic, shaking his gory locks over legislative halls and family prayers."[27] "Not an actual physical being of flesh and bones and blood," this terrifying racial specter was not – could not be – human.[28]

Whether exploiting or exposing the era's medico-legal discourse of racial alterity, Grey and McCune Smith registered how that discourse participated in a broader Romanticism, which in turn further complicated views of black and especially slave humanity. A shrill proslavery conservative like Grey shared with a strident abolitionist radical like Frederick Douglass a penchant for evoking slavery's excesses in gothic portrayals of grotesque cruelty and psychological terror.[29] Its insistent documentary facticity notwithstanding, the *Narrative of the Life of Frederick Douglass* (1845) introduces the brutal whipping of young Frederick's Aunt Hester as "the blood-stained gate, the entrance to the hell of slavery."[30] If sensationalism could serve propagandists on either side of the slavery debate, Gothicism posed particular rhetorical dangers for literary abolitionists. Portraying their fellow enslaved African Americans as eaten alive by rats, ripped to pieces by dogs, or clawed to death by cats, North Carolina "slave girl" Harriet Jacobs and Alabama slave "driver" James Williams risked degrading such brutalized slave victims from "the human rank" by "class[ing them] with those irrational animals which fall under the legal denomination of property."[31]

With their preference for the ideal over the real, Romantic portrayals could go to the other extreme as well, depicting enslaved African Americans as almost superhuman in their sublime capacity to endure – and transcend – suffering. Harriet Beecher Stowe's internationally best-selling antislavery novel, *Uncle Tom's Cabin* (1852), climaxes with a scene in which the eponymous hero, mortally beaten by the haunted, satanic slaveholder, Simon Legree, uses his final moments to plead with his tormentor. Tom pleads:

> Mas'r, if you was sick, or in trouble, or dying, and I could save ye, I'd *give* ye my heart's blood; and, if taking every drop of blood in this poor old body would save your precious soul, I'd give 'em freely, as the Lord gave his for me. O, Mas'r! don't bring this great sin on your soul! It will hurt you more than 't will me![32]

Rather than brutalized into abject or vengeful subhumanity by his own or others' gothic violence, Stowe's Christ-like Tom is etherealized by his exemplary martyrdom. Tom's death allegorizes Stowe's Romantic racialist hopes for transformed geopolitical race relations.[33] The Preface to the novel's first edition envisions an "Africa" that "began the race of civilization and human progress in the dim, gray dawn of early time, but . . . for centuries, has lain bound and bleeding at the foot of civilized and Christianized humanity, imploring compassion in vain" (xiii). Displaced to America by the slave trade, members of this "exotic race . . . brought with them, and perpetuated to their descendants, a character so essentially unlike the hard and dominant Anglo-Saxon race, as for many years to have won from it only misunderstanding and contempt" (xiii). Through the very patience, generosity, and Christian love displayed by Tom for Legree, Stowe suggests, the long-suffering black collective might now, at long last, model for (and thereby redeem) their racial opposites a softer, more yielding – indeed, feminized – human "character." For, idealized as her enslaved protagonist is, Stowe leaves no doubt about the shared humanity that he represents. Stepping back from Tom's final beating to offer an aside to the reader, the narrator laments: "What brother-man and brother-Christian must suffer, cannot be told us . . . , it so harrows up the soul! And yet, oh my country! these things are done under the shadow of thy laws!" (376).

The shadow cast by American slave law grew even deeper when, five years after Stowe had published *Uncle Tom's Cabin*, the Supreme Court handed down its landmark decision in *Scott v. Sandford* (1857). Purportedly seeking to determine whether Dred Scott had the standing to sue for his freedom on the basis of his master having voluntarily moved him for an extended period from a slave jurisdiction (Missouri) to a free one (first the State of Illinois and then the Wisconsin Territory), Chief Justice Roger B. Taney seized the opportunity to do much more.[34] Not content with merely denying the enslaved Scott the requisite personhood to bring suit in a court of law, Taney rewrote American legal history so as to call into question the rights claims of *all* African Americans, not just civilly dead slaves like Scott. Thus, the case is infamous for Taney's gratuitous observation (*obiter dictum*) that by the time of the nation's founding, Americans of African descent had "been regarded as . . . so far inferior, that they had no rights which the white man was bound to respect."[35] Historically inaccurate, legally heterodox, and politically devastating as it was, Taney's explosive statement created immediate outrage by effectively reducing all African Americans to the level of the slave – hitherto understood, in Douglass's words, as "a human being, divested of all rights."[36] Less well remembered is that the very blurring of legal terminology that allowed Taney to reach this remarkable conclusion also led him, in the same decision, to do what no other national legal authority had ever done in U.S. history: to found doubts about blacks' humanity in the denial of their personhood and citizenship.

Taney's revisionist history accomplishes the retrospective and retroactive denial of African Americans' civil rights through a misleading narrative that pits the racially progressive present against a (falsely) benighted past. Crucially, Taney's dubious account rests upon his insistence that "the words 'people of the United States' and 'citizens' are synonymous terms and mean the same thing" (404) – although, as Justice Benjamin R. Curtis noted in his dissent (576), this was far from true in his own era, much less in the early national period in which he grounded his argument. Taney's conflation of "people" and "citizens" enabled Taney to insert a dualistic logic of inclusion and exclusion in place of the finely calibrated gradation of civil standing and political membership that had structured American society since the Founding.

To support the Court's ruling that Scott "could not be a citizen of the State of Missouri, within the meaning of the Constitution of the United States, and, consequently, was not entitled to sue in its courts" (406), Taney maintained that it was necessary, first, to "inquire who, at that time [the Founding], were recognized as the people or citizens of a State" (407). Taney ignored both legal usage and the Constitution's own clear distinction between a state's "people" (divisible into "free persons" and "other persons") and its citizenry (comprising only a smaller portion of the former – almost certainly excluding "those bound to Service for a Term of Years" and, most likely, those "Indians" subject to be "taxed"). Such imprecision allowed him to assert that "the legislation and histories of the times, and the language used in the Declaration of Independence, show, that neither the class of persons who had been imported as slaves, nor their descendants, whether they had become free or not, were then acknowledged as a part of the people, nor intended to be included in the general words used in that memorable instrument" (407). Specifically, Taney went on to quote the Declaration's famous assertion of self-evident truths ("that all men are created equal; that they are endowed by their Creator with certain unalienable rights; that among them is life, liberty, and the pursuit of happiness"), explaining that the "words . . . would seem to embrace the whole human family, and if they were used in a similar instrument at this day would be so understood" (410). "But," Taney maintained of that earlier period, having invoked Americans' already beloved myth of racial progress, "it is too clear for dispute, that the enslaved African race were not intended to be included, and formed no part of the people who framed and adopted this declaration," given that "the negro race, . . . by common consent, had been excluded from civilized Governments and the family of nations, and doomed to slavery" (410).

Taney's sweeping rejection of black civil rights in the present required a fictive past in which "the unhappy black race were separated from the white by indelible marks, and laws long before established, and were never thought of or spoken of except as property" (410). Like Frederick Douglass but for very different reasons, Taney ignored James Madison's early national emphasis on the foundational importance of slaves' "mixed character" as persons and property – not merely to the composition of the House of Representatives but to that of the Constitution itself. Taney's segregationist rhetoric – of being "included" or "excluded," "acknowledged as a part" or "separated from" – conveniently obscures what Madison and Douglass took for granted: the way in which law "bestowed" a different legal and political "character" on different classes of people. In his mixed character as civilly dead property and criminally culpable person, the criminous slave resembled other Americans in that his or her recognizability as a person in the eyes of the law arose from a minutely calibrated range of statuses and conditions: free, indentured, apprenticed, or enslaved; male or female; adult or minor; foreign or native-born; able-bodied and sound-minded or incapacitated; white, black, mulatto, Indian, or Chinese; propertied or poor; and so on.[37] The nation was full of human beings: some could, on various occasions, appear as persons of various capacities in law; some could be counted as citizens; and some few of these could activate their citizenship through formal political rituals such as voting and office holding. Personhood and citizenship had never been a matter of being in or out – or of being human or not.

Taney found it harder to overlook the present than to rewrite the past. Unable to ignore completely the sliding scale of civil standing and political membership along which most Americans were distributed, Taney conceded that "a person may be a citizen, that is, a member of the community who form the sovereignty, although he exercises no share of the political power, and is incapacitated from holding particular offices" (422). Here, unlike with Douglass, the masculine pronoun was ill chosen, for Taney had in mind those "[white] women and minors, who form a part of the political family" and "cannot vote . . . yet . . . are citizens" (422). Conversely – and quite perversely – Taney went on to maintain, suffrage at the state level did not make "free negroes and mulattoes . . . citizens of the State, and still less of the United States" (422). It is at this point that Taney's purposive terminological imprecision yields its most pernicious effects. Invoking as citizens those disfranchised persons most closely associated with domesticity – women and children – Taney makes membership in the community of the tacitly white family coextensive with that of the polity, whether state or nation.[38] (Little surprise that he cites laws against intermarriage to support his broader argument.) No matter that women and minors, precisely as a result of participating in conventional families as wives and children, often ceded their legal and political rights to the male citizen who represented them as husband and father.[39] (For much of the nineteenth century, unmarried adult women could claim a legal personhood unavailable to their married counterparts.) Yet, rather than acknowledging such gradations of status, Taney throughout the *Dred Scott* decision speaks of inclusion or exclusion from a series of normally distinct but here overlapping, communities: the individual "State" and "the United States," as well as "civilized Governments and the family of nations" and, ultimately, "the white [race]." In his repeated recourse to the word "family" to characterize these various groupings at different moments in the decision, Taney is able to conflate the fictive legal persons and citizens comprised by the polity with those natural persons – human beings, with or without civil or political rights – comprised by the conventional family. The result of Taney's promiscuous mixture of terms is the U.S. Supreme Court's unprecedented but authoritative expression of legal doubt about blacks' membership in the entire "human family" due to their exclusion as persons and citizens from the domestic community of the (white) nation and thus the family of nations. Contrary to the ruling's myth of national racial progress, it was neither the Declaration of Independence nor the U.S. Constitution that had removed "the enslaved African race" from the "embrace" of "the whole human family" but, rather, a legal "instrument" of Taney's own "day" – in his own hand, in fact – that introduced that wholesale racial exclusion into American law and culture.

III. Emancipation and abolition

Perhaps the most powerful evidence – polygenists and the *Dred Scott* decision notwithstanding – that Americans continued to have little doubt about slaves' humanity lies in the reunited nation's post–Civil War response to emancipation and abolition. Rather than finding courts and legislatures struggling to recognize and accommodate the newly declared humanity of some four million formerly enslaved African Americans in the aftermath of the Civil War, we see lawyers, judges, and politicians, along with everyday people, striving to understand how the end of slavery had transformed personhood and citizenship for *all* Americans.

The touchstone for these efforts were the Reconstruction Amendments. Speaking of "persons" and "citizens" – not "humans" – the Thirteenth, Fourteenth, and Fifteenth Amendments to the U.S. Constitution seemed to eliminate some of the status confusion that had arisen from the legal fact of race slavery. By abolishing "slavery" and "involuntary servitude" ("except as a punishment for crime"), the Thirteenth Amendment (1865) ratified the abolitionist axiom that "human property" was an oxymoron.[40] (This state of affairs is once again changing, however, with the rise of biotechnology and the new medico-legal discourse of property rights in the human body and its component parts.) Introducing birthright citizenship, the Fourteenth Amendment (1868) made that status applicable at the federal as well as state levels. The amendment continued to distinguish between citizens and persons, protecting only the former from having their "privileges or immunities" abridged by a state, while shielding "any person" from being "deprive[d] . . . of life, liberty, or property, without due process of law" and being denied "the equal protection of the laws."[41] The Fifteenth Amendment (1870) concerned itself only with citizens – and adult male ones at that – affirming that "the right of citizens of the United States to vote shall not be denied or abridged by the United States or by any State on account of race, color, or previous condition of servitude."[42]

These changes to the federal Constitution occurred against the backdrop of widespread racial repression on the state level. Across the United States, emancipation and abolition were curtailed by so-called Black Codes designed to deny African Americans many of the duties and rights associated not just with citizenship but with the most basic legal personhood.[43] A succession of state and local laws excluded blacks from fulfilling civic duties such as voting, serving on juries and militia, or holding office while denying them the freedom of movement, assembly, or contract. Against this trend, the Civil Rights Acts of 1875 represented an effort to concretize the principles set forth in the Reconstruction Amendments. Yet it was not long before a series of precedent-setting court cases effectively withdrew federal protection from African Americans, rendering them vulnerable to hostile local actors, municipal authorities, and state governments. This litigation reached its nadir with *Plessy v. Ferguson* (1896), which upheld the constitutionality of "equal but separate accommodations" for what were characterized as distinct black and white races.[44] The extralegal analogue to these developments was the campaign of racial terrorism in which white supremacists across the nation enthusiastically took up lynching and other forms of violent repression to counteract whatever legal, political, and social gains African Americans had achieved in the Civil War and Reconstruction.

For the most part, postwar legislation and litigation continued to speak of "persons" and "citizens." Yet the assumption of a shared humanity was unsettled by the increasing prevalence of quasi scientific allusions to "race," which underwrote distinctions among "persons" and "citizens" that seemed less in keeping with the egalitarian thrust of the Reconstruction Amendments than with the status quo antebellum. Indeed, Supreme Court Justice Henry Billings Brown, writing for the majority in *Plessy*, looked back to *Roberts v. Boston* (1850), an antebellum school segregation case, to affirm Massachusetts Supreme Court Chief Justice Lemuel Shaw's ruling that "all persons, without distinction of age or sex, birth or color, origin or condition, are equal before the law." Crucially, however, Brown went on to quote Shaw's proviso: "But, when this great principle comes to be applied to the actual and various conditions of persons in society, it will not warrant the assertion that men and women are legally clothed with the same civil and political powers, and that children and adults are legally to have the same functions and be subject to the same treatment"—and so on, implicitly, down the list of statuses.[45]

Billings' retrograde ruling prompted former Kentucky slaveholder Justice John Marshall Harlan to dissent. Harlan reminded the court – and the nation – that the Reconstruction Amendments "removed the race line from our governmental systems," yielding a Constitution that "is color-blind, and neither knows nor tolerates classes among citizens," ensuring that "the law regards man as man, and takes no account of his surroundings or of his color when his civil rights as guaranteed by the supreme law of the land are involved."[46] Earlier, dissenting in the *Civil Rights Cases* (1883), which struck down the Civil Rights Act of 1875, Harlan was prompted by the postwar nation's growing tendency toward a race-based "class tyra[n]ny" to maintain that "if the constitutional amendments be enforced according to the intent with which . . . they were adopted, there cannot be, in this republic, any class of human beings in practical subjection to another class."[47]

Harlan's turn from the legal language of "man," "person," and "citizen" to a philosophical – indeed, ethical – invocation of "human beings" speaks to the seriousness of the racial crisis facing the nation. This discursive turn was even more pronounced in the literature of the period. In *The Red Record* (1895), an early pamphlet in her influential antilynching campaign, investigative journalist Ida B. Wells regularly refers to "persons." Yet she far more frequently and urgently deploys some version of the word "human" to protest the extrajudicial torture and killing of her fellow African Americans, usually men falsely accused of interracial sexual harassment or assault. "Humanity abhors the assailant of womanhood, and this charge upon the Negro at once placed him beyond the pale of human sympathy," Wells notes before offering case-by-case rebuttals of the rape pretext.[48] Repeatedly, she strives to bring her victimized subjects back into the pale by evoking "the sight of a human body being burned to ashes," "human beings burnt alive," or the torture of "a human being by burning his eyes out [and] by thrusting a red-hot iron down his throat."[49]

It is not just moderates and liberals whom we find introducing "humanity" into discussion of the racial crisis that preoccupied turn-of-the-century America. Thomas A. Dixon, apparently as committed to defending lynching as a method of white supremacist social control as Wells was to opposing it, joined her in acknowledging the era's new understanding of the "negro" as "place[d] . . . outside the pale of a human being."[50] Rather than challenge this comparatively recent view of African Americans, however, the conservative novelist seemed to affirm it. Early in *The Leopard's Spots* (1902), the first volume in his Ku Klux Klan trilogy, Dixon has Baptist minister Rev. John Dunham admonish the avowedly racist Confederate veteran Tom Camp, "Tom, it's a funny thing to me that as good a Christian as you are should hate a nigger so. He's a human being. It's not right" – only to have the heroic Camp demur, "He may be human, Preacher; I don't know. . . . I have my doubts" (28). Camp's doubts seem to prevail when, toward novel's end, the Preacher himself insists that "the Negro is a human donkey" – capable of training but ineligible for mating with the superior race (464).

IV. Conclusion

Taking the term "human" to be synonymous with "person" makes it easy to condemn the slaveholding United States – an undemanding and largely unproductive moral exercise. But detaching "human" from "person" requires us to think far more deeply about not just slavery but the complex interrelationship of nineteenth-century American law and culture. For if Americans did not define "slave" by simply opposing that concept to "human," they *did* tend to understand "citizen" and even "person" in definitive opposition to "slave." With the end of slavery came the urgent need to reconstruct, in the most fundamental ways, the meanings of personhood and citizenship for all Americans. Not surprisingly, perhaps, African Americans' formal, collective entry into the legal statuses of person and of citizen was accompanied – indeed, countered – by an increasingly virulent scientific discourse of race that cast aspersions on black humanity as never before, from the brutal mob violence of lynching to legally sanctioned segregation.

If one legacy of abolitionism is our tendency to see "human" and "property" as mutually exclusive categories, another may be our ongoing tendency to view law through a critical lens. For antebellum Americans, to know how the slave appeared in "the eye of the law" was by no means to adopt the law's perspective. Quite the contrary, to have such knowledge was to direct incisive popular scrutiny toward law, its sources of authority, representatives, procedures, and effects. In a nineteenth-century United States in which law and culture were interanimate, the nature of slavery lay not only in legal artifice but in cultural arts. The inseparably "legal and social relation of master and slave" articulated itself not merely through statute books, judicial decisions, and municipal ordinances but in novels, poems, tracts, plays, magazines, newspapers, and sermons. The challenge was not simply to change American law so profoundly that it would no longer tolerate having slavery in its sight; it was also to change American views of those racially identified with slavery – African Americans – in order to recognize them not merely as humans or even as legal persons but as fellow citizens, fully vested with natural as well as civil rights. That challenge continues today.

Notes

1 *United States v. Amy*, 24 F. Cas. 792, 797 (C.C.D. Va. 1859). On the importance of humanity to enslavement, see Saidiya V. Hartman, *Scenes of Subjection: Terror, Slavery, and Self-Making in Nineteenth-Century America* (New York: Oxford University Press, 1997); Ariela J. Gross, *Double Character: Slavery and Mastery in the Antebellum Southern Courtroom* (Princeton, N.J.: Princeton University Press, 2000); and Edlie L. Wong, *Neither Fugitive nor Free: Atlantic Slavery, Freedom Suits, and the Legal Culture of Travel* (New York: New York University Press, 2009), 77–182.

2 See Phillip Lapsansky, "Graphic Discord: Abolitionist and Antiabolitionist Images," in *The Abolitionist Sisterhood: Women's Political Culture in Antebellum* America, ed. Jean F. Yellin and John C. Van Horne (Philadelphia: Library Company of Philadelphia, 1998), 203–9.

3 Philip Gould, *Barbaric Traffic: Commerce and Antislavery in the Eighteenth-Century Atlantic World* (Cambridge, Mass.: Harvard University Press, 2003). As the current volume was in press, Walter Johnson made a similar point in "To Remake the World: Slavery, Racial Capitalism, and Justice," *Boston Review*, 26 October 2016, http://bostonreview.net/race/walter-johnson-slavery-human-rights-racial-capitalism.

4 On the slave's indispensability to nineteenth-century thinking about these purportedly opposite but interdependent legal concepts, see Stephen M. Best, *The Fugitive's Properties: Law and the Poetics of Possession* (Chicago: University of Chicago Press, 2004).

5 See, however, Justinian's distinction of the law of nations (*ius gentium*) from both natural law and civil law, as law 'common only to human beings among themselves.' Justinian, *The Digest of Justinian*, ed. Alan Watson (Philadelphia: University of Pennsylvania Press, 2009), I: 1.

6 John Bouvier, *Law Dictionary: Adapted to the Constitution and Laws of the United States of America and of the Several States of the American Union*, rev. 4th ed. (Philadelphia: Childs & Peterson, 1852), s.v. "person."

7 William Blackstone, *Commentaries on the Laws of England*, 4 vols., ed. Wilfrid Prest (1765–69; Oxford: Oxford University Press, 2016), 1: 284–5, 1: 84.

8 John F. Hume, *Abolitionists, Together with Personal Memories of the Struggle for Human Rights, 1830–1864* (New York: Putnam, 1905).

9 The strict "legalistic" understanding of "person" as a metaphor for law's subject is necessarily permeated, however, by philosophical, religious, and scientific discourses identifying personhood with humanness; see Ngaire Naffine, *Law's Meaning of Life: Philosophy, Religion, Darwin, and the Legal Person* (Portland, Ore.: Hart, 2009).

10 Alexis Tocqueville, *Democracy in America*, trans. Henry Reeve (1835; New York: Bantam-Random House, 2000), 323–4.

11 Frederick Douglass, *My Bondage and My Freedom*, ed. Henry Louis Gates Jr. (1855; New York: Library of America, 1994), 103–452, 419.

12 Frederick Douglass, *Narrative of the Life of Frederick Douglass, an American Slave* (1845; New York: Penguin, 1985), 107.

13 In some jurisdictions, law made human beings into chattels, or movable personal property; in others, real estate. Thomas Morris, *Southern Slavery and the Law, 1619–1860* (Chapel Hill: University of North Carolina Press, 1999), 61–80.

14 U.S. Const. art. 1, §2.

15 James Madison, Alexander Hamilton, and John Jay, *The Federalist Papers* (New York: Penguin, 1988), 332. Hereafter cited parenthetically.

16 John Bouvier, *Law Dictionary* (Philadelphia: Johnson, 1839), s.v. "person."

17 See Jeannine M. DeLombard, *In the Shadow of the Gallows: Race, Crime, and American Civic Identity* (Philadelphia: University of Pennsylvania Press, 2012).
18 Cotton Mather, *Tremenda. The Dreadful Sound with Which the Wicked Are to Be Thunderstruck. In a Sermon Delivered unto a Great Assembly, in Which Was Present, a Miserable African, Just Going to Be Executed for a Most Inhumane and Uncommon Murder* (Boston: Green, 1721).
19 Cotton Mather, *The Negro Christianized: An Essay to Excite and Assist That Good Work, the Instruction of Negro-Servants in Christianity* (Boston: Green, 1706), 23. Hereafter cited parenthetically.
20 See Daniel A. Cohen, *Pillars of Salt, Monuments of Grace: New England Crime Literature and the Origins of American Popular Culture, 1674–1860* (New York: Oxford University Press, 1998).
21 Mark S. Weiner, *Black Trials: Citizenship from the Beginnings of Slavery to the End of Caste* (New York: Knopf, 2004), 33–50.
22 Mather, *Tremenda*, 27.
23 Karen Halttunen, *Murder Most Foul: The Killer and the Gothic Imagination* (Cambridge, Mass.: Harvard University Press, 1998); Caleb Smith, *The Prison and the American Imagination* (New Haven, Conn.: Yale University Press, 2009).
24 David J. Rothman, *The Discovery of the Asylum: Social Order and Disorder in the New Republic*, rev. ed. (Boston: Little, Brown, 1990).
25 Thomas R. Gray, "The Confessions of Nat Turner, the Leader of the Late Insurrection in Southampton, VA," in *The Confessions of Nat Turner and Related Documents*, ed. Kenneth S. Greenberg (Boston: Bedford-St. Martin's, 1996), 54.
26 Ibid., 41.
27 James M. Smith, *The Works of James McCune Smith: Black Intellectual and Abolitionist*, ed. John Stauffer (New York: Oxford University Press, 2006), 86.
28 Ibid.
29 See Teresa Goddu, *Gothic America: Narrative, History, and Nation* (New York: Columbia University Press, 1997).
30 Douglass, *Narrative*, 51.
31 See Harriet A. Jacobs, *Incidents in the Life of a Slave Girl, Written by Herself* (1861; Cambridge, Mass.: Harvard University Press, 2000), 49; James Williams, *Narrative of James Williams, an American Slave* (1838; Baton Rouge: Louisiana State University Press, 2013), 40–1.
32 Harriet Beecher Stowe, *Uncle Tom's Cabin: Authoritative Text, Backgrounds, and Contexts, Criticism* (1852; New York: Norton, 2010), 376. Hereafter cited parenthetically.
33 George M. Frederickson, *The Black Image in the White Mind: The Debate on Afro-American Character and Destiny, 1817–1914* (Middletown, Conn.: Wesleyan University Press, 1987), 97–129.
34 See Don E. Fehrenbacher, *The Dred Scott Case: Its Significance in American Law and Politics* (New York: Oxford University Press, 2001).
35 *Dred Scott v. Sandford*, 60 U.S. 393, 407 (1856).
36 That enslaved as well as other African Americans retained, as legal persons, the right to due process when formally charged of a crime is evident from Taney's ruling in *United States v. Amy*, possibly the most thorough legal examination of slave personhood on record. *United States v. Amy*, 24 F. Cas. 792 (C.C.D. Va. 1859).
37 Barbara Y. Welke, *Law and the Borders of Belonging in the Long Nineteenth Century United States* (Cambridge, UK: Cambridge University Press, 2011).
38 See Priscilla Wald, *Constituting Americans: Cultural Anxiety and Narrative Form* (Durham, N.C.: Duke University Press, 1995), 42; for a groundbreaking analysis of humanness and personhood in *Scott v. Sandford* and *Cherokee Nation v. Georgia* (1831), see 20–47.
39 This dynamic was oddly reproduced in the case itself, where the hitherto separate freedom suits of Harriet Scott and Etheldred Scott were consolidated under that of the latter, who was also father of the couple's two daughters, Eliza and Lizzie. The fact profile of Harriet Scott's case was the stronger of the two and, as a woman, she was more representative of Missouri's often successful freedom suit litigants, whose change in status could extend to their children, in keeping with the legal doctrine which derived an enslaved child's status from that of the mother. Lea VanderVelde, *Mrs. Dred Scott: A Life on Slavery's Frontier* (New York: Oxford University Press, 2009), 231, 258, 277.
40 U.S. Const. amend XIII, §1.
41 U.S. Const. amend XIV, §1.
42 U.S. Const. amend XV, §1.

43 Eric J. Foner, *Reconstruction: America's Unfinished Revolution, 1863–1877* (New York: HarperCollins, 2002).
44 *Plessy v. Ferguson*, 163 U.S. 537, 540 (1896).
45 Id. at 544.
46 Id. at 555, 559.
47 *Civil Rights Cases*, 109 U.S. 3, 62 (1883).
48 Ida B. Wells-Barnett, *A Red Record. Tabulated Statistics and Alleged Causes of Lynchings in the United States, 1892–1893–1894* (Chicago: Donohue and Henneberry, 1895), 1.
49 Ibid., 60, 95, 40.
50 Thomas Dixon, Jr., *The Leopard's Spots: A Romance of the White Man's Burden – 1865–1900* (New York: Doubleday, 1902), 395.

3
THE CORPORATION AND THE TRANSFORMATION OF AMERICAN CULTURE

*Aaron Ritzenberg**

In the second half of the nineteenth century, as the corporation was becoming a dominant force in American life, American writers responded to its torrid growth with praise and trepidation. One of the most pervasive manifestations of the corporation – the railroad – was both celebrated and feared.[1] In 1868, Walt Whitman sang of the "mighty railroad" as one of "the great achievements of the present," a wonder that "spann'd" the New World.[2] But in his 1901 novel, *The Octopus*, Frank Norris described the corporate railroad as "the soulless force, the iron-hearted power" – an unrelenting monster that ravaged and consumed the landscape "from horizon to horizon."[3] Whitman's railroad symbolizes not only industry but "modern" expansiveness. For Norris, the railroad stands as the "symbol of a vast power" that has no soul and an unfeeling heart. Both writers suggest that the railroad's significance resides in its capacity as an organized structure that offers unprecedented reach and unrelenting growth. Put another way, the railroad is the corporation made visible, a creation symbolizing the energy and power of a new age, yet also looming with the presence of an impersonal, menacing giant. Chroniclers of the nineteenth century like Whitman and Norris tempt us to examine the corporation by studying its most spectacular examples – like the railroad – as organizations to be revered or condemned. But the story of the corporation requires a far more complex accounting than what is revealed by such apparently polarized responses.

If we focus only on narratives of corporate progress and corporate doom, we risk losing sight of the more deeply embedded cultural shifts generated by the corporation. If we examine only the most visible aspects of the corporation – the mighty industries controlled by robber barons – we miss the way that the technical instrument of incorporation led to an organizational culture that became naturalized in the practices of ordinary individuals. The corporation brought forth not only the loud and steady hum of American big business, with its tales of heroism and villainy, but also new notions of personhood and agency. The daily rhythms, habits of mind, and personal yearnings of working individuals were all influenced by a structural change so pervasive and fundamental that, like the atmosphere itself, it often went unnoticed and unnamed. Individuals, it seems, could apprehend the corporation only by its effects. As the literature of the time reveals, Americans often struggled to find the words to describe the corporate age.

In 1869, the prominent writer and railroad regulator Charles Francis Adams Jr. wrote that "the system of corporate life . . . is a new power, for which our language contains no name. We know what aristocracy, autocracy, democracy are; but we have no word to express government by moneyed corporations."[4] Adams sensed that his culture was experiencing radical transformations, but he recognized that no one could articulate the inscrutable ways of the force driving these changes. "[C]orporate life" is a "system" that exists beyond language; Adams' America had not yet come to terms with this sublime power. Adams was well aware, though, that this "new power" was not only changing business structure but also shaping "government" and "life." He realized that the corporate form – the mode of organizational structure designed to administrate modern businesses – was transforming the deep ways that Americans conceived of themselves and their places in the world.

At the beginning of the nineteenth century, only decades before Adams wrote, the United States was an agrarian society with a dispersed population whose daily interactions were typically intimate and familiar. By the end of the century, America was an industrialized nation where people were concentrated in major urban centers and relationships were often structured by bureaucratic networks. Business corporations permeated the nation; corporate form and logic not only governed the financial and industrial worlds but also organized the entire social order. The legal and economic entity of the corporation established new hierarchies and systems of power, changed the roles of government and families, forged new forms of relationships among individuals, and altered basic notions of time and selfhood. The United States was on its way to becoming the world's first corporate society.

I. The corporate form

The word "corporation" (from the Latin *corporare* – to embody) referred, at first, to any group of people united as a body for a single purpose. In Europe, early forms of nonbusiness corporations – guilds, colonies, and townships – go back to classical times. In the Middle Ages, universities and churches organized themselves as corporations. The public charters of these early corporations granted life to the organizations beyond the death of their founders. This relative immortality would become one of the hallmarks of the modern corporation. By the early seventeenth century in Britain, the word "corporation" gained the legal sense of "an artificial person created by a royal charter, prescription, or act of legislature, and having authority to preserve certain rights in perpetual succession."[5] British common law, which underlies much of American law, makes careful distinction between "natural person" and "artificial person."[6] While the category of "natural person" referred to human beings, "artificial person" was a category deployed so that governments, churches, and corporations might enter into contracts, pay taxes, and be accountable to the law. Early business corporations owed their artificial personhood to a sovereign power that granted them specific legal rights in return for serving the public good. With a charter, business was conducted under the name of the corporation, and the law dealt with the entity rather than with the individuals who formed it.

In the United States, even before corporations gained constitutional rights over the course of the nineteenth century, they had distinct advantages over family businesses and partnerships. The special charters issued by the government often granted monopoly power to corporations, freeing them from competitive pressures. Because the corporation existed as a separate entity from its owners, it could outlive them and stay intact through multiple generations. Most important, corporations were usually granted limited liability, meaning that individual owners and investors were not personally responsible for the debts of the business. When individuals invested in a corporation, they risked only the money they invested, not their personal assets. Owners could escape responsibility for a corporation's financial obligations, errors, negligence, or malfeasance.

The corporate form would eventually allow single business firms to contain and control many of the operations that had previously been performed by multiple firms and governed by an unpredictable market. The corporate form began proliferating among American businesses in the 1790s and early decades of the nineteenth century.[7] The movement toward widespread incorporation started in the North and became a national phenomenon by the 1830s.[8] Corporate businesses innovated sophisticated forms of financing to raise huge amounts of capital. Corporations issued stocks, bonds, and hybrid securities; they took out bank loans, bought government bonds, secured insurance policies, and invested in other corporations. Corporate businesses were soon able to benefit from their size. Beginning around 1840, large corporations used the newly built railroad and telegraph systems to profit from economies of scale: when dealing in large volumes, corporations decreased the unit costs of production. Corporations expanded even more through vertical integration, growing the scope of their business by acquiring suppliers and distributors. The corporate form thus facilitated a firm's capacity to marshal a larger and more disparate set of resources than previously feasible. Increasingly profitable corporations were also able to extend their investments in research and development, yielding new manufacturing processes and new materials.[9]

Changes in the organizational structure of American businesses brought changes in the way that capitalism functioned. As the influential business historian Alfred Chandler wrote, "[T]he visible hand of management replaced what Adam Smith referred to as the invisible hand of market forces."[10] For Adam Smith, market fluctuations occurred beyond the influence of any individual actor; in a modern corporate system, however, managers could manipulate production and distribution in such a way that economic forces were no longer beyond the reach of human influence. Managers designed systems that were newly powerful and profitable, yet many of the individuals caught within these systems – managers and workers alike – felt alienated by their abstract relationship to a network whose hierarchical structure would outlive any individual within it. When individuals tried to weigh the economic benefits of corporations against their social costs, their considerations extended beyond the realm of business. While American producers were concerned that they might not be able to compete with large corporations, so, too, were owners and workers afraid that the corporation might degrade the dignity of the American laborer.[11]

II. Corporate expansion in nineteenth-century America

To fully understand the tension between the promise of economic progress and the fear of social doom that characterized American attitudes toward corporations in the nineteenth century, it is important to understand the role of the corporation in America before 1800. From its earliest days, America had an unsettled relationship with corporations: corporate operations contained the seed of democratic practice, but they also relied on undemocratic systems of exploitation. The colonies were themselves "conceived in corporation," as one historian puts it.[12] The Virginia Company – incorporated by King James I in 1606 – settled the New World with the Jamestown Colony in 1607. This corporation created the first governing legislative body of Europeans in America; its members voted on leadership and company policy, and the corporation thus became a template for procedural democracy. The Massachusetts Bay Colony, too, began as a trading corporation under a 1629 charter issued by Charles I. When John Winthrop turned stockholders into voting subjects, company meetings operated with the rudiments of representative government. As historian Stephen Innes writes, "[A] commercial charter metamorphosed into the frame of government for a state."[13] Massachusetts Bay was never a democracy, but it did reject hereditary and feudal governance.[14]

Yet even as corporations provided a framework for democratic governance, they also epitomized the ways that wealth and power fed off society's most vulnerable individuals. Many of the settlers in Virginia were conscripted from among Britain's dispossessed tenants, imprisoned vagrants, and petty criminals.[15] The Virginia Company had a corporate formation that "made conditions for servants worse in Virginia than in England," resulting in servants who frequently died working for abusive landowners who did not abide by the customs and laws that controlled the British system of servitude.[16] The historian Edmund Morgan writes that Virginia in the early seventeenth century used "a system of labor that treated men as things," setting the stage for slavery.[17]

If the American system of governance has corporate roots, its origins also lie in the revolt against corporate power. In colonial America, most businesses were owned and run by families or partnerships that opposed corporations for fear that the corporations monopolized commodity markets. Leading American intellectuals followed their British and French counterparts in holding anticorporate views.[18] The Boston Tea Party arose from economic opposition to the East India Company – a transnational corporation that had successfully influenced the government to deny local competitors a fair market.[19] American Revolutionaries conflated massive corporate power with the crown and aristocratic privilege. The defeat of the British was, for many Americans, not just a victory over political tyranny but also a triumph over British corporate control.[20]

Conveners at the Constitutional Convention knew that the politics and economics of the new nation would be intertwined. American leaders viewed corporations as both necessary engines of the economy and potentially undemocratic entities. They debated whether or not the new federal government should have the power to grant corporate charters, yet the United States Constitution makes no mention of corporations.[21] What emerged was a system in which state legislatures issued special charters to incorporate businesses that would serve the public good.[22]

State-issued corporate charters often granted monopoly power and limited liability for a specific amount of time; in return, the corporations were highly regulated.[23] Just as the British monarchy had granted charters to massive trading companies in order to further the colonial ends of the British government, states granted corporate charters to advance government projects. The historian William G. Roy explains that the state depended on external resources to fund its much needed infrastructure: "While fledgling American governments were limited by both the low level of commercialization and the strong antitax sentiment that had helped fuel rebellion against colonial rule, the corporate form gave them access to the resources of the world of finance capitalism."[24] Granting corporate charters allowed state governments to navigate the narrow path that lay between their citizens' mistrust of centralized authority and the clear need for public works projects. Achille Murat, a French observer of American culture, wrote in 1833:

> [M]anufactures, mines, and improvements of every sort . . . roads, canals, bridges, railroads, – in short, all public works are constructed and carried into effect in the same manner. All these societies are corporations, having a civil and political existence . . . All of them employ lawyers, engravers, engineers, &c., &c., and become an immense source of prosperity.[25]

Murat noticed that the corporation was both a public good and a profit-making enterprise. Impediments that might have checked corporate growth in other countries – unwieldy centralized governments, landed aristocracy, the church – did not exist in the United States. Before 1790, state governments had incorporated about thirty businesses; by 1861, state governments had incorporated over twenty-two thousand businesses.[26]

Commentators in the early nineteenth century realized the uniqueness of the corporate form that was shaping the American economy; they were often eager to articulate the various ways that American systems of law and economy differed from those of England. In 1832, the American legal scholars Joseph Angell and Samuel Ames wrote:

> What is done by England by combination is most generally done by a combination of individuals, established by mere articles of agreement. On the other hand, what is done here by the co-operation of several persons, is, in the greater number of instances, the result of a consolidation effected by an express act or charter of incorporation . . . [W]e cannot but be impressed with a deep sense of the importance of this law in our own country [because] in no country have corporations been multiplied to so great an extent, as in our own.[27]

The American corporation gave Angell and Ames senses of distinction and national pride. The historian Kenneth Lipartito explains that American "openness to the corporation was no simple legal quirk. . . . Corporations came to be seen as little republics in the tradition of voluntary self-rule."[28] The corporate form symbolized not only the importance of the American economy on a global scale but also the strength of a political system built not on inherited custom but on the written word of explicit law.

However, consumers did not always feel the benefits of the corporate form. In the first half of the nineteenth century, debates about corporations grew in intensity and frequency. These debates frequently involved questions of whether or not a corporation provided a sufficient public good in return for the special legal dispensations it received. For example, in 1818, the Pennsylvania Senate passed an act incorporating the Lehigh Navigation Company, granting it sole jurisdiction on the Lehigh River for mining and transportation purposes. The Company served a public good by opening up mountain streams that had been difficult to navigate. But ten years later, critics accused the Company of using its monopoly powers to discourage competition in coal mining. The legislature engaged in a fierce debate, arguing whether or not a charter granting a virtual monopoly remained necessary for a business that was stable enough to secure private funding.[29]

American consumers were especially wary of corporations that seemed to use "monopoly" power to influence prices.[30] In 1835, a group of journeyman artisans in Newark, New Jersey, declared:

> We entirely disapprove of the incorporation of Companies, for carrying on manual mechanical business, inasmuch as we believe their tendency is to eventuate and produce monopolies, thereby crippling the energies of individual enterprise, and invading the rights of smaller capitalists.[31]

The artisans use the language of the American revolutionary spirit, pitting "individual" "smaller capitalists" against the "invading" imperial force of the corporation. These artisans, like many American producers who struggled to compete against corporations, were not antibusiness; rather, they feared that corporations were functioning mainly to concentrate power and help the rich grow richer.

The 1820s and 1830s saw the rise of conflicts over corporate charters.[32] The anticorporate spirit of Andrew Jackson's party stemmed from an objection to the privileges and corruption that permeated a system of special incorporation. In his 1835 book, *What Is a Monopoly?*, the attorney Theodore Sedgwick declared:

> Every corporate grant is directly in the teeth of the doctrine of equal rights, for it gives to one set of men the exercise of privileges which the main body can never enjoy. Every such grant is equally adverse to the fundamental maxim of free trade for it carries on its face that no one but the corporators are free to carry on the trade in question, with the advantages which the charter confers.[33]

Sedgwick suggested that special incorporation was un-American at its core – an affront to both "equal rights" and "free trade." But even with the widespread distrust of the charter system, many wage earners "clamored for shares" of stock, eager to invest in powerful companies.[34]

Instead of seeking an end to corporations in the United States, many critics sought to restore fairness by allowing universal access to the corporate form.[35] Even some of the harshest critics thought that the problems of corruption and monopolism might be solved by making the process of incorporation more democratic. George Taylor, a critic of coal corporations, wrote in 1833, "Let us all be placed upon an equal footing. The door must either be thrown wide open or be entirely closed."[36] After continued public pressure from critics, the door to incorporation opened slowly with laws of general incorporation.[37] The laws – which most states adopted by 1875 – conferred corporate status on any organization that abided by certain rules.[38] Instead of granting special charters one at a time, state governments detailed the circumstances under which individuals could incorporate. Under laws of general incorporation, any privileges or immunities that came with incorporation had to be available to anyone willing to file with the state. General incorporation laws reduced the image of special privilege and often made industries more competitive by making the corporate form's many legal and financial benefits available to those who would compete.

The relationships between the corporation and the state and between the corporation and the public changed dramatically under laws of general incorporation. In the age of special incorporation, when corporations existed to serve the public good, the state granted a corporation authority and purpose. Laws of general incorporation eventually removed the state from the inner workings and objectives of corporate businesses; in turn, corporations became increasingly widespread and autonomous.[39] Gradually, states replaced the limited terms of corporations with perpetual terms. As the legal scholar Gregory Mark puts it, "[T]he transformation of the private law of corporations from 1819 to the 1920s is best described as a move from a circumstance in which a corporation could do only those things specifically allowed by its charter to one in which a corporation could do anything not specifically prohibited by it."[40] Whereas corporations once had to demonstrate a "clear benefit to the larger community," the new belief was that "the larger community was served by strengthening the individuals who formed corporations."[41] Under laws of general incorporation, corporations moved from the realm of public franchise to the realm of private interest. The American legal system encouraged the growth of a national market through its hospitality toward American business interests. So hastened, too, the tremendous growth of corporate political power.

III. The evolution of corporate personhood

By the end of the nineteenth century, corporations began to be assigned constitutional rights that on their face had been written for individuals. Because the Constitution makes no mention of corporations, it was up to the states and the courts to determine their legal status. Legal cases defined and clarified corporate power; among the most important were *Dartmouth College v. Woodward*[42] (1819) and *Santa Clara v. Southern Pacific Railway*[43] (1886). In *Dartmouth College v. Woodward*, the Supreme Court limited the states' power to regulate or dissolve corporations. At issue was whether the state of New Hampshire could alter the charter granted to Dartmouth College by King George III in 1769. The New Hampshire government sought to turn the private college into a public one so that the governor could appoint trustees. Dartmouth sued the state, and the Supreme Court sided with the college. New Hampshire, effectively, could not convert corporate private property to public property, even if that private property was originally intended to serve the public good.

The *Dartmouth College* case set the precedent that a corporate charter has the status of a legal contract. Historian James Willard Hurst writes that the case

> extended the protection of the contract clause of the Federal Constitution not only over a donor's gift and the college's existing assets but also over the frame of organization and powers of the institution as created by the original charter, as against later intruding legislation. What the corporate charter gave and what the Constitution protected was thus not only an official license but also a pattern for organizing certain human relations.[44]

Governments could not interfere with existing corporate charters.[45] In his famous ruling on the *Dartmouth* case, Chief Justice John Marshall used words that would carry special resonance in subsequent cases regarding corporations:

> A Corporation is an artificial being, invisible, intangible, and existing only in contemplation of law. Being the mere creature of law, it possesses only those properties which the charter of its creation confers upon it, either expressly, or as incidental to its very existence.[46]

Marshall insisted that corporations are subordinate to state power; yet his ruling also raised the legal status of the corporation, allowing for the eventual erosion of state control over corporations. Most important, Marshall's view that the corporation is "an artificial being" offers later jurists the basis to decide that the corporation is entitled to a measure of constitutional protection and suggests that this "creature of law" has private rights.

When Marshall declared that the corporation was an "artificial being," he meant that it was a creation of the state: the corporation was not a natural being, which would exist independent of the state. But as Mark suggests, "[T]he rise of general incorporation laws and the general elimination of the special privileges that accompanied special charters played major roles in making the corporation appear to be a natural way to organize property."[47] Put another way, as corporate values and functions were no longer under control of the state through specific charters, the corporate form became a common way of organizing business, and the corporation was considered less and less a creation of the state. By the 1880s, in fact, corporate property was no longer considered artificial.[48] The corporation was no longer primarily a creature fashioned by the government for purposes of administration and regulation. Instead, the corporation was swiftly becoming the normal way for private firms to organize labor, management, and financial capital.

Corporate personhood naturalized the corporation. What might otherwise have seemed ghostly and abstract – a corporate body both immortal and unlocatable – became more human.[49] Mark writes:

> [P]ersonification has been vital because it (1) implies a single and unitary source of control over the collective property of the corporation's members, (2) defines, encourages and legitimates the corporation as an autonomous, creative, self-directed economic being, and (3) captures rights, ultimately even constitutional rights, for corporations thereby giving corporate property unprecedented protection from the state.[50]

At the moment that corporations became increasingly dissociated from their shareholders, they began to gain the powers and rights guaranteed to individuals. Where corporations were once empowered by the state to act in its service, they became empowered by individual investors and were increasingly protected from state intervention. Mark puts it succinctly: "The corporation, once the derivative tool of the state, had become its rival."[51]

In 1886, the Supreme Court granted corporations explicit constitutional protection. In *Santa Clara v. Southern Pacific Railway*, the Court ruled that corporate property was protected as the private property of the corporators. The Court asserted that a corporation was a legal person and that its property must be regulated in a way that conformed to the equal protection and due process provisions of the Fourteenth Amendment.[52] The Fourteenth Amendment, of course, was written to address one of the central ethical, legal, and moral crises in United States history. As one of the Reconstruction Amendments, it was intended to guarantee the citizenship and rights of former slaves.[53] But following *Santa Clara*, the Fourteenth Amendment was used most frequently to procure rights for corporations. Chief Justice Hugo Black, in a 1938 dissent, remarked:

> [O]f the cases in this Court in which the Fourteenth Amendment was applied during the first fifty years after its adoption, less than one-half of 1 percent invoked it in protection of the negro race, and more than 50 percent asked that its benefits be extended to corporations.[54]

The invocation of the Fourteenth Amendment on behalf of corporations would be used to invalidate hundreds of statues designed to limit corporate power, including child labor laws, safety standards, worker compensation for injuries, and work week limitations.[55] While corporations were gaining the guaranteed rights of personhood, the labor force itself became increasingly impersonal and disempowered.

IV. Work, opportunity, and the language of critique in corporate America

Even as courts granted corporations some of the same rights as humans, corporate organizations gained power beyond the grasp of any individual human. Corporations became increasingly depersonalized: instead of being guided by cultural norms and traditions, businesses abided by bureaucratic rules designed to maximize utility. As Chandler explains, a new figure emerged at the heart of the American economic landscape: the career manager.[56] Managers owned little or no equity in the firm, but as full-time, salaried executives, they made administrative choices usually designed for the long-term benefit of the enterprise. Managers did not themselves buy, sell, or move products but monitored and coordinated production and distribution, and they soon monitored and coordinated other monitors and coordinators. As many theorists have remarked, the mechanical and inflexible constraints of bureaucracy threatened human agency. The structure of the workplace considered employees anonymous cogs in giant machines, connected to other humans only in an abstract flowchart of operations. The anguish of individuals in a bureaucratized firm stemmed not only from the possibility of exploitation but also from the depersonalization of the workplace. When personal relationships gave way to functionalized, systematized, and bureaucratized relationships, individual workers commonly felt atomized and alienated.

American literature of the nineteenth century often reflected the cultural anxiety that pervades a society in which relationships could be defined by their organizational status above all else.[57] The literary critic Susan Mizruchi writes, "Next to the American legal system, there was perhaps no other cultural domain more interested in the affairs of business than American literature."[58] As if in response to Charles Francis Adams, American writers endeavored to find a language to describe the emerging corporate culture.

One of the first pieces of American fiction to take place in an office is Herman Melville's 1853 novella, "Bartleby, the Scrivener: A Story of Wall Street." Bartleby is an office worker who moves from being an effective scrivener who does his work "silently, palely, mechanically" to one who eventually declines to do any work at all, declaring at every request, "I would prefer not to."[59] Bartleby refuses to be a productive member of the Wall Street business, and, more crucially, he refuses to be humanized despite the narrator's frantic efforts. As a figure who deflects all attempts at sympathy, Bartleby might stand for the alienated worker in a culture where personal relationships are being replaced by corporate ones.[60] Indeed, in the middle of the nineteenth century, the rise of banks and insurance companies allowed businesses "both to raise capital and to distance themselves from the kinds of personal obligation that the existing credit system entailed."[61] With the growth of the American economy came the breakdown of intimate business connections.[62] For Melville, as for Americans anxious about cultural change, the office is a place of inscrutability. What should be the site for rational action is actually laden with mystery.

Bartleby is a member of the emergent white-collar labor force made up of interchangeable figures. After all, when a corporation had a personhood distinct from its constituent members, the lives of the members themselves were not as important as they would have been in a partnership or family-owned business. The historian Barry Shank explains that the new labor demands of corporate culture created new social relations:

> Large-scale business organizations were forced to hire such large numbers of managers that they had to reach beyond their immediate circle of family members and close acquaintances. Forced to deal with the contradictory needs of competitive capitalism and social affiliation, the modern corporation fostered the development of particular sensibilities and subjectivities.[63]

Shank describes the emergence of a corporate sensibility that had to navigate between modes of "affiliation" and "calculation."[64] Social relations in corporate America were shaped by what appeared to be a conflict between sympathy and profit.

As corporations became more pervasive and more powerful, critics felt new urgency in their endeavor to find the language of resistance. In 1871, Elizabeth Stuart Phelps published her novel *The Silent Partner* in response to what she perceived as the malignant values of corporate culture.[65] She explains in her prefatory note, "Had Christian ingenuity been generally synonymous with the conduct of manufacturing corporations, I should have found no occasion for the writing of this book."[66] Phelps's protagonist is Perley Kelso, a young woman who inherits a factory with hellish working conditions. She must overcome her role as "the silent partner," a manager in name only who is relegated to silence in the business realm. The novel charts the restorative effects of her female influence on working conditions and labor unrest; she acts as a counter to the destructive, inhumane treatment imposed by the male managers. Perley refuses marriage – she does not want to become "a silent partner" in matrimony – but she brings a feminine sense of domesticity and care to her public work on behalf of laborers.[67]

The Silent Partner describes woeful labor conditions, yet it also narrates a tale of new possibilities for women in the corporate age. Thousands of women moved from their farms to work in factories like the ones in Waltham and Lowell, Massachusetts. Millwork for women was exhausting and often dangerous, yet many women left their families for the factory. An 1858 article in *The Atlantic Monthly*, "Farming in New England," declared that "farmer's daughters . . . contemn the calling of their father, and will nine times out of ten marry a mechanic in preference to a farmer. They know that marrying a farmer is a serious business. They remember their worn-out mothers."[68] The article describes a generational change that was shocking to many Americans.

As the historian Thomas Dublin shows, the letters of mill women in the 1840s reveal their desires to leave rural life for the excitement of cities.[69] Women wrote of new degrees of independence and freedom, as well as new expectations of friendship and love.

Corporate life seemed to offer unprecedented opportunity. Amidst the populist and reformist voices decrying corporate power were individuals eager to take advantage of new routes of social mobility. The historian Martin Sklar writes, "For many Americans, the corporation became the new frontier of opportunity that the western lands had once symbolized."[70] Large business organizations dwarfed traditional social institutions in their power and reach. The middle class was divided between those who contributed to corporate growth and those who "clung to proven, and presumably more fulfilling, ways of doing business."[71] The women who left for the factories and the men who chose professional positions over traditional vocations dramatized an embattled cultural shift – away from the family, the church, the small farm, the local community – and toward the corporation.

V. Corporate space and corporate time

The simultaneous anxiety and attraction that many Americans felt for an emergent corporate culture is given poetic form by Walt Whitman in his poems "Crossing Brooklyn Ferry" (1855) and "Passage to India" (1868). Whitman recognizes that American corporate culture has rendered a new physical and spiritual landscape. But where some critics saw only the dismantling of tradition, Whitman yearned to discover new, inclusive forms of humanity. As if responding to the etymological roots of "incorporation," Whitman repeatedly returns to the human body as he ponders new forms of intimacy in a corporate world. In "Crossing Brooklyn Ferry," the poet declares his wonder at the commuting masses and suggests an unbridgeable psychological distance from them: "Crowds of men and women attired in the usual costumes! How / curious you / are to me!"[72] Human relations are strained in the corporate age: physical closeness seems not to yield intimacy. The poet ominously notes the "fires from the foundry chimneys / burning high / and glaringly into the night." But he also begins to feel deep sympathy for these crowds of Americans and resolves the poem triumphantly: "Burn high your fires, foundry chimneys! Cast black / shadows at nightfall! Cast red and yellow light / over the tops of the houses!" The poet feels doubt and hesitation toward a potentially alienating culture, but he is overcome by the promise of what one critic calls "the technological sublime."[73]

Whitman's exuberance toward the technology of American progress resonates even more powerfully in "Passage to India." The poem opens: "Singing my days, / Singing the great achievements of the present, / Singing the strong light works of engineers, / Our modern wonders, (the antique ponderous Seven / outvied,) / In the Old World the east the Suez Canal, / The New by its mighty railroad spann'd, / The seas inlaid with eloquent gentle wires; / Yet first to sound, and ever sound, the cry with thee / O soul, / The Past! the Past! the Past!"[74] The poet yearns for "the Past!" even as he celebrates "the great achievements of the present" – the Suez Canal, the Union-Pacific railroad, the Atlantic cable. As in "Crossing Brooklyn Ferry," the poet's hesitation is countered by the uplift of industrial promise: "I hear the locomotives rushing and roaring, and the / shrill steam-whistle, / I hear the echoes reverberate through the grandest / scenery in the world." For Whitman, corporate technology seems not to disrupt the natural landscape so much as it opens up this pastoral utopia for all to experience. Yet there remains in the poem an undercurrent of doubt, a vision of the "unloving earth, without a throb to answer ours, / Cold earth, the place of graves." The railroad and the telegraph transcend space and time, but the poet cannot help but sense a deathly gap between man and earth created by these technologies.

The railroad and telegraph enterprises epitomized American corporations; not only did they innovate modern corporate practices, but they also spread these bureaucratic innovations as they expanded. The railroad moved an unprecedented quantity of goods across great distances on a precise schedule. The telegraph allowed, for the first time ever, nearly instantaneous communication between distant locations. Prior to these technologies, owners generally managed their businesses personally. But the massive investment required for the construction and operation of rail and telegraph systems resulted in "the separation of ownership from management."[75] The operational requirements of the railroads demanded the first administrative hierarchies in the business world. Their financial requirements "brought trading and speculation on the New York Stock Exchange in its modern form."[76] In the 1850s and 1860s, managers of large American railroads "invented nearly all of the basic techniques of modern accounting."[77] By the 1880s, railroad managers constituted a recognizable business class, "the first professional business managers in America."[78] The railroad and telegraph systems assured businesses a continuous supply of raw materials and up-to-date information. The revolution in transportation and communication allowed for revolutions in production and distribution, making the American marketplace more efficient than ever before. On a deeper level, the railroad and telegraph brought with them new senses of space and time.

The sprawling geography of America, once thought to be virtually endless, became overlaid by a national system of commerce.[79] In 1803, Thomas Jefferson had declared that it would take one thousand years for people to fully settle the region east of the Mississippi.[80] By 1850, American settlers had reached the Pacific Ocean. And in 1869, the transcontinental railroad connected the coasts. A new view of the American landscape emerged: as the country made a push toward turning vast natural resources into manufactured consumer products, natural space became a commodity to be exploited for corporate profit. The historian Olivier Zunz describes the effect of national markets on Americans' sense of space: "Each place became more readily identified as part of a network of places and relied increasingly on the network's existence for its life."[81] Markets were no longer ruled by local merchants selling regional goods. Rather, corporations distributed brand-name products on a national scale as centers of commercial power became more concentrated. According to Lipartito, "[T]he tendency of modern business to sever the connection between the firm and its location" caused widespread consternation.[82] As communities became more dependent on one another, many community members felt anxious about losing a sense of local belonging.[83]

Corporations not only governed where and when workers would be employed but also changed their "inward apprehension of time."[84] Prior to the late nineteenth century, communities adhered to Local Mean Time, abiding by solar readings: when the sun was overhead, the local clocks and bells struck noon. Historian Alan Trachtenberg explains, "Local life arranged itself in relation to the most influential community timepieces: church bells and steeple clocks, and after the 1840's, the cupolas and stark brick bell towers of mills and factories."[85] The public signals of time testified to the influence of industrial labor, but localities retained control over the community's sense of daily time until corporations became powerful enough to institute a new system. In 1883, railway networks became sufficiently large to warrant a national timetable, and the railroad corporations introduced Standard Railway Time. Most cities quickly adopted the four uniform standards of time that the railroads agreed upon, and soon the Eastern, Central, Mountain, and Pacific Standard Time zones "transcended the railroad world" and were broadly accepted by Americans.[86] The sociologist Eviatar Zerubavel explains that this shift in understanding time engendered a shift in American values: "What seems to have replaced nature as a temporal referencing anchor is the principle of rationality, long viewed as one of the key characteristics of modern civilization."[87] National systematization brought with it a new mode of consciousness, shaping how individuals conceived of their place in the world. Space and time may have felt natural, but they were corporate.

VI. Managerial culture

In the final decades of the nineteenth century, individual Americans began to adhere rigidly to quantified time. According to historian T. J. Jackson Lears, "the 'pace of modern life,' a staple of popular sociology, is a direct result of the bureaucratic imperative in organized capitalism – the demand for disciplined, systematic work."[88] Thinkers such as Frederick Winslow Taylor developed management philosophies designed to increase the efficiency of labor. Managerialism spread rapidly at the end of the nineteenth century when Taylor and others brought into the factory the administrative structure that governed the railroad corporations.[89] Though Taylor did not write *The Principles of Scientific Management* until 1911, his work ushering in the scientific management movement began in the 1880s. He wanted to end the "wastes of human effort" caused by the "awkward, inefficient, or ill-directed movements of men."[90] Taylor's solution was to break down every factory task into a series of elements and prescribe precise movements in order to optimize each worker's performance. Managers sought to design systems of labor that were fully comprehensive; in Taylor's vision, every work detail would be dictated and controlled. The stopwatch and the flowchart became emblematic of a system in which managers timed and directed each labor task.[91]

This is the age when corporations turned "artisans into workers," to use historian Bruce Laurie's resonant phrase.[92] Laurie describes not only a shift in responsibility for laborers but also a dramatic transformation of identity. As late as the 1870s, the American economy was controlled by local merchants who worked with master craftsmen to produce and distribute goods.[93] But as the labor historian David Montgomery writes, "[N]ew methods of industrial management undermined the very foundation of craftsmen's functional autonomy. Job analysis through time and motion study allowed management to learn, then to systematize the way the work itself was done."[94] In the new administrative system, knowledge was to be held by management, not by laborers. Workers were valued insofar as they adhered to the precise guidelines of a bureaucracy that claimed to be scientific. The ideal worker in a Taylorized business used hands that were dissociated from the head; managers saw workers as brainless and compliant. Managers had always controlled work to a certain extent, but now they controlled the decisions made during the course of work. The business historian Peter Drucker writes, "Scientific management is all but a systematic philosophy of worker and work. Altogether it may well be the most powerful as well as the most lasting contribution America has made to Western thought since the federalist papers."[95] Even if managers did not explicitly subscribe to Taylorism, scientific management provided the bedrock principles that governed the relationship between management and labor in most corporations.[96] Although Taylor's own efforts at scientific management never had the effect he intended, the once radical idea of treating human workers as so many parts of a vast machine quickly became normal practice, even outside the factory.

The quest for corporate efficiency took its toll on the American labor force. The financial distress of workers was compounded by what many experienced as new forms of social and cultural disorientation. Historian Robert H. Wiebe describes the alienating effects of corporate managerial culture on many American workers:

> As the pace of industrialization quickened early in the eighties, the incomprehensible ways of the corporation were also alienating a multitude of wage earners. Rapidly losing control over their working lives, they knew only that decisions made somewhere else pushed them about like so many cattle.[97]

Highly systematized labor forms crystallized into increasingly regulated social forms. Significantly, the anxieties brought about by this cultural change were not limited to individuals directly involved with big businesses. Even those who at one time appeared to live beyond the reach of corporate power felt its grasp.[98]

As a number of literary critics have remarked, the literature of the late nineteenth century responded to prevailing senses of alienation and dislocation.[99] Many individuals felt that the nation was not living up to its promise, that Americans were not leading lives that followed the republican ideals of individualism and independence. Not only had the great fissure of the Civil War not been repaired – the devastating sacrifice never fully redeemed and a system based on racial exploitation never fully destroyed – but the emerging culture made many individuals question the possibility of self-determination in their daily lives. A number of writers believed that the end of the nineteenth century required a literary response that was clear-eyed, unromantic, and unsentimental. The novel might act as a cultural corrective. Leading literary spokesman William Dean Howells advocated literary realism, declaring, "[L]et fiction cease to lie about life; let it portray men and women as they are, actuated by the motives and the passions in the measure we all know."[100] For Howells, morally complex men and women were often submerged in situations beyond their full control, beyond, even, their powers of comprehension. Trachtenberg writes of the literary movement, "On the whole, realism portrayed the old American credo of a community of autonomous natural beings as a sad illusion."[101] For many Americans, life and work were no longer secure or reliable.

Howells' 1884 novel, *The Rise of Silas Lapham*, is among the first of many American works to feature a businessman as its central character.[102] Howells reveals the social upheaval wracking individuals like Silas Lapham, a paint manufacturer who has risen from the family farm to "colossal fortune."[103] Lapham realizes he lives in a new age, declaring, "The day of small things was past, and I don't suppose it will ever come again in this country."[104] But Lapham's millions won't buy him cultural capital, and he struggles with the moral choices he must make in order to maintain his fortune. When Lapham loses his wealth because he abides by his conscience in a business decision, the novel suggests that business interests and morality are not compatible. Howells punctures the myth of the American self-made man in the age of big business, and his narrative charts the painful choices of unheroic citizens in a newly corporatized world. The business world crunches onward, precipitating social uncertainty and operating without morality.

Perhaps the American writer who was most enthralled with the business world at the end of the nineteenth century was Mark Twain. He was a key figure in the commercialization of the literary profession, eager to connect himself to patrons and freely admitting his own money lust.[105] Yet his novels are far from celebrations of the culture brought forth under corporate regimes. In *The Adventures of Tom Sawyer*, for instance, Tom is a young schemer who manipulates boys into paying him for a chance to fulfill his chore of whitewashing a fence. In a day, Tom experiences a microcosmic version of the American dream: "And when the middle of the afternoon came, from being a poor poverty-stricken boy in the morning, Tom was literally rolling in wealth."[106] Tom learns a fundamental rule of capitalism: "[I]n order to make a man or a boy covet a thing, it is only necessary to make the thing difficult to attain."[107] Readers are taught to be even more suspicious of Tom Sawyer in *Adventures of Huckleberry Finn*, when Tom plays at being a young boss. He is the comical leader of a gang, leading with a paternal power upon which F. W. Taylor might nod his approval. Huck tells us that, "Tom superintended. He could out-superintend any boy I ever see."[108] As Huck and Jim find out, though, Tom is a cruel parody of a manager, inflicting pain in the name of control. Our last view of Tom, after he has led Huck and Jim in a violent, humiliating scheme, is with his watch: "Tom's most well, now, and got his bullet around his neck on a watch-guard for a watch, and is always seeing what time it is."[109] In reminding himself of his adventures, the boy fantasizes about being a corporate manager, keeping watch over a systematized world, retaining precise command.

Tom's bullet watch symbolizes the confluence of violence and time management, two themes that come together in Twain's next novel, *A Connecticut Yankee in King Arthur's Court.* Hank Morgan, the Yankee, is the "head superintendent" of a massive arms factory that makes "guns, revolvers, cannon, boilers, engines, all sorts of labour-saving machinery."[110] Embedded in Twain's joke – that the machinery saves labor by killing it – is a serious critique of the alienation facing workers whose jobs were fully dictated by a detached managerial system. To save labor through models of pure efficiency is to destroy the humanity of the labor force. The Yankee finds himself in Camelot in the sixth century, where he quickly becomes known as "the Boss" and sets out to industrialize the country stuck in the "ungentle" codes of medieval aristocracy.[111] Twain's mockery of a ridiculous chivalric culture turns into a devastating critique of a Taylorized system in which Hank, like a grown-up and professionalized Tom Sawyer, plays out an unchecked fantasy of managerial domination. Hank thinks of the country as a "corporation" and molds individuals in a "Man-Factory."[112] Hank systematizes and mechanizes the world, fashioning himself into a managerial class dictator who commands mass violence. The Boss's vision of progress ends, finally, in an electrified apocalypse.

A Connecticut Yankee was published with over 200 illustrations by Dan Beard, the most famous of which is titled "The Slave Driver" (see Figure 3.1). It features a caped man holding a whip in triumph and standing on the neck of a shackled young woman. The man's face is unmistakably that of Jay Gould, the most powerful and infamous speculator of the era.[113] Beard literalizes Twain's allegory: yesterday's slave drivers are today's corporate titans. Indeed, for much of the American public, corporate power at the end of the century felt tyrannical.[114] It is notable that the stepped-on "slave" is a white woman; the illustration suggests that white workers experienced their labor exploitation as racial degradation.

Much of the public resentment toward corporations was a response to what historian Naomi Lamoreaux calls the "great merger movement" of 1895 to 1904, when "hundreds of firms vanish[ed] suddenly into horizontal consolidations," and the nation "transformed overnight from a nation of freely competing, individually owned enterprises into a nation dominated by a small number of giant corporations."[115] At the end of the century, the economy lacked any strong countervailing forces to the corporation: consumers had few buying choices, the government was friendly to corporate power, and militias violently overpowered the frequent strikes of unions.[116] Historian Roland Marchand writes, "For all the legal legitimacy" of corporate personhood, "the great corporation of the early twentieth century still conspicuously lacked a comparable social and moral legitimacy in the eyes of the public."[117] The staggering size and power of big business led many individuals to believe that corporations were cold, corrupt, immoral behemoths. As Frank Norris wrote in 1901, the railroad corporation was "the leviathan, with tentacles of steel clutching into the soil, the soulless Force, the iron-hearted Power, the monster, the Colossus, the Octopus."[118]

But to think of corporate power in the nineteenth century only as a cruel industrialist standing on the necks of innocents or as a voracious monster consuming the nation is to miss the quieter story of bureaucracy and regulation. As Jean-Christophe Agnew suggests, capitalism took command not by fiery force but through a "flatland of ordinary material practices that habituated Americans to the new, systemic rules of capitalism as a market form of life and that did so in ways of which most Americans at the time were only dimly and bemusedly aware."[119] The corporation transformed the American economic system in the nineteenth century, but its deepest effects were felt on levels of culture that, for many Americans, were not obviously connected to modes of capitalist exchange. As Agnew suggests, most Americans did not realize the extent to which corporations governed their sense of agency, structured their feeling, and formed their notions of

Figure 3.1 Dan Beard, "The Slave Driver," from *A Connecticut Yankee in King Arthur's Court* (New York: Webster, 1889), 465

space and time. It took many years for critics and writers to find language that might accurately describe "the system of corporate life," as Charles Francis Adams called it. By the time American individuals might have had the language and vision clear enough to weigh the benefits of corporate life against its costs, the corporate form had already pervaded their identities.

Notes

* I am grateful to many people for helping me with this chapter, including Simon Stern, Nan Goodman, Caleb Smith, Raphael Rajendra, Catherine Steindler, Nicole Wallack, Karin Gosselink, Daniella Gitlin, Zachary Roberts, Thomas MacMillan, Briallen Hopper, and Sue Mendelsohn.

1 Due to the size and complexity of their operations, railroads were pioneers in corporate innovation. Alfred Chandler writes, "[T]he rail and telegraph companies were themselves the first modern business enterprises to appear in the United States." Alfred Chandler, *The Visible Hand: The Managerial Revolution in American Business* (Cambridge, Mass.: Belknap Press, 1977), 79.

2 Walt Whitman, "Passage to India," in *Leaves of Grass and Other Writings*, ed. Michael Moon (New York: Norton, 2002), 345–53 (p. 346).

3 Frank Norris, *The Octopus* (1901; New York: Penguin, 1994), 51.

4 Charles F. Adams Jr., "A Chapter of Erie," in *Chapters of Erie and Other Essays*, ed. Charles F. Adams, Jr. and Henry Adams (Boston: Osgood, 1871), 97. Alan Trachtenberg opens his important study *The Incorporation of America* with this famous quote.

5 "Corporation," Def. 3a, *Oxford English Dictionary*, 2nd ed., 1989; online version November 2010.

6 On the subject of personhood, the English jurist Sir William Blackstone wrote:

> Persons are divided by the law into either natural persons or artificial. Natural persons are such as the God of nature formed us; artificial are such as are created and devised by human laws for the purposes of society and government, which are called corporations or bodies politic.

William Blackstone, *Commentaries on the Laws of England*, 4 vols., ed. Wilfrid Prest (1765–69; Oxford: Oxford University Press, 2016), 1: 84.

7 For a quantitative analysis of corporate reach and wealth in the United States through 1860, see Robert E. Wright, "Capitalism and the Rise of the Corporate Nation," in *Capitalism Takes Command: The Social Transformation of Nineteenth-Century America*, ed. Michael Zakim and Gary J. Kornblish (Chicago: University of Chicago Press, 2012), 145–68.

8 Ibid., 148.

9 Ibid., 156.

10 Chandler, *Visible Hand*, 1.

11 For an example of concern about unfair competition, see George Taylor, *Effect of Incorporated Coal Companies upon the Anthracite Coal Trade of Pennsylvania* (Pottsville, Pa.: Bannan, 1833), 19–22. For an example of concern about the degradation of labor, see Nathan Appleton, *Introduction of the Power Loom and Origin of Lowell* (Lowell, Mass.: Penhallow, 1858), 15–16.

12 Jack Beatty, *Colossus: How the Corporation Changed America* (New York: Broadway Books, 2001), 9.

13 Stephen Innes, *Creating the Commonwealth: The Economic Culture of Puritan New England* (New York: Norton, 1995), 206.

14 Ibid., 208.

15 In a 1622 sermon, John Donne urged British investors by promising that the Virginia Company "shall sweep your streets, and wash your dores, from idele persons, and the children of idle persons, and imploy them." John Donne, *The Sermons of John Donne*, ed. George R. Potter and Evelyn M. Simpson (Berkeley: University of California Press, 1953), 4: 272.

16 Ted Nace, *Gangs of America: The Rise of Corporate Power and the Disabling of Democracy* (San Francisco: Berrett-Koehler, 2003), 34.

17 Edmund S. Morgan, *American Slavery, American Freedom: The Ordeal of Colonial Virginia* (New York: Norton, 1975), 129. Slavery would drive wealth not only in the American South but in all of the United States. The historian Bernard Bailyn writes, "Slavery was the ultimate source of the commercial economy of eighteenth-century New England. Only a few of New England's merchants actually engaged in the slave trade, but all of them profited by it, lived off it." Bernard Bailyn, "Slavery and Population Growth in Colonial New England," in *Engines of Enterprise: An Economic History of New England*, ed. Peter Temin (Cambridge, Mass.: Harvard University Press, 2002), 255.

18 Adam Smith, for example, was a staunch critic of corporations, believing that they were unnecessary and yielded monopolies that would harm the public. In *The Wealth of Nations*, he wrote:

> Being the managers rather of other people's money than of their own, it cannot well be expected that they should watch over it with the same anxious vigilance with which the partners in a private guild frequently watch over their own.

Adam Smith, *The Wealth of Nations* (1776; New York: Modern Library, 2000), 800. Franklin and the framers of the Constitution, influenced by Smith and other moral sense philosophers, were skeptical of concentrated power, whether financial or political. They considered monopolies an economic and moral evil.

19 See Benjamin W. Labaree, *The Boston Tea Party* (New York: Oxford University Press, 1964).

20 Pauline Maier writes, "[C]orporations were considered so much a part of the old order that in 1791 revolutionary France outlawed them altogether." Pauline Maier, "The Revolutionary Origins of the American Corporation," *William and Mary Quarterly*, 3rd ser., 50 (1993): 51–84, 51.

21 James Madison argued for putting the federal government in charge of corporations, but many delegates wanted to keep the power to grant charters in local hands. Some delegates were skeptical of the concentrated power and wealth of centralized institutions, arguing that the potential outsized power of corporations could be a threat to democracy. See Bruce R. Scott, *Capitalism: Its Origins and Evolution as a System of Governance* (New York: Springer, 2011), 252–3.

22 For example, a 1781 charter incorporating the Massachusetts Medical Society said it would help the "health and lives of many valuable individuals"; a 1789 charter incorporating the Beverly Cotton Manufactory explained that "the promotion of useful manufactures" would increase the "happiness and welfare" of the Commonwealth by "increasing the agriculture and extending the commerce of the country." Quoted in Maier, "Revolutionary Origins," 55.

23 The device of the charter "assumed that corporations were legally privileged organizations that had to be closely scrutinized by the legislature because their purpose had to be made consistent with public welfare." Ronald Seavoy, *The Origins of the American Business Corporation, 1784–1855* (New York: Greenwood, 1982), 5.

24 William G. Roy, *Socializing Capital: The Rise of the Large Industrial Corporation in America* (Princeton, N.J.: Princeton University Press, 1997), 48.

25 Achille Murat, *Moral and Political Sketch of the United States* (London: Wilson, 1833), 337–8.

26 Wright, "Capitalism," 148. Wright lists some of the many business sectors that included corporate firms before 1861: infrastructure, banking, insurance, manufacturing, transportation, mining, utilities, education, cemeteries, and entertainment.

27 Joseph Angel and Samuel Ames, *A Treatise on the Law of Private Corporations Aggregate* (Boston: Hilliard, 1832), v–vi.

28 Kenneth Lipartito, "The Utopian Corporation," in *Constructing Corporate America: History Politics, Culture*, ed. Kenneth Lipartito and David B. Sicilia (New York: Oxford University Press, 2004), 94–119, 105.

29 Louis Hartz, *Economic Policy and Democratic Thought: Pennsylvania 1776–1860* (Cambridge, Mass.: Harvard University Press, 1948), 58–62.

30 As Robert Wright points out, "[E]arly Americans did not possess the vocabulary to express market power with precision, so they labeled as 'monopoly' every business that did not function in . . . perfectly competitive markets." Wright, "Capitalism," 157.

31 Quoted in Susan Hirsch, *Roots of the American Working Class: The Industrialization of Crafts in Newark, 1800–1860* (Philadelphia: University of Pennsylvania Press, 1978), 86.

32 According to the historian Martin Horwitz, special incorporation was the right form for an "underdeveloped society, with little available private capital" that required "that the legal system provide legal arrangements that guaranteed private investors certainty and predictability of economic consequences." "But as development proceeded," Horwitz continues, "the early monopolistic strategy for encouraging economic growth soon became a legal barrier to further growth." Martin J. Horwitz, *The Transformation of American Law, 1780–1860* (Cambridge, Mass.: Harvard University Press, 1977), 111.

33 Theodore Sedgwick, *What Is a Monopoly?* (New York: Scott, 1835), 13.

34 Wright, "Capitalism," 161. As Wright explains, with new mutual savings banks, "indirect corporate stock and bond ownership [were] available to the poor." See also John Majewski, who writes that "ordinary Americans owned far more shares in corporations than historians might expect." John Majewski, "Toward a Social History of the Corporation: Shareholding in Pennsylvania, 1800–1840," in *The Economy of Early America: Historical Perspectives & New Directions*, ed. Cathy Matson (University Park: Pennsylvania State University Press, 2006), 294–316, 296.

35 Many Americans believed that their economy depended on corporate strength. In 1858, the powerful textile merchant Nathan Appleton wrote, "[M]anufactures cannot be carried on to any great extent in this country in any other manner than by joint stock companies. A large capital is necessary to success." Nathan Appleton, *Introduction of the Power Loom and Origin of Lowell* (Lowell, Mass.: Penhallow, 1858), 30.

36 Taylor, *Effect of Incorporated Coal Companies*, 26.

37 The first statute offering general incorporation was passed by New York State in 1811. By 1902, any individual in the U.S. "could receive a corporate charter merely by filing some papers with the state." Nace, *Gangs of America*, 72.

38 See L. Ray Gunn, *The Decline of Authority: Public Economic Policy and Political Development in New York State, 1800–1860* (Ithaca, N.Y.: Cornell University Press, 1988), 222–45.

39 Naomi Lamoreaux points out that when states began passing laws of general incorporation in the mid-nineteenth century, corporations were not immediately given free rein by the government: "[E]ven after the passage of general incorporation laws, public mistrust of corporations meant that firms that adopted this form of organization were exposed to a greater degree of public intervention than that borne by partnerships." Naomi Lamoreaux, "The Partnership Form of Organization: Its Popularity in Early-Nineteenth-Century Boston," in *Entrepreneurs: The Boston Business Community, 1700–1850*, ed. Conrad E. Wright and Katheryn P. Viens (Boston: Massachusetts Historical Society, 2005), 273.

40 Gregory Mark, "The Personification of the Business Corporation in American Law," *University of Chicago Law Review* 54 (1987): 1441–83, 1455.

41 Ibid., 1454.

42 17 U.S. 518 (1819).

43 118 U.S. 394 (1886).

44 James W. Hurst, *The Legitimacy of the Business Corporation in the Law of the United States, 1780–1970* (Charlottesville: University of Virginia Press, 1970), 16–17.

45 State legislatures responded to the Dartmouth ruling by immediately reasserting their sovereignty, adding clauses to charters that would allow the states to revoke or alter the charters. See Lawrence M. Friedman, *A History of American Law* (New York: Simon & Schuster, 1985), 197–8.

46 *Dartmouth College*, 17 U.S. at 636.

47 Mark, "Personification of the Business Corporation," 1455.

48 Ibid., 1457.

49 A number of scholars have suggested that the shifting idea of corporate personhood over the course of the nineteenth century determined the corporation's role in economic, political, and social life. See, especially, Mark, "Personification of the Business Corporation," and Daniel Lipton, "Corporate Capacity for Crime and Politics: Defining Corporate Personhood at the Turn of the Twentieth Century," *Virginia Law Review* 96 (2010): 1911–64.

50 Mark, "Personification of the Business Corporation," 1443.

51 Ibid., 1482.

52 Technically, the ruling itself says nothing about corporate personhood. Instead, it was the court reporter, J. C. Bancroft Davis, who wrote in his "Headnotes," "The defendant Corporations are persons within the intent of the clause in section I of the Fourteenth Amendment to the Constitution of the United States, which forbids a State to deny to any person within its jurisdiction the equal protection of the laws." The Supreme Court historian David M. O'Brien wrote:

> There is perhaps no better illustration of the consequence of a headnote than in *Santa Clara v. Southern Pacific Railroad Company* (1886). There, after consulting Chief Justice Waite, the Reporter at his own discretion decided to note in an otherwise uninteresting tax case that the Court considered corporations "legal persons" entitled to protection under the Fourteenth Amendment. Corporations, like individual citizens, could thereafter challenge the constitutionality of congressional and state legislation impinging on their interests.

David O'Brien, *Storm Center: The Supreme Court in American Politics* (New York: Norton, 1986), 149.

53 Section 1 of the Fourteenth Amendment reads:

> All persons born or naturalized in the United States, and subject to the jurisdiction thereof, are citizens of the United States and of the state wherein they reside. No state shall make or enforce any law which shall abridge the privileges or immunities of citizens of the United States; nor shall any state deprive any person of life, liberty, or property, without due process of law; nor deny to any person within its jurisdiction the equal protection of the laws.

54 *Connecticut General Life Ins. Co. v. Johnson*, 303 U.S. 77 (1938).
55 See Carl J. Mayer, "Personalizing the Impersonal: Corporations and the Bill of Rights," *Hastings Law Journal* 41 (1990): 577–667.
56 Chandler, *Visible Hand.*
57 See Aaron Ritzenberg, *The Sentimental Touch* (New York: Fordham University Press, 2012).
58 Susan L. Mizruchi, "Corporate America," in *The Cambridge History of American Literature, Volume 3: Prose Writing 1860–1920*, ed, Sacvan Bercovitch (New York: Cambridge University Press, 2005), 666–709 (p. 668).
59 Herman Melville, *Bartleby, The Scrivener* (1853; New York: Melville House, 2010), 16.
60 See Leo Marx, "Melville's Parable of the Walls," *Sewanee Review* 61 (1953): 602–27.
61 Christopher Clark, "The Agrarian Context of American Capitalist Development," in *Capitalism Takes Command*, 13–37, 25.
62 See Jonathan Levy, who explains the rise of impersonal systems in the world of finance and agriculture:

> Until the middle of the nineteenth century there existed a direct, personal link between many mortgage lenders and borrowers. Most farmers knew who owned their mortgage. With the rise of mortgage-backed securities and new forms of financial intermediation, this was no longer the case. The relationship between lender and borrower became attenuated.

Jonathan Levy, "The Mortgage Worked the Hardest: The Fate of Landed Independence in Nineteenth-Century America," in *Capitalism Takes Command: The Social Transformation of Nineteenth-Century America*, ed. Michael Zakim and Gary J. Kornblith (Chicago: Chicago University Press, 2012), 39–67, 41.

63 Barry Shank, *A Token of My Affection: Greeting Cards and American Business Culture* (New York: Columbia University Press, 2004), 119.
64 Ibid., 120.
65 The historian William F. Taylor remarks that Phelps is "the first American novelist to treat the social problems of the Machine Age seriously and at length." William F. Taylor, *The Economic Novel in America* (Chapel Hill, N.C.: University of North Carolina Press, 1942), 58.
66 Elizabeth S. Phelps, *The Silent Partner* (1871; New York: The Feminist Press, 1983), "Note."
67 Ibid., 262.
68 "Farming Life in New England," *Atlantic Monthly* (August 1858), 341; also quoted in Thomas Dublin, *Women at Work* (New York: Columbia University Press, 1981), 55.
69 Dublin, *Women at Work*, 55–7.
70 Martin Sklar, *The Corporate Reconstruction of American Capitalism, 1890–1926: The Market, the Law, and Politics* (New York: Cambridge University Press, 1988), 26.
71 Olivier Zunz, *Making America Corporate 1870–1920* (Chicago: University of Chicago Press, 1992), 13.
72 Walt Whitman, "Crossing Brooklyn Ferry," in *Leaves of Grass and Other Writings*, ed. Michael Moon (New York: Norton, 2002), 135–40.
73 Leo Marx, *The Machine in the Garden: Technology and the Pastoral Ideal in America* (New York: Oxford University Press, 1964), 222.
74 Whitman, "Passage to India," in *Leaves of Grass*, 345–53.
75 Alfred Chandler, *Scale and Scope: The Dynamics of Industrial Capitalism* (Cambridge, Mass.: Belknap Press, 1990), 1.
76 Chandler, *Visible Hand*, 92.
77 Ibid., 109.
78 Ibid., 132.
79 See Maier, "Revolutionary Origins."
80 See *The Boisterous Sea of Liberty*, ed. David Brion Davis and Steven Mintz (New York: Oxford University Press, 2000), 325.
81 Zunz, *Making America Corporate*, 12.
82 Kenneth Lipartito, *The Bell System and Regional Business: The Telephone in the South, 1877–1920* (Baltimore: Johns Hopkins University Press, 1989), 209.
83 See Thomas Bender, *Community and Social Change in America* (Baltimore: Johns Hopkins University Press, 1978).
84 Edward P. Thompson, "Time, Work-Discipline, and Industrial Capitalism," *Past & Present* 38 (1967): 56–97, 57.
85 Alan Trachtenberg, *The Incorporation of America: Culture & Society in the Gilded Age* (New York: Hill & Wang, 1982), 59.

86 Eviatar Zerubavel, "The Standardization of Time: A Sociohistorical Perspective," *American Journal of Sociology* 88 (1982): 1–23, 10.
87 Ibid., 21.
88 T.J. Jackson Lears, *No Place of Grace: Antimodernism and the Transformation of American Culture 1880–1920* (New York: Pantheon Books, 1981), 11.
89 According to Lyndall Urwick and E.F.L. Brech, Taylor's work was a culmination of a trend: "What Taylor did was not to invent something quite new, but to synthesize and present as a reasonably coherent whole ideas which had been germinating and gathering force in Great Britain and the United States throughout the nineteenth century." Lyndall Urwick and E.F.L. Brech, *The Making of Scientific Management, Vol. 1.* (London: Management Publications Trust, 1945–8), 17.
90 Frederick W. Taylor, *The Principles of Scientific Management* (1911; New York: Harper, 1914), 5.
91 Henry Ford, for one, was obsessed with timepieces. In *My Life and Work*, he remembers that one of the biggest events of his youth was "getting a watch" when he was twelve years old. The year would have been 1875. Henry Ford in collaboration with Samuel Crowther, *My Life and Work* (New York: Doubleday, 1923), 22.
92 Bruce Laurie, *Artisans into Workers* (New York: Hill & Wang, 1989).
93 Zunz, *Making America Corporate*, 13.
94 David Montgomery, *Worker's Control in America* (New York: Cambridge University Press, 1979), 26.
95 Peter F. Drucker, *The Practice of Management* (New York: Harper, 1954), 280.
96 Harry Braverman writes:

> If Taylorism does not exist as a separate school today, that is because, apart from the bad odor of the name, it is no longer the property of a faction, since its fundamental teachings have become the bedrock of all work design.

Harry Braverman, *Labor and Monopoly Capital* (New York: Monthly Review Press, 1974), 87.
97 Robert H. Wiebe, *The Search for Order: 1877–1920* (New York: Hill & Wang, 1967), 47.
98 The historian Louis Galambos offers an example of the widespread, pervasive influence of business culture when he describes the predicaments of Southern farmers in the 1890s. Galambos writes:

> [W]hile the cotton farmer (especially if he lived east of the Mississippi) was trapped in a painful cost-price squeeze, his economic plight alone does not provide an adequate explanation of his growing animosity toward the trusts. The anxiety grounded in economic interests was, in his case, bound up with a general sense of social disorganization.

Louis Galambos, *The Public Image of Big Business in America, 1880–1940* (Baltimore: Johns Hopkins University Press, 1975), 62.
99 See, especially, Louis J. Budd, "The American Background," in *The Cambridge Companion to American Realism and Naturalism: Howells to London*, ed. Donald Pizer (1995; New York: Cambridge University Press, 1999), 21–46; Eric J. Sundquist, "Introduction: The Country of the Blue," in *American Realism: New Essays*, ed. Eric J. Sundquist (Baltimore: Johns Hopkins University Press, 1982), 3–24; and Gregg Camfield, "A Republican Artisan in the Court of King Capital," in *A Historical Guide to Mark Twain*, ed. Shelley F. Fishkin (New York: Oxford University Press, 2002), 95–126.
100 William D. Howells, "A Call for Realism," in *The Rise of Silas Lapham: An Authoritative Text, Composition and Backgrounds, Contemporary Responses, Criticism*, ed. Don L. Cook (1891; New York: Norton, 1982), 496–500, 500.
101 Trachtenberg, *The Incorporation of America*, 202.
102 The realist ambition to treat the most prevalent forms of American life tells us that the businessman had become a recognizable and pervasive figure in American culture. Other prominent early examples of works that feature businessmen include Andrew Carnegie's *Gospel of Wealth* (1889), Henry Blake Fuller's *The Cliff Dwellers* (1893), Orison Swett Marden's *Pushing to the Front* (1894), Frank Norris's *The Pit* (1903), Robert Herrick's *Memoirs of an American Citizen* (1905), and Theodore Dreiser's *The Financier* (1912).
103 William D. Howells, *The Rise of Silas Lapham* (1884–5; New York: Norton, 1982), 18.
104 Ibid., 15.
105 Twain's notorious speculation in the Paige Typesetter, for instance, suggests his obsession with schemes that might save time and make money.
106 Mark Twain, *The Adventures of Tom Sawyer* (1876; New York: Norton, 2007), 20.
107 Ibid., 20–1.

108 Mark Twain, *Adventures of Huckleberry Finn* (1885; New York: Norton, 1999), 266.
109 Ibid., 295.
110 Mark Twain, *A Connecticut Yankee in King Arthur's Court* (1886; New York: Norton, 1982), 8.
111 Ibid., 44, 4.
112 Ibid., 68.
113 Chandler writes, "No man had a greater impact on the strategy of American railroads than Jay Gould." Chandler, *Visible Hand*, 148.
114 See Roland Marchand, *Creating the Corporate Soul* (Berkeley: University of California Press, 1988).
115 Naomi Lamoreaux, *The Great Merger Movement in American Business, 1895–1904* (New York: Cambridge University Press, 1985), 159.
116 For an explanation of how employer associations combated the growth of labor unions, see Kim Voss, *The Making of American Exceptionalism: The Knights of Labor and Class Formation in the Nineteenth Century* (Ithaca, N.Y.: Cornell University Press, 1993).
117 Marchand, *Creating the Corporate Soul*, 7.
118 Frank Norris, *The Octopus* (1901; New York: Penguin, 1994), 51.
119 Jean-Christopher Agnew, "Anonymous History," in *Capitalism Takes Command*, 277–84, 279.

4

DEVIANCE IN NINETEENTH-CENTURY AMERICAN LAW AND CULTURE

Tal Kastner

Viewing slavery as a defining phenomenon of the American nineteenth century, this chapter traces the unstable and evolving relation in this era between norm or law and deviance or crime. The dynamic negotiations of the parameters of normativity of this period, not least as embodied in the law and in relation to slavery, significantly shaped American culture and society. As norms became the subject of dispute, shifting figures of deviance emerged. It is not until the end of the nineteenth century, as Michel Foucault observed, that certain practices, such as homosexual acts, come to constitute a deviant identity.[1] Indeed, the deviant as an identity determined by an individual's divergence from a norm does not enter into American usage until the twentieth century.[2] Nonetheless, slavery – itself a contested legal and social phenomenon in this period – significantly shaped the ways normative social structures, including race, gender, and sexuality, are constructed through law in the course of the nineteenth century.

Dubbed the South's "peculiar institution" – in the sense of its distinctiveness to this particular society – slavery figures at the heart of the normative debate and resulting legal and social transformations of the nineteenth century. At mid-century, the contest over slavery precipitated discussion among abolitionists about the normative status of the Constitution.[3] Adherence to the dictates of the law – a purported site of normativity – came to be seen by some as criminal, impacting the ongoing negotiation of the bounds of deviance. The following discussion explores how works of literature, along with legal developments and cultural constructs, reflect and participate in the negotiation of normativity in the nineteenth century, as informed by the transforming figure of slavery. In addition, it traces the normative social models and countermodels precipitated by slavery, such as the penitentiary, the ideal of contract, and marriage. Before doing so, however, I consider the mutability of signs of law/crime or norm/deviance and look to literature, in which tensions in signification are often cultivated rather than repressed, in order to expose the possibilities of meaning that signs of law and deviance can engender. Specifically, I examine Nathaniel Hawthorne's iconic American origin story, *The Scarlet Letter*, and then trace the indirect impact of slavery on Ralph Waldo Emerson's influential vision of the archetypical American individual.

I. The individual as deviant and as American paradigm

The Scarlet Letter (1850) demonstrates the dynamic relations among the literal and figurative letters of the law, the criminal (or deviant), and the individual as American hero. A few months after the novel's publication, Congress passed the Fugitive Slave Act of 1850, mandating punishment of individuals hindering the return of escaped slaves. As part of the Compromise of 1850, the Act was viewed as an effort to reconcile competing interests of the Northern and Southern states. In its effective extension of slavery to the North, however, for some it also became a salient site of cleavage between normative and legal standards.[4] In this context, Hawthorne's protagonist, Hester Prynne – a convicted adulterer, forced by the magistrates of mid-seventeenth-century Puritan Boston to wear a scarlet letter A on her chest – might be read as a reformed deviant who ultimately heralds the promise of conciliation. An insistent outsider to the community, Hester travels to Europe following the revelation that Rev. Arthur Dimmesdale is the father of her illegitimate child, Pearl. However, in the end Hester returns, taking it upon herself to counsel the "wounded" or "erring" women of her community and pointing toward a brighter collective future.[5] In this role, she serves as a champion of hope if not a point of social coherence. Hester's reform, such as it is, also involves the transformation of the law from a mark of shame to a foundational sign, perhaps prefiguring a cohering nation, reconciled though marked by its crime. By the end of the novel, contrary to what might have been imposed by even "the sternest magistrate of that iron period," Hester takes up "of her own free will" the emblem that once "not merely estranged, but outlawed, [her] from society."[6] In doing so, she changes the resonance of the letter of the law – it "cease[s] to be a stigma," and is instead "looked upon with awe" and "reverence," if not without sorrow.[7]

The process leading to this refiguring suggests the dynamic and mutually constitutive relationship between the mark of the law and the individual in society. Thus, for example, in light of Hester's access "as a rightful inmate, into household[s] darkened by trouble," the letter comes to be read by some as a badge of charitable strength and ability.[8] Later in the novel, when Hester meets the as yet unexposed Reverend Dimmesdale in the forest, she throws off the A insisting, "With this symbol, I undo it all and make it as it had never been!"[9] The novel thereby suggests the potential of law or its expression to serve as an instrument of its own erasure.

This function of law as the source of its own undoing is contemporaneously evidenced in Hawthorne's mid-century Massachusetts – especially in connection with the Fugitive Slave Act of 1850. Notwithstanding the support from Daniel Webster and others in the state for the Compromise of which the statute was a part, the statute's passage and attempted enforcement highlighted its contested normative status. For example, mob law in the form of an antislavery crowd facilitated the escape from the courthouse in Boston of the first individual captured under the law in February 1851,[10] thereby undermining the authority of both the edict and the edifice of the law. When alleged fugitive slave Thomas Sims (who asserted he had been freed as a child) was taken into custody in Boston a few months later,[11] the fraught legal landscape reflected the contentious status of slavery: to comply with Massachusetts's 1843 so-called Latimer Law prohibiting detention of accused fugitive slaves in state prisons,[12] federal agents held Sims in the jury room of the federal courthouse instead.[13] In light of the physical challenges posed to enforcement agents in preceding months, the courthouse itself was secured by chains, creating a spectacle and requiring Lemuel Shaw, chief justice of the Massachusetts Supreme Judicial Court, to bow beneath the fetters on entering the premises.[14] In line with this symbolic act, Shaw's decision in the *Sims* case (1851), refusing to grant Sims's petition for habeas corpus and upholding the constitutionality of the statute,[15] manifested his perceived capitulation to formal constraints of law.

Shaw's adherence to legal precedent along with the accompanying expressions of the legal mandate precipitated further refiguring of the law. An abolitionist poster, for example, dated just a couple weeks later, warned "Colored people of Boston . . . to avoid conversing with the Watchmen and Police Officers of Boston . . . [who] are empowered to act as Kidnappers and Slave Catchers."[16] With its directive to "[k]eep a Sharp Look Out for KIDNAPPERS,"[17] the poster transforms agents of law into would-be criminals. The law, in the form of its mandate, instruments, and agents, can thus be seen to undermine its own authority, much in the spirit of Hester's sentence.

In a manner related to the constraint imposed on Shaw by his understanding of the dictates of the law, in the novel, Pearl, Hester's daughter, "the scarlet letter endowed with life," prompts Hester's initial reclaiming of the sentence, insisting that Hester once again "take [the letter] up!"[18] In Pearl's reflection, "so close upon the margin of a stream" that also reflects the "gold embroidery" of the discarded letter,[19] Sacvan Bercovitch read the "demands of social conformity . . . conveyed through an impassioned willfulness . . . the letter of the law conceived in the spirit of resistant individuality, and vice versa."[20] A manifestation of Hester's creative vision, Pearl both reflects and shapes Hester's identity. At times "wild, desperate, defiant" but also a "half-fledged angel of judgment," Pearl resists but also embodies legal and social norms.[21] In her ultimate development into a woman who would cease to "do battle in the world," Pearl escapes the social realm of the novel, finding her home in an "unknown region" abroad. The novel thereby suggests that in relinquishing her deviant identity, she also gives up her place in the developing nation.[22] The meanings of signs in this novel transmute in relation to one another, pointing to the ever changing position of the individual in society.

In "The Custom House," the frame-story for *The Scarlet Letter*, Hawthorne's alter-ego narrator uncovers the material remnants of the tale, underscoring this dynamic relationship among social norms, legal doctrine, and the individual. Channeling Hester and perhaps inverting her social trajectory, as he takes up and then "involuntarily" drops her scarlet badge, the narrator alternates between normativity and conciliation, on the one hand, and deviance, on the other.[23] By his own account, "adjudged guilty" of "atrocities" in his depiction of the Custom House, the author-narrator, who has been discharged from his position as Surveyor with the election of a Whig government, insists that "the public disapprobation" of his description of the Custom House officials "weigh[s] heavily on him."[24] "[D]isclaim[ing] motives" of "enmity," however, he finds himself "constrained . . . to republish his introductory sketch without the change of a word."[25] Like Hester, once "beyond the scope of generally received laws," who conjures an "angel and apostle of the coming revelation,"[26] Hawthorne's narrator-author suggests the special place of the individual as both the deviant and visionary of American society.

The self-conscious deviance of nineteenth-century Transcendentalist Ralph Waldo Emerson contrasts with Hawthorne's conciliatory posture.[27] Emerson's idea of the individual, however, also reflects the contingent process through which the deviant and the idealized American figure in relation to law. In addition, this notion of the individual indirectly reflects the impact of slavery in the countermodel it engages. Specifically, in Emerson's mobilization of self-reliance to unsettle cultural norms, the evolving paradigm of individual consciousness bears the imprint of the material reality of the criminal in the reformed prison cell of the early nineteenth century.[28] The penitentiary reform movement of the early nineteenth century, a counterpoint to the slave system, envisioned criminals as containing the seeds of their own social reform.[29] By enabling prisoners to turn inward to confront their guilt and repair themselves, reformers sought to renovate the soul of the convict.[30] In this way, Caleb Smith argues, "The Northern convict, trained and disciplined for factory work in the modern prison, was imagined in opposition to Southern slaves, a mass of bodies laboring in the fields."[31] A parallel to the Southern slave, the convicted criminal was to be a key economic component in the system of reform, supplying the factory labor that offset the cost of the prison and at times generated a profit. However, by the 1830s, once-model prisons were overcrowded and mismanaged, and as Emerson came to imagine the idealized individual as deviant, he turned the vision of the penitentiary inside out.[32] Rejecting the paradigm of the flawed self-repairing soul, Emerson instead identified the "conformity" of "[s]ociety everywhere in conspiracy against the manhood of every one of its members."[33] For

Emerson, Smith asserts, "Deviancy, the contemptuous disregard of social strictures, is the method and the sign of self-reliance."[34]

Although the key to redemption for Emerson is pushing one's "deviant individuality" beyond the constraints of social control, Emerson's ideal individual retains the imprint of the solitary cell of penitential architecture ("the . . . man . . . who in the midst of the crowd keeps with perfect sweetness the independence of solitude").[35] With Hester and Hawthorne's Custom House narrator, Emerson's transcendent nonconformist takes up and refigures contingent manifestations of the law – in this case, the solitary penitential cell, which itself bears a negative imprint of slavery: the solitary cell served as "an instrument of counterdefinition . . . by which the North declared its modernity and humanity against the retrograde brutality of the South."[36]

As this chapter shows, in the nineteenth century, the reality and specter of slavery in America shape the ways in which laws on the books register – or fail to register – as norms and, in doing so, frame the ways deviance is imagined and recast over time.

II. "Bartleby": critiquing the penitentiary and prefiguring the limits of contract freedom

If, at the beginning of the nineteenth century, the prison reflected a Northern response to slavery – conceptualizing the deviant prisoner as redeemable from within and simultaneously precipitating an American paradigm of the transcendent individual – in the mid-nineteenth century, contract emerged in contrast to slavery as the mark of the free individual in Northern discourse. Presciently evoking the limits of contract and emancipation to come, Herman Melville's mid-nineteenth-century tale, "Bartleby, the Scrivener" (1853), offers a portrait of individuality that illuminates various figures of deviance as they emerge at this time.

In this story, Bartleby, a Wall Street "law-copyist," refuses to participate in the nineteenth-century nexus of law and capitalism, insisting in variations on his now-famous phrasing that he "would prefer not to" copy the legal documents or otherwise undertake the tasks of his employment in the lawyer-narrator's "snug [legal] business."[37] Bartleby's intentions and character resist easy interpretation by the narrator and readers.[38] When he enigmatically refuses to quit the space that was his employer's law office, Bartleby is taken to prison, where he ultimately dies.[39]

In one reading, Bartleby figures as a prisoner, who initially undertakes the industrial labor of the penitentiary[40] "silently, palely, mechanically."[41] Prized by his employer as a "valuable acquisition," Bartleby also evokes the chattel slave, and his "ghost"-like presence in the office points to the liminal space between life and death that both slave and prisoner inhabit in nineteenth-century America.[42] North Carolina Judge Thomas Ruffin's opinion in *State v. Mann* (1829) demonstrates the tension created by the chattel slave's status as property. In this case, Judge Ruffin overturned a jury's determination that a hired slave had been subject to battery. Judge Ruffin "lament[s]" the circumstance, finding that cruel and unreasonable battery on a slave is not in fact indictable, but he asserts that

> [w]ith slavery . . . [t]he end is the profit of the master, his security and the public safety to live without knowledge, and without the capacity to make any thing his own, and to toil that another may reap the fruits.

As such, "the power of the master must be absolute, to render the submission of the slave perfect."[43] As articulated a few decades later by the Supreme Court of Appeals of Virginia, the criminal as prisoner forfeits

> all his personal rights except those which the law in its humanity accords him . . . [becoming] for the time being the slave of the State. He is *civiliter mortuus*; and his estate, if he has any, is administered like that of a dead man.[44]

Although felons retained citizenship, unlike slaves, the distinction between them blurs given that the slave's social death and the felon's civil death both entail a loss of personal rights, divestment of property, and dissolution of marriage; in the erosion of equal protection of rights toward the end of Reconstruction, former slaves came to inhabit a comparable status of incomplete citizenship.[45]

While the early nineteenth-century carceral structure sought to mobilize the convict's humanity, in civil death it subjected the prisoner to the ritual practice of mortification.[46] Bartleby not only evokes the prisoner in his "cadaverous" demeanor and "solitude" but also challenges the humanizing ideal of criminal law in his "passive resistance."[47] He refuses to work, eat, or grant the narrator a sense of interpersonal connection or even satisfaction in granting aid; as the narrator muses, "I might give alms to his body; but his body did not pain him; it was his soul that suffered, and his soul I could not reach."[48] The way Bartleby dies in prison, failing to find a place in society and unredeemed through legal process, cuts at the heart of the vision of criminal reform and invokes the figures of prisoner and slave in the liminal space created by the law.[49]

The character of Bartleby brings into focus various figures of deviance that are to emerge after Emancipation. In so doing, this quintessential "other," described by the perplexed narrator as "the strangest" of a "singular set,"[50] not only rebuts the imagined transcendence of the incarcerated criminal but also presciently critiques the structure of contract that figures as a counterpoint to slavery in the second half of the century. Bartleby thereby prefigures notions of deviance precipitated by the ideal and laws of contract.

Assuming a predominant role in American law over the course of the nineteenth century, contract reflected the belief in market economics and in the law as facilitator of private autonomy.[51] By the 1840s, when most of the action of "Bartleby" seems to take place,[52] contract had also become the common trope among abolitionists of different goals and approaches.[53] Nineteenth-century wage labor epitomized the exercise of free contract, even as it was understood to reflect a hierarchical "relation of authority and subordination."[54] Following Emancipation, contract emerged in opposition to slavery: it functioned as the manifestation of the status of freedom and autonomy, both as a transaction and as a social relation grounded in notions of "self ownership, consent and exchange."[55] Describing contract as "the meeting of the minds of the contracting parties," courts enforced agreement in the context of objective and formal constraints.[56] "Bartleby" presciently highlights the limits of contract as a sign of freedom, which among other things threatened to naturalize inequality.[57] In doing so, the tale implicitly marks contract as a normative boundary beyond which various nineteenth-century figures are forced to inhabit a space of deviance.

Bartleby's refusal to participate in the material production of contracts or to explain himself in the related language of capitalism marks him as beyond the norm. Rather than help copy and "verify" the various "rich men's bonds, and mortgages, and title deeds" that drive his employer's "pleasantly remunerative" business,[58] Bartleby eschews the framework of individual will, declining to engage in wage labor or to give a reason for doing so.[59] The contracts he is asked to produce document "assumptions" of debt and "preference" of creditors, as reflected in the language of nineteenth-century legal form books and case law. For example, the New York Chancery Court, of which the narrator was appointed for a time a Master of Chancery, handled cases involving "preference in payment" and "preferred debt" in the period ostensibly covered by the story.[60] The lawyer-narrator's perspective, indeed his sense of Bartleby as "unaccountable," reflects his immersion in this legal environment.[61] Bartleby, however, upends the lawyer-narrator's assumptions[62] and the language of contract with his reworking of "preference" into an insistence that he "would prefer not to." Bartleby thereby transforms the structure and language of contract into a form of resistance to the very framework of employment that contract underpins.[63]

In illuminating the bounds of contract freedom, Bartleby conjures other figures of deviance, precipitated by the structure of contract as a rebuttal to slavery following Emancipation. Bartleby is ultimately taken to prison, for example, "as a vagrant" (though the narrator continues to struggle with the challenge of classifying Bartleby).[64] With the increasing predominance of wage labor and the difficult economy of the second half of the nineteenth century, workers struggled to support themselves. Despite or as a result of this, new statutes identified begging as a crime punishable with forced labor; the beggar was seen as a loathsome "suspect figure" of deception who shirked hard work.[65] In Massachusetts, the first Northern state to pass stricter vagrancy statutes, "An Act Concerning Vagrants or Vagabonds" punished "persons wandering abroad and begging" with forced labor of up to six months. In the next twenty years, vagrancy statutes were enacted across the Northern states.[66] Those individuals deemed vagrants were thereby transformed into prisoners by the law, their coercion into forced labor validated by the principle of the free market.[67]

Eschewing options for wage labor suggested by the lawyer, Bartleby invokes this figure of the "common trespasser" in his reluctance to leave the office premises.[68] However, he also leaves untouched the additional handout his employer offers,[69] refusing charity and thereby challenging the stereotype of the dependent beggar. Again, by opting out of the paradigm of contract entirely, Bartleby is left nowhere to go: he dies in the "Tombs" or, as the narrator notes, "the Halls of Justice."[70] In this way, Bartleby embodies the ultimate deviant: subverting language in general as well as the particular language of contract.[71] In the process, he eschews the norm and also the posited role of the criminal. As such, Bartleby performs a wide-ranging critique of the social structure so deeply informed by contract, pointing forward to the challenges that freedmen and -women would face when they sought to support themselves in wage labor arrangements that replicated the demands of slavery.[72] In addition, Bartleby epitomizes the overlap and slippage at times between particular parameters of deviance, which becomes even more evident in the intersection and mutual framing of racial, gender, and sexual norms.

III. Incidents in the Life of a Slave Girl: the elusive space of normative law and sexuality

Inhabiting the office space, Bartleby blurs the bounds between the circumscribed domestic and public spheres that constituted the normative nineteenth-century worldview in both the North and the South. Thus, he points to yet another figure of deviance both constructed by the limits of contractual freedom and invoked as a sign of the degeneracy of the market – that of the prostitute. Whereas the character of Bartleby offers an oblique critique of the normative order, the prostitute served as a symbol of social ills. Described even by those sympathetic to her plight as "the extremity of abomination,"[73] the prostitute, along with the slave, comes to be appropriated in varying ways, demonstrating the instability of the contested space of social norms.

Although prostitution itself was not necessarily illegal, the act of soliciting money led police and courts to conceptualize it as criminal dependence akin to begging.[74] New York's Code of Criminal Procedure, enacted in 1881, included the "common prostitute, who has no lawful employment, whereby to maintain herself" in the definition of a "vagrant," who could be punished by fine and/or imprisonment of up to a year.[75] As early as the 1830s, prostitution was invoked by Northerners and Southerners as the symbol of the degeneracy of the social system of the other.[76] By commodifying sex in a market, the prostitute figured as the specter of abolition and free market relations.[77] Thus, in the antebellum South, the prostitute threatened the domestic order of relations of dependency between master and slave as well as between husband and wife.[78] In the antebellum North, the public became fascinated with the figure of the sexually transgressive woman, generating a movement of reform. In the process, the prostitute came to signify to abolitionists the structure of slavery.[79] Deriding slavery's impact on "domestic society," abolitionists viewed "slave states [as] one vast brothel," while Southern defenders of slavery pointed to the "prostitution of the North."[80] In this way, the prostitute as an antebellum figure of deviance highlights the contested normative space that slavery creates. The invocation of the prostitute to define normativity also draws upon and reinforces other accepted significations of deviance or degeneracy and, in the process, pathologizes women in general, women of color, nonheterosexual behavior, and sexual intercourse outside marriage, to name a few.

Harriet Jacobs' account of her experience escaping slavery, *Incidents in the Life of a Slave Girl* (1861), serves as another example of the way slavery and the laws facilitating it shaped the shifting figures of deviance. Jacobs's text, presented as a first-person chronicle, aligned itself for the most part with the vision of Garrisonian nonviolent reform. Edited by abolitionist and women's rights activist, Maria Child, the narrative gestures toward Christianity's higher law to justify civil disobedience, such as subversion of the Fugitive Slave Act.

Completed soon after John Brown's raid at Harper's Ferry,[81] Jacobs' restrained indictment of slavery reflects the degree to which the normative status of certain laws was not only actively contested but also highly dynamic.[82] The outcome of the soon to be fought Civil War might be viewed as the most significant normative shift, upending the seemingly radical framing of slavery as an actionable crime. Yet *Incidents* reveals the particular complexity of the American negotiation of the dialectics of law/crime or norm/deviance and foreshadows the impact of slavery on the figuring of deviance into the later nineteenth and early twentieth centuries.

Jacobs's narrative mobilizes the specter of illicit sexual behavior to mark the structure of slavery as depraved and also to highlight the perils of the urban Northern landscape for a woman. From the outset, the narrative uses antebellum code for "illicit female sexuality"[83] in the epigraph's promise of an account "of the depth of *degradation* involved in . . . Slavery."[84] Similarly, the term "slave girl" announced a narrative of a fallen woman to antebellum Northern readers – familiar with the threat of sexual transgression in plantations and industrialized cities from popular print culture.[85] As such, the narrative highlights the trend of pathologizing the figure of the black woman, who comes to be associated with the prostitute by the end of the century.[86] In doing so, Jacobs' narrative also presumes a paradigm of heteronormativity that enables her to link slavery with, and thus reinscribe the deviance of, "freak[ish]" sexual behavior.[87]

Jacobs' narrative underscores the centrality of the slave woman's sexual availability to the perpetuation of slavery.[88] Slave women, she explains, "are considered of no value, unless they continually increase their owner's stock."[89] Slave laws imposing a mother's status on her child created property incentives for sexual relations between masters and slaves. The law thereby situated illicit sexual behavior as a key component of the social structure. The earlier "archetypal slave narrative,"[90] *Narrative of the Life of Frederick Douglass, an American Slave, Written by Himself* (1845), depicted sexual violence as the "original generative act" of slave formation in an opening scene of Douglass's aunt being "stripped . . .from neck to waist" and whipped by the master.[91] Identifying "this terrible spectacle" of abuse as "the blood-stained gate, the entrance to the hell of slavery, through which [Douglass] was about to pass," Douglass's narrative bolsters the metaphoric suggestion of the production of slavery via rape with its description of the aunt forced to stand "fair for [the master's] infernal purpose" unclothed to the waist with her hands tied to a hook.[92] In relating the rumor that he had a white father, along with the suggestion of the aunt as a substitute mother, Douglass presents interracial rape as his own origin story and the mechanism of slave creation generally.[93]

In this context of the slave woman's requisite involvement in illicit sexual acts and against the backdrop of urban gothic fiction exploring illicit sex in developing cities,[94] Jacobs' narrative takes pains to relocate the subject of deviance. She identifies slavery itself as the pathology. Having spent "twenty-one years in that cage of obscene birds," Linda Brent, Jacobs' pseudonymous protagonist, "testif[ies] from . . . experience and observation," about "the all-pervading corruption produced by slavery": it "makes the white fathers cruel and sensual; the sons violent and licentious . . . contaminates the daughters, and makes the wives wretched," leaving it all but impossible for her "to describe the depth of [the] degradation [of "the colored race"]."[95]

Endeavoring to resist the advances of her master, Dr. Flint, and seeking to explain her seemingly transgressive decision to enter into a sexual relationship with an unmarried white man in the hope of securing her own and, ultimately, her children's freedom, Jacobs' narrator highlights her victimization by the law. She entreats the "virtuous reader" to "pity" and "pardon" her, "entirely unprotected by law or custom" and "reduce[d by the laws] . . . to the condition of a chattel, entirely subject to the will of another."[96] Indeed, under North Carolina statutes, the rape of a slave woman constituted a crime only to the extent it involved a trespass on a master's property.[97] Jacobs repeatedly returns to the failure of the legal structure to protect the innocent,[98] stressing its deviation from a notional higher law and thereby undermining its normative status. In addition, invoking a common abolitionist trope of slave law enforcers as criminals, Jacobs' narrator openly challenges laws establishing her and her children's status as "property": "I regarded such laws as the regulations of robbers, who had no rights that I was bound to respect."[99] In this way, the narrative characterizes as lawbreakers those enacting and adhering to laws enabling slavery, reframing the slave woman as innocent victim rather than as paradigmatic deviant-criminal.

Jacobs does not go so far as the overtly militant abolitionist movement to name slavery as a "crime" explicitly,[100] yet her discussion of the Fugitive Slave Act of 1850 in connection with particular horrors of slavery links this law to the deviant subject.[101] In pathologizing slavery, the narrative tars the legal institutional framework on which it is predicated along with, by implication, certain sexual behavior. Outlining the way this "iniquitous law" upends "humble homes" and threatens to separate "[m]any a wife," "husband," and the "children of his love," Jacobs affirms a normative baseline of domestic relations threatened by the law.[102] In contrast to the domestic idyll she invokes, her account of the experiences of a former slave named Luke paints a picture of homosexual desire in the slave system as "freak[ish]" pathology, which owes its power to and contaminates the law.[103] In doing so, Jacobs' narrative also prefigures the interrelation of racial and sexual normative categories, which emerge in the conception of deviant identity at the end of the century.[104]

Although Jacobs' narrative aims to establish a conceptual normative space of decency for women threatened with slavery, shifting the focus to the deviance of slavery-enabling law and homosexual acts, it concludes by marking the limits of this endeavor in practice. Jacobs explains, "Reader, my story ends in freedom; not in the usual way with marriage."[105] This disjunction between freedom and marriage points a reader back toward gender relations and sexual practice as a related site of evolving and contested normativity in the nineteenth century. Jacobs' narrative concludes with the compromised position of the narrator's daughter. As a servant in a Northern home subject to moral corruption and abuse, the daughter reminds readers of a related narrative of deviance and illicit sexuality, the urban gothic tale of white slavery in emerging cities (also suggesting the reality of women, lacking other means of support, caught up in charges of vagrancy and prostitution).[106] As such, *Incidents* points to the limited options for women in a corrupted social structure.

IV. Postbellum normative negotiations: suffragists, free-lovers, and polygamists

Whereas Jacobs introduces marriage as the unattainable space of normativity if not freedom in antebellum society, postbellum reform discourses take up the figure of slavery in framing prostitution and at times marriage.[107] As the substance of the law shifts during and after Reconstruction, so too do the rhetorical strategies available for women seeking equality under the law. The way deviance and norms are variously figured evolves as well. With abolition, by midcentury the idea of women's political participation had moved into the mainstream.[108] Even as women failed to secure equal rights of citizenship with the amendment of the Constitution, the contested meaning of the Constitution suggested to reformers new normative possibilities, including women's suffrage and political participation. For a time, reformers present the black woman as the model for inclusion.[109]

Yet as the meaning of the law, in courts and on the ground, became crystalized, some activists reframed their position in more conservative terms while others figured in popular discourse as patently aberrant. Victoria Woodhull, one of the most salient nonconforming figures of this period, made history as the first female candidate to run for president in 1872. In addition to labor rights, Woodhull advocated both women's suffrage and "free love" – a woman's right to establish and dissolve sexual relations at will – on the basis of the "sovereignty of the individual."[110] Divorced and sexually active, Woodhull established her reputation as an outlier. She stood on the radical edge of the women's suffrage movement, which had refigured a woman's role in the polity in terms that resonated with the traditional family structure established in marriage.[111] An 1872 cartoon in *Harper's Weekly* portrays Woodhull as an archetype of deviance, tapping into the enduring normative benchmark of traditional family roles. Depicted in the foreground of a rocky landscape with Satanic wings and a suggestion of horns, Woodhull holds a placard stating, "BE SAVED BY FREE LOVE." Over her shoulder, receding into difficult terrain, a woman makes her way along a precipice carrying on her back the burdens of small children and a man pouring rum into his mouth. The caption reads, "Get Thee Behind Me (Mrs.) Satan," with underneath: "Wife (with heavy burden) 'I'd rather travel the hardest path of matrimony than follow your footsteps.' "[112]

Along with a trend in scientific thought toward essentialist conceptions of race and gender, some women's rights rhetoric repositioned black men in the space of deviant sexuality. Elizabeth Cady Stanton tapped into the language of "degradation," and "humiliation," describing the plight of disenfranchised women in the context of the elevation of the "lowest orders of manhood."[113] In the arena of changing legal norms, however, activists soon found themselves marked as criminals. Federal agents arrested Woodhull for obscenity and Susan B. Anthony for "criminal voting," under the Enforcement Act, which had not long prior been understood to protect these actions under law.[114] In *Minor v. Happersett* (1874),[115] the Supreme Court unanimously asserted that the Constitution did not confer the right to vote on citizens, closing the door on the right to vote for women and on the protection of black men's ability to exercise their existing right to vote.

Henry James's novel *The Bostonians* (1886) captures the figures contending for normative status around this time, suggesting the trajectories of social critique. Set in this period of postbellum rights activism, the novel portrays the relationship of three potentially deviant characters: Olive Chancellor, an unmarried wealthy Bostonian committed to women's rights modeled after contemporary activists;[116] her bachelor cousin, Basil Ransom, a former Confederate soldier, whose family has been "ruined" by the war and who holds fast to traditional Southern views;[117] and the object of each's attention, Verena Tarrant, a beautiful, charismatic women's rights speaker, granddaughter of an abolitionist and raised among free-lovers.[118]

Olive Chancellor, "unmarried by every implication of her being" – "essentially a celibate," troubles the gender norm of the woman as the keeper of the hearth of the republican family.[119] At the same time, the relationship between James's "peculiarly . . . constituted" activist[120] and her protégée did not necessarily resonate in terms of illicit sexual intimacy in the late nineteenth century. Yet if deep friendships involving bourgeois women making passionate commitments to one another were culturally accepted, the assertion in the narrative that "[i]t was a very peculiar thing, their friendship" also resonates in terms of emerging sexual identities at the end of the century. The narrative explains that Verena's friendship with Olive "had elements that made it probably as complete as any (between women) that had ever existed. Of course it had been more on Olive's side than on hers, she had always known that; but that, again, didn't make any difference."[121] The novel thereby evokes a scenario of asymmetrical love interest of one woman in another, which storyline emerges explicitly in sensational news just a few years later, framed as an anomaly. Specifically, the 1892 murder of Freda Ward by Alice Mitchell, who claimed to love Ward too much to lose her, was depicted by lawyers and medical experts as unique and almost incomprehensible (resulting in Mitchell's commitment to the Tennessee State Insane Asylum).[122]

In *The Bostonians*, the potential emergence of Verena – or possibly Olive in the novel's final moments – as a speaker in the public sphere offers a counterpoint to Ransom's traditional domestic vision. Ransom dismisses Olive's pleas to let Verena complete her public speaking engagement – for which, the interested agent, Mr. Flier, points out, tickets have been sold, reflecting Verena's place in the public realm of contract and commerce. Ransom insists, "She's mine or she isn't, and if she's mine, she's all mine!"[123] By mid-century, many states had passed Married Women's Property Acts, enabling women to inherit property and at times keep separate earnings. The statutes thereby attenuated the existing common-law convention of subsuming a married woman's legal rights and obligations to those of her husband under coverture. Yet the increasing rights of married women also remained tied to judicial discretion.[124] Thus, for example, in the case of *Cole v. Van Riper* (1897), the Supreme Court of Illinois asserted that the Illinois Married Women's Act of 1861 "cannot receive a literal interpretation."[125] The opinion of Justice Charles B. Lawrence, writing for the majority of the court, explained:

> It is simply impossible that a woman married should be able to control and enjoy her property as if she were sole, without leaving her at liberty practically to annul the marriage tie at pleasure; and the same is true of the property of the husband, so far as it is directly connected with the nurture and maintenance of his household.

Ransom's seduction of Verena reflects the degree to which the traditional structure retained some hold on American consciousness but was also not without critics. For Ransom, a woman in marriage would be properly subsumed into the legal identity of her husband as a *feme covert* – a status he causes to be enacted in the novel's final scene: Ransom "wrenche[s]" Verena away from Olive, her family, and an awaiting public audience "by muscular force" and "thrust[s] the hood of Verena's long cloak over her head, to conceal her face and identity."[126]

The novel depicts the re-entrenchment of certain normative gender roles, though cast against the backdrop of an evolving sensibility being negotiated in courts and beyond. Peripheral characters of the novel reinforce the particular contours of contemporaneous debates around women's rights and roles. For example, the character of Dr. Mary Prance, an unmarried doctor who eschews the rhetoric of women's rights reform, reflects the late-nineteenth-century reality of women practicing medicine. At the same time, the field of law and, with it, the act of public speaking remained restricted on the basis of gender. Denied membership to the Illinois Bar as a married woman, Myra Bradwell appealed her case to the Supreme Court. Rejecting her claim, the Supreme Court made clear in *Bradwell v. Illinois* (1872) that a woman's right to practice law was not among her privileges and immunities as a citizen protected by the Fourteenth Amendment.[127] *Bradwell* immediately follows the *Slaughter-House Cases* (1872), in which a view of a history of slavery underpins the majority's limited reading of the privileges and immunities protected under the Fourteenth Amendment (and from which Justice Joseph P. Bradley dissented). Justice Bradley's concurring opinion in *Bradwell*, invoking a married woman's inability to contract without her husband's consent as a justification for women's exclusion from the bar, suggests the normative framing of women as presumptively married. While conceding "that many women are unmarried," Justice Bradley's opinion insists that "the rules of civil society must be adapted to the general constitution of things, and cannot be based upon exceptional cases." "[I]n view of the peculiar characteristics, destiny and mission of woman," Justice Bradley was willing to validate the state power to restrict women from professions.[128]

James renders the costs experienced by some in the trend toward reestablished gender spheres and refuses to grant that normative debates have been settled. Rather, observing "this union [with Ransom], so far from brilliant," the novel leaves Verena "in tears," "beneath her hood."[129] In addition, James ultimately positions Olive as his heroine, who in the novel's final moments, departs to take the stage and perhaps speak at the risk in her account of being "hissed and hooted and insulted."[130] In terms of race, the terrain remains equally if not more fraught. Abolitionists register as the activists of an earlier generation who can no longer read the terrain, and Ransom imagines the feelings of "a young man . . . who, waiting in a public place, has made up his mind . . . to discharge a pistol at the king or the president."[131] In this way, Ransom channels the iconic Reconstruction-era criminal/presidential assassin, while his tracts "on the rights of minorities," invoking "doctrines . . . about three hundred years behind the age," seem to be gaining new purchase as he finally secures an offer for publication.[132] As such, the novel depicts the trend toward "racial extremism in law, in science, and in literature" that lays the groundwork for the nation's "propensity to define equal protection under the Constitution in such a way as to render the black population invisible" by the end of the century.[133]

The Supreme Court's decision in the case of *Reynolds v. United States* (1878),[134] placing polygamy beyond the bounds of religious protection accorded by the First Amendment, suggests the complexity of the process by which racialism develops at the end of the century. In particular, *Reynolds* demonstrates the way in which slavery, by contrast, is used to entrench both the normativity of traditional marriage and marriage as the normative space of women. In the process, other sexual practices come to be placed in a racialized space of deviance. Presenting marriage as "a sacred obligation" as well as a "civil contract . . . regulated by law" upon which "society may be said to be built," the Supreme Court's opinion in *Reynolds* tied polygamy – "an overt act made criminal by the law of the land" and "subversive of good order" – to the shadow of slavery.[135] *Reynolds* echoed contemporary popular writings that framed polygamy as "degrading bondage" and mobilized images of illicit sexuality and pathology shared by urban gothic pulp and abolitionist narratives.[136] The Court asserted that "polygamy leads to the patriarchal principle . . . which . . . fetters the people in stationary despotism."[137] Antipolygamy rhetoric depicting free-love advocacy as the gateway to the degradations of polygamy also bolstered the marginalization of women's rights activists.[138] Thus, while the antipolygamy legal and cultural discourse categorized polygamy with slavery as degenerate acts, it simultaneously preserved marriage as the normative paradigm. As such, affirming a jury instruction to consider the crime of polygamy's "innocent victims" – "pure-minded women and . . . innocent children"[139] – the Court reinscribes the separate sphere of domestic dependence properly populated by married women.

In this context, slavery, as the central space of contested norms and crimes in the nineteenth century, serves to precipitate a nexus of purported deviancy around gender, sexual relations, and race. By naming certain practices criminal, *Reynolds* both contributes to and offers a glimpse of the evolving dynamic through which sexual deviance is marked with the implied pathology of race. It does so by situating polygamy and thus deviant practices in terms of an implicit geographic and racial hierarchy. The Court asserts, polygamy has "always been odious among . . . nations of Europe," being "almost exclusively a feature of the life of Asiatic and of African people."[140] *Reynolds* thereby illustrates the process of crystalization of racial distinctions in law and society toward the end of the century.

V. *Plessy v. Ferguson* and the emerging identity of the deviant

The re-entrenchment of a cultural vision of white superiority implied in *Reynolds* was similarly reflected in the postbellum prevalence of school segregation laws.[141] Nearly as popular, miscegenation laws marked a normative boundary, "embod[ying] the very essence of" Southern whites' "beliefs . . . that whites were racially superior to blacks and that any mixing of the two groups was bound to sully the whites."[142] In addition, notwithstanding the contingency of the particular legal developments of this period, rulings empowering states' rights significantly reduced the rights and protections of "colored" citizens.[143] The Supreme Court's holding in the *Civil Rights Cases* (1883) that the Fourteenth Amendment did not prohibit racial discrimination by private actors gave legal support to the view of private comingling among people regarded as racially distinct as non-normative.[144] In this case, the Supreme Court invalidated the provisions of the 1875 Civil Rights Act granting "colored citizens, whether slaves or not, and citizens of other races . . . the same accommodations and privileges as are enjoyed by white citizens," with respect to "inns, public conveyances, and places of amusement." Similarly, fears of sexual mobility and of the sexual threat of the black man to the white woman underpinned the segregation of rail cars.[145] The Supreme Court's validation in *Plessy v. Ferguson* (1896) of a state statute mandating "equal but separate accommodations for white, and colored races" in rail cars came, at least retrospectively, to mark the entrenchment of racial boundaries in nineteenth-century law and culture, reflecting the belief in social intermingling among perceived races as a deviant activity.[146]

Homer Plessy, the plaintiff in whom it was asserted that "the mixture of colored blood was not discernable"[147] belied the notion of "discrete markers of racial difference."[148] Nonetheless, the assertion of the majority opinion of the Supreme Court that the "legal distinction between the white and colored races" relies upon "a distinction . . . founded in the color of the two races, and which must always exist so long as white men are distinguished from the other race by color"[149] demonstrates a process of naturalizing racial identities in the law and in society. With discourses of scientific racism,[150] a surge of mob law in the form of lynchings in the final decades of the century[151] challenged the meaning of legal institutional pronouncements of racial equality. The pathologization of "colored" bodies also marked nonheterosexual behavior as deviant, and Jim Crow segregation eroticized racial distinctions.[152] This cultural and legal process opened the door to the notion of the homosexual as deviant in the early twentieth century and the subsequent distinct criminalization of homosexual behavior,[153] as well the ongoing criminalization of citizens of color.

From this perspective, a search for notions of deviance in nineteenth-century America reveals a contingent dynamic relation between law and figures of normativity. In nineteenth-century America, as a defining cultural flashpoint, slavery serves as a significant prism through which to view the negotiation of normative roles. As slavery receded into history as a once contested though legally supported practice, it laid the groundwork for the emergence of particular identities of deviance in the less volatile constitutional landscape of the twentieth century and beyond.

Notes

1 Michel Foucault, *The History of Sexuality, Vol. I* (New York: Vintage, 1990). Siobhan Somerville discusses the change in the conceptualization of identity and bodies in Siobhan B. Somerville, *Queering the Color Line: Race and the Invention of Homosexuality in American Culture* (Durham, N.C.: Duke University Press, 2000).
2 "deviant, n." *Oxford English Dictionary*, 2nd ed., 1989; online version November 2010.
3 For radical abolitionists, the Constitution was seen as a "pro-slavery instrument." Frederick Douglass's writings in *The North Star*, his Rochester weekly paper, reflect the ongoing debate as to whether the Constitution ought to be viewed as a "divine" mandate or a "human" one, "with all its vice and crimes." Frederick Douglass, "The Constitution and Slavery," *The North Star*, March 16, 1849.
4 Activist and abolitionist Lydia M. Child, for example, challenged the normative status of this law in *The Duty of Disobedience to the Fugitive Slave Act: An Appeal to the Legislators of Massachusetts* (Boston: American Anti-Slavery Society, 1860).
5 Nathaniel Hawthorne, *The Scarlet Letter and Other Writings*, ed. Leland S. Pearson (New York: Norton, 2005), 165–6.
6 Ibid., 165, 128.
7 Ibid., 165.
8 Ibid., 105–6.
9 Ibid., 130.
10 Leonard W. Levy, "Sims' Case: The Fugitive Slave Law in Boston in 1851," *Journal of Negro History* 35 (1950): 41; Brook Thomas, *Cross-Examinations of Law and Literature: Cooper, Hawthorne, Stowe, and Melville* (Cambridge, UK: Cambridge University Press, 1987), 95–6.
11 According to reports, as he was captured, Sims screamed out, "I'm in the hands of kidnappers!" (Levy, 44), thereby evoking a common trope of criminality in connection with the Fugitive Slave Act. Compare the following discussion concerning Harriet Jacobs's and others' framing of the Act in terms of robbery.
12 Laws of the Commonwealth of Massachusetts (Boston, 1843), 1843, chap. LXIX, cited in Levy, 45–6.
13 Levy, "Sims' Case," 43, 45–6.
14 Ibid., 46–7.
15 *In re Sims*, 7 Cush. 285 (Mass. 1851). Section 6 of the Fugitive Slave Act provided for summary judgment rather than determination of an alleged fugitive slave's status by jury trial.
16 http://commons.wikimedia.org/wiki/File:Slave_kidnap_post_1851_boston.jpg#filehistory (accessed November 24, 2014).
17 Ibid.
18 Hawthorne, *The Scarlet Letter*, 69, 135.
19 Ibid., 135.
20 Sacvan Bercovitch, *The Office of the Scarlet Letter* (Baltimore: Johns Hopkins University Press, 1991), 10 note *.
21 Hawthorne, *The Scarlet Letter*, 62, 69.
22 Ibid., 162, 165.
23 Ibid., 26.
24 Ibid., 5.
25 Ibid.
26 Ibid., 128, 166.
27 Bercovitch, *Office*, 127.
28 Caleb Smith, "Emerson and Incarceration," *American Literature* 78 (2006): 208–34.
29 For more on the prison and reform, see John Barton's chapter 14 in this volume.
30 Smith, "Emerson and Incarceration," 210.
31 Ibid., 209 note 4.
32 Ibid., 209.
33 Ibid., 222, citing Ralph Waldo Emerson, "Self-Reliance," in *Selected Essays*, ed. Larzer Ziff (New York: Penguin, 1982), 178. As Smith shows, Emerson inverts the figure of the criminal looking inward for reform and liberation, asserting in "Self Reliance": "[M]an as it were clapped into jail by his consciousness. As soon as he has once spoken with *éclat* he is a committed person, watched by the sympathy or hatred of hundreds, whose affections must now enter into his account."
34 Smith, "Emerson and Incarceration," 222.

35 Ibid., 223, 225, citing Emerson, "Self-Reliance," 181.
36 Smith, "Emerson and Incarceration," 223, 209 note 4.
37 Herman Melville, "Bartleby, The Scrivener," in *Melville's Short Novels*, ed. Dan McCall (New York: Norton, 2002), 4, 10–11, 15.
38 Gilles Deleuze, for one, sees neither metaphor nor symbol in Bartleby. He discusses the "agrammaticality" of Bartleby's response, through which Bartleby performs his resistance and "exhaust[s] language." Gilles Deleuze, "Bartleby; Or, The Formula," in *Essays Critical and Clinical*, trans. Daniel W. Smith and Michael A. Greco (Minneapolis: University of Minnesota, 1997), 68, 70.
39 Melville, "Bartleby," 31, 33.
40 Caleb Smith, "Detention without Subjects: Prisons and the Poetics of Living Death," *Texas Studies in Literature and Language* 50 (2008): 243–67, 256; Smith, "Emerson and Incarceration," 212.
41 Melville, "Bartleby," 10.
42 Ibid., 15. For a discussion of the status of slave and prisoner as "living dead," see Joan Dayan, "Legal Slaves and Civil Bodies," in *Materializing Democracy: Toward a Revitalized Cultural Poetics*, ed. Russ Castronovo and Dana D. Nelson (Durham, N.C.: Duke University Press, 2002), 69, and Smith, 246.
43 *State v. Mann*, 2 Dev. 263 (N.C. 1829), 264, 266.
44 *Ruffin v. Commonwealth*, 62 Va. 790, 796 (1871).
45 Dayan, 55–6, 67–9.
46 Smith, "Detention without Subjects," 248.
47 Melville, "Bartleby," 20, 17, 13.
48 Ibid., 19.
49 Smith, "Detention without Subjects," 255–60.
50 Melville, "Bartleby," 4, 3.
51 Amy D. Stanley, *From Bondage to Contract* (Cambridge, UK: Cambridge University Press, 1998), 13, 10.
52 Barbara Foley explains how the tale makes it difficult to date the story. Barbara Foley, "From Wall Street to Astor Place: Historicizing Melville's 'Bartleby,'" *American Literature* 72 (2000): 87–116, 89.
53 Stanley, *From Bondage to Contract*, 18.
54 Ibid., 83.
55 Ibid., x.
56 *Murray v. Bethune*, 1 Wend. 191 (N.Y. 1828). For an invocation of this principle by a New York Chancery Court contemporaneous with the plot of "Bartleby," see *Cammeyer v. United German Lutheran Churches*, 2 Sand. Ch. 186 (N.Y. Ch. 1844).
57 The marriage contract is another example of the limits of notions of contract as an expression of autonomy: Once married, women no longer had a right to contract or enter into a position of ownership and a husband had a property right in his wife's labor. Nineteenth-century "domestic relations" entailed a husband's or master's rights and a wife's or servant's obligation of obedience, and these subordinate roles of wives and servants were not considered inconsistent with contract principles of contract by nineteenth-century legal thinkers. Stanley, *From Bondage to Contract*, 16.
58 Melville, "Bartleby," 10, 4.
59 In postbellum America, contract was a "relation of voluntary exchange . . . It was an axiom of Enlightenment philosophy that contract derived from and governed individual will and that free will was intimately connected to rights of proprietorship." Stanley, *From Bondage to Contract*, 3. When Bartleby refuses his employer's request that he "just step around to the Post Office," he responds to the lawyer's query, "You *will* not?" with "I *prefer* not." Melville, "Bartleby," 14–15.
60 *Johnson v. Corbett* (N.Y. Ch. 1844).
61 Melville, "Bartleby," 16.
62 In liberating the language of preference from its legal framework, Bartleby foils the narrator's assumptions in the colloquial sense. The narrator asserts, "I *assumed* the ground that depart he must; and upon that assumption built all I had to say . . . The great point was, not whether I had assumed that he would quit me, but whether he would prefer so to do. He was more a man of preferences than assumptions." Melville, "Bartleby," 21.
63 For a discussion of the way contract language figures in this story, see Tal Kastner, "'Bartleby': A Story of Boilerplate," *Law and Literature* 23 (2011): 365–404. The discussion of "Bartleby" in relation to contract draws in large part on this article.
64 Melville, "Bartleby," 27–8. The narrative subtly draws attention to the conceptual limits of vagrancy laws. When Bartleby expresses his preference not to quit the office space, the lawyer-narrator reviews available legal remedies, asking himself,

> [S]urely you will not have him collared by a constable and commit his innocent pallor to the common jail? And upon what ground could you procure such a thing to be done – a vagrant is he? What! . . . a wanderer who refuses to budge? It is because he will not be a vagrant, then, that you seek to count him as a vagrant. That is too absurd."
>
> *Ibid., 27–8.*

65 Stanley, *From Bondage to Contract*, 99, 101–9.
66 Ibid., 109.
67 Ibid., 109, 137.
68 Melville, "Bartleby," 30, 28.
69 Ibid., 22–4.
70 Ibid., 33, 31. In the narrator's account, "[b]eing under no disgraceful charge," Bartleby is "permitted . . . freely to wander about the prison, and especially, in the enclosed grass-platted yards thereof." Ibid., 31. Although the narrator seems unaware of the irony of freedom thus circumscribed, the description suggests the naturalization of constraint inherent in contract as a sign of freedom.
71 Bartleby's phrase "I would prefer not to," which enables him to respond without a response, has been read as "foreign to every other human language." Jacques Derrida, *The Gift of Death*, trans. David Willis (Chicago: Chicago University Press, 1996), 74.
72 For a discussion of this predicament, see Stanley, *From Bondage to Contract*, 45.
73 Ibid., 222.
74 Ibid., 219–20.
75 N.Y. Code Crim. P. ch. 504, tit. VI, §887, 1881 N.Y. Laws. This statute reflected the main antiprostitution measure undertaken by the state. William N. Eskridge, Jr., "Law and the Construction of the Closet: American Regulation of Same-Sex Intimacy, 1880–1946," *Iowa Law Review* 82 (1997): 1007–136, 1033.
76 Stanley, *From Bondage to Contract*, 240.
77 Ibid., 218.
78 In the nineteenth-century framework of separate spheres, rights of contract were denied women within the marriage contract under laws of coverture. Ibid., 59.
79 Jennifer R. Greeson, "The 'Mysteries and Miseries' of North Carolina: New York City, Urban Gothic Fiction, and *Incidents in the Life of a Slave Girl*," *American Literature* 73 (2001): 277–309, 280.
80 Stanley, *From Bondage to Contract*, 209, 240.
81 Caleb Smith, "Harriet Jacobs among the Militants: Transformations in Abolition's Public Sphere, 1859–61," *American Literature* 84 (2012): 743–68, 743.
82 In Caleb Smith's words, "readers [of *Incidents*] were invited to constitute themselves as normative communities by making judgments about the legitimacy of law." Ibid., 746.
83 Greeson, "Mysteries and Miseries," 271.
84 Harriet A. Jacobs [Linda Brent, pseud.], *Incidents in the Life of a Slave Girl, Written by Herself*, ed. L. Maria Child (1861; reprint, ed. Jean Fagan Yellin (Cambridge, Mass. Harvard University Press, 2002)).
85 Greeson, "Mysteries and Miseries," 278, 287–8.
86 Sander L. Gilman, "Black Bodies, White Bodies: Toward an Iconography of Female Sexuality in Late Nineteenth-Century Art, Medicine, and Literature," *Critical Inquiry* 12 (1985): 204–42; Aliyyah I. Abdur-Rahman, "'The Strangest Freaks of Despotism': Queer Sexuality in Antebellum African American Slave Narratives," *African American Review* 40 (2006): 224.
87 Jacobs, *Incidents*, 192. See Abdur-Rahman, 231–3. The discussion that follows also draws on Abdur-Rahman.
88 Abdur-Rahman, "The Strangest Freaks," 229.
89 Jacobs, *Incidents*, 49.
90 Abdur-Rahman, "The Strangest Freaks," 227.
91 Frederick Douglass, *Narrative of the Life of Frederick Douglass, an American Slave, Written by Himself* (1845; New Haven, Conn.: Yale University Press, 2001), 16. Saidiya V. Hartman, *Scenes of Subjection: Terror, Slavery, and Self-Making in Nineteenth-Century America* (New York: Oxford University Press, 1997), 3.
92 Douglass, *Narrative*, 16.
93 Abdur-Rahman, "The Strangest Freaks," 227–8.
94 Greeson, "Mysteries and Miseries," 278.
95 Jacobs, *Incidents*, 51–2. Indeed, as Jennifer Greeson notes, the "episodic accounts" Jacobs presents

> read as a veritable urban gothic catalogue of explicit vice, including the forced and observed copulation of field hands (49), breast torture (13, 122), the selling of mulatta women into prostitution

(23, 85, 105), the implied homosexual rape of a male slave chained to his master's couch (192), as well as abortion, infanticide, and lingering deaths in illegitimate childbirth (13–14, 52, 58, 122).

Greeson, "Mysteries and Miseries," 294.

96 Jacobs, *Incidents*, 55.

97 See ibid., 27 note 2.

98 Similarly, Jacobs describes her predicament as a mother unable to protect her children from being bought and sold as "[t]here was no protecting arm of the law for [her] to invoke." Ibid., 138.

99 Ibid., 187.

100 In contrast, for example, in his commemoration of Harper's Ferry, John Brown disciple James Redpath seeks to "fan the holy flame that [Brown and his followers'] action kindled, until, becoming a consuming fire, it shall burn up, with thoroughness and speed, every vestige of the crime of American Slavery." James Redpath, *Echoes of Harper's Ferry* (Boston: Thayer & Eldridge, 1860), 5.

101 See Smith, "Harriet Jacobs among the Militants," 759–60.

102 Jacobs, *Incidents*, 191.

103 See Smith, "Harriet Jacobs among the Militants," 759–60.

104 Abdur-Rahman, "The Strangest Freaks"; Somerville, *Queering the Color Line*. See for example, Hunter McGuire and George F. Lydston, *Sexual Crimes among the Southern Negroes, Scientifically Considered* (Louisville, Ky.: Renz & Henry, 1893).

105 Jacobs, *Incidents*, 201.

106 Greeson, "Mysteries and Miseries," 300–3.

107 Stanley, *From Bondage to Contract*, 249, 258.

108 Ellen C. Dubois, "Outgrowing the Compact of the Fathers: Equal Rights, Woman Suffrage, and the United States Constitution, 1820–1878," in *The Constitution and American Life*, ed. David Thelen (Ithaca, N.Y.: Cornell University Press, 1988), 180–1.

109 Indeed, beginning in 1868 for a brief time, women's rights activists, including black women in South Carolina, voted with the support of election officials in some areas. Dubois "Outgrowing the Compact," 186–7, 193.

110 Ibid., 196.

111 Dubois, "Outgrowing the Compact," 191, 197. Reflecting, however, the extent to which the meaning of the Constitution remained open to debate during this dynamic period, Woodhull called on Congress to pass legislation clarifying women's enfranchisement under the Constitution, making her claim to the House Judiciary Committee at the invitation of Committee member Massachusetts Republican Benjamin Butler. Ibid., 194.

112 A reproduction of Thomas Nast's cartoon from *Harper's Weekly*, February 17, 1872, 140, can be seen in Dubois, "Outgrowing the Compact," 198.

113 Ibid., 190–1.

114 Ibid., 191, 197.

115 88 U.S. 162 (1874).

116 Sara De Saussure Davis has traced Olive's resemblance to Susan Anthony in "Feminist Sources in *The Bostonians*," *American Literature* 50 (1979): 570–87, 580.

117 Henry James, *The Bostonians* (Oxford: Oxford University Press, 2009), 10.

118 Ibid., 78.

119 Ibid., 79. See Michael Grossberg, *Governing the Hearth: Law and the Family in Nineteenth-Century America* (Chapel Hill: University of North Carolina Press, 1985), 7–8. Along similar lines, Ransom observes, "She had absolutely no figure, and presented a certain appearance of feeling cold." James, *The Bostonians*, 15.

120 James, *The Bostonians*, 73.

121 Ibid., 372.

122 Lisa Duggan, "The Trials of Alice Mitchell: Sensationalism, Sexology and the Lesbian Subject in Turn-of-the-Century America," *Signs* 18 (1993): 791–814. Duggan identifies the women's social status and plan for Mitchell to assume a male identity as combined factors that underscored the popular reaction to this case as deviant.

123 James, *The Bostonians*, 428.

124 Grossberg, *Governing the Hearth*, 282–3.

125 *Cole v. Van Riper*, 44 Ill. 58 (1867).

126 James, *The Bostonians*, 434.

127 *Bradwell v. Illinois*, 83 U.S. 130 (1872).

128 Ibid. at 141–2 (Bradley, J., dissenting).
129 James, *The Bostonians*, 435.
130 Ibid., 434.
131 James, *The Bostonians*, 414.
132 Ibid., 180.
133 Eric J. Sundquist, "Mark Twain and Homer Plessy," *Representations* 24 (1988): 102–28, 103.
134 98 U.S. 145 (1878).
135 Ibid. at 165–6, 162, 164.
136 Sarah Barringer Gordon, "A War of Words: Revelation and Storytelling in the Campaign against Mormon Polygamy," *Chicago-Kent Law Review* 78 (2003): 739–72, 756. These narratives described the "[m]urders, seductions, thefts, [and] all manner of iniquity," and "largely stocked harems" of a polygamous society. Ibid., 750, 754.
137 98 U.S. at 166.
138 Gordon, "A War of Words," 770.
139 *Reynolds*, 98 U.S. at 167–8.
140 98 U.S. at 164. Focusing on notions of deviance created in relation to slavery, I have not addressed characterizations of other marginalized groups, such as other religious minorities, Asians, or Native Americans, for example. The language in *Reynolds*, however, suggests the broader hierarchy of racial status. Chinese citizens were considered paradigmatic outsiders, as Justice John Marshall Harlan suggested in his dissent in *Plessy v. Ferguson*, writing that the "Chinese race" was "so different . . . that we do not permit those belonging to it to become citizens of the United States." *Plessy v. Ferguson*, 163 U.S. 537, 561 (Harlan, J., dissenting).
141 William Cohen, *At Freedom's Edge: Black Mobility and the Southern Quest for Racial Control 1861–1915* (Baton Rouge: Louisiana State University Press, 1991), 216. As conceptual precursor to the validation of equal but separate in *Plessy v. Ferguson*, in 1849, Lemuel Shaw, chief justice of the Massachusetts Supreme Court, upheld school segregation. The court deferred to the city committee on schools, positing that "prejudice, if it exists, is not created by law, and probably cannot be changed by law." *Roberts v. City of Boston*, 5 Cush. 198, 209 (Mass. 1850). For a discussion, see Sundquist, "Mark Twain and Homer Plessy," 107.
142 Cohen, *At Freedom's Edge*, 216. Thus, for example, the 1866 Penal Code of Alabama prohibits "[m]arriages between white persons and negroes" in its chapter on "Offenses Against Public Morality and Decency." The statute specifies that intermarriage or "adultery or fornication" by "any white person and any negro, or the descendent of any negro, to the third generation inclusive," is punishable by imprisonment or hard labor "for not less than two, nor more than seven years." Penal Code of Alabama, ch. 5, sec. 61 (Montgomery, Ala.: Reid & Screws, 1866), 29, 31.
143 For example, in addition to the impact of the *Slaughter-House Cases*, *United States v. Reese*, 92 U.S. 214 (1876) and *United States v. Cruikshank*, 92 U.S. 542 (1876), the Supreme Court, in *United States v. Harris*, 106 U.S. 629 (1883), invalidated federal penalties for private persons conspiring to deprive citizens of equal protection of the laws, leaving blacks vulnerable to Southern mobs.
144 109 U.S. 3 (1883).
145 Somerville, *Queering the Color Line*, 35.
146 163 U.S. 537, 540 (1896). The case of *Williams v. Mississippi*, 170 U.S. 213 (1898), upholding a poll tax and literacy test making on its face no distinction by race, arguably had a more immediate impact than *Plessy* in practice.
147 163 U.S. 537, 541.
148 Somerville, *Queering the Color Line*, 7. Albion Tourgée, the lawyer overseeing Plessy's case, argued for Plessy's property right in his apparent "whiteness," attempting to reshape the relationship between property and bodies that slavery established. Ibid., 9.
149 163 U.S. at 543.
150 For a discussion of how questions of race and sexuality implicated one another, especially in late nineteenth-century medical and scientific discourse, see Somerville, *Queering the Color Line*, chap. 1, "Scientific Racism and the Invention of the Homosexual Body."
151 Ibid., 1.
152 Ibid., 17, 35. As Somerville points out, the sexual threat of the black man to the white woman invoked in cases like *Plessy* presupposed a heterosexual normativity. Ibid., 35.
153 Before the 1880s, formal regulation of same-sex intimacy took the form of crime-against-nature statutes aimed in part at furthering procreative marriage. With urbanization in the last decades of the century, arrests for such crimes increased, but the numbers remained a small fraction of urban arrests. William N. Eskridge Jr., "Law and the Construction of the Closet: American Regulation of Same-Sex Intimacy, 1880–1946," *Iowa Law Review* 82 (1997): 1007–136, 1012, 1015–16.

5

COMPARATIVE RACIALIZATION AND AMERICAN INDIAN IDENTITY IN NINETEENTH-CENTURY AMERICA

Cheryl Suzack[*]

The lithograph "American Progress" depicts a central tension that runs through nineteenth-century legal and cultural texts concerning the political status of American Indian communities (see Figure 5.1). First circulated in 1873, the lithograph, based on a painting by John Gast and titled "Westward, the Course of Destiny," was commissioned by George A. Crofutt, a New York–based publisher and author of periodicals and travel guides. It portrays the figure of an angelic woman elevated above a teeming wilderness inhabited by wild animals, pioneering settlers, and "Indian" peoples seemingly driven to the edge of extinction by the onslaught of Western progress. A stage coach in the middle section draws the eye upward to a covered wagon and two steam locomotives that energize the print mid-frame, animating signs of culture and technology that direct the gaze toward ships in the east and mountains in the west, both of which are brought together by the figure of a woman who carries a book in one hand and telegraph wires in the other. The Indians, in scanty garb on horseback and on foot, appear doomed by the encroachment of Western technologies that exemplify colonial expansion. They are harried from the land mid-frame, apparently about to take the final plunge into an oblivion that is outside the frame of the print.

The caption, written by Crofutt to support sales of his periodicals and guides,[1] reiterates the problem of the geographical boundaries that separated settlers from tribal peoples – boundaries that brought into tension a conflict between Congress and the states in determining political jurisdiction and governing authority over tribes. Crofutt's descriptive language enacts the "us–them" binary logic that pervades this period as he strives to locate the existence of tribal peoples, their political powers, and their rights to territories firmly in the past. He writes:

> This rich and wonderful country – the progress of which at the present time, is the wonder of the old world – was, until recently, inhabited exclusively by the lurking savage and wild beasts of prey. . . . How has this change been wrought, and by whom, is illustrated by our Chromo, "AMERICAN PROGRESS." Purely National in design, this beautiful painting represents the United States' portion of the American continent in its beauty and variety, from the Atlantic to the Pacific Ocean, illustrating at a glance the grand drama of Progress in the civilization, settlement, and history of our own happy land.

Figure 5.1 George A. Crofutt, "American Progress" (1873)

Source: Library of Congress, Prints and Photographs Division

As a manifestation of "American progress" exemplified by vanquishing tribal communities and erasing their presence from U.S. society, the lithograph is more hopeful than prophetic. In the period from the early 1830s to the late 1880s, American courts sought to resolve the Indian's "peculiar status under Federal law"[2] and to manage the dual meaning of Indians' tribal identities both as "domestic dependent nations, owing allegiance to their tribe[s]" and as "subjects of the United States," lacking full citizenship rights under U.S. law.[3] The Supreme Court's decisions in *Cherokee Nation v. Georgia*[4] and *Worcester v. Georgia*[5] established limited tribal sovereignty over tribal lands that existed in principle until the passage of the Dawes General Allotment Act in 1887,[6] which dismantled tribal sovereignty by disbanding control of collectively held tribal lands. In the intervening period, federal courts applied the principles of tribal sovereignty brought into effect through Chief Justice John Marshall's characterization of tribal communities as "domestic dependent nations,"[7] but tribes' unwillingness to abide by their status as either "domestic" or "dependent" made this characterization faulty, even distracting, as it invariably forced the courts to engage, yet again, in deciding a legal and political status that both Congress and the Supreme Court believed they had laid to rest.

Because the political status of tribal peoples as "members"[8] within states was unclear, the presence of both "major tribes" and "Indians who had been annexed by and incorporated into non-Indian communities and made part of the body politic"[9] raised "hard legal questions"[10] concerning jurisdiction over major tribes and the "remnants of tribes" within state boundaries. According to Robert N. Clinton and Margaret Tobey Hotopp, Congress's frustration with constantly quelling states' attempts to wrest authority over tribal communities from federal control prompted James Madison to opine in the *Federalist*, following the Constitutional Convention of 1787, that:

> [w]hat description of Indians are to be deemed members of a State, is not yet settled, and has been a question of frequent perplexity and contention in the federal councils. And how the trade with Indians, though not members of a State, yet residing within its legislative jurisdiction, can be regulated by an external authority, without so far intruding on the internal rights of legislation, is absolutely incomprehensible.[11]

Challenges brought by Indian plaintiffs exploited these tensions. In seeking naturalization, they exposed the practices of racialization that courts used to settle individual claims, through cases that illustrated the double edge of legally enforced social segregation of tribal communities, on the one hand, and through discourses of racial inferiority that made explicit the logic of racial dependence that recast American Indian plaintiffs as "political aliens" lacking citizenship rights within their former homelands, on the other.

In this chapter, I analyze a line of federal cases concerning the question of naturalization for American Indians, a question that brought together the problem of tribal communities' unresolved legal status and individual Indians' political status in choosing U.S. citizenship over their tribal identities and collective rights.[12] Legal determinations of tribal sovereignty and American Indian political rights were implicated in wider debates in post-revolutionary America about how to develop a "theoretical foundation for sovereignty" within a divided nation. This tension focused the broader question of how sovereign institutions would govern autonomously and enable the formation of political identity through U.S. federalism, while at the same time instituting a governing structure that could account for "a federal system where power was diffuse" and a system of government in which "neither the states nor the United States had absolute power."[13] The doctrine of "divided sovereignty"[14] provided the necessary framework. It constituted "legal sovereignty" as "vested in the various concrete organs and agents of government" and expanded "political sovereignty [as] ultimately rest[ing] with the people."[15] Legal claims by American Indian plaintiffs seeking naturalization threatened to collapse these distinctions. When plaintiffs sought citizenship through naturalization, they accepted the government's objective of assimilation, but when courts of law denied them their claims to citizenship rights, plaintiffs stood in for tribal communities, occupying a liminal, alien status to which they were accorded neither collective rights nor individual entitlements. In crossing between competing political statuses, plaintiffs brought into view law's ambiguous political effects: on the one hand, its capacity to enact structural injustice toward tribal communities; on the other, its furtherance of "new social relations of dominance" that made necessary novel forms of legal regulation and administrative control.[16] The cases in question – *McKay v. Campbell*,[17] *United States v. Elm*,[18] *United States ex rel Standing Bear v. Crook*,[19] *United States v. Osborn*,[20] and *Elk v. Wilkins*[21] – arose during the "nationalist/federalist"[22] era to parody the federal government's benchmark of consent.[23] They exposed how the courts engaged in discourses of racialization by making visible an underlying logic through which law distinguished between tribal peoples according to a comparative lens, one that implicitly hierarchized tribal communities as those that were worthy of protected sovereign status and those that were not. Each case illustrates the discourses of racialization that courts entered into in order to secure racial boundaries. They mark out a legal pedagogy that shows how courts engaged in practices of "racialization" that Neil Gotanda describes as "the inscription of an ascribed subordination on a raced body linked to a racial category."[24] As these discourses were negotiated through the courts, they were also circulated in the periodical press and engaged by Francis LaFlesche's fictional autobiography *The Middle Five*.[25] A writer, scholar, and legally trained anthropologist who observed the allotment of reservation lands for the Omaha Indian Tribe of Nebraska, of which he was a member, LaFlesche makes apparent the changing conceptions of American Indian identity and the implications of these changes for individuals both within and beyond their tribal homelands. His attempt to cast a different understanding of nineteenth-century practices of legalized racialization participated in wider social debates concerning individual rights that arose in the periodical press during this period. Yet his attention to showing how race identity functioned as a legal pedagogy and how it was revised by tribal members suggests that cultural texts were a necessary corrective to widely held cultural beliefs about how American Indian communities ought to behave as they struggled to retain and enact their understanding of tribal identity and citizenship values in ways that challenged their legal and institutional nonrecognition.

Scholars of nineteenth-century federal Indian law note the essential role that the Supreme Court's reasoning played in *Cherokee Nation* and *Worcester v. Georgia* in establishing the benchmark of tribal sovereignty. Considered "companion cases"[26] that affirmed Indian tribes' sovereign powers as "continued in existence after relations with Europeans and the United States were established,"[27] these cases, together with *Johnson v. M'Intosh*,[28] form the so-called Marshall Trilogy of decisions that validated tribal sovereignty and set out "how the framers attempted to accommodate tribes within the nation's constitutional structure."[29] Their method of incorporation has been described as a "checkerboard pattern . . . of jurisdiction."[30] Prior to Felix Cohen's pronouncement of a tribal sovereignty doctrine in 1942,[31] which held that "tribes initially possessed complete sovereignty, they lost some of those powers to a more powerful nation, and they retain all powers not lost," courts regarded Indian tribes as occupying "a truly anomalous position,"[32] as neither foreign nations nor subject states.[33] When tribes appealed to law, they were viewed as "separate nations" but without the legal standing to "invoke the jurisdiction of the federal courts" due to the "precarious" ways in which tribal sovereignty rested on "the whims of Congress."[34] As a consequence of the Supreme Court's "extraordinary deference to the political branches . . . in their dealings with the Indians,"[35] nineteenth-century case law existed in a state of "disarray,"[36] which meant that, in practice, a tribe's designation as "sovereign" implied "a kind of dignity and respectability"[37] that tribes themselves could not enact. The Supreme Court's failure to protect tribal sovereignty manifested in unjust outcomes[38] that demonstrate the distance between the Court's recognition of sovereign status, in theory, and its attribution of this status, in practice.[39] As Sidney L. Harring observes, "Chief Justice John Marshall's 'domestic, dependent nations' language of *Worcester* . . . failed either to release a white missionary from a Georgia prison or to save the Cherokees from the loss of their lands."[40] Tribal sovereignty has since that time been regarded as an "inherent" or "retained" legal capacity that guarantees the autonomous status of tribes, permitting them to enact "governmental arrangements [that] protect and limit personal liberty through social control."[41] This capacity and status are held to be distinct from both civil rights and minority rights claims because their political attribution to tribes recognizes and validates a broader constitutional framework that empowers tribal governmental authority, sanctioning the legal view that "Indian law is based primarily on tribal status, not on racial status."[42]

Despite this view, however, tribal sovereignty is implicated with racial identity through practices of racialization that were resonant in legal decisions dating from the "treaty-federalism era."[43] These decisions equated tribal sovereignty with political allegiance in the determination of Indian character to establish a legal and social meaning for race that socially sustained what Ariela Gross describes as a "racial common sense."[44] During this period until well into the Allotment era, tribal status and individual Indian identity stood in for each other in complex ways that required American Indians to demonstrate legal "performance[s]" of fitness with displays of "moral character," "civic duty,"[45] and law-abiding behavior that measured their tribal identity according to the paradigm of tribal sovereignty established through *Cherokee Nation* and *Worcester*. This paradigm distinguished among tribes according to a racial hierarchy of sovereign status that worked in politically exclusionary ways. *Cherokee Nation* and *Worcester* gave meaning and validity to two linked principles of judicial reasoning that these cases make apparent: one, that the distinct status of Indian nations is premised on upholding tribal sovereignty because "individually they are aliens, not owing allegiance to the United States,"[46] and, two, that within this status were Indian nations made up of two "class[es] of Indians":[47] those that have a "distinct government of their own" and thus retain sovereignty and those that "consist[ ] of the mere remnants of tribes, which have become almost extinct."[48] When individual Indian plaintiffs sued for citizenship rights, they brought these distinctions into conflict. Behaving neither as autonomous tribes in a domestic-dependent state nor as the remnants of tribes existing at the discretion of state governments, individual plaintiffs exhibited an alien status that required new characterizations of American Indian identity through law in order to protect racial classifications already in place. These legal categories performed the work of securing racial boundaries that were popularized through the periodical press, permitting public access to a discourse of racial difference that was necessary to limiting how Indian plaintiffs could participate in American society. The social effect of these discourses was to educate the public about its role in restraining or disputing nonconforming behavior. This chapter highlights how *Cherokee Nation* and *Worcester* establish the Court's two-classes-of-Indians thesis in order to demonstrate the political implications associated with the racial logic that emerged in the key sovereignty cases from this period and to explicate their legal meanings for plaintiffs seeking naturalization.

I begin with a discussion of *Cherokee Nation* and *Worcester* to illustrate the racial hierarchy embedded in these decisions in order to show how the Supreme Court's two-classes-of-Indians thesis laid the groundwork for the later application of a "racial formation project," a project concerned with using race categories "to signify difference and structure inequality"[49] so as to differentiate between tribal nations based on their autonomous or assimilated political state. Next, I show how the Court's two-classes-of-Indians distinctions arose in cases involving Indian plaintiffs seeking naturalization. In the final section, I analyze how Francis LaFlesche's *The Middle Five* intervenes in social discourses about tribal identity that circulated in the periodical press during this period.

II. Comparative racialization in the Supreme Court's Cherokee Nation cases

Cherokee Nation[50] set the bar for the distinct status of tribal nations and the characterization of tribal sovereignty according to a racial formation project that subsequent courts affirmed through Chief Justice John Marshall's defense of the Cherokee Nation's unique identity and his characterization of their domestic-dependent political status. The well-known case concerned a bill brought by the Cherokee Nation for an injunction to restrain the state of Georgia from implementing laws passed in 1828 by its legislature, which permitted the state to annex Cherokee territories lying within state boundaries and to extend state laws over the Cherokee Nation's lands.[51] These laws proposed to nullify all "Indian customs and laws," deny "Indians the right to testify in cases involving whites," and "punish[ ] any persons or groups who tried to prevent Indians from emigrating from the State."[52] The Cherokee Nation's suit also sought federal protection from state aggression. In defiance of a writ of error issued by the Supreme Court, the state of Georgia incarcerated and sentenced to hang a member of the Cherokee Nation, George Corntassel, for the murder of an Indian man in Cherokee Territory.[53] When the state defied the writ and carried out the sentence, the Cherokee Nation sought the protection of the Supreme Court.[54]

In weighing the Cherokee Nation's claim to a political status as a "foreign nation"[55] under the authority of the United States Constitution, which gave the Supreme Court jurisdiction to decide controversies between "a state of the United States . . . and a foreign state,"[56] the chief justice attributed to the Cherokee Nation a tribal identity and political status necessitating a novel form of legal recognition that reconfigured prior relations as they existed between the United States and tribal nations. The Court's reconfiguration of these prior relations depended on its imposition of a racial hierarchy that distinguished its relations with the Cherokee Nation as distinct from its relations with all other nations. The chief justice stated: "[T]he condition of the Indians in relation to the United States is perhaps unlike that of any other two people in existence" and "the relation of the Indians to the United States is marked by peculiar and cardinal distinctions which exist no where else."[57] The Cherokee Nation's unique status, he argued, as a "distinct political society, capable of managing its own affairs and governing itself"[58] did not permit an injunction restraining the state of Georgia and its officers from enforcing the laws of Georgia within Cherokee territory,[59] but it did require the Supreme Court's recognition that the tribe's dependent political and legal status were as yet undefined and necessitated protection.[60] Not only did the Cherokee Nation exist "in a state of pupilage" and "look[ed] to our government for protection,"[61] but it also embraced a different legal path from other Indian tribes anticipated by the framers of the Constitution. The Cherokee Nation's "idea of appealing to an American court of justice for an assertion of right or a redress of wrong" amplified their "distinct appellation"; they were unlike the "Indian" or his "tribe" who appealed "to the tomahawk, or to the government" and unlike "foreign states."[62] Instead, they were "entirely distinct."[63]

What made the Cherokee Nation distinct was not only their elevation above and moral distance from other tribal nations. They were also the exception to "that class of Indians" that, according to Justice Smith Thompson, "consist[ed] of the mere remnants of tribes, which have become almost extinct; and who have, in a great measure, lost their original character, and abandoned their usages and customs, and become subject to the laws of the state."[64] In a "triangulation" of racial identity,[65] in which the Cherokee Nation was valorized for its capacity to endure as "an independent people," which "innumerable treaties formed with them acknowledge,"[66] the Court distinguished the Cherokee Nation from other tribal nations according to an ascending scale of tribal political statuses in which "two distinct classes" of Indian nations existed:

> those who are considered members of the state within which they reside, and the other not; the former embracing the remnant of the tribes who have lost their distinctive character as a separate community, and . . . become subject to the laws of the states, and the latter as still retained their original connexion as tribes and live together under their own laws, usages and customs, and, as such, are treated as a community independent of the state.[67]

The Cherokee Nation fulfilled the latter "condition" and "character" of a nation that was "numerous," "distinct," and "independent . . . living under the government of [its] own laws, usages, and customs, and in no sense under the ordinary jurisdiction of the state of Georgia."[68] They were thus the exception to a succession of tribal nations that existed in various forms of autonomous and assimilated states. What made the Cherokee Nation unparalleled was their capacity to "transcend the particular"[69] status of this racialized group. They existed as "[a] people once numerous, powerful, and truly independent,"[70] meriting "the protection of the United States, with a solemn guarantee by treaty of the exclusive right to the possession of their lands."[71]

Decided by the Supreme Court one year later, *Worcester v. Georgia*[72] reaffirmed the Cherokee Nation's distinct status as a "sovereign nation" under the protection of the United States and "[under the protection] of no other power"[73] but aligned their need for protection from state intrusions with the consolidation of their political identity as existing in a "domestic dependent"[74] state. This alignment permitted the Court to establish the political relationship represented by a "ward to his guardian"[75] and to essentialize the Cherokee Nation's political status through an inferior condition that was ascribed through their dependency.

Worcester summoned the Cherokee Nation as a party involving the dispute between the federal government and the state of Georgia because Cherokee laws and territorial autonomy were violated by the arrest and imprisonment of two missionaries, Samuel A. Worcester and Elizur Butler, who resided with the Cherokee Nation at the town of New Echota in Cherokee territory, where they preached the gospel and translated the scriptures into the Cherokee language. Worcester and Butler were charged and found guilty, with nine other missionaries, of trespassing in Cherokee Territory without a license from the state, which had passed laws requiring that "all white persons residing within the limits of the Cherokee nation" who did so without a license or permit from the Governor or his representatives, and who did not swear an oath of fealty to Georgia, were guilty of "high misdemeanor," and, if convicted, punishable "by confinement to the penitentiary, at hard labour, for a term not less than four years."[76] Nine missionaries swore the oath of allegiance, promised to leave Cherokee territory, and were pardoned by Georgia for their offenses.[77] Worcester and Butler refused.

When the case appeared before the Supreme Court, Chief Justice Marshall explained that the indictment and plea raised two issues concerning Georgia's right to impose its laws in Cherokee Territory and to claim jurisdiction over the missionaries' behavior and Cherokee lands: first, did the Supreme Court have jurisdiction to prevent the state of Georgia from extending its laws over Cherokee lands and over persons residing therein, and, second, did Georgia's laws violate the Constitution, laws, and treaties of the United States?[78] In affirming the Supreme Court's right to decide the case, the chief justice argued not only that Georgia's legislative acts were reviewable by the court whose power was conferred by Congress[79] but also that tribal nations existed in a state of pupilage to the United States, which had "succeeded to all claims of Great Britain, both territorial and political," and retained the "pre-emptive privilege" of determining relations between "the Europeans and natives" based on "power, war, [and] conquest" which "give rights . . . after possession" through the principle of "discovery."[80] Because Georgia's legislative acts sought not only to "seize on the whole Cherokee country" but also to "annihilate its political existence,"[81] they violated the federal government's exclusive jurisdiction in regard to Indian tribes and were thus "void"[82] of legal standing.

In deciding the second issue, the chief justice invoked the Court's prior stance of defending the Cherokee Nation's right to align itself with a more powerful nation while existing as an independent state[83] but ascribed a subordinate role to that stance based on the Cherokee Nation's need for guardianship and dependence. The chief justice stated that Indian nations were "necessarily dependent on some foreign potentate for supply of their essential wants, and for their protection from lawless and injurious intrusions into their country."[84] Although that dependence was initially invested in "Great Britain," it had been acquired by "the establishment . . . of the United States in its place," which "led naturally" to a "declaration, on the part of the Cherokees, that they were under the protection of the United States, and of no other power. They assumed the relation with the United States, which had before subsisted with Great Britain."[85] The Treaty of Hopewell and its articles, the chief justice claimed, guaranteed these relations. They "established a solid peace" based on an arrangement of "mutual consent."[86] "From the commencement of our government," the chief justice argued, "congress has passed acts to regulate trade and intercourse with the Indians; which treat them as nations, respect their rights, and manifest a firm purpose to afford that protection which treaties stipulate."[87] Protection, according to the Court, meant improving the Indians' condition. Not only did Congress "pass . . . an act for promoting those humane designs of civilizing the neighbouring Indians," an act "providing against the further decline and final extinction of the Indian tribes adjoining to the frontier settlements of the United States," but the "president of the United States," where he should see fit and "*with their own consent*," could "employ capable persons, of good moral character, to instruct them in the mode of agriculture suited to their situation; and for teaching their children in reading, writing, and arithmetic; and for performing such other duties as may be enjoined, according to such instructions and rules as the president may give and prescribe for the regulation of their conduct in the discharge of their duties."[88] The Act's "settled purpose," the chief justice stated, was "to fix the Indians in their country by giving them security at home."[89] The Cherokee Nation's dependence on the United States thus made Georgia's acts "repugnant to the constitution, laws, and treaties of the United States," and "in direct hostility with the treaties . . . which recognize the pre-existing power of the nation to govern itself."[90]

Cherokee Nation and *Worcester* illustrate how the Supreme Court, in determining the tribal communities' "unique status" but "dependent state," relies on attributions of jurisdiction, dependency, protection, and moral obligation: the Court thus enacts a distinct status for tribal nations in their dependent state, while also distinguishing among "two classes of Indians" so as to differentiate between "major tribes" and "remnant tribes" based on a hierarchy of unequal political statuses. These acts of redefinition occur through racial ascriptions propagated by law in characterizations that authorize and make available the language associated with a racial formation project. Racial formation projects, according to Shu-Mei Shih, depend on the "politics of recognition" and the granting of "exceptional" status to the "particular" in order for this subject status to transcend the particular and "approach the universal."[91] The granting of this status, Shih notes, defines how a racialized subject becomes inscribed within a hierarchy of racial attributes that cannot be easily inverted or undone because the objective of the recognition and hierarchy are to establish the "exceptional" as the "singular," as the "nonrepetitive" status that "set[s] a precedent" and "does not open a path for other particulars."[92] The bestowal of exceptional status permits selective racial criteria to escape the local and masquerade as the universal attributes of a racial identity. Because such projects emerge from "sociohistorical processes by which racial categories are created, inhabited, transformed, and destroyed,"[93] their goals are to "create or reproduce structures of domination based on essentialist categories of race."[94] By asserting the Supreme Court's right to define, protect, and oversee the Cherokee Nation's dependent state, the Court justified Congress's right to engage in race projects designed to civilize tribal nations by using the defense of tribal sovereignty as a political condition that enabled the law to transform the Cherokee Nation's status from an independent state to a dependent one. Its dependent state made legally comprehensible and socially normative a racial hierarchy of Indian identity that justified Indian tribes' ongoing social and political segregation.

III. Comparative racialization in federal naturalization cases

In cases that followed after Chief Justice John Marshall's formulation of tribal status as a "domestic, dependant state," American courts embraced the Supreme Court's racial formation project by weighing each plaintiff's claim to citizenship rights through the rationale provided by the Supreme Court's reasoning. Triangulating identity[95] according to Justice Thompson's two-classes-of-Indians thesis, the cases show how federal courts not only deployed a racial hierarchy that situated plaintiffs according to an ascending hierarchy of ascribed racialized differences but also how plaintiffs stood in for their tribal nations in legally and politically limiting ways.[96] Through their characterizations of Indian tribes according to a racializing logic, the cases brought into wider effect a multileveled arrangement of disempowerment that resonated both within the law through precedent and in the wider social sphere through periodical press debates that took up the racial ascriptions that these cases constructed. Their "racial common sense"[97] shows how the courts struggled to make tribal identity and individual positions consistent with law's authority to regulate both tribal and individual citizen's national allegiances.

A. *McKay v. Campbell*[98]

William McKay's suit appeared before the District Court of Oregon and called into question the stability of the Supreme Court's racialization of Indian tribes as "domestic dependent nations" existing for their protection in a segregated state when McKay challenged a state officer's authority to refuse him the right to vote in a state election. McKay argued that the election judge, James A. Campbell, denied his claim to be a citizen of the United States, subject to its authority and allegiance, and authorized to vote both under the Fifteenth Amendment of the Constitution and under the state laws of Oregon, which empowered Campbell to administer an oath to McKay that would thereby qualify him to vote, should his citizenship be called into question.[99] McKay claimed that Campbell's refusal was "on account of his being an Indian," "an alien," and "not a citizen of the United States."[100] He asserted that he was authorized to vote by means of the Fifteenth Amendment, which he claimed

> appl[ied] to and include[d] Indians . . . born within the limits of the United States . . . [and] that an Indian, whether of the whole or half blood who is a citizen of the United States, is entitled to vote, or . . . cannot be excluded from this privilege on the ground of being an Indian, as that would be to exclude him on account of race.[101]

The Court weighed McKay's suit by deliberating two questions concerning how birth and ancestry determined allegiance. It considered: "was the plaintiff born subject to the jurisdiction of the United States – under its allegiance,"[102] if his father was born a subject of Great Britain,[103] and was McKay a citizen of the United States and by his actions within the jurisdiction of the Fifteenth Amendment of the Constitution, which "enforce[s] the rights of citizens of the United States to vote in the several states of the Union, and for other purposes?"[104]

To determine McKay's political allegiance, the Court engaged in an extended analysis of McKay's family history, arriving at the conclusion that, based on his parentage, the nationality of his father and grandfather, and their marriage choices, he was, by the Court's reckoning, "seven sixteenths white and nine sixteenths Indian blood," with "the Indian blood predominating," due to his father's marriage to a "Chinook woman."[105] Citing *Worcester* to argue that Indian tribes within the United States have always been held to be "distinct and independent political communities, retaining the right to self-government, though subject to the protecting power of the United States," the Court speculated that McKay could "in legal contemplation" be considered "an American Indian, by virtue of his mother being a member of the Chinook tribe," or he could be considered "a British subject, without reference to his race, by virtue of being the son of Thomas McKay."[106] However, he could not be recognized as a citizen of the United States because having been born a member of "an independent political community – the Chinook – he was not born subject to the jurisdiction of the United States – not born in its allegiance,"[107] nor was he "a half-breed, as claimed . . . by his counsel."[108] The Court set aside McKay's claim to citizenship rights and advised him that he could become a citizen by "complying with the laws for the naturalization of aliens."[109] It went one step further to distinguish McKay's political status, for having been "born a member of 'an independent political community' – the Chinook,"[110] from other racialized communities. Inscribing a comparative hierarchy that segregated Indians from other racialized groups, the Court lamented the fact that McKay could not "be admitted [to] citizenship because he [was] neither a 'white alien' nor a person of 'African nativity or descent' " but resolved that this "matter" was within the "exclusive cognizance of congress" and not within the court's authority to "remedy."[111]

B. *United States v. Elm*[112]

Abraham Elm's suit explicitly shows the federal court's adoption of the Supreme Court's two-classes-of-Indians thesis. In determining Elm's political allegiance and right to vote, the court characterized Elm's tribe, the Oneida Indians of Madison County, as the "remnants" of the Oneida Tribe, the "main body" of which had been removed to Wisconsin from New York State in the 1830s through the enforcement of the state's removal policies.[113] Elm was indicted for illegal voting in the State's national elections in 1876. He was charged, tried, and convicted, but on a motion for a new trial, his sentence was suspended when the court upheld his claim that "the Oneida Indians [were] citizens of the United States" and "subject to the jurisdiction thereof."[114] The Court affirmed Elm's assertion that not only were the Oneida Indians "citizens" but, by reference to "the history of the Oneidas,"[115] the "remaining" families "[did] not constitute a community by themselves," did not live autonomously but rather inhabited "dwellings" that were "interspersed with the habitations of whites," and did not practice Indian customs because "[i]n religion, in customs, in language, in everything but the color of their skins, they are identified with the rest of the population."[116] Elm, although Indian by birth, ancestry, community residence, and tribal affiliation was considered to be "a citizen within the meaning of the fourteenth amendment" because his tribe "had ceased to maintain its tribal integrity," and he himself was considered to have "abandoned his tribal relations" by living similarly to "Indians in this state [who] are subject to taxation" and were regarded as "citizen[s] within the meaning of the fourteenth amendment."[117] The court granted Elm voting rights because he, like his tribe, "had ceased to maintain its tribal integrity,"[118] and thus Elm's allegiances were subject to the jurisdiction of the United States.

C. *United States ex rel. Standing Bear v. Crook*[119]

The political status of "remnant tribes" figured strongly in *Standing Bear v. Crook*, a case that enlarged the Supreme Court's racial hierarchy by augmenting its view that "remnant" tribes could not only be considered assimilated because they had diminished in numbers or had been removed to other territories and states but also because they exemplified the ascribed characteristics of waning nobility, degeneracy, and anticipated decline. The *Standing Bear* case concerned the arrest and incarceration of Chief Standing Bear and twenty-five members of the Ponca Indian tribe, who were detained on the Omaha Indian Reservation by General George Crook, acting under orders from the United States government to imprison the members for leaving Oklahoma Indian Territory without the government's permission. The Ponca Indian members filed a writ of habeas corpus seeking their discharge from custody and preventing their return to Indian Territory.[120] They claimed that they were confined and held unlawfully as "Indians who . . . formerly belonged to the Ponca tribe of Indians, now located in the Indian territory; that they had . . . withdrawn from the tribe, and completely severed their tribal relations therewith;" that they had "adopted the general habits of whites," and that they were attempting to "maintain themselves . . . without aid or assistance from the general government."[121] While engaged in lawful behavior and "without being guilty of violating any of the laws of the United States,"[122] they were arrested and imprisoned "in violation of a provision of their treaty."[123] They appeared before the court "praying for the allowance of a writ of habeas corpus"[124] because, as members of a tribe, they lacked the legal authority to prevent their "apprehen[sion] . . . and remov[al] . . . by force to the Indian Territory, from which it [was] alleged they [had] escaped."[125]

In describing the Ponca Indians capture and incarceration by U.S. authorities, the court engaged in an epic narrative style that not only made explicit the underlying logic that tribal nations resisting authority would be subject to "utter extermination"[126] but also that the court considered the Ponca members "representatives of . . . [a] wasted race,"[127] on the brink of extinction, as an essential condition of the confrontation between tribal Indian and American identity. Attributing the Ponca Indians' decline to their being prevented from adopting the habits of civilized life because of their social segregation to Indian Territory, Judge Elmer Scipio Dundy engaged in a comparative analysis that weighed American society and its influences against the values of Indian society, tribal customs, and associations. He stated:

> On the one side, we have the representatives of this wasted race coming into this national tribunal of ours, asking for justice and liberty to enable them to adopt our boasted civilization, and to pursue the arts of peace, which have made us great and happy as a nation; on the other side, we have this magnificent, if not magnanimous, government, resisting this application with the determination of sending these people back to the country which is to them less desirable than perpetual imprisonment in their own native land.[128]

The court characterized the Ponca Indians as members of a "weak, insignificant, unlettered, and generally despised race,"[129] that, although not "citizens," could still be characterized as " 'persons,' or 'parties,' who may be entitled" to a writ of habeas corpus, and therefore considered to be "unlawfully restrained of liberty under color of authority of the United States."[130] Citing the definition of "person" from "Webster," the Court found it "comprehensive enough . . . to include even an Indian."[131]

In determining the question of the Ponca Indians' claim that they had severed their tribal relations and were living lawfully and without government aid, the Court argued that the precariousness of tribal life and its eventual extinction meant that Indians retained the right to divest themselves of tribal identity if they so choose. Judge Dundy stated: "It can make but little difference . . . whether we accord to the Indian tribes a national character or not, as in either case I think the individual Indian possesses the clear and God-given right to withdraw from his tribe and forever live away from it, as though it had no further existence."[132] The Court found that because the United States was not at war with the Ponca tribe of Indians,[133] a tribe it considered "amongst the most peaceful and friendly of all the Indian tribes,"[134] no authority existed for keeping Standing Bear and his companions in custody, and they were ordered released.[135] The United States appealed their release in May 1879, but as the Ponca Indians were not present, the appeal was dismissed.[136]

D. *United States v. Osborn*[137]

"Joe Miller," an Indian from an unknown tribe on the Warm Spring Reservation in Oregon, purchased a pint of alcohol from Frank Osborn, who was charged by the Indian agent in violation of a statue prohibiting the "dispos[ing] of spirituous liquors" to an Indian.[138] The court held that despite "Joe's" residence off-agency, serving as a "domestic" and occasionally making his home with "an Indian living in the vicinity upon a portion of the public land under the homestead act," Joe subsisted under the authority of "Agent Smith," who claimed the "right to return him to [the Agency] whenever he thinks proper."[139] By reason of his dependent state under the authority of the Agent and because of the precedent set by *McKay*,[140] which held that "no Indians in Oregon were born subject to [the jurisdiction of the United States]," [141] the court upheld the charge against Osborn and fined him one dollar for his violation of the statute. The court stated that contrary to the public belief that "Indians . . . who live off the reservation and among, and more or less after, the manner of white people," they are not "a portion of the political community called the 'People of the United States.' "[142]

E. *Elk v. Wilkins*[143]

John Elk appeared before the Supreme Court of the United States to protest the refusal of his right to register to vote in a general election by Charles Wilkins, the registrar for the city of Omaha. In a suit similar to William McKay's and Abraham Elm's, Elk argued that he was deemed ineligible to vote because of his Indian identity. Like the court record in *McKay* and *Elm*, no details are provided in the published case to indicate how the voting officer reached the conclusion that Elk was an Indian.

Elk argued that Wilkins "refuse[d] to register [him] . . . for the sole reason that . . . [he] was an Indian, and therefore not a citizen of the United States, and not, therefore, entitled to vote," in violation of "his rights . . . under [the] fourteenth and fifteenth amendments to the constitution of the United States, on account of his . . . race and color."[144] Unlike McKay and Elm, however, Elk claimed that he was "an Indian . . . born within the United States" who had, for more than a year prior to his grievances, "severed his tribal relation to the Indian tribes, and had fully and completely surrendered himself to the jurisdiction of the United States."[145] Elk asserted as "a citizen of the United States . . . [he was] entitled to the right and privilege of citizens of the United States."[146] He sought damages in the sum of $6,000, with the costs of his suit, against Wilkins, for "carrying out his willful and malicious designs" in "declar[ing] him an Indian, . . . [declaring him] not a citizen of the United States, and [declaring him] not entitled to vote."[147] His petition raised the following issue: could an Indian "born a member of one of the Indian tribes within the United States . . . voluntarily separate[e] himself from his tribe . . . and tak[e] up his residence among white citizens, [as] a citizen of the United States, within the meaning of the first section of the fourteenth amendment of the constitution"?[148] Unlike the Court's reasoning in the *Standing Bear* case, the Supreme Court held that an Indian could not.

In a split decision, the Court determined that "the alien and dependent condition" of members of Indian tribes "could not be put off at their own will without the action or assent of the United States."[149] Such an action, it stated, did not conform to prior acts of granting citizenship established by the United States through the provisions of "treaty or statute to that effect" or by "application to a court of the United States for naturalization and satisfactory proof of fitness for civilized life."[150] Because the United States Constitution contemplated only two forms of citizenship – "birth or naturalization" – "Indians [were] not taxed . . . [and] formed no part of the people entitled to representation."[151] Although Elk asserted that, because he paid taxes, he demonstrated allegiance to the United States, the Court held, that Elk did not have the authority to divest himself of his tribal allegiance because "the question whether any Indian tribes, or members thereof, have become so far advanced in civilization that they should be let out of the state of pupilage, and admitted to the privileges and responsibilities of citizenship, is a question to be decided by the nation whose wards they are and whose citizens they seek to become, and not by each Indian for himself."[152] In what reads as a growing sense of legal confidence in the court's authority to determine how individual Indians fit within different racialized hierarchies of tribal political community, the Court relied on *Elm*[153] to argue that "the Indian" in that case "derived his origin" from a tribe whose "fragments"[154] resembled the "condition of those Indian nations" whom Justice William Johnson referred to in *Fletcher v. Peck*[155] as those that have "totally extinguished their national fire, and submitted themselves to the laws of the state."[156] It also cited *McKay*[157] and *Osborne*[158] to assert that the law "upon the question has been well stated,"[159] that "an Indian cannot make himself a citizen of the United States without the consent and cooperation of the government."[160]

IV. Comparative indigeneity in the periodical press

These cases show how nineteenth-century legal practices of racialization relied on multiple, intersecting discourses that appealed to a hierarchy of racialized differences to determine questions of political allegiance and to resolve claims to citizenship status for American Indian plaintiffs. The racial hierarchy that courts relied on to situate Indian tribes according to the Supreme Court's two-classes-of-Indians thesis, established through *Cherokee Nation* and *Worcester*, determined individual Indian identities in keeping with the assessment of their tribal status. Tribes, such as the Oneida and the Ponca, represented by the *Elm* and *Standing Bear* cases, that were considered the mere "remnants" of a once powerful people seemingly posed no threat to the American public such that courts could allow American Indian members entry into American civil life. Indians from tribes that were held to retain their political status as independent political communities or who lived under the charge of an Indian agent, as in *Osborne*, were barred from securing these privileges. When necessary, courts could invoke broader categories of classification, as in *McKay*, to distinguish Indian plaintiffs from "aliens" and persons of "African ancestry" who were permitted citizenship rights, while also maintaining the separate status of Indian peoples according to a hierarchy that distinguished between these communities in racialized terms. As a consequence of these imposed categories, the court could triangulate racial identity according to different classifications of tribal political statuses and different categories of "otherness," as aliens or persons of African ancestry. This capacity establishes that American courts engaged in racial formation projects during this period not only to withhold rights from individual Indians but also to educate the public about the rights that Indians, tribal nations, and other racialized groups were entitled to. Two observations bear out this conjecture.

First, none of the naturalization cases cited here contest the racial identity of the applicants or their status as members of a tribal nation. This omission implies that race identity based on physical appearance and ancestry was self-evident. However, tribal status as a measure of political allegiance was not. Thus, the political status of individual tribes who were considered "domestic dependent nations" and tribes that were viewed as the "remnants" of nations had to be determined in a manner that could uphold racial distinctions that were in flux during the post-Reconstruction era (i.e., through removal policies) while also maintaining barriers to citizenship. In a contradictory way, Abraham Elm's case demonstrates this predicament. By engaging in a selective history of political relations between the Oneida Nation and New York State,[161] the case made visible the characteristics of tribal assimilation that established the terms by which an acculturated political status could be known and subsequent courts could model in their reasoning in order to distinguish between classes of Indians that existed as "distinct political communit[ies]" or as "native[s] . . . ow[ing] no allegiance other than to the government of the United States."[162] If race was visible but political status was not, then hierarchies of racialization could also secure the goal of educating the public about their responsibilities in maintaining racial boundaries and intervening, when necessary, to prevent Indian applicants from attaining citizenship rights. The court's capacity to educate the public through case summaries and social reform articles that provided a legal pedagogy for the public served this second objective.

Periodical press debates from this period demonstrate the educative purpose through which published case summaries, debates about the value and protection of rights to American citizenship, and descriptions and interpretations about the meaning of racialized Indian identity circulated. Coverage of the *Standing Bear* case was by far the most extensive. No case gripped the public's imagination more thoroughly, with mention of it appearing in more than twenty newspapers. One reason for the case's sustained attention was that the Ponca tribes' key advocate, Thomas H. Tibbles, served as the assistant editor of the *Omaha Herald*.[163] His paper became a hub for the entire case, from Tibbles' initial meeting with the imprisoned Standing Bear, through the trial, to the subsequent lecture and fund-raising tour. Other papers reprinted coverage of the story, stressing the "Ponca issue" and the tribe's plight and dividing media responses according to stereotypes about Indian nobility or barbarity: were the Ponca Indians "child[ren] of nature" or "barbaric savages"?[164] The *Chicago Daily Tribune* openly criticized Judge Dundy's decision in granting the Ponca Indian's release from custody, which the newspaper argued "virtually declares Indians citizens, with the right to go where they please, regardless of treaty stipulations."[165] It argued that the release of the Ponca Indians dealt the Government's Indian system a "heavy blow" and that "If the power of the Government to hold Indians upon their reservations or to return them when they escape, is denied, the Indians become a body of tramps, moving without restraint wherever they please."[166] *The New York Tribune*, in contrast, praised the court's decision for declaring that "an Indian is a man with human rights, and not a mere head of live stock, to be shipped from place to place and imprisoned at the whim of military officers."[167] In calling attention to the Ponca's degraded state as a "tribe enfeebled by death, disease, and imprisonment,"[168] it conveyed the opinion that if their humanity was not in question, their status as a civilization certainly was because the tribe existed on the brink of extinction.

Coverage of *Elk v. Wilkins* was much more emphatic in drawing attention to the jurisdictional boundary that prevented Indians from having rights to vote. "Indians not Citizens"[169] appeared in several periodicals alongside the question, "Can Lo' Vote?"[170] Press commentary repeated the terms of racialization that the courts constructed. Statements such as "there are no Indians in Oregon that were born subject to its jurisdiction,"[171] and "they are not citizens of the United States,"[172] educated the public about its right to intervene and to prevent American Indians from asserting rights and entitlements to which they claimed access, maintaining a boundary that protected "white" interests while upholding American Indian political and social segregation.

V. Francis La Flesche's *The Middle Five*

On the one hand, these cases make apparent the logic of racial inferiority through which the courts justified withholding citizenship rights from American Indians; on the other, they also demonstrate the ways in which American Indians behaved in unexpected and unruly ways that challenged legal institutions as they struggled to maintain their grip on tribal nations. Their actions brought into view individual Indians' behavior as "racial anomalies who crossed over the racial divide,"[173] drawing into conflict competing legal statuses and racial identities that courts were subsequently forced to decide among, and making visible the ways in which seemingly progressive legislation reinscribed the social and political segregation of American Indian communities. Periodical press coverage arbitrarily drew attention to these issues, often participating in discourses of racialization that contributed additional stereotypes to public discourses about tribal identity or limiting the terms of intervention to debates about social reform.[174] Despite these public statements that purport to prevent tribal peoples from active political participation, literary texts propose an alternative framing of tribal political identity and of the humanity of American Indian communities. An exemplar in this regard is Francis La Flesche's fictional autobiography, *The Middle Five*.

Set on the Omaha Indian Reservation of Nebraska in the mid-1860s, the book depicts the time period following the removal of the Winnebago Indians from Minnesota to the Omaha Reservation in 1865,[175] the same year that the federal government signed a treaty with the Ponca Indians of Standing Bear's Tribe for their removal to lands along the Niobara River in Nebraska.[176] La Flesche was born on the Omaha Reservation in 1857 and grew up among the communities of Winnebago, Ponca, and Omaha Indians that resided on the reservation. He participated in the ceremonial life of the community and in the annual buffalo hunt that the Omaha Tribe took part in. In his early twenties, he accompanied Standing Bear during his Eastern tour, serving as an interpreter and orator in presenting the cause of the Indians.[177] Although he worked in the Office of Indian Affairs for most of his life, he also studied anthropology and law, earning an LLB. and an LLM from National University in 1892 and 1893.[178] His fictional autobiography, *The Middle Five*, published in 1900, depicts his experience of the "mission school," which he attended until it closed in 1869.[179]

Considered a playful narrative about young boys living "between cultures," the fictional autobiography not only critiques the school's civilizing mission, it also expresses La Flesche's goal to alter dominant views about American Indians and tribal life. In the Preface, he states that "the object of the book is to reveal the true nature and character of the Indian boy."[180] His concern to do so is both ethical and political. "I have made this choice not because the influences of the school alter the qualities of the boys," he writes, but rather because the "[t]he paint, feathers, robes, and other articles that make up the dress of the Indian, are marks of savagery to the European, and he who wears them . . . finds it difficult to lay claim to a share in common human nature."[181] The series of sketches that follow depict the antics of the boys as they engage in various tasks of teaching one another how to acclimatize to the rules by which the school is run and how to set aside their desires to escape to their neighboring village.

One of the ways in which they thrive is by forming "gangs" through which they establish status and hierarchies for their protection. La Flesche's gang is known as the "middle five" and is made up of the remnants of boys excluded from other gangs because they do not have the tribal status to join the "Ponka" group (109) since they are Omahas (35) and because the capacity to move between groups depended on each boy's standing within the tribe itself. If a boy could not accommodate the members of the group during periods when they were free to return to the village, he could not join a gang of a higher status (36). Each boy's reasons for joining "the middle five" differ, but each reason is related to their loss of status within the village itself, either through the death of family members through war with settlers, which impoverishes families, or through the "deserting of a sacred charge," which results in the diminishment of one's relations within the tribe. La Flesche shows how these changes result from the village's struggle against invading forces and changes in its political and cultural identity through colonization.

In a scene in which La Flesche has returned home, he discovers a crowd of boys and young men "swarming" about a figure who is struggling to escape from them. The boy is described as a "pitiful object," with legs and feet that are bare and a crust of bread in his hands. As La Flesche stands and watches, the boy escapes, and he is able to see that "[h]e belonged to the Winnebago tribe, against whom at that time there was much prejudice amongst the Omahas."[182] No information is given to explain the crowd's behavior, but when La Flesche returns home, his father strongly rebukes him for not intervening. He states, "The persecution of the poor, the sneer at their poverty is a wrong for which no punishment is too severe."[183] The reprimand serves to heighten his sense of responsibility to the other members of the gang in ways that call attention to the misguided objectives of the school's civilizing mission. They are taught to regard themselves through the status hierarchies arranged by the school that regulate their identities in singular terms and that disregard collective histories and identities that existed prior to the imposition of the school's authority. These practices serve to ostracize historically recognized community members and former traditions of inclusion.

Other scenes depict lessons in acquiring English and surviving the "industrial" school system where education and labor were undertaken side by side.[184] These sketches draw attention to LaF-lesche's more explicit comparison of the mission school to the Indian reservation. The much cited reference that La Flesche invokes, declaring that the "reservation itself is in the nature of a school," refers to Judge Dready's statement in *United States v. Clapox*, in which he states, "[T]he reservation itself is in the nature of a school, and the Indians are gathered there, under the charge of an agent, for the purpose of acquiring the habits, ideas, and aspirations which distinguish the civilized from the uncivilized man."[185] Likening the school to a prison, La Flesche engages in an act of creative triangulation that shows how the boys, brought together from many tribes then residing on the reservation, adapted and resisted their indoctrination into Western habits of life. In so doing, his book suggests that other cultural forms were necessary sites of resistance to law's overreaching attempts to control both tribal political culture and American Indian identity during this period.

Scholars of comparative racialization argue that "racialization is inherently comparative, [as] a psychosocial and [a] historical process," involving the "recognition and activation of relations that entail two or more terms."[186] The objective of comparison is to go beyond the collapse of historical differences into binary language that obscures the ways in which the "field of racial positions" is made up of different trajectories of "interracial solidarit[y]" and racial injustice through social and political practices that amplify a "sanctioned ignorance" that "persists regarding how issues of Native American rights, land, and cultural preservation must unsettle the framing and articulation of minority issues."[187] By analyzing how American courts used discourses of racialization to establish a link between tribal sovereignty and naturalization, we see the complex and ambivalent interchangeability of tribal and individual Indian identities established through legal paradigms, justifying the political undermining of both tribes and individuals. This identification is crucial to understanding a particularly elusive aspect of "the Indian" in nineteenth-century Anglo-American consciousness: on the one hand, the legal construction of the Supreme Court's two-classes-of-Indians thesis that established through legal precedent an all but unreachable bar in the determination of tribal sovereignty, a bar that has important implications for how we think about tribal sovereign status today; on the other, the broader negotiation and construction of an Anglo-American "racial common sense" that educated and empowered the public to determine which tribes and individuals retained their political status and identity. What we learn from the law's deliberations about tribal sovereignty and naturalization is the necessary role that the "Indian race" played to ensure that tribal and individual positions were consistent with major social issues of the time, not only the relationship between federal and state power but also anxieties concerning the individual citizen's national allegiances. Literary texts such as Francis La Flesche's *The Middle Five* indicate how tribal communities negotiated and spoke back to these racialized identities in ways that demonstrate their psychosocial and historical effects and how they were resisted through alternative ways in which both stories of racialization and the human story needed to be told.

Notes

* I am indebted to Simon Stern and Nan Goodman for essential feedback that improved the coherence, argumentation, and insights of this chapter. I offer genuine thanks to the anonymous reviewer for the press whose comments helped me to streamline my claims. For outstanding research assistance, my sincere thanks are extended warmly to Julia Boyd.

1 See *Crofutt's Western World*, a New York periodical that ran from July 1872 until June 1873, directed to "Tourists, Miners, and Settlers beyond the Mississippi," and *Great Trans-Continental Tourist's Guide* (New York: Crofutt, 1870).

2 Felix S. Cohen, *Handbook of Federal Indian Law* (Washington, D.C.: United States Government Printing Office, 1942), 154. Chief Justice John Marshall stated in *Cherokee Nation* that "the condition of the Indians in relation to the United States is perhaps unlike that of any other two people in existence" and that "the relation of the Indians to the United States is marked by peculiar and cardinal distinctions which exist no where else." *Cherokee Nation v. Georgia*, 30 U.S. (5 Pet.) 1, 5 (1831).
3 Cohen, *Handbook of Federal Indian Law*, 155. Citizenship rights, according to Cohen, were governed by various methods of acquisition determined by treaties, allotment practices, "fitness," and special statutes between tribes and the United States (153). Other mechanisms, Cohen notes, included "adopting the habits of civilized life, becoming self-supporting, and learning to read and speak the English language" (153). With the ratification of the Fourteenth Amendment, several tribes were also "naturalized" (153), which guaranteed that "the Indian ceased to be a member of the tribe and his land was subject to levy, taxation and sale." Ibid., 154.
4 30 U.S. (5 Peters) 1 (1831).
5 31 U.S. (6 Pet.) 515 (1832).
6 Act of February 8, 1887, ch. 119, 24 Stat. 388 (1887) (codified as amended at 25 U.S.C. §348 (2006)).
7 Id. at 13.
8 Robert N. Clinton and Margaret T. Hotopp, "Judicial Enforcement of the Federal Restraints on Alienation of Indian Land: The Origins of the Eastern Land Claims," *Maine Law Review* 31 (1979): 17–90, 24, 29.
9 Ibid.
10 Ibid., 26.
11 Ibid., 29, citing *The Federalist*, ed. Jacob E. Cooke (Middletown, Conn.: Wesleyan University Press, 1961), 284.
12 In the legal context, "naturalization," the action of admitting or investing the position and rights of citizenship, was barred to Indians, who were regarded as "domestic subjects or nationals." Ibid., 144.
13 Charles F. Wilkinson, *American Indians, Time, and the Law: Native Societies in a Modern Constitutional Democracy* (New Haven, Conn.: Yale University Press, 1987), 54. Wilkinson is quick to explain that the idea of absolute sovereignty or "absolute power" does not exist and is largely considered defunct. Ibid.
14 Ibid.
15 Ibid.
16 Elizabeth A. Povinelli, "The State of Shame: Australian Multiculturalism and the Crisis of Indigenous Citizenship," *Critical Inquiry* 24 (1998): 575–610, 580.
17 16 F. Cas. 161 (D. Or. 1871).
18 25 F. Cas. 1006 (N.D.N.Y. 1877).
19 25 F. Cas. 695 (C.C.D. Neb. 1879).
20 406, 2 F. 58 (D. Or. 1880).
21 112 U.S. 94 (1884).
22 David E. Wilkins characterizes this era as "nationalist/federalist" because it was dominated by the judiciary's concern with "national unity" and strong legal deference to the legislative branches of government, which "adopted policies and laws focused on the detribalization and assimilation of Indians into American society." David E. Wilkins, *American Indian Sovereignty and the U.S. Supreme Court: The Making of Justice* (Austin: University of Texas Press, 1997), 66. Wilkins argues that the United States' primary goal during the "nation-building process" was to achieve the "imposition of a single view of political democracy" that applied to "dominant" and "subordinate groups" alike (67). Tribes accorded "extraconstitutional" status suffered the diminishment of their "sovereignty, property, and civil and political rights" through a series of congressional acts and policies. These included the reconfiguration of Indian agencies as "religious societies; the establishment of the Courts of Indian Offenses; the Major Crimes Act of 1885; the General Allotment Act of 1887; the 1891 amendment to the General Allotment Act; the Curtis Act of 1898; and the Burke Act of 1906" (66).
23 Francis Prucha, *American Indian Policy in the Formative Years* (Lincoln: University of Nebraska Press, 1962), notes that Andrew Jackson's Indian Policy stressed voluntary removals (238). Joseph C. Burke, "The Cherokee Cases: A Study in Law, Politics, and Morality," *Stanford Law Review* 21 (1969), argues that Jackson's opponents did not disagree with his removal policies; rather, they wanted them enacted but with tribal consent (504).
24 Neil Gotanda, "The Racialization of Islam in American Law," *Annals of the American Academy of Political and Social Science* 637 (2011): 184–95, 187.

25 Francis LaFlesche, *The Middle Five: Indian Schoolboys of the Omaha Tribe* (1900; Lincoln: University of Nebraska Press, 1963).

26 Sidney L. Harring states that *Cherokee Nation* and *Worcester* "are always seen as companion cases" even though they "arose around singular events" and "any doctrinal meaning of the original *Cherokee Nation* has been entirely subsumed by *Worcester*." Sidney L. Harring, *Crow Dog's Case: American Indian Sovereignty, Tribal Law, and the United States Law in the Nineteenth Century* (New York: Cambridge University Press, 1994), 7. N. Bruce Duthu argues that *Worcester* represents a "landmark case" that "affirmed both the territorial integrity of tribal homelands and the primacy of tribal authority within those lands." N. Bruce Duthu, *American Indians and the Law* (New York: Viking/Penguin, 2008), 8. Nell Jessup Newton situates the case as launching the "plenary power era . . . which lasted until the 1930's" (228), an era that was supported by the rationale of the "perceived racial and cultural inferiority of Indians." Nell Jessup Newton, "Federal Power over Indians: Its Sources, Scope, and Limitations," *University of Pennsylvania Law Review* 132 (1984): 195–288, 236.

27 Wilkinson, *American Indians, Time, and the Law*, 55.

28 21 U.S. (8 Wheat.) 543 (1823).

29 Duthu, *American Indians and the Law*, 197.

30 Wilkinson, *American Indians, Time, and the Law*, 9. Wilkinson's metaphor describes the haphazard way in which the administration of tribal lands occurred in a jurisdictional vacuum without the benefit of "consolidating doctrine" (ibid.) until well into the modern era, the period following the allotment of tribal lands through the General Allotment Act of 1887 (ibid., note. 4). "Checkerboard jurisdiction," he notes, lead to extensive problems of land title, resource ownership, and administrative authority with the result that "Indian country today" is composed of several categories of land: "tribal land, allotted trust land held by individual Indians, fee land held by individual Indians, fee land held by non-Indians, federal public land, and state and county land" (ibid.). In some areas, Wilkinson argues, "the surface estate" is owned by individuals, while the "subsurface estate" may be owned by "the tribe, the United States, or a private entity" (ibid.). The recovery of land by tribes in the modern era is hindered by the injustice of land takings from this period. Modern-day courts, N. Bruce Duthu argues, rely on "frontier-era" and "frozen in time" formulations of tribal identity (ibid., 23, 24) that are extended to characterizations of land to justify their appropriation by the state or federal government. When tribal lands are deemed too acculturated through development, trespass, or settlement, they are held to have lost their "Indian character" and consequently to no longer express tribal sovereignty in its cultural form. Duthu argues that both the Termination era (1950s–1960s) and the Self-Determination era (1960s–present) (xvi–xvii) are dominated by decisions that draw "distinctions based on the status of the land" to develop "limiting principles" (44) that justify the erosion of tribal sovereignty by characterizing tribal communities as always-already assimilated. These legal decisions mirror the historical loss of tribal lands through earlier decisions that sustained colonization and settlement during this earlier period.

31 Wilkinson, *American Indians, Time, and the Law*, 58 (citing Cohen, *Handbook of Federal Indian Law*, 122–3). Wilkinson argues that the founding of the Marshall-Cohen sovereignty formulation "effectively stemmed the tide of opinions that threatened to bury the doctrine of tribal sovereignty in the name of changed circumstances." He explains that Cohen's "essential paradigm" of tribal sovereignty was so astute that it "attained something of the weight of a Supreme Court opinion" (58).

32 Newton, "Federal Power over Indians," 204.

33 Burke, "The Cherokee Case," *Cherokee Nation*, 30 U.S. at 33.

34 Newton, "Federal Power over Indians," 205.

35 Ibid.

36 Wilkinson, *American Indians, Time, and the Law*, 57.

37 Ibid., 55.

38 Harring explains, "All of the Cherokee cases arose from the same tragic violation of tribal rights." Harring, *Crow Dog's Case*, 26. "Modern scholars of Indian law," he continues, "look at *Cherokee Nation* as the beginning of a long chain of federal efforts to assert power over Indians." Ibid., 32.

39 Burke, "The Cherokee Cases," 501. Burke argues that *Cherokee Nation* and *Worcester v. Georgia* confronted the Supreme Court with the "difficult task of forging legal principles to reconcile theory and reality in dealings with the Indians" (501). Because legal claims to date had been brought by "white men with conflicting claims to land that once belonged to Indians" rather than "between states and Indians nations with rival claims," the Court had yet to address directly the question of the "political and property rights of the tribes" (502), which, Burke argues, were the "novel" (502) questions at issue in these cases.

40 Harring, *Crow Dog's Case*, 4–5 (parenthesis omitted).

41 Wilkinson, *American Indians, Time, and the Law*, 55. See also Duthu, *American Indians and the Law*, chap. 7, which argues that tribal governing systems "walk a fine line in balancing the tribes' communal interests as sovereign governments with individual rights of personal autonomy" (137–8).

42 Harring, *Crow Dog's Case*, 18. See also Duane Champagne, "Sovereignty to Minority: As American as Apple Pie," *Wicazo Sa Review* 20 (2005): 21–36, arguing against the incorporation of Native Studies into Ethnic Studies departments to preserve recognition of "the political and legal status of Native Americans" (22), and Duthu, *American Indians and the Law*, observing that "[t]he Supreme Court has isolated the field of federal Indian law from challenges grounded in racial discrimination on the theory that federal classifications among and distinctive treatment of Indians and tribes are in fact political, not racial, classifications" (139) (footnotes omitted).

43 Duthu designates this period from the 1780s to the 1870s beginning with the Trade & Intercourse Act, which established that transactions relating to Indian lands required congressional approval, and ending with the Allotment era beginning in the 1870s, which divided collectively held tribal lands into individual allotments. Ibid., xv–xvi.

44 Ariela Gross, *What Blood Won't Tell: A History of Race on Trial in America* (Cambridge, Mass.: Harvard University Press, 2008), 296.

45 For a theory of comparative racialization as requiring the "performance" of race through law in the creation of socially-mediated understandings of its "common sense," see Gross, *What Blood Won't Tell*, 296.

46 *Cherokee Nation*, 30 U.S. at 12.

47 Id. at 45.

48 Id.

49 Michael Omi and Howard Winant, *Racial Formation in the United States: From the 1960s to the 1990s*, 2nd ed. (New York: Routledge, 1994), 57.

50 30 U.S. (5 Peters) 1 (1831).

51 Id. at 4.

52 Burke, "The Cherokee Cases," 503.

53 30 U.S. at 7. The case is dealt with in historical detail and legal complexity by Harring, who argues that the offence represented an "intratribal crime" that was "within Cherokee jurisdiction." Harring, *Crow Dog's Case*, 28.

54 Ibid., 29–30. Two events appear to have exacerbated Georgia's hostility toward the Cherokee Nation: first, the failure of the United States to "extinguish the Indian title to lands within the state," in regard to a compact signed between the United States and Georgia for lands ceded by the state in 1802, and, second, the Cherokee Nation's adoption of a written constitution modeled after the United States' constitution, which asserted that "the Cherokees were one of the sovereign and independent nations of the earth with complete jurisdiction over their territory." Prucha, *American Indian Policy*, 225, 231. Scholars who debate the proper response that the Cherokee Nation should have taken to Georgia's aggression overlook the key insight that Francis Prucha notes as constitutive of Indian Policy during this period. Tribal nations who did not comply with the assimilation plans of the federal government or the states confronted three options: "extermination," removal to Indian Territory, or assimilation. Prucha, *American Indian Policy*, 220, 221.

55 30 U.S. at 11.

56 Id.

57 Id. at 12.

58 Id.

59 Prucha, *American Indian Policy*, 14. The court decided so because the nation did not comprise a "foreign state" according to the United States constitution and thus could not "maintain an action in the courts of the United States" (14). It held that the court's interference in "restrain[ing] a state from the forcible exercise of legislative power over a neighbouring people, asserting their independence; their right to which the state denies . . . savours too much of the exercise of political power to be within the proper province of the judicial department" (14, 15).

60 Its dependent status, categorized as "that of a ward to his guardian," in looking to the United States "for protection," in no way undermined its recognition "as a state," which "[l]aws . . . enacted in the spirit of these treaties . . . plainly recognize" (16).

61 30 U.S. at 13.

62 Id. at 13.

63 Id. Even Justice Johnson, whose reasoning most explicitly engages in a racist logic that characterizes Indian tribes as existing in a degraded state, calls attention to the Cherokee Nation as an exception to this condition when he writes:

> I cannot but think that there are strong reasons for doubting the applicability of the epithet *state*, to a people so low in grade of organized society as our Indian tribes most generally are. I would not here be understood as speaking of the Cherokees under their present form of government; which certainly must be classed among the most approved forms of civil government.

Id. at 15.

64 Id. at 50.

65 Shu-Mei Shih, "Comparative Racialization: An Introduction," *PMLA* 123 (2008): 1350.

66 30 U.S. at 39.

67 Id. at 43. Justice Thompson's wording of the two-classes-of-Indians thesis may have been informed by Justice Johnson's reasoning in *Fletcher v. Peck*, 10 U.S. (6 Cranch) 87, 147 (1810), in which Justice Johnson distinguished his opinion that "a just view of the state of the Indian nations" matters to the correctness of the court's decision: "Some have totally extinguished their national fire, and submitted themselves to the laws of the state; others have, by treaty, acknowledged that they hold their national existence at the will of the state within which they reside; others retain a limited sovereignty, and the absolute proprietorship of their soil. The latter is the case of the tribes to the west of Georgia" (34).

68 30 U.S. at 50.

69 Shu-Mei Shih, "Global Literature and the Technologies of Recognition," *PMLA* 119 (2004): 16–30, 26.

70 30 U.S. at 12.

71 Id. at 45.

72 31 U.S. (6 Pet.) 515 (1832).

73 Id. at 21, 29.

74 30 U.S. at 13.

75 Id.

76 Id. at 15.

77 Harring, *Crow Dog's Case*, 32.

78 31 U.S. at 13, 15.

79 Id. at 15.

80 Id. at 16, citing *Johnson v. M'Intosh* 21 U.S. (8 Wheat.) 543, 573. The case concerning the status of title conferred by an Indian tribe to a party brought into law two principles concerning title to tribal lands and the reconfiguration of Indian title as occupancy: one, that "discovery gave an exclusive right to extinguish the Indian title of occupancy, either by purchase or by conquest" and, two, that

> an absolute title to lands cannot exist, at the same time, in different persons, or in different governments. An absolute, must be an exclusive title, or at least a title which excludes all others not compatible with it. All our institutions recognize the absolute title of the crown, subject only to the Indian right of occupancy.

21 U.S. at 587–8.

81 *Cherokee Nation*, 31 U.S. at 15.

82 Id. at 13.

83 Id. at 29–30. The chief justice stated, "This relation was that of a nation claiming and receiving the protection of one more powerful."

84 Id. at 24.

85 Id.

86 Id. at, 29, 30.

87 Id. at 30.

88 Id. at 30, 31.

89 Id. at 31.

90 Id. at 33.

91 Shih, "Global Literature," 25–6.

92 Ibid., 26.

93 Ibid.

94 Omi and Winant, *Racial Formation in the United States*, 71 (emphasis in original omitted).

95 Shih, "Comparative Racialization," 1350. "Racial triangulation," according to Shih, "represents a key 'heuristic device' that brings other relational terms, meanings, and identities into view that are often displaced or obscured by binary models." Ibid., 1351.
96 The suits that follow were brought by individual plaintiffs rather than by collectives of tribal members. Clinton and Hotopp argue that tribes were not in a position to enforce their rights because many were "ignorant of American legal processes and were still politically organized in traditional fashions" (ibid., 46). They also indicate that following the Cherokee Nation's outcome that the Cherokees were not "a foreign state . . . that decision . . . had a chilling effect that discouraged [other] tribes from bringing suit." Clinton and Hotopp, "Judicial Enforcement of the Federal Restraints," 46.
97 Gross, *What Blood Won't Tell*, 296.
98 16 F. Cas. 161 (D. Or. 1871).
99 Id. at 161.
100 Id.
101 Id. at 166.
102 Id. at 163.
103 Id. at 162.
104 Id. at 161.
105 Id. at 166.
106 Id.
107 Id. at 167.
108 Id. at 166.
109 Id. at 167.
110 Id.
111 Id.
112 F. Cas. 1006 (N.D.N.Y. 1877).
113 Id. at 1008.
114 Id. at 1006.
115 Id. at 1008.
116 Id.
117 Id. at 1007.
118 Id. at 1007.
119 25 F. Cas. 695 (C.C.D. Neb. 1879).
120 Id. at 696.
121 Id. at 695.
122 Id.
123 Id. at 697.
124 Id. at 695.
125 Id. at 700.
126 Id. at 697. The court states that should they have resisted arrest, rather than seek a "writ of habeas corpus." Despite there existing no "record in which an Indian has been permitted to sue out and maintain a writ of habeas corpus in federal court," they would "readily see that any serious resistance on their part would be the signal for their utter extermination" (697).
127 Id. at 695.
128 Id.
129 Id.
130 Id. at 697.
131 Id.
132 Id. at 699.
133 Id. at 700.
134 Id.
135 Id. at 701.
136 Id.
137 406, 2 F. 58 (D. Or. 1880).
138 Id. The name "Joe Miller" appears to be an alias imposed by the court.
139 Id. at 59.
140 16 F. Cas. 161 (D. Or. 1871).
141 Id. at 60.

142 Id. at 59.
143 112 U.S. 94 (1884). For an important reading of this case, together with the briefs that support it, to illustrate its establishment of the "racial borders of citizenship," see Bethany Berger, "Birthright Citizenship on Trial: Elk v. Wilkins and United States v. Wong Kim Ark," *Cardozo Law Review* 37 (2016): 1185–1258.
144 Id. at 42.
145 Id.
146 Id.
147 Id.
148 Id. at 44.
149 Id.
150 Id.
151 Id. at 45, 46.
152 Id. at 48. In his dissent with Justice Woods, Justice Harlan argued that Elk's status was analogous to the "domestic dependent" state that Justice Marshall characterized in *Cherokee Nation v. Georgia*, existing in a state of "pupilage" and "completely under the sovereignty and dominion of the United States" (56). He stated that if Elk did not acquire citizenship "on abandoning his tribe," becoming resident of a state, and becoming "subject to the complete jurisdiction of the United States," then

> the fourteenth amendment has wholly failed to accomplish in respect of the Indian race, what, we think, was intended by it; and there is still in this country a despised and rejected class of persons with no nationality whatever . . . who are yet not members of any political community, nor entitled to any of the rights, privileges, or immunities of citizens of the United States.

Id. at 56.
153 F. Cas. 1006 (N.D.N.Y. 1877).
154 Id. at 48.
155 10 U.S. (6 Cranch) 87 (1810).
156 Id. at 48.
157 16 F. Cas. 161 (D. Or. 1871).
158 406, 2 F. 58 (D. Or. 1880).
159 Id. at 49.
160 Id.
161 Id. at 1008. The court reckoned that although the supreme court of the state had designated the "Indian residents . . . citizens," a status that was subsequently reversed, social and political relations between "the Indians and the body of citizens at large" had changed because treaties between the United States and the Six Nations, the Menominees, and the Winnebagoes had led to land cessions in Wisconsin, to which the main body of Oneidas had removed.
162 F. Cas. 1006, 1008 (N.D.N.Y. 1877).
163 "The Poncas Again," *New York Tribune*, May 16, 1879.
164 Valerie S. Mathes and Richard Lowitt, *The Standing Bear Controversy: Prelude to Indian Reform* (Urbana: University of Illinois Press, 2003); *Omaha Herald*, May 4, 1879.
165 "Indian Rights," *Chicago Daily Tribune*, May 15, 1879.
166 Ibid.
167 "The Poncas Again," *New York Tribune*, May 16, 1879.
168 Ibid.
169 *Frank Leslie's Illustrated Newspaper*, November 15, 1884.
170 *Omaha Herald*, January 15, 1881.
171 Editorial, *New York Times*, May 10, 1880, 4.
172 *Cherokee Advocate* (Tahlequah, Okla.), November 21, 1884.
173 Gotanda, "The Racialization of Islam," 193.
174 For an extended analysis of Tibbles' role in bringing public attention to the *Standing Bear* case, a suggestion that the court speeches attributed to Standing Bear may have been written by Tibbles, as well as an extensive treatment of Ponca tribal history, see James A. Lake, Sr., "Standing Bear! Who?" *Nebraska Law Review* 60 (1981): 451–503.
175 Communication from the Superintendent of Indian Affairs, "Winnebago Reservation," 39th Congress, 1st Session, Senate. February 8, 1866.
176 M. Leb Goddard, "The Story of the Poncas," *International Review* 9 (October 1880): 391–404.

177 Hartley B. Alexander, "Francis La Flesche," *American Anthropologist* 35 (1933): 328–31, 328.
178 Joan Mark, "Francis La Flesche: The American Indian as Anthropologist," *Isis* 73 (1982): 496–510, 504.
179 Ibid., 498.
180 La Flesche, *The Middle Five*, xv.
181 Ibid.
182 Ibid., 126.
183 Ibid., 128–9.
184 Ibid., 68–9.
185 *United States v. Clapox*, 35 F. 575, 577 (D. Or. 1888). Although the comparison is referenced by La Flesche, the case's depiction of the open defiance by tribal members from the Umatilla Reservation is overlooked. Following the incarceration of a tribal member named "Minnie," charged with committing the crime of adultery, tribal members "unlawfully and with force and arms" broke open the jail, rescued her, and "set [her] at liberty." Id. at 576.
186 Shih, "Comparative Racialization," 1350.
187 Ibid., 1351.

6
THE LEGAL PERSON
Tracing the history of a forensic fiction

Susanna L. Blumenthal

> Where-ever a Man finds, what he calls *himself*, there I think another may say is the same *Person*. It is a Forensick Term appropriating Actions and their Merit; and so belongs only to intelligent Agents capable of a Law, and Happiness and Misery.
>
> *John Locke (1689)*

> If personal identity consisted in consciousness, it would certainly follow, that *no man is the same person any two moments of his life*; and as the right and justice of reward and punishment are founded on personal identity, no man could be responsible for his actions.
>
> *Thomas Reid (1785)*

> Our law of persons is pre-eminently the law of liberty.
>
> *Timothy Walker (1838)*

The search for the essence of the legal person has inspired all manner of analysis on the part of philosophers and jurists to no conclusive end. "There is no general agreement regarding the nature *in se* of the jural subject," John Dewey observed in a well-known 1926 *Yale Law Journal* article, finding that "courts and legislatures do their work without such agreement, sometimes without any conception or theory at all regarding its nature."[1] And so scholars of the subject continue to note, some with consternation or alarm, others with knowing acceptance, and still others with studied bemusement. Much of the writing in the recent past has concerned the propriety of conferring legal personality on "artificial" entities as corporations while denying it to fetuses and nonhuman animals, beings some contend have greater claims to personhood because they are more "like us."[2] Such assertions are unsurprisingly read as question begging raising abstruse and thorny issues about the metaphysics of personhood and the bounds of humankind. The persistence of controversy engenders the impression that the legal person remains as indeterminate as Dewey found it nearly a century ago. The appearance of continuity is deceiving, however, resulting from a want of sustained and systematic inquiry into the historical dimensions of this problematic concept, as a matter of lived experience as well as a forensic term.

Studying the history of an abstraction presents formidable challenges, particularly one that has been invested with so many different meanings. This chapter nonetheless attempts to sketch a biography of sorts for this figure within the confines of American law. It points to the nineteenth century as a formative era in the life of the legal person and emphasizes the ways and means it became a site of cultural contestation. The chapter begins by taking notice of the fact that the law that the young republic inherited from England spoke in the *plural* of person*s*, organizing them hierarchically, in accordance with a more basic set of presuppositions about a divinely preordained chain of being. Defining themselves against this "feudal" way of arranging the subjects of law, early republican jurists forged a republican alternative, one premised upon a novel doctrine of popular sovereignty, which located the source of all legitimate earthly authority in "the free and independent man." Who had the capacity for self-government was, of course, a controversial issue in this expanding market society, as historians of class, gender, race, and ethnicity, and disability have amply documented in a variety of contexts, both within and outside of formal legal institutions. Yet such accounts have tended to overlook the extent to which there was a consensus at the level of the psychological – a common sense of the *self* in self-government. Melding Enlightenment ideals of rationality and autonomy with Protestant moralism, the self as they understood it was an entity endowed by God with the rational faculties of intellect, volition, and moral sense, enabling its possessor to shape his or her own destiny, in this world and the next. Here, in other words, was the concept of the person nineteenth-century Americans had in mind as they contended about the rights and duties of individuals as a matter of law.

In figuring the legal person in these psychological terms, early republican jurists did much to solidify their own cultural authority. However, the more legal personhood came to turn upon a set of mental qualities, the more courts became staging grounds for capacity challenges that proved exceedingly vexing, both in their nature and numbers. In these trials – civil as well as criminal – claimants submitted reasons for thinking that a given individual had lost or never possessed the intellectual, volitional, or moral power to be a self-determining self, contending that he or she had become legally insane. The ensuing courtroom contests routinely featured medical men who claimed expertise in diagnosing and treating mental illness, though they confronted a skeptical bench, increasingly doubtful of the doctors' ability to "dive into the mind." Attending to the "medical jurisprudence of insanity" that these trials generated, this chapter illustrates the various ways doctors and lawyers endeavored to articulate coherent rules of capacity and responsibility, focusing in particular on their efforts to reconcile subjective and objective points of view in thinking about what it was to be a legal person. The chapter concludes with some reflections about the cultural significance and distributive consequences of the law's presumption of sanity, finding in the treatise literature a studied ambiguity about the place of consciousness in the structure of liability, expressive of a deeper ambivalence about the status of mental disability as an excusing condition.

I. The American law of persons

Animated by the revolutionary principle of self-government, American jurists started from the premise that "men may be trusted to govern themselves without a master." In speaking in these terms, they marked a profound shift in ideas about legitimate authority, rejecting inherited forms of government, particularly those justified on grounds of birth and status rather than free and knowing consent. The Supreme Court justice James Wilson marked the distance his countrymen had traveled from their English past in his inaugural law lecture at the College of Philadelphia in 1790 before an illustrious audience that included President George Washington and the First Lady. He first likened the jurist's search for the basis of sovereignty to that of the intrepid explorer seeking the source of the Nile, noting that both had been shrouded in mystery for centuries and had been believed by poets to be "something more than human: it was impiously asserted to be divine." But in this enlightened age, Wilson observed, "the inquiry has been recommenced with a different spirit, and in a new direction," leading explorers to the discovery that the stupendous stream had its beginnings in "a collection of springs small, indeed, but pure." Similarly, jurists in the young republic had arrived at "the first and fundamental principle in the science of government": "The dread and redoubtable sovereign, when traced to his ultimate and genuine source, has been found, as he ought to have been found, in the free and independent man."[3]

This identification of sovereignty with independence had potentially radical implications, which Wilson seemed to sense as he proceeded with his lecture. As if to contain the explosive possibilities of locating sovereign authority in man as an individual, he rather immediately recast self-government as a collective endeavor, summoning up biblical imagery as he associated the late war for independence with the Israelites' deliverance from Egyptian bondage. "We have passed the Red Sea in safety: we have survived a tedious journey through the wilderness: we are now in full and peaceable possession of the promised land," Wilson pronounced, sounding a common refrain among patriots, who had found, in the Exodus story, divine sanction for rebelling against their English "taskmasters." Without quite claiming the mantle of Moses, he emphasized the importance of law in the new nation, proudly trumpeting the superiority of the federal and state constitutions as compared with that of England. Conceiving of the American character as "eminently distinguished by the love of liberty, and the love of law," the latter ensuring the former did not degenerate into "licentiousness," Wilson celebrated the boldness of his countrymen in defying conventional wisdom, as exemplified by Sir William Blackstone. In his celebrated *Commentaries on the Laws of England*, Blackstone had dismissed the popular right of revolution as "a political chimera," submitting that it was patently self-destructive for any legal system to recognize the supreme power of "the citizens at large" to "change their constitution and government whenever they pleased." Establishing their polity upon this "vital principle" of popular sovereignty, the newly united "States of America" not only exposed the errors of learned men like Blackstone but also provided "a foundation of human happiness, broader and deeper than any that has heretofore been laid." Yet this was no guarantee that the inhabitants of this new Canaan would continue to enjoy their hard-won freedom. For "the revolution principle" had to be instilled in and acted upon by the rising generation of Americans, and Wilson saw worrying signs of backsliding all around him, most obviously in the form of undue deference to English texts and authorities like Blackstone and his *Commentaries*. "Must we, after all, return to the flesh pots of Egypt?" he pointedly queried his audience. "Is there not danger, that when one nation teaches, it may, in some instances, give the law to another?" Exodus was for him ultimately a cautionary tale, carrying with it the implication that self-government did not come naturally, that the people had to be taught what it meant to be free.[2]

This was the problem of the self in post-revolutionary America, where analogies were so readily and ambiguously drawn between persons and states, often but not always implying that the legitimacy and viability of the national government rested upon "man's individual capacity to govern himself." The confidence with which many revolutionary leaders spoke on this score in the heat of the imperial crisis belied their conduct in the critical period that followed the war. While the self-evidence of the principle of self-government was bluntly proclaimed in such foundational documents as the Declaration of Independence, the self itself obtruded in ever more troubling ways in the decades that straddled 1800. The leading men who convened in Philadelphia in 1787 constructed a system of constitutional government designed to counterbalance the passions and interests of the citizenry and to call forth a "natural Aristocracy" of "Virtue and Talents" as distinguished from an "artificial" one, premised upon "Birth and Wealth." But it was far from clear that these legal structures would be sufficient to stabilize "the free, self-owning, rights-bearing, sovereign individual" who was supposed to stand at the foundation of this new nation, not least because its leaders had formally repudiated so many of the traditional props of social order. By the turn of the nineteenth century, high federalists like Fisher Ames were sounding alarms about "The Dangers of American Liberty," reasoning that if the people "have in fact no government but such as comports with their ever-varying and often inordinate desires, then there is anarchy." A similar worry animated the moderate Jeffersonian Benjamin Rush, who documented the downside of victory in the late war in a profusion of essays and public lectures, in which he lamented the extent to which his countrymen had redirected their "passion for liberty" into trade and speculation. Such activities "unhinged the judgment, deposed the moral faculty, and filled the imagination, in many people with airy and impracticable schemes of wealth and grandeur" that "could not be removed or restrained by government," essentially amounting to "a form of insanity which I shall take the liberty of distinguishing by the name of *anarchia*." This was a medical diagnosis with sociopolitical implications, which Rush drew out with increasing urgency, emphasizing that the Peace of 1783 "did not terminate the American revolution" – that "it remains yet to establish and perfect our new forms of government, and to prepare the principles, morals, and manner of our citizens for those forms of government after they are established and brought to perfection."[3]

The autonomy of the individual thus figured as an inalienable right and an ever present threat to the visions of ordered liberty projected by the nation's founders. To realize the ends of the Revolution, these leading men insisted, the citizenry of the young republic had to be properly educated. Indeed, Wilson went so far as to suggest that the primary object of the constitutional government lately ratified was "the cultivation and improvement of the human mind," and Rush devoted the remainder of his career to the task of transforming his countrymen into "republican machines." Conceiving of character formation as a national imperative, they drew upon Enlightenment mental and moral philosophy as they endeavored to render the people fit for their new freedoms. These systems of thought figured the human mind as composed of a collection of native faculties that could be developed or degraded through use and disuse over the course of a lifetime. Particularly influential were the mental models of the Scottish Common Sense philosopher Thomas Reid and his popularizers, who affirmed the existence of a unitary "I." This was offered as a corrective to John Locke's account of personal identity, which was grounded in consciousness, inspiring sceptics like David Hume to unnervingly contend that "what we call our self" was "nothing but a bundle or collection of different perceptions, which succeed each other with an inconceivable rapidity, and are in perpetual flux and movement." Appealing to "the common sense of mankind," Reid submitted that no one in his or her right mind could live in conformity with such a self-contradictory conception of the self, trenchantly observing that the sceptic was compelled to rely on the veracity of his mental faculties even as he placed them into question. One needed only to turn inward to see that human beings were, in fact, endowed with a set of "powers and principles of action" of three distinct sorts: the "rational" powers of intellect, will, and moral sense; the "animal" appetites, desires, and affections; and the "mechanical" instincts and habits. While arranging them in hierarchical order, with the implication that the rational powers were supposed to reign supreme over the animal and mechanical ones, Reid emphasized that this mental model could be maintained only through concerted effort; the mind had to be carefully nurtured in childhood by parents and teachers in the first instance and subjected to vigilant self-discipline ever after. Understood as divine gifts indicating "the intention of our being," these mental capacities rendered their possessors moral and accountable agents, answerable to "our Maker" and to "our fellow-men in society" for the "right use" of them.[4]

Armed with such insights about the "laws of the mind," post-revolutionary Americans founded and pursued new organizations and initiatives in order to channel the creative mental energies of this democratizing, increasingly market-oriented society without compromising the ideal of individual liberty. Colleges incorporated the Common Sense school of thought into the curriculum, according it particular prominence in the courses in mental and moral philosophy required of their young male students, teaching them about the powers of the human mind and the concomitant duties to self, family, state, and God that flowed from such endowments, thereby preparing them for positions of leadership. Educators within and outside these institutions – including doctors as well as ministers and lay moralists – also composed treatises, manuals, and magazine articles on character formation for popular consumption, promoting the enterprise of self-improvement to a broader audience of women as well as men. Yet gendered understandings of human nature pervaded this prescriptive literature even as its authors preached an egalitarian ethos, reflecting deeper tensions in the Enlightenment mental science that informed their reform activities. Following the convention of Common Sense philosophers like Reid, they tended to use "man" in the generic sense to refer to humankind. Most took for granted the existence of sexual differences, treating the feminine side of this binary as particular and problematic; they tended to accord women special treatment "as a designated *branch* of humanity," though they varied considerably as to whether "the fairer sex" was naturally endowed with the same intellectual faculties as her male counterpart and the extent to which her observed capacity to cultivate morals and manners was inborn or the product of social conventions. Whiteness also operated as a presumptive norm from which deviations were measured and found wanting, with doubts increasingly registered as to the capacity for "civilization" and self-rule among the Native and African American populations. Here, too, there were conflicting views as to whether these deficiencies were innate or the result of environmental causes. For answers, many drew upon a new transatlantic discourse of racial science produced by a widening array of naturalists, physicians, and anthropologists who undertook to systematically compare the skull sizes and other physical features of various subgroups within the "human family" in order to test assumptions about the mental and moral attributes of nonwhite racial groups as well as women, children, and idiots. Their findings nonetheless did more to inflame than to resolve debates about the sources and significance of human difference and inequality, intensifying controversies as to whether humankind was a single "unit of creation," as the Bible indicated, or instead composed of biologically distinct species that naturally fell into a graded sequence, with Caucasians enjoying pride of place, especially but not only on account of their intelligence, and "Ethiopians" relegated to the lowest rung, just a step above the orangutan.[5]

Early republican lawyers struggled to reconcile these conflicting understandings of the meaning and implications of American independence, as they elaborated the ground rules of everyday life in the new polity. Working from Common Sense premises about human nature, they endeavored to bring their English legal inheritance into greater alignment "with the genius and spirit of our constitution and government." The strains associated with this project are most evident in the annotated American editions of Blackstone's *Commentaries* published in the early decades of the nineteenth century, which were soon followed by works on the English jurist's model, retaining the basic division between persons and things as they elaborated the developing jurisprudence of the United States. While Blackstone was credited with bringing a measure of "order out of chaos" with his systematic arrangement of the laws of England, effectively placing "the study of law in the rank of the sciences," American jurists found it rather too elementary and obviously inadequate as a means of mapping the laws of their own country, not least because the latter were grounded in popular consent. As was characteristic of the age, they aimed at improvement, appreciating the perils and possibilities of their historical situation, presented as they were with the Adamic opportunity to begin anew. " 'The world is all before us where to choose,' " wrote David Hoffman at the outset of his 1829 *Legal Outlines*, a volume of lectures published with the aim of broadly disseminating knowledge about the moral science of law, seeking to enlighten and thereby secure the rights, liberties, and obligations of the citizenry.[6]

Nonetheless his intended audience was not as all-encompassing as it may have sounded, nor was the "universal jurisprudence" Hoffman elaborated – one premised on the idea that all human beings were divinely endowed with the capacity for moral freedom and (therefore) responsibility – necessarily incompatible with the maintenance of the patriarchal, status-based hierarchies of the English common law. The rising generation he and other law writers addressed in these didactic works was implicitly white and male, and they were expected to become heads of households – responsible providers for their wives and children, who were defined as dependents rather than fully autonomous persons as a matter of law. The existence of slavery and the civil incapacities of free blacks proved considerably more difficult for them to square with the animating principles of the late Revolution, moving a few to invoke the new racial science and many more to rely on arguments from necessity and to hope for the gradual emancipation of those in bondage, though few could see how "this unhappy class of people" was to be incorporated into the nation once they were liberated. "The early impressions of obedience and submission, which slaves have received among us, and the no less habitual arrogance and assumption of superiority, among the whites, contribute equally to unfit the former for *freedom*, and the latter for *equality*," observed the Virginia jurist St. George Tucker in his 1803 notes to Blackstone's *Commentaries*. Invoking the Exodus story to evoke darker premonitions than Wilson, he recalled:

> We have in history but one picture of a similar enterprize, and there we see it was necessary not only to open the sea by a miracle, for them to pass, but more necessary to close it again to prevent their return.[7]

This sense of foreboding continued to shadow the subject even as the American law of persons came into its own. An especially prominent illustration of this point is Timothy Walker's widely circulating *Introduction to American Law*, which was first published in 1837, earning him accolades as "the American Blackstone." This Ohio jurist underscored "the fundamental difference there is between personal relations in this country and in England, in consequence of our entire abolition of privileged orders." A simpler scheme prevailed in the United States: "With us, in theory at least, all men start equally; they are born with equal rights; and their distinctions in after-life, are mainly made by themselves." Indeed, the primary divisions of persons could be described "in half the space" required in Blackstone's *Commentaries*, which Walker demonstrated by reducing them to a single paragraph:

> 1. Persons are either natural or artificial. 2. They are either public or private. 3. They are either citizens or aliens. 4. They are either males or females. 5. They are either infants or adults. 6. They are either sane or insane. 7. They are either freemen or slaves, masters or servants, principals or agents. 8. Indians sustain relations different from any other persons. 9. The death of persons creates the relations of ancestors and heirs, devisors and devisees, and executors or administrators.

Seeking to bring theory and practice still closer together, Walker's treatise also vaguely but passionately pointed toward needed reforms, particularly concerning married women and slaves. While the denial of political rights to women was rooted in inveterate custom and "the most refined and enlightened" among them "would be the last to desire a change, which would involve them in the turmoil of politics," the law on the books governing the marital relation degraded wives – at least in theory – "almost to the level of slaves." "The torch of Hymen serves but to light the pile, on which these rights are offered up," he lamented, insisting there was "no foundation in reason or expediency, for the absolute and slavish subjection of the wife to the husband"; were she "the abject thing which the law in theory considers her to be when married," he submitted, "she would not be worthy of the companionship of man." Far more distressing, however, was the condition of the actual slaves in the Southern states who suffered a complete deprivation of their natural right of liberty, which could be "justified upon no principle but that of uncontrollable necessity." Presented with a "choice of evils," the framers reluctantly and ambiguously wrote slavery into the Constitution, a compromising compact "without which the Union could not have been formed, and cannot now be preserved." All but ruling out the notion that slavery would gradually wither away with the advance of American civilization, Walker acknowledged that "its extinction baffles all calculation," anxiously observing that "shadows, clouds and darkness rest upon the prospect." Whether the nation could withstand the intensifying strife between slaveholders and their foes, "which threatens to be carried on with increasing violence," he deemed a "fearful question, which only time can answer." And the legal status of blacks who were free or freed from slavery was likewise left unresolved, though he did note, with acceptance if not approval, that the laws of his own state were designed "to discourage them as much as possible from coming here, without absolutely excluding them."[8]

Walker's democratized law of persons thus bore the imprints of Jacksonian America. Writing from the standpoint of a native New Englander who had converted from orthodox Calvinism to a Unitarian faith and migrated westward in 1831, after studying law at Harvard, to a booming Cincinnati, placing him on the edge of the slaveholding South, this jurist bore witness to the intensifying social, economic, and racial conflicts of the antebellum era. Aligned with the Whig Party in matters of politics, his concerns about the excesses of popular government would crescendo over the course of his career. While he took to giving lyceum lectures in order to propagate a "profitable common sense . . . which the least educated of us can understand and appreciate, and which the best educated cannot despise," he privately confessed to a visiting Alexis de Tocqueville his growing apprehensions about the " 'democracy' without limits" his countrymen were pursuing. By mid-century, Walker had become convinced that the "reform spirit of the day" was animated by a dangerously distorted understanding of the constitutional principles of liberty and equality, typified by Amazonian women's rights advocates, who were no longer satisfied with the influence they wielded at home and now organizing conventions to secure political rights so that they could be "voters, legislators, governors, judges, and, for aught I know, generals and commodores." He urged audiences North and South to be wary of demagogues who propounded leveling principles and incited mob rule under the guise of popular sovereignty, for they threatened to undermine the rule of law that best protected individual liberty. Failing to discriminate between mere innovation and actual improvement, they only made matters worse by projecting illusory visions of a future earthly state where "the human condition could be perfectly equalized, so that there should be no high or low, no rich or poor, no master or servant." Equality rightly understood required only that the law deal evenhandedly with "all persons similarly situated," which to his mind was why "our numerous *corporations*," accorded the status of artificial persons enabling them to enjoy "special privileges and franchises, are not unconstitutional, so long as their charters exclude no class of persons from becoming members." What was worrying was not the proliferation of such legal entities, authorized as they were for the eminently republican purpose of "concentrating or perpetuating individual ability" but instead "the insane ardor with which we pursue wealth as the end of all endeavor." In a country where everything old was deemed questionable and money rather than knowledge was coming to be the measure of the fitness to rule, where a "gush of seeming prosperity" threatened to upend their democratic experiment, Walker sounded ever more embattled as he valorized moderation and sought the institution of "a real aristocracy," in the sense of "a *government of the best*," one helmed by men of virtue and intelligence, "which would, at the same time, be the most perfect democracy."[9]

In speaking in this register, Walker anticipated, informed, and echoed Tocqueville's rendering of American lawyers in his multivolume *Democracy in America* (1835–1840). But this vision of the legal profession as "the most cultivated portion of society," deserving of elevated social and political authority on account of their learning and integrity rather than wealth, proved difficult to sustain over the course of the antebellum era, owing in no small part to the renovations of the traditional English law of persons made by leading men like Walker. Having explained and justified these changes by reference to the commonplaces of Common Sense, they increasingly found themselves on the defensive, as the vocabularies of the self they put into circulation were infused with new meanings and turned to a variety of ends that were not easily harmonized with one another. To be sure, the advice writers who peddled their wares in this expanding market society continued to promote self-*discipline* among aspirants and occupants of the middling classes, projecting a gendered ideal of propertied independence, a well-ordered society composed of male-headed households, enjoying "a competency" in the economic sense: the material means to make a living "without superfluity" or the need to work for others. And this message was reinforced in many respect by politicians of both Jacksonian and Whig persuasions, for in the very act of trading the insults of "aristocrat" and "leveler," they converged a common precept of equal opportunity, which entailed a relative but not absolute equality of condition, so that success in life was determined by talent and industry rather than by birth, law, or patronage. Yet this egalitarian ethos contained the seeds of its own destruction, as Tocqueville trenchantly observed, for it paradoxically awakened towering ambitions and insatiable desires as it "opened the door to universal competition," which explained "this strange unrest of so many unhappy men, restless in the midst of abundance," apparently unable to "enjoy their independence without anxiety and without impatience." Nor was he first to notice the problem. By the time his travelogue was published, it had become almost proverbial among Americans themselves that "the very freedom of our institutions, by creating universal strife, and increasing the mental activity of all classes, causes much insanity." In other words, Rush's nightmare vision of *anarchia* seemed on the verge of becoming a lived reality in antebellum America, calling into question the moralists' teachings about individual freedom and responsibility and prompting reconsideration of the jurists' ways of modeling legal personhood as well as the philosophical premises upon which they were built.[10]

Standing amidst the remains of the English law of persons, these statesmen-lawyers elaborated a republican replacement that would prove to be a rather shaky structure as it was repeatedly tested over the course of the nineteenth century. This was in large part because they made mental ability rather than social status the primary determinant of legal capacity and responsibility. With the Common Sense philosophers they shared a belief in the innate capacity of most – if not all – human beings to master their passions and act in accordance with higher dictates of reason. Though individual efforts to realize this ideal might be frustrated by defects in education and environment, such unfortunate circumstances would not, as a rule, be accepted as excusing conditions as a matter of law. While sheer practicality alone might have dictated this rule, jurists of the day rationalized it on didactic grounds, tending to view the law as a socializing agent and expecting that the imposition of liability would serve a character-building function, teaching the nonconforming how to become responsible subjects. The lessons they hoped the law would teach nonetheless reveal the limits of their egalitarianism; not only were they gender specific, but race and ethnicity also became ever more salient as markers of difference in the decades between the American Revolution and the Civil War. Notions of independence and capacity were increasingly associated with being white and male, while African Americans and women found their status as rights bearers questioned, qualified, or denied, not just because they were actually or potentially slaves and wives but more generally on account of the mental peculiarities and deficiencies presumed to attach to their race and sex, whether innate or as the result of external circumstances.[11]

Yet attending as well to the anxious discourse about the prevalence of insanity in democratizing America adds an important twist to this well established storyline about the exclusions built into nineteenth-century liberalism. For the disease was associated with *advanced* societies even as it chipped away at the progressive ideology of improvement; it was said to be "part of the price we pay for civilization," with doctors and lay reformers finding an odd sort of consolation in statistical studies purporting to show that Native Americans, blacks, and other "primitive" and "barbarous" peoples rarely suffered from this sort of "mental alienation." According to the new medical psychology, those most vulnerable were the self-determining individuals directly and regularly exposed to the mental strains and emotional tumults of modern America, even and perhaps especially the propertied white men taken by jurists to constitute the prototypical legal person. Insanity was thus recast in democratic terms, bearing a haunting resemblance to the open and fluid society it shadowed. A condition long thought to be "the exclusive province of the raving lunatic and the total incompetent," permanently deprived of reason, was now reconceived as "a state of mind in which anyone could find themselves, and from which they could return." To assert that this was a fact of everyday life, as an emergent profession of "alienists" proceeded to do as they carved out a new field of "medical jurisprudence," would have profound legal, political, and social implications, fueling serious doubts about the revolutionary proposition "that man is actually capable of governing himself."[12]

II. The jurisprudence of insanity

The emergence of the new medical psychology marked the growing interest in comparing and relating "normal" and "disordered" mental operations. To be sure, American alienists fully recognized the importance of becoming "acquainted with the human mind in its sane state," drawing liberally on "our British Psychologists," referring to those following in the tradition of Locke and Reid. In line with them, most alienists would affirm that every individual was "endowed by the Deity with an equal gift of mind" and that the "exactness" of its operations essentially depended upon "physical organization," mental cultivation, and self-discipline. Yet it was the very fact of this original equality that spurred these mental pathologists to explore the "diversity of different natures," confident that their inquiries would yield new insights into disease processes and methods of cure. Traversing the expansive and largely unexplored territory between "perfect mental health" and "total insanity," they took pains to distinguish their scientific approach from that of "metaphysician," who was "directed in his course solely by his own self-consciousness." If the powers and limitations of the human mind were to be fully comprehended, they insisted, it was necessary to quit the "narrow circle" of one's own reflections and become "conversant" with the subject of mental disorder, ideally through clinical observation and treatment of afflicted individuals. This many of them were able to do as they assumed the superintendence of a growing number of specialized hospitals designed "to re-create fixity and stability to compensate for the irregularities of the society," providing physical and psychic asylum from the "cares and anxieties" of business as well as the agitating entanglements of religious, political, and family affairs.[13]

Professing to possess specialized knowledge of "the laws of mind and body," American alienists proceeded with almost missionary zeal to dispel superstitions about the supernatural origins of insanity. In the burgeoning medical literature on the subject – directed both to general practitioners and to the broader public – madness was recast as a physical disease of the brain rather than a metaphysical affliction of the soul or mind, and it was said to be caused by a host of hereditary, environmental, and "moral" causes, including mental overexertion and unregulated passion. Indeed, it was now insisted that men and women were entirely capable of going mad on their own, with little help from God and none from the devil. Yet while affirming that man had "power over himself to prevent or control his insanity," these doctors more than suggested they were indispensable to the healing process. Sounding alarms about "the unparalleled frequency of insanity in our country" and casting this as a public health crisis, they not only campaigned for public and private funding of asylum care but also took it to be part of their civic duty to expose and redress deficiencies in the law's treatment of insane persons. Presented in ever more elaborate treatises on medical jurisprudence of insanity, they summoned up patient case histories to illustrate what was wrong with traditional legal classification schemes, which were shown to be underinclusive in theory and inconsistently applied in practice. Judges tended to remain "enslaved by the thraldom of precedent and great names," according undue deference to "ancient" categories and definitions of Coke and Hale, which divided persons *non compos mentis* into four sorts: idiots, lunatics, and those who lost their memory and understanding from sickness or overindulgence in alcohol, all of which were understood to import a total deprivation of sense and reason. This was to view sanity and insanity as dichotomous conditions, failing to recognize the advances made by modern investigators, who revealed mental illness to be a disease of brain, "the best and latest writers" underscoring its varied shades, seldom if ever leaving their victims wholly bereft of their reason. The class of insane persons was expanded considerably by medical jurists as they delineated the physical and psychological symptoms as well as the behavioral signs of mental disease, which they tended to reduce to four main types: dementia, idiocy, mania, and monomania. This last type was a noteworthy innovation on the alienists' part, referring to partial and often quite circumscribed derangements, sometimes confined to a single topic, like religion, politics, or the fidelity of one's spouse, and/or affecting a particular faculty of the mind, such as the intellect, will, emotions, or moral sense. Although this might be read as a medicalization of human perversity, these physicians remained quite adamant that insanity was distinguishable from mere eccentricity or depravity, though this required the eye of an expert, one who had made mental disease "a special object of study."[14]

One of the earliest and most outspoken of these medical specialists was the American physician Isaac Ray, an asylum superintendent who would become one of the leading forensic psychiatrists in the Anglo-American world. His views were presented most comprehensively in *A Treatise on the Medical Jurisprudence of Insanity*, first published in 1838, and enjoyed a wide transatlantic readership as it went through six editions before his death in 1881. It was at once a practical manual and a searing diatribe, in which the decisions of contemporary judges were dissected for the benefit of the reader, so that he could "see for himself how little of true philosophy has presided over the department of criminal jurisprudence" and how many insane defendants were unfairly placed "on the same footing with men of the soundest and strongest minds" and sent to the gallows, though they displayed only the "the slightest vestige of rationality." This state of affairs was rendered all the more galling as the alienist turned to the civil side of the docket, where "one note sounding to folly" might provide grounds for stripping an individual of control over his property and person. Ray could find no "physiological or psychological ground" for this civil-criminal distinction. Indeed, it appeared to him that the common law had gotten the matter exactly backward. The making of a deed or will was, after all, a rather routine affair, usually having "nothing in it, to deprive the mind of all the calmness and rationality of which it is capable." The same could hardly be said of most criminal acts. Even if "abstractly wrong," still they might be "right and meritorious" under certain circumstances, and "if strongest and acutest minds have sometimes been perplexed on this point, what shall we say of the crazy and distorted perceptions of him, whose reason shares a divided empire with the propensities and passions?" The ease with which guilty verdicts were affirmed in such cases compelled the conclusion that the common law took "more account of property than life."[15]

Although ostensibly concerned with critiquing the common law of capacity and responsibility, medical jurists like Ray also brought to the surface unarticulated premises about the constitution of the legal person, unwittingly exposing ambiguities and strains in the liberal Enlightenment conception of the autonomous self that they shared with members of the bench and bar. Like their legal brethren, they understood human nature to be "essentially good, rational, free, and capable of self-government" but they did not as readily conclude that those who deviated from this norm were morally and legally responsible for their failings. To the contrary, alienists suggested that they might be manifestations of an underlying somatic disease, especially if the deviation was out of character, constituting an abrupt and marked "departure from the ordinary habits, feeling, and acting, without any adequate external cause." Because their science had not yet advanced far enough to provide visual evidence of the underlying physical locus of the disease, they made due with such behavioral signs, contending that they provided compelling evidence of mental alienation, of the intrusion of a "controlling" disease that took possession of the sufferer's self. In positing the existence of this "alien persona," Karen Halttunen has argued, they did more than simply exonerate afflicted individuals of culpability for their transgressive acts. They also created "a kind of moral quarantine" that contained the threat such behavior posed to "the liberal faith in human nature." Yet even as they set the insane apart as a social type, distinguishable both from criminals and from the indigent and the eccentric, the alienists chipped away at any sense of security their categories might have provided, redrawing the social geography so as to underscore that everyone was vulnerable to this mental scourge. In works directed toward popular as well as professional audiences, they filled this vast borderland between perfect sanity and total derangement with scientific categories and accompanying descriptions, drawings, and daguerreotypes that challenged traditional ways of seeing the insane in relation to everyone else. Their writings were replete with references to the "thin partitions" separating the sane from the insane, underscoring a common vulnerability: "Every man is interested in this subject; for no man can confidently reckon on the continuance of his perfect reason." Indeed, insanity was all but identified with the human condition as readers were reminded that "no one is of perfectly sound mind but the Deity." In so doing, alienists extended the jurisdiction of their profession to encompass the whole of the population, which not only begged the question of responsibility but pointed toward the paradoxical (and unworkable) conclusion that the only *fully* accountable agents were those who were constitutionally incapable of violating the laws of God and man.[16]

So it was that in a nation built upon the ideal of self-sovereignty, courts were ironically besieged with claims of mental incapacity, testing the traditional common-law presumption of sanity. The uses that criminal defendants made of the insanity plea attracted considerable attention and controversy across the nineteenth century, particularly but not only in high-profile murder trials, the reports of which were published as dramatic narratives intended for popular consumption, usually in a fashion that served only to heighten the mystery and horror of the accused violent acts. The reading public was also fed a steady diet of harrowing stories about men and women who were "railroaded" into asylums, with the wrongful commitment case of Elizabeth Packard becoming into an especially prominent cause *célèbre*, as she proceeded to expose the peculiar vulnerabilities of married women under the existing legal rules and asylum practices, ultimately securing the passage of "personal liberty" laws in a number of states. But these headline-grabbing tales about "homicidal mania" and "enchained reason" were just the tip of the iceberg, for the mind was routinely placed "in issue" by private litigants in a wide array of civil cases. Some proved all too eager to assert their own incompetence in order to escape liability for their deeds, contracts, and torts. Many more brought claims with respect to the incapacity of others, typically grantors and testators who had made eccentric dispositions that were not challenged until after their death. The proceedings that ensued could rival criminal insanity trials in their length and notoriety, generating voluminous transcripts and commanding front-page coverage, especially when a large estate was involved. Moreover, even in the common run of civil cases, each side entered the courtroom flanked by medical men and an army of lay witnesses, who offered dueling biographies of the alleged incompetent. Though undeniably skewed in various ways, these legal contests provide a telling window onto the processes of identity formation and social sorting during the formative era of American law, as well as the profession of psychiatry. Put differently, these trials constitute defining moments in the history of legal personhood. For the arguments, testimony, decisions, news accounts, and critical commentaries produced about what it was to be a self-governing self stand as concrete and revealing instances of what Ian Hacking has provocatively described as "making up people": the phenomenon of naming, describing, and accumulating knowledge about different kinds of individuals, effectively introducing new ways to be – or not to be – a person.[17]

To say that participants in these trials were "making up" categories of persons is not to imply they were imaginary or entirely of their own creation. It is instead to underscore the historicity of our ways of comprehending mental difference and disease and to call attention to the roles played by patients, their families, newspaper reporters, and the broader public, as well as doctors, lawyers, and judges in determining "who are really insane." The word "insane" and its cognates had been around for centuries, of course, along with lived experiences of mental difference and disorder. But "monomania" and "moral insanity" cannot be simply read as novel labels for diseases that had an objective existence in nature long before they were discovered and so named by the nineteenth-century alienists. While these specialists drew upon and were greatly influenced by the very legal doctrines and folk beliefs they purported to "explode," their classification schemes did not exactly map onto the territory covered by previous definitions and diagnoses. To the contrary, their tendency to conceive of these forms of insanity as disease entities, as pathological deviations from a normal state that were curable by scientific means, was expressive of a more general reorientation toward human *nature*, which was increasingly viewed as dynamic and malleable rather than fixed and embedded in a divinely determined universe. Indeed, the concept of "normality" gradually displaced nature in discourse about human kinds in the middle decades of the century as evolutionary ideas began to take hold, marking "a shift in the locus of faith from a God-centered to a human-centered world, from a culture that looked within to a core and backward to lost Edenic origins toward one that looked outward and forward to a perfected future." The alienists' disease entities came to operate as "social realities, actors in complex and multidimensional negotiations that configure and reconfigure the lives of real men and women." As medicalized concepts, they worked not only to naturalize and legitimate conventional ways of understanding and treating human difference and deviance. They were also prone to destabilize and problematize them, particularly insofar as they gave credence to new social and biological determinisms, ones that challenged the notion of self-making itself. Thus, as the alienists' taxonomies became part of the cultural lexicon, they profoundly altered "the space of possibilities for personhood," inducing changes in the self-conception and behavior of the people classified. The responsiveness of the labeled to this labeling process made them "moving targets" from the standpoint of clinicians, who were tasked with continually revising their classifications and theories as a result of these dynamics, a vivid illustration of what Hacking refers to as "the looping effects" of the human sciences.[18]

The *law* of persons added another layer of complexity to these efforts to organize oddity. Though manifestly impacted by the new medical psychology, as well as broader social, political, and economic forces, this body of judicial decisions, statutes, and learned commentaries constituted a distinct conceptual scheme, one with its own purposes, logics, and instrumentalities. Moreover, the modernization of the law of persons *non compos mentis* was inextricably bound up with legal controversies about other traditional status regimes, most notably those concerning slavery and marriage. It is surely no coincidence that the legal definition of insanity underwent a marked expansion in the so-called age of emancipation, supplying conservative elites with new means of rationalizing racial and gender hierarchies and legitimating their own privileged position within a liberalizing legal order. Alienists could be cited to support the proposition that African Americans were not fit to withstand the trials of freedom, especially those with asylum statistics at the ready, going to show that abolition had yielded "a beautiful harvest of mental and physical degeneration," that the freedman was "now becoming a martyr to an heredity thus established," fated to die off or revert back to a primitive savagery. Nor was it difficult to summon up similar medical evidence about women, who could not participate in "active life" without running the risking mental disorder, though their exclusion from the political arena was usually cast by conservatives as "a noble sort of disenfranchisement," wholly unlike that of "the pauper, the criminal, the insane," who were "set aside as persons not human." But these group-based theories of mental difference and deficiency were eminently contestable, and the moral valence and legal significance to be attached to the fact of insanity remained exceedingly ambiguous, not least because "the insane" was not as determinate a category of persons as it was sometimes made out to be, nor were they simply identified with "the dangerous and defective classes," exiled from the human family or pronounced civilly death. To be sure, the linkages between insanity, poverty, and crime gained credence with the spread and popularization of the evolutionary theories of Charles Darwin and Herbert Spencer, especially those who ominously spun them out in terms of degeneracy.[19] Yet all the while insanity remained complexly intertwined with civilization, ironically assuming "epidemic" proportions among the white propertied men and women who seemed to have worked the hardest in their separate spheres to conform to the moral prescriptions set out in antebellum textbooks and advice manuals. They were the ones whose minds were most often placed in issue in postbellum capacity contests, slowly but surely chipping away at the certitudes of Common Sense and begging the question of whether human nature was as morally free and mentally capable as was implied by the law's presumption of sanity.

Rather than confront the ultimate questions posed by such trials, American judges and jurists equivocated on the subject of legal personhood, pronouncing in one breath that "medical science is part of the common law of the land" only to insist in the next that "the law is not a medical or metaphysical science." Standardizing the legal person would prove ever more challenging in an industrializing nation that continued to celebrate its diversity and to privilege the ideal of the autonomous individual, even as it centralized and bureaucratized its systems of governance, erected new barriers to immigration, and absorbed the deterministic teachings of a new generation of neurologists, psychologists, social scientists, and criminologists, many of whom were downright derisive about the concept of free will. Proceeding in a positivistic spirit, these students of human behavior focused their inquiries on observable phenomenon with the aim of generating empirically verifiable principles that were of practical utility, commanding assent, forging consensus, and reliably guiding social policy. Those trained in these disciplines repudiated the faculty psychology upon which the field of medical jurisprudence was founded, casting philosophical efforts to construct an "Ideal Standard Man" as quixotic at best and favoring laboratory techniques and statistical methods as the most promising means of measuring and making sense of mental abnormality. This way of being scientific appealed to more than a few Gilded Age jurists, with Oliver Wendell Holmes providing an especially prominent and illuminating example. His 1881 tome on *The Common Law* approvingly chronicled the evolution of the law from subjective forms of liability rooted in vengeance toward objective, external rules of conduct, ones that took "no account of the infinite varieties of temperament, intellect, and education which make the internal character of a given act so different in different men," instead determining civil and criminal liability by reference to what was blameworthy in "the average man." Indeed, the man of "ordinary intelligence and reasonable prudence" was arguably the hero of Holmes's story, signifying the historical movement of American law from "barbarism to civilization."[20]

Yet even the Holmes of 1881 would admit that there were certain exceptions to this rule, epitomized by the blind man, the infant, and the madman. The first was "not required to see at his peril," nor was the second obliged to exercise the discretion of an adult – he could only be expected to "get as near as he can to the best conduct possible for him." When it came to the subject of madness, however, the jurist equivocated, finding it difficult to state any general rule because many insane persons remained "perfectly capable" of exercising ordinary prudence in their daily affairs. He nonetheless seemed to contemplate the existence of a threshold of mental ability, implying that those who fell below it were not legally bound to act the part of the reasonable man. But there the matter was left in *The Common Law*, which remained centrally concerned with reasonableness as an objective norm rather than as a psychological condition.[21]

In the everyday legal culture lying just outside the jurist's imagination, the problem of insanity was not so easily managed. Indeed it is worth recalling that 1881 was the year of the sensational insanity trial of the assassin Charles Guiteau – an event that vividly exhibited how divided legal, scientific, and public opinion remained regarding the bases of legal personhood and human responsibility. As intellectuals, scientists, and popular writers wrung their hands about the human condition – projecting nightmarish visions of the "degeneration" of "civilized man" and a physically determined universe even as they skewered the forensic uses of the insanity "dodge" – common-law judges continued to be called upon to make determinations of legal responsibility.[22] This they did, mindful of all the disintegrative forces around them operating to undermine Enlightenment faith in the benevolence of God, the autonomy of the will, and the basic intelligibility of the universe. Yet the Gilded Age courtroom was, in fact, a place where epistemological and metaphysical worries were actually more likely to be allayed than confirmed. For experience taught judges the perils of following the logic of Common Sense and deferring to the alienists' expertise. Such lines of thought led in deterministic directions, pointing toward outcomes that were not only impracticable but psychically unappealing as well. Judges had also come to see that "what is rational to one is highly irrational to another," accepting that there was much that could not be known about another mind. These realizations did not, however, move judges toward the extreme of subjectivism, allowing every person to make the law for himself. Nor did they embrace the opposite extreme of objectivism, conclusively presuming everyone was as competent as the reasonable man. Instead, judges in this era eschewed abstract speculation, scientific jargon, and high-toned moralizing, recasting the legal person along more pragmatic lines. They developed an autonomously "legal sense" of what it was to be sane or insane, free or coerced, capable or incapable – distinct from their meanings in philosophical and medical discourses. In the closing decades of the century, judges worked to strengthen the common-law presumption of sanity through a variety of procedural means, and they grew only more resolute in rejecting insanity pleas that were based upon what they saw as "mere eccentricity of conduct, harshness of temper, revengefulness of heart, or a depraved, cruel, and malicious disposition." As they admitted an ever widening array of perverse behavior within the bounds of the "normal," the legal person underwent a change of character. Once held out as a realistic ideal, this "standard man" increasingly came to be viewed as a sort of forensic fiction, practically necessary in a world without absolutes.

III. Conclusion

"For the greater part of a century American courts strove valiantly but vainly to put the whole law in terms of the will," wrote Roscoe Pound in 1954, obscuring as much as he revealed about his legal forebears in casting them as "metaphysical jurists."[25] Contrary to Pound's characterization, members of the bench in this period were rather pragmatic in their thinking about human agency and accountability. Though they reasoned from Common Sense premises, they did not cling dogmatically to an individualistic ethos that was inattentive to the constraints of heredity and environment. Instead they entertained all manner of capacity disputes, which raised more fundamental questions about the sources and significance of human difference and inequality, the bounds of individual freedom and responsibility, and the processes of identity formation. The law reports collecting their decisions record their struggles to square their Enlightenment conceptions of human nature with the actualities of nineteenth-century American life as they were revealed in everyday litigation. In placing the mind in issue, petitioners called upon courts to make determinations of liability not only with respect to alleged crimes and misdemeanors but also with a wide variety domestic and commercial transactions and altercations. The adjudication of these matters was a complex cultural process, each trial providing a new occasion for judges, lawyers, litigants, medical men, and lay witnesses to renegotiate the basic constitution of legal personhood. The final judgments rendered in these trials provided a certain sort of closure to these troublesome matters, though most did not admit of complete resolution. Accordingly, the judges' opinions may best be read as anxious meditations on the meaning of mental health and the bounds of human potential in the United States. Just as importantly, however, this study emphasizes that the legal system did not simply reflect contemporary concerns about sanity and selfhood. Case by case, nineteenth-century American judges performed important cultural work, elaborating a conception of legal personhood that worked to dispel the specters of solipsism and determinism that haunted the philosophical and literary discourse of the era. This conception would prove remarkably resilient both within and beyond American legal culture, exerting a powerful hold on lawyers, judges, and the general public even as a new century brought new insights from such fields as psychoanalysis, behavioral psychology, and neuroscience.

The pragmatic turn of the nineteenth-century bench has nonetheless proved double-edged in its implications. For in strengthening the presumption of sanity even as they widened the legal definition of insanity, disparities in mental ability were rendered less salient as a matter of law. The protective role of courts was correspondingly diminished, leaving individuals freer, in a certain sense, to act on their own ideas and impulses, however eccentric, perverse, or foolish. This judicial tendency might be interpreted as part of the general movement toward abstraction and generalization in the jurisprudence of the period, which historians have long seen as essentially antiredistributive in spirit. But when the trial transcripts and opinions of the court in everyday capacity contests are read alongside the treatise literature, it becomes apparent that there was no straightforward path from subjective to objective principles of liability. Though fin de siècle jurists attempted to standardize the rules of law applicable to "normal" as opposed to "abnormal" persons, their contemporaries on the bench never fully embraced this style of categorical thinking. To the contrary, most judges continued to treat insanity as a matter of degree, with each case to be considered "on its own special and peculiar circumstances." Indeed, to this day there remains a gray area between the uncontested competence of the reasonable man and the clear incompetence of the individual falling below the threshold set by the default legal person. Those who populate this murky middle ground continue to beguile and bedevil judges and jurists alike, as its inhabitants invite and yet resist objective measure. This is perhaps only to be expected within a legal system that treats mental weakness with such ambivalence, its officers seemingly unable to make up their minds whether and when mental abnormality ought to be pitied or penalized.

Notes

1 John Dewey, "The Historic Background of Corporate Legal Personality," *Yale Law Journal* 35 (1926): 655–73, 660.

2 See, e.g., Ngaire Naffine, *Law's Meaning of Life: Philosophy, Religion, Darwin and the Legal Person* (Oxford and Portland, OR: Hart Publishing, 2009); Sheryl N. Hamilton, *Impersonations: Troubling the Person in Law and Culture* (Toronto and Buffalo, NY: University of Toronto Press, 2009).

3 Thomas Jefferson to David Hartley, July 2, 1787, in *The Papers of Thomas Jefferson*, vol. 11, 1 *January–6 August 1787*, ed. Julian P. Boyd (Princeton: Princeton University Press, 1955), 525–6; James Wilson, "Of the Study of the Law in the United States," in *The Works of James Wilson*, ed. Robert Green McCloskey (Cambridge, Mass.: Harvard University Press, 1967), 1: 81.

4 Ibid., 70, 72, 77, 79, 82. For discussions of the ways the Exodus story was invoked by American revolutionaries, see John Coffey, *Exodus and Liberation: Deliverance Politics from John Calvin to Martin Luther King, Jr.* (Oxford: Oxford University Press, 2014); James P. Byrd, *Sacred Scripture, Sacred War: The Bible and the American Revolution* (Oxford: Oxford University Press, 2013); Eran Shalev, *American Zion: The Old Testament as a Political Text from the Revolution to the Civil War* (New Haven, Conn.: Yale University Press, 2013); see also Michael Walzer, *Exodus and Revolution* (New York: Basic Books, 1985). On sovereignty and independence, see David Armitage, *The Declaration of Independence: A Global History* (Cambridge, Mass.: Harvard University Press, 2007), 20–1, which sees the American patriots' 1776 Declaration of Independence as primarily intended "to express the international legal sovereignty of the United States."

5 Joyce Appleby, "The Radical *Double-Entendre* in the Right to Self-Government," in *The Origins of Anglo-American Radicalism*, ed. Margaret C. Jacob and James R. Jacob (Atlantic Highlands, NJ: Humanities Press International, 1991), 304–12, 305; Barbara Young Welke, *Law and the Borders of Belonging in the Long Nineteenth Century United States* (Cambridge: Cambridge University Press, 2010), 3; Fisher Ames, quoted in Louis P. Masur, "'Age of the First Person Singular': The Vocabulary of the Self in New England, 1780–1850," *Journal of American Studies* 25 (1991): 189–211, 194; Benjamin Rush, "An Account of the Influence of the Military and Political Events of the American Revolution upon the Human Body," in *Medical Inquiries and Observations* (Philadelphia: Dobson, 1794), 263–78; Benjamin Rush, "Address to the People of the United States on the Defects of the Confederation," *American Museum* 1 (January 1787): 8–11; Benjamin Rush to Richard Price, May 25, 1786, in Benjamin Rush, *Letters of Benjamin Rush*, ed. L. H. Butterfield (Princeton, NJ: Princeton University Press, 1951), vol. 1, 388–90.

6 James Wilson in Max Farrand, ed., *The Records of the Federal Convention of 1787* (New Haven, Conn., 1911, rev. ed., 1937), I, 605; Benjamin Rush, "On the Mode of Education Proper in a Republic," in *Essays: Literary, Moral, Philosophical*, ed. Michael Meranze (Schenectady, NY: Union College Press, 1988), 7–9; David Hume, *A Treatise on Human Nature*, ed. Mary J. Norton and David Fate Norton (Oxford: Clarendon, 2007), vol. 1, 164–5; Thomas Reid, *An Inquiry in to the Human Mind on the Principles of Common Sense*, ed. Derek R. Brookes (1764; reprint, Edinburgh: Edinburgh University Press, 1997), 163; Thomas Reid, *Essays on the Intellectual and Active Powers of Man* (1768; reprint, Philadelphia: Young, 1793), vol. 2, 399–401. For a wide-ranging historical treatment of the idea of common sense as it has figured in elite politics since the eighteenth century, see Sophia A. Rosenfeld, *Common Sense: A Political History* (Cambridge, Mass.: Harvard University Press, 2011).

7 John Carson, *The Measure of Merit: Talents, Intelligence, and Inequality in the French and American Republics, 1750–1940* (Princeton, N.J.: Princeton University Press, 2007), 38–60, 75–97. For other studies documenting the pervasive influence of the Scottish Common Sense philosophy in antebellum America, see especially Daniel W. Howe, *Making the American Self: Jonathan Edwards to Abraham Lincoln* (Cambridge, Mass.: Harvard University Press, 1997); Donald H. Meyer, *The Instructed Conscience: The Shaping of the American National Ethic* (Philadelphia: University of Pennsylvania Press, 1972); Terence Martin, *The Instructed Vision: Scottish Common Sense Philosophy and the Origins of American Fiction* (Bloomington: University of Indiana Press, 1961). On the dissemination of racial science in post-revolutionary America,

see Winthrop D. Jordan, *White over Black: American Attitudes toward the Negro, 1550–1812* (1968; Chapel Hill: University of North Carolina Press, 2012); Bruce R. Dain, *A Hideous Monster of the Mind: American Race Theory in the Early Republic* (Cambridge, Mass.: Harvard University Press, 2002); for leading accounts extending into the antebellum era, see William R. Stanton, *The Leopard's Spots: Scientific Attitudes toward Race in America, 1815–1859* (Chicago: University of Chicago Press, 1960) and Ann Fabian, *The Skull Collectors: Race, Science, and America's Unburied Dead* (Chicago: University of Chicago Press, 2010).

8 St. George Tucker, *Blackstone's Commentaries* (Philadelphia: Birch and Small, 1803), vol. 3, 119; St. George Tucker, *Commentaries on the Laws of Virginia* (Winchester, VA: Office of the Winchester Virginian, 1831), vol. 1, p. II; David Hoffman, *Legal Outlines: Being the Substance of a Course of Lectures Now Delivering in the University of Maryland* (1829; London: Miller; Baltimore: Neal, 1836); see also David Hoffman, *A Course of Legal Study, Addressed to Students and the Profession Generally* (1817; Baltimore: Neal, 1836).

9 Hoffman, *Legal Outlines*, viii; Tucker, "The Editor's Appendix," *Blackstone's Commentaries*, vol. 2, 63, 70 (quoting the Massachusetts lawyer James Sullivan). On the forms of liberation and domination the Enlightenment promised and provoked in post-revolutionary America, see Robert A. Ferguson, *The American Enlightenment, 1750–1820* (Cambridge, Mass.: Harvard University Press, 1997), 22–43; on the implications for law see Susanna L. Blumenthal, *Law and the Modern Mind: Consciousness and Responsibility in American Legal Culture* (Cambridge, Mass.: Harvard University Press, 2016), chap. 1.

10 Timothy Walker, *Introduction to American Law* (Philadelphia: Nicklin & Johnson, 1837), 163, 165–166, 202–3; 211, 222–223, 650–651. Revised second and third editions appeared in 1846 and 1854, respectively after his death in 1856, the work was reprinted nine times, the last in 1905.

11 Timothy Walker, *The Reform Spirit of the Day. An Oration before the Phi Beta Kappa Society of Harvard University* (Boston: Munroe, 1850), 5–38, 16–17, 19, 20, 22, 24, 37; Walker, *Introduction*, 180, 204; Gordon A. Christenson, "A Tale of Two Lawyers in Antebellum Cincinnati: Timothy Walker's Last Conversation with Salmon P. Chase," *University of Cincinnati Law Review*, 71 (2002): 457–92, 467–8. The strains in Walker's thought reflect "the uneasy union of theological liberalism and social conservatism," incisively discussed in Jeffrey Sklansky's *The Soul's Economy: Market Society and Selfhood in American Thought, 1820–1920* (Chapel Hill: University of North Carolina Press, 2002), 33–72.

12 Alexis de Tocqueville, *Democracy in America*, vol. II (Boston: Little, Brown, 1841), chap. 13; Henry W. Bellows, "The Influence of the Trading Spirit upon the Social and Moral Life of America," *The American Review: A Whig Journal of Politics, Literature, Art, and Science* 1 (1845): 94–8; Richard B. Latner, "Preserving 'the Natural Equality of Rank and Influence': Liberalism, Republicanism, and the Equality of Condition in Jacksonian Politics," in *The Culture of the Market: Historical Essays*, ed. Thomas L. Haskell and Richard F. Teichgraeber III (Cambridge, UK: Cambridge University Press, 1993), 189–230. On the shifting connotations of "competency," see Daniel Vickers, "Competency and Competition: Economic Culture in Early America," *William and Mary Quarterly*, 3d ser., 47 (1990): 3–29.

13 Laura F. Edwards, *The People and Their Peace: Legal Culture and the Transformation of Inequality in the Post-Revolutionary South* (Chapel Hill: University of North Carolina Press, 2009), 205–98; Welke, *Law and the Borders of Belonging*, 21–94.

14 David J. Rothman, *The Discovery of the Asylum: Social Order and Disorder in the New Republic* (Boston: Little, Brown, 1971), 123; Alison Winter, *Mesmerized: Powers of Mind in Victorian Britain* (Chicago: University of Chicago Press, 1998), 46–7; Benjamin Reiss, *Theaters of Madness: Insane Asylums & Nineteenth-Century American Culture* (Chicago: University of Chicago Press, 2008), 1–22; Joyce Appleby, "The Radical *Double-Entendre* in the Right to Self-Government," 304 (quoting John Stevens).

15 Alexander Crichton, *An Inquiry into the Nature and Origin of Mental Derangement* (London: Cadell and Davies, 1798), 1: xxvii; Philippe Pinel, *A Treatise on Insanity* (Sheffield, UK: Todd, 1806), 51; Benjamin Rush (Ed.), "On the Study of Medical Jurisprudence," in *Sixteen Introductory Lectures* (Philadelphia: Bradford and Innskeep, 1811), 363–95; John Haslam, "Medical Jurisprudence as It Relates to Insanity, According to the Law of England," in *Tracts on Medical Jurisprudence*, ed. Thomas Cooper (Philadelphia: Webster, 1819), 291; John Conolly, *An Inquiry Concerning the Indications of Insanity* (London: Taylor, 1830), 39–40, 68–9, 92; Isaac Ray, "Criminal Law of Insanity," *American Jurist and Law Magazine* 14 (1835): 253–74.

16 Mary A. Jimenez, *Changing Faces of Madness: Early American Attitudes and Treatment of the Insane* (Hanover, N.H.: University Press of New England), 28–9, 65–79; Norman Dain, *Concepts of Insanity in the United States, 1789–1865* (New Brunswick, N.J.: Rutgers University Press, 1964), 3–27; Ray, "Criminal Law of Insanity," *American Jurist and Law Magazine* 16 (1837), 54. On the complexities entailed in the process of medicalization as an historical phenomenon, see Blumenthal, *Law and the Modern Mind*, 62–6.

17 Isaac Ray, *A Medical Jurisprudence of Insanity* (Boston: Little, Brown, 1838), vii, 256, 234; Ray, "Criminal Law of Insanity," 273.

18 Conolly, *An Inquiry Concerning the Indications of Insanity*, 8, 59, 171; Ray, *Medical Jurisprudence of Insanity*, 142; Joseph Chitty, *A Practical Treatise on Medical Jurisprudence*, 2nd American ed. (Philadelphia: Carey, Lea, 1836), 353; Karen Halttunen, *Murder Most Foul: The Killer and the American Gothic Imagination* (Cambridge, Mass.: Harvard University Press, 1998), 227, 239; Blumenthal, *Law and the Modern Mind*, chap. 2.

19 Charles E. Rosenberg, *The Trial of the Assassin Guiteau: Psychiatry and the Law in the Gilded Age* (Chicago: University of Chicago Press, 1968); Halttunen, *Murder Most Foul;* Peter McCandless, "Liberty and Lunacy: The Victorians and Wrongful Confinement," in *Madhouses, Mad-Doctors and Madmen*, ed. Andrew Scull (London: Athlone, 1981), 339–62; Hendrik Hartog, "Mrs. Packard on Dependency," *Yale Journal of Law & the Humanities* 1 (1989): 79–103; Blumenthal, *Law and the Modern Mind*; Ian Hacking, "Making up People," in *Reconstructing Individualism: Autonomy, Individuality, and the Self in Western Thought*, ed. Thomas C. Heller, David E. Wellbery, and Morton Sosna (Stanford: Stanford University Press, 1986), 222–36.

20 Douglas C. Baynton, "Disability and the Justification of Inequality in American History," in *The New Disability History: American Perspectives*, ed. Paul K. Longmore and Lauri Umansky (New York: New York University Press, 2001), 33–57, 35–6; Charles E. Rosenberg, "The Tyranny of Diagnosis: Specific Entities and Individual Experience," *Milbank Quarterly* 80 (2002): 237–60, 250; Ian Hacking, "Kinds of People: Moving Targets," *Proceedings of the British Academy* 151 (2007): 285–318; Ibid., "The Looping Effects of Human Kinds," in *Causal Cognition: An Interdisciplinary Approach*, ed. Dan Sperber, David Premack, and Ann J. Premack (Oxford: Oxford University Press, 1995), 315–83. On the interfaces between folk psychology, medical knowledge, and legal doctrines, see Joel Eigen, *Witnessing Insanity: Madness and Mad-Doctors in the English Court* (New Haven, Conn.: Yale University Press, 1995).

21 Baynton, "Disability," 35–45; Cynthia Eagle Russett, *Sexual Science, The Victorian Construction of Womanhood* (Cambridge, Mass.: Harvard University Press, 1989); Gail Bederman, *Manliness & Civilization: A Cultural History of Gender and Race in the United States, 1880–1917* (Chicago: University of Chicago Press, 1995); Robert J. Richards, *Darwin and the Emergence of Evolutionary Theories of Mind and Behavior* (Chicago: University of Chicago Press, 1987).

22 Robert B. Warden, *A Familiar Forensic View of Man and Law* (Columbus, Ohio: Follett, Foster, and Co., 1860), 208; Oliver Wendell Holmes, Jr., *The Common Law* (Boston: Little, Brown, 1881), 5, 51, 108.

23 Holmes, *The Common Law*, 50, 109.

24 Rosenberg, *Trial of the Assassin Guiteau*; on the broader cultural debates about blame and responsibility in this period see Nan Goodman, *Shifting the Blame: Literature, Law, and the Theory of Accidents in Nineteenth-Century America* (Princeton, N.J.: Princeton University Press, 1998).

25 Roscoe Pound, "The Role of Will in Law," *Harvard Law Review* 68 (1954): 1–19, 7.

PART II

A new archive

INTRODUCTION

Nan Goodman and Simon Stern

The legal archive expanded during the nineteenth century in ways that American lawyers noted with satisfaction and concern and in ways that went unnoticed at the time but that have had profound significance for historians. Published case reports, at the beginning of the century, were scant and expensive. In the course of the century, a regular series of published reports became available in every state and for all federal courts, the quality of case reporting rose significantly, and legal libraries proliferated, making law books more available to lawyers and to the public. In addition, treatises appeared on every imaginable subject, along with hornbooks, books of forms, and police manuals that epitomized state criminal laws; a new kind of casebook for students was created, in tandem with the new pedagogy that was inaugurated at Harvard; legal magazines and newspapers began to appear in major cities; and crime reporting became a regular feature of daily and weekly papers.

Even as lawyers congratulated themselves on the improvements to law reporting, they looked with alarm at the increasing volume of published decisions, which in turn created heightened expectations about how attorneys should prepare their cases and allowed judges to place greater emphasis on the importance of abiding by precedent. The Supreme Court of Georgia, in an 1866 decision, addressed both issues in a somewhat aggrieved minilecture, explaining that:

> [w]hen a question has once been decided by this Court, we desire it to be distinctly understood that such a decision is, with us, *authority*. . . . Counsel will, we hope, from this understand the importance of investigating *thoroughly* the decisions of this Court, touching any case which may be brought before it. He will thus be much more likely to gain his case, and will do both us and the State service.[1]

These comments reflect a set of assumptions about access to prior decisions that would not have been warranted even a few decades earlier.

As may be seen from the chapters in this section, the growing library of officially approved and formally edited case reports, as well as of professional legal commentaries on them, hardly accounts for the many new dimensions that the American legal archive acquired in the nineteenth century. Michael Hoeflich's contribution shows how both lay and how professional commentary became increasingly available in periodicals during the course of the century, creating new means of spreading information – and misconceptions – about legal events and doctrinal changes. Jon Blandford's chapter explores a range of visual media that taught Americans about criminality, formal and informal legal processes, and the brutality of extralegal violence in the form of lynch law. Through prints, lithographs, frontispieces, leaflets, newspaper engravings, photographs, and postcards, Americans absorbed legal norms, announced verdicts, and denounced legal atrocities. Robert Tsai's examination of the changing cadences of legal language shows how vernacular and professional forms of law-speak circulated throughout the country, creating a uniquely American legal idiom characterized by efficiency and precision, while also ranging into romantic, emotional, and poetic strains that informed fictional treatments of legal questions, popular and political advocacy, and even courtroom argumentation. The various registers in which Americans recorded, examined, and challenged the developing law come into dialogue throughout this section, most explicitly in the last two chapters. Norman Spaulding shows how practices and sites conventionally described as "extralegal" – namely, lynching, dueling, and wildcat strikes – complement and participate in the formal legal archive rather than constituting its alternative, and Robert Ferguson takes up the competing stories told about the *Somers* mutiny of 1842–43 and its translation into questions about democracy and national security in both elite and popular legal discourse.

Note

1 *Gray v. Gray*, 34 Ga. 499, 501 (1866).

7

LAW IN NINETEENTH-CENTURY AMERICAN PERIODICALS

Michael H. Hoeflich

Introduction

Law and lawyers have been an integral part of American periodical publishing since the beginning. In 1740, Benjamin Franklin announced that he would publish the first true American magazine, *The General Magazine, and Historical Chronicle, for All the British Plantations in America*. He chose John Webbe, a Philadelphia lawyer, as the first editor.[1] As it happened, Webbe's loyalties lay with another publisher, Andrew Bradford, and Webbe decided to serve as editor of Bradford's competing magazine, the *American Monthly*, whose first issue saw the light of day in February 1741.[2] The choice of a lawyer to edit a general circulation magazine was sensible, for these earliest American magazines were dedicated to improving the circulation of literature in the colonies, as well as to carrying political news and commentary. Colonial lawyers were part of the educated elite and were active both in literary and political circles. In the years following the establishment of Franklin's and Bradford's magazines (Bradford published only three issues and Franklin, six),[3] dozens of additional magazines were founded (many were equally short-lived), and other lawyers, notably Noah Webster and Francis Hopkinson, took up the editorial pen.[4] The tradition of lawyers serving as editors of general circulation magazines continued well into the nineteenth century, as witnessed by the activities of such notable lawyers as the South Carolinian lawyer Hugh Swinton Legare, who served for a time as the editor of the *Southern Literary Messenger*.[5]

In order to understand the role of law and lawyers in the publication of periodicals in the nineteenth century, one must recognize that law was conceived to be a branch of general literature and that law and legal writing were not seen as the province only of trained legal professionals.[6] The specialization and professionalization of law and the legal profession that occurred during the latter part of the nineteenth century were notably absent during the early national period. Those trained in the law often sought alternate employment in literary endeavors, and even those who earned their living at the law did not hesitate to be active as writers and public orators. Joseph Story, for instance, was both a lawyer and a poet.[7] Francis Hopkinson, a Philadelphia jurist, was also a poet.[8]

Even a cursory survey of general magazines of the period reveals that legally themed articles and notices were a staple of their content.[9] Of course, the antebellum period also saw the rise of specialist legal periodicals. When surveying these, it is important to recognize that there is no clear line of demarcation between actual magazines as we understand the term today and what we would consider newspapers or serialized books.[10] In part, this fuzziness in classification arises from a peculiarity of antebellum U.S. postal regulations. Until 1851, periodicals enjoyed significant privileges over books in terms of postal service.[11] Thus, many publishers chose to issue books in parts, often in monthly installments, to take advantage of the postal preferences.[12] Often the shaky financial foundations of specialist legal periodicals resulted in irregular publication schedules. In this chapter, however, I have adopted the standard that a periodical will be discussed if it was issued on a monthly or quarterly basis and contained diverse content rather than appearing as a coherent whole more like a single book.

I. Specialist legal periodicals in antebellum America

Between the Revolution and the start of the Civil War, something on the order of thirty legal journals were created and published in at least one issue.[13] Of these, only six survived past 1865.[14] Some of these journals lasted for only a few issues. Others, such as John Hall's *American Law Journal*, the Cambridge-based *American Jurist and Law Magazine* published by Freeman and Bolles in Boston, and the Philadelphia-based *Legal Intelligencer*, first published by Henry Wallace, a Philadelphia lawyer, lasted longer. The *American Law Journal* survived for nine years (1808–17), the *American Jurist* was published for twelve years (1829–41), and the *Legal Intelligencer* was the sole antebellum law journal not only to survive the period but to continue to the present day, albeit under different names.[15] The failure of so many of these journals attests, as we shall see, to the financial risk involved in publishing specialized periodicals in the period, as well as to the hesitancy of many lawyers to invest in subscriptions to these journals at this time.

The antebellum law journals were spread out geographically throughout the new nation both North and South, although most were published in the major Northern urban centers. Even the West had its own law journal. Timothy Walker, a Cincinnati lawyer and judge, founded the *Western Law Journal* in 1843 and published it for ten years (1843–53).

The format and contents of these antebellum specialist law journals were quite similar and so helped to establish a standard format for the journals, which came to dominate the market. These journals all published case opinions that they believed would be of interest to their readers. In many cases, these opinions were of courts within the region in which the journal was published, but a number of journals, such as the *American Law Journal* and the *American Jurist*, also published opinions from throughout the United States as well as from abroad.[16] In publishing these case opinions, the law journals were in direct competition with the earliest published law reports. The reason for doing so was simple: lawyers needed, above all things, access to case reports. Although by publishing these reports the journals had to compete with published volumes of reports, they offered several advantages to the subscriber. The first advantage to subscribers was that they could get a selection of opinions from different courts and jurisdictions without purchasing multiple volumes of reports. Second, journals, since they were published on a regular and frequent basis, provided the reports more quickly than they could be provided in book format. The disadvantage was that significantly fewer opinions were included in the journals than in the reports. One may imagine that the typical law journal subscribers most likely purchased the published reports for their own jurisdiction but depended upon the law journals to supply selected foreign opinions of interest.

Other than the case opinions, the early law journals published significant additional material and thereby added value to the case reports they published. One may look, for example, at the third number of the *American Jurist and Law Magazine*, published in 1829, as an example of what was published in a typical antebellum journal. That number contained the text of a speech given by C. P. Sumner, Sheriff of Sussex County, Massachusetts, comparing the office of sheriff in Massachusetts and in England; a review of Angell's *Treatise on the Common Law of Water Courses*, published in Boston in 1824; an essay on the civil law in the form of a review of two recently published books on civil law; "remarks on the Review of Jackson on Real Actions in the Second Volume of the *American Jurist*"; a review of two books recently published in New York on damages relating to bills of exchange; and an essay on corporate law. These articles were followed by the full text of an unreported Massachusetts case on derelict property, which the editors introduced with the statement that it had been "elaborately discussed by the bar and by the court" and that it was being published because "it will not appear in any volume of reports."[17] Following this opinion, the journal contains thirty-six pages of case digests arranged alphabetically by subject, the opinions being drawn from Massachusetts and Connecticut court reports. There then follow eleven pages of digests of state legislation from Vermont, Connecticut, Kentucky, Missouri, Georgia, and Louisiana. The next section is titled "Intelligence" and contains an account of the establishment of the Dane Professorship of Law at Harvard, a reprint of Samuel Dickinson's prospectus for a new law school at Amherst, Massachusetts, a note on a case from the Michigan Territory, a note on English law reform, a notice on Jeremy Bentham, a note on a jury trial in The Netherlands, notes on recently published law books, an abstract of an English case on checks drawn on bankers, and notes on recent judicial appointments. The volume finishes with a "Quarterly List of Law Publications."

The first number of the second volume of *The American Law Journal* contained the "documents accompanying the message from the President of the United States at the commencement of the second session of the Tenth Congress"; a report on the English statutes then in force in Pennsylvania; reports of cases decided in the federal, state, and county courts in Pennsylvania; a report of a Massachusetts case; a report of a case decided by the French Court of Cassation; a report of several English cases; a report of a case from the Vice-Admiralty Court in Antigua; and a report from the Vice-Admiralty Court in Halifax. These reports were followed by a section labeled "Adversarial," containing brief essays on the law of nations, and, finally, a review of an American reprint of Espinasse's *Reports*. In later numbers, one finds a selection of biographies of eminent judges and lawyers, as well as translations from foreign legal works.[18]

Not all of the antebellum law journals contained as much material as did the *American Jurist* and the *American Law Journal*. For instance, the first number of the second volume of the *Quarterly Law Journal*, edited by A. G. Guignon and published by J. W. Randolph in Richmond, Virginia, in 1857, contained a report of a case from the U.S. District Court for the Eastern District of Virginia, followed by reports of cases from North Carolina and Virginia courts, followed by a report of a case in the United States Court of Claims, nine pages of digests of English cases, reports of two additional Virginia cases, a report of a Massachusetts case (on disbarment of a lawyer), followed by more Virginia and North Carolina cases. These case reports are followed by a section titled "Editorial Miscellanies," which includes brief notices of dueling laws in Virginia as well as a longer essay on usury laws, based in large part on English decisions. The volume concludes with two pages of book notices.

The November 1845 number of the Boston-based *Law Reporter* begins with a biographical essay on Sir Samuel Romilly, followed by fourteen pages of digests of recent Massachusetts cases, followed by nine pages of digests of recent U.S. Supreme Court cases. The volume then continues with two pages of short notices of recently published books, a section of "Intelligence and Miscellany" containing a discussion of a recent case from New Orleans, a long notice of the death of Justice Story, a section labeled "Hotch-Pot" containing notices of the deaths of English lawyers, a discussion of a recent case on drunkenness heard in Boston Municipal Court, a brief notice of an article in the *Western Law Journal*, and notices of recent court appointments in Boston, as well as of a recent visit to Boston by an English author. The volume is concluded with an obituary of

Judge Hitchcock in New Haven, Connecticut, and eight pages of advertisements by publishers and a one-page advertisement for the Harvard Law School.

The additional material included in the various law journals just listed served several purposes for the readers. First, the journals were providing current news about the legal profession to the subscribers. In many cases, law journals were the only source for such specialized professional news. Second, the inclusion of foreign news and reports not only provided access to material that would not otherwise be easily available to subscribers and that might well be useful to them as sources of authority in a period in which American law was still in its formative stage but also appealed to those readers who saw themselves as part of a transatlantic community of lawyers and jurists.[19] Third, for most antebellum lawyers, books were a significant expense. and they wanted to purchase only those that were essential to their practice. By printing lists of new books and reviews of the most important, the law journals enabled their readers to make intelligent and informed decisions about book purchases. By saving a reader from making even one unwise purchase, a journal could easily justify its annual subscription price. Fourth, the inclusion of legal and judicial biographies not only helped to solidify a reader's sense of belonging to a professional community but also provided professional role models that readers could emulate.[20]

One of the most interesting law journals published in the antebellum period was *Livingston's Monthly Law Magazine*, published by the New York attorney and legal entrepreneur John Livingston,[21] which flourished during the 1850s and early 1860s. Livingston wisely decided not to begin publication of the journal until he had a sufficient number of advance subscriptions in hand to assure its financial solvency[22] and in so doing avoided the early failure of so many of his predecessors. Even more significantly, the *Monthly* was only one of a number of related publishing ventures in which Livingston engaged. He also published *Livingston's Law Register*, a national listing by state and city of practicing attorneys. He published, as well, collections of legal biographies, biographies that he solicited from lawyers across the republic.[23]

The interconnections between these three publishing ventures assured financial success for the *Monthly*. Lawyers who chose to be included in the *Law Register* almost certainly also subscribed to the *Monthly*, since the two were published in tandem. Further, biographies that were published in the biographical volumes were also eligible for inclusion in the *Monthly*.[24] Livingston also operated as a law bookseller, publishing catalogues and offering his merchandise through the mails. Many of these books were advertised in the *Monthly* as well.[25]

The *Monthly* itself was initially not radically different from its predecessors and competitors in content. It contained case reports, particularly reports of commercial cases that might be of national interest, as well as scholarly and general articles about the law. Livingston made it clear that he intended to have a "national" audience.[26] The journal also carried "biographical and miscellaneous notices" until 1853. In that year, Livingston abandoned this practice on the grounds that these were not popular with his subscribers, thereby demonstrating his good business sense.[27] As a result of all of this, the *Monthly* achieved and maintained a large national subscription base, one that it kept through the 1860s, when it ceased publication.

Although the various antebellum law journals varied somewhat in format, all were more similar than not. The bulk of these journals was comprised of court opinions. They all featured opinions from the jurisdiction in which they were published, as well as from geographically contiguous jurisdictions where their readers were likely to have some business. Most featured some English reports, no doubt because English reports continued to be a prime source of American law in the antebellum period.[28] A number of the journals, such as the *American Law Journal*, also carried reports from European countries. We may attribute this to two factors. First, such reports would appeal to readers who practiced in areas in which civil law was important, such as admiralty and international trade. Thus, these journals carried these reports for much the same reason they contained translations of foreign works on the law of the sea and commercial law. Second, the elite members of the antebellum Bar considered some knowledge of Roman and civil law to be the mark of a *learned lawyer*, a status to which some subscribers clearly aspired.[29] Beyond the reported and unreported decisions these journals published was information useful to lawyers, including news and reviews of recently published books, notices of legislation, and general gossip about the law and legal profession. Biographical articles, too, served an important purpose, for these articles provided lawyers not only with knowledge of their fellow lawyers and judges but also with models from which lawyers could glean information on how to succeed in practice and achieve both professional eminence and celebrity.[30]

Why did the vast majority of these antebellum law journals fail after only a few issues? This question has confounded modern scholars.[31] First, a number of these journals were founded by lawyers rather than legal publishers, and their failure may simply have been attributable to the lawyers' business ineptitude or loss of interest in favor of more lucrative activities such as law practice. Second, the journals that were founded by law publishers were often created as a vehicle by which the publishers could advertise their legal publications.[32] If these publishers decided that their journals were not justifying the cost of publishing, this alone would have led to the journals' cessation. Third, all of the journals were on shaky financial grounds without a large subscriber list or subscribers who paid their subscriptions in a timely fashion. Many of the journals were unable to acquire large numbers of subscribers, and even those that did suffered from massive nonpayment of annual subscriptions by readers.[33] In spite of the many failures, lawyers and publishers continued to attempt new journals. Why? One may speculate that the reasons were twofold. First, lawyers who began these journals often did so not simply in order to make a profit but out of a desire to promote the profession and their place within it. As to the publishers, the answer may simply be that they saw a market niche and thought that they could succeed where others failed. The fact that some law journals did succeed no doubt helped to foster this optimism.

There may have been another, far more fundamental problem faced by the antebellum legal publications. Ross Davies speculates that antebellum lawyers had too many options available for published materials when looking at the large number of law books, case reports, and other materials all directed at the legal market in the antebellum period.[34] Certainly, there were a limited number of lawyers with limited funds for books and journals. But given this competition, one must ask whether these law journals would have been a top priority for the lawyers to whom they were directed. For many lawyers, in relatively simple practices doing the journeyman's labor of the law (wills, trusts, real estate, simple litigation), the intellectual content of these journals would have seemed superfluous and the case reports duplicative of what they already purchased in book form. In short, for many antebellum lawyers, purchasing law journals was a luxury that many could choose to do without.

II. Law in general circulation magazines

The early nineteenth century saw a "proliferation" of general circulation magazines, so that nearly every town of any consequence in America could boast a weekly literary miscellany of some kind.[35] The period from 1825 to 1850 has been called the "golden age" of such magazines in America.[36] During this period, the number of magazines published increased from 100 in 1825, to 600 in 1850.[37] Most of these magazines were designed to entertain and instruct readers, and they often included fiction, factual articles, news, and current affairs, as well as biographies of prominent persons. Not surprisingly, law was a common subject of these articles. One can look at several issues of almost any of these magazines at random and find articles with a legal theme. The magazines publish fictional accounts of lawyers and the law and frequently included serious disquisitions on the subject. However, the targeted readers of these general circulation magazines were not professionally trained lawyers, and so there was little interest in actual legal decisions or technical accounts of areas of the law. Instead, the legally themed fiction often fell within the typical range of romance and mystery included in the periodicals, and the law was simply the setting for the story. The more serious nonfiction articles tended to focus on areas of the law that would be of special interest to the periodicals' readers and tended to explain these areas in nontechnical terms. A brief study of two of the more popular magazines of the period demonstrates this quite clearly.

Godey's Ladies Book was one of the first and certainly one of the most popular nineteenth-century magazines. It was published from 1830 until 1898, and during much of its life, its editor was the famous Sara Josepha Hale, one of the first successful American woman editors.[38] With women as its target audience, it featured articles on domestic economy, on childrearing, on fashion (and included fashion plates to accompany these articles), on music suitable for home performance, as well as on fiction and factual articles designed for the literate, well-to-do American housewife.[39]

In 1832 *Godey's* ran a series of short fiction under the title "Reminiscences of a Jurisprudent," recounting the adventures of a lawyer who also was an amateur detective. The first of these stories involves a lost will and a plot to disinherit a rightful heir.[40] It is a well written mystery reminiscent of the later works of Edgar Allan Poe and Arthur Conan Doyle. It is just the sort of fiction that would have appealed to a literate readership, and the legal details are accurate. In the volume for 1837, the magazine ran a story titled "The Two Light-Houses," in which a lawyer figures prominently.[41] The volume for 1841 includes a philosophical essay, "Justice," by Henry F. Harrington, which was commissioned for the magazine.[42] The level of the discussions in this article of the legal system is first-rate and undoubtedly served the educational mission of the magazine. Also in 1841, *Godey's* published a brief notice of a new book recently released by Carey & Hart, a noted Philadelphia publisher of both legal and general works: *Law and Lawyers; or, a Sketch and Illustrations of Legal History and Biography.* The notice characterizes the book as a "pleasant" collection of anecdotes about the law and the legal profession.[43]

In January 1842, the magazine published "Wilton Harvey," a story involving a Wall Street lawyer that has an interesting section on lawyers' retainers.[44] The volume for 1849 includes another account of a fictional lawyer, "The Travelled Monkey."[45] This story, like several of the earlier ones printed in the magazine, is critical of the legal profession and describes one character, Lawyer Heston, by recounting that he "had his hands in the pockets of a good many of our unquiet villagers," a sentiment reflective of the popular distrust of the legal profession during this period.[46] This was a theme that runs throughout nineteenth-century American literature and it is not at all surprising to find it here.[47]

Similar legally themed articles and stories continued to appear in the pages of *Godey's* after the Civil War as well. For instance, the magazine published a short obituary of Chief Justice Salmon P. Chase in 1873.[48] In 1874. the magazine featured one of a series of short stories titled "The Polycarp Papers," which contains a long disquisition on law and justice from the Quaker perspective. Finally, in 1883 *Godey's* printed another legally themed story, "A Case in Law."

For half a century *Godey's Lady's Book* published both fiction and factual articles about the law and lawyers. Many of the fictional pieces recounted the interactions of women, often young women of some social status, with lawyers. For the most part, the portrayal of lawyers is positive, although some of the pieces are critical of the legal profession. While legally themed articles do not constitute a large percentage of the content of the magazine over the half century surveyed, they also are not infrequent. One must conclude that the inclusion of such legally themed pieces reflected the editors' judgment that their readers would be interested in them.

The *Southern Literary Messenger* was the preeminent antebellum Southern literary magazine from its founding in 1834 until it ceased publication in 1864, a casualty of the Civil War.[49] It numbered among its editors some of the greatest intellects of the antebellum South, including lawyer and United States Attorney General Hugh Swinton Legare. The magazine was targeted at the intellectual and literary elite of the South, including lawyers. Its articles and stories reflected the interest of the antebellum Southern elite, and so the magazine published a significant number of articles on law and lawyers during its three decades of publication.[50]

The legally themed articles in the *Messenger* tend to be more serious and more instructional than those found in *Godey's*. The *Messenger* published a number of articles on legal education, for instance, including the text of letters by William Wirt and Thomas Jefferson on the study of law.[51] In 1856, the magazine carried a notice of the law school at the College of William and Mary focused on the eminent law faculty members of that institution, including George Wythe, St. George Tucker, and Beverly Tucker.[52]

The *Messenger* published an article responding to popular criticisms of the Bar in its volume for 1847.[53] The magazine also published a number of articles on law reform. In the fourth volume, one finds a series of articles by "a member of the Alabama Bar" arguing for the abolition of Bar Associations because by establishing minimum fee schedules, they led to higher fees.[54] Another article called for a reform of legal reporting and argued for publication of digests of reported cases rather than full texts as a means of reducing the growing burden that the increasing number of reported cases placed on lawyers.[55] The use of the *Messenger* to promote legal reform is not surprising since its editors, especially H. L. Legare were very reform-minded.[56]

Like *Godey's*, the *Messenger* published reviews of recent law books, as well as obituaries of prominent judges and lawyers.[57] The magazine also published legally themed fiction, though not as often as *Godey's*, a fact explained by the *Messenger*'s different target audience.[58] Indeed, the magazine occasionally even published legally themed poetry, most notably a reprint of Sir William Blackstone's "The Lawyer's Farewell to His Muse."[59]

As with *Godey's Lady's Book*, the legally themed articles and stories in the *Messenger* not only reflected the editors' judgment as to what would interest their readers but also demonstrated the extent to which law and lawyers were a subject of considerable popular importance. The range and selection of articles and stories published in these two magazines also represent the content of other nineteenth-century general circulation of American periodicals. Surveys of such magazines as *Grahams,* the *North American Review*, and *Harper's* show an equal interest in legally themed materials.

Even nonlegal specialist magazines in the nineteenth century published articles about the law and lawyers. A prime example is the popular magazine, *Scientific American*, aimed at Americans with interests in engineering and science, especially at would-be inventors. In the nineteenth century. the lone inventor was king in the United States, and *Scientific American* was the inventor's publication.

Scientific American was founded in 1845 as a weekly magazine, primarily to report current filings in the Patent Office and patents granted.[60] Rapidly, it expanded its coverage to new articles about the sciences and engineering in general, as well as to patent law both in the United States and abroad.[61] Thus, it was a magazine with significant coverage of a narrow area of the law: patents, but it also included brief notices of patent litigation and a number of short notices on the law and lawyers in general, which could just as easily have been included in the notices section of legal periodicals. These notices ranged from short notices on new legislation to comic pieces satirizing the law and the legal profession.[62] Thus, even the young inventors who read *Scientific American* got a fair dose of the law in their reading.

III. Specialist legal journals and the rise of student-edited law journals after the Civil War

After the Civil War, we continue to find a number of specialist law journals. A few, such as the Philadelphia-based *Legal Intelligencer*, were survivors of the antebellum period. Others, such as the *Albany Law Journal* and the *Green Bag*, were postwar creations. Such specialist law journals, however, pale in significance to a new type of legal periodical that began to appear in the postwar period: student-edited law reviews affiliated with university-based law schools.

From the end of the Civil War to the beginning of the twentieth century, specialist law journal publishing flowered. In addition to the surviving antebellum law journals, a whole new generation of periodicals targeted at practicing lawyers came into being. Some of the most notable were the *American Law Review*, published in Boston by Little, Brown & Company, one of the most important legal publishing houses; the *Albany Law Journal*; the *Central Law Journal*, published in St. Louis, Missouri; the *Western Law Journal*, published in Des Moines, Iowa; and other similar journals published in New Orleans, Louisiana, Cincinnati, Ohio, Pittsburgh, Pennsylvania, Bloomington, Illinois, and Washington, D.C.[63] These postwar journals did not differ much from their antebellum predecessors, although the geographic move westward demonstrates the growing strength and importance of the legal profession in the western United States. In addition to these new general content legal periodicals, new journals addressed to practitioners in specialist areas of the law like bankruptcy, taxation, and insurance also began to appear.[64] The appearance of these specialty law journals has been attributed to the increase in the number of new lawyers who were focused on particular areas of practice.[65] In addition, a number of specialized industries were becoming sufficiently important and lucrative in the postwar period to generate enough legal business to justify some lawyers specializing to the extent that they believed that it was necessary to maintain their knowledge in these specialty practice areas. Another characteristic of these journals was that they could not maintain a local or regional focus because the industries served by them, such as insurance and taxation, were of national scope. Thus, the journals needed to focus on these areas of law within the national arena.

The most important development in legal periodicals in the postwar period was the decision by several law schools to begin publishing their own law reviews. The first of these, the *Albany Law School Journal*, began publication in 1875. Unfortunately, it ceased publication within the year.[66] Ten years later, students at Columbia law school made an attempt to publish a law school–based journal, but, again, this venture failed, and the *Columbia Jurist* ceased publication after only three years.[67] After these ill-fated ventures into law school–based law journals, the true beginnings of such journals may be ascribed to the founding of the *Harvard Law Review* in 1886.

The *Harvard Law Review* was founded by student members of one of the law school's forensic clubs, the Langdell Society, named after C. C. Langdell, the reforming dean of Harvard Law School appointed in 1870.[68] Langdell transformed the Harvard Law School by instituting the case method of studying law and abandoning the lecture and recitation method of teaching, by publishing the first casebook (on contract law), and by appointing full-time, nonpracticing law faculty, of whom the first, James Barr Ames, succeeded Langdell as dean.[69] Interestingly, however, neither Dean Ames nor the law school faculty directly involved themselves in publication of the new journal.[70]

Nevertheless, the journal's avowed purpose was to publish "faculty scholarship."[71] This fit perfectly with the evolving concept of the law professor championed by Langdell and Ames, a full-time professor who taught and produced scholarship aimed at improving the law and the legal profession, as well as enhancing the reputation of the law school.[72] It also fit well with the law school's almost evangelical zeal to spread the gospel of the Harvard case method to other law schools across the nation. The *Law Review* became the principal showcase for the work being done by the Harvard faculty, helped to spread their legal and pedagogical ideas nationally and internationally, and became a model for law professors around the globe.[73]

The *Law Review* also became a showcase for the work being done by Harvard Law students. In addition to scholarly articles, the *Review* also published book notices, summaries of lectures, and, most important, case notes and comments written by student editors.[74] The notes were about cases related to the lectures printed elsewhere in the *Review*. These notes were of immense importance to both the authors and the law school.[75] They highlighted the writing and analytic talents of the students, and they also went a long way toward making the cases discussed into "leading cases" that would be relied upon and cited by lawyers who read the *Review*.[76]

The success of the *Harvard Law Review* is best measured by its imitators. Within a few years virtually every elite law school had established its own student-edited journals.[77] This success continued throughout the twentieth century so that every American law school could boast at least one law journal, and many had several. Such was the success of the student-edited law journal that these had substantially displaced and replaced commercial legal periodicals by the middle of the twentieth century. Within a few decades, student-edited law reviews became the principal venue for the publication of legal scholarship in the United States. Law faculty could not achieve tenure without being published in these law reviews. In effect, student law review editors became the arbiters of legal scholarship and could make or break professorial careers. This, in turn, gave rise to a backlash by law professors who believed that these law reviews and their editors had become too powerful.[78]

One other postwar law journal deserves separate notice because of its unique mission. The *Green Bag* first appeared in 1889 and continued to be published until 1914. It was a commercial journal not affiliated with any law school. Its first editor, Horace Fuller, sought to produce a journal that would entertain rather than enlighten its readers. According to the advertisement for the first issue:

> A useless but mildly entertaining magazine for lawyers, to be edited by Horace W. Fuller, is announced by Charles C. Soule, Boston. It is to be a monthly, intended to interest and entertain lawyers. It will cover legal history, antiquities, biography, news, gossip, and facetiae, together with correspondence and book notices. The first number, to be published this month, will contain an excellent portrait of Chief Justice Fuller in his robes of office. Each subsequent number will contain the portrait of some distinguished judge or lawyer. There will also be illustrated articles, among them a series of papers upon the leading American law schools.[79]

The *Green Bag* quickly captured the imagination not only of potential subscribers but also of potential authors. The first issue featured an article on the Harvard Law School by Brandeis, as well as a piece by James Barr Ames.[80]

The *Green Bag* quickly became the "official" journal of levity and fun of the American Bar. It featured articles on judges and law schools, humorous verse, including verse renditions of important cases, gossip about the law and lawyers, and pieces on legal history and jurisprudence. Its appearance and success were notable for several reasons. First, this marked, in many ways, a coming of age for the American Bar and a sign that the legal profession was finally able to take itself less seriously in public.[81] Second, although legal history was a subject treated in student-edited law journals, these articles tended to focus on the history of legal doctrine treated abstractly, the subject then most current in legal academic circles, rather than on the social or political history of the law or the legal profession. The *Green Bag* published both original sources and articles on the history of legal education and of the legal profession, subjects that had barely penetrated the academic cloisters of American law schools.

IV. Conclusion

Throughout the nineteenth century, a number of legal publishers as well as lawyers and law schools made attempts at publishing legal periodicals for the practicing Bar. While the majority of the journals begun before the Civil War did not survive into the postwar period, they still were of immense importance, for they established the template for law journals that was to be followed into the twentieth century. They also are a significant source for those interested in the culture and business of the Bar in the antebellum period and stand as an important witness to the practicing Bar's attempts to upgrade their social and intellectual standing as well as to become a national force.

After the Civil War, law journals that targeted members of the Bar continued to be established at a brisk pace. Some of these survived for substantial periods, and others, like their antebellum predecessors, disappeared after only a few issues. It was also in this period that specialized journals targeting practitioners in newly important subject areas like bankruptcy and taxation began to appear and flourished. Finally, at the end of this period, the *Green Bag* made its first appearance and provided something new for the practicing Bar and legal academia: a journal that looked at the lighter side of the law and the legal profession. Its success over nearly two decades speaks to the growing maturity of the American Bar and the ability of lawyers to laugh at themselves.

During the final two decades of the nineteenth century, the form of law journal that still exists today first appeared: the law school–affiliated, student-edited law journal. The two earliest of these, the *Albany Law School Journal* and the *Columbia Jurist*, survived for only short periods. But the latter inspired a group of students to found the *Harvard Law Review* in 1886, one of the greatest law publishing successes of the nineteenth and twentieth centuries. Within a few decades, law schools across the nation were founding their own law journals in imitation of and competition with the *Harvard Law Review*, and the pattern for twentieth-century legal periodicals was set.

As outlined, writing about law and lawyers was not confined to specialist law journals in the nineteenth century. Rather, these were frequent topics in the general circulation magazines throughout the century. From the earliest literary magazines like the *North American Review* and the *Southern Literary Messenger* to *Harper's* and *Godey's*, throughout the century articles, book notices, and fiction about the law and the legal profession were common. The frequency with which legally themed pieces appear in these general circulation magazines reflects the American public's perpetual fascination with the law and lawyers and its willingness to purchase magazines that slaked this literary thirst.

Notes

1 James P. Wood, *Magazines in the United States* (New York: Ronald Press, 1956), 10. On early American periodical literature, see also John W. Tebbel and Mary E. Zuckerman, *The Magazine in America* (New York: Oxford University Press, 1991); Algernon Tassin, *The Magazine in America* (New York: Dodd, Mead, 1916); Neal L. Edgar, *A History and Bibliography of American Magazines, 1810–1820* (Metuchen, N.J.: Scarecrow, 1975); Steven Lamazow, *American Periodicals. A Collector's Manual and Bibliography* (West Orange, N.J.: Lomazow, 1996.

2 Wood, *Magazines in the United States*, 10.

3 Ibid., 14.

4 Webster became editor of *The Herald* in New York; Hopkinson became editor of *The American Museum*, published in Philadelphia by Matthew Carey, who was to become one of the leading law booksellers in the early national period. Ibid., 14–17.

5 Ibid., 14.
6 Ibid., 14–17; see also Richard Squibbs, *Urban Enlightenment and the Eighteenth Century Periodical Essay* (New York: Palgrave-Macmillan, 2014) and Richard Squibbs, "Lawyers, Republicanism and the Eighteenth-Century Periodical Essay in the *Port Folio*," *Huntington Library Quarterly* 75 (2012): 69–93.
7 Wood, *Magazines in the United States*, 14–17.
8 Ibid.
9 Ross E. Davies, "The Original Law Journals," *Green Bag 2d* 12 (2009): 187–217.
10 Ibid., 198.
11 Michael H. Hoeflich, *Legal Publishing in Antebellum America* (Cambridge, UK: Cambridge University Press, 2010), 95.
12 Ibid., 45.
13 Davies, "The Original Law Journals," 187; Michael I. Swygert and Jon W. Bruce, "The Historical Origins, Founding, and Early Development of Student-Edited Law Reviews," *Hastings Law Journal* 36 (1985): 739–91; Frederick Charles Hicks, *Materials and Methods of Legal Research*, 3rd ed. (Lawyers Co-operative Pub. Co., 1942), 204–7.
14 Davies, "The Original Law Journals," 187.
15 Ibid., 187.
16 On this important aspect of these early journals, see Zoey F. Orol, "Reading the Early American Legal Profession: A Study of the First American Law Review," *NYU Law Review* 87 (2012): 1523–69, 1552–3.
17 Luther S. Cushing, "Derelict Property," *American Jurist and Law Magazine* 2 (1829): 119–39.
18 For an excellent analysis of the contents of Hall's *American Law Journal*, see Orol, "Reading the Early American Legal Profession." On antebellum legal translations, see Hoeflich, *Legal Publishing in Antebellum America*, 1; Michael H. Hoeflich, "Translation and the Reception of Foreign Law in Antebellum America," *American Journal of Comparative Law* 50 (2002): 753–75.
19 See Michael H. Hoeflich, *Roman and Civil Law and the Development of Anglo-American Jurisprudence* (Athens: University of Georgia Press, 1998), *passim*.
20 See Michael H. Hoeflich, "Legal Ethics in the Nineteenth Century: The Other Tradition," *University of Kansas Law Review* 47 (1999): 793–817.
21 This journal began life as the *U.S. Monthly Law Magazine* in 1850, but its publisher soon changed its name to reflect his ownership; on the history of this journal and Livingston's related enterprises, see Hoeflich, *Legal Publishing in Antebellum America*, 145–70.
22 Ibid., 146.
23 Hoeflich, *Legal Publishing in Antebellum America*, 145.
24 Ibid., 149–52, 157–62.
25 Ibid., 162–5.
26 Ibid., 154.
27 Ibid., 156.
28 Ibid., 40.
29 See Hoeflich, *Roman and Civil Law*; Hoeflich, *Legal Publishing in Antebellum America*, 86; Orol, n. 16, above.
30 The most extensive use of biographical material is to be found in the journal conducted by John Livingston of New York, first published during the 1850s and 1860s under the title the *American Law Register* and then renamed *Livingston's Law Register*. See Hoeflich, *Legal Publishing in Antebellum America*, 145.
31 Davies, "The Original Law Journals," 187; Swygert and Bruce, "Historical Origins," 739.
32 Hoeflich, *Legal Publishing in Antebellum America*, 101.
33 Davies, "The Original Law Journals," 1523.
34 Davies, "The Original Law Journals," 1523. See also Hoeflich, *Legal Publishing in Antebellum America*, 101, on the drastic increase in the number of law books published in the 1830s and beyond.
35 Tebbel and Zuckerman, *The Magazine in America*, 9.
36 Ibid., 11.
37 Ibid.
38 *Godey's Lady's Magazine* (Philadelphia: Godey, 1830–98); see also Ruth E. Finley, *The Lady of Godey's* (Philadelphia: Lippincott, 1931).
39 Tebbel and Zuckerman, *The Magazine in America*, 27–39.
40 *Godey's* 4 (January 1832), 1–4.
41 *Godey's* 15 (December 1837), 265–74.
42 *Godey's* 22 (March 1841), 136–9. Harrington had been the editor of the *Boston Herald* during the 1830s.

43 *Godey's* 23 (November, 1841), 238.
44 *Godey's* 24 (January 1842), 12–18.
45 *Godey's* 39 (July 1849).
46 Tebbel and Zuckerman, *The Magazine in America*, 11.
47 See Maxwell Bloomfield, *American Lawyers in a Changing Society. 1776–1876* (Cambridge, Mass.: Harvard University Press, 1976); Michael H. Hoeflich, "Lawyers, Fees and Anti-Lawyer Sentiment in Popular Art, 1800–1925," *Green Bag 2d* 4 (2001): 147–56.
48 *Godey's* 87 (July 1873), 92.
49 *Southern Literary Messenger* 14 (1848): 255; on the *Messenger*, see Benjamin B. Minor, *The Southern Literary Messenger* (New York: Neale, 1905) and Michael O'Brien, *A Character of Hugh Legare* (Knoxville: University of Tennessee Press, 1985).
50 I would like to acknowledge the research of Ms. Laura K. Brooks, KU Law Class of 2004, whose research forms a basis for this section.
51 *Southern Literary Messenger* 1 (1834): 33; *Southern Literary Messenger* 14 (1848): 88.
52 *Southern Literary Messenger* 23 (1856): 276.
53 "The Legal Profession," *Southern Literary Messenger* 13 (1847): 356–9.
54 *Southern Literary Messenger* 4 (1838): 581.
55 *Southern Literary Messenger* 14 (1848): 255. On this theme in antebellum America, see C. Clark and Michael H. Hoeflich, "Oceana Juris" (lecture, University of Edinburgh, Scotland, UK, March 2007).
56 On Legare, see, above all, O'Brien, *A Character of Hugh Legare.*
57 See, for instance, *Southern Literary Messenger* 3 (1837): 464; *Southern Literary Messenger* 7 (1841): 865; *Southern Literary Messenger* 20 (1854): 636.
58 See, for instance, "Circumstantial Evidence: A Tale Founded on Fact," *Southern Literary Messenger* 1 (1834): 141–4.
59 Sir William Blackstone, "The Lawyer's Farewell to His Muse," *Southern Literary Messenger* 1 (1835): 316. Legally themed poetry was common throughout the nineteenth century; see the online bibliography of such poetry maintained by Professor James R. Elkins, *Strangers to Us All*, http://myweb.wvnet.edu/~jelkins/lp-2001/intro/.
60 "The Press Room," *Scientific American*, www.scientificamerican.com/pressroom/about-scientificamerican/.
61 See, for instance, "Law of Patents in Prussia," *Scientific American* (1849), 306.
62 See, for instance, "Advantages of Law," *Scientific American* (1847), 43; "Law and Art," *Scientific American* (1848), 1.
63 Swygert and Bruce, "Historical Origins," 8–11.
64 Ibid.
65 Ibid., 12.
66 Ibid.
67 Ibid., 13–14; The authors suggest that the *Columbia Jurist* had one lasting effect: it inspired the law students at Harvard to begin their own journal, the *Harvard Law Review.*
68 Ibid., 14.
69 Ibid.
70 Ibid., 15.
71 Ibid.
72 Ibid., 14.
73 Ibid., 16.
74 Ibid.
75 As Swygert and Bruce noted, ibid., 17. The notes gained authority from the fact that the selection of student editors for the *Review* was done on a "democratic and meritocratic" basis; i.e., the student editors were the most academically successful students at the law school.
76 Ibid.
77 Ibid., 18–21.
78 Fred Rodell, "Goodbye to Law Reviews," *Virginia Law Review* 23 (1936): 28–35.
79 "Among the Publishers," *Science*, May 31, 1889, 429.
80 Davies, "The Original Law Journals," 1–2.
81 As opposed to the Bar's very serious self-image during the antebellum period, a reaction to strong public antilawyer sentiment; see Bloomfield, *American Lawyers in a Changing Society.*

8

SPECTACULAR JUDGMENTS

Law and disorder in the nineteenth-century visual imagination

Jon Blandford

In his *Theory of Moral Sentiments* (1759), Adam Smith characterizes the remorseful criminal as someone who "dares no longer look society in the face" and would "be glad to fly to some inhospitable desert, where he might never behold the face of a human creature, nor read in the countenance of mankind the condemnation of his crime." Only the "horror of solitude drives him back into society, and he comes again into the presence of mankind, astonished to appear before them, loaded with shame and distracted with fear, in order to supplicate some little protection from the countenance of those very judges, who he knows have already all unanimously condemned him."[1] Aligning the moral sense with the sense of sight, this passage is typical of the emphasis on looking that pervades Smith's moral philosophy. In this case, it is not punishment itself that Smith's hypothetical criminal dreads but "look[ing] society in the face" and seeing on its countenance "the condemnation of his crime." Indeed, Smith describes here what we might call the ideal relationship between spectacle and justice in the legal imagination. The public, represented by Smith's "impartial spectator," looks on criminals in judgment, and criminals internalize that disapproving gaze, coming to see themselves as they are seen by others, "unanimously condemned."

If this is what the spectacle of the law looks like in theory, the practice is significantly more complex. Criminals do not always see themselves as the law that condemns them does, nor does the public always see from the law's perspective or regard its pronouncements as just. Far from "impartial" or "unanimous," the spectators of the law may sympathize or even identify with those singled out for judgment, turning their scrutinizing gaze on the law itself. The spectacle of the law too might serve purposes other than those for which it was intended, functioning as entertainment or as an incitement to further subversion of the dominant order. It is a tool that can be wielded by the state but also against the state as a means of making visible popular resistance to the law's dictates. In short, as integral as spectacle is to the law, it is also highly unstable, capable of generating a range of responses and effects that exceed the control of those in power.

This chapter explores these and other ambivalences as they pertain to spectacle in nineteenth-century U.S. law and culture. The chapter's first section addresses the controversy over capital punishment, which during this period transformed from a public ritual into an exercise of power that took place out of public view. Although nineteenth-century opponents of capital punishment were unsuccessful in eliminating the practice, changing attitudes conspired to relocate punishment behind the walls of newly erected penitentiaries, where it was administered in solitude, unobserved by a putatively healthy body politic. Seen from this angle, the operations of power became less spectacular over the course of the nineteenth century, the rituals of the scaffold replaced by Foucauldian regimes of discipline that derived much of their force from their lack of visibility.

Yet the spectacle of crime and punishment did not go away. It simply migrated to different venues that allowed for other kinds of mass witnessing. One such venue, the focus of this chapter's second section, is the popular crime literature that flourished during the nineteenth century, as the published execution sermons and confessions that dominated earlier decades came to be supplanted by an increasingly secular and generically varied array of representations. This new textual corpus inherited the representational instability of the rituals that public execution used in order to inscribe meaning on the body of the condemned. Just as the spectators who gathered before the gallows or the whipping post could come away with divergent interpretations – interpretations that were sometimes at odds with the official script authored by the representatives of the law and the clergy – so too did the crime literature of this later period invite mixed, even contradictory responses, often opposing the defiant words of criminals and dissenters to the authoritative discourse of the law and serving as an arena in which larger social issues of the day were contested.

Along with the printed page, the emergence of the courtroom as the literal and symbolic center of the practice of the law changed the way Americans saw crime and punishment. Prior to the late eighteenth century, court was held in spaces such as taverns and town houses, the construction of courthouses at the end of the century coinciding with the professionalization of the law. Not only did these courthouses – which grew in size and number throughout the nineteenth century – legitimize the legal profession by setting it apart from other public activities, they also created a new theater of judgment. As Robert A. Ferguson has pointed out, although much of the practice of the law would still take place elsewhere, it is the courthouse – and more specifically, the courtroom – that would come to occupy a privileged place in the popular imagination, precisely because it opened up the law to public scrutiny.[2] The third section of this chapter examines the new types of spectacle that this development made possible by analyzing the architecture of nineteenth-century courthouses and courtrooms, along with the concomitant development of courtroom fiction, a genre that first appeared in the mid-nineteenth century and that illustrates, in particularly dramatic fashion, how print culture and courtroom space functioned as mechanisms through which the public could observe the spectacle of the law.

Lastly, the chapter concludes with a discussion of lynching, an extralegal spectacle that took up the display of violence that the state openly disavowed. Beginning in the eighteenth century and persisting into the twentieth, lynching operated at the margins of power, often implicitly condoned or even encouraged. Although lynchings took place throughout the nineteenth century in all areas of the United States, the practice intensified during the eras of Reconstruction and post-Reconstruction, when African Americans were targeted by white mobs seeking to reaffirm their authority. Advertised in newspapers and drawing large crowds, sometimes in the thousands, the lynchings that terrorized and brutalized African Americans at the end of the century recall in important ways the public executions common at the century's beginning. Putatively about the punishment of crime, they were also about the control of populations deemed threatening to dominant interests. Lynchings also shared public execution's essential ambiguity: seen by many as a tool for maintaining order, they were seen by many others as spectacular, undeniable proof of gross injustice.

I. Capital punishment: from scaffold to prison yard

Public executions in America up through the early nineteenth century adhered to a highly conventionalized form, holding up the condemned as a negative example of the consequences of sin. The prisoner was led to the gallows before a crowd of onlookers, who, prior to the execution itself, heard remarks delivered by a minister or magistrate, followed by, in most instances, the condemned's own confession. Taken together, these speeches from the scaffold shaped a narrative of transgression and repentance. This interpretation was further reinforced by print material that included formulaic records of the lives of criminals which, purportedly in the criminals' own words, emphasized where and how they went wrong and pleaded for forgiveness. Seeing condemned criminals acknowledge the justice of their fate afforded the audience that gathered to witness the execution, as well as those who read about it after the fact, the opportunity for moral self-reflection, lest their own actions lead to a similar end. The ceremony of execution also affirmed the authority of the church and the state, reconciling the sinner to the larger community of believers and asserting the power of the secular government to punish those who violated the terms of the social contract. The latter was an especially salient feature of execution day during the tumultuous early years of the new nation when, as Louis Masur observes, "civil and religious leaders argued that only public executions could control the disordering effects of independence, war, and the establishment of government."[3]

An execution broadside titled *God's Judgment upon Murder* (1812), published to coincide with the hanging of Samuel Tulley and John Dalton, two sailors convicted of murder after participating in a mutiny aboard the *George Washington*, exemplifies the message that the execution ritual was designed to convey (Figure 8.1). The text begins with two quotations from scripture (Job 36:17 and Job 36:14) and then states, "When society is called upon to perform the painful yet necessary duty of punishing with death the violated laws of God and man, the mind is necessarily led into a train of unpleasant, though not unprofitable reflections." Exactly what these reflections should be and why they are "not unprofitable" get spelled out for the audience in the remainder of the text. We are told how "the commission of one crime leads to that of another" and are instructed to shed tears for the widow and children of Tulley, who, along with Dalton, the "awful moment" of their execution having commenced before a "gazing" and "mute" crowd, will "soon appear before the judgment seat of Christ." The "fate of these unhappy men," depicted in the illustration at the top of the page, will "be a warning beacon to others," especially "all our youth," a reminder that "the paths of vice, which though for a time they may appear flowery and pleasant, will most assuredly lead to the dark and gloomy abyss of irretrievable ruin." Representative of the cultural and ideological work performed by public executions more generally, this example is particularly interesting for the extent to which it layers the political, the economic, and the theological: a mutiny on a commercial schooner named after the nation's first president, mere months before the onset of the War of 1812, is denounced in language derived from the Puritan execution sermons of the eighteenth and seventeenth centuries. "God's Judgment upon Murder" thus demonstrates how the ritual of execution worked to contain various threats to dominant interests – against property, religious values, or civil authority – by corralling those threats within a predictable structure.

Actual executions, however, did not always fit neatly within this discursive scaffolding. Although Tulley was executed, Dalton was granted a last-minute presidential pardon, spared in life the fate he suffered in print.[4] Other convicted criminals used the scaffold as a platform from which to proclaim their innocence or their mistreatment at the hands of the law. Sentenced to hang for robbery in 1789, Rachel Wall reportedly framed her last words, in keeping with convention, as "a solemn warning and caution to every one, . . . especially those of my own sex," but also insisted that she was "entirely innocent" of the specific crime for which she was to be executed. Wall protested that she "never saw Miss *Bendar* [*sic*] (the person I was charged with robbing that evening) and was quite surprised when the crime was laid to my charge. The witnesses who swore against me are certainly mistaken; but as a dying person I freely forgive them."[5] The deviation of Wall and other criminals from their prescribed role effectively flipped the execution

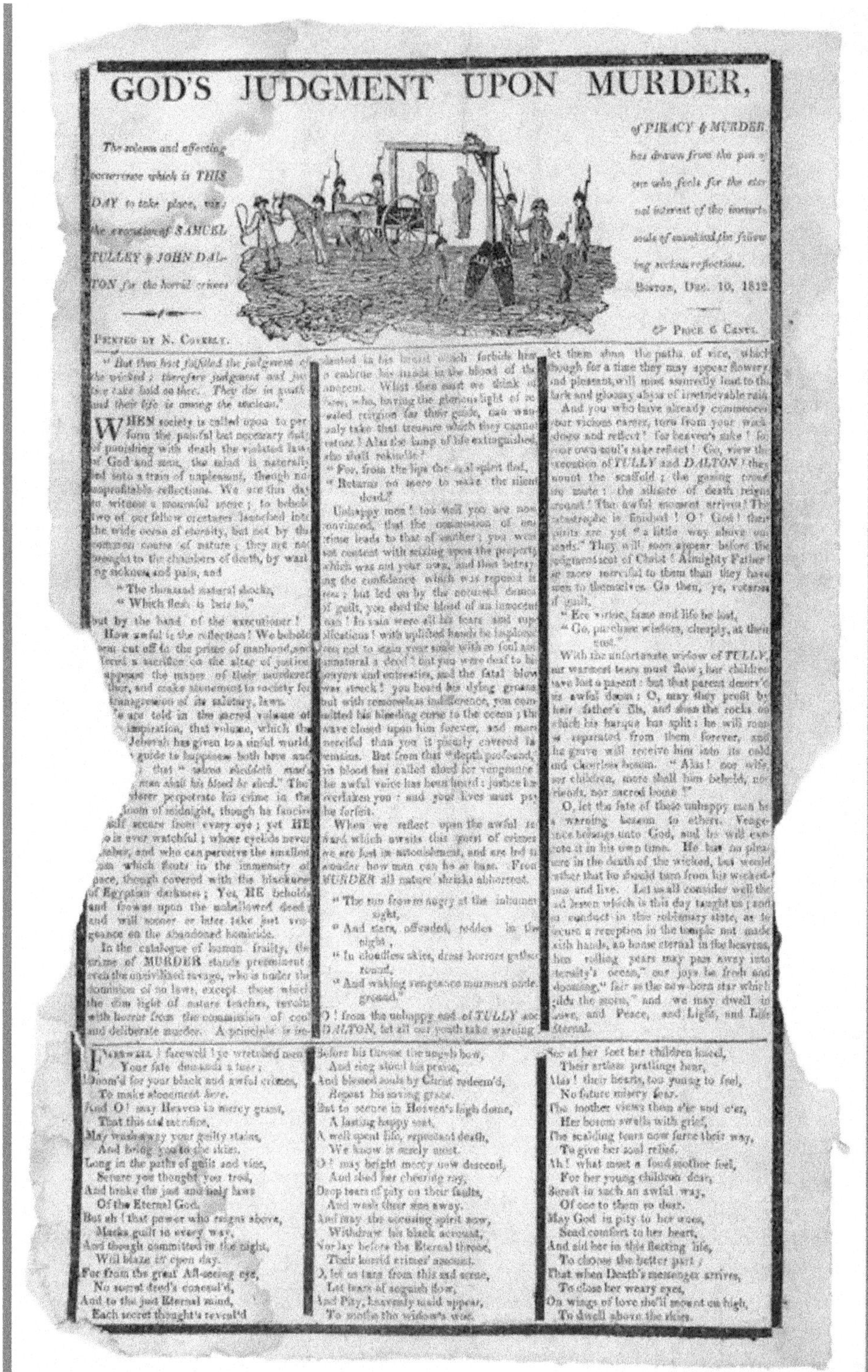

GOD'S JUDGMENT UPON MURDER,

The solemn and affecting occurrence which is THIS DAY to take place, viz: the execution of SAMUEL TULLEY & JOHN DALTON for the horrid crimes of PIRACY & MURDER, has drawn from the pen of one who feels for the eternal interest of the immortal souls of mankind the following serious reflections.

BOSTON, DEC. 10, 1812.

PRINTED BY N. COVERLY.

☞ PRICE 6 CENTS.

"But thou hast fulfilled the judgment of the wicked; therefore judgment and justice take hold on thee. They die in youth and their life is among the unclean."

WHEN society is called upon to perform the painful but necessary duty of punishing with death the violated laws of God and man, the mind is naturally led into a train of unpleasant, though not unprofitable reflections. We are this day to witness a mournful scene; to behold two of our fellow creatures launched into the wide ocean of eternity, but not by the common course of nature; they are not brought to the chambers of death, by wasting sickness and pain, and

"The thousand natural shocks,
"Which flesh is heir to,"

but by the hand of the executioner!

How awful is the reflection! We behold men cut off in the prime of manhood, and offered a sacrifice on the altar of justice to appease the manes of their murdered brother, and make atonement to society for transgression of its salutary laws.

We are told in the sacred volume of inspiration, that volume, which the Jehovah has given to a sinful world, a guide to happiness both here and [illegible], that "whoso sheddeth man's [blood, by] man shall his blood be shed." The [mur]derer perpetrate his crime in the gloom of midnight, though he fancies [him]self secure from every eye; yet HE who is ever watchful; whose eyelids never slumber, and who can perceive the smallest atom which floats in the immensity of space, though covered with the blackness of Egyptian darkness; Yes, HE beholds and frowns upon the unhallowed deed, and will sooner or later take just vengeance on the abandoned homicide.

In the catalogue of human frailty, the crime of MURDER stands preeminent; even the uncivilized savage, who is under the dominion of no laws, except those which the dim light of nature teaches, revolts with horror from the commission of cool and deliberate murder. A principle is implanted in his breast which forbids him to embrue his hands in the blood of the innocent. What then must we think of those, who, having the glorious light of revealed religion for their guide, can wantonly take that treasure which they cannot return! Alas the lamp of life extinguished, who shall rekindle?

"For, from the lips the [illegible] spirit fled,
"Returns no more to wake the silent dead."

Unhappy men! too well you are now convinced, that the commission of one crime leads to that of another; you were not content with seizing upon the property which was not your own, and thus betraying the confidence which was reposed in you; but led on by the accursed demon of guilt, you shed the blood of an innocent man! In vain were all his tears and supplications! with uplifted hands he implored you not to stain your souls with so foul and unnatural a deed! but you were deaf to his prayers and entreaties, and the fatal blow was struck! you heard his dying groans but with remorseless indifference, you committed his bleeding corse to the ocean; the wave closed upon him forever, and more merciful than you it [illegible] covered his remains. But from that "depth profound," his blood has called aloud for vengeance! the awful voice has been heard: justice has overtaken you: and your lives must pay the forfeit.

When we reflect upon the awful reward which awaits this [illegible] of crimes we are lost in astonishment, and are led to wonder how man can be so base. From MURDER all nature shrinks abhorrent.

"The sun frowns angry at the inhuman sight,
"And stars, offended, redden in the night,
"In cloudless skies, dread horrors gather round,
"And waking vengeance murmurs under ground."

O! from the unhappy end of TULLY and DALTON, let all our youth take warning! let them shun the paths of vice, which though for a time they may appear flowery and pleasant, will most assuredly lead to the dark and gloomy abyss of irretrievable ruin.

And you who have already commenced your vicious career, turn from your wickedness and reflect! for heaven's sake! for your own soul's sake reflect! Go, view the execution of TULLY and DALTON! they mount the scaffold; the gazing crowd are mute; the silence of death reigns around! The awful moment arrives! The catastrophe is finished! O! God! their spirits are yet "a little way above our heads." They will soon appear before the judgment seat of Christ! Almighty Father! be more merciful to them than they have been to themselves. Go then, ye, veterans of guilt,

"Ere virtue, fame and life be lost,
"Go, purchase wisdom, cheaply, at their cost."

With the unfortunate widow of TULLY, our warmest tears must flow; her children have lost a parent: but that parent deserv'd his awful doom: O, may they profit by their father's ills, and shun the rocks on which his barque has split: he will soon be separated from them forever, and the grave will receive him into its cold and cheerless bosom. "Alas! nor wife, nor children, more shall him behold, nor friends, nor sacred home!"

O, let the fate of these unhappy men be a warning lesson to others. Vengeance belongs unto God, and he will execute it in his own time. He has no pleasure in the death of the wicked, but would rather that he should turn from his wickedness and live. Let us all consider well the sad lesson which is this day taught us; and so conduct in this probationary state, as to secure a reception in the temple not made with hands, an house eternal in the heavens, when rolling years may pass away into eternity's ocean," our joys be fresh and blooming, "fair as the new-born star which gilds the morn," and we may dwell in Love, and Peace, and Light, and Life Eternal.

FAREWELL! farewell! ye wretched men
Your fate demands a tear;
Doom'd for your black and awful crimes,
To make atonement *here*.
And O! may Heaven in mercy grant,
That this sad sacrifice,
May wash away your guilty stains,
And bring you to the skies.
Long in the paths of guilt and vice,
Secure you thought you trod,
And broke the just and holy laws
Of the Eternal God.
But ah! that power who reigns above,
Marks guilt in every way,
And though committed in the night,
Will blaze in open day.
For from the great All-seeing eye,
No secret deed's conceal'd,
And to the just Eternal mind,
Each secret thought's reveal'd

Before his throne the angels bow,
And sing aloud his praise,
And blessed souls by Christ redeem'd,
Repeat his saving grace.
But to secure in Heaven's high dome,
A lasting happy seat,
A well spent life, repentant death,
We know is surely meet.
O! may bright mercy now descend,
And shed her cheering ray,
Drop tears of pity on their faults,
And wash their sins away.
And may the accusing spirit now,
Withdraw his black account,
Nor lay before the Eternal throne,
Their horrid crimes' amount.
O, let us turn from this sad scene,
Let tears of anguish flow,
And Pity, heavenly maid appear,
To soothe the widow's woe.

See at her feet her children kneel,
Their artless pratlings hear,
Alas! their hearts, too young to feel,
No future misery fear.
The mother views them o'er and o'er,
Her bosom swells with grief,
The scalding tears now force their way,
To give her soul relief.
Ah! what must a fond mother feel,
For her young children dear,
Bereft in such an awful way,
Of one to them so dear.
May God in pity to her woes,
Send comfort to her heart,
And aid her in this fleeting life,
To choose the better part;
That when Death's messenger arrives,
To close her weary eyes,
On wings of love she'll mount on high,
To dwell above the skies.

Figure 8.1 "God's Judgment upon Murder" (Boston: N. Coverly, 1812)

Source: Library of Congress, Rare Book and Special Collections Division, Printed Ephemera Collection

day script, granting the condemned the power to accuse and, in Wall's case, to forgive those who had wronged *her*. The large crowds that assembled on execution day likewise often refused to fulfill their assigned part in the drama of crime and punishment. As early as 1770, the Reverend Moses Baldwin saw it necessary to remind those in attendance at the execution of William Shaw that it was "not a day for rioting and vain merriment" but "rather for fasting, humiliation, and prayer," an admonition that, as Scott Seay points out, reflects how the execution ritual had become something other than what authorities wanted it to be.[6]

Anxieties about whether public executions served an instructive purpose or were occasions for "rioting and vain merriment" informed the debate on capital punishment that took place during the late eighteenth and early nineteenth centuries. Defenders of the practice, often drawn from the ranks of the orthodox clergy, stressed its value as a deterrent to crime and its consistency with Biblical precedent. Antigallows activists, by contrast, argued that the display of violence ran contrary to Christian and republican values, that it disregarded the environmental causes of crime and the possibility of reforming criminals, and that it had a corrupting influence on public morality.[7] For both sides of the argument, the spectacular dimension of public execution was crucial. Where *God's Judgment upon Murder* and other broadsides and pamphlets like it imagine a "gazing" and "mute" crowd receptive to the "warning beacon" of the ritual of execution, Benjamin Rush, in a famous essay first delivered in the company of Benjamin Franklin's Society for Promoting Political Enquiries, contended that any manner of public punishment, whether whipping, forced labor, or death, risked sending the wrong message to spectators, prompting admiration (for criminals who bear their suffering with dignity), sympathy (for criminals in distress), or possibly even distrust and contempt for humankind in general. Worse still, for "spectators [who] are themselves hardened with vice," as well as for those who are "too young, or too ignorant, to connect the ideas of crimes and punishments together," public punishments may seem "mere arbitrary acts of cruelty," which, Rush reasons, could in turn inspire such spectators to "exercise the same arbitrary cruelty over the feelings and lives of their fellow creatures."[8]

In the nineteenth century, a number of reformers and writers embraced the antideath penalty cause. Societies dedicated to the abolition of capital punishment formed in Philadelphia (1842), New York (1844, the founding members of whom included *New York Tribune* editor Horace Greeley and *Democratic Review* editor John O'Sullivan), and Massachusetts (1845); a national society, headed by then U.S. Vice President George M. Dallas, was organized in 1845. Prominent among these reformers was Charles Spear, whose antigallows newspaper *The Hangman* (Figure 8.2) began publication in 1845 and was retitled *The Prisoner's Friend* in 1846. Spear's periodicals featured a mix of editorials, calls for petitions and other interventions on behalf of specific criminals, profiles of penitent convicts and benevolent reformers, and poetry, some of which, such as Samuel Hanson's "The Convict to His Bible" (Figure 8.3), was written by prisoners themselves. Spear was far from alone in using print publicity to advocate for an end to capital punishment. Among others, John Greenleaf Whittier, John Neal, Lydia Maria Child, and William Gilmore Simms authored poems and fictional works critical of the death penalty, summoning a counterpublic of readers in opposition to the public that, earlier in the century, had gathered before the gallows.[9]

Ultimately, the nineteenth-century opponents of capital punishment could claim only partial success, with just five states abolishing the death penalty altogether: Michigan in 1846, Rhode Island and Wisconsin in 1853, Maine in 1876 (and again in 1887, after it was reintroduced in 1883), and Colorado in 1897, which reestablished the practice a mere four years later. Far more representative was Pennsylvania, which, in 1794, eliminated the use of execution for all crimes except murder, and, in 1834, became the first state to stop holding executions in public. As Michael Meranze has shown, the path Philadelphia took from public display to the segregation

THE HANGMAN.

"I shall ask for the Abolition of the Penalty of Death until I have the infallibility of Human Judgment demonstrated to me."—Lafayette.

Vol. I.] Boston, (Mass.,) Wednesday, August 13, 1845. [New Series—No. 20.

Appointment of the time for the execution of Orrin De Wolf.

The friends of suffering humanity have now only a few days more to labor in behalf of Orrin De Wolf. On Tuesday, the 26th inst. the Governor and Council of this Commonwealth will meet in this city for the transaction of executive business. They will then appoint the day and the hour when John W. Lincoln, the Sheriff of Worcester County, shall take Orrin De Wolf from his cell, and hang him up by the neck, until he is dead. Shall this unnecessary and inhuman work be done in this ancient Commonwealth in the year 1845? Is it not full time to discontinue forever this horrid practice? Let all those who do not desire to have De Wolf hung, make great exertions to save his life by circulating petitions immediately asking for a commutation of punishment. Now is the time to work for the prisoner, for him 'who is appointed unto death.' Send petitions to our office. We will forward them to the Executive.

Figure 8.2 *The Hangman*, 1:20 (Boston: Charles Spear, 1845)

of criminals in the penitentiary was uneven and riddled with obstacles. In between the use of the gallows and whipping post and the opening of Eastern State Penitentiary in 1829, the city experimented with a system of public labor, eventually abandoned in part out of fears that the too-visible presence of criminals amidst the general population would engender "mimetic corruption."[10] While not everywhere in the United States followed this exact trajectory, the outcome

PRISONER'S FRIEND.

DEVOTED TO THE ABOLITION OF CAPITAL PUNISHMENT, AND THE IMPROVEMENT OF PRISON DISCIPLINE.

VOL. I....No. 14. BOSTON, WEDNESDAY, APRIL 8, 1846. (OLD SERIES, Vol. II.

THE PRISONER'S FRIEND, PUBLISHED EVERY WEDNESDAY

CHARLES SPEAR, JOHN M. SPEAR, Editors and Proprietors.

Memoirs of Mrs. Elizabeth Fry.

THE CONVICT TO HIS BIBLE

Figure 8.3 *The Prisoner's Friend*, 1:14 (Boston: Charles Spear, 1846)

was generally the same, the penitentiary replacing the gallows as the site of punishment, concealing that punishment from outside spectators.

Confinement in the penitentiary was, according to Masur, a solution "supple enough to satisfy both those who dreamed of reforming criminals and those who wanted to terrorize them."[11] Out of sight, the ambiguous space of the prison could be imagined as a Gothic dungeon where offenders suffered horribly for their crimes or as a hospital of sorts that cured criminals of ill habits and behaviors, preparing them for successful reintroduction into society. The rise of the penitentiary also robbed the antideath penalty movement of part of its rationale by removing executions from public view. The executions that occurred from the 1830s on took place in the prison yard, before an invited audience of spectators much smaller and more homogeneous than the ones that had assembled to witness public punishments. Some prison yard executions, such as the hanging of Alexander Anderson and Henry Richards in 1858, still drew crowds: as Karen Halttunen notes, having unsuccessfully petitioned for a temporary suspension of the Pennsylvania law prohibiting public execution, would-be spectators nevertheless turned out in droves on Anderson and Richards' execution day, with some buying tickets to watch from nearby buildings and others bringing ladders or climbing trees so that they could see inside the walls of the prison.[12] Overall, though, those eager to see such things increasingly had to settle for reading about them after they had occurred, helping to create a demand for mediated spectacle that the authors and publishers of the era's proliferating corpus of crime literature were more than happy to fulfill.

II. Crime literature and mass mediation

Although the cloistering of executions and other punishments behind prison walls limited their audience to a few elite spectators, the bourgeoning popular print culture of the nineteenth century held up more criminals and crimes than ever before to public view. Technological and infrastructural changes throughout the first part of the century contributed to an explosion in the number and variety of printed texts, many of which fed the public's seemingly limitless appetite for representations of crime and punishment.[13] In place of the execution sermon and its endorsement of clerical and civic authority, a veritable rogue's gallery of unruly genres vied for readers' attention, including biographies and autobiographies that romanticized the lives of criminals, trial reports that implicitly called into question the very verdicts they recorded, and sensational narratives, common in the penny press, that often featured lurid depictions of sex and violence. As Daniel Cohen argues, these insurgent forms were part of a larger epistemological shift, "impl[ying] a conception of truth not as the pronouncement of a single authoritative voice but as the collaborative product of a multiplicity of independent speakers and viewpoints."[14]

Some of these viewpoints belonged to criminals themselves. While criminals' biographies and last words figured prominently in earlier American crime literature, the authoritative words of ministers and other representatives of the dominant order almost always framed such utterances. Moreover, the narratives themselves were frequently so formulaic as to be indistinguishable from one another, offering essentially interchangeable iterations of the same themes. By contrast, the criminals-turned-authors of the late eighteenth and early nineteenth century often defiantly spoke for themselves, using publication, as Ann Fabian points out, "to police speech outside [their] cell[s], to check the spread of malicious rumor and mean gossip, and to admit to some misdeeds but deny others."[15] Confidence man Stephen Burroughs, whose best-selling *Memoirs* (1798) appeared in multiple editions over the course of the century, was especially unrepentant, portraying himself as besieged by tyrannical and corrupt forces intent on ruining his good name. Rather than submit to the generic requirements of contrition and negative exemplarity, Burroughs repeatedly and emphatically insists that only he is qualified to pass judgment on his own life; recounting how he was caught hiding in a barn after having escaped from the proto-Alcatraz of Castle Island, he laments that his captors "knew not my feelings, [and] therefore could not judge with regard to that conduct which I thought they ought to exercise toward me. They had never been in my situation, hence could not view it in its proper light."[16] Print provided a mechanism for Burroughs and others like him to seize control of their own representation, to dispute competing published reports, and to attempt to persuade curious readers to see them and their actions in the "proper light."

In addition to creating a market for criminals to tell their stories, the popular interest in crime fueled the emergence of the penny press. Karen Halttunen has analyzed how the cheap, abundant crime literature of the nineteenth century trafficked in a "pornography of violence" that reexposed to an eager public gaze subject matter that had been privatized or rendered taboo by recently emergent humanitarian sensibilities.[17] Much of this exposure involved graphic descriptions of bodies, violated bodies, and in particular the violated bodies of women. The sordid story of murdered New York City prostitute Helen Jewett in 1836 provided ample fodder for upstart penny papers such as the *Sun*, the *Transcript*, the *Herald*, and the *Ladies Morning Star*, forcing more established six-cent papers like the *Evening Post* to redefine what counted as news worthy of the public's attention.[18] Five years later, the violent and unsolved death of "Beautiful Cigar Girl" Mary Rogers similarly drove newspaper sales, inviting readers to leer at explicit renderings of Rogers's ravished corpse, which, Amy Gilman Srebnick explains, came to embody anxieties about female sexuality, the working class, and the intersection of private and public life in the nation's new urban environments.[19] The coverage of these and other sensational crimes tended to be highly speculative in nature, indicative of the porous boundaries between fact and fiction. Rogers's story in particular inspired fictionalizations by J. H. Ingraham and, more famously, Edgar Allan Poe, whose "The Mystery of Marie Roget" (1842) relocates the crime to Paris, where, in what Mark Seltzer reads as an early example of crime writing's reflexivity, his detective character Dupin solves the mystery by reading about it in the papers.[20]

Published trial reports also blurred the lines between crime fact and crime fiction, recording attorneys' conflicting interpretations of the same events and prompting readers to join in the imaginative act of translating evidence into narrative.[21] Further complicating matters, high-profile cases often generated multiple such reports; the trial of Methodist minister Ephraim Avery for the alleged murder of pregnant mill worker Sarah Maria Cornell, for example, saw the publication of transcripts skewed in favor of the defense alongside ones more favorable to the prosecution.[22] The Avery trial reports were supplemented with a range of other texts, including a narrative from Deputy Sheriff Harvey Harnden, who pursued the suspect across three states when he fled arrest; a set of lithographic reproductions of letters introduced as evidence at the trial; a *Vindication* written by the minister and his Methodist allies; and even a phony confession that claimed Avery as its author. Avery and Cornell's story also inspired numerous newspaper editorials, poems, two different stage plays, and Catharine Williams's *Fall River* (1833), an important early work of true crime remarkable for its generic hybridity.[23] Acquitted in his trial, Avery found himself condemned in the court of public opinion and, his reputation ruined, was eventually forced to move from the area.

A print depicting Avery strangling Cornell, unambiguously titled "A Very Bad Man," illustrates the spectacular nature of the trial and the tension between the legal verdict and popular judgment (Figure 8.4). The murderer and his victim are surrounded by cartoon devils that appear to stand in for the widespread fascination with the case – one of the devils asks, "Do you see what is going on here," and another remarks, "I never sleep on such occasions." A third devil wonders, "How will this be managed if it should go to a jury," to which a fourth replies, "A jury ye young fools is nothing. What's to be done with PUBLIC OPINION?"

Their attitude somewhere between vigilance and prurience, the audience of devils in this image mirrors the mass audience that consumed the print publicity surrounding the case. Indeed, the presence of these observers at the scene of the crime itself reflects the paradoxical promise of nineteenth-century crime literature, which, through the technology of mass mediation, offered to bring readers closer to criminals and crimes so that they could see and judge for themselves, all the while allowing those same readers to maintain a safe distance.

Figure 8.4 "A Very Bad Man" (New York: Henry Robinson & Company, 1833)

Source: Library of Congress, Prints and Photographs Division

III. The theater of the courtroom

The Avery case is suggestive of the degree to which the locus of spectacle in the popular legal imagination shifted, over the course of the nineteenth century, from the site of punishment to the site of judgment. As the administration of executions and other punishments moved out of the public square and into the prison, the courthouse became an increasingly prominent part of the cultural landscape, focusing attention on the judicial process. Martha McNamara has detailed how the transition in the late eighteenth and early nineteenth century from conducting legal proceedings in multiuse structures such as taverns to holding them in courthouses built solely for that purpose helped to establish lawyers and architects as professional classes with distinct, specialized areas of expertise. Often imposing in size, these new courthouses were segregated yet still visible from commercial spaces, sequestering the operation of the law – in theory if not in practice, of course – from potentially corrupting outside influences while maintaining its position at the center of civic life.[24]

The Allegheny County Courthouse in Pittsburgh, erected in 1841 and destroyed by fire in 1882, typifies the Greek Revival style popular during the period. Situated atop Grant's Hill and later flanked by an Episcopal church and a Roman Catholic cathedral (both built during the 1850s), its Doric portico and massive dome signified its status as a secular temple

Figure 8.5 Allegheny Court House, stereograph (Pittsburgh: S. V. Albee, 1882)

Source: Library of Congress, Prints and Photographs Division

of reason and order (Figure 8.5). It was replaced by an even more elaborate Romanesque structure constructed on the same site, designed by architect Henry Hobson Richardson and finished in 1888 (Figure 8.6). Still standing today, this courthouse – Allegheny County's third – was joined to an adjacent jail by a so-called Bridge of Sighs, a striking reminder, visible from the street, of the connection between judgment and punishment. Richardson's design, Martin Aurand observes, took full advantage of the area's natural and civic topography: the rough stone masonry of the courthouse and jail mimicked the surrounding terrain, and the 325-foot courthouse tower, more than twice as tall as the 148-foot dome of the courthouse that preceded it, "dominated the skyline as an emphatic center point for the entire city and a visible expression of the *axis mundi*."[25] Though not all were as spectacular

Figure 8.6 South view of Allegheny County Courthouse and Jail, photocopy of lithograph (Pittsburgh: photographer unknown, 1890)

Source: Library of Congress, Prints and Photographs Division

as Richardson's achievement, other courthouses throughout the United States sent very much the same message, enshrining the law as both integral to and apart from the rest of communal life.

The courthouses built during the nineteenth century are notable too for their interiors, which were subdivided into spaces with discrete functions: jury rooms; law libraries; judges' chambers; rooms housing deeds and probate records; and, of course, courtrooms, often more than one dedicated to different purposes. Courtrooms themselves, while varied in design, were further subdivided so as to differentiate spectator from practitioner, accused from accuser, juror from judge. The division between the bar and gallery, the elevation of the witness stand and the judge's bench, the positioning of the jury box and lawyers' tables – all combined to create a hierarchized, segmented division of space that distributed individuals according to their assigned roles.

Perhaps above all else, the courtroom became a theatricalized venue, a place where the law was performed and spectatorship of it was organized and given shape. According to the *Philadelphia Inquirer*, before the poisoning trial of Ellen Wharton began in 1871, "Large crowds of anxious and curious persons . . . constantly assembl[ed]" outside of Wharton's home in the hopes of catching a glimpse of the accused, "greatly blocking up the streets, requiring, at times, to be forcibly driven away."[26] As an illustration of the trial shows (Figure 8.7), the courtroom also drew a number of spectators but more effectively managed the potential for disorder. Although comprised of both men and women, the audience in the image is more genteel than the crowds that might have assembled in the street – or, earlier in the century, before the spectacle of the scaffold. In the estimation of a later *Inquirer* report, while "every seat and foot of standing room appropriated to the public had been occupied," the spectators were hardly representative of a general public, consisting of "ladies occupying the first social positions in the land," along

Figure 8.7 "Maryland – Scene in the Court-House at Annapolis – Trial of Mrs. Wharton on the Charge of Murdering General Ketchum by Poison – From a Sketch by Jas. E. Taylor" (*Frank Leslie's Illustrated Newspaper*, December 23, 1871, 236)

with "professional gentlemen representing almost every branch of science, eminent clergymen, doctors, lawyers, chemists and legislators."[27] The courtroom as we know it today may, as Robert Ferguson puts it, "temper authority with the promise of access through strategic doorways and other symbols of democratic identity," but it also both limits access and, through a combination of spatial design and explicit rules, exerts control over those allowed entry.[28]

The elevated prominence of the courthouse and the courtroom is evident, not only in the popularity of published trial reports and the voluminous newspaper coverage of trials such as Ellen Wharton's but also in fiction written during the latter part of the century. Metta Fuller Victor's pathbreaking detective novel *The Dead Letter* (1866) – the first, according to Catherine Ross Nickerson, to appear in the United States – features a lawyer turned sleuth for its narrator, as does Anna Katherine Green's influential *The Leavenworth Case* (1878), a device that anticipates countless later legal thrillers and that indicates the success lawyers had distinguishing themselves as a profession worthy of respect and even admiration.[29] James Fenimore Cooper's last work, *The Ways of the Hour* (1850), predicts many of the now familiar features of the Perry Mason–style courtroom whodunit: a wrongly accused defendant, a heroic defense attorney, witnesses whose stories fall apart under cross-examination, and a series of dramatic courtroom revelations and reversals of judgment, the most dramatic of which being the surprise appearance of a man believed to be dead just moments after the jury finds the defendant guilty of his murder. Although the trial itself occupies less than half its length, the novel as a whole is shot through with the adversarial dialectic of courtroom discourse, earlier chapters consisting largely of a series of lengthy, essayistic dialogues in which one character – usually but not always Thomas Dunscomb, the aforementioned heroic defense attorney – attempts to convince another of the superiority of his or her opinion on a political or social issue of the day. As such, in spite of its frequent and explicit criticisms of the jury system and the codification movement, Cooper's novel evinces a strong attraction to the form of courtroom discourse, which it sets in opposition to the spread of misinformation through gossip and newspapers. Cooper thus imagines the courtroom novel as a structure that, like the new courthouses of the nineteenth century, can contain the messy energies of popular judgment, delivering conviction through a carefully regulated set of forms and conventions.[30]

IV. Lynching and extralegal violence

During the same period in which courthouses were erected as monuments to the law's rationality and Cooper and others helped buttress the courtroom's status as a privileged site for the resolution of social disorder, the spread of lynching exhibited a very different version of justice in the form of bloody, spectacular death meted out on the margins of the law. The origins of "lynch law" are bound up with the origins of the United States itself, the practice supposedly taking its name from either Colonel Charles Lynch or William Lynch, two Virginians reputed to have taken the law into their own hands to punish Tories during the final years of the American Revolution.[31] More precisely, although mob justice is, of course. not unique to the United States, the extralegal collective violence that would come to be known as lynching was, as Michael Pfeifer puts it, "shaped with reference to particular American conditions, most notably the violent libertarian tradition bequeathed by the Revolution and the mobile, fractious settings of the early- to mid-nineteenth-century cotton, mining, and agrarian frontiers."[32] Contrary to popular opinion, lynching in the nineteenth century was not strictly a black/white issue. Nor was it confined to the post–Civil War South. As several recent studies have emphasized, lynchings took place throughout the United States, the targets of its violence including whites, Native Americans, Latinos and Latinas, and Chinese immigrants.[33] Mob violence against African Americans in particular did, of course, increase in frequency and intensity in the years leading up to the Civil War, with lynching reaching the height of its nineteenth-century infamy after the war, when it came to symbolize the failures of Reconstruction and post-Reconstruction.[34]

In many ways, lynching imitated the state-sponsored executions that nineteenth-century reforms removed from public view. As Amy Louise Wood explains, lynchings "appropriated many rituals of public executions – the declarations of guilt, the confessions, the taking of souvenirs and photographs – to confer legitimacy on their extralegal violence."[35] Crucially, much as public executions circulated beyond the scaffold as broadsides, engravings, and woodcuts, print media and the new technology of photographic reproduction preserved the scene of lynching, disseminating its violent imagery throughout the United States. Photographic images often emphasized the size of the crowd, making the spectators into the object of the spectacle. In a photo taken at the 1882 lynching of Frank McManus, for example, although the figure of the hanged body is the focal point of the image, its presence in the background is dwarfed by the spectators in the foreground, many of whom are turned to face the camera, their gaze confronting the viewer's (Figure 8.8).

In a similar way, the extensive coverage of lynchings in newspaper reports served to enlarge the audience of spectators to include readers not present to see the violence firsthand. Under the front-page headline "Another Negro Burned," the *New York Times* described the 1893 lynching of Henry Smith by a white mob in Paris, Texas. Wanted for what the *Times* deemed "the most atrocious murder and outrage in Texas history," Smith was apprehended in Arkansas, and, according

Figure 8.8 "Lynching of McManus" (H.R. Farr, 1882)

Source: Library of Congress, Prints and Photographs Division

to the report, the train returning him to Texas was met by 5,000 people in Texarkana and then by "a surging mass of humanity 10,000 strong" upon its arrival in Paris, where Smith was "placed upon a carnival float, in mockery of a king upon his throne, and, followed by the immense crowd, was escorted through the city so that all might see." The report goes on at considerable length, recreating the spectacle in all of its gruesome, awful detail: it tells of how Smith was "placed upon a scaffold six feet square and ten feet high, securely bound, within the view of all beholders," how he "was tortured for fifty minutes by red-hot irons being thrust against his quivering body," how he in vain "begged for protection" from the law, and how the crowd took pieces of his clothing and coals from the fire as souvenirs. It concludes by widening the scene from the streets of Paris, Texas, to the streets of cities across the United States, claiming that "[w]hen the news was flashed over the wire at every town, anvils boomed forth the announcement."[36]

If, as Benedict Anderson has theorized, newspapers enabled far-flung individuals to imagine themselves as part of the same nation, the imagined community of the late nineteenth-century United States was in part consolidated around the grotesque spectacle of violence inflicted on the bodies of African Americans who were denied inclusion in that community.[37] Newspapers helped to convene this imagined community by publicizing lynchings in advance, as in a report from 1892 of "A Mob Seeking to Lynch a Negro at Montgomery for Assaulting a White Lady" that appeared in the *Durham Daily Globe* (Figure 8.9). This notice, typical of many from the period, panders to racialized fears of black male sexuality, which is indicative of how mass media culture promoted and even incited mass violence against African

THE DURHAM DAILY GLOBE, MONDAY, FEBRUARY 15.

THE NAVAL BATTALION FLAG.

Arrived Yesterday—It Is the Handsomest in the State.

The Charlotte Chronicle says: The handsomest flag in the state, or this entire section for that matter, is the naval battalion flag which arrived here yesterday. It was on exhibition at the mint, Lieutenant Commander Cramer's home, and there a Chronicle reporter had the pleasure—for such it was—of looking at it. The dimensions are 5x6 feet. The material is heavy navy blue silk, in one piece, bordered with yellow silk knotted fringe, it costing $5 extra to have the fringe knotted so as to prevent raveling. In the center of the flag is the state coat of arms, hand painted, surrounded by a pretty circular design. Over the coat of arms is a red scroll with the words "First Battalion," in gilt lettering. Underneath is a corresponding scroll with the words "Naval Artillery." To the left of the coat of arms the initials "N. C." and to the right, "S. G." In the corners are the crest of the batallion—crossed cannon and anchor. The flag pole is surmounted with a gold eagle, underneath which is tied a heavy yellow silk cord and tassels.

The flag cost $80, and was made by the M. C. Lilly company, of Columbus, Ohio. It is the most costly and handsomest flag the battalion could procure, and its choice is in thorough keeping with the elegant taste of the personnel of the battalion. Color bearer Harvey Bryan may "furl that banner" with proud consciousness that in beauty and elegance it is unsurpassed by that of any regiment in the South.

Charlotte's naval battalion has excited considerable interest throughout the state, and emulous Wilmington has decided to "go and do likewise," and is now agitating the formation of a similar

AFTER HIM.

A Mob Seeking to Lynch a Negro at Montgomery for Assaulting a White Lady.

MONTGOMERY, Ala., Feb. 13.—The negro Wm. Webb, captured last night for rape of Mrs. Crump here about a week ago, was identified by her this morning. Her husband identified the pistol in the negro's possession as one the latter grabbed out of a trunk and used to make Mrs. Crump comply with his wishes. Crump said the pistol lock had rubber in it in place of a spring, and opening the lock the rubber was found. The negro had tried to conceal the pistol. When Mrs. Crump identified him the officers instead of bringing him back to jail, went off into the country with him to Waynesville, out of harm's way.

Large crowds of people are in the streets about the jail now, awaiting the return of Webb; but growing weary, have concluded possibly that the officers have secreted him in police headquarters, and have gone there to search. It is also rumored that another crowd are trying to go down the railroad to Mobile in hope of intercepting the officers with the prisoner.

The negro is just out of the penitentiary, where he had served ten years for a similar offence. The officers will have great trouble to prevent a lynching.

We Are With You.

[Franklin Times.]

THE DURHAM GLOBE is making strong and earnest efforts to raise a creditable sum, by subscription, to defray the expense of an exhibit of the state's resources at the World's fair, which is to be held in the city of Chicago. THE GLOBE heads the list with $250, and urges all patriotic people in the state to join in. While the bank account of the Times will not bear a very large subscription, we desire to

The North Carolina and

CAPITAL STOCK,

Par value $100 per share, fully pai

OFFICE

B. L. DUKE, President. Durham

LEO D. HEARTT, Treasurer. Durham

Chartered under the Laws of the

Having purchased outright 178 of the
Newport News, for a short time only the
number of its shares of stock on the following
cash, $5.00 in one month, $5.00 in two months.
per share every two months until $60.00 shall ha

Investment Safe, Attractive

For Prospectus and particulars apply to

J. S

Office up stairs, Mangum building.

"Seeing is Belie

must be simple; when it is
not good.
words mean much, but to see
will impress the truth more
tough and seamless, and made
it is *absolutely safe* and
of old, it is indeed a

Figure 8.9 "After Him: A Mob Seeking to Lynch a Negro at Montgomery for Assaulting a White Lady" (*Durham Daily Globe*, February 15, 1892)

Source: University of North Carolina at Chapel Hill, Library

Americans. Situated alongside a number of advertisements – including an ad for a lamp, which promises that "Seeing Is Believing" – the report invites its readers in North Carolina to bear mediated witness to an act of retributive violence elsewhere in the South, to join in sympathy with the "[l]arge crowds of people . . . in the streets" eagerly awaiting a lynching it suggests is inevitable and just.

At the same time, the technologies of mass mediation provided a forum in which to decry the horrors of lynching. Shocked by the murder of three African American businessmen in Memphis, Ida B. Wells began her antilynching campaign in 1892 in the pages of *Free Speech*, attacking not just the lynching itself but also the misrepresentation of its violence and the motives behind it by other local media, a powerful call for justice that was then echoed and amplified in newspapers elsewhere such as the *Chicago Conservator*.[38] Photographs of lynchings, often mass-produced and disseminated as postcards, became another site of struggle. Originally intended to "substantiate the very ideals of white supremacy and white solidarity that the lynching itself effected,"[39] lynching photographs were recirculated by the NAACP in the early decades of the twentieth century in order to undermine those very same ideals.

As such, lynching is emblematic of the radical instability of the visual grammar of violent spectacle that it deployed for purposes of racial terror. Like the spectacles of the law it imitated, the spectacle of extralegal violence was received not by a unified public gaze but rather by a multiplicity of perspectives capable of generating a range of interpretations. To be sure, spectacles of crime and punishment throughout the nineteenth century could and did serve the interests of those in power. And yet such spectacles also allowed for new ways of seeing the law, providing spectators with visible evidence they could use to make the case for social and political change.

Notes

1 Adam Smith, *The Theory of Moral Sentiments* (Indianapolis: Liberty Fund, 1984), 84–5.
2 Robert A. Ferguson, *The Trial in American Life* (Chicago: University of Chicago Press, 2007), 1.
3 Louis P. Masur, *Rites of Execution: Capital Punishment and the Transformation of American Culture, 1776–1865* (New York: Oxford University Press, 1989), 29. For other accounts of public executions, including detailed analyses of the execution sermon genre, see Scott D. Seay, *Hanging between Heaven and Earth: Capital Crime, Execution Preaching, and Theology in Early New England* (DeKalb: Northern Illinois University Press, 2009); Karen Halttunen, *Murder Most Foul: The Killer and the American Gothic Imagination* (Cambridge, Mass.: Harvard University Press, 1998), 7–32; Daniel A. Cohen, *Pillars of Salt, Monuments of Grace* (New York: Oxford University Press, 1993), 83–114; Daniel E. Williams, "Introduction," to *Pillars of Salt: An Anthology of Early American Criminal Narratives*, ed. Daniel E. Williams (Madison: Madison House, 1993), 1–63; and Caleb Smith, *The Oracle and the Curse: A Poetics of Justice from the Revolution to the Civil War* (Cambridge, Mass.: Harvard University Press, 2013), 67–77.
4 For an account of the trial, along with an appendix that discusses Tulley's execution and Dalton's reprieve, see *The Trial of Samuel Tulley & John Dalton, on an Indictment for Piracy and Murder* (Boston: Belcher, 1812).
5 *Life, Last Words, and Dying Confession of Rachel Wall* [1789], in Daniel E. Williams, *Pillars of Salt: An Anthology of Early American Criminal Narratives* (Madison: Madison House, 1993), 284, 285–6. Wall, apprehended on the streets of Boston after she allegedly tried to steal another woman's bonnet, holds the distinction of being both the first woman in Massachusetts executed for highway robbery and the last woman executed in that state for any offense. See Alan Rogers, *Murder and the Death Penalty in Massachusetts* (Amherst: University of Massachusetts Press), 50–2.
6 Quoted in Seay, *Hanging*, 35.
7 For a fuller discussion of the arguments made for and against the death penalty during the nineteenth century, see Masur, *Rites of Execution*; and Paul C. Jones, *Against the Gallows: Antebellum American Writers and the Movement to Abolish Capital Punishment* (Iowa City: University of Iowa Press, 2011).
8 Benjamin Rush, "An Enquiry into the Effects of Public Punishments upon Criminals, and upon Society," in *Essays, Political, Moral, and Philosophical*, Benjamin Rush, ed., 2nd ed. (Philadelphia: Thomas and William Bradford, 1806), 145.
9 For analyses of how these and other literary writers engaged the death penalty debate, see Jones, *Against the Gallows*; and John C. Barton, *Literary Executions: Capital Punishment and American Culture, 1820–1925* (Baltimore: Johns Hopkins University Press, 2014).
10 Michael Meranze, *Laboratories of Virtue: Punishment, Revolution, and Authority in Philadelphia, 1760–1835* (Chapel Hill: University of North Carolina Press, 1996).
11 Masur, *Rites of Execution*, 6.
12 Halttunen, *Murder*, 73.
13 For a thorough history of this transformative period in U.S. print culture, see Robert A. Gross and Mary Kelley, eds., *An Extensive Republic: Print, Culture, and Society in the New Nation, 1790–1840*, vol. 2, *A History of the Book in America* (Chapel Hill: University of North Carolina Press, 2010).
14 Cohen, *Pillars*, 34.
15 Ann Fabian, *The Unvarnished Truth: Personal Narratives in Nineteenth-Century America* (Berkeley: University of California Press, 2000), 58. In a fascinating recent study, Caleb Smith classifies many such texts under the rubric of the "curse," a category of discourse that answered and opposed the oracular statements of the law. See Smith, *Oracle*, especially 77–86. For more on how criminal authors of the late eighteenth

and early nineteenth centuries pushed back against dominant values and elicited readers' sympathies, see Cohen, *Pillars*, 117–63.

16 Stephen Burroughs, *Memoirs of Stephen Burroughs* (Boston: Northeastern University Press, 1988), 128, 150.

17 Halttunen, *Murder*, 60–90.

18 Patricia Cline Cohen, *The Murder of Helen Jewett: The Life and Death of a Prostitute in Nineteenth-Century New York* (New York: Vintage, 1998), 20–37.

19 Amy G. Srebnick, *The Mysterious Death of Mary Rogers: Sex and Culture in Nineteenth-Century New York* (New York: Oxford University Press, 1995). Sexual violence as a metaphor for urban corruption was also a defining feature of the city mystery genre popularized by works such as George Lippard's *The Quaker City; or, The Monks of Monk Hall* (Philadelphia: Leary, Stuart & Company, 1845) and George Foster's *New York by Gas-Light* (New York: Dewitt & Davenport, 1850).

20 Mark Seltzer, *True Crime: Observations on Violence and Modernity* (New York: Routledge, 2007), 61–74. Dating at least back to Charles B. Brown's *Wieland; or, The Transformation* (New York: H. Caritat, 1798) – based in part on the story of William Beadle, who killed his wife and four children before taking his own life – U.S. fiction-writers have mined "true" accounts of crime for material. Other notable examples include William G. Simms's *Beauchampe, or The Kentucky Tragedy: A Tale of Passion* (Philadelphia: n.p., 1842); and George Thompson's *Life and Exploits of the Noted Criminal, Bristol Bill* (New York: M. J. Ivers & Co., 1851).

21 For a classic treatment of the relationship between legal evidence and storytelling, see Alexander Welsh, *Strong Representations: Narrative and Circumstantial Evidence in England* (Baltimore: Johns Hopkins University Press, 1995).

22 The definitive history of the Avery trial remains David R. Kasserman, *Fall River Outrage: Life, Murder, and Justice in Early Industrial New England* (Philadelphia: University of Pennsylvania Press, 1986). See also Ian C. Pilarczyk, "The Terrible Haystack Murder: The Moral Paradox of Hypocrisy, Prudery, and Piety in Antebellum America," *American Journal of Legal History* 41 (1997): 25–60; and Kristin Boudreau, *The Spectacle of Death: Populist Literary Responses to American Capital Cases* (Amherst, N.Y.: Prometheus, 2006), 37–65.

23 Of all of the contemporaneous accounts of this case, Williams's fascinating text has drawn the most attention from recent scholars. See, for example, Patricia Caldwell, "In 'Happy America': Discovering Catharine Williams's *Fall River* for the Women Writers Project," *South Central Review* 11 (1994): 79–98, and Jeanne E. DeWaard, "'Indelicate Exposure': Sentiment and Law in *Fall River: An Authentic Narrative*," *American Literature* 74 (2002): 373–401.

24 Martha J. McNamara, *From Tavern to Courthouse: Architecture & Ritual in American Law, 1658–1860* (Baltimore: Johns Hopkins University Press, 2004).

25 Martin Aurand, *The Spectator and the Topographical City* (Pittsburgh: University of Pittsburgh Press, 2006), 34–5.

26 "Maryland: The Poisoning Case – Latest Facts," *Philadelphia Inquirer*, July 15, 1871, 1.

27 "The Wharton Trial," *Philadelphia Inquirer*, January 18, 1872.

28 Ferguson, *Trial*, 69–70.

29 For discussion of the importance of Victor and Green, along with other late nineteenth-century American women writers, to the development of the detective novel, see Catherine R. Nickerson, *The Web of Iniquity: Early Detective Fiction by American Women* (Durham, N.C.: Duke University Press, 1999). For analysis of the historical codevelopment of detective fiction and case method, see Simon Stern, "Detecting Doctrines: The Case Method and the Detective Story," *Yale Journal of Law & the Humanities* 23 (2011): 339–87.

30 In spite of the significant generic precedent it sets, *The Ways of the Hour* has received scant attention from critics. Robert Ferguson reads the novel as signaling the end of an earlier partnership between law and letters, with Dunscomb standing as a "last figuration for the predicament of the lawyer as republican spokesman in American culture." Robert A. Ferguson, *Law and Letters in American Culture* (Cambridge, Mass.: Harvard University Press, 1984), 303. Other sources that consider the novel and its legal contexts include Charles Hansford Adams, *"The Guardian of the Law": Authority and Identity in James Fenimore Cooper* (University Park: Pennsylvania State University Press, 1990), 135–48; and Barbara Bardes and Suzanne Gossett, "Cooper and the 'Cup and Saucer' Law: A New Reading of *The Ways of the Hour*," *American Quarterly* 32 (1980): 499–518.

31 For the facts and mythology surrounding these two supposed originators of lynch law, see Christopher Waldrep, *The Many Faces of Judge Lynch: Extralegal Violence and Punishment in America* (New York: Palgrave Macmillan, 2004), 15–21.

32 Michael J. Pfeifer, *The Roots of Rough Justice: Origins of American Lynching* (Urbana: University of Illinois Press, 2011), 4.
33 On lynching in the Midwest and West, see the essays collected in Michael J. Pfeifer (ed.)'s *Lynching beyond Dixie: American Mob Violence outside the South* (Urbana: University of Illinois Press, 2013), and Ken Gonzales-Day, *Lynching in the West, 1850–1935* (Durham, N.C.: Duke University Press, 2006).
34 On mob violence against African Americans and abolitionists during the antebellum period, see David Grimsted, *American Mobbing, 1828–1861: Toward Civil War* (New York: Oxford University Press, 1998).
35 Amy L. Wood, *Lynching and Spectacle: Witnessing Racial Violence in America, 1890–1940* (Chapel Hill: University of North Carolina Press, 2009), 24. See also Jacqueline Goldsby, *A Spectacular Secret: Lynching in American Life and Literature* (Chicago: University of Chicago Press, 2006). Instead of seeing lynching as a residual practice at odds with modernity, Goldsby contends that lynching made visible the contradictions central to modern life, while at the same time disavowing this connection (which she characterizes as lynching's "secret").
36 "Another Negro Burned: Henry Smith Dies at the Stake," *New York Times*, February 2, 1893, 1.
37 Benedict Anderson, *Imagined Communities: Reflections on the Origin and Spread of Nationalism*, rev. ed. (New York: Verso, 2006).
38 Paula Giddings, *Ida: A Sword among Lions* (New York: Amistad, 2008), 188–210.
39 Wood, *Lynching and Spectacle*, 85.

9

LEGAL LANGUAGE

Expansion, consolidation, resistance

*Robert L. Tsai**

Legal language in America, a species of the political discourse of popular sovereignty, underwent significant changes during the nineteenth century. Overall, the rhetorical development of the law was characterized by several overlapping patterns: popularization and fragmentation on the one hand, and increasing specialization and sophistication on the other, as elites sought to tame the revolutionary features of America's early democratic culture. The colonists, a fairly homogeneous and literate population, inherited a revolutionary tradition with British and continental antecedents. That rhetorical tradition emphasized limits on bureaucratic authority, fair process, a distinction between higher law and ordinary law, and the people as sovereign. Beyond certain cultural proclivities, several other factors contributed to the rapid spread of legal language in the United States and made it difficult for elites to dictate the law's development.

One indispensable force involved technological innovation, which spurred the dissemination of law, rendering it less hierarchical, more accessible, and often eclectic in substance. The rise of print capitalism ushered in the age of nationalism, as populations recreated themselves into "imagined communities" bound by a common literary heritage.[1] For Americans, that was a nation constituted by written law and the popular language of political liberty.[2] A cultural emphasis on writing improved the durability of legal language, linked disparate communities, and made it possible to make elaborate plans for family and nation.[3]

Technological improvements from the typewriter to the rotary printing press facilitated the emergence of the book trade in America, the spread of private and institutional law book collections, and the establishment of legal training as a science.[4] At the same time, technological change also hastened the emergence of partisan newspapers and editorial writing, the spread of pamphlets, and periodicals catering to ethnic and partisan interests. Dissent, too, would have its literary voice. With these technological advancements, legal language thus developed along dual tracks: an official version recorded in bound volumes, cited in court documents, and spoken by trained specialists in formal settings, and a popular dialect bursting through the rough-and-tumble debate of popular media and sustained in the literature and everyday interactions of ordinary people. As a result, the evolution of legal language overall trended toward democratization and diversification – regardless of the actual justifications and dominant ideology associated with any particular issue.

Beyond dramatic changes in the technologies of language, two major sociolegal dynamics of political development drove linguistic innovation during the nineteenth century: expansion and consolidation. For a significant period of time, an unruly vernacular in property rights, self-governance, and individual liberty fostered the destabilization of borders and the breaking of treaties, the rapid acquisition of land, and the forging of newfound civic identities. At the same time, official renderings of law facilitated a rush for political integration, institution building, and the displacement of older folkways with a common national heritage and set of Anglo-American laws. This more sophisticated view took most visible hold in property, torts, and contract law, helping industrialists and corporations take increasing risks in the economy by altering social expectations of responsibility and blame.[5]

The push and pull of these objectives produced a profound sense of anxiety in the American polity, and those conflicted feelings and shifting values were often worked out in courtroom discourse and through popular literature. As Tocqueville observed, the rise of the legal profession in America served as a bulwark "against the excesses of democracy."[6] The "love of order and of formalities" instilled in lawyers "naturally render them very hostile to the revolutionary spirit."[7] A scientific logic and rhetorical preference for efficient, detached analysis conducted by experts typified legal conversation.[8] Yet a space for oral argumentation was preserved in the trial court, often before a jury of one's peers, allowing for an emotional appeal to communal experiences.[9] This performative relationship between lawyer and jury intensified through reforms restricting a judge's ability to comment on testimony and oral advocacy.[10]

Arguments over the meaning and application of higher law became prevalent within the legal system, but, through contest and resolution, the language of liberty and equality also became routinized and domesticated. Revolutionary arguments and methods were consistently frustrated through legal rules and discredited in the courtrooms; the most radical constitutional theories were rejected as so much rubbish. As opportunities within legal proceedings for wide-open discourse diminished, the major sources for the innovation of legal language had to be discovered and nurtured elsewhere: in secondary legal writings and treatises, political writings and orations, newspapers, and novels.

Nationally, legal efforts to manage the growth of the American nation produced both linguistic fragmentation and consolidation. The discourse of settler sovereignty, seen as a natural outgrowth of colonial self-rule, was the first to have its way in the nineteenth century. In the age of nation building, the pioneer served as a romantic ideal of citizenship: hardy, curious, self-sufficient, and virtuous. Whether it was in the mastery of nature, as some depicted it, or in the battlefield conquest of indigenous peoples, as others saw it, there can be little doubt that settler-made law became an engine of America's fledgling democracy.[11]

Walt Whitman's poetry paid tribute to this ideal citizen and mythologized the migratory experience. In "Pioneers! O Pioneers," he casts Americans as a "restless race" and describes people living on the frontier in energetic, masculine terms: "impatient, full of action, full of manly pride and friendship."[12] They are "[c]onquering, holding, daring, venturing as we go the unknown ways." In the process of felling "primeval forests," settlers build a civilization for the "followers" who "in embryo wait behind." To be first is to face untold danger but also to be heroic, for "all the rest on us depend." Whitman portrays a society united in the frenetic task of political development: "all the workmen at their work / All the seamen and the landsmen, all the masters with their slaves."

But America's budding legal rhetoric could also be used to subvert the social order. Determinist movements employed legalistic language associated with the pioneer ideal to challenge basic social tenets and to reorganize existing communities. From the breakaway Republic of Indian Stream and Dorr's Rebellion in the Northeast to the secession of the Republic of Texas from Mexico in the Southwest, citizens forged legal rights by controlling land and asserting a natural right to rule.[13] The 1836 Texas Declaration of Independence illustrated this trend.[14] Its signatories claimed that Mexico encouraged migration and created expectations of political liberty, promises upon which settlers had relied:

> The Mexican government, by its colonization laws, invited and induced the Anglo-American population of Texas to colonize its wilderness under the pledged faith of a written constitution, that they should continue to enjoy that constitutional liberty and republican government to which they had been habituated in the land of their birth, the United States of America.

Moreover, Mexican officials could not be counted on to protect settlers' rights, for they had "acquiesced in the destruction of their liberty" and the instigation of martial rule. Mexico could hardly complain now that Americans had "taken up arms in defence of the national constitution" and severed their "political connection with the Mexican nation."

Yet the vernacular of liberty, property, and destiny used by settlers and prodevelopment policy makers had a double-edged quality. In an age of territorial expansion, pioneer sovereignty proved to be a potent language of power, uniting a youthful citizenry around dreams of discovery, systematic rationality, and the irrepressible right to rule. Nevertheless, the rhetoric of pioneer sovereignty could not be allowed to go unchecked, for its very logic disrupted legal boundaries and made it difficult to institutionalize a society's hard-won gains. As unorganized and indigenously populated lands became territories, and as territories turned into states, a more systematic rule of law displaced the more unruly discourse of popular sovereignty, driving more adventurous ideas ever into alternative texts and underground communities.

Religious revivals and political reform movements, including a number of utopian projects, spread the language of liberty and popular consent as groups migrated west. Such dissenting communities depended on the language of liberty in creating their own legal texts and belief systems. For example, the Icarian immigrants from France created law-like institutions, even as they organized themselves according to socialist principles. Some alternative communities played with more democratic procedures; others tried more autocratic ones. In doing so, these groups instrumentally used American legal language in the service of their own narrow goals, but their actions also often revealed, at a profound level, a kinship with America's democratic culture.[15] Religious groups and reform movements played a significant role in keeping the higher-law tradition alive, preserving space for a robust vernacular for criticism and legal change. In this manner, legal language became broader, thinner, and more available to a wide array of persons, and compatible with a shocking range of ideologies and policy objectives. Law, as a "vulgar tongue," gained the power to resist existing hierarchies and impart new forms of social order.[16] At times, states blessed these radical projects; at other times, these religious experiments were merely facilitated by available constitutional idioms and the law of contract. Social groups not only challenged existing property rights regimes by recycling existing legal modalities but also tried different rules to promote the equality of women and racial minorities, as well as expressive and religious freedoms. When these experiments ended, state law often intervened to liquidate communal holdings and reintegrate their members into American society.

Perhaps the most dramatic shifts in legal discourse took place around slavery. Opponents of slavery appropriated the language of liberty against traditionalists, racial nationalists, and even the very authors of America's legal texts. Through forceful counteruse and agitation, they enlarged a young nation's vocabulary of power. Sermons, books, and newspaper editorials forcefully stated the case for abolition, argued that slavery entailed illegal kidnapping and battery, and defended resistance to slavery as an exercise of the natural right of self-defense.[17] Americans fought over conceptions of equality and liberty, veering between communal understandings of these fundamental ideas and more individualistic formulations.

Uncle Tom's Cabin, published in 1852, was a runaway best seller, described by reviewers as "a necessity of the age . . . [that] had to be written," with readers expressing "doubt if abler arguments have ever been presented, in favor of the 'Higher Law' theory, than may be found here."[18] At one point in the tale, Tom watches as a slave trader hands over a slave woman's sleeping boy to a buyer without her knowledge or consent. The casual nature of the transaction, juxtaposed with the mother's horrified reaction upon learning of the sale and departure of her son, leads Tom to describe a mix of feelings about the law:

> Tom had watched the whole transaction from first to last, and had a perfect understanding of its results. To him, it looked like something unutterably horrible and cruel, because, poor, ignorant black soul! He had not learned to generalize, and to take enlarged views. If he had only been instructed by certain ministers of Christianity, he might have thought better of it, and seen in it an every-day incident of a lawful trade; a trade which is the vital support of an institution which an American divine tells us has "no evils but such as are inseparable from any other relations in social and domestic life." But Tom, as we see, being a poor, ignorant fellow, whose reading had been confined entirely to the New Testament, could not comfort and solace himself with views like these. His very soul bled within him for what seemed to him the wrongs of the poor suffering thing that lay like a crushed reed on the boxes; the feeling, living, bleeding, yet immortal thing, which American state law coolly classes with the bundles, and bales, and boxes, among which she is lying.

In this passage, Tom openly struggles with competing visuals and legal principles, weeping over what he has witnessed. Tom's Bible-based learning matches his feelings of disgust and sympathy, along with his powerful sense of injustice arising from the lived experience of slavery. Stowe contrasts the potency of higher law joined by human experience from ordinary "state law," which (though reflecting community judgment) denied the reality of human suffering by classifying slaves with other nonsentient commodities that are bought and sold. The next day, the trader learns that the mother had drowned herself in sorrow while others slept. His response is merely to shrug and write off his business loss as a "little incident[ ] of lawful trade."

The sensational 1829 pamphlet known as *Walker's Appeal* turned America's language of political liberty against the slave trade.[19] David Walker, a former slave, directed his words primarily to the colored people of the United States, urging them to "assert their rights as men" by revolting against their slave masters. Toward the end of his pamphlet, Walker recited the Declaration of Independence, using its ringing words to raise a charge of hypocrisy on the part of republicans nevertheless devoted to a brutal and unequal practice and to show that legal slavery's manifold cruelties gave rise to a "right . . . [and] duty, to throw off such government."

In a similar vein, the radical abolitionist John Brown wrote an editorial justifying his armed rescue of slaves as an enforcement of individual "liberty"; he later authored a Declaration of Liberty on behalf of the enslaved people of America.[20] In that declaration, likely written in 1859, Brown called for defenders of the "Slave Code," whose "laws are no laws," to be dethroned and for "universal freedom" and the "natural equality of rights" to be restored. To Brown, elites had warped the meaning of the Constitution for selfish and dehumanizing ends. In order to both publicize an alternative rhetoric of liberty and imbue it with the force of popular sovereignty, Brown held a convention of "friends of freedom," namely, abolitionists and former slaves. In Chatham, Canada, Brown and his followers elaborated upon the principles announced in the Declaration by approving a Provisional Constitution. The rotting remnants of the 1787 Constitution now had a direct competitor in a text sanctified by freedmen and their allies.

Slaveholders, too, claimed America's legal language as their own, employing it to entrench their economic interests and value system. On the other side of the contentious question, pamphlets and newspapers played a prominent role in rationalizing slavery in terms of man's social nature, property rights, and the prerogative of white citizens as sovereigns.[21] Though stressing the equality of citizens, the rhetoric of civic republicanism presumed that not all individuals were fit for self-rule. Moreover, slavery preserved federalism, or the structure of constitutional governance, and its proponents used the rhetoric of equality to advance the political equality of states rather than what they called the "equality of the enslaved." Slaveholders contended that the people of each state enjoyed the basic rights of nullification and disunion when they became despondent about their political future.[22] By contrast, the North's war justifications, issued in presidential speeches, proclamations and other public documents, offered a theory of constitutional self-government that rejected the right of states to leave the "perpetual" Union and called secession an act of rebellion.[23]

An increase in the use of proclamations and public orations offered American presidents fresh means by which to present a striking vision of the law and themselves as guarantors of liberty.[24] In this reprisal of older models of charismatic leadership, a president is called from among the people and claims to be uniquely capable of protecting the rights of the community. In fulfilling this literary-historical role, the oral and the written interacted in dynamic fashion: speeches were given with an eye toward memorialization; the most important legal texts might also be announced live for dramatic effect. Presidential discourse therefore straddled the official and the popular, at times reinforcing the law as given by judges and at other times capitalizing on broader idioms to resist juridic formulations of the law in the name of the people.

Perhaps the most famous presidential writing of all – the Emancipation Proclamation – had its formal function as a legal document justifying the liberation of slaves in the seceding states overtaken by its function as a vehicle popularizing the language of resistance to slavery.[25] After President Abraham Lincoln affixed his signature, the five-page document was sent by telegraph to concerned parties and published widely in newspapers. The U.S. Supreme Court's *Dred Scott v. Sanford* decision in 1857 had read the Constitution's protection of slavery in absolutist terms, excluding slaves and former slaves from the America political community as "beings from an inferior order" forever incapable of the duties of citizenship. Chief Justice Roger Taney's ruling privileged the individual slaveholder's right of property in the slave, reading the Due Process Clause of the Fifth Amendment in such a way as to short-circuit local and state movements toward emancipation and citizenship and to disrupt congressional efforts to manage the slavery dispute.[26]

Lincoln's January 1, 1863, wartime proclamation pushed back against this juridic formulation of political equality as an idea reserved for white men alone. That winter in Gettysburg, Lincoln rewrote the nation's founding so as to emphasize the birth of "a new nation . . . dedicated to the proposition that all men are created equal."[27] Lincoln freed the slaves as a "fit and necessary war measure" but also called it an "act of justice, warranted by the Constitution." Some abolitionists were not satisfied by the technical and limited scope of the statement, but others hailed it as a strong moral signal from the presidency – one that would ultimately make the Emancipation Proclamation and Gettysburg Address more famous than the Thirteenth Amendment later abolishing slavery.[28]

In one sense, defenders of the Union utilized the popular language of justice, liberty, and equality to demoralize the South and win the war. In another sense, Lincoln deployed war-dependent arguments about freedom to rhetorically create a new political community during a time of great upheaval: a polity based no longer on condition of servitude (past or present) but rather on mutual sacrifice and acceptance of ideas of equality and freedom. Legal language was thus deployed by the administration to knit together soldiers, abolitionists, slaveholders in states that had not seceded, escaped slaves, and anyone willing to resist the Confederate theory of law and politics. Though Lincoln would not live long enough to see the realization of this legal vision, his speeches and writings helped Americans imagine a future in which the rule of law once again constituted a pluralistic citizenry concerned with happiness and good order.

Though sanitized of the strongest forms of racial sovereignty, Lincoln's powerful vision of American law recapitulated the view that a strong, undivided nation-state was the best vehicle for political community. Valuing unity of purpose and belief above all, his prose failed to acknowledge that differences, too, could be an enormous source of strength and respect for law. Additionally, Lincoln's short-term reliance on war to move citizens to embrace racial equality, while instrumentally brilliant, left equality arguments vulnerable in the long run to counterarguments that the problems of racial discrimination were historically contingent ones that had mostly been solved at war's end.

The Confederate theory of law, in particular, had to rely on alternative media as the political fortunes of slaveholders changed for the worse.[29] On this front, popular legal language fostered a regional lifestyle based on the plantation and later helped forge a national identity based on shared economic and cultural ties. Having abandoned the institutions associated with the Union, secessionists tried to recreate their own legal culture, by transforming what had previously been a dissident belief system into a governing framework and new laws. The founders of the Confederacy sought popular authorization for their linguistic enterprise by following the precedent established by the framers of the 1787 U.S. Constitution: calling for conventions in the slaveholding states where grievances could be aired, publishing statements justifying Southern independence, and then drafting and ratifying a constitution to govern a slave-owning republic.[30] Pro-slavery newspapers and pamphlets waged an ideological battle against abolitionist writings, giving as good as they got and encouraging other states to flee what they believed to be a despotic legal order.[31]

After the Civil War, the Reconstruction Amendments codified an antislavery legacy, one that imposed new obligations on states while strengthening and clarifying the terms of national citizenship.[32] As written, the Amendments promised the franchise, due process, and equal protection of the laws to every member of the polis. Still, it did not take long for linguistic conflict over the meaning of equality to resume. In the *Slaughterhouse Cases*,[33] the Supreme Court read these provisions narrowly to forbid Congress from enacting a civil rights public accommodation law. This highly technical interpretation of the Fourteenth Amendment's Privileges and Immunities Clause was met with public outrage and warred with a broader understanding of the nation's commitment to ensuring racial equality. It also represented an effort by elites – judges in particular – to assert control of linguistic development over the rights of citizenship (and deny Congress that power except as to a narrow range of rights).

As Reconstruction ended, other tropes reemerged to frustrate broad application of the Constitution's promise of equality. The ordinary language of "civil" and "political" life – nowhere mentioned in the Bill of Rights but an active element of republican ideology – became a potent way of limiting the Constitution's reach as legal strategies of exclusion became increasingly discredited. Thus, through the ordinary operation of the justice system, the juridic grammar of equality became routinized and particularized. Phenomena defined as involving only the "social" sphere, even though governmental regulation might be involved, could thus be defined beyond the scope of the Fourteenth Amendment. Such terms, coupled with formulations extolling the traditional "police power" of each state to ensure public order and regulate the moral welfare of the people, thus became the legal discourse for creating new racial hierarchies. Local ways of life reasserted and retrenched themselves, despite the imperatives of national citizenship.

It is in this light that the *Plessy v. Ferguson* decision upholding racially segregated railroad cars is best understood.[34] The U.S. Supreme Court's majority opinion stressed the ineradicable quality of social differences – differences that by themselves gave rise to no right of action: "A statute which implies merely a legal distinction between the white and colored races – a distinction which is founded in the color of the two races and which must always exist so long as white men are distinguished from the other race by color – has no tendency to destroy the legal equality of the two races."[35] Draining race-based laws of the presumption of ill motive or effect, Justice Henry Billings Brown wrote that

> [l]aws permitting, and even requiring, [racial] separation in places where they are liable to be brought into contact do not necessarily imply the inferiority of either race to the other, and have been generally, if not universally, recognized as within the competency of the state legislatures in the exercise of their police power.[36]

Using the "social" as a category that delimited legal remedies, the Court ironically then turned a blind eye to the sociological reality of a community stratified by race-based regulations and norms. The "social" became an anticategory, a widening lawless zone (at least by higher law standards).

Plessy was not merely a product of a rhetorical clash involving individual rights on the one hand and state prerogatives on the other. Through its manipulation of social and legal categories, the decision also licensed an atomistic and antagonistic set of rhetorical practices that both justified and obscured practices that systematically dehumanized racial minorities.

Life within the system of legal slavery and racial segregation was highly fraught, filled with contradictions and having many unintended consequences. Justice John M. Harlan's famous *Plessy* dissent pointed out that, under Louisiana's racial code, Chinese passengers who in many formal respects enjoyed a lesser legal status were treated better than blacks. But a more wide-ranging critique of the law could be found in literature. Mark Twain's *The Tragedy of Pudd'nhead Wilson* not only dramatized the absurdities inherent in America's system of racial apartheid but also toyed with the legal spaces for defiance.[37] A major plot line involves a slave girl, Roxy, who is charged with taking care of a slave master's son. To protect her own son from being sold, she decides to switch the two boys, raising her own fair-skinned son as the heir to the plantation and the inattentive slave master's boy as a slave. This shocking subversion of the racialized legal order reveals not only a mother's desperation living under slavery but also the depravity of a legal system that could so callously separate family members. Yet the mother's microresistance to slavery is ultimately unsuccessful, for her son grows up passing for white but also becomes spoiled, cruel, reckless, and violent. This turn of events reveals the apparent superiority of cultural forces over inborn traits, though the legal system theoretically turns on the innate characteristics that differentiate human beings. Worse, the young man ends up robbing and killing his "uncle," a local judge. When two innocent people are tried for murder, fingerprint evidence leads to the discovery of Tom, the real killer, as well as his true identity as Roxy's son. His fate is not only to be convicted of murder but also to be pardoned by the Governor (at the request of his "father's" creditors) and sold down the river to satisfy the slave master's debts – a poignant reminder of the inescapable quality of legal slavery. Meanwhile, the real Tom, raised culturally as a slave, is restored to his place as a free man and the heir to a fortune, but his manners remain "vulgar and uncouth," and he simply "could not endure the terrors of the white man's parlor." When Twain hands down these moral-legal judgments, Roxy finds her own "heart was broken" and "the voice of her laughter ceased in the land."[38]

Beyond recurring issues over race, arguments about security, war making, and the needs of a national economy spurred the growth of a language of power that consolidated ideas of belonging and authority. The rule of law – extended in a series of judicial rulings to every subject matter in which the federal government might be said to have an enumerated or implied interest – enhanced the influence of political actors and judges alike over land, institutions, and identity.[39] After the Civil War, the needs of political development continued to shape the terms of civic membership and how the state dealt with noncitizens and populations perceived to comprise imperfect citizens. On the one hand, a young nation-state's impetus to expand allowed advocates to use the language of equality to push for more inclusive terms of participation. On the other hand, while formal rules for immigration and voting were relaxed for most of the nineteenth century, a host of procedures and informal practices arose by which to regulate the lives of minority communities.[40] Rather than simply exclude or banish all undesirables, the law turned toward strategies of partial integration and management.[41]

As the nineteenth century came hurtling to a close, new disintegrating forces worked against national efforts at linguistic consolidation. The law appeared to many Americans as too confining, overly partisan, and highly susceptible to corruption. Once again, the law seemed to serve the interests of the few over the many, and the rhetoric of liberty and equality would have to be refitted for a new age. The excesses of capitalism and big government continued to generate adaptations of the rhetoric of equality and sovereignty. Those who did not organize their own alternative communities tried to reform economic and social policies. Some tax resistors, who could be found among the business class and working class alike, tried to dismantle the system of taxation that had emerged to fund major war efforts and internal improvements of the nineteenth century; others labored to frustrate tax reforms such as progressive taxation. Tax resistors not only recycled revolutionary-era idioms involving taxation without adequate representation, they also claimed that broad tax powers had to be tied to specific exigencies and that certain taxation programs violated individual rights to equality and property.[42] During the Civil War, onerous taxes by the Confederacy in its final, desperate months had helped erode support for the Southern cause. Far from ending such defiance, the conclusion of the war merely merged older forms of tax skepticism with newer concerns about the size of government and how it was financed. As the justifications for expanded governmental power grew, so too did popular legal arguments seeking to check or reverse these developments.

Urbanization, industrialization, and economic dislocation in the waning decades of the nineteenth century produced fiery rhetoric levied against Gilded Age excesses. Populists unleashed the republican language of virtue and equality against electoral fraud, the monopolization of natural resources ("a heritage of the people"), exploitation of labor by management, and unchecked immigration. Outraged farmers and their allies turned property rights rhetoric against rich owners and speculators, insisting that "wealth belongs to him who creates it" rather than to those who amass it. The most strident and conspiratorial Populists complained that corporations had "enslaved" the American people.[43]

Tapping into fears about the demise of the agrarian economy, the ascendance of an impersonal industrial order, and a latent strain of nativism, the platform of the People's Party in 1892 called for the realization of "equal rights and equal privileges," the unionization of workers, and the return of government to "the hands of the 'plain people.' "[44] Believing sovereignty and territorial control to be inextricably linked, leaders of this farmers' revolt demanded that any land held by corporations "in excess of their actual needs" and all lands owned by aliens be reclaimed by the government and given to "actual settlers only." Four years later, at the height of its influence, the Populist Party embarked on efforts to regain "our financial and industrial independence" by wresting power from "European moneychangers" and corrupt politicians.[45] The platform advocated the referendum as a vehicle for direct lawmaking, the direct election of senators, and the establishment of term limits for public officials. Expressing explicit disapproval of recent Supreme Court decisions on taxation, Populists reiterated their support for a graduated income tax.

Popular sentiment also led to the redrawing of the design of the judiciary throughout the country. In a burst of legislative activity during the mid-nineteenth century, citizens demanded that judges be directly accountable to the people to guard against cronyism and subservience to other branches of government – a phenomenon that tugged against the federalist legacy of indirect governance.[46] Populists extended this older critique against a new political aristocracy, seeking to dismantle what William Jennings Bryan called an "office-holding class [that] excludes from participation in the benefits the humbler members of our society."[47]

Bryan's electrifying "Cross of Gold" speech at the Democratic National Convention bore all the hallmarks of a popular assault on elite formulations of law. He cast the problems facing the yeoman farmer as a matter of collective "liberty," for "[t]he individual is but an atom; he is born, he acts, he dies; but principles are eternal; and this has been a contest of principle." Bryan then deployed the rhetoric of equality to lift up the agrarian laborers represented by the populist movement:

> But we stand here representing people who are the equals before the law of the largest cities of Massachusetts. . . . The farmer who goes forth in the morning and toils all day, begins in the spring and toils all summer, and by the application of brain and muscle to the natural resources of this country creates wealth, is as much a businessman as the man who goes upon the Board of Trade and bets upon the price of grain.

He assailed the Supreme Court for striking down tax reform legislation, thundering, "the principles upon which rest Democracy are as everlasting as the hills; but . . . they must be applied to new conditions as they arise." From there, Bryan described the Populist surge as an effort to stand "against the encroachments of accumulated wealth."

While potent regionally, the angry class-driven rhetoric of pitchfork liberty eventually stumbled against the harsh demographic realities of urban existence at the national level. This is not to say that dissatisfaction dissipated with Bryan's loss in the 1896 presidential election, but rather that such appeals had to be broadened before lasting policy changes could be made. To the ears of many citizens, Populist exhortations seemed overly radical, narrow, and insufficiently attentive to modern American life in the cities. Though Bryan disclaimed any desire for ideological "conquest," his strident attack on the gold standard and major features of the national economy sounded positively revolutionary to voters who desired more modest corrections.

Because Populism was primarily an agrarian and sectional experience, sex equality did not figure as a prominent concern; women had to clamor for recognition and autonomy separately. The women's rights movement enjoyed a galvanizing moment in Seneca Falls, where attendees of a convention prepared the *Declaration of Sentiments* in 1848.[48] With Elizabeth Cady Stanton as its primary author, the document cited Blackstone for the proposition that natural law is superior to human law and that the "true and substantial happiness of woman" is the ultimate purpose of government. Then, playing on the words of the 1776 Declaration of Independence, the Seneca Falls document listed a series of "injuries and usurpations on the part of man toward woman." Unlike separatist movements, however, women's rights leaders used the ancient language of liberty and self-determination to promote reform within the existing legal order. They demanded the franchise, equal opportunity in the workplace, and fair treatment in the areas of property rights, marriage, religion, and education. Legal language served several functions for reformers: identifying subjects for reevaluation, marking the importance and urgency of these issues vis-à-vis other matters, and inspiring collective political action. Tactically, the women's rights movement looked to the precedent established by abolitionists. Substantively, however, the connections were more strained. Sex equality arguments were highly fraught, with considerations of sex entangled with those of race and nationality. For many, women's rights emerged seamlessly from more established forms of antislavery rhetoric. But for others, racial equality was little more than a convenient foil, reminding white men that their wives and daughters should not be treated worse than black citizens and recent immigrants.[49]

In this same vein, it may be instructive to consider briefly the nineteenth-century experience of the indigenous population, whose own interactions with Anglo-American law began in serious antagonism and moved into a more complicated phase of linguistic adaptation and political assimilation. Early on, American law treated indigenous populations as foreign nations. Defeat of Indians on the battlefield led to banishment on a massive scale to the outer edges of the polity. Even so, native tribes, forcibly relocated west of the Mississippi in the 1830s, pushed for greater autonomy during the latter part of the nineteenth century.[50] They did so in the face of efforts to organize the land and extend the rule of law over Indian affairs. At first, the federal government directed inhabitants of the region to establish a single government with an eye toward territorial status and eventual statehood. Soon thereafter, Congress enacted a series of laws apportioning Indian lands and requiring individuals to register for a share of real property. These laws attacked tribal sovereignty by destroying its territorial basis and, along with other measures, subsumed much of Indian governance within a federal framework.

In response, tribal leaders not only demanded that treaties with the federal government be honored, they also increasingly resorted to the language of American law in making their appeals.[51] Indian leaders tried to turn the rhetoric of political liberty against elites who they believed wanted nothing more than to steal ancient lands, destroy indigenous culture, and abrogate valid agreements. From the perspective of liberal nationalists, the Civil War had proven the importance of creating a strong national legal order and civic identity, coupled with a commitment to individual rights and liberties. For such theorists, the connection between the citizen and the nation-state had to be profound and as direct as possible, uncomplicated by the claims of competing sovereigns.

To resist this dominant vision of the law, legal writing again served as a tool for the oppressed. The so-called Five Civilized Tribes (Cherokee, Choctaw, Seminole, Creek, and Chickasaw) met in 1870 and drafted the Okmulgee Constitution, in response to a federal directive that "all the nations and tribes in Indian territory be formed into one consolidated government." Drawing on previous native constitutions and laws, as well as the white man's legal instruments (including the Tennessee Constitution), representatives of these Indian nations proposed a republican form of government for Indian Territory. The Okmulgee Constitution envisioned a confederacy ruled by a government with three branches, including a governor, general assembly, and judicial department. A Declaration of Rights secured to each inhabitant of Indian Territory Anglo-American trial rights, as well as familiar expressive rights of assembly, speech, and religion.[52] Although this instrument was never ratified according to its own terms, the document framed future conversations over Indian independence, the synthesis of competing legal systems and cultures, and the scope of minority political rights into the next century.

Much had changed during the nineteenth century. Territory had been acquired, annexed, and mapped. Early forms of American politics had matured into an intricate system of bureaucracies across the land, administered by trained professionals. Through it all, legal language played a major role in shaping debates, inspiring risk taking and lawbreaking, and justifying changes in communal boundaries and civic identities. The most visible development involved the displacement of customary legal discourse by institutions and statutes over time. Nevertheless, legal vernacular retained a vitality in politics and literature, simultaneously nurturing widespread belief in the rule of law while preserving an oppositional democratic culture.

Notes

* Professor of Law, American University, Washington College of Law. Thoughtful advice from Nan Goodman and Simon Stern improved this contribution immensely. My thanks to Laura Klick and Amy Yoon for their fine editorial assistance.

1 Benedict Anderson, *Imagined Communities: Reflections on the Origins and Spread of Nationalism* (London: Verso, 1991); see also Eric Hobsbawm, *Nations and Nationalism since 1780: Programme, Myth, Reality* (Cambridge, UK: Cambridge University Press, 1990).

2 Robert L. Tsai, *America's Forgotten Constitutions: Defiant Visions of Power and Community* (Cambridge, Mass.: Harvard University Press, 2014); Pauline Maier, *Ratification: The People Debate the Constitution, 1787–1788* (New York: Simon & Schuster, 2010); Christian Fritz, *American Sovereigns: The People and America's Constitutional Tradition before the Civil War* (New York: Cambridge University Press, 2009); Larry D. Kramer, *The People Themselves: Popular Constitutionalism and Judicial Review* (New York: Oxford University Press, 2004); Gordon S. Wood, *The Creation of the American Republic, 1776–1789* (Chapel Hill: University of North Carolina Press, 1969); Edward S. Corwin, *The "Higher" Law Background of American Constitutional Law* (Ithaca, N.Y.: Cornell University Press, 1967).

3 Peter M. Tiersma, *Parchment, Paper, Pixels: Law and the Technologies of Communication* (Chicago: University of Chicago Press, 2010), 13–32.

4 Michael H. Hoeflich, *Legal Publishing in Antebellum America* (New York: Cambridge University Press, 2010), 10–29.

5 Nan Goodman, *Shifting the Blame: Literature, Law, and the Theory of Accidents in Nineteenth-Century America* (Princeton, N.J.: Princeton University Press, 1998); Morton J. Horwitz, *The Transformation of American Law: 1780–1860* (Cambridge, Mass.: Harvard University Press, 1977).

6 Alexis de Tocqueville, *Democracy in America*, trans. Henry Reeve (1835; New York: Gryphon, 1992), Book I, chap. 16, 254–5.

7 Ibid. Tocqueville astutely notes that "[a] portion of the tastes and of the habits of the aristocracy may consequently be discovered in the characters of men in the profession of the law." Ibid., 255.

8 Peter M. Tiersma, *Legal Language* (Chicago: University of Chicago Press, 1999), 51–151, 203–10.

9 Laura H. Korobkin, *Criminal Conversations: Sentimentality and Nineteenth-Century Legal Stories* (New York: Columbia University Press, 1998).

10 Renee L. Lerner, "The Transformation of the American Civil Trial: The Silent Judge," *William & Mary Law Review* 42 (2000): 195–264, 233–9.

11 Christopher Tomlins, *Freedom Bound: Law, Labor and Civic Identity in Colonizing English America, 1580–1865* (New York: Cambridge University Press, 2010); Frederick J. Turner, *The Frontier in American History* (New York: Holt, 1921); Tsai, *America's Forgotten Constitutions*, 18–33.

12 Walt Whitman, "Pioneers! O Pioneers," *Leaves of Grass* (Brooklyn: Eakins Press, 1855).

13 Fritz, *American Sovereigns*, 246–76; Tsai, *America's Forgotten Constitutions*, 18–82.

14 *The Unanimous Declaration of Independence Made by the Delegates of the People of Texas*, March 2, 1836.

15 Tsai, *America's Forgotten Constitutions*, 49–82; Diana M. Garno, *Citoyennes and Icaria* (Lanham, Md.: University Press of America, 2005); Carol Weisbrod, *The Boundaries of Utopia* (New York: Pantheon, 1980); Albert Shaw, *Icaria: A Chapter in the History of Communism* (New York: Putnam's, 1884); Emile Péron, *Brief History of Icaria. Constitution, Laws and Regulations of the Icarian Community* (Corning, Iowa: Office of Publication, 1880); Etienne Cabet, *The History of the Colony or Republic of Icaria in the United States of America* (Nauvoo, Ill.: Icarian Print, 1852).

16 In calling law a "vulgar tongue," Tocqueville remarked that the "whole people contracts the habits and the tastes of the magistrate" and that law is fashioned to suit the purposes of the legal profession. Tocqueville, *Democracy in America*, 261. In fact, legal language proved to be far more dynamic than the Frenchman believed, not merely domesticating revolutionaries but also inspiring average citizens to take up radical projects.

17 See, e.g., Lysander Spooner, *A Plan for the Abolition of Slavery and to the Non-Slaveholders of the South* (New York: Lysander Spooner, 1858); Lysander Spooner, *The Unconstitutionality of Slavery* (Boston: Bela Marsh, 1845). During this period, William L. Garrison's newspaper *The Liberator* and *Uncle Tom's Cabin* (London: Cassell, 1852) by Harriett Beecher Stowe became literary influences on the slavery debate.

18 Review, *London Times*, September 1852; Review, *The National Era*, April 15, 1852; Review, *Frederick Douglass' Paper*, April 1, 1852.

19 David Walker, *Walker's Appeal* (Boston: David Walker, 1829).

20 John Brown, "Old Brown's Parallels," *New York Tribune*, January 28, 1859; A Declaration of Liberty by the Representatives of the Slave Population of the United States of America, July 4, 1859; *Provisional*

Constitution and Ordinances for the People of the United States, 1858; Robert L. Tsai, "John Brown's Constitution," *Boston College Law Review* 51 (2010): 151–207. See also Brian McGinty, *John Brown's Trial* (Cambridge, Mass.: Harvard University Press, 2009); F. B. Sanborn, ed., *The Life and Letters of John Brown: Liberator of Kansas and Martyr of Virginia* (Boston: Roberts Bros., 1885).

21 Eric Walther, *The Fire-Eaters* (Baton Rouge: Louisiana State University Press, 1992); William W. Freehling, *The Road to Disunion, vol. 2: Secessionists Triumphant, 1854–1861* (New York: Oxford University Press, 2007); John C. Calhoun, Speech, January 10, 1838, in Eric L. McKitrick, ed., *Slavery Defended: The Views of the Old South* (Englewood Cliffs, N.J.: Prentice-Hall, 1963); George Fitzhugh, *Cannibals All! Or, Slaves without Masters* (Richmond, Va.: Morris, 1857); George Fitzhugh, *Slavery Justified* (Fredericksburg, Va.: Recorder Print Office, 1850).

22 Michael T. Bernath, *Confederate Minds: The Struggle for Intellectual Independence in the Civil War South* (Chapel Hill: University of North Carolina Press, 2010); Eric Foner, *Free Soil, Free Labor, Free Men: The Ideology of the Republican Party before the Civil War* (New York: Oxford University Press, 1970); Laura A. White, *Robert Barnwell Rhett: Father of Secession* (Gloucester, Mass.: P. Smith, 1965).

23 President Jackson's Proclamation Regarding Nullification, December 10, 1832. On the different uses of a citizenry's war experiences to justify constitutional change, see Robert L. Tsai, "Three Arguments about War," *Constitutional Commentary* 30 (2015): 1–59.

24 Jeffrey K. Tulis, *The Rhetorical Presidency* (Princeton, N.J.: Princeton University Press, 1987).

25 Eric Foner, *The Fiery Trial: Abraham Lincoln and American Slavery* (New York: Norton, 2010); Paul Finkelman, "Lincoln, Emancipation, and the Limits of Constitutional Change," *Supreme Court Review* 9 (2008): 349–87; Sanford Levinson, "Was the Emancipation Proclamation Constitution? Do We/Should We Care?," *University of Illinois Law Review* (2001): 1135–58.

26 *Dred Scott v. Sanford*, 60 U.S. 393 (1857). See generally Mark Graber, Dred Scott *and the Problem of Constitutional Evil* (New York: Cambridge University Press, 2006); Don E. Fehrenbacher, *The* Dred Scott *Case: Its Significance in American Law and Politics* (New York: Oxford University Press, 1978).

27 Abraham Lincoln, Address, Gettysburg, Pennsylvania, November 19, 1863.

28 John H. Franklin, "The Emancipation Proclamation: An Act of Justice," *National Archives*, January 4, 1993, reprinted in *Prologue Magazine* 25 (1993).

29 Jon L. Wakelyn, ed., *Southern Pamphlets on Secession, November 1860–April 1861* (Chapel Hill, University of North Carolina Press, 1996); William C. Davis, *"A Government of Our Own": The Making of the Confederacy* (New York: Free Press, 1994).

30 See, e.g., *Declaration of the Immediate Causes Which Induce and Justify the Secession of South Carolina from the Federal Union*, April 26, 1852; *Confederate States of America–Constitution for the Provisional Government*, February 8, 1861.

31 Tsai, *America's Forgotten Constitutions*, 120–34; Stephanie McCurry, *Confederate Reckoning: Power and Politics in the Civil War South* (Cambridge, Mass.: Harvard University Press, 2010).

32 Garrett Epps, *Democracy Reborn: The Fourteenth Amendment and the Fight for Equal Rights in Post–Civil War America* (New York: Holt, 2006); Bruce Ackerman, *We the People 2: Transformations* (Cambridge, Mass.: Belknap Press, 1998); John Hope Franklin, *Reconstruction: After the Civil War* (Chicago: University of Chicago Press, 1961); Eric Foner, *Reconstruction: America's Unfinished Revolution, 1863–1877* (New York: Harper & Row, 1988).

33 83 U.S. 36 (1873).

34 163 U.S. 537 (1896).

35 Id. at 543.

36 Id. at 544.

37 Mark Twain, *The Tragedy of Pudd'nhead Wilson* (1894; New York: Bantam, 1981). Spangler finds in the story a compelling critique of the importance of property rights in the Gilded Age. George M. Spangler, "*Pudd'nhead Wilson*: A Parable of Property," *American Literature* 42 (1970): 28–37; see also Lee C. Mitchell, "'De Nigger in You': Race or Training in *Pudd'nhead Wilson*?," *Nineteenth-Century Literature* 42 (1987): 295–312; Earl F. Briden, "Idiots First, Then Juries: Legal Metaphors in Mark Twain's *Pudd'nhead Wilson*," *Texas Studies in Literature and Language* 20 (1978): 169–80.

38 Ibid., Conclusion.

39 *Marbury v. Madison*, 5 U.S. 137 (1803); see also *Cohens v. Virginia*, 19 U.S. 264 (1821); *McCulloch v. Maryland*, 17 U.S. 316 (1819); *Martin v. Hunter's Lessee*, 14 U.S. 304 (1816).

40 For most of the nineteenth century, the states regulated immigration as waves of migrants arrived from European countries. In 1882, Congress enacted the Chinese Exclusion Act during a serious economic downturn in which legislators acceded to concerns about racial purity.

41 On the Puritan roots of the American rhetoric of banishment, see Nan Goodman, *Banished: Common Law and the Rhetoric of Social Exclusion in Early New England* (Philadelphia: University of Pennsylvania Press, 2012).

42 Romain D. Huret, *American Tax Resisters* (Cambridge, Mass.: Harvard University Press, 2014), 13–77. Recall that American colonists had castigated the Crown "For imposing Taxes on us without our Consent," listing tax policies among the "injuries and usurpations" justifying a complete political break. *Declaration of Independence*, July 4, 1776.

43 Mrs. Sarah E. V. Emery, *Seven Financial Conspiracies Which Have Enslaved the American People* (Lansing, Mich.: Smith & Co., 1887), reprinted in Jeffrey Ostler, "The Rhetoric of Conspiracy and the Formation of Kansas Populism," *Agricultural History* 69 (1995): 1–27.

44 *Populist Party Platform*, July 4, 1892; see generally Comer V. Woodward, *The Origins of the New South: 1877–1913* (Baton Rouge: Louisiana State University Press, 1951); Robert H. Wiebe, *The Search for Order, 1877–1920* (New York: Hill & Wang, 1967); Richard Hofstadter, *The Age of Reform: From Bryan to FDR* (New York: Knopf, 1955).

45 *People's Party Platform*, July 24, 1896.

46 Jed H. Shugerman, *The People's Courts: Pursuing Judicial Independence in America* (Cambridge, Mass.: Harvard University Press, 2012).

47 William J. Bryan, Speech, Democratic National Convention, Chicago, Illinois, July 9, 1896. See generally Rhys H. Williams and Susan M. Alexander, "Religious Rhetoric in American Populism: Civil Religion as Movement Ideology," *Journal for the Scientific Study of Religion* 33 (1994): 1–15.

48 *Seneca Falls Declaration of Sentiments and Resolutions*, July 19–20, 1848. See Sally G. McMillen, *Seneca Falls and the Origins of the Women's Rights Movement* (New York: Oxford University Press, 2008); Judith Wellman, *The Road to Seneca Falls: Elizabeth Cady Stanton and the First Woman's Rights Convention* (Urbana: University of Illinois Press, 2004); Kristin A. Olbertson, "Religion and Rights in Nineteenth-Century American Law: Reflections on the Work of Elizabeth B. Clark," *American Journal of Legal History* 53 (2013): 121–30. On the influence of the Declaration of Independence more generally, see Alexander Tsesis, *For Liberty and Equality: The Life and Times of the Declaration of Independence* (New York: Oxford University Press, 2012).

49 For instance, the Declaration of Sentiments itself decried, "[Man] has withheld from her rights which are given to the most ignorant and degraded men – both natives and foreigners." See Kathryn K. Sklar, *Women's Rights Emerges within the Anti-Slavery Movement, 1830–1870: A Brief History with Documents* (Boston: Bedford/St. Martin's, 2000); Linda K. Kerber, "From the Declaration of Independence to the Declaration of Sentiments: The Legal Status of Women in the Early Republic 1776–1848," *Human Rights* 6 (1977): 115–24.

50 Frank Pommersheim, *Broken Landscape: Indians, Indian Tribes, and the Constitution* (New York: Oxford University Press, 2009); Stuart Banner, *How the Indians Lost Their Land: Law and Power on the Frontier* (Cambridge, Mass.: Harvard University Press, 2005); Rennard Strickland, *Fire and the Spirits: Cherokee Law from Clan to Court* (Norman: University of Oklahoma Press, 1975); Angie Debo, *And Still the Waters Run: The Betrayal of the Five Civilized Tribes* (Princeton, N.J.: Princeton University Press, 1972); Grant Foreman, *The Five Civilized Tribes* (Norman: University of Oklahoma Press, 1934).

51 Tsai, *America's Forgotten Constitutions*, 152–60.

52 *Okmulgee Constitution*, 1870; Arrell M. Gibson, "Constitutional Experiences of the Five Civilized Tribes," *American Indian Law Review* 2 (1974): 17–45.

10
THE IMPERSONATION OF JUSTICE
Lynching, dueling, and wildcat strikes in nineteenth-century America

Norman W. Spaulding

I. Becoming modern

Transformation is by far the dominant theme in the historiography of nineteenth-century America. Over and over, the events and experiences of the period are represented in the language of change. This is, of course, as it should be. After all, rapid changes took place, and the archival remainders of the period are themselves replete with metaphors of change. In myriad ways, the nation at 1900 looked nothing like it was upon the election of Thomas Jefferson. This is particularly true of the geographic size of the country and the consequences of territorial expansion for the growth of an industrial economy, for the debate over slavery and the outbreak of the Civil War, and for the displacement of the population (indigenous, immigrant, and enslaved). It is also true of the law and conceptions of legality. As legal historians of early America are keen to remind us, there was an extensive system of law in place before the Revolution, but nineteenth-century reform movements dramatically affected the forms of legal action, training for the practice of law, and the organization of the bench and bar. As importantly, entirely new bodies of substantive law emerged to regulate new forms of social and economic action. As Christopher Tomlins has emphasized, "law became *the* paradigmatic discourse explaining life in America, the principal source of life's 'facts.' "[1]

If it should come as no surprise that twentieth- and twenty-first-century historians seek to locate the raw materials of what we have become as a nation in the period – that they look to the nineteenth century as the period in which the components of modern American life were assembled – the methodological risks attendant to such an approach should be equally obvious. Perhaps the gravest risk is that elements of continuity, remainders, and resistance to change in the nineteenth century may be lost to us. I refer here not to schools of legal and historical interpretation that seek to "discover" continuities by reducing the complexity of the past, asking the past to affirm mythical or foundational truths against the varied grain and the contradictions of lived experience.[2] Rather, the continuities we risk losing are those to which the people who experienced the transformations were themselves attached – the narratives, practices, rituals, nostalgias, and anxieties that mediated the experience of change. The power of these stabilizing and resistant features of social life should not be underestimated. Through them, after all, transformation can be experienced as continuity. A basic function of identity (personal, social, and national) is not only to frame changes that test the boundaries of the self, the community, and the state as affirmations of those very boundaries but to elide the status and experience of such tests as tests. Here again, the law plays a particularly salient role by defining change on terms that render it continuous with prior experience and first principles.

The problem of representing change and continuity in the period is captured vividly in a scene in Nathaniel Hawthorne's *The House of the Seven Gables*. Hawthorne describes the first train ride taken by Clifford and Hepzibah Pyncheon – "time stricken" New England siblings – on the then tantalizingly new mode of transportation:

> At last, therefore, and after so long estrangement from everything the world acted or enjoyed, they had been drawn into the great current of human life, and were swept away with it, as by the suction of fate itself . . .
>
> "Clifford! Clifford! Is not this a dream?"
>
> "A dream, Hepzibah!" repeated he, almost laughing in her face. "On the contrary, I have never been awake before!"
>
> Meanwhile, looking from the window, they could see the world racing past them. At one moment, they were rattling through a solitude; the next, a village had grown up around them; a few breaths more, and it had vanished, as if swallowed by an earthquake. The spires of meeting houses drifted from their foundations; the broad-based hills glided away. Everything was unfixed from its age-long rest, and moving at whirlwind speed in a direction opposite to their own.[3]

Hawthorne contrasts the astonishment of the Pyncheon siblings at the sensation of movement with the "tedium" of passengers already accustomed to the experience: "It seemed marvelous how all these people could remain so quietly in their seats, while so much noisy strength was working in their behalf."[4] Clifford's dialogue with a "gimlet-eyed old gentleman" about the virtues of innovation (trains, electricity, telegraphs) and being able to "live everywhere and nowhere" ensues.[5] For Hepzibah, however, "[f]ast and far as they had rattled and clattered along the iron track, they might just as well, as regarded [her] images, have been passing up and down Pyncheon Street."[6] The house on Pyncheon Street from which they were trying to escape "transported its great, lumbering bulk with more than railroad speed, and set itself phlegmatically down on whatever spot she glanced at."[7]

Ultimately, both Clifford and Hepzibah return home to confront their past, and that confrontation brings new displacements. The train ride nevertheless serves as a synecdoche for the dizzying technological, economic, and social transformation of the period – the ways in which everything had become "unfixed from its age-long rest, and moving at whirlwind speed." Clifford's euphoria, his exclamatory language, his (well-founded) feeling of liberation, all come close to overwhelming other elements of the scene – most significantly, Hepzibah's disorientation and constant recourse to the stability of hearth and home, as well as the monotony experienced by those for whom the train was already just another form of commuting, its "noisy strength" but a background hum.

Tedium and stability in the context of rapid transformation are remarkably difficult to represent. Even Hawthorne has to divide elements of the experience among characters on the train in order to draw these elements into relief. What exactly is Hepzibah dreaming? How does her dream, chased as it is by the overpowering memory and moral force of the family home, arrest and even reverse the momentum of the train?

These questions address elements of the experience of transformation that the very study of transformation – particularly transformation as a process of becoming, of becoming modern – can easily miss. The task is even more daunting for historians. Consider, for instance, the difficulties of representing violent labor strikes and the emergence of a genuine labor movement in the latter half of the nineteenth century against the tedium of increasingly routinized labor. Is the more important historical question how and why the strikes emerge (and lead to the legal reforms associated with the labor "movement") or why the tedium was otherwise tolerated by so many for so long? Or how the conditions of late nineteenth-century labor and labor law incorporated and extended the oppressive conditions of preindustrial labor in the antebellum period?[8]

For historians of law, some of the most intriguing questions about the experience of transformation in the nineteenth century have been missed in the effort to frame legal reforms as changes and to trace the law's relationship to the transformative power of capitalism. What happens when we turn our attention from how the law changed to areas in which it failed to change, in which legal change was steadfastly *resisted*, or in which discrete legal reforms appear not to have altered the social practices they were designed to regulate? These questions are not trivial. A remarkably wide array of "extralegal" practices associated with dispute resolution became entrenched in the nineteenth century – dueling, lynching, courthouse burning, barn burning, jailbreaks, strikes, and riots. Most had antecedents in the revolutionary period, if not earlier, and most reached their apotheosis and ended late in the nineteenth century (the most obvious exceptions are lynchings and strikes, though one can find evidence of jailbreaks, attacks on courthouses, and other such conduct well into the twentieth century).

Whether and to what extent legal reforms were responsible for ending these "extralegal" practices or channeling them into less violent iterations is an important and open question – the standard fare of historical analysis. But before periodizing these practices in relation to what we take to be the modern legal order – before, that is, the question of transformation – it's worth inquiring what may have unified these practices, how they bear upon nineteenth-century understandings of legality, and why they persisted for so long alongside what we take to be the ordinary operation of law.

In what follows I hope to show that if we attend to the organization of what is conventionally considered "extralegal" space, it quickly becomes apparent that the forms of social expression, protest, and dispute resolution occurring there were anything but extralegal. Resort to "extralegal" action was neither irregular, nor wholly irrational, nor always a response to failures in the ordinary operation of law. Adversarial and so-called extralegal spaces were in many ways homologous and overlapping. The point is not simply that the rule of law was understood to be more than the actions of an Austinian sovereign, more than the laws on the books, and more than what the courts say it is, though it is well to remember how deeply we modern Americans have internalized the view that the law belongs in the first instance to formal legal officers working in the enclosures of formal legal spaces. Rather, my purpose is to show that the movement of law between formal, judicial settings, and less formal spaces for dispute resolution involved the people – quite literally the bodies of the people asserting and defending legal claims – in the action of the law. Modern American law obviously still acts quite violently upon the body, and resistance to law often still demands putting the body at risk, but it is remarkable just how closely bodily risk was associated with the process of rights definition and the various forms of social power that flowed from this process in the nineteenth century.

II. The enclosure of justice

What were the basic features of formal legal process in the nineteenth century? At the level of form, content, and organization of space there is no denying that American adversarial procedure experienced significant transformations in the nineteenth century. I have elsewhere argued that enclosure was the organizing principle.[9] Architecturally, adjudication increasingly occurred in specialized purpose-built courthouses rather than in the community buildings designed for public affairs and commerce that were common before the Revolution. By mid-century, the neoclassical Roman Templar style (a stone pedimented portico with six or eight columns) was standard. Law was our civic religion, so façades were increasingly built to reflect and inspire the requisite faith. Inside, courtrooms borrowed from and repurposed the features of churches that delineated sacred space – elevating and decorating the judge's bench while dividing and cordoning off the adversarial area for parties, counsel, the jury, and testifying witnesses from the more distant seating for press and the public.

Procedurally, adjudication was transformed by intense popular democratic reform movements. Laypeople consistently objected to the cost, delay, and complexity of the writ system and all the aspects of pleading and practice that made access to justice turn on access to a lawyer skilled in the intricacies of common law and equity litigation. However, the most significant populist reform measures were quickly colonized by the legal profession. A movement that began by seeking to lower or eliminate barriers to admission to the bar, to make judicial office elective, and to eliminate the common law in favor of a democratically enacted and simplified code of rights, was first blunted by Whig-Federalist lawyers who defended the legal profession as an embodiment of republican virtue ("public sentinels" was Justice Story's favorite term) and the niceties of common-law adjudication as a valuable counterpoint to majoritarian politics.[10] By the middle of the century, lawyers simply took charge of the codification movement, ensuring their presence and voice in states that adopted simplified procedural rules and attempted legislative revisions of substantive common-law rights.[11] By the end of the century, elite lawyers had developed a successful model of formal postgraduate legal education to replace the apprentice system, thus raising barriers to admission. They also promulgated a scientific theory of legal reasoning tailored to rebut countermajoritarian objections to adjudication, and they began forming voluntary state bar associations that would eventually become mandatory and regulate both entry into (through licensure) and exit (through disbarment) from the profession.[12]

The contest between popular and elite professional control of adjudication can be seen in the transformation of specific procedural rules for adjudication as well. On the one hand, parties to a case secured the right to testify as the traditional common-law rules on witness competence gave way to the demand for participation and increased dependence upon the jury to resolve conflicting testimony.[13] On the other hand, judges gradually amplified their authority to regulate juries in other ways. Judges not only disaggregated questions of law from questions of fact and restricted the decision-making authority of the jury to the latter, they modified procedural tools such as the motion for judgment as a matter of law to permit cases to be removed from the jury where "no reasonable juror" could fail to find for the movant.[14] These incursions on the traditional prerogatives of the jury by judges not only altered the balance of power at the trial phase, they amplified the authority of appellate judges by increasing the quantity and scope of occasions for them to review the rationality of trial proceedings.

Thus even as pleading practice became somewhat simpler and jury trial more participatory, and even as the traditions of viva voce exchange and courtroom oratory persisted, adversary adjudication also became more strictly regulated and enclosed. The trend toward enclosure is in some respects even more pronounced in criminal adjudication, where physical enclosure in the form of incarceration displaced other forms of punishment, capital punishment went from being a public affair to an event occurring almost exclusively behind prison walls, and, as in civil cases, the balance of power between judge and jury shifted toward judges.[15]

III. Lynching as "unwritten" law

As historians have confronted violent nineteenth-century social practices such as lynching, dueling, strikes, riots, and courthouse burnings, the temptation has ever been to yoke them, sometimes explicitly, to the same narrative of transformation that is thought to explain the enclosure of justice. In this way, improvements in the physical security, efficiency, and rationality of the administration of justice by courts draw the irrationality, brutality, and anachronism of violent dispute resolution practices into relief. On the one hand, violent dispute resolution is framed as a threat to the rule of law, where the rule of law is already coded in terms of formal adversarial adjudication. Amy Louise Wood claims that lynch mobs' "flagrant disregard for legal order and authority . . . shocked and terrified because they struck against common notions of what civilized people could or should be capable of."[16] Michael J. Pfeifer similarly contends that lynching "was an aspect of a larger cultural war over the nature of criminal justice waged between rural and working-class supporters of 'rough justice' and middle class due process advocates."[17]

On the other hand, the persistence of violent dispute resolution practices is framed as an understandable and sometimes legitimate, if regrettably uncontrollable, community response to failures of formal adversarial adjudication. For instance, dueling is explained by Barbara Holland and Peter De Seve in terms of the failure of antebellum courts to recognize civil claims for libel and defamation.[18] Richard Maxwell Brown sees vigilantism in general and lynching in particular as expressions of a deep-seated feeling of responsibility to regulate criminality.[19]

The difficulty with the first argument is that closer examination of violent dispute resolution practices reveals that they were in many instances *highly* ordered. An extensive literature documents the "structured order of activities" that rendered the "nightmare choreography" of lynchings, including efforts to appropriate "some of the trappings of an actual trial," a discrete kind of "performance phenomena" notwithstanding important local and regional variations in the practice.[20] Moreover, lawyers, judges, jurors, law enforcement officers, and other public officials were frequently complicit in "extralegal" violence; indeed, they were sometimes quite active participants. The difficulty with the second argument is that the alleged failings of formal adversarial adjudication were frequently more imagined than real. At least, the real failings were commonly not those alleged. Whites anxious to lynch black people on trumped-up charges, for instance, knew perfectly well that their local prosecutors, judges, and juries would reliably convict.[21] And in the case of dueling, even when libel and defamation claims were eventually recognized, they did not impose liability for the offenses to honor that most commonly resulted in challenges to duel.[22]

Historians can be forgiven for some of the confusion. Research examining the broad class of violent dispute resolution practices *as a class* is rare, with the consequence that some of the commonalities and contradictions that define the class are missed.[23] As importantly, the archives themselves are rich with seemingly contradictory claims. Over and over, duelists, participants in lynchings, striking workers, and contemporary commentators conceded that the practices were barbarous and uncivilized but also necessary means to important social ends, constrained by rational principles and somehow also the spontaneous result of overpowering moral outrage or innocent suffering – sentiments that, as the *Atlanta Constitution* put it in defending the 1899 lynching of a black man in Palmetto, Georgia, "dethroned the reason of the people."[24] The modern mind understandably reels at the grotesque, sanguinary excesses, the seemingly senseless loss of life and destruction of property, the chilling terror of white supremacy wearing the mask of community justice, and the seemingly comic absurdity of duelists, animated by honor culture, drawing pistols over petty verbal slights.

The temptation to salute the enclosure of justice in studying "extralegal" violence is thus hard to resist. The risk, however, is that we may obscure the very nature of legality we are trying to understand. In a word, violent nineteenth-century dispute-resolution practices appear "extralegal" because they were extra*judicial* and/or because they violated written law. Once having embraced these dichotomies, we naturally focus on periodizing the violence in relation to the enclosure of justice rather than on the intriguing question of what kind of legal order those who engaged in such violence were trying to establish, protect, or upend. As importantly, we also obscure the interest and role of the legal profession in protecting and expanding its power by making the dichotomies seem Manichean – insisting that extrajudicial violence is always a threat to the rule of law and that a democratic society must therefore depend for social control upon an elite class of dispute-resolution experts following set procedures in an enclosed space subject to their control.

On the latter point, consider the 1894 essay "The True Remedy for Lynch Law," published in the *American Law Review* by Walter McKenzie Clark, a prominent lawyer, newspaper editor, and former Confederate officer who had just been appointed to the North Carolina state Supreme Court. Clark soberly notes national data showing that in 1892, "there were 107 executions by process of law and 236 by lynching. Taking the reports for ten years 1883–1892 the average has been more than two executed by lynching for one executed by law."[25] Legal efforts to reverse the trend by criminalizing lynch mobs "have had, and can have, no effect. It has always been murder to take the life, even of a criminal, without warrant of law, and no new law can make it any greater offense."[26] The remedy, Clark insisted,

> is to restore the confidence of society in the just, prompt, and efficient trial and punishment of criminals. . . . Let the trial be speedy, and the punishment, if there is a conviction, be prompt and certain. Remove the technicalities which render so many trials a travesty. Abolish the delays and continuances which baffle justice. . . . Do these things, and not only will lynchings disappear, but the grand annual total of over 10,000 capital offenses will shrink wonderfully.[27]

Notice that this was no solemn plea for due process of law. In Clark's view, criminal procedure was unduly solicitous of defendants' rights:

> [E]very possible advantage is given to the defendant and every possible disadvantage is imposed on the prosecution. . . . He has the great advantage that erroneous rulings of the presiding judge in his favor cannot be corrected; while a single erroneous ruling against him vitiates the whole proceedings. The sympathy of the jury in favor of a fellow being in jeopardy of his life is easily appealed to and readily invoked. . . . Our civilization has gone too far and has overdone itself in these matters.[28]

Strikingly, his reforms would have made criminal trials more like lynchings – summary, swift, and final.

> The principle . . . which instinctively actuates lynching mobs . . . is in itself right and just, and courts should act upon it and not leave it to be . . . a motive for the illegal execution of justice.[29]

Clark makes no reference whatsoever to the stark racial disparities that defined both late nineteenth-century lynchings and legal process, even though the essay was written as the number of annual lynchings peaked and as blacks became the primary targets.[30] As late as 1920, while serving as chief justice on the State Supreme Court, he would publicly deny that there was any racial disparity in the administration of justice in North Carolina.

> A colored man may have differences with a white man . . . but when they go into the courthouse to have it settled every man knows the colored men are at no disadvantage. The white men on the jury, with the pride of the Anglo-Saxon race, will see that equal and exact justice is done.[31]

The denial was patently contrary to fact.[32]

After the turn of the century, as the number of lynchings began to fall but spectacle lynchings amplified public experience of the practice, bar leaders anxiously repeated Clark's call. At the twenty-ninth annual meeting of the American Bar Association in 1906, Thomas J. Kernan, a prominent Louisiana lawyer, insisted in a speech provocatively titled "The Jurisprudence of Lawlessness" that "unwritten" and "lawless laws" such as lynching and dueling "are in full force and effect in some parts of this great and growing republic; and some of them in all parts of it."[33] This was a matter of grave concern not only for the peace and safety of the nation but for the bar. "Wherever they are effective, they are enforced with much greater certainty and celerity, than any written statutes or sacred constitutions. Their existence poses a problem for American lawyers."[34]

The problem for the profession, Kernan argued, was that these "lawless laws" were making a mockery of the administration of justice by courts, and hence a mockery of lawyers and judges.

> All of [these laws], in their last analysis, have their origin and source in some real or supposed failure, defect or injustice of the law itself; most of the lawless rights they establish are . . . counterparts of the real or supposed lawful wrongs which they are meant to compensate. The slow and painful process of the courts and the utter inadequacy of all legal remedy for certain crimes have given rise to all the rest.

The threat to society was grave, he believed, and it was incumbent upon the legal profession to respond.

> [Lawless laws] seem to be abnormal and malignant growths upon the body of the law, and they must either be excised or removed by constitutional treatment of the legal system itself. The indicated remedy is necessarily legal, and it is the first duty of American lawyers to discover and apply the remedy. . . . When the punishment of crime itself becomes a crime, all organized government is shaken to its foundation stones and the fabric of civilization is fast tottering to its fall.[35]

Like Clark, Kernan advocated no expansion of due process but rather something approaching summary justice to rival the spectacle of spectacle lynchings.

> The trial should be speedy, and there should be no appeal. The judgment of the court should be instantly executed. . . . [W]here the verdict is guilty with capital punishment, swift and inexorable death, in horrid form, should be the inevitable penalty. The convict should be executed in public by some form of death so supremely horrible as to strike terror even to the hearts of fiends themselves.[36]

Kernan then obliquely but provocatively refers to the racial element of lynching by invoking British colonial experience in India:

> The English in India found that the death penalty had no terrors for the mutinous Sepoys until they began to blow them into eternity from the mouths of cannon. It

> might be well legally to destroy our human fiends, by blowing them into atoms with dynamite, or by casting them into a burning pit, simulating as nearly as may be the popular conception of the fires of hell. . . . If it is not granted by the law, the wild cry for vengeance of a people writhing in dumb, helpless agony will continue to be heard and heeded by the mob, and lawless executions will increase in number and in horror.[37]

Kernan worried about the risk of innocents being lynched, but he insisted that "[t]he wound inflicted upon the law and upon society is even deeper and more ghastly."[38] Beyond those harms, there was the wound to professional authority:

> The flagrant violation and open defiance of law involved in the practice sets all law and authority at naught. It degrades the courts, debases the administration of justice, brings judges, juries and lawyers all into contempt and strikes at the very roots of all social order. . . . The situation is daily becoming more unbearable, and we lawyers must end it or cease boasting of our usefulness to civilization and society.[39]

If the enthusiasm of Kernan and Clark for summary justice seems contradictory coming from elites in the profession whose commitment to due process of law should have run deep, the contradiction was at least partly resolved by their desire to ratify and redirect long-standing popular critiques of the adversary system. That desire became feverish as spectacle lynchings proliferated and tested the principles of enclosure upon which the power of the profession turned.[40] Kernan's use of the term "unwritten law" is particularly revealing in this respect, for it was precisely the intricacies of "unwritten" common law – rules of practice and pleading known only to lawyers and judges – which populist Jacksonian supporters of codification had criticized as undemocratic. The contradiction was also partly resolved for contemporaries by public awareness of the very racial disparities Kernan and Clark sidestepped. With the exception of Kernan's endorsement of cruel and unusual public executions, their visions of summary justice dovetailed with the realities of the administration of criminal justice in courts under Jim Crow segregation.[41]

But the contradictions were never fully resolved. As Richard Maxwell Brown emphasizes, "[t]here is a wide range of evidence illustrating the collusion between law officers and vigilantes, the participation of lawyers and leading men in vigilante movements, and the sympathy with which members of the legal illuminati viewed vigilantism and lynch law."[42] Sheriffs, police officers, and justices of the peace not only leaked information about the movement of suspects to lynch mobs, they turned suspects over without resistance and failed to call for reinforcements necessary to suppress lynch mobs. "The open cooperation of officials with lynchers had become such a scandal that after 1892 a number of states adopted legislative or constitutional provisions designed to end the evil" by fining or removing from office law enforcement officers who "through fault or neglect lost prisoners to mob violence."[43] Prosecutors frequently refused to charge members of lynch mobs, and, when they did, juries frequently refused to convict.[44]

Brown also provides an extensive list of prominent lawyers who were members of vigilance committees, participated directly in lynchings, or counseled or applauded the practice of lynching during the nineteenth century. The list includes presidents (Andrew Jackson), governors, and a number of United States senators.[45] Joseph B. Wall, a prominent Florida lawyer, former Confederate soldier, graduate of the University of Virginia, brigadier general of the Florida national guard, and former state attorney in Tampa, "played an influential role in a lynching that took place at the doorstep of a sitting federal court" in 1882.[46] Wall and a mob of a hundred other people raided the courthouse jail during the lunch recess and hanged the black prisoner they seized "from an oak tree in front of the courthouse steps. . . . The judge returned from his meal to find the corpse dangling at the entrance to his court."[47] Wall was disbarred from practice in federal court, but he suffered no other penalty. He was not prosecuted for his role in the lynching, and five years after the incident he was elected "the first president of the newly founded Florida State Bar Association."[48]

Brown puts the participation of elite lawyers and other public officers in lynchings down to their commitment to a "dual system of legal and extralegal justice" rationalized "by adherence to the primary value of repression of crime with little regard for procedural safeguards."[49] On this "behaviorist" account of legality, however, it is hard to explain the use of lynching as a tool of white supremacy or as a tool for mere partisan politics. Yet it was frequently used for both purposes in ways that related tenuously, if at all, to the interest in regulating criminality.[50] It is equally difficult to understand how and why those interested in the repression of crime would have been so casual about the risk of executing innocent people or why, if the "dual system" was well understood, it should have been perceived as such a threat to the rule of law and professional authority. Further, if one examines other extrajudicial dispute-resolution practices, it is not at all clear that criminality was at issue, except in the sense that people were willing to commit crimes (murder in the case of dueling, trespass, and property damage in the case of strikes) in order to vindicate other interests.

The likelier explanation is that the legal profession itself was divided about the propriety of extrajudicial dispute resolution and that the profession's ambivalence was accentuated by long-standing public hostility to and ambivalence about the enclosure of justice. One of the most significant constants of the nineteenth century may have been precisely this contestation and uncertainty among lawyers and between the legal profession and the public about whether legality derived more or less exclusively from adjudication and other formal sources or from the people in some more organic sense – whether, that is, *extrajudicial* dispute resolution was always *extralegal* and, if not, whether and on what terms the practice of justice should be enclosed.

Closer examination of the relationship between dueling, strikes, and lynching may help illuminate this claim.

IV. The Adams-Richards duel: dueling to code

At 6:15 in the evening of July 9, 1877, two young, socially prominent Savannah lawyers raised pistols at each other at an abandoned plantation outside the city. Standing twelve paces apart, they waited for instructions to fire, shot at each other, missed, and then promptly negotiated a settlement of their grievances through their "seconds" (agents chosen by each "principal" to conduct all negotiations with one's adversary). After the agreement was signed, they shook hands, mounted a carriage together, and "returned to Savannah as friends and colleagues."[51] The settlement agreement was reduced to writing by the seconds and provided as follows:

> I. Samuel B. Adams retract any insulting language to Mr. R.R. Richards in the City Court where upon Mr. R.R. Richards allows the case of Ambrose and Puff vs. Hudson and Sullivan to be reinstated in the City Court.
>
> II. Mr. Samuel B. Adams apologizes for his language before the office of Captain McGowan to Mr. Richards.
>
> III. Mr. Richards withdraws all imputation of falsity against Mr. Adams.
>
> IV. Mr. Adams withdraws his motion against Mr. Richards [for disbarment] in the Superior Court and expresses his regrets therefore.[52]

This particular duel was unusual in a number of respects. To begin with, it is one of the latest nineteenth-century duels for which formal records exist. Dueling was widespread early in the antebellum period. Although not restricted to the south, Frank T. Wheeler notes that "[b]etween 1800 and 1825, dueling was a daily 'sport' in some southern cities. . . . New Orleans was the most active city for duels with one report indicating three or four duels per day in the early 1800s."[53] Dueling occurred in the North as well. The Hamilton-Burr duel is the most famous example, but it was not a unique occurrence among Northern politicians early in the century. Joanne B. Freeman has shown that "[i]n New York City . . . there were at least sixteen affairs of honor between 1795 and 1807," many of which served mixed political and personal purposes.[54]

> Politicians manipulated the affair of honor to serve their immediate political needs, but they also shared a profound respect for its personal dimension, its impact on their sense of self. The duel was a subtle blend of the strategic and the sincere, the self-interested and the selfless, the political and the personal, the public and the private. . . . Personal honor was a concern of politicians throughout the nation.[55]

Dueling was also common in the West and border states. "From the 1830s on . . . pro-slavery and abolitionist hotheads challenged each other regularly."[56]

Secondly, unlike many duels, the Adams-Richards duel was an almost completely secret event. We know about it only because the correspondence between the principals and their seconds and between the seconds, as well as the "Articles of Agreement" setting out the terms of the duel, were carefully preserved by Adams and his estate. In other duels, publicity was a central feature. Freeman observes:

> Often, the two seconds published conflicting newspaper accounts of a duel, each man boasting of his principal's bravery and mocking his opponent's cowardice. Fought to influence a broad public, synchronized with the events of the political timetable, political duels conveyed carefully scripted political messages.[57]

Even outside the arena of partisan politics, duels and the insults that sparked challenges to duel were frequently made public because the reputations of the principals were at stake. Both initial insults and formal challenges to duel were "posted" via formal written notices "in taverns and on street corners" and in newspapers.[58] Some duels were spectacles attended by substantial crowds. "In California in 1859 the former chief justice of the state supreme court, proslavery judge David Terry, killed antislavery senator David Broderick before a large crowd of fascinated spectators."[59]

Third, unlike some of the most famous duels, the Adams-Richards duel did not result in death or injury to either principal. The seconds for Adams and Richards could have negotiated a second volley. Instead, "Meldrim asked if Mr. Richards, as the challenger was satisfied," and after Mr. Hollis replied that a "courteous note" regarding the underlying offenses would receive a "courteous response . . . an agreement was drawn up and signed."[60]

A common misconception about dueling is that it was primarily "a ritual of violence."[61] Although duels could certainly result in death or grave bodily injury, Freeman emphasizes that "they were demonstrations of manner, not marksmanship . . . intricate games of dare and counterdare, ritualized displays of bravery. . . . A man's response to the *threat* of gunplay bore far more meaning than the exchange of fire itself."[62] In fact,

> [m]ost conflicts waned during negotiations and concluded when each principal felt that his honor had been vindicated. Such was the role of the principal's second, who acted as a sort of legal representative, attempting to defend his client's honor without necessitating a duel.[63]

Here we can see some of the ways in which the Adams-Richards duel was quite conventional. The seconds in the Adams-Richards duel not only advised Adams and Richards on whether to make and accept the challenge after the two had argued in court, they carefully negotiated Articles of Agreement setting the terms of the duel, and through a series of highly formal exchanges, they nearly succeeded in submitting the dispute to the arbitrament of two neutrals.[64] This is precisely the mediating role of seconds advocated in John Lyde Wilson's widely circulated 1838 booklet, *The Code of Honor: Rules for Principals and Seconds in Dueling*, which he modeled on standard European dueling codes. Wilson, a lawyer and former governor of South Carolina, insisted that "nine duels out of ten, if not ninety-nine out of a hundred, originate in the want of experience in the seconds."[65] Before a formal challenge has been made, a second should

> [u]se every effort to soothe and tranquilize your principal; do not see things in the same aggravated light in which he views them; extenuate the conduct of his adversary whenever you clearly see the opportunity to do so. . . . Endeavor to persuade him that there must have been some misunderstanding in the matter.[66]

Wilson's Code further prescribed that correspondence with an adversary's second should be "written in the style of a gentleman."[67] If "an accommodation is tendered, never require too much," and if the party offering it "wishes to give a reason for his conduct in the matter, do not, unless offensive to your [principal], refuse to receive it; by doing so you may heal the breach more effectually."[68] Finally, seconds were advised to

> search diligently into the origin of the misunderstanding; for gentlemen seldom insult each other, unless they labor under some misapprehension or mistake; and when you have discovered the original ground or error, follow each movement to the time of sending the note, and harmony will be restored.[69]

The seconds for Adams and Richards certainly achieved this in considering arbitrament by neutrals even after the challenge had been issued and, of course, by averting a second exchange of fire.

The Adams-Richards duel followed traditional rules in other respects as well. It originated from a disagreement that culminated in charges of dishonesty. Richards had objected to the introduction of certain evidence as untimely; Adams countered that Richards had violated a prior agreement between the two to allow the evidence and filed a motion to have Richards disbarred.[70] Further verbal insults were exchanged outside the courtroom. And the dispute arose between two social elites (gentlemen did not duel with social inferiors on the ground that an inferior could offer no insult to a gentleman's honor).[71] Carefully worded exchanges of correspondence approaching the formality of pleading in civil litigation preceded the duel, and, just as Wilson's Code prescribed, the duel itself was carefully orchestrated according to rules delimiting the appropriate use of force. "A fair duel was a game of chance that displayed the willingness of both principals to die for their honor, not their skill at inflicting pain or death." As one pamphleteer noted, the "polite" duelist fought "without any design to injure his adversary."[72] In fact, killing an opponent left "a duelist open to charges of bloodthirstiness and personal ambition."[73]

Significantly, those charges did not always stick. Although Aaron Burr's reputation was forever tarnished by the killing of Alexander Hamilton, Andrew Jackson was repeatedly charged with misconduct in duels and the charges appear rather to have amplified than diminished his reputation. Take, for example, his duel with John Sevier when they confronted each other in public in Knoxville, Tennessee. Sevier challenged him on the spot. "Both men pulled pistols and shot wildly," missing each other but injuring a bystander.[74] The men were separated and a formal duel was then arranged in Indian Territory bordering the state. Before they reached the arranged spot, Jackson drew on Sevier, Sevier fled, and "a growing crowd of onlookers rushed to stop Jackson from firing."[75] Three years later, in a famous public duel with another Tennessee attorney, Charles Dickinson, Jackson agreed to "a quick-draw duel" rather than the ordinary procedures of firing on a three count or taking designated turns firing. This gave Dickinson a considerable advantage as he was an expert marksman and something of a "trick shot artist" who claimed to have "shot through a string at twenty-four feet. He carried the broken string as a reminder of his skill and as a warning to would-be opponents."[76] Jackson decided "to let Dickinson draw and shoot first while he stoically stood his ground," faked that he had not been hit in the chest (if he revealed a wound the duel would have ended with Dickinson the victor according to the code of honor), and only then returned fire.[77] Dickinson had no occasion to object to the irregularity as he bled to death on the spot. A "large audience" attended the duel and "Jackson's notoriety rose as a result of the duel."[78]

A final commonality with traditional duels is that the dueling ground or "field of honor" in the Adams-Richards duel was a location well-known for that purpose – a plantation on the outskirts of Savannah that had been abandoned since the Civil War.[79] Holland and De Seve report that, in other cities, liminal spaces such as

> [i]slands and sandbars were popular because of their ambiguous jurisdiction. . . . Bloody Island served St. Louis. Memphis duelists often crossed the river to Arkansas to fight. . . . Most famous of all was the more-or-less official national dueling ground in Bladensburg, Maryland, a convenient mile or so beyond the District of Columbia line. Here, on 15 vine-choked acres a hundred or more duels were fought.[80]

In New York, "duelists ferried across the Hudson River to the more congenial (i.e., less prosecutorially aggressive) shores of New Jersey."[81]

Legal regulation of dueling was lax for much of the antebellum period. By "1859, nineteen states had banned dueling," but the prohibitions were ineffective.[82] They "proved hard to enforce, harder to prosecute and hardest to explain to a jury."[83] Freeman reports that even in well publicized political duels, "these lawyers and lawgivers were seldom charged. Sometimes police officers simply refused to tangle with men of influence; on those rare occasions when legal authorities made the law known, politicians often persisted in their duel negotiations regardless."[84] Even duels resulting in the death of a principal rarely ended in prosecutions for murder, and when charges were brought, elites came to the defense of the accused. Publicly reviled as he was, "when Burr faced murder charges after killing Hamilton, eleven sympathetic Republican senators signed a petition to New Jersey governor John Bloomfield, reminding him that political duels were *not* usually prosecuted."[85] They added that previous New York duelists at Weehawken "had not only been spared judicial proceedings but had later received judicial appointments."[86]

Seconds, attending physicians, and spectators sometimes followed elaborate rituals to observe or participate in the events without "witnessing" the crime of murder. Guns were concealed until the last minute, permitting observers to deny that they saw weapons, and boatmen who rowed duelists to dueling grounds stood with their backs to the duelists in order to "testify that they 'did not see the firing.' "[87] A doctor might be called out from a waiting place only after one party was injured and the other had left so that he could not identify the shooter.[88] "Surviving witnesses, usually just one of the principals and the two seconds, often swore that the shooting had been an 'accident.' "[89] Even without these precautions and dissimulation, as Wilson explained, prosecutors and jurors who understood honor culture were reluctant to charge or convict. "The severest penal enactments cannot restrain the practice of dueling, and their extreme severity in this state, the more effectually shields the offenders."[90] Wilson went even further, arguing just as defenders of lynching did, that dueling was a natural human response to inadequacies in the formal administration of justice.

> How many cases are there . . . where there is no tribunal to do justice to an oppressed and deeply wronged individual? . . . [I]n cases where the laws of the country give no redress for injuries received, where public opinion not only authorizes, but enjoins resistance, it is needless and a waste of time to denounce the practice. It will be persisted in as long as manly independence, and a lofty personal pride in all that dignifies and ennobles the human character, shall continue to exist.[91]

What caused dueling to end is a hotly contested question.[92] The salient point for present purposes is that it persisted through much of the nineteenth century, even among legal elites, notwithstanding the fact that it was plainly illegal as a matter of formal law. If one starts from the narrow premise that violent dispute resolution is extralegal whenever it takes place out of court, dueling is paradigmatically extralegal. It is premeditated murder – a most proper target for the enclosure of justice. Alternatively, if one emphasizes concern for reputation to the exclusion of other factors, dueling and honor culture can seem anachronistic and superficial even during the period in which they flourished. Consider the presentism and derision in Kenneth Greenberg's distinction between the emerging scientific rationalism of the nineteenth century and the backwardness of Southern honor culture.

> If a central concern of nineteenth-century scientific and intellectual activity was to penetrate into the secrets of nature, to move from the level of superficial appearance to a deeper and hidden reality, then it may have involved a sensibility alien to antebellum Southern white male culture. Many cultures concerned with honor highly value appearance. . . . The central issue of concern to men in such a culture is not the nature of some underlying reality but the acceptance of their projections.[93]

On this view, dueling seems irrational and daffy – again, a proper target for the enclosure of justice.

However, neither of these accounts fully captures the formality of the practice, the complex public response to deviations from those formalities, the capacity of seconds to avert violence by insisting on the formalities of the code, the frequency with which lawyers served as duelists and seconds, the role of lawyers, judges, prosecutors, and other public officials in exempting dueling participants from the ordinary operation of criminal law, and the analogues to dueling that proliferated among nonelites. On the latter point, notice that Andrew Jackson's controversial early nineteenth-century duels already contained elements of gunfighting and other extrajudicial modes of dispute-resolution practiced by non-elites later in the nineteenth century.[94] And neither account captures the ambivalence with which proponents of the code of honor publicly defended the practice.

That ambivalence is vividly reflected in Hamilton's famous decision not to fire on Burr. "Confident that he had saved his reputation" by accepting Burr's challenge, "Hamilton could . . . satisfy his religious and moral 'scruples' " by observing "all the expected dueling rituals on the field" *except* the injunction to shoot.[95] Even Wilson sensed the delicacy of the question of dueling's legitimacy. After stridently defending the practice, he added, "I would not wish to be understood to say, that I do not desire to see dueling cease to exist entirely, in society."[96] But he squarely rejected passive submission to insult and obloquy. Rather than attempt to abolish dueling by law or by teaching "a passive forbearance to insult and indignity," the "rising generation" should be taught that it "is more an act of heroism and bravery to repair the injury, than to persist in error, and enter into mortal combat with the injured party."[97] The Code was offered as an interim device to preserve high standards in the practice. "The teaching and preaching of our eloquent Clergy, may do some service, but is wholly inadequate to suppress" dueling.[98] "Under these circumstances, the following rules are given to the public, and if I can save the life of one useful member of society, I will be compensated."[99]

Wilson's ambivalence on moral and religious grounds is clearly nowhere near as acute as Hamilton's. The threshold he set for the administration of justice in courts and for moral and spiritual reform was plainly unrealistic. Even when the law of libel, slander, and defamation became more robust, they would not regulate the reputational harms that gave rise to dueling, and Christian moral education rather decisively favored "passive forbearance." But by condemning the practice of dueling even as he published and promoted a code for its proper execution, Wilson established terms for discriminating between "fair" duels and unruly analogues. The unruly analogues, on this view, were doubly condemnable, violating ordinary criminal law and the code of honor.

We are now in a position to appreciate the respects in which adversary adjudication and dueling not only impersonated each other but depended upon each other for legitimacy – where legitimacy is understood in the democratic sense of public acceptance or endorsement rather than in the positivistic sense of express legal sanction (law in action, as opposed to law on the books). To the extent that dueling actually resolved social disputes the courts could not effectively remedy, the courts were spared the embarrassment of their inadequacies. To the extent that dueling observed formalities that prevented it from becoming a mere "ritual of violence," it drew upon and complemented the principles of legality in adversary adjudication. Dueling further benefited not only from the complicity of courts, prosecutors, and juries but from the express endorsement and participation of lawyers as principals and seconds. Adjudication in court, for its part, continued to draw on a tradition of adversarialism that permitted attorneys, acting as seconds for parties, to "duel" on their behalf according to the formalities of common law and equity practice.

V. The Great Railroad Strike of 1877: dueling with the sovereign

The class element and elitism of Wilson's defense of dueling comes into sharp relief when that practice of judicial dispute resolution is contrasted with the street duels between labor and capital that became increasingly common later in the century. No one writes about strikes as affairs of honor. They are read as quintessential expressions of the pathologies of a market culture that is thought to have gradually displaced honor culture. This is a mistake. To begin with, all but the most unruly of wildcat strikes, and perhaps even these strikes too, were carefully staged confrontations in which honor, dignity, and reputation played as fundamental a role as brute financial interest. As a historian of dueling has observed, "Dueling for dollars replaced the pistol."[100] Nor, it is worth noting, were financial, political, and other base interests absent from the traditional affair of honor. Freeman reminds us that partisan credibility and electoral power were almost always at stake in political duels, litigation advantage was at the root of the Adams-Richards duel, and competition for a prestigious military appointment prompted the Jackson-Sevier duel. Economists, moreover, have argued that creditworthiness was frequently at stake in duels arising from accusations of mendacity.[101] Interest and honor continued to play intersecting roles not only in the sectional controversy of the mid-century and the Civil War to which it led but in the industrial economy that flourished in the Gilded Age.

Figure 10.1 "The Tournament of Today – A Set-to Between Labor and Monopoly" (*Puck*, August 1, 1883)

Source: Library of Congress, Prints and Photographs Division

Consider the double-page centerfold cartoon titled, "The Tournament of Today – A Set-to between Labor and Monopoly," published in *Puck Magazine* on August 1, 1883 (see Figure 10.1). *Puck* was an illustrated weekly satirical magazine founded by the artist Joseph Keppler in 1871. It published the first color cartoons in America, and the centerfold each week usually addressed a political topic. A "set-to" is a synonym for a duel, derived from the sport of boxing, meaning "[t]he action of 'setting to' . . . hence, a bout or round . . . Also, a bout, engagement, or match at some other sport."[102] In the cartoon, "Monopoly" is depicted as an enormous knight in gleaming gold armor, holding a lance called "Subsidized Press," and a shield labeled "Corruption of the Legislature," while mounted on a black locomotive. The figure advances toward a cowering, feeble horse labeled "Poverty," mounted by a gaunt man in threadbare clothes labeled "Labor," who is barely able to lift a mallet labeled "Strike." Just behind the knight of Monopoly and his train, wealthy spectators sit in an area "Reserved for Capitalists." In the background, hungry-looking children dangle from the fence where ordinary men and women look on as the tip of the knight's lance looms menacingly before the defeated face of Labor.

The image thus represents a strike as a duel between tragically unequal principals – quite the opposite of the duels contemplated in Wilson's Code. And the inequality was not just between capital and labor as distinct social classes but, crucially for our purposes, between the legal status of the two groups. If the result of the set-to was presented as a foregone conclusion in *Puck*, that was in no small measure a reflection of the experience of the Great Railroad Strike of 1877, the first national wildcat strike. While traditional duelists and lynch mobs counted on the tolerance and complicity of law enforcement officials in social action that was formally criminal and an affront to due process of law or simply defied them, the attempts of striking workers to draw their dispute into extrajudicial space for resolution were met not only by law enforcement working in concert with railroad executives and lawyers but by military forces drawn out to do the bidding of the railroads. Combined with the legal authority of corporations to fire striking workers and replace them with strikebreakers, the use of "yellow dog contracts," judicial criminalization of labor combinations, and the close relationship of state and federal officials to the railroad corporations they subsidized, strikers found themselves in almost completely extralegal space.[103]

The railroads' arrogation of sovereign power is captured in two famous cartoons by Frank Bellew for the *New York Daily Graphic*, both titled "The American Frankenstein." In the first, published March 18, 1873, a locomotive depicted as a mechanized monster with stereotypically exaggerated black facial features rises from a workbench and lifts a tattered copy of the United States Constitution over its head as a diminutive white male worker in a star-festooned shirt retreats in terror (see Figure 10.2). The caption reads: "When Frankenstein beheld the hideous monster he had created he started with terror and disgust." A year later, Bellew published the second cartoon (see Figure 10.3). Here a locomotive depicted as a giant black monster brandishes a spiked bat labeled "Capital" in one hand and the cape of a robe of state labeled "Judicial Ermine" in the other, as he tramples a small white family. The caption reads: "Agriculture, commerce and manufacture are all in my power. My interest is the higher law of American politics."

Although there had been earlier strikes in America, what made the strikes of 1877 unique and of central importance was the scale and breadth of the violence that ensued. When railroad workers decided to strike to protest wage cuts in the summer of 1877, they refused to allow strikebreakers to cross their lines, and they occupied railroad property in order to prevent the trains from running. Crucially, frustrated and sympathetic workers from other industries quickly joined their protests. Material and dignitary concerns combined to stiffen the strikers' resolve. The wage cuts were drastic and came on the heels of earlier cuts in the midst of one of the nation's worst industrial depressions even as the railroads continued to pay dividends to shareholders. Railroad managers not only refused to negotiate with employee "grievance committees" that inquired about wage relief but summarily fired the committee members.[104] There would be no negotiation between "seconds."

Instead, a cycle of strikes, military intervention, and violent clashes escalated into riots across ten states, with the initial epicenters along the Baltimore & Ohio Railroad in Martinsburg, West Virginia, and nearby Baltimore, Maryland, as well as the Pennsylvania Railroad's facilities in Pittsburg, Pennsylvania. The triggering events for violence related in each location to the strikers' decision not just to stop working but to stop the trains from running until the wage cuts were revoked. By occupying railroad property (trains, rail lines, bridges, roundhouses, and depots), the strikers orchestrated a direct challenge to the authority and status of the railroad owners as owners.

The challenge was promptly accepted. Working closely with the governor of West Virginia, the president of the B&O, John Garrett, placed armed militiamen on a cattle train and ordered it to leave Martinsburg where strikers had bottlenecked hundreds of B&O trains in mid-July. When the armed cattle train reached a switch that had been set to derail the train, a militiaman jumped off the train, rifle in hand, to confront a striker guarding the switch. The striker raised a pistol, shot the militiamen as he advanced, and was then shot three times himself by the militia.[105]

Although Martinsburg remained calm in the immediate aftermath of the shooting, in other cities the show of both state and federal military force was much greater. After the incident in Martinsburg, Garrett personally wrote to President Rutherford B. Hayes describing the situation along the B&O's lines as an "insurrection," even though no violence had followed the initial shooting, and insisting that "this great national highway can only be restored for public use by the interposition of the U.S. forces."[106] In Pittsburgh, John Scott, general counsel of the Pennsylvania Railroad, drafted a request for the governor to send state troops after local police proved

Figure 10.2 Frank Bellew, "The American Frankenstein" (*New York Daily Graphic*, March 18, 1873)

Source: Library of Congress, Prints and Photographs Division

Figure 10.3 Frank Bellew, "The American Frankenstein" (*New York Daily Graphic*, April 14, 1874)

Source: Library of Congress, Prints and Photographs Division

inadequate to open the lines there.[107] Strikers and sympathizers were shocked and offended by what they took to be an excessive government-sponsored show of force on behalf of the railroads. The initial scene in Martinsburg was thus repeated elsewhere but with much bloodier consequences – armed strikers blocked the rails, police and soldiers sought to break through with loyal railroad employees, violence broke out, and reprisals on both sides amplified as word of the deaths and injuries spread.

As the violence escalated into rioting, railroad property became a primary object of attack. Most dramatically, the roundhouse and Union Street Depot at Pittsburg were burned along with tracks, trains, machine shops, and entire sections of the city near the railroads.[108] "A large part of Pittsburg's population stayed up to see the show. Thousands made the hillside their grandstand. . . . Thousands more filled Liberty Street down to the Union Depot and beyond."[109] As "the spectator element watched quietly, almost raptly," new fires broke out "[a]ll along the car-packed yards," and as the night wore on, others began "pillaging."[110] The looting "began as a byproduct of the burning, then became an end in itself."[111]

The rallying cry and rebuke to officials who called for strikers to disband in Pittsburg was "Bread or blood!" an unmistakable reference to early nineteenth-century British food riots and the French Revolution.[112] Garrett soon got the very "insurrection" he falsely claimed was on hand in Martinsburg all along the B&O lines, just as Scott got the street war he sought to avert by calling state troops to the aid of the Pennsylvania Railroad in Pittsburg. In this way, the strikes became pitched contests over the impersonation of sovereignty – contests, that is, over who held rightful dominion over railroad property, who rightfully spoke for the public interests at stake in their construction, expansion, and efficient operation, and, as with all disputes over sovereignty, who controlled the rule of law and held a legitimate right to the use of force. Fifteen years later, during the Pullman Strikes, *Harper's Weekly* ran a cover image dramatizing these stakes, as well as the more powerful position of labor. Over the caption "King Debs," a larger than life Eugene Debs wearing a massive crown with his name and the name of his union etched into it, sat imperiously on a closed railway bridge labeled "The Highway of Trade," as lines of stalled rail cars extended into the distance behind him (see Figure 10.4).

Figure 10.4 W. A. Rogers, "King Debs" (*Harper's Magazine*, July 14, 1894)

Source: Library of Congress, Prints and Photographs Division

There were urban riots in the nineteenth century unconnected to labor unrest – most prominently, race riots in New Orleans in 1866, antidraft riots in New York City in 1863, and nativist riots in Philadelphia in 1844.[113] Any complete history of the 1877 railroad strikes would have to place them in the context of these events, as well as more violent labor protests like the Haymarket Riot of 1886 in Chicago, and militarized racial confrontations in the South during Reconstruction, such as the Colfax Massacre of 1873 in Grant Parish, Louisiana. The histories of urbanization, police professionalization, social movements, and the use of public space for nonviolent celebrations such as parades, military displays, and holiday celebrations is also deeply relevant.[114] Comparison to dueling and lynching is nevertheless useful because it reveals the sense in which the performance of a strike (and its repression) were addressed to law at a point of intersection with financial interests and personal honor.

Even in sensitive treatments of the cruelly paradoxical legal situation in which the strikers found themselves, this central attribute of the strikes as legal performances can be obscured in the association of violence with irrationality, particularly the supposed irrationality and incendiary nature of crowds.[115] The violence of the railroad strikes was certainly more unruly than the violence of duels among elites – at least those conducted according to code. But the stakes were different too – collective rather than individual and connected to the dignity of a living wage, or rather the indignity of being denied it and treated as disposable property. The morality of "passive forbearance" was distinctly unlikely to provide meaningful leverage in negotiations with the railroad owners, and the space for formal legal action was already monopolized by the railroads – companies that had in many ways mastered the art of impersonating the sovereign.[116]

VI. Conclusion: The unwritten law and the sovereignty of the body

What legal order were those who engaged in violent, extrajudicial dispute resolution in the nineteenth century dreaming of? Whatever the dream was, by the time of Bellew's eerie, racialized depiction of the railroad corporation as an American Frankenstein in 1873 and 1874, it had become a nightmare. America held itself out to the world as a beacon of liberty and evidence of accelerated "civilization" was everywhere – not just in technological advances and economic growth but in the second Great Awakening, the explosive growth of voluntary associations, the expansion and organization of the professions, and the seemingly providential conquest of the West. Extrajudicial violence nevertheless continued to "set itself down" in the line of progress and not just on the frontier or in the sectional bloodletting of the Civil War.

Bellew's cartoons draw explicitly from the gothic genre, depicting railroad corporations as monsters rather than using the more common postbellum caricature of capitalism in the form of a wealthy, morbidly obese white man in a black top hat.[117] Ominously, Bellew's monsters have seized the attributes of sovereignty. In the 1874 version, the "judicial" ermine and an oversized spiked bat represent the transformation of economic monopoly into a monopoly on the use of force. In the 1873 version, the monster has taken possession of the Constitution itself and wields it over its creator. The monsters are nothing less than mechanized Leviathans. Racializing them as black not only made them even more grotesque and menacing to a white audience still deeply attached to white supremacy; it also linked the corruption of crony capitalism to the perceived corruption of the project of Reconstruction.

If this was the nightmare – or at least a particularly vivid version produced for popular consumption on the heels of the Credit Mobilier scandal and flagging Northern support for Reconstruction – what was the dream? We know that striking workers would continue to launch their bodies into the maw of the Leviathans of the Gilded Age. We know as well that the body, not just reputation, was central to honor culture. As Andrew Jackson's mother reportedly advised him: "Indict no man for assault and battery or sue him for slander."[118] In questions of honor, Greenberg emphasizes, "[a] personal attack on the body could only be countered by a return attack on the body."[119] And we know that the black body would continue to serve as a displaced object of anger and anxiety regarding the social, economic, and legal power of whites long after Reconstruction ended.[120] Studies of spectacle lynching have revealed in intricate detail the symbolic significance of the visitation of violence upon the black body – the orchestration of that violence as a performance and the memorialization of the performance not only in the visual media of postcards and the textual media of sensationalized newsprint accounts but in the grotesque "souvenirs" pulled from the remains of the lynched bodies.[121] Close attention also has been paid to the audience constituted by the performance, the formal stages of a lynching process and variations thereupon, as well as the role of the spectacle in the vindication of white honor culture.[122]

Little, however, has been said about the relationship of the body of the victim to the bodies of the people who enacted and witnessed lynchings. As in strikes and duels, the extrajudicial violence of lynching involves the conversion of bodies into instruments of what Kernan called "unwritten" law. Members of a lynch mob ran down and personally seized the victim, faced off with or elicited the cooperation of law enforcement, and even stormed or burned courthouses and jails when necessary. Once seized, the body of the victim had to be physically restrained and then dragged by the mob to an appropriate scene – the nearest tree, the scene of the alleged crime, the town square, or, as commonly happened, a tree outside the local courthouse.

In a duel, the participants placed their bodies at risk on mutually agreed terms; in a lynching, by contrast, one body was trapped, physically disabled, dismembered, made an object of torture at the hands of a multitude of people, executed, and then dismembered even further. This radically asymmetrical relationship among the bodies involved was always present in a lynching. It was the central element in establishing the dishonor of the victim, and it became most symbolically acute when lynching shifted from frontier vigilantism and the early Ku Klux Klan tactic of dragging a black man from his home at night and lynching him from a nearby tree, to spectacles attended by thousands.[123] These differences matter to our assessment of violent extrajudicial dispute-resolution practices. Region, race, sexual politics, and class matter as well.

Still, the unifying element in violent extrajudicial dispute resolution practices of the nineteenth century remains the body – the effort, over and over in duels, lynchings, strikes, and other practices to invest the body with the force of law, to inscribe one's view of the legal order upon the body of one's adversary. This impersonation of justice could, of course, have profoundly undemocratic consequences. That is the legacy not only of crony capitalism and white supremacy but of the sometimes quite violent means used by unions to "organize" its membership. The impersonation of justice could also be staged in response to both real and imagined injustices. Only a partial, ideological reading can convert the impersonation of justice into an object of nostalgia. But none of these liabilities, grave as they are, fully distinguish the practices of impersonating justice either from the enclosure of justice, which has its own well documented antidemocratic pathologies, or from the more direct and pervasive means by which the modern state induces docility and "passive forbearance." In any democratic society, all the more so a pluralist one, the paradoxes of popular sovereignty and their roots in the terrifyingly violent practice of revolution always find expression in the practice of justice. We modern Americans simply pay in different ways for the division of adjudicative labor that has relieved us of the burden of impersonating justice on all but the days on which we vote and sit on juries.

Notes

1 Christopher Tomlins, *Law, Labor, and Ideology in the Early American Republic* (New York: Cambridge University Press, 1993), 20.
2 See Bernadette A. Meyler, "Towards a Common Law Originalism," *Stanford Law Review* 59 (2006): 551–600. On the longstanding historiographic debate about commonality and transformation in the South, see Howard N. Rabinowitz, "More Than the Woodward Thesis: Assessing the Strange Career of Jim Crow," *Journal of American History* 75 (1988): 842–56.
3 Nathaniel Hawthorne, *The House of the Seven Gables* (New York: Penguin Books, 1986), 256.
4 Ibid.
5 Ibid., 186–7.
6 Ibid., 185.
7 Ibid.
8 For especially insightful treatment of these issues, see Karen Orren, *Belated Feudalism* (Cambridge, UK: Cambridge University Press, 1991); Tomlins, *Law, Labor and Ideology*.
9 Norman W. Spaulding, "The Enclosure of Justice: Courthouse Architecture, Due Process, and the Dead Metaphor of Trial," *Yale Journal of Law & the Humanities* 24 (2012): 311–43.
10 Norman W. Spaulding, "The Discourse of Law in Time of War: Politics and Professionalism during the Civil War and Reconstruction," *William & Mary Law Review* 46 (2005): 2001–108.
11 Charles M. Cook, *The American Codification Movement: A Study of Antebellum Legal Reform* (Westport, Conn.: Greenwood, 1981); Amalia D. Kessler, *Inventing American Exceptionalism: The Origins of American Adversarial Legal Culture, 1800–1877* (New Haven, Conn.: Yale University Press, 2017).
12 See Spaulding, "Discourse of Law"; Thomas C. Grey, "Langdell's Orthodoxy," *University of Pittsburgh Law Review* 45 (1983): 1–53.
13 George Fisher, "The Jury's Rise as Lie Detector," *Yale Law Journal* 107 (1997): 575–713.
14 For discussion of the drift of power from judges to juries in civil cases, see the dissenting opinion of Justice Black in *Galloway v. United States*, 319 U.S. 372 (1943).
15 On the history of appellate review of criminal convictions, see David Rossman, "'Were There No Appeal': The History of Review in American Criminal Courts," *Journal of Criminal Law and Criminology* 81 (1990): 518–66, 525.
16 Amy Louise Wood, *Lynching and Spectacle: Witnessing Racial Violence in America, 1890–1940* (Chapel Hill: University of North Carolina Press, 2009), 1.
17 Michael J. Pfeifer, *Rough Justice: Lynching and American Society, 1874–1947* (Urbana: University of Illinois Press, 2004), 2–3.
18 Barbara Holland and Peter De Seve, "Bang! Bang! You're Dead," *Smithsonian* 28 (1997): 122–33; Alison L. LaCroix, "To Gain the Whole World and Lose His Own Soul: Nineteenth-Century American Dueling as Public Law and Private Code," *Hofstra Law Review* 33 (2004): 563.
19 Richard M. Brown, *Strain of Violence: Historical Studies of American Vigilantism* (New York: Oxford University Press, 1975), 146.
20 The seminal article is Kirk W. Fuoss, "Lynching Performances," *Text and Performance Quarterly* 19 (1999): 1–37; see especially 5–7, 14.
21 Stewart Tolnay and Elwood M. Beck, *A Festival of Violence: An Analysis of Southern Lynchings, 1882–1930* (Urbana: University of Illinois Press, 1995), 18, 92–3; cf. Brown, *Strain of Violence*, 160.
22 Holland and De Seve, "Bang! Bang! You're Dead." Cf. Barbara Holland, *Gentlemen's Blood: A History of Dueling* (New York: Bloomsbury, 2003), 280.
23 Though not concerned directly with the concept of legality, a notable exception is, of course, the work of Richard Slotkin. See his *Regeneration through Violence: The Mythology of the American Frontier* (Middletown, Conn.: Wesleyan University Press, 1973).
24 Philip Dray, *At the Hands of Persons Unknown: The Lynching of Black America* (New York: Random House, 2002), 4.
25 Walter Clark, "The True Remedy for Lynch Law," *American Law Review* 28 (1894): 801–7.
26 Ibid.
27 Ibid., 802.
28 Ibid., 803, 806.
29 Ibid., 807.
30 For data on the disparities, see Tolnay and Beck, *A Festival of Violence*, 29–30, 102–3.
31 Walter M. Clark, "The Negro in North Carolina and the South, His Fifty Years of Freedom and What He Has Done," Address at St. Augustine's School, Raleigh, North Carolina, May 26, 1920.

32 Decades later, the North Carolina criminal process continued to function in a racially discriminatory fashion. See *Brown v. Allen*, 344 U.S. 443 (1953) (habeas petition grounded in discriminatory exclusion of black people from both grand and petit juries).
33 Thomas J. Kernan, "The Jurisprudence of Lawlessness," Report of the 29th Annual Meeting of the American Bar Association, August 29–31, 1906, 453. Earlier commentators had noted the "close relationship between vigilantism and legality." Brown, *Strain of Violence*, 171. Brown cites an "English observer, Francis J. Grund," who wrote in 1837 that "'Lynch law, is not, properly speaking, an opposition to the established laws of the country, or, is at least, not contemplated as such by its adherents; but rather as a supplement to them, – a species of *common* law, which is as old as the country, and which . . . has . . . been productive of some of the happiest results.'" Ibid., 171.
34 Ibid.
35 Ibid.
36 Ibid., 457–8.
37 Ibid., 458.
38 Ibid., 455.
39 Ibid., 455, 458.
40 And they were not the only legal elites to advocate summary criminal trials. See ibid., 173, 176.
41 See David M. Oshinsky, *Worse Than Slavery* (New York: Simon & Schuster, 1996); Comer V. Woodward, *The Strange Career of Jim Crow* (New York: Oxford University Press, 2002).
42 Brown, *Strain of Violence*, 159.
43 Ibid., 161.
44 David Garland, "Penal Excess and Surplus Meaning: Public Torture Lynchings in Twentieth Century America," *Law & Society Review* 39 (2005): 793–833, 806–9.
45 Brown, *Strain of Violence*, 162–5.
46 Ibid., 166.
47 Ibid., 167.
48 Ibid.
49 Ibid., 148.
50 On lynching and white supremacy, see William F. Brundage, *Lynching in the New South, 1880–1930* (Urbana: University of Illinois Press, 1993); Wood, *Lynching and Spectacle*; Orlando Patterson, *Rituals of Blood: Consequences of Slavery in the Two American Centuries* (Washington, D.C.: Civitas, 1998). On lynching as a partisan political weapon, see Mary P. Ryan, *Civic Wars: Democracy and Public Life in the American City during the Nineteenth Century* (Berkeley: University of California Press, 1997).
51 Frank T. Wheeler, "Satisfaction due a Gentleman: Early Conflict Resolution," *Journal of Southern Legal History* 8 (2000): 1–27, 21.
52 Ibid.
53 Ibid. at 1; see also Holland, *Gentlemen's Blood.*
54 Joanne B. Freeman, *Affairs of Honor: National Politics in the New Republic* (New Haven, Conn.: Yale University Press, 2001), 167.
55 Ibid. at 167–8.
56 Holland and De Seve, "Bang! Bang! You're Dead."
57 Freeman, *Affairs of Honor*, 167.
58 Holland and De Seve, "Bang! Bang! You're Dead." After animosities arising from competition for military promotion in Tennessee broke out between Andrew Jackson and the attorney and former governor John Sevier, Jackson "posted" Sevier in the Knoxville Gazette in 1803:

> "Know ye that I, Andrew Jackson, do pronounce, public, and declare to the world, that his Excellency John Sevier . . . is a base coward and poltroon. He will basely insult, but has not the courage to repair." Sevier countered by publicly calling Jackson a "petty forging lawyer."

Robert P. Watson, *Affairs of State: The Untold History of Presidential Love, Sex, and Scandal* (Lanham, Md.: Rowman & Littlefield, 2012), 175.
59 Holland and De Seve, "Bang! Bang! You're Dead."
60 Wheeler, "Satisfaction due a Gentleman," 21.
61 Freeman, *Affairs of Honor*, 167.
62 Ibid.
63 Ibid., 177.
64 Wheeler, "Satisfaction due a Gentleman," 19.

65 John L. Wilson, *The Code of Honor* (Charleston, S.C.: Phinney, 1838). See also Holland and De Seve, "Bang! Bang! You're Dead," 122 (noting that Wilson's Code was a "big seller").
66 *Rule* 1.2.
67 *Rule* 1.3.
68 *Rule* 1.9.
69 *Rule* 2.2.
70 Wheeler, "Satisfaction due a Gentleman," 7–9.
71 Freeman, *Affairs of Honor*, 172.
72 Id. at 178.
73 Id. at 178.
74 Watson, *Affairs of State*, 175.
75 Ibid., 176.
76 Ibid.
77 Ibid., 177.
78 Ibid.
79 Ibid., 174.
80 Holland and De Seve, "Bang! Bang! You're Dead"; LaCroix, "To Gain the Whole World," 519.
81 LaCroix, "To Gain the Whole World," 511.
82 Holland and De Seve, "Bang! Bang! You're Dead."
83 Ibid.
84 Freeman, *Affairs of Honor*, 178.
85 Ibid.
86 Ibid.
87 Ibid.
88 Ibid.
89 Christopher G. Kingston and Robert E. Wright, "The Deadliest of Games: The Institution of Dueling," *Southern Economic Journal* 76 (2010): 1094–106, 1096.
90 Wilson, *Code*, introduction.
91 Ibid.
92 See Freeman, *Affairs of Honor*; LaCroix, "To Gain the Whole World."
93 Kenneth S. Greenberg, "The Nose, the Lie, and the Duel in the Antebellum South," *American Historical Review* 95 (1990): 57–74, 62.
94 See Slotkin, *Regeneration through Violence*.
95 Freeman, *Affairs of Honor*, 190.
96 Wilson, *Code*, introduction.
97 Ibid.
98 Ibid.
99 Ibid.
100 Holland, *Gentlemen's Blood*, 276.
101 Kingston and Wright, "The Deadliest of Games," 1095.
102 *Oxford English Dictionary*, 2nd ed., 1989; online version, November 2010.
103 Robert V. Bruce, *1877: Year of Violence* (Indianapolis: Bobbs-Merrill, 1959), 57; Philip S. Foner, *The Great Labor Uprising of 1877* (New York: Monad Press, 1977); Christopher L. Tomlins, *The State and the Unions: Labor Relations, Law, and the Organized Labor Movement in America* (Cambridge, UK: Cambridge University Press, 1985).
104 Bruce, *1877*, 57, 62.
105 Ibid., 78.
106 Ibid., 85.
107 Ibid., 132–4.
108 Ibid., 149–58.
109 Ibid., 156.
110 Ibid.
111 Ibid., 157.
112 Ibid., 135. See J.R. Dinwiddy, *Radicalism and Reform in Britain, 1780–1850* (London: Hambledon, 1992), 213: "During the famine of 1800 a sketch of the guillotine appeared on a handbill advocating taxation populaire at Maldon in Essex, and posters everywhere carried messages such as 'Peace and Large Bread or a King without a Head,' and 'Bread or Blood . . . Have not Frenchmen shown you a

pattern to fight for liberty.'" See also Sylvia Neely, *A Concise History of the French Revolution* (Lanham, Md.: Rowman & Littlefield, 2008), 224; Cynthia A. Bouton, *Interpreting Social Violence in French Culture: Buzançais, 1847–2008* (Baton Rouge: Louisiana State University Press, 2011), 62–3.

113 See David Grimsted, *American Mobbing, 1828–1861: Toward Civil War* (New York: Oxford University Press, 1998); Ryan, *Civic Wars.*

114 See Susan G. Davis, *Parades and Power: Street Theatre in Nineteenth Century Philadelphia* (Philadelphia: Temple University Press, 1986); Charles T. Goodsell, *The Social Meaning of Civic Space: Studying Political Authority through Architecture* (Lawrence: University Press of Kansas, 1988).

115 Bruce, *1877*, 104, 149.

116 For examples of the power and influence brokering of railroad lawyers, particularly the conversion of judges into railroad lawyers, see William G. Thomas, *Lawyering for the Railroad: Business, Law, and Power in the New South* (Baton Rouge: Louisiana State University Press, 1999).

117 See, e.g., "The Bosses of the Senate," *Puck* (January 23, 1889), 62–3.

118 Greenberg, "The Nose, the Lie, and the Duel," 73.

119 Ibid.

120 Patterson, *Rituals of Blood.*

121 Harvey Young, "The Black Body as Souvenir in American Lynching," *Theatre Journal* 57 (2005): 639–57.

122 Fuoss, "Lynching Performances."

123 Allen W. Trelease, *White Terror: The KKK Conspiracy and Southern Reconstruction* (New York: Harper & Row, 1971).

11

THE *SOMERS* MUTINY AND THE AMERICAN SHIP OF STATE

Robert A. Ferguson

I. Introduction

The *Somers* mutiny affair, which led the captain of an American naval vessel to execute three of his crew while at sea, usually comes to a reader through Herman Melville's last great masterpiece, the unfinished novella *Billy Budd, Sailor (An Inside Narrative)*.[1] The affair itself mesmerized the nation when it occurred in late 1842 and early 1843. Two legal events, a court of inquiry and then a court martial against the captain, divided antebellum Americans. In fact, the deepest source of conflict is still with us, one reason why history books and articles continue to explore the event on a regular basis.[2]

Melville had an intimate reason for being attracted. His first cousin was a central figure as second in command aboard the *Somers*, but half a century later, in transforming the *Somers* affair into fiction, the novelist emphasized a more philosophical source of conflict.[3] Always concerned as a former sailor about the abuse of seamen, Melville wrote instead of the plight of the punishers, of "that harassed frame of mind," "the urgency felt, well-warranted or otherwise," of the officers on the *Somers* who feared a mutiny in progress and punished preemptively to avoid it.[4]

Billy Budd as a story goes much further. It accentuates the unbounded nature of the punishers' fears, and it makes the mutiny a villain's lie rather than a discovered plot. The nature and legitimate extent of authority is its real subject. The Honorable Edward Fairfax Vere, the captain of the ship who orchestrates the execution of Billy Budd, puts the dilemma of his drumhead court in interrogatory form. "How can we adjudge to summary and shameful death a fellow creature innocent before God and whom we feel to be so? – Does that state it aright?"[5] Well, does it?

The condemned men aboard the *Somers* were not as popular or innocent in temperament as Melville makes his "Handsome Sailor." Even so, the same problem applies to the events of 1842 and 1843. Melville's overriding interest in ambiguity – "the urgency felt, well-warranted or otherwise" – helps to explain why the *Somers* affair can still vex communal consciousness. The affair produced the first sustained version of an uncertainty that would become a national anxiety. When in democratic culture should a claim of national security be allowed to override an accusation of crime against a government official? High-profile trials remain of interest when their resolutions contain an unanswered question. The *Somers* affair did more than that; it raised an unanswerable question.

Such trials, the ones that continue to absorb communal attention, are weakly characterized as political events even though any claim of national security, as in the *Somers* trial, will be openly political. Every trial is political in the sense that the state, along with the accused, is on trial for the fairness of its proceeding. Famous courtroom events are best understood through the characteristics that sustain longevity of interest: first, *a spread of conflict* (well beyond the original legal issue into common parlance); second, *cultural surprise* (a shock that reverberates then and later); and, third, *iconographic significance* (a sustaining visual element through the personalities involved).[6]

The *Somers* trials had all three of these elements with an intensity that deserves explanation.

The spread of conflict in the *Somers* court of inquiry and subsequent court martial was extraordinary even for a high-profile trial. Why did these events lead to such heated, widespread, and seemingly extraneous debate among the public intellectuals of that day? Why did so much of that debate turn on a familial narrative fixated on mothers when the episode occurred on the high seas entirely among men? Why did leading commentators take such counterintuitive ideological stances in exchange with one another, and why did they fight so personally to explain events that reached beyond everyone's knowledge and control?

S*urprise* and *iconographic significance* also apply. The *Somers* affair shocked everyone as the first claimed mutiny ever to take place in the United States Navy, and the central mutineer was none other than the son of the Secretary of War. Excitement over these elements forged a third focal point. The captain of the *Somers*, a federal officer, epitomized strong or weak governmental authority depending on whether the executions had been legally justified or not. Disputes over him grew fierce, with commentators weighing his strength or weakness in parallel with what they thought of the nation's problem and how those problems should be solved.

The United States of the 1840s were still discussed in plural form. They were regionally committed, separate states dealing with sectional strife, threats of disunion, weak political leadership, the growing slavery issue, and economic uncertainty after the devastating panic of 1837. How did one think of the still fragile union? Were the states – with new and very different entities spreading across the continent and clamoring for admission – a loose confederation or a unified nation-state? These questions dominated public discourse, and the *Somers* controversy gave them context and urgency. Instead of a proud "ship of state," the favorite metonymy for nationhood in nineteenth-century thought, the *Somers* had come apart on the open sea.

II. Fact and circumstance compete at trial

What happened aboard the *Somers*? What went wrong there? The first question is one of fact. The second, misunderstood even at trial, raised the nebulous realm of circumstance. These questions should first be separated at trial and then brought together for a court to act. The necessity of an early coming together in the *Somers* case is where controversy flourished. The facts received broad agreement. Why they happened depended on circumstance, and that was hotly disputed.

Fact and circumstance diverged over whether or not the Captain of the *Somers*, Alexander Slidell Mackenzie, had erred in summarily hanging aboard ship a midshipman, Philip Spencer, and two crewmen, Samuel Cromwell and Elisha Small, after accusing them of mutinous behavior. The legal stakes in an overreaction were high. If Mackenzie made his decision to execute the accused beyond the necessity of his situation, he could be held liable for murder in either a military or a civil court, and if you wanted him severely punished, you also wanted him removed from military understanding, where officers might protect their own. Opponents of Mackenzie sought trial in a civil jurisdiction.

The undisputed preliminary facts are these.[7] The *Somers*, a small brig but one of the fastest ships on the sea, was on a training mission for young sailors from New York to the coast of Africa and back, and it was overcrowded as it left New York on September 13, 1841. Built for a crew of 90, the *Somers* sailed with one hundred twenty. Just twelve aboard were officers. Of the one hundred twenty on the *Somers*, only twenty-five percent were beyond their teens, and two of the twelve imputed officers were sixteen years of age with several others almost as young; just eight officers or officers in training, counting the captain, were experienced enough to train younger protégés. Overcrowding also meant that Marines, the ultimate keepers of order aboard a naval vessel, had been left behind. The ship was too congested to maintain the customary physical separations between officers and men. Command structure had to rely on strict naval decorum to sustain order through lines of authority, and breakdown began here.

Although it was not a fighting ship in the most powerful sense, the *Somers* was a well gunned force on the open seas capable of outrunning bigger ships and devastating smaller ones. It had been designed to catch and punish slave ships and tariff-breaking commercial vehicles, which were part of a thriving black market in human cargo and goods. Of course, the *Somers* was also a naval vessel on an official mission. In the age of sailing ships, military standing came through the number and quality of warships a nation possessed. Everyone agreed that the *Somers* represented American honor *and* a gauge in the balance of power with other countries. It would be a national disgrace, as well as a serious danger, if the ship fell into the wrong hands.

A little over two months into its mission and on its way back across the Atlantic, after a stop in the island paradise of Madeira, the *Somers* experienced a noticeable drop in crew discipline with some of the difficulties traceable to the disruptive behavior of Samuel Cromwell, Chief Bo'sun's Mate in charge of administering punishment to sailors, and Acting Midshipman Philip Spencer, who fraternized openly with the sailors against orders and gave them forbidden tobacco, liquor, and money. Both transgressors spoke with open disdain of Captain Mackenzie and flaunted various rules of ship conduct. Both, in point, had been admonished but not punished.

In this deteriorating atmosphere and on the evening of November 25, Philip Spencer secretly approached the ship's steward, J. W. Wales, with a detailed plan of mutiny that he claimed to lead with a number of the ship's company already included. He meant to convert the *Somers* into a pirate ship at the first opportunity. The amazed Wales, threatened with immediate death if he divulged the plan, listened for two hours while Spencer spelled out the conspiracy in detail to make it credible. It is relevant that Wales felt himself under close surveillance by Spencer and a sailor that Spencer had claimed to be part of the conspiracy, Elisha Small, for the rest of that evening and night.

When Wales, afraid for his life, finally managed to get unobserved to a senior officer early the next day, that officer reported the conversation between Wales and Spencer through the ship's hierarchy to the *Somers*'s captain, and Captain Mackenzie pondered the matter for the better part of November 26, while asking his second in command, Lieutenant Guert Gansevoort, to watch Spencer and the crew for signs of suspicious behavior. Gansevoort did notice signs of insubordination and unfriendliness in Spencer, Cromwell, and some of the crew and reported what he had seen. Mackenzie, who had meanwhile reviewed a long history of infractions by Spencer previous to the voyage and aboard ship, decided to face the issue directly after first receiving that recommendation from Gansevoort.

So on that same evening, November 26, with all of his leading officers armed and mustered around him on the quarterdeck, Mackenzie formally challenged Spencer over the meaning of his meeting with J. W. Wales, and when Spencer admitted the conversation but declared "it was in joke," Mackenzie responded, "This, sir, is joking on a forbidden subject. This joke may cost you your life," and he had Spencer arrested and put in double irons on the quarterdeck, there being no secure place aboard the overcrowded *Somers* that might serve as a prison.[8]

The language used in this opening interview is instructive. Mackenzie was already contemplating drastic action, a fact substantiated by another. He ordered that Spencer be put to death if he attempted by word or sign to communicate in any way with other crew members. The captain's suspicions would develop into certainty when a search of Spencer's locker disclosed a ciphered message in Greek, that, when decoded, listed members of the ship's crew for a clandestine venture where some appeared under the heading "The certain," some under a separate heading "the doubtful," and others under a third heading "to be kept whether they would or not." The remainder, including all of the officers, were to be thrown overboard, Wales would testify. The lists and some of the names on them, but not all, corroborated what Wales heard the previous day.[9]

The arrest and ironing of Midshipman Spencer in plain sight naturally attracted crew interest, and attraction became alarm when, on November 27 – with considerable less evidence except for a questioned accident to the top-gallant mast – Samuel Cromwell and Elisha Small were also arrested and put in irons, and two other sailors were flogged for infractions that led Mackenzie to fear a general breakdown in discipline. In further response, on November 28, the captain gathered his crew to warn them that a mutiny had been contemplated and that he "was in the possession of the names of those who were implicated."[10]

Mackenzie meant for his speech to quell unrest, but it had the opposite effect, a twist in events that led many to question the captain's judgment as a leader. Officers and crew alike would later agree that alarm and some disorder among the crew became acute at this point, and it was easy to see why. Who would be next to be accused? By November 30, four other crewmen – Daniel McKinley Alexander McKee, Charles Wilson, and Benjamin Green – were in irons as well. In Mackenzie's own words, "each new arrest of prisoners seemed to bring a fresh set of conspirators forward," and he asked himself a question that showed the depth of his apprehensions: "If the most deeply implicated were ironed, would all the dangerous be in custody?" Fearing loss of control of his ship while still several weeks from home port, he ordered his seven senior officers to meet together to advise their captain on what should be done with the main conspirators.[11]

Meeting that day and on the next morning, December 1, the senior officers of the *Somers* unanimously reported that Spencer, Cromwell, and Small "have been guilty of a full and determined intention to commit a mutiny on board of this vessel" and recommended "they should be put to death, in a manner best calculated as an example to make a beneficial impression upon the disaffected." They at no point questioned or cross-examined the three accused men. The three, each at first protesting in his own way, were then hanged on Mackenzie's order with the armed officers ordered to cut down any sailor who failed to pull on the ropes that executed their condemned crewmates.[12]

In the aftermath, there would be a last element of consensus on the facts. Better order aboard the *Somers* followed the executions as the *Somers* made its way back to New York under round-the-clock vigilance of the fully armed and by then thoroughly exhausted and sleep-deprived officers of the ship. But why was there better order? The question leads back to circumstances aboard ship.

Circumstance molds the facts on the all-important issues of intent, justification, and blame at trial. Controversy during the naval inquiries centered on these contextual issues. There was no question about what Mackenzie did; plenty of questions about why he had done it and if it could be justified. Curiously, among all of the questions raised, one aspect of circumstance remained off limits. The experiment in educating new sailors aboard the *Somers* had failed. It had been benighted to believe beginners in sea life as young as thirteen should learn the integrity of their craft from hard-bitten older sailors and distant officers. The Navy would solve this problem of policy indirectly and very quietly. It established the United States Naval Academy at Annapolis, Maryland, in 1845.[13] Naval education would henceforth be a formal undertaking begun on land.

What is *not* expressed at trial in a forum where all things tend to be exposed is always of interest and a comment on the times. Some of what had happened aboard the *Somers* came from misguided naval policy. Organizationally, beyond Captain Mackenzie's control, the ship had been vulnerable to corruption of authority. Why, then, did no one speak of it? Institutions protect themselves first. Blame of official policy would have implicated the high command structure of the United States Navy, and none of the senior officers who ran inquiries in the *Somers* affair were about to raise that issue. The navy was managing a scandal that already touched everyone in the service. It saw no point in making matters worse.

The willed obliviousness of the naval inquirers shows what trials can do and what they cannot do. If circumstance explain events, individuals, not circumstance, are placed on trial. The officers of the naval inquiry and court martial proceedings could limit the scope of their investigations by narrowing their questions to the circumstances of the moment and calling them facts. Did specific conditions aboard the *Somers*, on December 1, 1842, justify Alexander Slidell Mackenzie's decision to execute three of his crew in response to a conspiracy of mutiny that threatened his ship? In the words of the judge advocate, who confused fact with circumstance in prosecuting the court martial, "whatever may have been the impressions and motives of the commander at the time cannot affect the question of fact, as to whether the necessity did in truth or not exist."[14]

Turning circumstances into facts appears in questions over the uncertainties involved. Could an extended joke about a conspiracy to commit mutiny, if joke it was, allow a captain to designate "three ringleaders" and declare them "three principal criminals" guilty of mutiny and subject to immediate execution in peacetime?[15] When does a ciphered list of names that supports indirect oral evidence of a mutiny constitute an act of mutiny? Did approaching the ship's steward, a petty officer, with a plan of mutiny under a threat of death constitute such an act? Were Cromwell and Small executed through guilt by association? Really hard evidence, evidence beyond the observation of their friendly contact with Spencer and minor insubordination, did not exist as to their guilt. Spencer had even said, in what he thought would be his "last words," that Cromwell was innocent, and Cromwell would insist on it right up to the moment of his execution.[16]

Worse, were the two sailors hanged with Spencer because, as Mackenzie observed, "the three chief conspirators alone were capable of navigating and sailing" the *Somers* without officers?[17] Could you hang three men in order to teach the rest of a suspected crew that they no longer had the means to carry out a successful mutiny? Worse still, how sure could the captain be that unrest in the crew had anything to do with mutiny when it was just as logical for that unrest to be keyed to anxiety over loose accusations coming in their direction? As more and more people were arrested and placed in irons on circumstantial evidence, wouldn't the average uneducated sailor fear he might share the same fate as the first three in irons?

The questions continue. What was one to make of Philip Spencer, the nineteen-year-old boy/man at the root of the problem? Captain Mackenzie did not help his case by admitting on the record that he told the doomed midshipman that "it was not in nature that his father [Secretary of War, John Canfield Spencer] should not have interfered to save him" if the *Somers* took the conspirators into port. Amazingly, Mackenzie added words repeated at trial and all across America: "for those who have friends or money in America there was no punishment for the worst of crimes"; hence, "the best and only service he [Philip Spencer] could do his father was to die."[18]

At trial, the hanged midshipman would figure either as a man or errant boy, depending on whether one stood for or against Mackenzie. Either way, the subject was a melodramatic one. Spencer had previously committed acts that amounted to conduct unbecoming an officer, including physical run-ins with other military officers, alcoholism, and breaches of duty in which he was the clear instigator, all of which would have led to severe reprimands and maybe even expulsion from the Navy but for the quiescence of higher authorities intimidated by the prospect of having to answer to the notoriously irascible secretary of war. Mackenzie had been impolitic but not wrong on this issue. John Canfield Spencer knew no limits in support of his wayward son and would throw all official propriety aside in seeking to prosecute Mackenzie in civil court for the murder of his son.

Philip Spencer had failed to progress in two different colleges, had been in and out of a series of drunken public scrapes, and had even stolen money and other items from his own family. Today, he might be classified as a juvenile delinquent who might grow out of adolescent difficulties. In 1842, he was an officer and a gentleman expected to behave as one with penalties levied if he did not.

But if the divide between man and boy worked well at sea, it became less clear on shore, in court, and in hindsight over the extremity of the penalty inflicted. At least one subsequent account would refer to "murder" of "the high-bred boy." Philip Spencer, according to William H. Seward, Governor of New York, must have been innocent of serious wrongdoing. "I should as soon have expected a deer to ravage a sheepfold." Seward relied on how "friends know our children."[19] What could these words mean against so much evidence of Philip Spencer's bad conduct?

The United States in the 1840s was on the cusp of changes in its thinking about how to raise its young. The shift, slow but inexorable, inched away from the hardheaded vocational apprenticeship of young children at an early age toward a romanticized concept of nurtured development in the home, not in the work force. The plan to educate juveniles through long sea voyages bespoke the earlier vocational orientation, but, as we have seen, the Navy had little interest in dwelling on that educational policy. Commentary about the trial would therefore emphasize a more sympathetic, tender, familial side in favor of Philip Spencer with help coming, oddly enough, from Mackenzie himself.[20] The reasons for that help are complicated and turn on a literary phenomenon with larger implications.

Mackenzie's rise in the Navy had been aided by an ancillary rise. He was a well-known author of naval history and travel books, and these publications won him gratifying friendships with such leading writers as Washington Irving and Henry Wadsworth Longfellow. From the other side of the lists, they made him a formidable enemy in James Fenimore Cooper, another literary titan. The two men had clashed earlier over accounts of the Battle of Lake Erie in the War of 1812. Recognitions within these lofty circles clearly mattered to the captain of the *Somers*. Indeed, they seemed to matter as much to Mackenzie as his naval rank.

Although the charges against the accused were serious ones, Mackenzie could not keep himself from taking advantage of the literary opportunity before him. As soon as he arrived on shore, he wrote out a passionate, highly sentimental account of mutiny aboard the *Somers* with his own agony as the centerpiece of concern. The mutiny became a soaring melodrama in his hands, and we need to understand why. The controlling example before this eager storyteller was an even greater story known to all who thought about ships: namely, the famous British mutiny of the *Bounty* in 1789. That mutiny in popular lore had been provoked by the harsh behavior of the notorious Captain William Bligh. Mackenzie wrote at such length to prove he was no Captain Bligh!

Thirteen thousand heartrending words in all would pour from Mackenzie's pen over his personal distress aboard the *Somers*. All of them were part of the court record, and they would lead his own counsel, Theodore Sedgwick, to lament every one of them. Sedgwick recognized "a diabolical document" when he saw one. He knew it would cause no end of legal difficulty, and it did for both lawyer and client.[21] From another perspective, however, that of the relation of courtroom to community in antebellum America, Mackenzie's account is a culturally grounded text of great significance. His instinctive reliance on the literary impulses of his day opens into the emotional registers of the time and into the shape that legal conflict would take.

The extraneous words of a defendant at trial have artifactual significance for both sides in a dispute, and this defendant's overly expedient account of a presumed mutiny lent itself to diametrically opposite conclusions. Was Mackenzie the kindly, caring leader who sacrificed himself to flag and country in the way he tried to represent himself, or was he something of a fool, an incompetent captain, a poor educator, and an inadequate parental surrogate who lost control of a ship full of youngsters?

Both versions fascinated a magazine readership steeped in patriotic discourse and domestic melodrama. Competing stories make a high-profile trial by occupying mutually exclusive discursive space in advocacy. Only one story can win, but both must intrigue for a community to fight over them with the prolonged enthusiasm that defines a high-profile trial. That happened in the *Somers* affair and continued long after legal closure.

Mackenzie wallowed in stereotypical thinking to explain his situation, and the power of the impulses he tapped would color the legal narrative and shape public understanding. Also in play were a national narrative, a bizarre familial narrative, and a prescient abolitionist narrative. The priorities given to each would divide social, intellectual, and political elites from Boston to the nation's capital with New York City at the epicenter. In effect, the legal narrative empowered the extraneous narratives that overtook it, and for that reason, we begin with it.

III. The legal narrative

The difficulties that the court of inquiry and court martial faced reached beyond law. Neither legal event could proceed on strictly statutory terms or case precedent. Captain Mackenzie had broken military law when he hanged Philip Spencer, Samuel Cromwell, and Elisha Small. The relevant articles of the naval code called for a formal court martial proceeding before anyone accused of mutiny could be put to death. Mackenzie's actions, based on the sought recommendation of his hastily convened senior officers aboard ship, did not meet the level of procedural integrity required.[22] Mackenzie realized as much himself when he wrote "in the necessities of my position I found my law."[23]

The questions that the initial inquiry and subsequent court martial had to answer were twofold, and both turned on a dimension of necessity that required speculation beyond the law. Was Captain Mackenzie justified in hanging his crewmen? If so, and backtracking in ways that implied some procedural confusion, what exactly could justification mean in killing others beyond established law? Mackenzie tried to answer these questions by wrapping his actions in patriotic discourse. "Their lives were justly forfeited to the country which they had betrayed, and the interests of that country, and the honor and security of its flag, required that the sacrifice, however painful, should be made."[24]

Easily said, but was wrapping oneself in the flag sufficient? Even Mackenzie worried about the answer. Just before his justification of necessity, Mackenzie raised prospects to alarm the court and the public beyond the court. The *Somers*, if turned into a pirate ship, would have roamed the seas bent on mayhem and plunder. Fear of piracy dogged the period, and Mackenzie knew how to give that fear maximal effect. In earlier language, he had warned that the conspirators in control of the *Somers* meant to attack commercial shipping and "destroy every vestige of the captured vessels, after having removed what was useful."[25]

The "useful" tag in this statement contained a salacious detail. Most crew and passengers of a captured vessel, like loyal members of the *Somers* crew, would be murdered directly or made to walk the plank, but not all! The conspirators planned "to select such of the female passengers as were suitable and after they had used them sufficiently to dispose of them."[26] Used them sufficiently? Not for the first or last time, females, nowhere in evidence aboard ship, occupied a position of great prominence in the *Somers* affair.

In the face of these horrendous details, could Mackenzie *think* these things could happen, or did he have to *know* they were *about* to happen? Those for Mackenzie assumed the first standard of proof, while those against demanded the latter, but neither standard lent itself to a straight legal answer. J. W. Wales's account of his two-hour conversation with Philip Spencer, relayed through the purser, Mr. H. M. Heiskill, then to Lieutenant Gansevoort, and on to the captain was hardly evidence of an imminent mutiny; it was evidence of the possibility. The message in code found in Spencer's locker was more evidence, but how much evidence and worthy of what reliance?

Alternative forms of explanation beyond the law were needed by both the prosecution and the defense to explain the difference between an overreaction and justified punishment. Did the captain and his officers panic by making a mountain out of a molehill, or, badly outnumbered by an increasingly recalcitrant crew, did they actually stop a mutiny that had begun to take place? A last fact, one of geography, made the question doubly important.

The *Somers* had been more than 500 miles from home port, two weeks sail away, at the time of the executions, but the ship had been close to an English port in the Caribbean Island of St. Thomas, where the *Somers* would dock for a matter of hours in the night just three days after the hangings. Captain Mackenzie did not seek to make the port in St. Thomas before executing the so-called conspirators. Nor did he ask for help from British authorities after arriving there in what he still conceived to be a dangerous situation aboard ship during his brief stop. Why not?

The law could not answer such a question. Left to itself, though, the military court might draw the conclusion that Mackenzie and his officers had misconstrued the degree of necessity and could be found culpable. Why had they acted so precipitously just three days from available assistance? There had to be answers to this question against the naval code with its insistence on an official trial instead of a summary sentence. "The law of necessity" covered only part of the distance to St. Thomas.

IV. The national narrative

Three answers were given at trial to explain why St. Thomas could not provide available succor. Mackenzie and his officers claimed first that the conspirators had chosen the days right before the scheduled arrival at St. Thomas to launch their mutiny.[27] Second, they argued that the ship could not have made port before the mutiny took place.[28] Well and good as claims of sincerity, but these replies merely echoed already questioned beliefs about an active mutiny in progress. Something more was needed, and the need took the officers of the *Somers* further and further afield from law in their third answer.

The honor of the Navy was in question, and it extended easily to the honor of the nation. "Why did you say you would sooner go overboard than seek protection in St. Thomas?" the prosecution asked acting master Lieutenant Matthew Perry. Part of Perry's answer reached back: "[because of the conspiracy] it would be an impossibility to take the vessel into any port," but a more important answer reached wildly beyond the situation. "Because I thought it would be a disgrace to the United States, the navy, and particularly the officers of this brig; my reasons were that if an American man-of-war could not protect herself, no use in having any."[29]

Such extreme logic led to correspondingly extreme replies. The naval judges on the court were just as quick to raise the ideal of honor. "After the discovery of the intended mutiny, and before the execution of the ringleaders," asked one judge, in a question that assumed what the court was supposed to prove, "was the Somers in a state to sustain the honor of the American flag, on the event of her going into action?" The answer? "She was not."[30] These comments and others like them, offered first by Captain Mackenzie, sold well in the military court.[31] Elsewhere they raised doubts.

The code of honor is never really law. Praise for the honor of officers, ship, and nation did not sound quite right against the sacrificed lives of three of its citizens. Nor was that all. Too much talk of naval honor suggested a military court protecting its own and itself. Just how far could a national narrative go in giving a credible explanation of events in court? Certainly Mackenzie was not above orchestrating unseemly use of it. Moments after the execution, when some of the crew had been in tears and while the warm bodies still swayed above him, Mackenzie demanded that all aboard "cheer the ship." "I gave the order, 'Stand by, to give three hearty cheers for the flag of our country;' never were three heartier cheers given."[32]

Today citizens save their highest respect for the military services when thinking about governmental authority, but in the antebellum period, most Americans still feared standing armies, military bustle, and the possibility of a Caesar subverting the republic.[33] The desire for civilian control in a libertarian legal tradition remained strong, and it led to calls for a civil trial of Mackenzie. Those calls would become action when John Canfield Spencer and Samuel Cromwell's widow, Margaret Cromwell, tried to have Captain Mackenzie charged with murder in federal and state courts. They failed but not before a great deal of energy was spent on the controversy in and out of courts of law.[34]

The jurisdictional controversy pulled the leading judicial figures of the nation into the fray. Associate Justice of the Supreme Court Joseph Story, the most eminent legal figure in the country in the early 1840s, thought "the circumstances would form a complete defence for a homicide on shore, in the view of an enlightened civil tribune; *a fortiori*, they would at sea, on shipboard, and under the stern laws of war."[35] Story's only challenger for preeminence in law agreed with him. Chancellor of New York James Kent "delivered an elaborate opinion that the circuit court of the United States for New York cannot lawfully take cognizance of the case."[36] "Military courts have traditionally enjoyed near immunity from the surveillance of the federal judiciary."[37]

Executive authority, in control of military power, remained eerily quiet. The overt antagonism between two powerful cabinet members, with an especially weak president presiding over them, made silence the best official policy. Enraged over the death of his son, the splenetic Spencer as secretary of war fought repeatedly with Abel Parker Upshur, secretary of the Navy, who was in charge of the proceedings in the inquiry and court martial of Mackenzie. Ostensibly over them, John Tyler, the tenth president, proved incapable of mediating this conflict.

Tyler, it has to be remembered, was the first vice president to succeed through the death of an incumbent, William Henry Harrison. He was known everywhere by the withering epithet "His Accidency." "A calculating and devious politician," one always "positioning himself to avoid political minefields," Tyler had been a Democrat who opportunistically joined the Whig ticket to run with Harrison, a war hero, on the winning campaign slogan "Tippecanoe and Tyler Too." An afterthought to balance the ticket and a party renegade, Tyler was a slaveholding Virginia aristocrat who had temporized on slavery and everything else to get to where he was. He pleased no one in the high office that he had so assiduously sought.[38]

Analogies were easily drawn in the national narrative. Tyler symbolized weak leadership in a country without a strong hand at the wheel of the ship of state. The nation as well as the *Somers* seemed adrift. The negative political parallels played well for those who wanted to see Mackenzie found guilty, but they inserted more heat than light into the debate. The national narrative was like the legal narrative subject to manipulation. Both were loudly invoked, but neither brought explanation or satisfaction to a puzzled nation. Enter a familial narrative that no longer seems bizarre when attached to the vexed question of leadership lost or gained.

IV. The familial narrative

Mothers figured with astonishing frequency aboard a ship without mothers anywhere in sight. The key to the discrepancy came first in Captain Mackenzie's narrative of events. "I have no respect for a base son of an honored father – on the contrary, I consider that he, who by misconduct sullies the lustre of an honorable name, is more culpable than the unfriended individual whose disgrace falls only on himself." How far did Spencer's disgrace reach beyond him and to whom? "The circumstance of Mr. Spencer being a son of a high officer of the government" had the effect of "enhancing his baseness" in Mackenzie's estimation.[39] Honor disgraced and base culpability would be touchstones in a familial narrative that carried to the issue of leadership.

Philip Spencer's behavior and the reasons for it were the ultimate puzzles to be solved in the *Somers* affair. Mackenzie's words forced this issue back on the family. If the honored but famously tough-minded father and busy secretary of war could not be held responsible for his son's "baseness," what of the despairing mother who might die when she heard what happened? About to be executed, Spencer invoked her in precisely these terms. "This will kill my poor mother." As the controlling melodramatist, Mackenzie falls away in stunned silence before this appalling knowledge. "I was not before aware that he had a mother."[40]

Really? Mackenzie knew full well of the honored father, and Elizabeth Spencer was an accomplished social leader and energetic hostess on the Washington scene as the wife of a leader in President Tyler's cabinet. In keeping with the familial narrative, Mackenzie staggers back, recovering slowly "from the pain of this announcement."[41] After all, devastation of a mother will always sell a sentimental tale. In support, we have the forlorn Elisha Small, who in Mackenzie's account announces, "I have nobody to care for me but my poor old mother, and I would rather that she should not know how I have died."[42]

Mothers in these and other passages are dangerously frail but mysteriously empowered. The feminine ruler of the domestic sphere was fixed in American understanding by 1842 even if the paradigmatic text that summarized its full connection to virtuous leadership came only in 1847 with Horace Bushnell's "Views of Christian Virtue," an essay and message already delivered many times, even endlessly, from American pulpits. Bushnell "probably the most influential American religious thinker of the nineteenth century," summarized what the nation had come to feel. He wrote of "domesticity of character," where the parent, and especially the mother, presided over "those humble, daily, hourly duties, where the spirit we breathe shall be a perpetual element of power and love bathing the life of childhood." Bushnell saw "the house, having a domestic Spirit of grace dwelling in it"; it was "the church of childhood."[43]

In the cult of domesticity, mothers were the natural keepers of that first church in the home.[44] So how had Elizabeth Spencer failed this her youngest child? Aboard ship, she came to represent unendurable despair by contributing to the loss of familial honor through her child. Her fate resided in Mackenzie's use of her son's words. In the logic of story, Mrs. Spencer would succumb for failing to nurture Philip Spencer in the Christian path of virtue that would have made him the leader he deserved to be.

The epigraph to Bushnell's "Views of Christian Virtue" came from Ephesians 6:4: "Bring Them Up in the Nature and Admonition of the Lord." Then this:

> But suppose there is really no trace or seed of holy principle in your children. . . . [H]ave you nothing to blame in yourselves, no lack of faithfulness, no indiscretion of manner, or of temper, no mistake of duty, which with a better and more cultivated piety, you would have been able to avoid?

Against this nightmare in child rearing, everything followed from "the moral agency of the parent."[45]

Mackenzie underlined his own version of this familial narrative with an accusation adroitly tied to the national narrative.

> I informed Mr. Spencer that when he had been about to take my life, and dishonor me as an officer . . . it had been his intention to remove me suddenly from the world in the darkness of the night . . . without a moment to utter one murmur of affection to my wife and children, one prayer for their welfare.

Full orchestration of the familial narrative came through the pressure of execution. Spencer's life "was now forfeited to his country," but he would be offered the opportunity not given Mackenzie in Spencer's plan of mutiny. "If there yet remained to him one feeling true to nature," Spencer would be allowed to leave proper word for his parents.[46]

What should that message be? Coming in his final hour to an acceptance of Christian virtue encouraged by Mackenzie and only after forgiveness had been urged and offered all around, Philip Spencer intoned, "I feel sincerely penitent, and my only fear of death is that my repentance may be too late." When specifically urged by Mackenzie "to send some words of consolation in so great an affliction" and especially "for any one whom he had injured to whom he could yet make reparation," Spencer complied by completing the circle in the family narrative. "I have wronged many persons, but chiefly my parents."[47]

With these counseled words successfully extracted, Mackenzie, the punisher, transformed himself into the guiding pastor, priestly confessor, evangelical converter, and surrogate parent of the familial narrative. Of course, one goal in this narrative would prove futile. Mackenzie sought to propitiate Spencer's "honored parents," particularly the "distinguished father, whose talents and character had raised him to one of the highest stations in the land." But once again the emotional Mackenzie did not know when to stop his cautionary tale:

> I spoke of the distinguished social position to which this young man had been born; of the advantages of every sort, that attended the outset of his career, and of the professional honors to which a long, steady, and faithful perseverance in the course of duty, might have raised him.[48]

The familial narrative explained the absence of leadership in Philip Spencer well enough, but it ended in waste, shame, regret, and implied blame for the family above him. There was, nonetheless, a nuance in all of this excess. Did Mackenzie realize how this narrative might help the naval officers who, in charging him, also sought to contain a naval scandal? The embarrassing question of a failed policy in naval education could be subsumed. It could be pushed back to the earliest period of character formation, back to Bushnell's "plastic nature of childhood."[49]

V. The abolitionist narrative

Watching these narratives unfold, sometimes sitting on the bench alongside the military judges who had invited him to join them, the renowned New York diarist Philip Hone came up with one of the shrewdest comments on the case. "There is no middle ground in this business; it was altogether right or altogether wrong."[50] Hone recognized the legal polarities against the middle ground of circumstance aboard ship. Mackenzie had to be found absolutely guilty or termed innocent, but his phraseology had other implications. It bespoke the dividing lines in a normative predicament that challenged the nation and entered the *Somers* affair.

The Missouri Compromise of 1820 had created middle ground over slavery while the nation argued over whether its peculiar institution was altogether right or altogether wrong. The compromise prohibited slavery north of the 36′ 30″ parallel except for the boundaries of the proposed state of Missouri. Yet no one really accepted the artificiality involved. The compromise left the country nervously half slave and half free. Soon enough, the ideological hypocrisies in the arrangement would come apart. A temporary solution, really a running sore in the body politic, the Missouri Compromise caused sectional strife to fester into the 1840s, and that strife took the form of growing abolitionist opposition to slavery in the North.

The ensuing political instability explains one of the puzzles in the *Somers* affair. Figures like Charles Sumner and Richard Henry Dana Jr. would normally have sided with the sailors in such a case. Both antislavery men drew analogies between the treatment of sailors and slaves, and Dana in 1840 had published his mesmerizing account of the misery of common sailors under the absolute sway of sea captains in *Two Years before the Mast.* The practice of flogging sailors automatically raised the specter of the same punishment in slavery. Yet both men were among the staunchest supporters of Captain Mackenzie at trial despite his use of flogging as a form of discipline aboard the *Somers.* They insisted that Mackenzie had been justified in his actions, and they rose to his defense. Dana's experience and knowledge of sea life made him an especially forceful and popular advocate in discussions of the case.

Several factors explain the support of Sumner and Dana and that of other noted antislavery figures, such as Theodore Sedgwick, Mackenzie's lawyer, and Catharine Maria Sedgwick, a novelist who wrote of republican motherhood in the domestic sphere.[51] Like Mackenzie, many members of the social and intellectual elite thought Philip Spencer had deserted his class through the "baseness" that Mackenzie had identified. Spencer, they felt, deserved the punishment he had received. "Among the educated people, in the professions, and in what we call in America, the upper classes" Dana wrote Mackenzie, "you were (you must excuse me the indelicacy of a direct compliment to a stranger), a hero, and not a hero of the sword, but the hero of moral conflict."[52]

The move from martial to normative identifications in these words is telling. If there was no social excuse for Philip Spencer in falling so far below the behavior expected of his class, a broader accusation clinched the elite's opposition on more absolute moral grounds. Spencer was more than a gentleman turned pirate. He planned to use the *Somers* to profit from the slave trade. He wanted to subvert the very purpose of the ship, which had been created to prevent that illegal trade.

Nothing could justify these motives in abolitionist thought. Again and again, in recognition of a class opprobrium that reached the issue of slavery, Mackenzie and his officers overrode the objections of the prosecution by connecting the charge of mutiny to the conspirators' interest in slavery.[53] The power of this tactic in a trial that reached a national audience can hardly be overemphasized.

Slavery was the forbidden governmental subject. Congress received over 130,000 petitions calling for the end of slavery in the 1830s, and the divided House of Representatives responded by barring discussion of such petitions in session after session with renewals into the 1840s. These "gag rules" turned trials into an important default forum. Courts of law, unlike legislatures and executives, had no choice. They had to deal with slavery as cases came before them. The contradiction of owning human beings in a democratic rule of law took hold here. Fugitive slave trials fueled abolitionist thought until the trial of John Brown in 1859 made it an overwhelming political force in the northern states.[54]

Here, in essence, was the third and most compelling reason for vibrant support of Mackenzie among the abolitionist elite. The unwelcome compromise and general paralysis in Congress, alongside a weak and detested slave-owning president, caused figures like Sumner and Dana to deplore the lack of authority and action in the federal government. Those against slavery had no reason to expect state action against the institution anywhere in the South, and they rightly feared its spread into the territories. Their hope lay in federal executive and judicial authority. Only a constitutional amendment guided by a strong president would bring down slavery and, in their view, save the union. Not until 1865 would that happen.

Everyone for Captain Mackenzie needed a normative claim that could rise above the suspect argument of necessity, and abolitionism supplied one. Mackenzie's strong action could stand for the kind of federal authority needed to save a ship of state sinking under the taint and divisions of slavery. The threatened rebellion aboard ship had its parallel in the threatened secession of the South over slavery. From a different direction, abolitionists, like nationalists and naval officers in court, coupled their theme to the honor of the flag.

Richard Henry Dana Jr., among others, saw the importance of establishing Captain Mackenzie as a moral and intellectual force beyond his feckless actions and the sentimental story that he told the court:

> [T]his case is one which receives its complexion very much from the character of the chief actor. . . . He has every mark of a calm, self-possessed, clear-minded man, entirely free from that dashing, off-hand or assuming manner which sometimes attends the military button . . . he is more noted for conscientiousness, order and thoroughness, than for imagination or enthusiasm.[55]

A rather different captain of the *Somers* emerges in this description than found in the melodramatic writer. For Dana, any "open defiance of authority," including a temporary refusal of men to muster aboard the *Somers*, "was of itself a mutiny" and the "definition of mutiny." The crisis was therefore real. "If the officers were morally certain of an outbreak," they had to act. Priority belonged to "their solemn duty as public officers, at all hazards to prevent this vessel's becoming a pirate, in the hands of men who would have the power and the will to commit the most dreadful atrocities of which we can form any imagination." As in abolitionist thought against slavery, moral certainty justified action.[56]

Charles Sumner wrote in a similar vein. "It is sufficient, if it be shown that the Commander, in taking the steps that he did towards the suppression of the mutiny, acted in good faith, even supposing subsequent knowledge may have made it evident that he erred in judgment." Mackenzie *thought* he was right, so "*actual* guilt of each one of the three persons executed" did not have to be found. "It seems to us, most clearly," wrote Sumner, "that this is not essential to his justification in any point of view; certainly it is not requisite to his legal justification." Most clearly? Certainly? So certain is Sumner that "we have forborne all inquiry into the guilt of Spencer, Cromwell, and Small, believing that it is irrelevant to the determination of the merits of the defence."[57] How could unsubstantiated and even erroneous belief by the captain of a ship justify the execution of three men? The answer came in many paragraphs, but it could be summarized in two words: national security.

Sumner's version of American vulnerabilities, like so many later ones, sought to scare a citizenry into passive acceptance of the power needed. It culminated in a nightmare vision of the *Somers* as a pirate ship. "Like a baleful meteor, it shoots over the troubled ocean, with unwonted fears perplexing the navigation of the world." "It arrests the commerce of the country, floating on every sea." It then destroys everything in sight. "It fastens upon one of those stately ships . . . the gentle vessel, gay with the beautiful and the cherished of the land, bearing to foreign shores wives in the fresh morning of a husband's love, and maidens the light and joy of happy household hearths." All who encounter the *Somers*, and especially the American woman, become "the pirate's prey."[58]

Mutiny aboard the *Somers* worked on the public mind much like potential terrorist thefts of an intercontinental ballistic missile or nuclear weapon does today. People of different persuasions can be brought together through fear of the unknown. Consider again Richard Henry Dana Jr.'s dread of the possibilities aboard the *Somers*: "men who would have the power and the will to commit the most dreadful atrocities of which we can form any imagination."[59] The claim of national security can carry all before it, including legality. This happens when official language cloaks authority with new power by positing an intolerable risk that is not unlikely.[60]

In Sumner's finale, Mackenzie's acquittal is like "the country's flag revealed in the smoke of battle." The simile demands confirmation of federal authority. "Does any one in his heart believe that the conduct of the Commander was not justified by the circumstances in which he was placed?"[61] Well, yes, many in their hearts *did* question the conduct of Captain Mackenzie.

VI. The quest for certainty

What strikes a reader today is how both supporters and detractors of Captain Mackenzie could so passionately claim they were right amidst so many uncertainties and confusions aboard the *Somers*. Why was the need for belief so strong? From the other side of the case, James Fenimore Cooper dismissed Mackenzie's written defense out of hand: "such a medley of folly, conceit, illegality, feebleness and fanaticism was never before assembled in a public document." Expansive worries supported this angry denunciation. Cooper wrote, "I regard the affair of the *Somers* as one of the darkest spots on the national escutcheon."[62]

How each party thought about the country mattered a lot in disputes over the *Somers* affair. Cooper, an idealistic republican who thought his country was heading in the wrong direction, was an experienced seaman in his own right, and he spent much time and energy using his expertise to bring Mackenzie down. Such were his powers of persuasion that his own negative assessment of the case appeared *with* the publication of the court's decision.[63] As inappropriate as this conjunction may seem today, it had its own relevance. The stark and continuing divisions in the case forced both sides of the story into the official record.

Cooper thought Mackenzie had magnified an adolescent's harebrained fantasy into a full-blown mutiny through his own lack of control of the *Somers*. Authority was again the issue – this time in the poor exercise of it. Mackenzie had been wrong about everything. Belief in a mutiny had been a confusion and failure in leadership. "The act was, unquestionably, one of high moral courage, one of the basest cowardice, one of deep guilt, or one of lamentable deficiency of judgment."[64]

Competing stories remained passionately aloft in public exchange. Either Mackenzie had forcefully put down a major challenge to authority, or he had panicked in his incompetent exercise of that authority. Who was right? Why had command of the ship become so tenuous? These were questions that could stop with Mackenzie or reach far beyond him, but, either way, expressions of certainty depended on extraneous considerations.

Consider two comments from opposing leading intellectuals. "The better opinion is everywhere against him," Cooper insisted, "though there is a desperate effort making to get Mackenzie out of the scrape."[65] Henry Wadsworth Longfellow countered just as forcefully in a letter to the accused: "the voice of all upright men – the common consent of all the good – is with you."[66] Phrases like "the better opinion is everywhere," "all upright men," and "the common consent of all the good" assumed a consensus on normative grounds beyond legal deliberation. Each side asserted a communal cohesion that did not exist. No one could be as sure as they wanted to appear and claimed.

Even the judges making the decision hesitated. If they acquitted Mackenzie, it was on the grudging vote of 9 to 3, controversial numbers that were revealed only after opponents, unwilling to give up the fight, wrote that Mackenzie had been cleared by a single vote. The court martial judges had been a worried group. They stopped short of finding Mackenzie "not guilty." Each of thirteen charges against him received the same meager qualification: "not proved," hardly a sturdy declaration of innocence.[67]

Rhetoricians explain the vehemence in conflict by "the field-dependence of our standards." Opponents often argue from popular cultural positions away from the actual interests that dictate their positions. Reconciliation demands a deeper level of realization.[68] Why did that spirit of reconciliation fail in the *Somers* affair? The narratives employed – legal, national, familial, and abolitionist – competed with one another over priorities even as they came together in changeable combinations. Variations in these combinations led proponents to disagree vehemently, and vehemence moved them away from a similarity of truer interests.

Yet everyone's main concern was arguably the same. Americans shared an anxiety over the validity, integrity, and course of the United States of America in a moment when both the *Somers* and the nation seemed out of control. Disputants essentially fought over what the country meant to them and what it was supposed to mean without identifying the gap between those two levels of concern. Their differences were really uncertainties that became bewilderment and then anger when filtered through the legal controversy. Each side insisted on its own certainties against the fraught symbolism of the *Somers*.

Something had gone terribly wrong aboard the ship, and terms like "honor," "the flag," and "sacrifice" implied a disgrace that had to be met. Where was blame for that disgrace to be assigned? The need to find fault brought everyone back to the meaning of the country and the country's danger. Had established authority failed, or had the rising new generation of Americans run amuck? There was no commensurate answer to questions that raised different angles in national anxiety, and the disparities forced discussion toward a frustrating conundrum. Should national honor and authority triumph no matter what?

High-profile trials rarely ease this conundrum. The law demands an answer and gives one, but the spread of conflict defies that answer by raising unsettled issues in the body politic. This happened in the *Somers* affair, and therein lies a difficulty that applies to the legal and the historical study of high-profile trials.

Legal analysts need to remember that advocates under pressure in the adversarial process will use whatever is at hand. Divisive cultural narratives become tools of exploitation in the legal trade with no limits placed on their use in the desire and need to win. In the *Somers* affair, adversaries reached for rhetorical extremes that trumped commonalities that might have led to a useful public discussion. The unbridled desire for victory through courtroom oratory can divide a country beyond the necessities of the situation. That is the danger in all high-profile trials.

Historical analysts look for something different. The narratives aloft in the *Somers* affair reveal how antebellum Americans used ideas in the 1840s. There may be no better barometer of thought than a high-profile trial that forces a community to debate with itself over an outcome. A comity is defined by the language people wield in conflict with one another. The mutiny became such a concern because everyone who looked at the troubled *Somers* found an equally troubled country on land. Coming into port raised more questions than answers.

Notes

1 Melville, who died in 1891, left the unfinished manuscript in his desk. It was kept with his papers but ignored for more than a quarter of a century and published almost by accident in 1924.

2 See Philip McFarland, *Sea Dangers: The Affair of the* Somers (New York: Schocken, 1985); Buckner F. Melton, Jr., *A Hanging Offense: The Strange Affair of the Warship* Somers (New York: Free Press, 2003). For an exhaustive list of other sources, see Melton, *A Hanging Offense*, 285–91.
3 Newton Arvin, "A Note on the Background of *Billy Budd*," *American Literature* 20 (1948): 51–5. First Lieutenant Guert Gansevoort is the cousin who was second in command.
4 Herman Melville, "Chapter 21," in *Billy Budd, Sailor (An Inside Narrative)*, ed. Harrison Hayford and Merton M. Sealts Jr. (Chicago: University of Chicago Press, 1962), 113–4.
5 Ibid., 110.
6 Robert A. Ferguson, *The Trial in American Life* (Chicago: University of Chicago Press, 2007), 2–3.
7 I take the preliminary facts in this and the next four paragraphs from the two modern accounts of the *Somers* affair: McFarland, *Sea Dangers*, 48–9; Melton, *A Hanging Affair*, 82, 88–9, 103–10.
8 *Proceedings of the Naval Court Martial of Alexander Slidell Mackenzie* (New York: Langley, 1844), 194–7. I rely on the official court record, hereinafter *Proceedings* in the text and later notes. I rely, as well, on a definitive collection of primary materials in Harrison Hayford, ed., *The Somers Mutiny Affair: A Book of Primary Sources* (Englewood Cliffs, N.J.: Prentice-Hall, 1959). All further references to *Proceedings* are given parenthetically in the text.
9 Ibid., 197–8.
10 Ibid., 199.
11 Ibid., 200–1.
12 Ibid., 203, 206–7.
13 For a direct connection between the *Somers* affair and the establishment of the United States Naval Academy, see Melton, *A Hanging Offense*, 255–6.
14 Ibid., 257–8.
15 Ibid., 202–3.
16 Ibid., 203.
17 Ibid., 74–5, 143, 203.
18 Ibid., 204.
19 Gail Hamilton, "The Murder of Philip Spencer," *Cosmopolitan* 7 (1889): 133–40, 248–55, 345–54.
20 For the nineteenth-century transformations in child rearing, see Joseph F. Kett, *Rites of Passage: Adolescence in America, 1790 to the Present* (New York: Basic Books, 1977).
21 Theodore Sedgwick to Charles Sumner, July 6, 1843, quoted in McFarland, *Sea Dangers*, 181, 281.
22 See Fifth Congress, Session III, Ch. 24. 1799, *An Act for the Government of the Navy of the United States*, March 2, 1799, Ch. XXIV, Stat. 1, 24, at 709, 711:

> Any officer, seaman, mariner, or other person who shall disobey the order of his superior, or begin, excite, cause or join in any mutiny or sedition in the ship to which he belongs, or in any other ship or vessel in the service of the United States, on any pretence whatsoever, shall suffer death, or such other punishment *as a court martial shall direct*; and further, any person in any ship or vessel belonging to the service aforesaid, who shall utter any words of sedition and mutiny, or endeavour to make any mutinous assembly on any pretence whatsoever, shall suffer such punishment *as a court martial shall inflict.*
>
> *(Emphasis added)*

See also Sixth Congress. Session I, Ch. 33. 1800. *An Act for the Better Government of the Navy of the United States*, April 23, 1800, Article XIII, at 47.

> If any person in the navy shall make or attempt to make any mutinous assembly, he shall *on conviction thereof by a court martial*, suffer death; and if any person as aforesaid shall utter any seditious or mutinous words, or shall conceal or connive at any mutinous or seditious practices, or shall treat with contempt his superior, being in the execution of his office, or being witness to any mutiny or sedition, shall not do his utmost to suppress it, he shall be punished *at the discretion of a court martial.*
>
> *(Emphasis added)*

Both statutes imply that Philip Spencer, if understood to be merely uttering mutinous words, might have been subject to a lesser penalty than death.
23 Melton, *A Hanging Offense*, 203.
24 Ibid.

25 Ibid., 203, 195.
26 Ibid., 195, 11.
27 Ibid., 42, 65.
28 Ibid., 16, 35, 41, 51, 54, 58, 61, 62, 66, 76, 78, 131, 158.
29 Ibid., 66.
30 Ibid., 56.
31 Ibid., 20, 39, 40, 72, 158, 211, 240, 258.
32 Ibid., 207.
33 See Robin Toner, "Trust in the Military Heightens among Baby Boomers' Children," *New York Times*, May 27, 2003, A1; and Edwin A. Miles, "The Whig Party and the Menace of Caesar," *Tennessee Historical Quarterly* 27 (1968): 361–79.
34 For the full record of legal skirmishing in attempting to charge Captain Mackenzie in civil courts, see Melton, *A Hanging Offense*, 212–17.
35 Charles Sumner to Lieutenant Charles H. Davis, Boston, January 3, 1843, in Edward L. Pierce, ed., *Memoir and Letters of Charles Sumner* (London: Low, Marston, 1878), II: 225.
36 *Niles National Register* 64 (March 11, 1843), 32. See also Melton, *A Hanging Offense*, 216.
37 "Collateral Attack on Courts-Martial in the Federal Courts," *Yale Law Journal* 57 (1948): 483–96. See also Edward F. Sherman, "The Civilianization of Military Law," *Maine Law Review* 22 (1970): 3–103; *Feres v. United States*, 340 U.S. 135 (1950); *Chappell v. Wallace*, 462 U.S. 296 (1983); and *United States v. Stanley*, 483 U.S. 669 (1987).
38 Edward P. Crapol, *John Tyler, the Accidental President* (Chapel Hill: University of North Carolina Press, 2006), 2, 26, 27, 36–7, 56.
39 Ibid., 196.
40 Ibid., 204.
41 Ibid.
42 Ibid.
43 Horace Bushnell, "Views of Christian Virtue," in *The American Intellectual Tradition*, 3rd ed., 2 vols., ed. David A. Hollinger and Charles Capper (New York: Oxford University Press, 1997), I: 363, 365–6, 368, and generally 363–73.
44 See Gillian Brown, *Domestic Individualism: Imagining Self in Nineteenth-Century America* (Berkeley: University of California Press, 1990).
45 Bushnell, "Views of Christian Virtue," 304–5, 372.
46 *Proceedings*, 203. See *Proceedings*, 56 for comparable suggestions of familial leave-taking offered to Cromwell.
47 Ibid., 204.
48 Ibid., 207.
49 Bushnell, "Views of Christian Virtue," 369.
50 "December 29, 1842," in *The Diary of Philip Hone, 1828–1851*, 2 vols., ed. Allan Nevins (New York: Dodd, 1927), II: 642.
51 For the ardent support of Dana, Sumner, and the Sedgwicks, see Hayford, ed., *The Somers Affair*, 75–6, 83, 87–9, 102–6, 117, 129, 163–4. Dana's long letter in support of Mackenzie to Catharine M. Sedgwick on January 11, 1843, was published in the New York *Evening Post* on January 13, 1843. It was widely reprinted and contested. Sumner published his own impassioned defense of Mackenzie in "The Mutiny of the Somers," *North American Review* 57 (1843): 195–241.
52 Richard Henry Dana Jr. to A. S. Mackenzie, April 16, 1843, in Hayford, ed., *The Somers Affair*, 159.
53 Ibid., 26, 80, 90, 91, 112, 113, 152, 153.
54 See Don E. Fehrenbacher, *The Slaveholding Republic: An Account of the United States Government's Relations to Slavery* (Oxford: Oxford University Press, 2002), Albert J. Von Frank, *The Trials of Anthony Burns: Freedom and Slavery in Emerson's Boston* (Cambridge, Mass.: Harvard University Press, 1998), and Ferguson, "John Brown: Defendant on the Loose," in *The Trial in American Life*, 117–52.
55 Richard H. Dana Jr., to Catharine M. Sedgwick, January 11, 1843, in *Richard Henry Dana*, ed. Charles Francis Adams (Boston: Houghton Mifflin, 1890), I: 52.
56 Ibid., I: 55–7.
57 Sumner, "The Mutiny of the Somers," 236–9.
58 Ibid., 239.
59 Richard H. Dana Jr. to Catharine M. Sedgwick, in Adams, ed., *Richard Henry Dana*, I: 56.

60 For a recent leading political figure who worried about national security justification of illegal action, see Daniel P. Moynihan, *On the Law of Nations* (Cambridge, Mass.: Harvard University Press, 1990), 169–77, and [Moynihan] *Report of the Commission on Protecting and Reducing Government Secrecy* (Washington, D.C.: Featured Senate Publications: Y.1.1/3: 05–2: December 31, 1997).
61 Sumner, "The Mutiny of the *Somers*," 238–9.
62 James Fenimore Cooper to Susan de Lancey Cooper [his wife] (January 4, 1843), and James Fenimore Cooper to William Sturgis (September 17, 1843), in James Fenimore Cooper [grandson], ed., *Correspondence of James Fenimore-Cooper* (New Haven, Conn.: Yale University Press, 1922), II: 487–8, 510.
63 Cooper's criticism of the court martial proceedings is so integral that the publication of *Proceedings* continues without a break in pagination from page 263 to page 344.
64 Ibid., 343–4.
65 James Fenimore Cooper to Paul Cooper [his son] (January 28, 1843), in Cooper, ed., *Correspondence*, II, 491.
66 Henry W. Wadsworth to A. S. Mackenzie, July, 1843, quoted in Hayford, *The Somers Mutiny Affair*, 177.
67 Ibid., 243. See also Melton, *A Hanging Offense*, 252, 243.
68 Stephen E. Toulmin, *The Uses of Argument*, updated ed. (Cambridge, UK: Cambridge University Press, 2003), 15, 33–6, 154, and Roger Fisher and William Ury, "Focus on Interests, Not Positions," in *Getting to Yes: Negotiating Agreement without Giving In*, 2nd ed. (New York: Penguin, 1991), 40–55.

PART III

Managing the human

INTRODUCTION

Nan Goodman and Simon Stern

The law tends to express itself in a limited number of ways: it issues permissions, requirements, and prohibitions, followed by rewards or punishments. These expressions in turn help to manage human behavior, motivating people to do certain things and refrain from others. If the form of legal expressivity is limited, however, the implications for human behavior are not. It's important to remember that humans created the laws that manage their behavior to begin with and that they respond to the law and its efforts to manage them in a variety of ways. In the broadest sense, the law offers ethical norms to which people are always responding, by either complying with or violating them, ignoring or revising them, forming creative paralegal alternatives to them or overturning them entirely. On some level, then, to understand how the law manages human behavior, all we need do is to watch people interacting with one another in the social sphere. Yet the law seems to play a particularly salient role in certain areas of human life, areas that are explicitly in dialogue with the law and its system of rewards and punishments, pleasures and pains. The chapters in this section cover those areas.

In Milette Shamir's chapter on privacy we learn how the public face of American law, where legal intervention is routine and expected, has wittingly or unwittingly contributed to the development of a private sphere, where the law ostensibly has limited entry. Similarly, in the chapters by Simon Cole and Trinyan Mariano, we see how one of the most fundamental behavioral functions of the law – to name and define a society's citizens – creates and interacts with the technologies that have over time come to make human identification more difficult and more troubling. Criminal behavior, criminal reform, and the carceral state are, arguably, among the most visible areas of legal management; these are the areas in which the law comes down hard on individuals who explicitly defy its norms, and this is the topic of human behavior covered by John Barton. Finally, in the chapters by Andrea MacDowell and Edlie Wong, we see how the law manages or fails to manage the growth of the community beyond its original borders (MacDowell) or beyond its original population (Wong). In both cases, human behavior revolves around a legal threshold that separates those who are in or subject to legal management from those who are out, or beyond the law's reach. As all the authors in this section demonstrate, however, nineteenth-century efforts to manage human behavior in these terms only proved how ineffective such a binary view of legal management was. In demonstrating these limitations, these chapters also reveal the myriad ways in which the lines drawn by nineteenth-century American jurists for containment and management shifted over time as people moved, regrouped, and reidentified – in essence, did what people always do, exemplifying the moving target that is law and the humanities.

12

THE EMERGENCE OF A RIGHT TO PRIVACY

Milette Shamir

In November 2013, Google's chief internet evangelist created a media stir when he argued that "privacy may actually be an anomaly." Responding to worries about the internet goliath's misappropriation of personal emails and other digital self-expressions, Vint Cerf said that our expectations of privacy are but a recent fad. Privacy has not been eroded by new technologies, he claimed; new technologies actually created the demand for privacy. In the small town of old, "where the postmaster saw who everyone was getting mail from," the right to privacy was never a concern.[1]

These extempore comments were since criticized widely, but Cerf was certainly right in this respect: the right to privacy has a history. While anthropologists have argued that every society marks off some zones as private, the notion that privacy is the realm of authentic selfhood and that its protection is a social priority is a modern one. In many cultures and for much of Western history, privacy connoted the condition of being sadly disconnected, reduced to sameness, lacking in full humanity. The word's origin is from the Latin verb *privare*, meaning to deprive or to bereave.[2] In Ancient Rome, privacy was associated with property and the body, a realm of materiality and necessity inferior to the business of the *res publica*.[3] It is safe to assume that for Cerf's contemporary American audience "privacy" has very different connotations. It is a privileged realm ("privilege" is another word derived from the same root), a site of freedom, unique individuality, and intimate relations. Indeed, privacy is considered a legal right, some claim the most fundamental right Americans possess; one authority famously called the right to privacy "the underlying theme of the Bill of Rights."[4]

When did privacy turn into a right in the United States? Analysts offer different accounts. Those who understand privacy in terms of control over personal information tend to regard its protection as a current issue, a response to the recent multiplication of information technologies and to post-9/11 government surveillance. Others, who associate privacy with domesticity, intimacy, and sexuality, trace that right back to a series of Supreme Court decisions of the second half of the twentieth century: *Griswold v. Connecticut* (1965), *Eisenstadt v. Baird* (1972), and *Roe v. Wade* (1973).[5] Most commonly, analysts date the birth of the right to privacy back to 1890, the year Samuel Warren and Louis Brandeis published a *Harvard Law Review* article titled "The Right to Privacy," which some describe as "the foundation of American privacy law."[6] In such accounts, the century prior to Warren and Brandeis's publication is considered a time when privacy was either not sought after – as in Cerf's nostalgic comment on the small town with its panoptic postman – or so self-evident that it required no protection at all.[7]

In fact, however, it is in the nineteenth century that privacy began to emerge in the United States as a right, though, as we shall see, this emergence was slow and fraught with tension.[8] By the middle of the century, law, literature, and other discourses have begun to articulate and distinguish a right to privacy. Here, for example, are the words of an actual postman. In 1855, J. Holbrook, a special agent to the U.S. Postal service, published *Ten Years among the Mail Bags*, a series of anecdotes drawn from his professional experience. That such anecdotes are bound to interest the readers, he wrote, is because "a mailbag is an epitome of human life."[9] The personal thoughts, delicate sentiments, and small domestic stories that are written down and then "flow[ ] among the privacies of domestic circles" are of supreme importance.[10] Such an assertion would not have made much sense a few decades earlier. For early-Republic thinkers, who patterned their ideals on ancient Rome's, public action, not private affairs, were considered the "epitome of human life." The writing of a much better known postmaster illustrates this. Benjamin Franklin's *Autobiography* (1791) – though written in part as a personal letter and though the words "Private Life" appeared in the title of early editions – focuses almost exclusively on the public sphere, paying scant attention to family intimacies or the inner workings of the spirit. Although, like Holbrook, Franklin understands life as a story – a text with "errata" he wishes he could correct – that story is generated by public achievements.

By the time *Ten Years among the Mail Bags* was published, private life came to be thought of as both precious and immensely significant. As such, it required legal protection. "The laws of the land," Holbrook writes, "are intended not only to preserve the person and material property of every citizen sacred from intrusion, but to secure the privacy of his thoughts, so far as he sees fit to withhold them from others. Silence is as great a privilege as speech."[11] At present, he lamented, law protects from intrusion into a private realm understood only in material terms – property and the body (as in the republican model). But it needs to expand its definition and recognize an aspect of the private that transcends the material. Although Holbrook was likely not aware of this, similar arguments began to be raised in courtrooms as well. In an 1851 trespass case, for example, a New York judge recognized that a remedy would compensate not just for the infringement on property rights but also for "injury, insult, invasion of the privacy, and interference with the comfort of the plaintiff and his family."[12]

Such early articulations of a right to privacy invite many questions. For example, why should thoughts and feelings belonging to an individual not be subsumed under property rights? Does a right to privacy protect an individual person, or a family, or both? And if privacy involves the stories one tells of his or her personal life, why does it also involve the privilege of silence, of *refusing* to share stories?

Such questions were inherent in the modern understanding of privacy from its inception. In *The Structural Transformation of the Public Sphere*, the most influential analysis of the distinction between public and private as it emerged with the rise of liberalism and the bourgeoisie, Jürgen Habermas described the tension between property and interiority, personhood and domesticity, and expressing and withholding the self. The bourgeois private sphere, he explained, came into being as property owners, newly experiencing a degree of freedom in the marketplace, came to believe that this freedom signals also subjective freedom. They projected this notion of an emancipated interiority on domestic space. But this projection clashed with other features of home: its economic function and its role as the realm of intimate exchange and sociability. Moreover, bourgeois subjects expressed their emancipated interiority on paper – eventually in autobiographies and novels, but first in the form of personal letters. "In the age of sentimentality," writes Habermas, "letters were containers for the outpourings of the heart," but since letters are always addressed to an other, "subjectivity, as the innermost core of the private, was always already oriented to an audience."[13] Private interiority, in other words, was created by the act of self-narration, but this act dissolved that interiority's privacy.

By the nineteenth century, modern conceptions of privacy travelled across the Atlantic and took roots in American soil. To better understand the complexities that characterize the right to privacy in the United States, we need to consider the three bedrocks in which it grew: liberalism, romanticism, and sentimentalism. The three combined to support the creation of a right to privacy. But since each emphasized different values associated with the private, they also chafed against one another, producing frictions that persist to this day.

Classic liberalism understood privacy in negative terms. Liberalism grew out of opposition to state interference, and within this context privacy came to be defined as "the right to be let alone." Furthermore, since this opposition "found its best argument in the intertwined freedoms of trade and conscience," privacy came to be associated with both property and interiority. As Michael McKeon put it, liberalism conjoined "on the one hand, the material freedom of unrestrained industry and absolute ownership; on the other hand, the 'spiritual' freedom of unrestrained belief, opinion, and expression."[14] As it entered American political thought, gradually taking over republicanism, liberalism charted the boundaries of privacy around both the mind and real estate. The U.S. Bill of Rights, for example, recognized interior privacy in the First Amendment's freedom of thought and conscience, as well as in the Fifth Amendment's self-incrimination clause and proprietary privacy in the Third Amendment's prohibition against the quartering of soldiers without the consent of the owner, as well as the Fourth Amendment's prohibition of unreasonable searches and seizures. Indeed, these two zones of privacy reinforced and legitimized one another. Liberalism's ideal subject, the "possessive individual," owned the self as he owned his house.

Alongside liberalism, the invention of the right to privacy drew from romantic sources. Like liberalism, romanticism gained in influence in the United States in the first decades of the century. But the two worldviews did not necessarily coexist harmoniously. As Nancy Rosenblum points out, "Liberalism is legalistic. It values regularity, impersonality, and impartiality." Romanticism, by contrast, is artistic and literary. It is concerned with "individuality, spontaneity, and expressivity."[15] While liberalism understood privacy negatively, hiding the particulars of private life behind a "veil of ignorance," romanticism injected the private with positive value. Privacy (for the romantics, the term was often exchangeable with "solitude") is not simply a place where one is let alone; it provides space for the creative cultivation of authentic selfhood, away from society's coercive influence. On this account, individuals are not possessive but *expressive*: each of us is unique, and we require privacy to express that uniqueness against constraints and conventions.[16] Henry David Thoreau, for example, isolated himself in the privacy of his cabin both to explore "the private sea" of his interiority and to express his findings in writing.[17] As liberalism was joined by romanticism, then, the right to privacy was shaped both as "the right to conceal one's conduct, thoughts, feelings and beliefs; and [as] the right to disclose that same conduct, those same thoughts, feelings and beliefs." The former "considers privacy a matter of protecting one's home and one's self from outside intrusions, while the latter construes privacy as a matter of safeguarding, even promoting, liberty of expression and autonomy of personhood."[18]

Further complexity was introduced as sentimentalism contributed its own understanding of privacy. Growing in influence with the strengthening of the middle-class and the conjugal family, sentimentalism focused on the right to privacy of the home. Home, for sentimentalists, meant neither property nor solitude. It meant, first and foremost, a haven of spiritual values blossoming in intimate relations, a haven that required protection from a public realm driven by materialist and egotistic interests. Cohering in conduct books, home magazines, and popular novels, sentimentalism conflated privacy with domesticity. As one magazine writer put it,

> the disposition to pry into the privacy of domestic life is, unfortunately, very common, and is always dishonorable. . . . A family have a sacred right to privacy. In guarding the delicate relations of the household, secrecy becomes a virtue.[19]

The sentimental subject – most typically a woman – was defined neither by possession (as Habermas points out, the domestic sphere's economic function is what sentimentalism repressed) nor by solitary self-expression (which, as the example of the reclusive Thoreau illustrates, draws one *away* from the family circle), but through "delicate relations" with intimate others.

Hence, as the concept of privacy shed the last vestiges of its negative republican connotations in the first half of the nineteenth century, its value was associated with three distinct but overlapping zones: the laissez-faire realm of economic privilege and freedom, the space of authentic interiority and irreducible difference, and the sphere of domestic relations and emotional intimacy.[20] As such, the right to privacy emerged to offer the fullest protection to the subject who inhabited comfortably all three zones: the property owner who is not only a member of a conjugal family but also assumed to harbor a unique and profound private self. Those who did not – say, who refused marriage, or were powerfully subjected to social convention, or had no property – found it more difficult to claim that right. An article in the *Spectator* on "The Privilege of Privacy" made this point, noticing that the poor

> do not live as the richer classes do; they are fenced in by no conventional guards to their privacy, and have no protection against intrusive curiosity . . . The poor have no privacy; that is the privilege of the rich the well-to-do.[21]

In the sections that follow, I look at legal and literary expressions of that privilege, going deeper into the complexities resulting from the meeting point of liberalism, romanticism, and sentimentalism. But I consider also the resistance to and yearning for the right to privacy by those for whom it did not promise to offer much protection.

II. Expressing and hiding the self

Associating privacy with the expression of a unique subjective core, the romantic writer encountered a conundrum. In "Self Reliance," Emerson writes his manifesto of expressive individualism: "In this pleasing, contrite wood-life which God allows me, let me record day by day my honest thought." Privacy allows us to express ourselves sincerely, remote from the conventionalizing effects of society. But Emerson adds that others may understand this expression better than even we can. Emerson compares character to "an acrostic or Alexandrian stanza; – read it forward, backward, or across, it still spells the same thing." Ironically, this simile suggests that, once our inner essence is expressed, it is immediately shaped by convention, since Emerson likens character to two of the most rigid and binding poetic forms. More importantly, he now claims that as a text, one's interiority is always open to an other, who reads it "forward, backward, or across." As in the case of the Habermasian letter, where the sentimental outpourings of the heart that are "always already directed at an audience," the Emersonian character is always already exposed to a reader. "We pass for what we are," writes Emerson. The privacy that ensures the expression of "honest thoughts" is compromised by the very act of expression.[22]

American romantics strove to overcome this tension by developing a style of writing that incorporated elements of the liberal understandings of privacy. As we mentioned, liberalism's negative idea of privacy meant that private particulars are hidden behind a veil of ignorance, replaced by universal abstractions. Romantic writers recreated this veil in language. Nathaniel Hawthorne, for example, proclaimed his refusal to share with the reader private facts about his life, insisting that "so far as I am a man of really individual attributes, I veil my face."[23] In *Walden* (1854), Thoreau likewise sought to conceal his personal life even as he recorded it. While the book's subject is the private "I," not the public actor of Franklin's *Autobiography*, *Walden* is surprisingly silent about details of intimate life, even more so than Franklin's book. Substituting intimacy with intimation, Thoreau designed a rhetorical style that allowed him to write about the private without exposing it. "You will pardon some obscurities," Thoreau apologizes, "for there are more secrets in my trade than in most men's . . . inseparable from its very nature." Writing the private self leads "inseparably" to secrecy, so as to protect that self from exposure to the reader. When Thoreau writes in the next paragraph that he "long ago lost a hound, a bay horse, and a turtledove, and [is] still on their trail," the reader senses that he is alluding to some deeply felt and intensely personal experience of loss. But what that experience actually was is never revealed. To both express and protect the private, Thoreau writes "obscurely," the rhetorical equivalent of liberalism's veil of ignorance.[24]

Thoreau sees the desire to conceal as particular to his "trade," but romantic writers were not alone in confronting the tension between self-expression and secrecy. Lawrence Friedman has shown how staggering rates of mobility in nineteenth-century America meant that self-expression became an important aspect of modern life. When Americans moved from east to west or from the small town to the city, they had the opportunity to build their reputation anew by reinventing themselves in narrative. In the absence of traditional ways of knowing a person – through his family or community – that narrative is what determined social standing. Through it, people could pass for what they wanted to be. "Passing," writes Friedman, "was more than a racial phenomenon. It was a phenomenon of a mobile society."[25] The romantic idea that "we pass as what we are" gained further connotations in a society of self-made men on the move.

For such men, measures for the protection of privacy were crucial. If a person's success relied upon the persuasiveness and coherence of his self-narration, information that could undermine that story needed to be kept private. This became a particularly urgent concern as new print genres developed devoted precisely to the exposure of skeletons in the closet. The newspaper exposés and the urban exposé novel gained the biggest popularity among lower-class readers, since what they capitalized on was often the secrets of the propertied. In 1850, journalist and author George Foster, who specialized in such writing, wrote this about the nouveau riche:

> their fathers made shoes, dug ditches, tended stables, sold pins . . . But neither dares expose his neighbor's origin, for he is, alas! aware of his own; and exposure from *any* source would be certain ruin . . . Not one of these who would not pay, and pay roundly, rather than be exposed.[26]

Some social passers no doubt purchased privacy, but others preferred to take the exposer to court. Friedman mentions the increase in blackmail litigation in this period, pointing out that, tellingly, antiblackmail laws did not punish the transgressor but the person who threatened to reveal the transgression, although it was unclear why what the latter did was a crime.[27] In such cases, the notion that the protection of privacy supersedes other considerations began to surface.

Victims of exposure could also sue for slander or libel; indeed, defamation law is another legal area within which a right to privacy emerged. Courts could not be said to be protecting privacy as long as truth constituted a defense in libel and slander suits. If unpleasant facts about a person can be revealed with immunity as long as they are true, then privacy considerations do not carry much weight. From the first decades of the nineteenth century, however, courts began to reconsider this defense. In criminal libel cases such as *Commonwealth v. Clap* (1809), truth was sometimes rejected as a defense, although not in order to protect personal privacy but to secure public peace (as judges worried that offensive statements would lead to violent revenge).[28] This rationale, however, gradually changed. In *Commonwealth v. Blanding* (1825), a judge ruled against a newspaper editor who claimed in his defense that the allegedly libelous article he published was true. The judge did so, however, not just to protect the public but also in the interest of privacy. The very need to establish the truth or falsity of the article, he explained, would violate the plaintiff's rights. The judge used the standard liberal language of privacy: if a man is "liable to censure for private vices, irregularities of temper or unaccommodating manners, they should be left, as the law leaves them, to the correction of conscience."[29] By the 1840s, the rejection of truth as defense entered civil libel cases as well. In England, a committee headed by Lord Campbell recommended that Parliament eliminate truth as absolute defense, and "from then on, in England as well as in America, judges seem[ed] to increasingly favour privacy over truth, and exhibit increasing empathy to those whose acts are exposed by truthful statements."[30]

Like the romantics, then, liberal courts recognized the need to protect privacy within a culture of self-expression. Like the romantics, moreover, they recognized the connection between the protection of privacy and a specific mode of language. Thoreau, we have seen, used "obscurities" to shield his privacy. In defamation cases, too, vagueness was recognized as a way of talking about the private without violating it. If a defendant's words were characterized by "innuendo," they were not actionable; that is, if the meaning of the words could not be readily understood without the help of external information, the defendant could not be found guilty of defamation. A plaintiff needed to prove the availability of this external information to secure a conviction. Just as *Walden* readers could not know what particular loss Thoreau hinted at with the symbol of the hound, the bay horse, and the turtle dove in the absence of information external to the book, so the reputation of a plaintiff could not be said to have been damaged by mere innuendo, unless it was accompanied by external information.[31]

This coming together of the legal and the literary is illustrated in Hawthorne's Preface to *The House of the Seven Gables* (1852). At the end of this Preface appears a disclaimer that has since become standard in works of fiction: Hawthorne "trusts not to be considered as unpardonably offending, by laying out a street that infringes upon nobody's private rights, and appropriating a lot of land which has no visible owner." The events narrated in his book, that is, do not violate the privacy of any real person. Hawthorne's distinct genre of writing, moreover, makes possible this disclaimer. In the same Preface, he famously defines "romance," by which he means a style of writing that, while committed to expressing "the truth of the human heart," will do so not by "minute fidelity" to reality, as novels do (say, the urban exposé novel or the sentimental novel, to which I will return). Instead, romance is crafted by "fancy-pictures" that are not "in positive contact with the realities of the moment." Truth of the heart will be revealed, that is, but only indirectly, nonmimetically, without reference to actual facts. Romance thereby avoids what Hawthorne calls "an inflexible and exceedingly dangerous species of criticism" – the kind of libelous interpretation that aims to substitute oblique references with particularized contents. Romance, like innuendo, is thus not actionable – it speaks about the private without violating "private rights."[32]

III. Privacy and property

In *The House of the Seven Gables'* Preface, another aspect of the emergent right to privacy momentarily surfaced: its connection to property rights. When Hawthorne likens the exposure of privacy to "appropriating a lot of land" from its rightful owner, he evokes liberalism's connection between ownership of property and ownership of self. His contemporary, essayist Gail Hamilton, summed up this connection: "the law awards to a man the right to his own possessions through life; and the personal facts and circumstances of his life have usually been considered among his closest, most inalienable possessions."[33] One's personal story is a valuable piece of property and should be protected as such. Romantic writers sometimes used ideas of possessive individualism, but they often resisted them in the name of a sacred, metaphysical interiority. Despite the metaphor of personal story as real estate in the Preface, what the hero of *The House of the Seven Gables* will need to learn by the end of the romance is that the inviolability of the self supersedes any property claims. The mesmerist Holgrave has the power to infiltrate the pure soul of his beloved but learns to resist doing so. For romantics, treating the self as property meant its contamination. "Trade curses everything it handles," writes Thoreau.[34] While the value of property is created only through exchange, for romantics the value of the private self is secured in self-contained solitude, by *resistance* to exchange.

In the legal domain, the liberal tethering of self and property was standard. Bound by a long and powerful tradition, judges repeatedly subsumed claims that today we would recognize as involving privacy under the paradigm of property rights. But as romantic ideas of the inviolable self-saturated mid-century culture, a frustration with the limitations of that paradigm began to surface in courtrooms, and judges began to identify a need for a new paradigm.

One area that signaled that shift takes us back to personal letters. As we have seen, mailman Holbrook referred to the events and sentiments expressed in letters as the "epitome of human life"; in cases involving unauthorized publication, judges were called upon to determine to whom exactly these events and sentiments belong. In *Hoyt v. MacKenzie and Others* (1848), the plaintiff, whose personal correspondence was pilfered and published by the defendants, argued that "he alone had the right to publish the letters he had written." The chief justice of the New York Court of Appeals, however, cancelled a lower court's injunction, claiming that "this court cannot restrain and punish crimes, or enforce the performance of moral duties, except so far as they are connected with the rights of property." Although as early as in *Pope v. Curl* (1741), a precedent was set for regarding the words of letters as the property of the author, this applied only if these words had "literary value"; a writer's ownership depended on the letter's potential value in the literary marketplace. Since Hoyt's letters were private in nature and not intended for publication, they could not be protected under property rights. The paradox is that the more private a letter was, the less literary value it had (since it was not written for publication) and therefore the more *vulnerable* it was to public exposure. Something was missing that would protect private contents that do not come with a price tag.[35]

A few years later, the same court heard *Woolsey v. Judd* (1855). The plaintiff in this case charged that the New York *Chronicle* got hold of a copy of "a certain letter – wholly private in character" and intended to publish it. The judge voiced concern that the letter "may involve whole families in great distress from the public display of facts and circumstances," such that were originally intended to "remain forever inviolable secrets." But he was not able to find a basis for the protection of their privacy other than by stretching to its limits the right of property. He explained that the exposure of privacy is a moral issue that has not yet been recognized by the law: "A court of equity is not the general guardian of the morals of society. It has not an unlimited authority to enforce the performance, or prevent the violation, of every moral duty." The judge looked forward to a day when "the jurisdiction is established" for the protection of privacy. But for now, "we must be satisfied," he wrote, "that the publication of private letters, without the consent of the writer, is an invasion of an exclusive right of property which remains in the writer, even when the letters have been sent." As things stand, "[t]he exclusive right, which alone a court is bound to protect . . . is [the] right of property in the words, thoughts and sentiments, which [the] manuscript embodies and preserves." Here the court no longer considered literary value the only criterion for protection, conceding that the privacy of feelings and domestic events is what is at stake. But it had to settle for the right of property as its only available tool.[36]

Similar sentiments were expressed in a much more famous case, this time in England. In *Prince Albert v. Strange* (1849), the plaintiff pleaded with the court to prevent the publication of the royal couples' "Sunday etchings." The defendant's lawyer responded:

> it has been argued that privacy is the essence of property . . . [but] the notion of privacy is a notion altogether distinct from that of property. That a thing belongs to a man constitutes property. That another man should or should not see it is not property . . . it might be well if a rule could be laid down by which the invasion of that which is strictly private could be prevented; but that is not now the law and never can be.[37]

He was wrong to predict that a right to privacy would never become a legal reality, but in distinguishing privacy from property he voiced a timely dissatisfaction with their conflation in liberal courts.

IV. Sentimentalism, domestic privacy, and the strategy of exposure

Like that of the romantics, the sentimentalists' view of the domestic sphere – as a haven of spirituality, morality, and emotional intimacy that requires protection from the public sphere of politics and trade – both drew on liberal ideas of possessive individualism and resisted them. An anonymous ladies' magazine writer, in defending the "sacred right to privacy," warned that "the turpitude of a betrayal of family history by a visitor is far greater than theft would be. The ear is the open market where the tongue sells its ill-gotten wares."[38] This writer concurred, then, with the liberal view that private stories are a kind of property, "wares" that can be exchanged in the marketplace. But she or he implied also that the value of familial privacy transcends the material, since its violation is "far greater than theft would be."

The notion that family life requires protection from intrusion was long supported in courtrooms through the property paradigm. The idea that "a man's house is his castle" has been central to common law for centuries and was given an extra boost by liberalism. With the rise of the middle class and its idealization of family life, however, courts began to uphold a right to domestic privacy even when that right clashed with property rights. This was true, for example, in trespass litigation. *State v. Armfield* (1822) affirmed a householder's right of shutting his door even in the face of the justified property claims of others. Over the next three decades, courts questioned the right of landlords to enter their property without consent of residents and the right of property owners to retrieve it from the house of others without permission, and they also asserted the right of occupiers to domestic privacy even if they were mere tenants or lodgers. "The purpose of the law" wrote one judge, "is to preserve the repose and tranquility of families within the dwelling house" even if those contradicted property rights.[39]

But this thickening of the protective walls around the home also presented an enormous challenge to sentimentalists. Law did not just bar intrusive landlords or nosey neighbors from entering the home; increasingly, it also blocked the entrance of state authorities, even when intervention in family matters was morally justified. If an owner's house is his castle, the liberal reasoning went, then whatever he chooses to do in this castle is his "business" only, even if those deeds are reprehensible or hurtful to other members of the household. Historian Elizabeth Pleck has shown that during the middle decades of the century, many instances of "domestic tyranny" were let alone by authorities, including sexual misconduct, wife mistreatment, abuse of children, and, in the South, cruelty to slaves.[40] Indeed, "the courts were 'loath' to intervene in 'trivial complaints arising out of the domestic relations.' The 'evil of publicity would be greater than the evil involved in the trifles complained of.' "[41] A North Carolina court opined that "if no permanent injury has been inflicted, nor malice nor dangerous violence shown by the husband, it is better to draw the curtain, shut out the public gaze, and leave the parties to forgive and forget."[42]

As a result, often the most ardent supporters of the ideal of domesticity were at the same time enemies of the liberalist right to privacy. If this right enabled the destruction of the family in the name of the home owner's right to be let alone, the sentimentalists' redress was to expose his private conduct to public condemnation. This strategy of exposure was wielded most forcefully by women activists working in the temperance movement, moral reform societies, and the abolition movement. Reformer Zena Fay Peirce summed it up in a speech before the New York City Woman's Parliament in 1869: "Bad morals will exist only as long as virtuous women do not choose to look at all they see, to understand all they hear, and to tell all they know." Reformer Mary Putnam Jacobi called on women to "[l]ive in the open air! A thing that one is not willing the whole world should know is wrong." As William Leach points out, women like Jacobi were so adamant in their attack on the "veil of ignorance" that they came close to repudiating the core of liberalism, the freedom of the private conscience, insisting that "the essence of personal life – its private character – be open to public inspection."[43]

The conflicting desire to protect domestic privacy and to expose it was everywhere evident in sentimental novels. Mid-century best sellers, such as Sarah Parton's *Ruth Hall*, Susan Warner's *The Wide, Wide World*, and Maria S. Cummins's *The Lamplighter*, all idealized the sanctity of home and cherished its intimate relations, especially that of a mother to her children. But at the same time, they also exposed the cruelties of home life to the eyes of the reader. A home that fell short of sentimentalism's glossy ideal lost its privileges. These novels' literary style, moreover, enforced the strategy of exposure. The sentimentalists adopted a mimetic, realistic style of writing, and often their novels were thinly disguised exposés of actual domestic events. *Ruth Hall*, for example, was an autobiographical roman-à-clef that revealed to the readers the abuse inflicted upon Sarah Parton by her family. Despite its enormous popularity, the book was condemned by reviewers precisely because of the dangerous precedence it set for the exposure of privacy. "As we wish no sister of ours, nor no female relative to show toward us, the ferocity she has displayed toward her nearest relatives," one reviewer wrote, "we take occasion to censure this book that might initiate such a possibility."[44]

This period's most successful novel, Harriet Beecher Stowe's *Uncle Tom's Cabin*, told its readers that the gruesome pictures of slavery it offered are facts, not fiction. Stowe made clear in her "Concluding Remarks" that the novel is based on "her own observations, or that of her personal friends"; the "terrible incidents" reported have "their parallel in reality" and are "sketches drawn from life." They are part of a bloody corpus of private facts that, despite legal restrictions, "occasionally force their way to the public ear."[45] This insistence on factuality is diametrically opposed to Hawthorne's "imaginative latitude." While the Hawthornian romance strove not to infringe on anybody's private rights and avoided the conflation of fact and fiction, the sentimental novel made intrusion its agenda and hence adopted that conflation.

Indeed, *Uncle Tom's Cabin* is a detailed indictment of law's failure to protect the weak because of its liberal reasoning. Cruel slave owners rebuff interventionary attempts by saying: "I know my own business, sir . . . It's a free country, sir."[46] Even benevolent slave holders assume that proprietary privacy supersedes ethical obligation. Commenting on the torture and murder of a female slave, one Southerner explains: "the best we can do is to shut our eyes and ears, and let it alone . . . If we are to be prying and spying into all the dismals of life, we should have no heart to anything."[47] The slaves themselves recognize law's unscrupulous withdrawal from the private sphere: "[n]ot a white person here, who could testify, if you were burned alive . . . There's no law here, of God or man, that can do you . . . the least good."[48]

But where law fails, the sentimental novel steps in to issue a corrective. If the slave owner cannot be brought to justice, he certainly can be judged in fiction. It was not quite surprising, then, that this strategy earned Stowe the threat of a lawsuit. One of the supporters of slavery that she mentioned in *Uncle Tom's Cabin* was Dr. Joel Parker, a Philadelphia Presbyterian minister. Parker's reaction was to threaten her with a $20,000 libel suit, charging her: "After painting a scene of shocking inhumanity you hold me up to the public, in an odious light, by representing me as uttering sentiments that seem to justify or, at least to palliate the cruelties which you have described." Stowe's reaction was typical of the strategy of exposure. While she (rather ironically) pleaded the feminine obligation to remain silent in public, in her next novel she included the unpleasant character of Dr. Packthread, a thinly disguised portrait of Dr. Parker, in revenge. "While other people look upon words as vehicles for conveying ideas," she wrote, "Dr. Packthread regarded them only as mediums for concealment. His constant study, on every controverted topic, was to adjust language that, with the appearance of the utmost precision, it should always be capable of a double interpretation." Stowe's criticism of Dr. Packthread's language of concealment captures the epistemological difference between sentimental and romantic genres of writing and positions on privacy. While the latter often used language to "conceal" and create "double interpretation," thus producing regions of protective privacy, the sentimental novel used mimesis to deny any fallible man's right to be let alone.[49]

As it met and at times confronted liberal and romantic notions of privacy, the sentimentalist position gave rise to some disturbing questions. For one, if only perfectly regulated families and morally impeccable subjects can claim the right to privacy, why is that right needed at all? In Stowe's novel, the one domestic interior that truly deserves to be let alone is the Quaker home, ruled by a pure and angelic matriarch. Ironically, then, privacy is the reward of those who would never claim its protection, since their closets are clean of skeletons. Here sentimentalism's distance from romanticism is salient. The romantic subject desires personal privacy to cultivate his uniqueness unthreatened by social convention; the sentimental subject is conventional through and through: there is nothing unique or particular about the female paragon of virtue, and it is precisely her conforming to the conventions of the domestic ideal that makes her deserving of the right to be let alone. But that domestic ideal renders personal privacy superfluous, since the sentimental subject exists only in the context of intimate family relations.

Moreover, if in sentimentalism it is the virtuous woman who deserves the protection of personal privacy, by the very act of claiming that protection, she risks undermining her virtue (recall reformer Jacobi's claim that "a thing that one is not willing the whole world should know is wrong"). Lawrence Friedman's discussion of breach of promise and seduction laws illustrates this. Within these two types of lawsuits, women could be compensated for romantic and sexual exploitation by men, despite liberalism's withdrawal from the private domain, but this compensation depended on the women's perception as "chaste" by the courts. Without an unblemished reputation, a woman could not claim to have suffered a loss by being seduced. But the fact that a plaintiff was willing to expose herself in a public courtroom in itself threatened to undermine her reputation. A letter in *Ladies' Magazine and Literary Gazette* explained: "Law it is true provides against breaches of promise; but shall the shrinking delicacy of woman, lay open the inmost recesses of her heart before a court of Justice?"[50] Once again, if under sentimentalism the morally pure woman is most deserving of protection, her mere seeking of that protection could imply that she is not, in fact, morally pure.

In light of such complications, sentimentalists sometimes ended up wishing for the kind of privacy that liberalism envisioned, the very type of privacy they frequently deplored. As *Uncle Tom's Cabin* illustrates, sentimentalists occasionally used liberal formulations to argue for the extension of full humanity to African Americans, women, other excluded subjects. Stowe recognized, for instance, that in order to turn a slave from property to person, she needs to turn him into a *proprietor* and that to qualify as a free human being, he needs a space in which to be let alone. As one of her deserving slaves put it, being in bondage means that he has "not a cent of money, nor a roof to cover [him], nor a spot of land to call [his] own" and what he most yearns for "is to be let alone" in a house of his own (which, at the end of the book, he gets).[51]

Such longing for privacy is found also in mid-century African American writing. In the context of the abolitionist movement, the private experience of the slave was turned into narrative and used as one of the most powerful tool in the movement's arsenal. But these slave narratives, although based on autobiographical fact, cannot be read in romantic terms – in the terms, say, *Walden* is read – as the authentic expression of a unique interiority. Nor do they fall under the liberal paradigm of story-as-inalienable property. Heavily edited and rigidly conventionalized by abolitionist editors, these narratives were cleansed of much of their particularized contents and then used as currency in the political marketplace. African American writing sometimes allude to this problem of self-alienation and expresses a yearning for the kind of privileged privacy that propertied whites enjoy. Harriet Wilson's *Our Nig* (1859) includes a minor African American character who makes a living by pretending to be an escaped slave, peddling his narrative around the country, much like the white man-on-the-make who constructs an autobiography for profit and success. This character claims for himself ownership of a narrative that typically the abolitionists would appropriate. In *Incidents in the Life of a Slave Girl* (1861), Harriet Jacobs finds relief from both the sexual advances of her master (shielded by the privacy of his home) and from the sentimental conventions of female chastity by constructing what she calls a "loophole of retreat," an actual space of hiding that also symbolizes her right to privacy. In the "Heroic Slave" (1852), Frederick Douglass adopts techniques of representation similar to Thoreau's and Hawthorne's to create a space of privacy for his protagonist. While the novella begins with the slave displaying his conventionally moral interiority to a white abolitionist, by the end he retreats into obscurity, the narrator shielding him from the reader by refusing to expose his thoughts or feelings any longer.

Like their African American counterparts, white, middle-class woman writers sometimes expressed a wish for the kind of privileged privacy we have been associating with romanticism and liberalism. As we have seen, sentimental ideology both linked women with the private sphere and deprived them of meaningful privacy. Some women responded by asking for a room of their own (decades before Virginia Woolf did). An article in *The Lady's Repository* observed that in the typical family the son has "his room . . . his sanctum, and mothers or sisters hesitate to break in upon [his] privacy" and wondered "where is the corresponding privacy in most girls' lives?"[52] Charlotte Perkins Gilman complained that

> such privacy as we have at home is family privacy, an aggregate privacy, and this does not insure – indeed, it prevents – individual privacy . . . the home is the one place on earth where no one of the component individuals can have any privacy . . . this affects women more than men, because men live very little in the family and very much in the world.[53]

By the time the nineteenth century drew to a close, such claims to privacy by those long excluded from its privileges were heard in the highest courts. In *DeMay v. Roberts* (1881), a woman from an economically modest background sued her physician for allowing his friend, who was not a doctor, to accompany him into her home as she was giving birth. While the two men's lawyers argued that their conduct broke no existing law and that they should not be legally charged for actions "involving solely the question of taste or propriety," the Michigan Supreme Court stated that the "plaintiff had a legal right to the privacy of her apartment at such a time."[54] This was the earliest legal case to name explicitly the right to privacy as the basis for a conviction. Importantly, Caroline Danielson has shown that the woman was seen as deserving the protection of privacy based not on sentimental notions of female chastity (as in seduction and breach of promise litigations) but rather on the romantic notion of "authentic experience," now extended to encompass a lower-class woman's interiority.[55]

Less success was met by the African American Homer Plessy in the landmark *Plessy v. Ferguson* (1896). Lawyer and civil rights activist Albion W. Tourgée based his justification of his client's violation of the Louisiana code of segregation on the liberal equation of selfhood and property. By passing as white, he claimed, Plessy constructed a reputation for himself, one that has material value. The officer who arrested him for using a whites-only train coach, exposed his black origins and thereby deprived Plessy of (self) property. Tourgée thus claimed for Plessy the privileges we have discussed earlier as those of the mobile white man, who "passes" by constructing a profitable autobiography. Unlike the latter, though, Plessy could not claim the right to conceal personal facts that interfered with his reputation. The U.S. Supreme Court rejected Tourgée's argument, ironically by confirming its basis – the equation of reputation with property. Plessy was regarded by the court as a thief "since he is not lawfully entitled to the reputation of being a white man." The freedom of self-expression and the privileges of self-concealment, the court ruled, did not cross the color line.[56]

By the time Warren and Brandies published "The Right to Privacy," then, this concept has been evoked, discussed, and debated in the United States for decades. Rather than creating a new right, as they are sometimes credited with having done, the pair may be said to have brilliantly combined the various approaches to privacy we have discussed here. Their article pulled together rhetorical strands from the liberal, romantic, and sentimental archives. They pointed out that "[t]he common law has always recognized a man's house as his castle, impregnable, often, even to its own officers engaged in the execution of its commands" and equated privacy with "the right to be let alone."[57] But they also evoked the sentimental context, arguing that "a man's family relations became a part of the legal conception of his life"[58] and pausing on examples drawn from domesticity. They echoed romanticism in arguing that "[t]he principle which protects . . . personal productions," is "in reality not the principle of private property, but that of an inviolate personality."[59] By "personal productions" Warren and Brandeis referred explicitly to written texts and works of art; and, indeed, throughout the article the right to privacy is inextricably tied to nineteenth-century law cases involving unauthorized publication of the kind we have surveyed. They made explicit that what should be protected in a letter is not the literary value of the text but "the domestic occurrence" reported in it.[60] They detached the private contents of a letter from its material aspect and argued that rights be given not to the writer or publisher but to the person or family whose private life it depicted. This is the right to privacy that Holbrook and his contemporaries wished for in 1855.

If this article is indeed "the foundation of American privacy law," then this foundation is impressively wide but also somewhat shaky. Warren and Brandeis bequeathed to the twentieth century a legal right that rests on multiple philosophical and cultural traditions and therefore harbors tensions that have not been resolved in over a hundred and twenty years. Legal scholars still debate, for instance, whether the right to privacy is distinct from property rights, whether it is indeed relevant to issues involving of intimacy and sexuality, and whether what privacy protects is our self-expressions or our silences. In the age of Gmail and Facebook, the latter question is especially unavoidable. Our digital lives are marked by constant self-narration, as the letters of old have transformed into emails, blogs, and tweets. The current obsession with telling our personal story and attendant anxiety over that story's vulnerability and alienability predates Google, as we have seen, by two centuries; our demands for privacy are not, *pace* Vint Cerf, an "anomaly" at all. Most of us can still identify with the words of the nineteenth-century author who wrote: "betwixt the love of hearing on the one side, and the love of telling on the other, small space remains on which one may adventure to set the sole of his foot and feel safe from the spoiler."[61]

Notes

1 "Google's Chief Internet Evangelist Says 'Privacy May Actually Be an Anomaly'," last modified November 20, 2013, http://www.theverge.com/2013/11/20/5125922/vint-cerf-google-internet-evangelist-says-privacy-may-be-anomaly.
2 Ferdinand D. Schoeman, *Privacy and Social Freedom* (Cambridge, UK: Cambridge University Press, 1992), 116.
3 See discussion of Arendt's *The Human Condition* in Bonnie Honig, "Toward an Agonistic Feminism: Hannah Arendt and the Politics of Identity," in *Feminism, the Public and the Private*, ed. Joan Landes (New York: Oxford University Press, 1998) 100–32.
4 Quoted in Mary A. Glendon, *Rights Talk: The Impoverishment of Political Discourse* (New York: The Free Press, 1991), 56.
5 *Griswold v. Connecticut*, 381 U.S. 479 (1965), ruled that the Constitution protected a right to privacy in a case involving a married couple use of contraceptives; *Eisenstadt v. Baird*, 405 U.S. 438 (1972), extended the same rights to unmarried couples; *Roe v. Wade*, 410 U.S. 113 (1973), applied the right to privacy to a woman's decision to have an abortion.
6 Samuel Warren and Louis Brandeis, "The Right to Privacy: [The implicit made explicit]," in *Philosophical Dimensions of Privacy*, ed. Ferdinand Schoeman (Cambridge, UK: Cambridge University Press, 1984), 74–103. The quote is Neil M. Richards' from "The Puzzle of Brandeis, Privacy, and Speech," *Vanderbilt Law Review* 63 (2010): 1295–352.
7 Among those who argue that the nineteenth century was blessed with privacy are Rochelle Gurstein, *The Repeal of Reticence* (New York: Hill & Wang, 1996), e.g., 32.
8 A detailed discussion of nineteenth-century legal cases involving the right to privacy can be found in "The Right to Privacy in Nineteenth Century America," *Harvard Law Review* 94 (1981): 1892–910.
9 James Holbrook, *Ten Years among the Mail Bags; Or, Notes from the Diary of a Special Agent of the Post Office Department* (Philadelphia: Cowperthwait, 1855), xv.
10 Ibid., xvii.
11 Ibid., xviii.
12 *Ives v. Humphrey*, 1 E.D. Smith 196, 201–02 (N.Y. Ct. C.P. 1851).
13 Jürgen Habermas, *The Structural Transformation of the Public Sphere: An Inquiry into a Category of Bourgeois Society*, trans. Thomas Burger (Cambridge, Mass.: MIT University Press, 1992), 49. For an excellent analysis of Habermas's description of the private sphere, see Elizabeth M. Dillon, *The Gender of Freedom: Fictions of Liberalism and the Literary Public Sphere* (Stanford, CA: Stanford University Press, 2004), chap. 1.
14 Both quotes are from Michael McKeon, *The Secret History of Domesticity: Public, Private, and the Division of Knowledge* (Baltimore: Johns Hopkins University Press, 2005), 49.
15 Nancy L. Rosenblum, *Another Liberalism: Romanticism and the Reconstruction of Liberal Thought* (Cambridge, Mass.: Harvard University Press, 1987), 2, 103.
16 The term "expressive individualism" was coined by Robert N. Bellah, Richard Madsen, William M. Sullivan, Ann Swidler, and Steven M. Tipton in *Habits of the Heart: Individualism and Commitment in American Life* (Berkeley: University of California Press, 1985); it was recently taken up by Charles Taylor in *A Secular Age* (Cambridge, Mass.: Harvard University Press, 2007), 473–95. Both works are interested in the term in a contemporary society, but both trace its roots back to romanticism.
17 Henry David Thoreau, *Henry David Thoreau: A Week, Walden, etc.* (New York: Library of America, 1985), 578.
18 Jeffrey Insko, "The Logic of Left Alone: *The Pioneers* and the Conditions of US Privacy," *American Literature* 81 (2009): 664; Insko discusses here recent privacy cases, but he goes on to trace this duality to the nineteenth century.
19 "The Family Circle," *Ladies' Repository* 30 (n.s. 4) (1869): 393–5, 394.
20 See Seyla Benhabib, "Models of Public Space: Hannah Arendt, the Liberal Tradition, and Jürgen Habermas," in *Feminism, the Public and the Private*, ed. Joan B. Landes, 65–99, 86–7.
21 "The Privilege of Privacy," *The Spectator* (November 19, 1892), 29–30, 29.
22 Ralph Waldo Emerson, "Self-Reliance," in *Emerson: Essays and Lectures* (New York: Library of America, 1983), 266. For an analysis of this passage in relation to privacy, see John P. Schlueter, "Private Practices: Washington Irving, Ralph Waldo Emerson, and the Recovery of Possibility," *Nineteenth-Century Literature* 66 (2011): 283–306, 302.
23 Nathaniel Hawthorne, "The Old Manse: The Author Makes the Reader Acquainted with His Abode," in *Nathaniel Hawthorne: Tales and Sketches, etc.* (New York: Library of America, 1982), 1143.
24 Thoreau, *Walden*, 336.

25 Lawrence M. Friedman, *Guarding Life's Dark Secrets: Legal and Social Controls over Reputation, Propriety, and Privacy* (Stanford, CA: Stanford University Press, 2007), 77.
26 George Foster, *Celio or, New York Above Ground and Under Ground* (New York: Dewitt and Davenport, 1850), 49.
27 Friedman, *Guarding Life's Dark Secrets*, chap. 5.
28 *Commonwealth v. Clap*, 4 Mass. 163, 169 (1809).
29 *Commonwealth v. Blanding*, 20 Mass. (3 Pick.) 304 (1825).
30 Diane L. Zimmerman, "Requiem for a Heavyweight: A Farewell to Warren and Brandeis's Privacy Tort," *Cornell Law Review* 68 (1983): 292–302.
31 See, for example, *McCuen v. Ludlum*, 17 N.J.L. 12 (1839).
32 Nathaniel Hawthorne, *Collected Novels* (New York: Library of America, 1983), 351–3.
33 Gail Hamilton, "The New School of Biography," in *Skirmishes and Sketches* (Boston: Ticknor and Fields, 1865), 332.
34 Thoreau, *Walden*, 378. On the complex relation of American romantic authors to the free market, see Michael T. Gilmore, *American Romanticism and the Marketplace* (Chicago: University of Chicago Press, 1985).
35 *Hoyt v. MacKenzie*, 3 Barb. Ch. 320, 324–5 (N.Y. Ch. 1848). This and the following court case are described in detail in Morris L. Ernst and Alan U. Schwartz, *Privacy: The Right to Be Let Alone* (New York: Macmillan, 1962), 24–43.
36 *Woolsey v. Judd*, 11 How. Pr. 49 (N.Y. Sup. Ct. 1855).
37 *Albert v. Strange* (1849) 64 Eng. Rep. 293, 306, quoted in Ernst and Schwartz, *Privacy*, 12.
38 "The Family Circle," 394.
39 *State v. Armfield*, 9 N.C. (2 Hawks) 246, 247 (1822); *Wien v. Simpson*, 2 Phila. 158, 158–9 (Pa. Dist. Ct. 1857); *Hobbs v. Geis*, 13 Serg. & Rawl. 417, 418–9 (Pa. 1826); *Ilsley v. Nichols*, 29 Mass. (12 Pick.) 270, 277 (1832); *Oystead v. Shed*, 13 Mass. 520, 523 (1816). The quote is from the latter.
40 Elizabeth Pleck, *Domestic Tyranny: The Making of Social Policy against Family Violence* (New York: Oxford University Press, 1987).
41 Friedman, *Guarding Life's Dark Secrets*, 70.
42 Maryhelen C. Harmon, "Soul Murder and Other Crimes of the Heart: Familial Abuse in Nathaniel Hawthorne's Fictional Psychodramas," in *The Aching Hearth: Family Violence in Life and Literature*, ed. Sara Munson Deats and Lagretta Tallent Lenker (New York: Insight Books, 1991), 119–34, 122.
43 Both quotes are from William Leach, *True Love and Perfect Union: The Feminist Reform of Sex and Society* (New York: Basic Books, 1980), 40–3.
44 Reviews of *Ruth Hall* are quoted and discussed in Joyce W. Warren's "Introduction," to *Ruth Hall and Other Writing*, ed. Fanny Fern and Joyce W. Warren (New Brunswick, N.J.: Rutgers University Press, 1986), ix–xvii.
45 Harriet Beecher Stowe, *Uncle Tom's Cabin or, Life among the Lowly* (1852; New York: Library of America, 1982), 511.
46 Ibid., 25.
47 Ibid., 259.
48 Ibid., 419–20.
49 For a discussion of the Parker controversy see Joan D. Hedrick, *Harriet Beecher Stowe: A Life* (Oxford: Oxford University Press, 1994), 225–30, 261.
50 Quoted in Friedman, *Guarding Life's Dark Secrets*, 116.
51 Stowe, *Uncle Tom's Cabin*, 220–3.
52 "The Education of Girls," *Ladies' Repository* 2 (1868): 40.
53 Quoted in Anita L. Allen, *Uneasy Access: Privacy for Women in a Free Society* (Totowa, N.J.: Rowman and Littlefield, 1988), 84.
54 *De May v. Roberts*, 46 Mich. 160, 165 (1881).
55 Caroline Danielson, "The Gender of Privacy and the Embodied Self: Examining the Origins of the Right to Privacy in US Law," *Feminist Studies* 25 (1999): 311–44.
56 Amy Robinson, "Forms of Appearance and Value: Homer Plessy and the Politics of Privacy," in *Performance and Cultural Politics*, ed. Elin Diamond (London: Routledge, 1996), 237–61.
57 Warren and Brandeis, "The Right to Privacy," 74.
58 Ibid., 75–6.
59 Ibid., 82.
60 Ibid., 79.
61 Hamilton, "The New School," 331.

13
THE SCIENCE OF IDENTITY

Simon A. Cole

In 1892, a Washington, D.C.–based attorney named George E. Harris published a four-hundred-some-odd-page *Treatise on the Law of Identification.*[1] While there are many famous treatises on the law of evidence and on medico-legal matters more generally, Harris's appears to be the only nineteenth-century American legal treatise specifically on the law of identification. Harris seemed aware of this, as he subtitled his work *A Separate Branch of the Law of Evidence.* Indeed, Aubrey Moriarty, the British author of short pamphlet on the subject, noted that identification was "a subject of considerable difficulty, and which has hitherto received less attention, than from its importance, it would seem to merit. I have been unable to discover any substantive Essay or Treatise in any modern language upon the subject."[2] Moriarty went on to claim that "[i]n the whole range of judicial inquiry there is notoriously no class of cases with which courts of justice have so much difficulty dealing" and that

> [i]t is only in reference to this class of cases that large sections of society fling aside their habitual reverence for the law, and those entrusted with its administration, and refuse to subordinate their personal convictions to the judgments of judges or the findings of juries.[3]

The resulting compilation reads to modern eyes as a somewhat incongruous, perhaps even Borgesian hodgepodge of topics. Harris's treatise covers the identification of both persons and things and therefore ranges from murder cases to real estate disputes (333) to the identification of patented articles (447). The treatise also contains a number of other legal topics, such as the reversal of felony convictions because of typographical errors in stating the names of the victims (97), disputes over the identity of horses and other livestock based on written descriptions of their color (357), and the bringing of a dog into court to assist the jury "in judging of his temper and disposition" (386). Another issue is the compulsory examinations: the inspection of the body of a defendant for tattoo marks (410) and the compulsory placement of the defendant's foot in footprints (413–14). Another is nonexpert testimony:

> as to the identity (in the case of murder) of the accused and the deceased; as to the identity of a pamphlet, in a case of slander; as to dangers of fire insurance; as to dangers in a railroad car; as to benefit to result from the construction of a ditch; as to comparison

> of footprints; as to the agility and power of fish to resist the ascent of a stream; as to the health of a slave.
>
> *(121)*

As to the identity of persons, the means of identification of persons discussed range widely. They include the identification of a murderer by the impression of a corduroy patch on his pants in the soil (8); a felon by the "remarkable shape" of his horse (36); and a murderer by the measurement of footprints nineteen days after the crime (88); the identification of a body "by his peculiar teeth, a carpenter's rule and a pair of shoes" (176); identification of persons on the basis of attire (186); the identification of a robber by the mark of key, with which the robber had been struck, in his face (198); and the identification of an assailant by a mark in the face from a kick by the victim (433).

I introduce Harris's treatise here primarily to illustrate the near complete absence in it of my subject matter, "the science of identity," as the nineteenth century drew to a close. There is no mention of "science" in the context of identification in the treatise, but my point is larger than a historical shift in nomenclature. A "science of identity," as I conceptualize it here, has several qualities lacked by the identification practices discussed by Harris: general utility and independence. First, although a science of identity may not claim to be applicable to all identification problems, it does claim to be applicable to many. As such, it claims to be a solution to identification problems as a general matter rather than, say, merely the solution to an identification problem in a single case. Second, a science of identity claims to solve identification problems without help from other identification practices. It purports to offer a self-contained solution to identification problems. Third, a science of identity claims a high degree of accuracy, if not infallibility. Fourth, a science of identity roots all these claims in an appeal to the authority of "science" as an epistemically privileged form of knowledge that therefore supports these claims to general utility, independence, and accuracy.

In this sense, Harris's treatise may be viewed as a remarkable document in that it records something very close to the last historical moment in which there was *no* science of identity. Today, of course, we are well aware of accelerating technological means of identifying not only persons, through biometrics, but also things, through such affordances as radio frequency identification (RFID) tags.[4] These technologies are based on improvements in the ability to detect, capture, store, index, and store variable physical attributes (like fingerprints, genetic profiles, retina vein patterns, and so on). We, as a society, are wrestling with complex questions about the social consequences of such technologies and whether and how any limits can or should be placed upon them.[5] But whatever social decisions are made, it seems unlikely that it will be possible in the foreseeable future to deny that a "science of identity" exists.

Apparently unbeknownst to Harris, at the very moment of publication, seeds were being sown for this science of identity. The very year his treatise came out in print also saw the publication of Francis Galton's *Finger Prints*, a seminal work in developing that paradigmatic identification technology.[6] Also that same year, Juan Vucetich, a police official in La Plata, Argentina, helped solve a murder case by examining bloody fingerprints, setting the stage for the establishment of the adjunct forensic application of this identification technology that would enhance the public's perception of its social utility.

Harris does not appear to have been aware of the changes that were coming. There is no mention of the anthropometric system of identification that was already in place in France and Argentina and, indeed, in some locales in the United States and Canada, even though anthropometric instruction manuals had already been translated into English, and anthropometry had been discussed in some recent legal literature.[7] There is, curiously, one use of the term "finger prints" (100). But this referred to the use of bloody marks found on a stick in the defendant's possession, presumably left by his fingers. The incriminating fact was that the stick with bloody marks was in the defendant's possession; there was no claim about determining that the defendant's fingertips were the source of the marks. Harris was able to use the term "finger prints" with no apparent awareness of the changes that were in the offing.

I. Treatises and texts

Problems of identification go back centuries.[8] The nineteenth century was no different, and legal treatises struggled with such problems and explored solutions. Wharton's *Treatise on Medical Jurisprudence* declared, "Identification of the person seen with the person accused is established by the testimony of witnesses who have known him long enough to have his appearance impressed firmly in their memory. Such is the evidence of neighbors, old acquaintances, and relatives." Unfortunately, they noted, "Numerous instances, however, have occurred in which such witnesses have been entirely mistaken."[9]

America, with its high immigration, seemingly "open" Western lands, decentralized criminal justice system, and ideological character as a "new world" that promised many a fresh start, may have been particularly vulnerable to problems of assumed and remade identities. As Tocqueville noted during his celebrated tour of American prisons in the 1830s:

> Where passports do not exist, nothing is easier than to change one's name. If, therefore, a delivered convict commits a new crime under a fictitious name, he can very easily conceal his relapse, providing he is not brought back to the prison where he underwent his first punishment. There are, besides, a thousand means of avoiding the chances of being recognized. Nothing is easier than to pass from one state to another, the ties between the various states being strictly political, there is no central power to which the police officers might refer to obtain information respecting the previous life of an indicted person: so that the courts condemn, almost always, without knowing the true name of the criminal, and still less his previous life.[10]

If the authors of legal treatises were oblivious to the coming of the science of identity, at least one science fiction author was not. Within a year of the publication of Harris's treatise, Mark Twain published his novella *The Tragedy of Pudd'nhead Wilson*, which evinced an awareness of a technology so new that he called it "the fad without a name . . . which dealt with people's finger-marks" (7).[11] Twain had, in fact, mentioned fingerprints six years earlier in a story in *Life on the Mississippi* and had written about "double or duplicitous identity" in numerous works, such as *The American Claimant* (1892).[12] But in *Pudd'nhead Wilson* he more fully explored the implications of having a science of identity. Twain, who was famously fascinated by technology and may be regarded as something of a proto–science fiction writer,[13] was remarkably prescient in capturing the central ethical and epistemological quandaries posed by the science of identity.

In this chapter, I focus on these two texts, published nearly simultaneously in this two-year period in the twilight of the nineteenth century, *A Treatise on the Law of Identification* and *Pudd'nhead Wilson*. I do not argue that these texts were necessarily representative of the nineteenth-century discourse on identification but rather that they capture a moment when modern society was on the brink of having a "science of identity." The former text was oblivious to the coming science of identity and thus allows us to understand nineteenth-century identification practice and identification law; the latter anticipated the new science of identity but still within the context of the nineteenth century.[14]

II. The law of identification in the nineteenth century

Twentieth-century sciences of identification claim high degrees of accuracy. Indeed, some, notoriously, claim infallibility. The claims for nineteenth-century identification practices were much more modest. As Harris noted, questions of identity "are fraught with their dangerous consequences, and difficult in their solution, and are of the greatest importance in the affairs of men. But where is the remedy?" For Harris, there was no technological solution. Rather, any solution "lies alone in caution and prudence. Observation and sad experience admonish courts and juries to the use of the utmost care, caution and prudence" (3). Harris's phrase "caution and prudence" illustrates the modesty typical of nineteenth-century identification practices. There was no process upon which Harris might rely to remove the sense of trepidation and doubt with which he clearly approached the various resolutions to the identification problems he detailed. Similarly, in Britain, Moriarty had described three types of what he called "tests of identity of person" – "physical," "mental," and "moral" – only to dismiss them as not "safe or reliable."[15]

As Harris's treatise illustrates, nineteenth-century identification was a multifaceted process, a sort of pastiche. Twentieth-century sciences of identification are self-contained: a single identification technology, like fingerprinting, genetic profiling, retina scanning, or hand geometry purports to solve all of a set of identification problems, like the maintenance of criminal records or access to a secure area. Rather than being a single technology, approach, or assay, nineteenth-century identification was composed of heterogeneous elements including but not limited to: names, physical features, documents, photographs, handwriting, letters, memories, knowledge, accents, tracks and traces, material objects, animals, attire, behavioral characteristics, family resemblances, wounds, prosthetics, and compulsory physical examinations. Identification had to be triangulated from these various elements, which often conflicted with one another. As Harris noted, identification used to be governed by "the doctrine that the identity of name was evidence of identity of persons" (1–2). "The identity of the name . . . is to be taken as *prima facie* evidence of the identity of the person. It raises a presumption which will stand until it is rebutted or overthrown by countervailing evidence" (58–59). By the close of the nineteenth century, however, Harris noted, this doctrine "has measurably exploded, except in the examination of titles to real estate," and the rule "is not now enforced" (2). According to Harris, identity of name was sufficient to shift the burden of proof to the opposing party but was not definitive proof of identity of persons (2, 58–59).

With names no longer definitive, identification problems were left open to other forms of evidence, none of which proved entirely satisfactory. Harris noted that personal appearance "may seem . . . free from difficulty in the estimation of those unaccustomed to reasoning on the subject" (2–3). In fact, he argued, "the subject is, on the contrary, perhaps one of the most difficult questions with which courts and juries are called to deal" (3). Identification by personal appearance was stymied by "[t]he change in the appearance of the person whose identity is in question, wrought by age, mode of life, hardships, toil and care, sometimes coupled with a skillful disguise" (3). Thus, "[t]he identity of persons by their appearance and by closest examination and scrutiny seems to be far from satisfactory" (4). Another contemporary legal treatise, after recounting a case of mistaken identity, opined:

> This adds another to the numerous recorded cases of mistaken identity, which are almost countless, and which are becoming so frequent of late as very much to impair the value of the clearest and most positive testimony as to whether a certain person was at a certain place at a certain time. If any testimony as to identity of person can be trusted, is it not that of a man as to the woman whom he has courted and just married, and whose face and other personal traits might be reasonably supposed to be clearly and indelibly fixed upon his memory?[16]

And yet all the other potential sources of information were similarly unreliable to varying degrees.

Systematically, nineteenth-century legal treatises raised and dashed whatever hopes of reliability might be imbued in all the available identification modalities. Attire, for example, was doubly pernicious, both unreliable and a distractor from perhaps more reliable information: "The sad comment is, that dress is sometimes more observed and noticed than the person who wears it, and often more easily identified, because more observed; and hence less reliable as a means of human identity" (187). As another nineteenth-century treatise remarked:

> [P]eculiar marks upon the body are a very important, perhaps much the most reliable means of identification. . . . Still such evidence is not always reliable, for a mark of such a nature may exist from exactly the same cause in two different persons.[17]

Yet it was necessary to use evidence, even of questionable reliability. As Harris noted, "While evidence of identity by merely hearing the voice, may not be the most reliable, it has been often received" (9).

What was weak alone, however, might gain strength in numbers. Harris suggested that combining various pieces of evidence could lead to almost certain identification:

> And yet there is an indescribable something by which you recognize him, from general characteristics, or family peculiarities or resemblances, and you may identify him with reasonable, but perhaps not absolute certainty. But if there are any distinctive marks about him, such as lameness, peculiar gait, carriage, manner, loss of a finger, scar on the face or hand, or artificial teeth, or blemish in the eye, these bring a corresponding increase of assurance, and he is identified with greater certainty. And then when he converses, you hear him narrate the incidents of your boyhood days, the reminiscences of youth, the schoolmates, the playgrounds, the teachers, the classes, the Sabbath-school, the church, the minister, the sermons, the playmates, the sports, the fishing, the hunting, the dogs and their names, the beaus and belles, who they married, where they lived, and how many children they had, and their names, the assurance is so full that you can identify him with almost absolute certainty.[18]

This general view of aggregated identification would not change by the time of the publication of Wigmore's much more famous treatise on evidence in 1904. Echoing Harris, Wigmore would note:

> Rarely can one circumstance alone be so inherently peculiar to a single object. It is by adding circumstance to circumstance that we obtain a composite feature or mark which as a whole cannot be supposed to be associated with more than a single object. The process of constructing an inference of identification thus consists usually in adding together a number of circumstances, each of which by itself might be a feature of many objects, but all of which together can conceivably coexist in a single object only. Each additional circumstance reduces the chances of there being more than one object so associated.[19]

Wigmore's treatise, like Harris's, contained no mention of fingerprinting, which was already laying claims to being that "one circumstance . . . so inherently peculiar to a single object" that Wigmore claimed did not exist.

The famous nineteenth-century cases of imposture and mistaken identification – Hoag and Parker, Luther Hause, and, most famously, "The great Tichborne case, which has furnished a small library to jurisprudence"[20] – all involved contradicting heterogeneous evidence of this type. In New York City in 1801, a court acquitted a married man named Joseph Parker of charges stemming from the accusation that he had committed bigamy by marrying again while posing as a man named Thomas Hoag. In an 1849 case in Bangor, Maine, a man named Luther Hause was convicted of conspiracy to obtain goods under false pretenses for having impersonated a man named James Hause.[21] Most famously of all, in 1866 a man appeared in England claiming to be the aristocrat Roger Tichborne, who had been lost at sea in 1854. Skeptics contended that "the Claimant," as he was called, was in fact a butcher from Wagga Wagga, Australia, named Arthur Orton. Sensational legal proceedings captivated England in the early 1870s, eventually ending with the Claimant's conviction for perjury.[22] Among others, the case clearly had an impact on Twain, most obviously in *The American Claimant.*[23] In the Hoag/Parker case, starkly contradictory testimony by numerous witnesses (4) was resolved by the examination of the prisoner for a scar, which witnesses recalled having seen upon Hoag (427–31). In the Hause case, however, seeming evidence of identity from a scar was later contradicted by eyewitness testimony.[24] In the Tichborne case, appearance, diction, accent, handwriting, manner, and knowledge of family lore were all fiercely contested.

In the famous Sally Miller case (1845), much discussed in nineteenth-century medico-legal treatises, Miller claimed that she was not a light-skinned African American born a slave but rather a German, Salomé Muller, who had immigrated as a child, lost both her parents, and been sold into indentured servitude.[25] Miller claimed that a malicious owner had transformed her from German indentured servant to black slave, essentially "enslaving" her, and she sued for her freedom. Phenotypically "white" slaves were so common in the American South generally – and in Louisiana in particular – that Miller's individual identity could not be resolved merely by inferring from her phenotypic features that she was German.[26] A legal determination of "whiteness," then, entailed far more than a simple phenotypic assessment. All the trappings of nineteenth-century identification were also involved: documents, memories, peculiar marks, family resemblances, behavior, accent, and so on. The first witness to "find" Salomé, Madame Karl Rouff, claimed that she could recognize her "among one hundred thousand persons."[27] There was also documentary evidence of Salomé Muller's movements. But the Supreme Court of Louisiana found particularly convincing evidence of peculiar marks, birthmarks on the inner thighs, about which it had been said "that if Salomé were ever lost, she could be identified 'at the end of a hundred years'."[28] Historians Ariela Gross and Carol Wilson have both noted that the evidence concerning Sally's race was not merely physical. It also concerned behavioral traits like "perseverance . . . good conduct . . . quiet and constant industry . . . moral power, and weight, and influence." Sally was described as "careful and prudent . . . neat in her person, simply in her array, and with no ornament upon her."[29] The court was convinced by all this evidence and concluded, dramatically:

> If they are mistaken as to the identity of the plaintiff; if there be in truth two persons about the same age, bearing a strong resemblance to the family of Miller, and having the same identical marks from their birth, and the plaintiff is not the real lost child, who arrived here with hundreds of others in 1818, it is certainly one of the most extraordinary things in history.[30]

However, John Miller, Sally's erstwhile owner, countersued for fraud, and in the second case he amassed strong counterevidence against Miller's claim to be Muller, evidence that has convinced most modern scholars.[31] Although Miller remained free, she was not able to win her suit to free her enslaved children under the argument that, as children of a white woman, they were free.

The issue of the interaction between individual and racial identification raised by this case will be discussed further later in the chapter.

Late nineteenth-century case law shows similar combinations of heterogeneous evidence. In *Udderzook v. Commonwealth*, a case noted for its early discussion of the evidentiary value of photographs, the court noted "happily" that "the proof of identity in this case is not dependent on the photograph alone" but also on handwriting, "a peculiar ring," recognition by witnesses, mail, and, most controversially, evidence concerning drinking habits. The court noted that "habits are a means of identification, though with strength in proportion to their peculiarity."[32] This allowed the photographic evidence to be considered while preserving the judicial doctrine that photographs constituted "illustrative" but not "independent" evidence.[33] *Udderzook* was only one of many life insurance cases that hinged on evidence of identity. The Hillmon case, better known for its doctrinal role in establishing an exception to the hearsay rule, pitted physical evidence of identity against documentary evidence in the form of (perhaps forged) letters.[34]

III. Sciences of identity

What was conspicuously absent from this assembling of identity from heterogeneous elements was any sort of identification modality that claimed to be dispositive or definitive, let alone "infallible." With hindsight, of course, we can see the contrast between these triangulated identification practices and biometric systems like anthropometry, fingerprinting, DNA profiling, and even voice and facial recognition which, to varying degrees, would later claim the ability to *stand alone* in determining identity, to be capable of fending off contradictory evidence of supposedly "lesser" types – of being, in essence, *sciences* of identity. Of course, there was such an identification modality in 1892: the anthropometric system of identification developed by Alphonse Bertillon in Paris around a decade earlier. And, another one, fingerprint identification, was just coming into being.[35]

Designed to detect repeat offenders who might escape recognition by employing an alias, the Bertillon system of identification was a three-part system. Best known was the recording of eleven anthropometric measurements of "osseous lengths" using fine calipers and rulers. The second part was the recording of physical attributes like hair color, eye color, nose, and, most famously, ear shape, using a rich predefined vocabulary of terms. The third part was the meticulous recording of "peculiar marks," such as scars, birthmarks, and tattoos. The anthropometric measurements served as the method of indexing the records; the description and especially the peculiar marks, served as the confirming evidence of hypothesized identification decisions.[36] Bertillon's identification procedure was thus triangulated identification too but within a self-contained "system." "Biometrics as we know it today can be viewed as [an] extension of Bertillon's anthropometric approach."[37]

By 1892, a number of developments in fingerprint identification had occurred. William Herschel had experimented with using fingerprints to combat fraud among pension claimants in colonial India. He had published a report in *Nature*, prompting a reply from the Scottish physician Henry Faulds, who, while serving in Japan, had recognized the potential of the technique for identification both civil and forensic.[38] The letters to *Nature* piqued the interest of Galton, who published his book in 1892, reporting a crude initial attempt at devising categories of fingerprint pattern types, as well as – not surprisingly considering Galton's eugenic interests – comparisons of the frequencies of the various pattern types among different ethnic groups.[39]

In contrast to the heterogeneous assemblages described by Harris, these new techniques made explicit claims to being science, to being infallible, and to being complete, wholly contained, solutions to the problem of identification. As the American historian Frank Morn observes, the Bertillon system "showed clearly the impact of developing science, specifically forensic science, in the nineteenth century and the struggles going on in the criminal justice system over adopting it."[40] In 1888, R. W. McClaughry, warden of the Illinois Penitentiary, told the National Prison Association that the Bertillon system "substitutes certainty for uncertainty – a thoroughly reliable identification for the shrewd guess of the detective, or the scarcely more reliable testimony of the photograph."[41] An American translation of Bertillon's manual *Signaletic Instructions* claimed a degree of certainty that legal treatise writers would not have attached to other single modes of identification: "the agreement of the figures [the anthropometric measurements] comes at last to constitute a *quasi-certitude of identity*."[42] The breadth of Bertillon's claims to be able to make identity permanent and mobile, at a level of discrimination down to the individual, were summed up by a quotation by Eduard de Ryckère, a Belgian prosecutor, a quotation that both Bertillon and Galton would appropriate as their own: "to fix the human personality, to give each human being an identity, a positive, lasting and an invariable individuality, always recognizable and easily demonstratable, such seems to be the broadest aim of this new method."[43] In 1896, in an address to the Prison Association of New York, McClaughry and Paul Brown, describing the Bertillon system, declared that "a practical, simple and absolutely certain method of identification has been devised, inexpensive in its operation and of unqualified usefulness."[44]

Rather than relying on an improvised collage of identity guided by common sense, it was hoped, at the close of the nineteenth century, that identification would become mechanical. As San Francisco Police Chief, F. H. DePue put it:

> Nature has furnished us with so much material of fixed or rigid character and mechanism has such a peculiar power for accuracy that it would seem we ought in time be released from the nightmares of horror caused by our too well grounded fears of the alarming possibilities of human fallibility. Nature has given to man in mechanism his best, because safest hand; therefore, by mechanism we hope to properly fix identity.[45]

Such statements reflect the notion of what historians of science Lorraine Daston and Peter Galison call "mechanical objectivity."[46]

Perhaps counterintuitively for contemporary readers, anthropometry had the easier claim to "scientific" status because it was a familiar tool of anthropology and thus "looked like" science. It took longer for fingerprinting to acquire the aura of science. Even into the twentieth century, skeptics continued to concede fingerprinting only a role in aggregated identification. For DePue, an idiosyncratic advocate of a facial identification system, the need for a science of identity was distinctly American. Dismissing the British colonial origins of fingerprinting,[47] he declared:

> But, surely finger impressions are not enough, unaided by any other means of identification. For indifferent Hindus and wandering Arabs it might answer. The English regime has not been considered too particular in the matter of identity of native suspects. We, in America, however, demand something scientifically reliable.[48]

To be sure, the body was crucial for identification in the nineteenth-century too: physiognomic appearance, tattoos, scars, brands, footprints, and so on.[49] But the sciences of identity were different. First, they brought rigor and system to the analysis of the body. Bertillon's page upon page of ear types was a far cry from laypersons' or even supposed experts' verbal attempts to characterize the niceties of the human face.[50] Second, they asserted, perhaps for the first time, that the body alone was sufficient for identification in all cases. The body was *identity*, and identity was nothing more than the body, an idea that still resonates today.[51] As Williams and Johnson put it:

> The marking of individuals to identify them as criminals – to literally incise a social identity into the flesh – may differentiate such bodies but it does not provide a method to tell one marked body from another. That specific practice, of subjecting a body to examination in order to differentiate it from all others, is founded in a range of techniques that culminate in the nineteenth century "science" of identification.[52]

More precisely, the sciences of identification hinged upon a specific claim of a one-to-one correspondence between body and identity: that an "identity" would be linked to a body but linkable to only one body and no other and, conversely, that a body be linkable to one and only one identity, or what Gowland and Thompson have called "one body=one individual."[53] To be sure, the claim was clearer for fingerprinting – which has become synecdoche for this notion of one body=one individual in popular culture – than it was for anthropometry. But Bertillon did make similar claims of one body=one individual for the entire, three-part system.

IV. The fad without a name

Having learned about fingerprints by reading Galton's book, Twain wove them into the plot of *Pudd'nhead Wilson*, which has been called "the first post-Galtonian novel."[54] *Pudd'nhead Wilson* takes place in Dawson's Landing, Missouri, in 1830. The plot concerns infants who are switched at birth. Both are phenotypically white, but one, Chambre de Valet ("Chambers"), is one-thirty-second part "Negro" and thus considered a slave under the doctrine of hypodescent.[55] Chambers' mother, Roxy, also a phenotypically white slave, switches him with the heir of the household, Thomas "Tom" á Becket Driscoll. The protagonist, David "Pudd'nhead" Wilson, is an attorney, recently relocated to Dawson's Landing. Wilson, a bit of dilettante, dabbles in "the fad without a name," fingerprint identification, recording and archiving the fingerprint impressions of townsfolk for his own amusement. As literary scholar Susan Gillman notes, Roxy gets the idea to switch the infants while Wilson is taking her fingerprints:

> Because the two incidents occur side by side, the reader is led to anticipate that if one system of personal identification in the novel – names, titles, clothing – is patently unreliable, the other – fingerprinting – may prove to have more accurate differentiating power.[56]

Fingerprints turn out to be dispositive of identity in *Pudd'nhead Wilson*. Two visiting Italian identical twins, Angelo and Luigi Cappello, mirror the ersatz "twins" who were switched at birth. The plot then turns to the murder of Tom's uncle, Percy Driscoll, and the false accusation of Luigi. Wilson represents them, and in the climactic trial scene, he proves their innocence by using fingerprints to show not only that "Tom Driscoll" murdered his uncle but also that "Tom" is not "Tom" at all but a slave.

Twain anticipated the claims that would be made on behalf of fingerprinting – that it transcended the weakness that dogged nineteenth-century identification practices. For example, as discussed, clothing was considered an element of nineteenth-century identification practice. But in *Pudd'nhead Wilson*, reliance on clothing leads the characters to false identifications. Twain writes:

> Even the father of the white child was able to tell the children apart – little as he had commerce with them – by their clothes: for the white babe wore ruffled soft muslin and a coral necklace, while the other wore merely a coarse tow-linen shirt which barely reached to its knees, and no jewelry.
>
> *(9)*

The father's identification is, of course, false because the infants were switched. As Gillman points out, the final trial scene of the novel is as much a trial of Wilson's expertise and the epistemological claims of fingerprinting as of the identity of the murderer.[57] In his climactic courtroom speech, Wilson extols the powers of the fingerprint:

> Every human being carries with him from his cradle to his grave certain physical marks which do not change their character, and by which he can always be identified – and that without shade of doubt or question. These marks are his signature, his physiological autograph, so to speak, and this autograph cannot be counterfeited, nor can he disguise it or hide it away, nor can it become illegible by the wear and the mutations of time.
>
> *(108)*

He then demolishes all of the canonical nineteenth-century markers of identity:

> This signature is not his face – age can change that beyond recognition; it is not his hair, for that can fall out; it is not his height, for duplicates of that exist; it is not his form, for duplicates of that exist, also, whereas this signature is each man's very own – there is no duplicate of it among the swarming populations of the globe.
>
> *(108)*

Here, then, we have the famous two "premises" upon which fingerprint identification, for the next century, would purport to rest. The first was "permanence," the cradle-to-grave stability of the pattern over time. While both fingerprinting and anthropometry posited one body=one individual, fingerprinting made the added claim of keeping this relationship stable across time. Whereas anthropometric measurements obviously remained stable only after anatomical growth was completed and, even then, was subject to some ill defined shrinkage due to aging, fingerprinting purported to keep identity stable from birth (a little earlier, even) through death (a little later, even). Pudd'nhead Wilson established permanence in the same way Herschel, Galton, and others did: "He liked to have a 'series' – two or three 'takings' at intervals during the period of childhood, these to be followed by others at intervals of several years" (9). The second was "uniqueness," the breathtakingly ambitious, never proven, and yet universally assumed claim that each fingerprinting pattern was without duplicate in the entire human population:

> To the untrained eye the collection of delicate originals made by the human finger on the glass plates looked about alike; but when enlarged ten times, they resembled the markings of a block of wood that has been sawed across the grain, and the dullest eye could detect at a glance, and at a distance of many feet that no two of the patterns were alike.
>
> *(105)*

These last seven words would become the mantra that supposedly supported the reliability of fingerprint identification for the next century.[58] Emphasizing the point, Wilson declared:

> I have the finger-prints of the court, the sheriff, and every member of the jury. . . . [N]ot one of them can so disguise himself that I cannot pick him out from a multitude of his fellow creatures and unerringly identify him by his hands. And if he and I should live to be a hundred I could still do it!
>
> *(109)*

Through these dramatic speeches, Twain presaged the extraordinary strength of the claims of this new science of identity. Far from being subject to the conflicts and contradictions that pervaded identification practices in the nineteenth century, fingerprinting claimed to be a unitary and universal identifier that would trump all other claims about identification. It also claimed to be "scientific"; its practitioner, Pudd'nhead Wilson, is mocked for his "scientifics."[59] More than that, it would claim to be "infallible," a word that became associated with fingerprinting in the popular imagination for the next century until such claims began to come under some derision.[60] *Pudd'nhead Wilson* alludes to this notion on its very first page, in establishing the setting of Dawson's Landing:

> When there was room on the ledge outside of the pots and boxes for a cat, the cat was there – in sunny weather – stretched at full length, asleep and blissful, with her furry belly to the sun and a paw curved over her nose. Then that home was complete, and its contentment and peace were made manifest to the world by this symbol, whose testimony is infallible.
> (3)[61]

Thus, Twain begins the story with supposedly infallible testimony that is absurd, but at the end of the book he "raises the possibility that the body really can be read infallibly."[62] As literary scholar Cathy Boeckmann puts it, "In a novel where character is most often improperly read . . . a means appears by which one who is trained in a supposed science of the body can arrive at a correct reading."[63] This supposed infallibility trumps not only all other supposed evidence of identity but also all other evidence in the criminal case. It resolves not only identity but the entire mystery:

> In *Pudd'nhead Wilson*, fingerprinting allows the detective to make the misleading signification of Tom's disguises and performances irrelevant. Wilson is thus able to pare away faulty metaphorical and physiognomic readings, leaving a single narrative line based on indexical certainty.[64]

This notion of certainty too is still very much present today.[65]

One key aspect of the marvelousness of these new sciences of identity was that they derived identity directly from the body. For both systems, the body "spoke." Bertillon's system of physical description was actually called the *portrait parlé*. The body betrayed itself.[66] And:

> With Wilson's reading of Tom's bodily gesture, there is no need for the final fingerprint in the indexical chain or for Tom to even speak his own confession. His body confesses for him just as the prints left inadvertently on the glass slide, the mute testimony of his body, previously allowed Wilson to crack the case.[67]

V. Twain and twins

In *Pudd'nhead Wilson*, fingerprinting correctly identified two individuals who had been mistakenly identified for more than two decades. Moreover, through his distinguishing of the visiting Italian twins, Luigi and Angelo, Wilson shows that fingerprinting can distinguish even the proverbial hardest case for identification: supposedly physically indistinguishable "identical" twins. Tom Driscoll makes a fool of himself when he declares, "The hand-print of one twin is the same as the hand-print of the fellow-twin" (49). Instead, Wilson later declares:

> The patterns of a twin's right hand are never the same as those on his left. One twin's patterns are never the same as his fellow-twin's patterns – the jury will find that the

> patterns upon the finger-balls of the accused follow this rule. . . . You have often heard of twins who were so exactly alike that when dressed alike their own parents could not tell them apart. Yet there was never a twin born into this world that did not carry from birth to death a sure identifier in this mysterious and marvelous natal autograph. That once known to you, his fellow-twin could never personate him and deceive you. *(108–9)*

The theme of twins pervades *Pudd'nhead Wilson* and Twain's work more generally. There are the black and white infants switched at birth, of course, and also the Italian identical twins, Luigi and Angelo. Twain's very pen name was, arguably, a reference to twins, and twins, *doppelgängers*, and imposters appeared frequently in his work. Susan Gillman observes that for Twain such doubles "raise a fundamental question: whether one can tell people apart, differentiate among them." She argues that Twain returned repeatedly, as he did in *Pudd'nhead Wilson*, to "the law as one agent of control that resolves confusions about identity, restoring and enforcing the fundamental distinctions of society."[68]

Over the next century, the ability of fingerprints to distinguish identical twins would be portrayed as the ultimate demonstration of its claim to being a science of identity, and many of these demonstrations would echo *Pudd'nhead Wilson*. Scotland Yard detective John Ferrier would display photographs and fingerprints of the Fox twins, Ebenezer Albert and Albert Ebenezer, in his celebrated exhibit on fingerprint identification at the 1904 Louisiana Purchase Exhibition in St. Louis.[69] The earliest British fingerprint trial, the so-called Deptford Murder Trial ended in the hanging of twin brothers, Alfred and Albert Stratton.[70] Harris Hawthorne Wilder, a professor of Anatomy at Smith College who would emerge as one of the leading American proponents of fingerprint identification in the early twentieth century, collected numerous examples of twins' photographs and fingerprints, supposedly illustrating the distinguishing power of fingerprints.[71] Two American vaudeville performers, Charles and Frank Terry were used to demonstrate the ability of fingerprints to distinguish twins, and they even appeared in one of the earliest fingerprint trials in the United States, *People v. Crispi*, in 1911.[72] The judge, Otto Rosalsky, overruled Crispi's defense attorney, Robert Moore's alliterative objection that presenting the vaudeville twins to the jury was "incompetent, immaterial, irrelevant and inadmissible in this case." Instead, the judge intoned, "Mr. Moore, this is a new science. In our country our law cannot be like a pool, permitted to become stagnant. It has to be flexible and we have to advance in accordance with the times."[73] "Identical" twins continue to present vexing identification problems to courts today, especially because genetic identification, as commonly practiced, does not claim that ability to distinguish twins.[74]

VI. Identity and race

Of course, the central interest in *Pudd'nhead Wilson* was not merely the distinguishing of identical twins but the simultaneous distinguishing of race: the distinguishing of the black and white "twins," Chambers and Tom. Race was, of course, a crucial theme for Twain. In Wilson's climactic courtroom speech, he emphasizes that the discriminating power of fingerprinting is indifferent to race: "There is hardly a person in this room, white or black, whose natal signature I cannot produce" (109).

"Tom" is able to pass for white because of his white phenotype and because his upbringing allows him to obtain the dress, manners, and accent to pass for white. But fingerprinting exposes the fraud and assigns each individual to his or her "proper" born "race." Fingerprints allow us to see racial identities previously invisible to us, which were obscured by the unreliable physical manifestations of what historian Evelynn Hammonds calls "embodied race."[75] Using fingerprints, Wilson is able to "see" that Tom is in fact "black" and that Chambers is in fact "white," even when this determination cannot be reached through a visual assessment. Twain is also able to distinguish the Italian twins, whose differences are repeatedly described in terms of color: "One was a little fairer than the other, but otherwise they were exact duplicates" (27). Elsewhere, they are described as "the blonde twin" and "the brunette one" (27, 55, 103).

Race was a common element in problems involving identifying people in nineteenth-century America. For example, Harris discusses a North Carolina case in which a woman was attacked by a "negro man." She and another witness both identified a free Negro as her attacker. However, "It so happened, as many other strange things happen, that there was a slave man or boy in the neighborhood, the very counterpart of the free negro as to color, face and form. . . . The slave boy confessed that it was him that committed the crime, and not the free negro." Both men were brought into court, and both witnesses still identified the free Negro. "Such is the tenacity with which people cling to first impressions, and originally expressed opinions," Harris comments (remarks that would not seem out of place in a contemporary discussion of the "hardening" of memory in eyewitness identification) (421).[76] To make matters worse, one of the attorneys also confused the two men. Eventually, the slave's confession trumped:

> The free negro was released, and the slave boy was hung. The evidence of the woman and the old man made such an impression against the free negro, that some were loth to believe but that it was him; but the slave persisted in his statement of his own guilt, and said just before he was hung that it was all right; he was the one, and not the free negro. *(422)*

This case illustrates the perception of physiognomic homogeneity of individuals of races other than white, especially American blacks, what Peter Hutchings calls "the colonialist Eurocentrism of the idea of indistinguishable natives."[77] It is also notable that the confused individuals are never named but merely described by a combination of legal status and race: "free negro" and "slave boy or man" (thereafter abbreviated as "boy"). In the next case, Harris discusses, however, names are prominent. The Greenwood case was a British case of multiple thefts. Greenwood was identified by multiple witnesses but had an alibi for most of the thefts and strong character evidence. Greenwood's attorney was able to find "another young man of the name of Greenwood, who awaited his trial on a capital charge of felony." The attorney brought this second Greenwood to court and placed him beside his client.

> The witness turned his head towards the dock, when beholding two men so nearly alike, he became petrified with astonishment, dropped his hat, and was speechless for a time, but at length declined swearing to either. The young man was of course acquitted. Greenwood was tried for another offense and executed, and a few hours before his death acknowledged that he had committed the robbery with which the other was charged. *(423)*

Thus, it is claimed that these two individuals had a remarkable resemblance in both physical appearance and name! The stubborn insistence upon the name as an identification technology would persist even into the twentieth century as physically based identification technologies became available. It would appear when fingerprinting supposedly "proved" that its discriminating power was superior to the nineteenth-century heterogeneous approach in the apocryphal 1903 "Will West case," in which two African American convicts, supposedly indistinguishable in physiognomy, anthropometric measurements, and *name* were distinguished by their fingerprints.[78]

The Wests, though apparently not twins, were often described as looking as similar as twins.[79] The West case echoes both of Harris's mistaken identity cases just discussed: the North Carolina case because of the theme of the supposed physiognomic homogeneity of American blacks and the Greenwood case because of the remarkable coincidence of resemblance in both physical appearance and name.

Twain's exploration of how "the appeal of fingerprints lies in their capacity to counteract the confusion presented by undifferentiated hordes of racialized bodies"[80] would also reappear in the 1911 *Crispi* trial, one of the first major American criminal trials involving fingerprint evidence, a trial in which both prosecutor and fingerprint expert adopted the theatrical tactics drawn directly from *Pudd'nhead Wilson*. Not only did the prosecutor present the Terry twins to the jury, the fingerprint expert, Lieutenant Joseph Faurot, duplicated Wilson's courtroom demonstration of having the jurors create fingerprints and then identifying which of them had touched a piece of glass.[81] Crispi's defense attorney, Robert Moore, in arguing that fingerprint evidence was not scientific enough to be used in court, protested that "there might be two other men whose faces would be as unlike as *dark and daylight*, and their finger prints might yet be as like as two peas."[82] Moore's comment reveals that at this historical moment, the question of which was the ultimate "identifier," the true "science of identity," was still in play. It was still possible for Moore to imagine the opposite of the scenario posed by Twain: perhaps there is a pair of individuals who are indistinguishable by fingerprint but distinguishable by "race."

In the twentieth century, paradoxically, the suppressing of the racial component of these intertwined acts of individual and racial identification would play a large role in supporting the claims of technologies, such as fingerprinting, to qualify as "science." As race became discredited as a topic of science over the course of the twentieth century,[83] it would be helpful rather than harmful for fingerprinting's claims to the mantle of "science" that it no longer made any claim be able to identify race and could thus claim to reveal only individual, not group identity.[84]

Conclusion

While periodization is always hazardous, this chapter posits the nineteenth century as a period in which identification practices, especially legal identification practices, moved toward what we might call a "science of identity." I define a "science of identity," as opposed to mere "identification practices," as a system of identification that purports infallibility or near infallibility, that is, independent in that it purports to solve a set of identification problems using a single identification modality – a "panacea for identity verification"[85] – and that invokes the authority of "science" in support of these claims. Defined in this way, "the science of identity" was a product of the twentieth century. Nineteenth-century identification practices offer a valuable glimpse – perhaps our last glimpse – of a world without a science of identity . . . a world that most likely is gone forever.

Notes

1 George E. Harris, *A Treatise on the Law of Identification: A Separate Branch of the Law of Evidence* (Albany, N.Y.: Parsons, 1892).

2 Aubrey Moriarty, *On Personation and Disputed Identity, and Their Tests* (London: Stevens and Haynes, 1873), 2.

3 Ibid., 5.

4 E.g., Roy Want, "RFID: A Key to Automating Everything," *Scientific American* (January 2004), 56–65.

5 E.g., Joseph Pugliese, *Biometrics: Bodies, Technologies, Biopolitics* (New York: Routledge, 2010); Irma Van Der Ploeg, *The Machine-Readable Body* (Maastricht: Shaker, 2005); Irma Van Der Ploeg, "Biometrics and the Body as Information: Normative Issues of the Socio-Technical Coding of the Body," in *Surveillance as*

Social Sorting: Privacy, Risk and Digital Discrimination, ed. David Lyon (London: Routledge, 2003), 57–73; Lisa S. Nelson, *America Identified: Biometric Technology and Society* (Cambridge, Mass.: MIT Press, 2011); Kelly A. Gates, *Our Biometric Future: Facial Recognition Technology and the Culture of Surveillance* (New York: New York University Press, 2011); Shoshana A. Magnet, *When Biometrics Fail: Gender, Race, and the Technology of Identity* (Durham, N.C.: Duke University Press, 2011).

6 Francis Galton, *Finger Prints* (London: Macmillan, 1892).

7 Alphonse Bertillon, *Instructions for Taking Descriptions for the Identification of Criminals and Others by the Means of Anthropometric Indications* (Chicago: American Bertillon Prison Bureau, 1889); "Identifying Thieves in Paris," *The Green Bag* (1890), 34–35; "The Identification of Criminals by Measurement," *The Green Bag* (1891), 526–27.

8 Valentin Groebner, *Who Are You? Identification, Deception, and Surveillance in Early Modern Europe*, trans. Mark Kyburz and John Peck (New York: Zone, 2007).

9 Francis Wharton, Moreton Stillé, and Alfred Stillé, *A Treatise on Medical Jurisprudence*, 2nd ed. (Philadelphia: Kay & Brother, 1860), 934.

10 Gustave de Beaumont and Alexis de Tocqueville, *On the Penitentiary System in the United States and Its Application in France* (Philadelphia: Carey, Lea & Blanchard, 1833), 101–2.

11 Samuel L. Clemens, *Pudd'nhead Wilson* (1894; New York: Norton, 1980).

12 Susan Gillman, *Dark Twins: Imposture and Identity in Mark Twain's America* (Chicago: University of Chicago Press, 1989), 151.

13 Mark Seltzer, *Bodies and Machines* (New York: Routledge, 1992); Mary McAleer Balkun, *The American Counterfeit: Authenticity and Identity in American Literature and Culture* (Tuscaloosa: University of Alabama Press, 2006), 43.

14 For a similar approach to another forensic technology, the lie detector, which "does not pit literature and science against each other, nor . . . attempt a simple reversal that would replace the primacy of science with the primacy of literature," see Melissa M. Littlefield, *The Lying Brain: Lie Detection Is Science and Science Fiction* (Ann Arbor: University of Michigan Press, 2011).

15 Moriarty, *On Personation*, 20.

16 Richard Harris, *Before and at Trial: What Should Be Done by Counsel, Solicitor, and Client* (Northport, N.Y.: Thompson, 1890), 375.

17 Wharton, Stillé, and Stillé, *Treatise on Medical Jurisprudence*, quoted in Harris, *Before and at Trial*, 426.

18 Harris, *Before and at Trial*, 25.

19 John H. Wigmore, *A Treatise on the System of Evidence in Trials at Common Law Including the Statutes and Judicial Decisions of All Jurisdictions of the United States*, 4 vols. (Boston: Little Brown, 1904), 1: 501–2.

20 "Personal Identity," *Criminal Law Magazine* (1881), 287–312.

21 Joel Munsell, *Cases of Personal Identity* (Albany, N.Y.: Munsell, 1854), 91–102.

22 Carrie Dawson, "'The Slaughterman of Wagga Wagga': Imposture, National Identity, and the Tichborne Affair," *Australian Literary Studies* 21 (2004): 1–13.

23 Gillman, *Dark Twins*, 150.

24 Munsell, *Cases of Personal Identity*, 91–102.

25 Wharton, Stillé, and Stillé, *Treatise on Medical Jurisprudence*, 444–5.

26 Carol Wilson, *The Two Lives of Sally Miller: A Case of Mistaken Racial Identity in Antebellum New Orleans* (New Brunswick, N.J.: Rutgers University Press, 2007), 63–5.

27 Ibid., 3.

28 Ibid., 12.

29 Ariela J. Gross, *What Blood Won't Tell: A History of Race on Trial in America* (Cambridge, Mass.: Harvard University Press, 2008), 58–63; Wilson, *The Two Lives of Sally Miller*, 72–3.

30 *Miller v. Belmonti*, 11 Rob. 339, 343–4 (1845).

31 Wilson, *The Two Lives of Sally Miller*, 100; Gross, *What Blood Won't Tell*, 58–63; John Bailey, *The Lost German Slave Girl* (New York: Grove, 2003).

32 *Udderzook v. Commonwealth*, 76 Pa. 340 (1874). For discussion, see Jennifer L. Mnookin, "The Image of Truth: Photographic Evidence and the Power of Analogy," *Yale Journal of Law & the Humanities* 10 (1998): 1–74, 23–4; Hillel Schwartz, *The Culture of the Copy: Striking Likenesses, Unreasonable Facsimiles* (New York: Zone, 1996), 96–7.

33 Mnookin, "The Image of Truth," 43–4.

34 Marianne Wesson, "'Particular Intentions': The Hillmon Case and the Supreme Court," *Law & Literature* 18 (2006): 343–402; Marianne Wesson, *A Death at Crooked Creek: The Case of the Cowboy, the Cigarmaker, and the Love Letter* (New York: New York University Press, 2013).

35 The seminal work comparing these two technologies is, of course, Allan Sekula, "The Body and the Archive," *October* 39 (1986): 3–64.
36 Alphonse Bertillon, *Signaletic Instructions: Including the Theory and Practice of Anthropometrical Identification* (Chicago: Sharp and Smith, 1896).
37 Damien Dessimoz and Christophe Champod, "Linkages between Biometrics and Forensic Science," in *Handbook of Biometrics*, ed. Anil K. Jain, Patrick Flynn, and Arun A. Ross (New York: Springer-Verlag, 2008), 425–59, 425.
38 William J. Herschel, "Skin Furrows of the Hand," *Nature* 23, no. 578 (1880): 76; Henry Faulds, "On the Skin Furrows of the Hand," *Nature* 22, no. 574 (1880): 605.
39 Galton, *Finger Prints.*
40 Frank Morn, *Forgotten Reformer: Robert Mcclaughry and Criminal Justice Reform in Nineteenth-Century America* (Lanham, Md.: University Press of America, 2011), 251.
41 National Prison Association Proceedings, 1888, 76, quoted in Morn, *Forgotten Reformer*, 93.
42 Bertillon, *Signaletic Instructions*, 23.
43 Ibid., 80.
44 Prison Association of New York, *Fifty-First Annual Report of the Prison Association of New York for the Year 1895* (Albany, N.Y.: Wynkoop Hallenbeck Crawford, 1896), 51–2.
45 F. H. De Pue, "The De Pue System of Identification," in *Proceedings of the International Association of Chiefs of Police* (Grand Rapids, Mich.: Seymour & Muir, 1902), 98–102.
46 Lorraine Daston and Peter Galison, "The Image of Objectivity," *Representations* 40 (1992): 81–128.
47 Chandak Sengoopta, *Imprint of the Raj: How Fingerprinting Was Born in Colonial India* (London: Macmillan, 2002); Radhika Singha, "Settle, Mobilize, Verify: Identification Practices in Colonial India," *Studies in History* 16, no. 2 (2000): 151–198.
48 De Pue, "The De Pue System of Identification."
49 E.g., Groebner, *Who Are You? Identification, Deception, and Surveillance in Early Modern Europe*; Edward Higgs, *Identifying the English: A History of Personal Identification, 1500 to the Present* (London: Continuum, 2011).
50 Bertillon, *Signaletic Instructions.*
51 Rebecca Gowland and Tim Thompson, *Human Identity and Identification* (Cambridge, UK: Cambridge University Press, 2013), 67–9.
52 Robin Williams and Paul Johnson, *Genetic Policing: The Use of DNA in Criminal Investigations* (Cullompton, UK: Willan, 2008), 26.
53 Gowland and Thompson, *Human Identity and Identification*, 67–9.
54 Ronald R. Thomas, *Detective Fiction and the Rise of Forensic Science* (Cambridge, UK: Cambridge University Press, 1999), 240.
55 Gillman, *Dark Twins*, 64; Robin West, *Narrative, Authority, and Law* (Ann Arbor: University of Michigan Press, 1993), 131.
56 Gillman, *Dark Twins*, 77.
57 Ibid., 89.
58 As I have discussed elsewhere, the issue of whether this claim is "proven" is of far less interest or importance than the fact that the claim is banal without further specification of what is meant by the term "unique." The validity of the "uniqueness" claim is entirely a consequence of the language rules chosen for defining objects as "the same" or "different." Simon A. Cole, "Forensics without Uniqueness, Conclusions without Individualization: The New Epistemology of Forensic Identification," *Law, Probability and Risk* 8 (2009): 233–55.
59 Gillman, *Dark Twins*, 87–8.
60 E.g., Sharon Begley, "Despite Its Reputation, Fingerprint Evidence Isn't Really Infallible," *Wall Street Journal*, June 4, 2004, B1; James E. Starrs, "Forensic Science on the Ropes: Procellous Times in the Citadels of Infallibility," *Scientific Sleuthing Review* 20 (Winter 1996): 1–3.
61 I am indebted to Cathy Boeckmann for pointing this out. See Cathy Boeckmann, *A Question of Character: Scientific Racism and Genres of American Fiction, 1892–1912* (Tuscaloosa: University of Alabama Press, 2000), 108.
62 Ibid., 100.
63 Ibid., 126.
64 Ibid., 128.
65 E.g., Corinna Kruse, "Producing Absolute Truth: *CSI* Science as Wishful Thinking," *American Anthropologist* 112 (2010): 79–91.

66 Carlo Ginzburg, "Morelli, Freud, and Sherlock Holmes: Clues and Scientific Method," in *The Sign of Three: Dupin, Holmes, Peirce*, ed. Umberto Eco and Thomas A. Sebeok (Bloomington: Indiana University Press, 1983), 81–118.
67 Boeckmann, *A Question of Character*, 130–1.
68 Gillman, *Dark Twins*, 5.
69 Simon Cole, "Fingerprints: An Archival Whodunit," *New York Archives* 1, no. 4 (2002): 12–15.
70 Anne Joseph, "Anthropometry, the Police Expert, and the Deptford Murders: The Contested Introduction of Fingerprinting for the Identification of Criminals in Late Victorian and Edwardian Britain," in *Documenting Individual Identity: The Development of State Practices since the French Revolution*, ed. John Torpey and Jane Caplan (Princeton, N.J.: Princeton University Press, 2001), 164–83, 178.
71 Harris H. Wilder, "Palms and Soles," *American Journal of Anatomy* 1 (1902): 423–41, 435.
72 *People v. Crispi*, trial transcript (Special Collections, Lloyd G. Sealy Library, John Jay College of Criminal Justice, City University of New York), 152–4 (1911); New York City Police Department, "Annual Report," (1921), 232.
73 *People v. Crispi*, trial transcript, 152–4.
74 Jess Bidgood, "New DNA Test Sought in Identical Twin's Rape Case," *New York Times*, September 16, 2014, A17; Richard Willing, "Identical Twins Complicate Use of DNA Testing," *USA Today*, June 3, 2004; Ken Kolker, "Lab Offers Free DNA Test of Twins in Rape Case," *Grand Rapids Press*, August 10, 2004.
75 Evelynn M. Hammonds, "New Technologies of Race," in *Processed Lives: Gender and Technology in Everyday Life*, ed. Jennifer Terry and Melodie Calvert (London: Routledge, 1997), 107–22, 118.
76 E.g., John C. Brigham, Adina W. Wasserman, and Christian A. Meissner, "Disputed Eyewitness Identification Evidence: Important Legal and Scientific Issues," *Court Review* 36 (Summer 1999): 12–5, 18.
77 Peter J. Hutchings, *The Criminal Spectre in Law, Literature and Aesthetics* (London: Routledge, 2001), 151.
78 Simon A. Cole, "Twins, Twain, Galton and Gilman: Fingerprinting, Individualization, Brotherhood and Race in *Pudd'nhead Wilson*," *Configurations* 15 (2007): 227–65.
79 Federal Bureau of Investigation, *The Identification Division of the FBI: A Brief Outline of the History, Services, and Operating Techniques of the World's Largest Repository of Fingerprints* (Washington, D.C.: Federal Bureau of Investigation, 1991), 7.
80 Hsuan L. Hsu, *Sitting in Darkness: Mark Twain's Asia and Comparative Racialization* (New York: New York University Press, 2015), 103.
81 *People v. Crispi*, 83–99.
82 Ibid., 152–4, emphasis added.
83 E.g., George W. Stocking, Jr., *Race, Culture, and Evolution: Essays in the History of Anthropology* (New York: Free Press, 1968); Jenny Reardon, *Race to the Finish: Identity and Governance in the Age of Genomics* (Princeton, N.J.: Princeton University Press, 2005); Jonathan Marks, *Human Biodiversity: Genes, Race, and History* (New York: de Gruyter, 1995).
84 Paul Rabinow, "Galton's Regret: Of Types and Individuals," in *DNA on Trial: Genetic Identification and Criminal Justice*, ed. Paul R. Billings (Plainview, N.Y.: Cold Spring Harbor Laboratory Press, 1992), 5–18; For a critique, see Cole, "Twins, Twain, Galton and Gilman: Fingerprinting, Individualization, Brotherhood and Race in *Pudd'nhead Wilson*."
85 Damien Dessimoz J. Richiardi, C. Champod, and A. Drygajlo, "Multimodal Biometrics for Identity Documents," *Forensic Science International* 167 (2007): 154–9, 154.

14
THE AMERICAN PRISON, 1786–1860

John Cyril Barton

The degree of civilization in a society can be judged by entering its prisons.

– Dostoevsky, *The House of the Dead, or Prison Life in Siberia (1862)*

Today, the United States incarcerates more people than any other country in the world. Our culture of incarceration, of course, directly impacts those imprisoned, but its influence goes far beyond the prison's walls, with its institutions and practices permeating various genres of popular music and literature, as well as providing a setting or backdrop for over 300 Hollywood films and several recent television series, such as HBO's *Oz* (1997–2003), Fox's *Prison Break* (2005–09), and Netflix's current *Orange Is the New Black*.[1] The American prison, as we now think of it, seems always to have been there, but it was born at the turn of the nineteenth century. Before then, prisons, or "gaols," served mainly as temporary holding facilities. Debtors were lodged there – more as a means to encourage payment than to punish – but so too, of course, were individuals charged with serious crimes. The latter were housed in local prisons until trial; those convicted then awaited punishment there, which usually took the form of corporal or capital punishment – or a public shaming based on such punishment, like the one to which Hester Prynne is subjected as she exits "the prison-door" and ascends the scaffold for a mock execution to begin Hawthorne's *The Scarlet Letter*.[2]

Developed in part as a response to social conditions and the politics of reform during the nineteenth century, the U.S. prison was also the product of eighteenth-century Enlightenment philosophies of crime and punishment propounded by Montesquieu, Beccaria, Voltaire, and Bentham as well as the practical work of British, French, and American reformers such as John Howard, Elizabeth Fry, Sir Thinas Beever, Jean Jacques Vilain, Benjamin Rush, and Thomas Eddy, each of whom advocated separating prisoners by gender and implementing a system of solitary confinement. Such theories and practices directly influenced penal reform in the United States. For instance, American reformers throughout the nineteenth century championed the pioneering work of Howard and Fry, whereas Philadelphia's Society for Alleviating the Miseries of Public Prisons (established 1786), near the turn of the century, published a description of Beever's work at the Wymondham Gaol in England that helped persuade Pennsylvania to pass legislation that brought about the Walnut Street Jail,[3] the first so-called penitentiary in the United States – if not the world. By 1800, eleven of the sixteen states comprising the newly formed republic had approved plans for constructing state penitentiaries like Pennsylvania's, and "prison discipline" – as this new practice would be called – became a hot-button topic for the next hundred years.[4]

Prior to the Civil War, discourse concerning prison discipline culminated in the 1830s and 1840s, making it one of the period's major reform initiatives, along with the movements to abolish slavery and capital punishment and the campaigns for both Temperance and Women's Rights. As David J. Rothman and other historians have noted, however, the first great wave of prison reform began a decade earlier. In 1821, for example, Edward Livingston published his landmark study for the Louisiana state legislature, *Report on a Plan of a Penal Code*, and New York established its seminal Auburn Penitentiary based on a new model of prison discipline. It was during this time, moreover, that numerous penal reform bills were introduced in states across the nation and that several major prisons (in addition to Auburn) and penal institutions were built, such as New York's House of Refuge (1825) for juveniles and state prison at Ossining, commonly known as Sing Sing (1826), Connecticut's Wethersfield (1827), Pennsylvania's famous Eastern State Penitentiary (1829), and New York's Mount Pleasant (1835) for women. Heated debates about the best methods and practices for running penitentiaries and correctional facilities thus played out across much of the nation (excluding the South, where reform lagged), and they came to center around two competing models: the "Pennsylvania" (or "Separate") system, exemplified by the Eastern State Penitentiary, and the "Auburn" (or "Congregate") system, named after New York's famed institution. Influential advocates of the former, such as Samuel Gridley Howe, Dorothea Dix, and Francis Lieber, argued for the continuous isolation of inmates, with periodic visits from ministers and positive role models, in order to encourage their reflection on and repentance of the crimes for which they were incarcerated; those who supported the latter, including Matthew Carey, Louis Dwight, and Francis Wayland, believed in isolating prisoners at night but having them work and worship together in strict silence during the day as a way to promote rehabilitation and to generate revenue for the state. The Auburn System, largely because it was deemed more practical and economically viable, ultimately won out, providing the model for new penitentiaries built in New Hampshire, Vermont, Maryland, Kentucky, Tennessee, Washington, D.C., Illinois, Indiana, Georgia, Missouri, Michigan, Texas, and Arkansas before the Civil War.

Engaging psychological, sociological, legal, and literary perspectives, this chapter surveys the prison and the campaign for its reform from the birth of the penitentiary in Pennsylvania through the eve of the Civil War, as the prison became the cornerstone around which the modern criminal justice system was constructed. With an emphasis throughout on the textuality of prisons, it begins by examining the historical and conceptual interconnections between the institution of imprisonment and that of capital punishment, whose campaign for abolition – like the movement for Temperance – was intimately connected to prison reform. If the death penalty in a democratic republic, as I've argued at length elsewhere,[5] dramatizes the confrontation between the citizen-subject and sovereign authority in its starkest terms, then incarceration complicates that relationship through its prosaic (as opposed to dramatic) structures and its principle aim of reforming (rather than destroying) the criminal. Moving from larger psycho-social concerns in the early history of the penitentiary, the chapter then turns to debates over prison discipline in antebellum America that played out in the popular press, giving special attention to representations of "The Prison" and responses to its reform in the *North American Review*, a prestigious, middle-of-the-road magazine with a national audience that probably did more to shape the common reader's perceptions of prison reform than any other periodical from the period. The stakes of that debate were dramatic, even if the prison itself became banal and routinized in its operations. For with the demise of the death penalty for many crimes in the early nineteenth century, the penitentiary became – quite literally – the most concrete expression of state authority as those convicted of serious crimes would, in lieu of execution, spend up to decades of their lives behind tons of cement and iron. I conclude the chapter with a brief look at a new category of the citizen-subject, the "discharged convict," and a discussion about it that emerges in two little-known periodicals dedicated to America's culture of incarceration at mid-century.

I. Capital punishment and incarceration, Pennsylvania and the penitentiary

Imprisonment and the death penalty, as forms of lawful punishment in the United States, are interconnected in obvious and important ways. To begin with, prolonged incarceration becomes a means of punishing serious crimes only as the separate states, starting with Pennsylvania in 1794, begin drastically to reduce the number of capital statutes and to substitute them with substantial prison terms. America, of course, was not alone in this transformation in penal practices, and the paradigm shift from the death penalty to the penitentiary over the long nineteenth century – from punishment to surveillance and disciplinary practices – has been famously theorized by Michel Foucault and studied by many others.[6] More so than in Europe, where most liberal governments and so-called republics were still monarchical in practice, in the United States the reformation of capital punishment and incarceration were closely interlinked in terms of the rights and liberties of citizens. As Louis P. Masur illustrates, a principled opposition to capital punishment was an important part of the republican politics of the Founding Fathers. William Bradford, John Jay, James Madison, Thomas Jefferson, and Benjamin Rush, for instance, all associated the death penalty with a King's prerogative,[7] thus making it anathema to a truly republican form of government in which the people themselves were sovereign. Speaking for this group, Rush denounced "Capital Punishments" as "the natural offsprings of monarchical governments" and powerfully equated "an execution in a republic" to a "human sacrifice in religion."[8] Rush – the nation's foremost physician, a signer of the Declaration of Independence, and the first great spokesperson for penal reform in America – made these statements in a 1792 essay on the "injustice" and "impolicy" of the death penalty. Five years earlier, he first broached those ideas in *An Inquiry into the Effects of Public Punishments* (1787), a groundbreaking essay on penal reform that, as we shall see, paved the way for the penitentiary to come. Such a political orientation extended its reach for decades, as the most influential opponents of the death penalty were often proponents of prison reform and the new penitentiary. For example, Edward Livingston and Robert Rantoul, Jr. – two of the most distinguished lawyers and legislators from the 1820s and 1830s respectively – each endorsed both causes in legal works that commanded large audiences in the court of public opinion. Whereas Livingston's *Report on a Plan of a Penal Code* (1821) focused on penal reform and plans for a new penitentiary system, it also included a lengthy section arguing for abolishing the death penalty. Likewise, Rantoul's influential *Reports on the Abolition of Capital Punishment* (1835–37) to the Massachusetts legislature made frequent appeals to imprisonment as a more appropriate and effective means of deterring crime and administering criminal justice.

In opposing the death penalty on political grounds, each of the figures – Rush, Livingston, and Rantoul – subscribed to we can call a "republican ideology" or "logic of republicanism," which sought to limit the government's powers and in which a citizen's inalienable right to life was sacrosanct.[9] For instance, echoing earlier arguments of Rush, Rantoul identified "protection" as "the only object of society" and belittled the notion that "any sane man has of his accord bartered away his original right in his own existence."[10] Taking aim specifically at Rousseau's model of the social contract, which he denounced as "anti-republican and slavish" insofar as it legitimated capital punishment, the Massachusetts lawyer and legislator went so far as to claim: "Not only has no man actually given up to society the right to put an end to his life, not only is no surrender of this right under a social compact ever to be implied, but no man can, under a social contract, or any other contract, give up this right to society, or to any constituent part of society, for this conclusive reason, that the right is not his to be conveyed.[11]

That right, for Rantoul, belonged to God alone. Rush, writing a half century earlier, anticipated Rantoul's argument here in his groundbreaking essay on prison reform, first delivered at the home of Benjamin Franklin on March 9, 1787: "The powers over human life," Rush reasoned in *Public Punishments*, "is the solitary prerogative of Him who gave it. Human laws, therefore, rise in rebellion against this prerogative where they transfer it to human hands."[12]

Rush begins that essay by addressing "the design of punishment," whose chief features he lists in order of importance: first, "to reform"; second, "to prevent crimes, by exciting terror in the minds of spectators"; and third, "to remove those persons from society . . . that are unfit to live in it" (4). Ranking the purposes of punishment in this way, Rush reveals an obvious but crucial difference between capital punishment and incarceration. For while both penalties intend to incapacitate offenders and to deter others from committing crime, only imprisonment can be seen as having a reformative effect on criminals themselves, as executions obviously terminate those subjected to it. Rush, however, was not primarily concerned with distinguishing these two kinds of punishment. Rather, his interests lie in exposing the deleterious effects of *all* "public punishments" (including executions), and his essay itself was occasioned by a particular penal practice: Pennsylvania's so-called wheelbarrow law, recently enacted September 15, 1786, which forced felons, chained together or to iron balls, to perform hard labor in the city streets. Such punishment, Rush claimed, degraded and harmed both prisoners and free citizens who witnessed it, "tend[ing] to make bad men worse, and to increase crimes, by their influence upon society" (5). In this way, Rush participated in a larger Enlightenment critique of crime and punishment that he and his audience would have associated with Cesare Beccaria, to whom Rush would twice refer in his later essay criticizing capital punishment. But lest one conclude he "wish[ed] to abolish punishment" in general, Rush clarified his position in his earlier 1787 essay: "I wish only to change the *place* and *manner* of inflicting [punishments], so as to render them effectual for the reformation of criminals, and beneficial to society" (emphasis original 10).

The "place" Rush imagines marks a pivotal moment in both the invention of the U.S. penitentiary and the "manner" of its operations. Calling attention to the effect that "secret" and "unknown" punishment has on the human mind, Rush insists that penal sentences must be carried out privately, behind prison walls, to have an optimal impact on both criminals and society. Moreover, what people value and fear losing most is *not* life itself – without which it is impossible to imagine one's existence – but rather "personal liberty," something anyone can imagine having confiscated; the "loss of it, for an indefinite time," Rush asserts, "is a punishment so severe, that death has often been preferred to it" (10). Hence, far from opposing punishment, Rush seeks the most effective way of administering it – one "calculated to diffuse terror thro' a community, and thereby to prevent crimes" (11). Rooted in a logic of deterrence but committed foremost to reform through the (temporary) confiscation of liberty, his argument for *private* punishment in *Public Punishments* provided the kernel out of which the nineteenth-century prison would grow.

Rush's invocation of the penitentiary to come reaches an apotheosis as he declares, like the Hebraic God of *Genesis* creating the world:

> Let a large house, of a construction agreeable to its design, be erected in a remote part of the state. Let the avenue to this house be rendered difficult and gloomy by mountains or morasses. Let its doors be of iron, and let the grating occasioned by opening and shutting them, be increased by an echo from a neighboring mountain, that shall extend and continue a sound that should deeply pierce the soul. Let a guard constantly attend at a gate that shall lead to his place of punishment, to prevent strangers from entering it.

> Let all the officers of the house be strictly forbidden ever to discover any signs of mirth, or even levity, in the presence of the criminals. To increase the horror of this abode of discipline and misery, let it be called some name that shall import its design.
>
> *(10)*

Conjuring the essential design and symbolic effect of later nineteenth-century prisons – massive gothic edifices of stone and iron, like Pennsylvania's own Eastern State Penitentiary built in the 1820s – Rush's proposition exemplifies John Bender's provocative thesis about eighteenth-century British novelists, such as Daniel Defoe and Henry Fielding, whose fictive descriptions of prisons inspired later generations of architects and penologists involved in their actual construction.[13] Indeed, the prison Rush envisions is fabulous and almost otherworldly, situated, as it were, in a "remote part of the state," entrenched by "mountains or morasses," and reverberating with the clanging of iron gates against a deafening background of silence. Externally designed to elicit terror and fear through its spectacularity, the penitentiary internally would reform through discipline, routine, and banality. Thus, to ground the poetic flights of his conjuration, Rush describes the prosaic terms of actual confinement: "punishments should consist of bodily pain, labor, watchfulness, solitude, and silence," he matter-of-factly states. "They should all be joined with cleanliness and simple diet. . . . The labour should be so regulated and directed, as to be profitable to the state" (12).

The prose and poetics of Rush's imagined penitentiary clearly influenced the theory and penal practices of both the Walnut Street Jail, reformed in 1790, and the Eastern State Penitentiary approved for construction through state legislation some thirty years later. Indeed, Rush's underlying principles of "solitude," "watchfulness" and "silence" in punishment, as well as his practical concerns for the prisoner's "simple diet" and labor "profitable to the state," are evinced through the day-to-day routines and rules that regulate confinement under the new laws governing Walnut Street Jail.[14] But so, too, are the horrors and sufferings of solitary confinement, especially evident in Pennsylvania's landmark *Report on the Penitentiary System* presented by a legislative committee before the state Senate in January 1821. The committee explained:

> To be shut up in a cell for days, weeks, months and years, alone, to be deprived of converse with a fellow being, to have no friendly voice to minister consolation, no friendly bosom on which to lean or into which to pour our sorrows and complaints, but on the contrary, to count the tedious hours as they pass, a prey to the corrodings of conscience and the pangs of guilt, is almost to become the victim of despair.[15]

Hardly reformatory in its appeal here, the committee's punitive emphasis must have proved effective, for its *Report* led to legislation that brought into being plans for the erection of Eastern State. Yet the intense suffering (albeit through nonphysical violence) that the committee describes had, in itself, a reformative purpose in its intent to make inmates "almost" – but not quite – "the victims of despair." Like the gallows' victim whose imminent demise was intended to elicit a conversion from the condemned – a transformation from, to use the common Puritan trope, "a Pillar of Salt" to "a Monument of Grace"[16] – the penitentiary's prey was meant to be brought to a similar reckoning but one they survived. Through this survival would come reformation, a process that unfolded as convicts were removed from evil associates and corrosive environmental factors, thereby forced to look inward or to turn to positive role models provided by the state for moral guidance.

If the state's 1821 *Report on the Penitentiary System*, like Rush's *Public Punishments*, was successful in part because it promised pain and suffering, it also emphasized reform as the primary purpose of punishment. In fact, the *Report* began by announcing that purpose, as Rush's essay does, in its case by rehearsing a "brief history of the Penitentiary in our state" – a history in which Rush played an integral role, not only in writing his essay but in helping to organize Philadelphia's Society for Alleviating the Miseries of Public Prisons. "On the 5th of April, 1790, a law was passed entitled '*An act to reform the penal laws of this state*,' " the 1821 *Report* stated, quoting from the bill that repealed the wheelbarrow law and approved the reforming of the Walnut Street Jail. Because prior laws "have in some degree failed of success, from the exposure of offenders employed at hard labor to public view," the *Report* continued in its citation, "and from the communication with each other not being sufficiently restrained with the places of confinement; and it is hoped that the addition of *unremitted solitude* to laborious employment, as far as it can be effected, will contribute as much to reform as to deter" (emphasis original, 2–3). Sounding a series of keynotes that reverberate throughout the *Report*, the legislative committee went on to underscore the state's failure to follow through with past laws such as the reformatory act of 1790, to reaffirm its commitment to reform, and to emphasize the essential principle of "solitary confinement," a key term to which the *Report* refers another six times in its twelve pages.

*Re*form, indeed, was desperately needed, because of the *form* the prison had assumed: "It seems to be generally admitted," the second document in the *Report* began,

> that the mode at present in use in the penitentiary does not reform the prisoner. It was intended to be a school of reformation; but it is now a school of vice. It cannot be otherwise where so many depraved beings are crowded together, without the means of classification or of adequate employment. There were in confinement, on the first instant, four hundred and twenty-four men and forty women, convicts. For want of room to separate them, the young associate with the old offenders, the petty thief becomes the pupil of the highway robber; the beardless boy listens with delight to the well-told tales of daring exploits and hair-breadth escapes of hoary headed villainy, and from the experience of age derives instruction which fits him to be a pest and terror to society. A community of interest and design is excited among them instead of reformation, ruin is the general result.
>
> (7)

Drawing from the trope of education – a commonplace in the literature of the penitentiary – the *Report* argues for reform by way of a negative example. The prison, regrettably, has become a "school of vice" with the petty thief as "pupil" and the "beardless boy" educated in criminal opportunities and regaled with sensational tales romanticizing crime. A system of separation, the *Report* reasoned, would enable the state to reclaim the prison as a pedagogical place and to reshape its inmates and improve *prison discipline* – a catchall for the methods, modes, strategies, and techniques through which the convict could be reformed into a productive citizen. But to work properly it had to be a "pure solitary system," a plan called for by earlier legislation and imagined by early reformers (such as Rush) but "never yet exhibited in Pennsylvania" (9). Such a system, as we shall see, had certain advantages. For one thing, it would help state officials regain control of narratives that circulated within and about "The Prison." After all, with prisoners isolated from one another, the "highway robber" could no longer instruct, and "hoary headed villainy," removed from an audience, could no longer entertain. The state could thus lay claim to counternarratives of reform, and the prison itself – in its Sphinx-like silence and intimidation – could generate narratives of deterrence through the mysteries of its horrors. Rush, in fact, had the latter effect in mind when he contemplated the psychological impact that a solitary, enigmatic penitentiary would have upon society, especially the young: "Children will press upon the evening fire in listening to the tales that will be spread from this abode of misery," Rush wrote in *Public Punishments*. "Superstition will add to its horrors, and romance will find in it ample material for fiction, which cannot fail of encreasing [*sic*] the terror of its punishments" (11).

The prison would indeed provide rich material for later fiction writers and romancers, as a survey of works from Philadelphia's own Charles Brockden Brown, through the gothic and city-mystery tales of Edgar Allan Poe, George Lippard, Ned Buntline, George Thompson, William Gilmore Simms, and countless others would attest. A source of intrigue and curiosity in its own right, the prison also served as a site in fiction for sentimental investigations into criminal subject formation, expertly rendered by Lydia Maria Child, E.D.E.N Southworth, and Elizabeth Oakes Smith, to name a few. The prison, indeed, figured powerfully in the minds of later nineteenth-century readers and writers alike. "How many images of sorrow, pain, and hope deferred, are raised by that one word, 'Prison!' "[17] began an 1832 article in a literary magazine some four decades after Rush penned *Public Punishments*. It is to that imagery, as it was refracted through the prism of the popular press, that I shall turn our attention in what follows.

II. Prison discipline in the court of public opinion

"The prisons of the United States are confessedly superior in the structure, economy, and reformatory influence, to those of any other nation on the globe," declared a writer, swelling with national pride, to start an 1845 essay in *The Democratic Review*.[18] To be sure, American prisons – especially those in Pennsylvania and New York – were deemed the world's best, and no fewer than five countries had recently sent dignitaries to tour U.S. penal institutions and to study its practices with an eye toward improving their own. Domestically, the United States bustled with interest in prison reform that went well beyond legislative halls and penitentiary walls. In addition to Philadelphia, New York City and Boston became hotbeds for the cause, each city with its own influential prison society and affiliated organizations. If New York, Massachusetts, and Pennsylvania constituted the major hubs of penal reform, news radiated throughout the country by way of the popular press – especially debates related to the nation's competing models: the Pennsylvania, or Separate, system versus the Auburn, or Congregate, system. As Rothman has put it: "If the literature on Auburn and Pennsylvania never quite matched the outpouring of material on the pros and cons of slavery, it came remarkably close."[19]

It would be an impossible task to survey even a fraction of this literature in an overview chapter. We can, however, get a sense of its contours and impact by tracing the discourse surrounding "prison discipline" in one journal, the *North American Review*, and putting it in dialogue with some of the institutions and individuals that helped shape the debate and were relevant to the journal's treatment of it. One of the first extended discussions of prison discipline in the *North American Review* occurs in an 1833 essay on Gustave de Beaumont and Alexis de Tocqueville's *On the Penitentiary System in the United States* (1833), a study commissioned by the French Government. Ostensibly a review, the article explicitly treats de Beaumont and de Tocqueville's work only in its final pages; instead, it spends most of its time providing an overview of penal reform and practices in England and America. Written with the general reader in mind and occasioned by "the general interest recently awakened among us on this subject,"[20] the article begins with John Howard's groundbreaking work in exposing the horrors of the British prison in the late eighteenth century. It then delineates a history of penal reform in Pennsylvania similar to the one I have sketched, emphasizing "the prejudices of the society of Friends against capital punishment first suggested at Philadelphia" (123) that instigated prison reform in the first place, as well as the law of 1790 that led to the state's Separate plan and the reformation of the Walnut Street Jail and the establishment, decades later, of Eastern State Penitentiary. What this chapter adds, however, are important details concerning the history of prison reform in New York: the state's imitation of the Walnut Street Jail in establishing Newgate Prison in 1797; "radical reform" (124) efforts in Auburn from 1816 to 1819, when plans for a state penitentiary were approved; and the state's early experimentations with "solitary confinement . . . night and day, *without labor*" (emphasis original 125), before settling in the early 1820s on a "Congregate" system exemplified at Auburn and later implemented at Ossining (Sing Sing) in 1826. If the principle of separation, as we have seen, served as the hinge on which the Pennsylvania model turned, readers of the *North American Review* learned that "silence" is the fundamental component "absolutely essential to the Auburn plan" and "that nothing but the scourge is found adequate to keep up the discipline of the prison in this respect" (133). More descriptive than analytic, the article closes by outlining the framework of de Beaumont and de Tocqueville's book and noting its imminent translation by esteemed legal scholar and advocate of Pennsylvania's Separate system, Francis Lieber, who would later draft the provisions of war for President Lincoln's administration.

The preceding sketch concerning prison reform in the United States was substantially fleshed out six years later in "Prison Discipline," the lead article of the July 1839 issue of the *North American Review*. Again, written for readers presumably unfamiliar with prison reform and recent developments in the field, the essay starts off by noting the profound "attention, which within the last fifty years, has been given to the subject of prison discipline."[21] This interest, readers are told, justified the journal in "devot[ing] a larger portion of our pages than usual, to a review of the origin, progress, and present conditions of the penitentiary system of the United States" (3). Like the earlier *North American Review* article on de Beaumont and de Tocqueville's work, this one begins its analysis by eulogizing British reformer John Howard, whose "labors must always be the groundwork of all that shall ever be done for the improvement of prison discipline" (6). Detailing the work of Howard for several pages, the article then provides lurid descriptions of the prison – in its pre-reform state – both at home and abroad. One description, certainly designed to titillate as much as to educate readers, is quoted at length from a 1783 account of Pennsylvania's Walnut Street Jail from G.S. Smith's *A Defence of the System of Solitary Confinement of Prisoners, adopted by the State of Pennsylvania*, one of the five books under review in the current article (another was *A Popular Essay on Subjects of Penal Law* by Lieber, identified in a *North American Review* article as a "warm friend of the Pennsylvania system" [34]). Highlighting "abuses in prison discipline" at that time, Smith characterizes the Walnut Street Jail as a "perfect pandemonium," a "den of abomination," wherein

> were mingled, in one revolting mass of festering corruption, all the collected elements of contagion: all *ages*, *colors*, and *sexes* were forced into one horrid, loathsome communion of depravity. Children, committed with their mothers, here first learned to lisp in the strange accents of blasphemy and execration. Young, pure, and modest females, committed for debt, here learned from the hateful society of abandoned prostitutes (whose resting-places on the floor they were compelled to share) the insidious lessons of seduction. The young apprentice, in custody for some venial fault, the tyro in guilt, the unfortunate debtor, the untried and sometimes guiltless prisoner, the innocent witnesses, detained for their evidence in court against those charged with crimes, were associated with the incorrigible felon, the loathsome victim of disease and vice, and the disgusting drunkard (whose means of intoxication were unblushingly furnished by the jailer!).
>
> *(7–8)*

Resonating with the bad example we examined earlier in Pennsylvania's 1821 *Report on Penitentiary System*, this portrait of profligacy instructs by way of a negative example, showing vice to promote the reform of this "nursery of crime" – one of several pedagogical metaphors for malfeasance taught in prisons of old found in the essay (another, developed by the article's author, is "seminaries, in which criminals could select and educate their associates" [15]). The importance of this scene is that it gave a national audience – no doubt, one much larger than what Smith's book alone would have had – a concrete image of what early American prisons were like, or it reinforced assumptions readers already had about them. In fact, the editor of New York's *The Knickerbocker* made special note of the *North American Review* article, calling it "an admirable dissertation upon the systems of prison discipline in the United States" *and* citing in full the excerpt from Smith's book that appeared in the *North American Review*, which *The Knickerbocker* dubbed a "shocking description" that "too accurately depicts the condition of the greater part of the prisons in this country in 1788–9."[22] Other periodicals, such as *The American Jurist and Law Magazine*, the *Boston Recorder*, *The New York Review*, the *Boston Weekly Magazine*, and *The American Almanac and Repository of Useful Knowledge* all referenced or acknowledged the *North American Review* "Prison Discipline" article, thus illustrating its impact in the court of public opinion.[23]

The *North American Review* article in question appealed to such a public court and threw its proverbial hat into the political ring in working through a history of American prison reform. With an image of the degraded and degrading prison graphically rendered for readers, the author of "Prison Discipline" would go on to ask: "What can be more inexcusably culpable, than for the intelligent, responsible citizens of a free country to suffer such abominations to go on, year after year, uncorrected?" (14–15). This rhetorical question – calling upon the duties of citizens in a democratic republic to care for a penal system administered in their names – sets up a discussion of the "responsible" response of two groups of citizens from different regions of the country: on the one hand, "the citizens of Philadelphia" who first organized the city's Society for Assisting Distressed Prisoners in 1776 and then, as we have seen, the Society for Alleviating the Miseries of Public Prisons, to which both Benjamin Franklin and Benjamin Rush belonged (16); and on the other, a coalition from Boston called the Prison Discipline Society, founded in 1825 by Reverend Louis Dwight who still controlled the group and served as its Secretary in 1839 (and did so until his death in 1854). If the origins of prison reform lie in Philadelphia, authority over its development and practices clearly shifted to Boston shortly after its prison society was founded. Under Dwight's influential leadership, the Boston group began touring the nation's prisons and writing comprehensive annual studies about them. These annual and quasi official Reports, "forming together a volume of twelve hundred and thirty four closely printed octavo pages" (17) when the 1839 *North American Review* article was published, were used by Massachusetts' and other states' legislatures in reforming their prison laws and implementing their penal practices. During its thirteen years of producing and circulating its authoritative Reports, Dwight's Prison Discipline Society consistently censured Pennsylvania's Separate system and repeatedly recommended New York's Congregate model, which had been implemented in nine other states since 1835 – including Massachusetts.[24]

In its analysis of these competing systems, the *North American Review* article squarely sides with the Congregate model. From an "examination of facts," its author concludes that

> the Pennsylvania system can claim no superiority over the other. It is not proved to be either more reformatory, more humane, more easy of management, or more healthy. Indeed, so far as the results can be compared, it appears to be in most of these respects decidedly, though not greatly, inferior.
>
> *(38–39)*

By criticizing the Pennsylvania plan in this manner, the *North American Review* joined a contentious debate that had developed between Boston and Philadelphia over the future of prison discipline. The impact that the *North American Review* article had in this debate is perhaps best registered through Philadelphia's response. Incensed by the article's negative assessment, the

Society for Alleviating the Miseries of Public Prisons convened a special meeting, as noted in the group's minutes for August 17, 1839, "to hear an article on the Pennsylvania System of Prison Discipline in reply to one in the North America Review (July, 1839)."[25] That response, a detailed treatise written by a Philadelphia lawyer, was published later that year as *A Vindication of the Separate System of Prison Discipline from the Misrepresentations of the North American Review, July, 1839*. From this moment through the mid-1840s, a veritable "quarrel" intensified between both cities that a later reviewer for the *North American Review* summed up in crude, partisan terms:

> "You drive the prisoners mad," cries Boston, "by the long continued horrors of solitary confinements"; "You subject the criminal to the cruel and degrading punishment of the lash," shouts Philadelphia. "Your own statistics," exclaims the former, "show a fearful amount of insanity and mortality in your prisons"; "Figures prove nothing, and there is a mistake in your calculations," retorts the latter.[26]

This caricatured exchange came from the journal's review of Samuel Gridley Howe's *An Essay on Separate and Congregate Systems of Prison Discipline; Being a Report Made to the Boston Prison Discipline Society*, one of the most impactful (and certainly most controversial) works on prison discipline published in the 1840s. Written by an influential Massachusetts legislator, abolitionist, and eminent physician best known for his work with the blind, Howe's *Minority Report* (as his essay was known) played a crucial role in the prison debate, not only because of its author's esteemed reputation but for the circumstances surrounding the report's publication. As explained in the preface, Howe had long taken for granted the accuracy and wisdom of the annual Reports produced by Boston's Prison Discipline Society, to which Howe himself belonged, but he began to question the society's consistent and "severe" censure of the Pennsylvania system, given that system's universal acclaim in European studies like de Beaumont and de Tocqueville's. This suspicion of inaccuracy and "unfairness," coupled with the "partisan character" of the Reports in their advocacy of the Congregate system, prompted Howe's "personal inspection of the principle prisons of the United States, and reflection upon the subject."[27] Sharing his views with Boston's society, Howe was appointed chair of a subcommittee to review the Society's *Reports*, whose primary author was Secretary Dwight, who also served on the subcommittee along with Charles Sumner and Horace Mann, both of whom were influential members of the Massachusetts state legislature, along with Howe. In its detailed comparison of the two systems, Howe's *Minority Report* argued for the "vast superiority" of the Pennsylvania system and basically accused the society and Secretary Dwight of manipulating data. As one might imagine, Boston's Prison Discipline Society suppressed the *Minority Report*, calling it "unjust to the Secretary and suicide to the Society" (vi) and claiming that the report itself "had no legal existence" (vii). In defiance, Howe, along with committee members Mann and Sumner, sought a larger audience for the report in the court of public opinion and thus "resolved to print it ourselves" (ix).

In addition to its publication context, Howe's *Minority Report* is valuable for its distillation of the key differences between, as well as the shared assumptions of, the Separate and the Congregate systems. Writing for the general reader and as if in response to pro-Auburn arguments like that of the *North American Review*'s "Prison Discipline," Howe demonstrates exactly how (from his perspective) the Pennsylvania system more effectively reforms and more humanely treats its convicts and how it is easier to manage and administer. It reforms more effectively, he argues, through its underlying principle of *continuous separation*, which disables any communication among prisoners themselves and leaves them, as noted earlier, only to self-reflection and to interaction with agents whom the state deems as positive influences. The system, moreover, is more humane insofar as it does not constantly tempt speech and nonverbal interaction among inmates through their close proximity to one another (sometimes within six inches) during the day or require a quick response from the lash for anyone who violates the Congregate system's policy of strict silence. Additionally, a system of complete isolation is easier to manage in its self-sufficiency – given that there is no silence to maintain through the threat or enactment of violence – just as a "machine," Howe reasons at one point, with fewer parts and a greater "simplicity" in design, is easier to operate and maintain (33).

Notwithstanding these distinctions, Howe emphasizes the shared principle of separation that undergirds each system. Indeed, the main difference is that "one attempts to do partially what the other attempts to do thoroughly" (17). Hence, Howe reasons, "the Auburn system is only a partial and imperfect Pennsylvania system" (18) – a point he drives home by comparing "moderate drinking" to "total abstinence . . . in the prevention of drunkenness" (19). By drawing such an analogy, Howe appeals to the lay reader and not to the professional penologist well versed in the niceties of prison discipline. Speaking to this audience, Howe, like the author of *North American Review*'s "Prison Discipline," calls upon the responsibilities of U.S. citizens for the convict, "stripped of his citizen's garb," both within and outside prison walls. That appeal cut to the core of civic duty, emphasizing the responsibilities of Americans compared to those of citizens (or rather subjects) of other nations who are *subjected* to the authority of their governments instead of meaningful participants of them: "In those countries where the citizens have no part or lot in the government," Howe writes in his preface, "they may wash their hands of this wrong; but here where we boast that our rulers are our servants, and their acts the expression of our will, how shall we answer for the treatment of our fallen brother?" (iv) Those responsibilities – concomitant with the rights and liberties of U.S. citizens – are especially important when the fallen are among the nation's youth: "When a government seizes upon a person, especially if he be young, and deprives him of all liberty of action, it assumes at once the office, and incurs the responsibilities, of a parent and guardian" (iv). Asking readers to imagine someone sentenced to death as their own son or daughter, as Howe does here of the individual committed to prison, was a common strategy employed by antigallows activists during the antebellum period.[28] Such paternalism, applied to the prison convict as opposed to the condemned, sentimentalized the criminal subject but in different ways; for the lawfully condemned, as I suggested to begin this chapter, ceased to be a citizen (or anything at all) after the law's sentence was enacted. The convict, in contrast, would likely reenter the world from which he or she was removed, albeit forever marked by the performative act of a past legal conviction – in spite of any reformation or positive change in character that might have occurred in the penitentiary. "We look with interest upon the reformed drunkard and the reformed gambler," Howe remonstrates at one point in his *Minority Report*; "but the poor convict, the prison-bird, is a Pariah for life" (44).

This peculiar afterlife brought into being a new category of the citizen-subject in the nineteenth century, once the exconvict – to appropriate Howe's metaphor – put *back on* the "citizen's garb." To be sure, for the first time in history, scores of individuals who had spent much (in some cases most) of their lives behind bars were reintegrated into society. What did such a life look like, especially for those who had served a "life" sentence or one extending a decade or more? What, if anything, did society (in a democratic, republic sense) owe to them once their debt was paid to it? And how and in what ways might society, in the first place, be responsible for criminal subject formation? Such were among the questions asked not only by Howe but by two periodicals dedicated to prison reform that began publication independently of each other the year before Howe's *Minority Report* appeared in the court of public opinion.

One of them was *The Pennsylvania Journal of Prison Discipline and Philanthropy*, which served as the official organ for Philadelphia's Society for Alleviating the Miseries of Public Prisons, later renamed "The Pennsylvania Prison Society." For the most part a professional journal, it printed penitentiary reports from around the country and abroad, socioeconomic studies of prisoners and criminal activities, letters from wardens and other penal officials, medical and psychiatric studies written by physicians, and treatises related to prison discipline from other professions and academic fields – including a series of forty-page technical reports on the ventilation systems at the Eastern State Penitentiary.[29] The *Pennsylvania Journal* also reached out to a broader audience. It attacked or defended itself against Boston's Prison Discipline Society and its allies in the propaganda war over prison reform, and it featured biographical sketches of famous reformers, as well as an occasional imaginative piece, such as "A Cell in a Separate Prison." Providing a virtual tour of Pennsylvania's "Eastern or Western State Penitentiaries," that piece walked readers through the prison's corridors and cells to show how humane, reasonable, and effective its practices were, thus disabusing the journal's general readers of the stereotypes and assumptions about the penitentiary's inhumane and barbarous practices that were popularized, no doubt, by Charles Dickens' censorious reflections about his visit to Eastern State in *American Notes for General Circulation* (1842). "All notions of ghosts and hobgoblins, madness and death," the article assured readers, "would at once be dissipated, or transferred from the separate to the congregate prison" upon such a visit.[30]

Articles like "A Cell in a Separate Prison" accounted for a larger percentage of the material printed in *The Prisoner's Friend: A Monthly Magazine Devoted to Criminal Reform, Philosophy, Literature, Science and Art*, the second periodical dedicated to the cause and also launched in 1845. Edited by tireless reformer Charles Spear, the Boston-based weekly (it would become a monthly in 1848) enjoyed an estimated readership of approximately 10,000 and published short articles and literature related to every – and *any* – aspect of prison reform and antigallows activism.[31] Truly a variety paper, *The Prisoner's Friend* printed excerpts from capital punishment and prison reports, descriptions of ongoing meetings related to both causes, as well as sermons, book reviews, biographical sketches, fiction, poetry, news reports, editorial correspondence, and advertisements concerning its interrelated interest in abolishing the death penalty and reforming the prison. It also developed a series of original columns based on developing issues in the field of penal reform.

One such column, perfectly pitched to address Howe's concerns about exconvicts, focused on "Discharged Convicts" and society's responsibility to them. In fact, in his first editorial on the topic, Spear echoed Howe by describing the *trans*formative and *re*formative moment when the discharged convict's prison "dress is removed" and a "citizen's dress resumed," emphasizing the potential of the exconvict – through society's "encouragement" (the subject of subsequent columns in the series) – to become a "useful citizen."[32] A week later in the second number of the series, Spear bolstered his case by enlisting statistical evidence provided in annual Reports from the Boston Prison Discipline Society, whose "best estimate" from data collected in 1840 was that "about six thousand [exconvicts] are now abroad in society" – a staggering number, from Spear's perspective, given how many more convicts must have been released nationally between 1840 and 1846, since Boston alone discharged about one hundred annually.[33] Appealing both to sentiment and to one's civic duties in a democratic republic, Spear wonders, "Who that has a son or brother, or father, or sister, in prison, can help feeling a deep interest in the subject on which we have now entered?" and concludes the column by reminding the reader of "his duty towards this unfortunate class of his fellow-beings."[34]

Lydia Maria Child – who wrote extensively about crime, punishment, and the penitentiary in her massively popular *New York Letters* and elsewhere – also advocated for the rights and welfare of exconvicts and indicted "Society," as she often would put it, for "mak[ing] its own criminals."[35] Child's work is often excerpted in *The Prisoner's Friend*, and the author herself is cited authoritatively in more than one of the magazine's dozens of articles on "Discharged Convicts." Similarly, Nathaniel Hawthorne and Herman Melville, if we follow Carol Coletrella and especially Caleb Smith's brilliant reading in *The Prison and the American Imagination*,[36] drew from the figure of the exconvict to create two of American literature's most memorable characters: the skittish, imbecilic Clifford Pyncheon in *The House of the Seven Gables*, released from a thirty-year prison sentence, and the inscrutable Bartleby, estranged from himself and the world at large in the tale that bears his name. Coletrella and Smith, in different ways, insightfully link the mannerisms of Hawthorne's and Melville's discharged convicts (again, if we assume the mysterious Bartleby to be one) to Dickens' 1842 portrayal of prisoners at Pennsylvania's Eastern State, whom the British writer sympathetically described as "secretly terrified," cadaverous men who appeared "buried alive."[37] Likely inspired by Dickens, Hawthorne and Melville may also have been drawing from sources closer to home and closer in time; for *The Prisoner's Friend*, whose Boston offices were not far from where each author lived in the late 1840s and early 1850s, published notable articles in the "Discharged Convict" series. One was "The Aged Criminal," which concerned a "feeble old man," recently released, who had "spent thirty-one years of his life in our State prison!"[38] Another recounted a perplexed businessman's (or lawyer's, the profession is not clear) encounter with a Bartleby-like figure: "a very tidily-dressed and well behaved man, who was out of employment, but competent and willing to labor, and seeking a place" and who "could write well."[39] The strange man, "a skillful accountant," we learn, who appears before the businessman's door is a "discharged convict" whom no one will employ despite his skills. "Is it not pertinent to inquire, through your Journal," the anonymous businessman asks in this letter originally written to the *Pennsylvania Journal of Prison Discipline* and reprinted in *The Prisoner's Friend* in 1850, "what is to be done with such a man? If he remains unemployed, he must beg, or steal, or starve. He will not beg while has a muscle to use, honestly or knavishly."[40]

Such an inquiry resonates with the larger question of social responsibility and civic duty that riddles "Bartleby" itself and that Samuel Gridley Howe and the contributors to both *The Prisoner's Friend* and *Pennsylvania Journal of Prison Discipline* often asked their readers. And such questions – not only about the reformation of convicts and the welfare of discharged prisoners but of "The Prison" as such – provide a rich context for reevaluating the literature of the American Renaissance, especially in terms of race and gender, important categories well beyond the scope of my investigation. Much work indeed remains to be done, as prison reform played a crucial role in the cultural context for the flowering of American literature at mid-century.

Notes

1 "Prisons," Peter Caster writes, "are a ubiquitous part of how contemporary U.S. culture imagines itself, as suggested by the more than 250 U.S. films featuring men in prison and almost 100 focusing on women in prison." Peter Caster, *Prisons, Race, and Masculinity in Twentieth Century U.S. Literature and Film* (Columbus: Ohio State University Press, 2008), xi.

2 Nathaniel Hawthorne, *The Scarlet Letter*, ed. William Charvat, Roy Harvey Pearce, and Claude M. Simpson (Columbus: University of Ohio Press, 1962), 36. Stuart Banner, referencing Hester's ascension on the scaffold, calls it a "simulated hanging" or "*symbolic* death, a penalty that mimicked some aspects of capital punishment without actually killing the defendant." See Banner, *The Death Penalty: An American History* (Cambridge, Mass.: Harvard University Press, 2002), emphasis in original, 54.

3 Negley K. Teeters, *The Cradle of the Penitentiary: The Walnut Street Jail in Philadelphia, 1773–1835* (Philadelphia: Pennsylvania Prison Society, 1955), 32.

4 My understanding of the history concerning the American prison draws from David J. Rothman's *The Discovery of the Asylum*, rev. ed. (Boston: Little, Brown, 1990) and his "Perfecting the Prison: United States, 1789–1865," in *The Oxford History of the Prison*, ed. Norval Morris and David J. Rothman (New York: Oxford University Press, 1995), 111–29; Michael Ignatieff's *A Just Measure of Pain: The Penitentiary in the Industrial Revolution* (New York: Pantheon Books, 1978); Walter D. Lewis's *From Newgate to Dannemora: The Rise of the Penitentiary in New York* (Ithaca, N.Y.: Cornell University Press, 1965); Blake McKelvey's *American Prisons: A History of Good Intentions* (Montclair, N.J.: Patterson Smith, 1977); Michael Meranze's *Laboratories of Virtue: Punishment, Revolution, and Authority in Philadelphia* (Chapel Hill:

University of North Carolina Press, 1996); and Adam J. Hirsch's *The Rise of the Penitentiary* (New Haven, Conn.: Yale University Press, 1992).

5 This claim accounts for one of the central theses of my book, *Literary Executions: Capital Punishment and American Culture, 1820–1925* (Baltimore: Johns Hopkins University Press, 2014). See, for example, the introduction, "The Cultural Rhetoric of Capital Punishment."

6 In addition to Foucault's *Discipline and Punish*, trans. Alan Sheridan (New York: Pantheon Books, 1977), see David Rothman's *The Discovery of the Asylum* and Michael Ignatieff's *A Just Measure of Pain* for authoritative accounts of this transformation from the eighteenth to the nineteenth centuries.

7 Louis P. Masur, *Rites of Execution: Capital Punishment and the Transformation of American Culture* (New York: Oxford University Press, 1989), 61–2.

8 Benjamin Rush, *Considerations on the Injustice and Impolicy of Punishing Murder by Death* (Philadelphia: Carey, 1792), 18–19.

9 These are Masur's productive terms for a broader ideology or logic of republicanism, in which opposition to death penalty played a fundamental role. See Masur, *Rites of Execution*, 61.

10 Robert Rantoul, Jr., *Memoirs, Speeches and Writings of Robert Rantoul, Jr.* ed. Luther Hamilton (Boston: Jewett, 1854), 442.

11 Ibid., 440, 443.

12 Benjamin Rush, *An Enquiry into the Effects of Public Punishments upon Criminals, and upon Society, in Two Essays: A Plan for the Punishment of Crime*, ed. Negley K. Teeters (Philadelphia: Pennsylvania Prison Society, 1954), 15. Hereafter cited parenthetically.

13 See John Bender, *Imagining the Penitentiary: Fiction and the Architecture of Mind in Eighteenth-Century England* (Chicago: University of Chicago Press, 1987), especially chaps. 1–3.

14 See, for instance, the descriptions of rules and protocols of Walnut Street Jail in Caleb Lownes's *An Account of the Alteration and Present State of the Penal Laws of Pennsylvania, Containing also an Account of the Gaol and Penitentiary House of Philadelphia and the Interior Management Thereof* (1793), appended to William Bradford's *An Enquiry How Far the Punishment of Death Is Necessary in Pennsylvania* (Philadelphia: Dobson, 1793). Those works are collected in *Reform of Criminal Law in Pennsylvania: Selected Enquiries: 1787–1819*, ed. Morton J. Horwitz and Stanley N. Katz (New York: Arno, 1972).

15 Pennsylvania General Assembly, Senate, Committee of the Penitentiary System, *Report on the Penitentiary System* (Harrisburg, Pa.: Buyers, 1821), 9. Hereafter cited parenthetically.

16 In the preface to a well-known execution sermon, Minister John Rogers describes the condemned woman's transformation, through confession and repentance, from guilty sinner to redeemed member of the Elect as "A Pillar of Salt Transformed into a Free Monument of Grace." See *The Declaration & Confession of Esther Rodgers* (1701) collected in Daniel E. Williams, ed., *Pillars of Salt: An Anthology of Early American Criminal Narratives* (Madison, Wis.: Madison House, 1993), 95. Cotton Mather also used the trope in the title of his collection of execution sermons, *Pillars of Salt* (1699), also collected in Williams. For discussions of this trope in early American crime literature, see, especially, Daniel Cohen's *Pillars of Salt, Monuments of Grace: New England Crime Literature and the Origins of American Popular Culture, 1674–1860* (Oxford: Oxford University Press, 1993). See also Karen Haltunnen's *Murder Most Foul: The Killer and the American Gothic Imagination* (Cambridge, Mass.: Harvard University Press, 1998).

17 Anon., "Seventh Annual Report of the Board of Managers of the Prison Discipline Society, Boston," *The New England Magazine* 3 (December 1832), 515–17, 515.

18 Anon., "The Clinton State Prison," *Democratic Review* 17 (November 1845), 345–53, 345.

19 Rothman, *The Oxford History of the Prison*, 117.

20 Anon., "De Beaumont and De Tocqueville on the Penitentiary System," *North American Review* 37 (1833): 117–38, 118. Hereafter cited parenthetically.

21 Anon., "Prison Discipline," *North American Review* 49 (July 1839), 1–43, 1. Hereafter cited parenthetically.

22 See Anon., "Editor's Table," *The Knickerbocker; or New York Monthly Magazine* 14 (August 1839), 184.

23 See, for instance, Professor Carl J. Anton Mittermaier, "On the Progress of the Penitentiary Improvement in Europe and North America," *American Jurist and Law Magazine* 28 (October 1842), 110–49; Anon., "Prison Discipline," *Boston Recorder*, July 19, 1839, 113; Anon. [untitled], *The New York Review* 6, no. 11 (January 1840), 12; Anon., "Weekly Record," *Boston Weekly Magazine* 1, no. 45 (July 13, 1849), 359.

24 McKelvy, *American Prisons*, 27–9.

25 Quoted in Negley K. Teeter, *They Were in Prison: A History of the Pennsylvania Prison Society* (Chicago: Winston, 1937), 194.

26 Anon., "Howe on Prison Discipline," *North American Review* 64 (1847): 257–60, 259.

27 Samuel G. Howe, *An Essay on the Separate and Congregate Systems of Prison Discipline; Being a Report Made to the Boston Prison Discipline Society* (Boston: Ticknor, 1846), iv, iii. Hereafter cited parenthetically.

28 Lydia M. Child and Sylvester Judd, for instance, make such appeals in their fiction. See Barton, *Literary Executions*, 92–4, 133. For a broader discussion of sentimentalism in antigallows writing, see also chapter 5 ("Women's Anti-Gallows Writing: The Sentimental Strategy of E.D.E.N Southworth") in Paul C. Jones's *Against the Gallows: Antebellum American Writers and the Movement to Abolish Capital Punishment* (Iowa City: University of Iowa Press, 2011).

29 For instance, see Articles II and III, both titled, "On the Ventilation and Warming of Prisons and Other Buildings," in *Pennsylvania Journal of Prison and Philanthropy*. The first appears in vol. 1, no. 3 (July 1845) and the second in vol. 1, no. 4 (October 1845).

30 Anon., "A Cell in a Separate Prison," *Journal of Prison Discipline and Philanthropy* 14, no. 2 (April 1859): 49.

31 Spear himself estimates this readership in an advertisement to subscribers to donate money or to help increase the paper's circulation. See *The Prisoner's Friend* 1, no. 44 (November 4, 1846): 174. I am indebted to Birte Christ for calling my attention to this article from Spear's magazine. See Christ, "Popular Thought and Public Faith: Anti-Gallows Poetry of the 1840s and 1850s" (unpublished manuscript), 14.

32 Charles Spear, "Discharged Convicts: Number 1," *Prisoner's Friend* 1, no. 1 (January 7, 1846): 2.

33 Spear, "Discharged Convicts: No. II Number Annually Discharged Statistics of Fifteen Penitentiaries from Reports of 1840, 1841," *Prisoner's Friend* 1, no. 2 (January 14, 1846): 6.

34 Ibid.

35 Lydia M. Child, "Kindness to Criminals – The Prison Association," *Prisoner's Friend* 1, no. 33 (November 12, 1845): 132.

36 See especially Caleb Smith, *The Prison and the American Imagination* (New Haven, Conn.: Yale University Press, 2009), 59–72. See also Carol Colatrella, *Literature and Moral Reform: Melville and the Discipline of Reading* (Gainesville: University Press of Florida, 2002), 35–52.

37 Dickens, *American Notes* (London: Chapman and Hall, 1910), 119, 129.

38 Anon., "The Aged Criminal," *Prisoner's Friend* 1, no. 16 (April 22, 1846): 1, 16, 62.

39 Anon., "Discharged Convicts: Article XI," *Prisoner's Friend* 3, no. 4 (December 1, 1850): 179. This story is reprinted in the magazine from *The Pennsylvania Journal of Prison Discipline*.

40 Ibid., 180.

15
HOW MEETINGS WON THE WEST

Andrea McDowell

On March 15, 1851, in the California gold rush town of Shasta City, Pearson Easterbrook was tried, convicted, and hanged for the murder of his messmate, Price. The citizens of Shasta held a meeting and ran the trial and the execution themselves because there were no courts in that part of the state. The Californians called this process "trial by Judge Lynch." It takes no imagination to see how it might go wrong, but, according to the transcript, Easterbrook's trial could hardly have been more methodical and formal. A Mr. Enos Dutton was appointed chairman, and a Robert Crenshaw, secretary. Then "[a] motion was made and seconded, to appoint a committee of three to select a jury of twelve men, to try the cause before the people," and this was carried unanimously. The committee was chosen, and it duly elected twelve men as jurors; the full names of all of these parties appear in the published transcript. Further motions were made, seconded, and carried: to allow the accused a fair and impartial trial; to call the witnesses; and to instruct the chairman to swear the jury and the witnesses. The witnesses testified at length and the jury retired, briefly, before returning a verdict of guilty.[1]

I have spared the reader the full account of Easterbrook's trial because, as one can tell from this summary, the process of electing a chairman and secretary, appointing a committee, making motions, seconding them, and voting was utterly conventional. The reporter could have been describing the proceedings of a new literary society. In fact, much of the trial procedure was *exactly* like a nineteenth-century meeting of a benevolent society, Young Men's Club, or a political party. The thesis of this chapter is that the men who tried Easterbrook, like most Americans on the frontier, were familiar with voluntary or political associations in their home towns in New York, Massachusetts, Texas, Missouri, or elsewhere, and they had a general knowledge of the rules of parliamentary procedure that we now know as Robert's Rules of Order. They came West with a shared model of how to run a meeting and the assumption that this was the way to make communal decisions, even in haste and at a time of great excitement, such as a trial for murder.

The rules they knew were basic. The organization has a chair who runs the meeting. Business is brought before the meeting by means of a motion, made and seconded, usually in the form of "*Resolved*: etc." Members then debate the motion. No member may speak until recognized by the chair, every member may speak unless two-thirds of the assembly vote to close the debate, the chair puts the question, and there is a vote. Some further specific rules will be discussed in this chapter.

Using these procedural rules, Americans formed joint stock companies for founding new settlements on the Great Plains, for traveling to Oregon and California, for engaging in large-scale mining projects, and for building huge flumes and tunnels to bring water from the mountains to the dry diggings. With the same tools, they enacted mining codes and tried and punished crimes like Easterbrook's. The widespread familiarity with one system of procedure enabled men on the frontier to organize themselves quickly and to have a reasonable expectation that everyone would respect majority decisions. It sometimes turned out that the rules drawn up in advance were unsuitable to the pioneers' needs or were rendered obsolete by changing circumstances. In such cases, they did not hesitate to dissolve their companies or devise new rules on the spot, and both dissolutions and the adoption of new rules took place at meetings run along parliamentary lines. The procedure itself was, in the end, as important as the constitution or company that it produced.

As the term "parliamentary rules" suggests, the procedure originated in the British House of Commons.[2] The British Parliament's rules were not codified but had evolved over centuries through usage and precedent, like common law.[3] The British brought this "common parliamentary law," as it was called, to America, where it was used by colonial bodies and, later, by Congress and the state assemblies, except when the body had enacted superseding rules.[4] The United States Senate, for instance, had officially adopted a few rules and referred all other questions of order to their president, who presumably applied the common law as he understood it.[5] Thomas Jefferson, who knew the deficiencies of this haphazard system from his term as vice president (1787–1801), sought to promote order and method by publishing a *Manual of Parliamentary Practice for the Use of the Senate of the United States* (1801).

Most educated British and American citizens were conversant with parliamentary procedure through their participation in voluntary associations formed to promote public improvements, education, poor relief, the advancement of religion, and, most often, camaraderie and mutual support.[6] Such societies were already widespread in the United Kingdom by 1710, and their numbers increased rapidly thereafter.[7] Their organization and procedures were clearly modeled on Parliament's. The simplest form of society had a president, a secretary, and a standing committee; large philanthropic societies might have dozens of officers and multiple committees.[8] When British citizens gathered to establish a new society, they followed the steps that would later be used by Americans on the frontier; an individual was called to the chair, a committee prepared a constitution, and resolutions were moved and voted upon.[9] What de Tocqueville and others would describe as a distinctive American trait, the ability to organize quickly for joint action, clearly originated in the United Kingdom.[10]

Americans founded societies on the British model from a very early date, and the number of societies surged after the revolutionary war, stimulated by urbanization, commerce, the growing number of newspapers, and a lack of government engagement in philanthropy and the promotion of agriculture and manufacturing.[11] Americans who joined these voluntary associations not only observed organizational procedures and skills in action but also became involved in running the societies. The 1810s and 1820s saw the foundation of nationwide political parties, Bible and missionary societies, and temperance movements. These were organized as a central committee with auxiliary branches around the country, again following a British model.[12] The centralized associations distributed annual reports to their subsidiaries, familiarizing Americans across the country with their procedures.[13]

Ever increasing participation in associations created a need for popular handbooks on parliamentary rules. Luther Stearns Cushing's *Manual of Parliamentary Practice: Rules of Proceeding and Debate in Deliberative Assemblies*, commonly known as *Cushing's Manual* (1845), was the first to fill the void.[14] Cushing's manual was based on Jefferson's but was intended for the average citizen.[15] An endorsement by the *Law Reporter*, included in the first pages of Cushing's book, states that "the necessity of such a work as this has been very generally felt in our country, where almost every citizen is occasionally called upon to exercise the duties of a presiding officer."[16] This is an astounding remark; it certainly could not be said of America today. But even if the writer was exaggerating, it was not by much. Henry M. Robert himself, author of *Robert's Rules of Order*, first interested himself in procedure in 1863, as a result of being unexpectedly asked to serve as chairman of a meeting. Too embarrassed to admit his ignorance, he muddled through, but he determined on the spot to teach himself parliamentary law before he attended another meeting.[17] In 1924, James W. Witham, the author of another handbook on procedure for the ordinary man, said that his aim was to equip even "the most inexperienced person of limited education" not only to participate in meetings but also "to act as chairman of the same and acquit himself with credit."[18]

In addition to rules for running established associations, there were rules for organizing on the spot to carry out a project or make a decision. Both Cushing and Robert devote sections of their manuals to a mass meeting, described by Roberts as a "public assembly called together to consider some special subject."[19] Such a meeting is like a temporary association whose rules are those of the "common parliamentary law." The meeting begins when one of the organizers calls the members to order and nominates a chairman or calls for nominations. The first name mentioned is put to a vote; if the response is negative, then another nomination is considered, and so on until they have a chairman; the chairman similarly presides over the election of a secretary; and the meeting can get started. The chairman explains the purpose of the meeting, and members either propose resolutions or move that a committee be appointed to draft resolutions suitable to carrying out the purpose of the meeting.[20] In the latter case, the committee retires and returns with a series of resolutions, which are moved and seconded and put to a voice vote.[21] The beauty of this system of self-organization – or rather, of everyone's familiarity with the system – is that a large group could coordinate quickly and efficiently for a common enterprise, such as to deal with an emergency. For example, when the citizens of New York met at the City Hotel on February 17, 1817, to raise funds "for the relief of the Poor, then suffering from the extreme inclemency of the weather, and other causes," they elected a general committee. This committee could not report back at once but directed the chairman, secretary, and treasurer to report their findings to the public.[22] Note how closely the miners who tried Easterbrook followed these same procedures.

Thirdly, parliamentary rules were used to create new long-lasting associations and joint stock companies. "The Organization of a Permanent Society," as described by Robert, begins, like a mass meeting, with the election of a chairman and secretary.[23] When the assembly has passed a resolution to form the proposed society, the chairman appoints a committee to draft bylaws.[24] The bylaws thus drafted are presented to the members and are discussed section by section and, if necessary, amended; the whole is then put to a vote.[25] Cushing's manual does not discuss the creation of a constitution but does say that, if more officers are desired, "it is the practice to organize temporarily, in the manner above mentioned, and then to refer the subject of a permanent organization . . . to a committee; upon whose report, the meeting proceeds to organize itself."[26]

It would be tedious to give multiple accounts of this model in action when a single example will suffice.[27] Parliamentary practice and the humanities come together in the foundation of the literary society, or Lyceum, of Greenwood, South Carolina, on March 25, 1842.[28] At a meeting of the people of Greenwood, "the Rev. William P. Hill was called to the Chair, and Geo. W. Curtiss appointed Secretary." A preamble and Constitution had been prepared in advance and were presented to the assembly. The preamble announced the purpose of the society: "to promote the advancement of Science and Literature" and for "securing the services of able lecturers." The Constitution consists of the form of and rules for the Lyceum, just as one would expect. The members are to elect a president, vice president, secretary, and treasurer at each annual meeting. As Theda Skocpol points out, this type of rotation in office familiarized many citizens with the inner workings of organizations, assuming, of course, that the members did not reelect the same officers every year.[29] The president's job is to preside at meetings, preserve order, and put the question for decision. A majority of the whole membership shall form a quorum, and amendments to the Constitution must be approved by two-thirds of the members present. "Which Constitution, on motion of Thos. L. Whitlock, Esqr, was unanimously adopted." In short, it was all very much according to form.[30]

Pioneers and frontiersmen employed all three of the aforementioned branches of parliamentary practice: creating new associations, conducting the business of such associations, and holding mass meetings. They used these tools to form companies for the westward journey and for mutual support and protection in their new homes; for establishing claim clubs to protect one another's rights to land before it was legally available for settlement; to adjudicate differences between themselves; to make rules for lead mines in Illinois and for gold and silver mines further west; to carry out joint endeavors; and to try and punish criminals.

The frontiersmen, who were beyond the reach of law or its agents, were fortunate that they all knew and recognized one set of rules for decision making. This was least important when a group of neighbors met in a living room in Massachusetts to plan their trip west, when it was relatively easy to achieve a consensus. The advantage of universally accepted rules was greatest in the mining camps where hundreds of men from every part of the country adopted law codes or held criminal trials. When the discoverers of a diggings passed rules favoring themselves, for example, newcomers had a recognized mechanism for decreasing claim sizes – and even the losers accepted the outcome as legitimate.

The great thing was that the rules were shared. As Thomas Jefferson wrote in his section on "The Importance of Adhering to Rules," it was "really not of so great importance" that the rules were the best of their kind: "[i]t is much more material that there should be a rule to go by, than what the rule is."[31] Nevertheless, writers on parliamentary law were advocates of this system in particular.[32] A recent edition of Robert's *Rules of Order* offers a well-honed case for parliamentary law: it is

> the best method yet devised to enable assemblies of any size, with due regard for every member's opinion, to arrive at the general will on the maximum number of questions of varying complexity in a minimum amount of time and under all kinds of internal climate ranging from total harmony to hardened or impassioned division of opinion.[33]

In other words, it is efficient, allows minority groups to be heard, and works for both reading groups and tumultuous crowds.

Self-organization began even before the pioneers left their homes in the East. Some emigrants moved westward on their own, of course, either as individuals or families, without drawing on parliamentary practice. Those who travelled as companies and whose journey was especially long or dangerous, however, required a consensus about the division of labor and mutual responsibilities. So too did expeditions to the far West for a joint venture such as mining or "claiming" land in anticipation of legislation authorizing such claims. Such groups used meetings, committees, constitutions, and so on, to form joint stock companies and then to run them.

One such emigrant group was the Western Emigration Company, conceived by a group of twelve friends in 1834 to secure land in Wisconsin before the government land sale, ideally at an "important point" where they could found a town.[34] They followed standard procedure for forming a new organization, first convening a committee to draft a constitution for the company and then calling a public meeting in a public place which "quite a large number attended." The proposed constitution must have been discussed and voted upon because we know that one of those present, J. Bullen Jr., moved that an article on temperance be added. (It was accepted at the time but removed from the final version.)[35]

The Western Emigration Company was a joint stock company, and the constitution served "as a contract between the parties thereto."[36] It was intended to be a money-making venture, although it did not, in fact, make any money; the reason for founding a town was that property in and around an urban center would appreciate quickly. The company issued 400 shares stock, at $10 each, to purchase land and hold it until prices went up. "Even poor persons, who either expected to remove West, or hoped to share in the large prospective gains, paid their money and took shares."[37] Because this was a business company, it is not surprising that it had officers and meetings and followed formal rules of procedure, but it goes to show that parliamentary procedure extended from living rooms to boardrooms and that constitutions and bylaws were common to both governments and contracts.

When representatives of the Western Immigration Company had reached Wisconsin, identified a suitable location at Pike River, and began making improvements, they were by no means in the clear. The government had not yet surveyed the land, let alone made it available for sale, so the settlers had no legal rights to their homesteads. They believed, however, that "as Government has heretofore encouraged emigration by granting pre-emption to actual settlers . . . our settling and cultivating the public lands is in accordance with the best wishes of Government."[38] The representatives of the Western Immigration Society and thousands like them therefore formed claim clubs – also known as claimants' unions or claim associations – to define and protect their rights until they could formalize them.[39]

These claim clubs were distinct from the immigration companies and were founded from scratch following the procedures for creating an association. The settlers at Pike River held a meeting at Bullen's store (the same Bullen who proposed the temperance amendment to the company constitution) and, as the chronicler of the meeting described the proceedings: "Austin Kellogg was chosen Moderator, and William C. Etheridge, Clerk," and a "preamble and constitution, presented by the committee appointed to draft the same, were unanimously adopted."[40] This was Cushing's formula in a nutshell, before the fact.

The claim club rules served two purposes. First, they defined the local claim system by setting maximum claim sizes, minimum improvements necessary to hold the claim, registration requirements, and a forum for resolving disputes between members of the club.[41] Second, they bound members to support one another when the federal government auctioned off the land. In the settlers' version of events, the claim members had to defend themselves against interlopers – "invidious wolves in human form" – who bought the claims that the settlors had improved and sold them at a profit to later arrivals.[42] In practice, some claim clubs acted like cartels, making bogus "improvements" (a ten-inch by twelve-inch cabin registered as "ten by twelve"), bullying bona fide settlors who were not members, lobbying the legislature to locate the capital on or near their claims so they could sell at much higher prices, and so on. Both genuine farmers and speculators formed clubs, and, in any case, the line between the two was vague.[43] "It seldom happens," de Tocqueville wrote, "that an American farmer settles for good upon the land which he occupies; especially in the districts of the far West he brings land into tillage in order to sell it again, and not to farm it; he builds a farmhouse on the speculation that, as the state of the population will soon be changed by the increase of population, a good price will be gotten for it."[44] The club constitutions were therefore part legislation (creating and running a property regime)[45] and part contracts for mutual protection in the absence of government institutions or even in defiance of United States law.

For emigrants to Oregon and California, the journey itself was the subject of many meetings and resolutions, whether or not the participants intended to stay together once they had reached their destination. Almost everyone who made the two-thousand-or-more mile trip to the West Coast in the 1840s and 1850s – overland or by sea – travelled with a group for mutual support, and all of those groups had some agreement regarding the expenses of the journey, division of labor, duties that members owed one another, and so on. The companies took different forms, including joint stock companies, whose members contributed capital and shared their wagons, animals, and supplies; groups who traveled together but held their property separately; passenger trains, whose members paid a leader to take them across; and employers with hired hands.[46] John Phillip Reed has described and analyzed these arrangements in meticulous detail, with the result that self-government on the overland trail is better documented than on any other part of the frontier.[47]

Before leaving the inhabited area of the United States, many, perhaps most, early joint-stock companies and travelling companies held meetings to draw up a compact to govern themselves on the trail.[48] For example, the "citizens of Jefferson county, who contemplate[d] emigrating to California early in the ensuing spring, met in the Iowa Drug Store" to begin the formation of the Fairfield Company. A chairman and secretary were chosen, and a five-man committee was asked to draft a code of rules, which were presented the following Monday to all who planned to go to California.[49] As always, the members debated the proposal, offered amendments, and finally voted to adopt the amended code as their constitution.

Reid questions whether the pioneers felt bound by their rules once they were on the trail, noting one writer's impression that it was impossible to legislate in advance for the situations that might arise on the trail. "[T]here is no use in setting to & forming a lengthy code of laws," wrote one, "for they will surely be broken – it is time enough to correct an evil when it appears that we have the evil to contend with among us."[50] Indeed, constitutions and bylaws fell out of favor after 1850. Reid suggests tentatively that the later companies learned from accounts by earlier emigrants, most notably Edwin Bryant, who wrote that the regulations previously adopted were "rarely enforced."[51] For example, when the officers or arbitrators convicted someone of breaking the rules or committing a crime, he almost always appealed directly to the company as a whole, and it reassessed his case.[52] In so doing, the company limited the authority of the officers and might also amend the rule itself. A majority vote could also change articles of the constitution, such as rules prohibiting Sunday travel.[53] Ultimately, Reid says, the emigrants valued majority rule over laws, "even laws to which they had consented."[54] Bryant wrote, "We are a pure democracy. All laws are proposed directly to a general assembly, and are enacted or rejected by a majority."[55] The *process* of voting on individual questions and enacting rules for the future replaced the constitution, which is what Bryant meant by a pure democracy, but the process was itself an exercise in parliamentary law.

Overland companies felt free to change individual rules, but very few actually disbanded so long as they were travelling. Those who were bound for the gold mines, however, broke up on arrival, even if they originally intended to continue operating in California, sharing their labors and pooling their profits. Once they reached the Golden State, they discovered that their members were pulled in different directions, some toward trade and others to mining; some lazy, others industrious and resentful about having to share their earnings with slackers. Miner Daniel Woods advised his readers that companies organized at home "work badly; they cramp your energies; they entangle all your operations."[56] Members could not quit unilaterally because that meant sacrificing their share of the company assets. They had to persuade a majority of members to dissolve the company; the final parliamentary act was the vote for dissolution.[57] Many would form new companies in the mines, enlisting once more the parliamentary methods that they had brought from the East Coast.

The need for self-government and collective action was greater in Gold Rush California than anywhere else on the frontier. California was an unusual sort of frontier, since it had some hundred thousand inhabitants in 1850 but no government until late 1849, and no courts until 1850.[58] It took several more years after *that* to get gold mining laws, police, or judges in the mountains where mining took place.[59] The miners therefore passed their own mining laws, ran their own criminal trials, and formed their own joint stock companies to carry out ambitious mining projects. All of these ventures relied on parliamentary procedure.

In every camp and on every bar, the miners adopted mining codes or rules and regulations that established maximum claim sizes, notice and work requirements, and a system for dispute resolution.[60] The rules resembled those of claim clubs but differed in that they applied to everyone in the relevant mining district, old hands and newcomers alike, rather than only members of a club. New arrivals could vote, and, if there were enough of them, they could change the rules. When the state courts were finally up and running, they treated the miners' codes as law.

The procedures for forming a mining district and enacting a code followed the familiar pattern, as is clear from Clarence King's compendium of California district mining laws in *The United States Mining Laws*.[61] Here is one particularly detailed account, regarding the formation of the Warren Hill Mining District:

> In pursuance of [a previously published] notice a large number of miners met at the House of J.M Jackman & Kidder at 7 p.m. Oct 21st 1853, and proceeded [*sic*] to Business by the election of J.H. Kilbourn as chairman.
>
> On Motion of Mr. Haymond the chairman appointed the following gentlemen as a committee to draft a constitution and Bye Laws [*sic*] viz: W.H. Lester C.M. Bosworth C. Bordwell C.F. Jackson Geo. McKelvey.
>
> On motion of W.H. Lester, the chairman was added to the committee and Creed Haymond appointed Secretary
>
> On motion of Mr R. B. Sigafoose, the meeting proceeded to elect a recorder.[62]

The office of recorder was contested; fifty-nine votes were cast, of which J. H. Kilbourn, the chairman, received thirty-seven, Jackson fourteen, and the remaining eight went to various candidates. (The recorder collected fees for his services.) On the following day, the miners reassembled and the Secretary read the committee's proposed constitution. "On Motion of Mr. A.A. Hayden it was taken up article by article and the following with its preamble was unanimously adopted."

This script is repeated over and over in the literature, sometimes with more detail and sometimes with much less;[63] it follows exactly the same parliamentary procedure used to found the Lyceum of Greenwood, South Carolina, as described, and any other kind of association in the United States. The Warren Hill account is distinctive only in that it reveals that a number of individuals were making motions, that there was a contest among the candidates for recorder, and that the meeting did in fact discuss each article of the proposed constitution. But other meetings may also have been less cut-and-dried than their reports suggest. It is, in a sense, unfortunate that the emigrants and miners were so familiar with the forms and language of meetings that their descriptions also follow the formula, and all regional color and language are smoothed over. For example, most accounts are in the passive voice and do not identify the individuals who propose candidates or offer resolutions. Hence it is interesting to see the process through the eyes of an outsider from Scotland, J. D. Borthwick, who reported the scene before him instead of taking minutes for the assembly. A "meeting was held one Sunday afternoon for legislative purposes," he wrote.

> The miners met in front of the store to the number of about two hundred; a very respectable-looking old chap was called to the chair; but for want of that article of furniture he mounted an empty pork-barrel, which gave him a commanding position;

> another man was appointed secretary, who placed his writing materials on some empty boxes piled up alongside of the chair.

This is all very rustic and amusing. When Borthwick comes to the actual proceedings, however, and records the words of the participants, we hear them following the parliamentary guidelines:

> The chairman . . . addressing the crowd, told them the object for which the meeting had been called, and said he would be happy to hear any gentleman who had any remarks to offer; whereupon some one proposed an amendment of the law relating to a certain description of claim, arguing the point in a very neat speech. He was duly seconded, and there was some slight opposition and discussion; but when the chairman declared it carried by the ayes, no one called for a division, so the secretary wrote it all down, and it became law.

How conversant all of the members were with the form of a deliberative assembly! From the fact that some miners came prepared with a proposed amendment and that others were ready and able to debate it, it appears that the meeting was truly participatory and not a piece of parliamentary theater run by the officers. We even learn that the vote was a voice vote with the possibility of a division if the numbers were close. This detail, too, goes to show that parliamentary rules were more detailed and allowed for more member participation than appears from the more laconic newspaper reports.

Borthwick evidently enjoyed the contrast between the formal proceedings and the primitive surroundings – the pork barrel dais and the storefront assembly. After a vote of thanks to the chairman, he said, "[t]he meeting was . . . declared to be dissolved, and accordingly dribbled into the store, where the legislators, in small detachments, pledged each other in cocktails as fast as the storekeeper could mix them." And then he adds a sentence that sums up the thesis of this chapter: "While the legislature was in session, however, everything was conducted with the utmost formality, for Americans of all classes are particularly *au fait* at the ordinary routine of public meetings."[64]

Dame Shirley, who as a woman was also an outsider in the mines, thought that Americans positively enjoyed making laws. She said, "Miners are as fond of playing at law making and dispensing justice as French novelists are of 'playing at Providence.' "[65] The American miners certainly held meetings and passed resolutions at every conceivable opportunity; some were law-related, others not at all, and yet others cloaked illegal activities in the mantle of legislation. Examples of the latter include numerous resolutions to expel foreigners from the mines or to form a military-type expedition to chase them out. The reports generally included some justification or pretext for the expulsions, such as alleged attacks on Americans, as at a meeting at Sonora on July 21, 1850. The proposal was,

> Whereas, The lives and property of the American citizens are now in danger, from the hands of lawless murderers of every clime, class and creed under the canopy of heaven . . . Resolved, That all foreigners in Tuolumne county (except persons engaged in permanent business and of respectable character) be required to leave.[66]

This charge against the foreigners was entirely trumped up; it was in fact the Americans who had bullied Mexicans and Chilenos off their claims and then blamed a series of robberies and murders on these same foreigners with no basis besides their own bad consciences. Somehow the whole business of meetings, resolutions, and votes was thought to make the shady dealings shipshape and aboveboard.

Just as travelers to California formed companies for the journey to California, so too did miners form companies to carry out large projects. Daniel Woods, who wrote that the companies formed back East were bound to fail, also said that, "In the mines, it will always be necessary for you to associate yourself with one or two, and sometimes twenty, or even fifty mining companions. These associations are formed and terminate with the necessity of the occasion."[67] The larger operations were joint stock companies; their members had equal shares, worked equal hours, and ran the company through meetings of the kind described.[68] They provide the best evidence of the advantage that familiarity with parliamentary procedure gave Americans.

As Woods suggested, the miners' joint operations ranged in size and complexity, including turning streams from their beds to get at the gold-rich ground beneath, deep shaft mining, quartz mining and milling operations, and water delivery companies. The larger ones "elect their officers, form their laws, and mutually share the expense and labor of the preparatory work, and also divide equally the profits."[69] Woods himself was a member of the Hart's Bar Draining and Mining Company, and he included its Articles of Agreement in his book. They were adopted at a meeting of the company and included a provision that it was the president's duty "to call all meetings of the company, and to preside at them. He shall put to vote all motions duly made, and, in all cases of a tie in voting, he shall give the casting vote."[70]

The apogee of the joint stock companies – in terms of the number of members, the complexity of the operation, and the capital investment – was the Columbia & Stanislaus River Water Company. Gold mining required water to separate the tiny flakes of gold from the vastly greater volume of earth and stones; so, as mining operations moved farther and farther from the rivers, delivery companies were formed to transport water from many miles away and sell it in the "dry diggings." The first such operations were joint stock companies, but in 1851, two bankers founded the Tuolumne County Water Company, funded by outside capital.[71] The miners were happy that this newly formed company opened new regions for gold mining, but over time, as mining became less profitable, they complained that it was taking advantage of its monopoly to charge extortionate rates. So a group of miners formed the Columbia and Stanislaus River Company as a joint stock company to supply water at a fair, miner-friendly price. It was a huge undertaking: sixty miles of wooden flumes and canals, enormous aqueducts spanning valleys, and a 3,100-foot tunnel. The joint owners did the work themselves and supplied their own provisions; other laborers and local merchants took their payment in stock. Unfortunately, the company ultimately had to borrow $150,000 in cash to complete the project, and since by then mining was beginning to fail, the company was not able to pay its debts. The investors foreclosed, and the Tuolumne County Water Company acquired its rival for a song.[72] As Donald Pisani writes, however, the Columbia & Stanislaus River Water Company's failure was not due to bad management but to the exhaustion of the gold fields: "Their aqueduct was a symbol of what free men in a free society could accomplish."[73]

More specifically, it was a symbol of what American joint stock companies, drawing on parliamentary procedure, could accomplish. Foreigners in California believed that Americans enjoyed a great advantage over miners from other countries because they were so adept at coordination. The Scot Borthwick wrote that the French were unable to form large mining companies, and even smaller combinations did not hold together, whereas the Americans

> are certainly of all people in the world the most prompt to organise and combine to carry out a common object. They are trained to it from their youth in their innumerable, and to a foreigner unintelligible, caucus-meetings, committees, conventions, and so forth, . . . while the fact of every man belonging to a fire company,

> a militia company, or something of that sort . . . accustoms them also to the duty of choosing their own leaders, and to the necessity of afterwards recognising them as such by implicit obedience.[74]

Similarly, Albert Bernard de Roushaile, a Frenchman who otherwise despised Americans, admired their behavior at meetings. "[T]hey are always orderly, quite unlike our meetings in France," he wrote. "If ten Frenchmen come together, they will be quarreling and insulting one another within five minutes."[75] The French *Journal des Débats*, quoted in the *Placer Times* of December 1, 1849, agreed that the American flair for self-government provided a useful lesson "for that laborious but timid population – enemies of anarchy, but who do not know how to unite and organize themselves – which forms the immense majority of the French Society."[76] It is unlikely that Americans could have carried out their largest mining and water turning operations *as equals*, as opposed to as employees of business, without their experience in group decision making and respect for majority rule.

This discussion began with a description of Pearson Easterbrook's trial by a meeting using parliamentary law that was in many ways exactly like the many meetings previously described, from the election of officers to votes on the rules of the body. Easterbrook's case was typical of criminal trials in the mines except in two respects. First, the proceedings were reported in vivid detail. Most accounts of popular trials, or trial by Judge Lynch, are laconic and formulaic. Second, the crowd managed every step of Easterbrook's trial, whereas it usually elected a judge to carry out routine duties like swearing the witnesses.[77] Easterbrook's trial was therefore even more like a typical meeting than the majority of lynch trials that had a judge instead of a chairman.

Nevertheless, all reports of trials by Judge Lynch or by the People's Court in California, of which I have collected at least one hundred fifty, share some of the features of the Easterbrook trial.[78] There were undoubtedly more lynch trials than these. Newspapers could report on a lynching only when someone happened to send in an account of the incident, and the *Placer Times* even said explicitly that it did not report on some trials that resulted in a whipping as opposed to an execution:

> If a man has committed a crime, been found guilty and received forty or fifty lashes, and then sent away not to return under penalty of death, we think the punishment quite sufficient . . . and it is useless to mortify innocent relatives and friends . . . by the publication of such proceedings.[79]

Accounts in diaries and letters are equally incomplete, since not all lynchings happened to be witnessed by a diarist. In the first five years of the gold rush, there may have been as many miners' meetings for criminal trials as there were for enacting mining codes. Because only the state has the authority to try and execute criminals, the assumption of this role was the ultimate form of government by popular assembly.

The miners and other frontiersmen wanted to replicate a proper American trial as closely as possible: there was always a jury, whose verdict was final, a judge (Easterbrook's trial was a rare exception), a prosecutor, and usually defense counsel for the accused. If the jury pronounced a verdict of guilty, the assembled miners voted on the sentence, which, since few defendants were acquitted, was the most important and sometimes most contentious stage of the process. The trials were a mix of traditional legal procedure and deliberative assembly.

At Easterbrook's trial, the assembled miners voted on whether to give him a jury and every other procedural question, including the selection of a chairman, secretary, and bailiff, appointment of a committee to choose the jurors, and the summoning of witnesses. Few reports of lynch trials provide such detail about technicalities, but even very concise accounts sometimes reveal the crowd's role in running the trial. Dame Shirley was awakened one morning by a deep and mighty, "Aye," followed by "the confused murmur of many voices and the rapidly succeeding 'ayes' and 'noes.'" It turned out to be the first stage of a miners' meeting to try a suspected thief; they were voting on whether they should hold their trial at Indian Bar or Rich Bar.[80] Presumably, since there were multiple votes, the meeting was also making other procedural decisions. It was common for the meeting to elect the judge, or the judge and a sheriff, for the trial.[81] The jury could be selected in several ways: by vote, selected by ballot, or selected by the accused from a list of fifty names chosen by committee.[82] The assembly might vote on whether the accused was to have counsel or might actually appoint counsel for the defense.[83] In short, the assembled miners micromanaged the trial not just in Easterbrook's case but in many, probably most cases.

If the jury found the accused guilty, then the assembly faced its most important decision: what punishment to impose. The penalty for murder was death, but thieves were either executed or, alternatively, whipped, had their heads shaved or their ears cut off, or branded – or some combination of these. Like all other questions, the sentence was put to a vote.[84] The motions and votes are seldom preserved; accounts report only that there was a debate and the outcome. In 1849, a sailor was sentenced to death for stealing $5,000 and a bag of silver coins, but "some opposition" was raised to "depriving him of his life and a milder punishment [was] suggested," namely, to give him a hundred lashes, cut off his ears, and shave his head. "This sentence gave general satisfaction."[85] Englishman Henry Clark, also convicted of theft, was sentenced to receive two hundred lashes, to be branded with an "R," and to have half his head shaved. "Many were in favor of hanging him, but on account of his youthfulness he received the above punishment instead."[86] It was here that respect for majority rule was most important as a peaceful means of settling disputes.

Even a mob on the point of hanging a suspect might be persuaded to hold a vote first. In one case,

> a large crowd took the prisoner from the hands of the authorities, and were about to hang him without judge or juryman, but through the influence and exertions of some of our citizens the excitement was allayed, and it was decided that he should be tried by a jury of the citizens, and that the people would abide by their decision.[87]

In another example, there

> were many persons present, and the nature of the charge was such as to produce an intense excitement among the crowd, some of whom were strongly disposed to bring to bear upon him the severest penalty of Judge Lynch's code. We understand that Mr. Sheldon assumed a most decisive course in favor of bringing the man to town for a regular trial, and his motion finally prevailed.[88]

"His motion" indicates that respect for a form of parliamentary procedure saved the man from immediate hanging. While, of course, there were plenty of mob killings and outrageous trials, *sometimes* the rowdies were outvoted.

Criminal trials are discussed here in the context of the gold rush because the evidence from that period is particularly rich, but they occurred everywhere on the frontier. John Phillip Reid presents an engrossing study of trials on the overland trail in his book *Policing the Elephant*.[89] The emigrants' trials were more conscientious and formal than the miners' – more like trials and less like meetings. There was no question of dispensing with a judge or counsel for the defense, but, then, the emigrants were new to the frontier and more careful than their counterparts in the mines. Other Western lynch trials, though less well documented than either those on the overland trail or in California, bear signs of the assembled populations' involvement in the proceedings.[90] In the murder trial of Patrick O'Connor in 1834, for example, the people of Dubuque "met, selected among themselves a judge and a jury, tried the man and, upon their own responsibility, hanged him."[91] And in the 1863 trial of George Ives in Nevada City, Montana, a crowd of several hundred debated before deciding to empanel a double jury of twenty-four men but reserved the right to decide any possible punishment.[92] Again, meetings using parliamentary procedure were ubiquitous on the frontier as the only imaginable means to concerted action.

Ultimately, we must ask whether parliamentary procedure made a substantive difference on the frontier. Since it was used for everything from criminal trials to Fourth of July celebrations, there is no single answer to whether the habit of holding meetings was essential, useful, or indifferent. It was a process for reaching decisions, and the value of those decisions depended largely on the participants and their goals. In the East, proslavery groups held meetings and passed resolutions; in the Midwest, claim clubs used their power to bully nonmembers off their claims; and in California, vigilance committees used parliamentary procedure in secret, while miners used it to expel non-English speakers from the diggings.[93] The capacity to coordinate was a powerful tool for good and bad.

Particularly with respect to lynch trials, to the extent that they were trials by parliamentary procedure, the verdict has to be mixed. No matter how earnestly frontiersmen explained the necessity of lynch trials, they met only condemnation from foreigners and other Americans.[94] Englishman Charles Murray wrote in his *Travels in North America* (1839) that it was "impossible to conceive a more horrible outrage upon law, justice, and social order, than this kind of self-constituted court, taking upon itself, in a civilized country, to decide upon life and liberty."[95] Certainly, once "the people" took the punishment of crime into their own hands, things could go badly wrong. The very "legitimacy" of the process gave the mining community confidence to try and punish criminals on very shaky ground, and it was impossible to hold the "people" to account when their actions were clearly unjust, as once when they hooted *down* the proposition to give the accused a trial and unanimously approved a motion to execute him at once.[96] When the courts were established, lynch law competed with actual law, and trials were speeded up to prevent the sheriff from intervening. There was still a trial, but it was *de minimis*: "the excited people seized the prisoners, took them to the top of an adjacent hill, selected a jury under a tree, tried and found them guilty, and sentenced them to be hung."[97] Lynch trials also illustrated the weakness of majority vote. There was a tendency toward compromise; some rowdies would push for a hanging, and those "more mildly disposed" were lucky if they could argue the hotheads down to mutilation.

But Murray was wrong when he said that it was impossible to conceive of anything worse than a lynch trial. Other modes of criminal punishment could be worse. Self-help was accepted if a suspect was caught in the act, as when, in the course of an argument, a certain "Bowen drew his revolver, and . . . *blew out the brains* of Mr. Boggs." Five or six bystanders, friends of the dead man, "immediately seized Bowen, placed a lasso around his neck, and after dragging him about eighty rods, hung him up to a frame, used by a butcher for slaughtering cattle."[98] The regular use of mob law would have been more chaotic than lynch law. On the other hand, if the miners had not been so comfortable with running their own trials, the reaction to such outrages might have speeded up the development of the state courts.

More generally, parliamentary law was not essential to the settlement of the West. It could have happened differently if, for instance, the federal government had taken control. In the Canadian and Australian gold rushes, the civil service kept authority firmly in its own hands, and the miners neither made their own rules nor held their own trials. In Victoria, the Gold

Fields Commissioners maintained order in the mines; they were civil servants of good families and on good salaries.[99] Similarly, in Canada on the Klondike, the authorities acted quickly to prevent miners' meetings from deciding claim disputes. When the authorities learned of these meetings and their "unfair decisions," they sent in the Mounted Police to inform the miners that their "proceeding was not legal and must not occur again," and that put a stop to the practice. According to the officer in charge: "This [was] the only occasion on which the miners in any way attempted to assert themselves."[100] Washington, on the other hand, not only failed to provide authority for regions beyond the organized territories, but through the Preemption Act of 1841 tacitly encouraged pioneers to stake claims in areas that were not officially opened for settlement. So Americans were thrown back on their own devices.

On the positive side, the mining codes, the claim clubs, and the joint stock companies brought order to the West. The companies, in particular, achieved amazing things, while the codes generated the law for a major industry both before and after the State of California acquired a government. But perhaps the greatest contribution of parliamentary procedure was something more nebulous: it channeled disagreements into a series of resolutions and votes and maybe even strengthened the hand of moderate but timid types who would otherwise not stand up to bullies, as, for example, when it came to expulsion of foreigners. H. H. Bancroft found that "[i]n several camps the more liberal-minded Americans interfered to annul the banishment,"[101] and we have a record of one such set of "resolutions unanimously adopted at a public meeting, and signed by Francis D. Clark, Chairman, and others":

1 Resolved, That all men shall have permission to live in this camp, without being in any way molested.
2 Resolved, That the civil law shall be sustained, and that all those under the civil law shall be supported.
3 Resolved, That two hundred and fifty copies of these resolutions be printed in English and Spanish, and distributed through the various diggings.[102]

No doubt the frontier could have been settled without parliamentary procedure, but given America's weak federal government and eager pioneers, as well as Americans' resistance to authority, the rules of procedure provided at least a modicum of stability in the wilderness.

Notes

1 "The Tragedy at Shasta City," *Sacramento Transcript*, April 3, 1851.
2 James W. Witham, *Fifty Years on the Firing Line* (Chicago: by the author, 1924), 177. Luther S. Cushing, *Manual of Parliamentary Practice: Rules of Proceeding and Debate in Deliberative Assemblies* (Boston: Reynolds, 1854), 13. This is the seventh edition, but the "Advertisement to the Seventh Edition" (p. 3) states that it uses the same plates as the first, except that this new edition included notes at the end.
3 There were unofficial compilations of past rulings on parliamentary law but nothing like a digest or manual before the nineteenth century. Michael Rush, *The Role of the Member of Parliament since 1868: From Gentlemen to Players* (Oxford: Oxford University Press, 2001), 57; *Robert's Rules of Order Newly Revised*, 10th ed. (Philadelphia: Perseus, 2000), xxv, xxviii–xxix.
4 On "common parliamentary law" see "Advertisement to the First Edition" in Cushing, *Manual of Parliamentary Practice* (p. 4) (the *Manual* "contains only what may be called the *common parliamentary law*," which every legislative assembly has modified by special rules); Henry M. Robert, *Robert's Rules of Order: Pocket Manual of Rules of Order for Deliberative Assemblies* (Chicago: Griggs, 1876), 10.
5 Thomas Jefferson, *Manual of Parliamentary Practice for the Use of the Senate of the United States* (Washington, D.C.: Davis & Force, 1820), v.
6 Peter Clark, *British Clubs and Societies 1580–1800: The Origins of an Associational World* (Oxford: Oxford University Press, 2000); Robert J. Morris, "Voluntary Societies and British Urban Elites, 1780–1850,"

Historical Journal 26, no. 1 (1983): 95–118: R. J. Morris, "Clubs, Societies and Associations," in *The Cambridge Social History of Britain, 1750–1950*, vol. 3, ed. Francis M.L. Thompson (Cambridge, UK: Cambridge University Press, 1990), 403–43. Widespread membership in associations is thought to have been exclusive to Britain, her colonies, and former colonies (Clark, *British Clubs and Societies*, 5, 18–19, 428); although some scholars suggest that French and German associations have merely been understudied (Stefan-Ludwig Hoffman, "Democracy and Associations in the Long Nineteenth Century: Toward a Transnational Perspective," *Journal of Modern History* 75 (2003): 269–99, 283–5).

7 On the early date, see Clark, *British Clubs and Societies*, 4; on the types of clubs, see ibid., 272.

8 Ibid., 213–14.

9 "Conference of the National Association of United Trades," *Northern Star, and National Trades Journal* (London, May 29, 1847), 5 (a description of the formation of the association states that at the first meeting to consider the formation of the association in 1845, it was resolved "that an Association should be formed, and a provisional committee was appointed, to whom the preparation of the constitution and laws was entrusted." The draft plan was submitted to "another delegate meeting . . . and after full consideration was finally adopted with various amendments"). "Anniversary of the British and Foreign Unitarian Association," *Monthly Repository and Review* (London, June 2, 1831), 412 (a report of a meeting of the society with resolutions moved, seconded and passed unanimously); George Browne, *The History of the British and Foreign Bible Society from Its Institution in 1804, to the Close of Its Jubilee in 1854*, vol. 1 (London: British and Foreign Bible Society, 1859), 9ff. (report of first meeting, March 7, 1804, at the London Tavern; 300 persons attended. Granville Sharp was unanimously called to the chair. The resolutions had been drafted in advance; they were adopted unanimously. The meeting elected a committee to nominated officers).

10 Alexis de Tocqueville, *Democracy in America*, trans. Henry Reeve (Oxford: Oxford University Press, 1952), 376.

11 Clark, *British Clubs and Societies*, 302–6 (ethnic societies from 1716); 400–4 (growth in societies in 1750s and 1760s); 407–20 (growth accelerated after the Revolution). See also Richard D. Brown, "The Emergence of Urban Society in Rural Massachusetts, 1760–1820," *Journal of American History* 61 (1974): 29–51, 38; Theda Skocpol, "How Americans Became Civic," in *Civic Engagement in American Democracy*, ed. Theda Skocpol and Morris P. Fiorina (Washington, D.C.: Brookings Institution Press, 1999), 27–80.

12 Johann Neem, *Creating a Nation of Joiners: Democracy and Civil Society in Early National Massachusetts* (Cambridge, Mass.: Harvard University Press, 2008), 81ff; see also Brown, "The Emergence of Urban Society," 37. The British and Foreign Bible Society in the United Kingdom established its first eleven auxiliaries in 1809 and 1810. See Browne, *History of the British and Foreign Bible Society*, 38–9.

13 Neem, *Creating a Nation of Joiners*, 90.

14 Cushing, *Manual of Parliamentary Practice.*

15 Ibid. 3.

16 Ibid., included in the Notices at the beginning of the volume, before the title page.

17 *Robert's Rules* (2000) (note 3), xxxv.

18 Witham, *Fifty Years on the Firing Line*, 175.

19 *Robert's Rules* (1876) (note 4), 101 (section 46); Cushing, *Manual of Parliamentary Practice*, 8 (on how to organize a deliberative assembly).

20 Cushing, *Manual of Parliamentary Practice*; *Robert's Rules* (1876) (note 4), 8–9.

21 *Robert's Rules* (1876) (note 4), 102–5.

22 *The National Advocate* (New York), March 3, 1817, col. E.

23 *Robert's Rules* (1876) (note 4), 108.

24 Ibid., 110.

25 Ibid., 112–13.

26 Cushing, *Manual of Parliamentary Practice*; 9, section 4. See also Witham, *Fifty Years on the Firing Line*, 177, for a more detailed description of a hypothetical "meeting to form a farmers' club."

27 Some further examples: "Reception of the Volunteers" *Boon's Lick Times* (Fayette, Mo.), June 26, 1847, 2 (Public meeting to plan for the reception of the Howard County volunteers, now on their way back from Mexico); "Fifth Annual Meeting of the American Anti-Slavery Society," *The Liberator* (Boston), May 18, 1838, 1; James Stuart, *Three Years in North America* (Edinburgh, UK: Cadell, 1833), 567 (the working men of New York organize an amazing procession to celebrate the recent French revolution).

28 Letter to the editor, *Edgefield Advertiser* (S.C.), April 27, 1842, 3, cols. 1–2.

29 Skocpol, "How Americans Became Civic," 68; Theda Skocpol, *Diminished Democracy: From Membership to Management in American Civic Life* (Norman: University of Oklahoma Press, 2003, republished 2013), especially chap. 7, "Joiners, Organizers and Citizens," 74 ff.

30 For a similar but terser summary of the founding of a Lyceum, see *The Highland Weekly News* (Hillsborough, Ohio), November 18, 1858, 3 col. 1.
31 Jefferson, *Manual of Parliamentary Practice*, 12.
32 Ibid.
33 *Robert's Rules* (2000) (note 3), xviii.
34 Western Historical Company, *The History of Racine and Kenosha Counties, Wisconsin* (Chicago: Western Historical Co., 1879), 343.
35 Ibid., 343–4.
36 Ibid., 344.
37 Ibid., 345.
38 Preamble to the Constitution of the Pike River Claimants' Union, in Western Historical Company, *History of Racine and Kenosha Counties*, 348. Allan G. Bogue, "The Iowa Claim Clubs: Symbol and Substance," *Mississippi Valley Historical Review* 45 (1958): 231–53, 236, notes that most preambles to claim club regulations in Iowa state that it had become customary for settlers to take claims as soon as Indian title was extinguished, and those claims were "respected by both the citizens and laws of Iowa."
39 See Benjamin H. Hibbard, *A History of the Public Land Policies* (New York: Macmillan, 1924), 200ff, for rules passed by claims clubs in Iowa, Kansas, and Wisconsin; 198–9, for a description of an early claim club in Alabama (1830); also Bogue, "The Iowa Claim Clubs," 236–8. Abner D. Jones, *Illinois and the West* (Boston: Weeks, Jordon & Co., 1838), 224–9:

> So soon as some half-dozen men have *settled* themselves down in a neighborhood, and laid claim to the soil, or more appropriately, to the right of pre-emption, they form themselves into an *association*, each member signing a constitution by which they pledge themselves to abide.

40 *History of Racine and Kenosha Counties*, 348.
41 Bogue, "The Iowa Claim Clubs," 236; see also claim club constitutions reproduced in Ilia Murtazashvili, The Political Economy of Claims Clubs (PhD dissertation, University of Wisconsin, Madison, 2009), 103–11.
42 The quotation is from "Pledge of the Madison County, Iowa, Claim Club" reproduced in Herman A. Mueller, *History of Madison County, Iowa, and Its People*, vol. I (Chicago: S.J. Clarke Publishing Company, 1915), 127.
43 Murtazashvili, The Political Economy of Claims Clubs, 99–100, 106.
44 De Tocqueville (note 10), 425–6.
45 Claim club rules were described as law by Willard Hurst, *Law and the Conditions of Freedom* (Madison: University of Wisconsin Press, 1956), 5: "these settlers all over the central and Midwestern states set up local governments in the form of "claims associations"; see also Hibbard (note 39), 203: "Although 'claim law' is no law derived from the United States or from the statute book of the territory, yet it nevertheless is the law, made by and derived from the sovereigns themselves."
46 John P. Reid, *Law for the Elephant* (San Marino, Calif.: Huntington Library, 1980), 128.
47 John P. Reid, "Governance of the Elephant: Constitutional Theory on the Overland Trail," *Hastings Constitutional Law Quarterly* 5 (1978): 421–43.
48 Fred V. Lorch, "Iowa and the California Gold Rush of 1849," *Iowa Journal of History and Politics* 30 (1932): 307–76, 314–15; Reid, "Governance of the Elephant," 422. The French companies also had "constitutions" of sorts, but it is less clear how they were drafted. See Malcom J. Rohrbough, *Rush to Gold: The French and the California Gold Rush, 1848–1854* (New Haven, Conn.: Yale University Press, 2013).
49 Lorch, "Iowa and the California Gold Rush," 340.
50 Ibid., 423 (quoting Joseph W. Wood, *Diaries of Crossing the Plains in 1849*, entry for May 14, 1849).
51 Quoted in Owen C. Coy, *California: The Great Trek* (Los Angeles: San Francisco Powell Pub. Co., 1931), 113.
52 John P. Reid, *Policing the Elephant* (San Marino, Calif.: Huntington Library, 1997), 110, quoting Edwin Bryant, *What I Saw in California* (New York: Appleton, 1848; rep. ed., Lincoln: University of Nebraska Press, 1985), 60 (entry for May 26, 1846).
53 Reid, "Governance of the Elephant," 437.
54 Ibid., 431.
55 Quoted in Coy, *California*, 113.
56 "[E]ven if they held a charter and were bound to each other under heavy liabilities," said Woods, "they soon fell to pieces on reaching the gold placers." Daniel Woods, *Sixteen Months* (New York: Harper, 1851), 170.
57 Kimball Webster, *The Gold Seekers of '49* (Manchester, N.H.: Standard Book Co., 1917), 96 ("The Granite State and California Mining and Trading Company was this day dissolved by a unanimous vote of its members").

58 Andrea McDowell, "Criminal Law beyond the State: Popular Trials on the Frontier," *Brigham Young University Law Review* (2007): 327–86, 335.
59 Andrea McDowell, "From Commons to Claims: Property Rights in the California Gold Rush," *Yale Journal of Law & the Humanities* 14 (2002): 1–72, 2–3.
60 Ibid., 1–72.
61 Clarence King, *The United States Mining Laws*, 47th Congress, 2nd Session, H.R. Misc. Doc 42, 279 (1885) Alternative title: *Tenth Census of the United States, 1880.* Vol. 14.
62 Ibid., 279.
63 Further examples, Ibid., 283, Surface and Ravine Mining Laws of Smith's Flat District, February 20, 1855; 284, Siskiyou County – Lower Humbug Creek Mining District Mining Laws, April 7, 1855; 286, Butte County – Oregon Gulch Mining District, Laws Regulating Placer Diggins [*sic*] Passed December 29th 1855; 291, Siskiyou County – Little Humbug Creek Mining District, April 8, 1856.
64 John D. Borthwick, *Three Years in California* (Edinburgh, UK: Blackwood, 1857), 156–7.
65 Louise A.K.S. Clappe, *The Shirley Letters from California Mines in 1851–52* (San Francisco: Russell, 1922), 114.
66 John Heckendorn and W. A. Wilson, *Miners & Business Men's Directory* (Columbia, Calif: Printed at the Clipper Office, 1856), 42.
67 Woods, *Sixteen Months*, 181.
68 Maureen A. Jung, "Capitalism Comes to the Diggings: From Gold: Rush Adventure to Corporate Enterprise," *California History* 77 (1998/1999): 52–77, 59.
69 Woods, *Sixteen Months*, 144.
70 Ibid.
71 Donald Pisani, *Water, Land and Law in the West* (Lawrence: University Press of Kansas, 1996), 25.
72 Ibid., 29.
73 Ibid., 28.
74 Borthwick, *Three Years in California*, 369.
75 Clifford H. Bissell, "The French Language Press in California," *California History Society Quarterly* 39 (1960): 1–18, 8 (quoting from the journal of Albert Benard de Roushaile).
76 See also Hypolite Ferry, *Description de la Nouvelle Californie: Géographic, Politique, et Moral* (Paris: L. Maison, 1850), 331, who wrote that there are no people who love order more than the Americans because they know that there is no liberty without order.
77 The only other example I know of is the trial of Rigler, Allen and Miller, "Confession of the Nevada Robbery," *Sacramento Transcript*, April 7, 1851.
78 McDowell, "Criminal Law beyond the State," 327–86.
79 Editorial, *Placer Times* (Sacramento, CA), September 15, 1849.
80 Clappe, *The Shirley Letters*, 121–2.
81 Herbert O. Lang, *A History of Tuolumne County* (San Francisco, Calif.: Alley, 1882), 13 (miners elected an *alcalde* (mayor) for the trial of Atkins, accused of theft); Clappe, *The Shirley Letters*, 123 (assembled miners voted in a president for the trial); "From the Mines," *Weekly Alta California*, February 8, 1849 (the citizens assembled and selected three judges).
82 Clappe, *The Shirley Letters*, 123 (the assembled miners voted in a jury); "From the Mines," *Weekly Alta California*, February 8, 1849 (twelve jurymen drawn by ballot); "Confession of the Nevada Robbery," *Sacramento Transcript*, April 7, 1851 (accused selected twelve jurors from a list of fifty).
83 "For the Marysville Herald Row at Park's Bar – Judge Bernard Stabbed," *Marysville Daily Herald*, May 31, 1851 (the meeting selected attorneys for the people and for the defendant); Clappe, *The Shirley Letters*, 123 (counsel appointed for the defendant); John Hovey, *Journal of a Voyage . . . Commencing*, January 23, 1849, and ending July 23, 1849 (unpublished manuscript, on file with the Huntington Library), 81 (citizens of Moquelumne supplied the defendants with "a young and smart Lawyer from the City of Boston").
84 "Summary Execution of Five Mexicans," *Sacramento Transcript*, May 2, 1851.
85 William R. Ryan, *Personal Adventures in Upper and Lower California, in 1848–9* (London: Shoberl, 1850), 62–3 (relating what someone told him) and also David A. Shaw, *Eldorado* (Los Angeles: Baumbardt, 1900), 143–4. Ryan was published in 1850 and Shaw in 1900: Shaw must have copied from Ryan.
86 "Lynched," *Sacramento Transcript*, January 30, 1851.
87 "Serious Affray at Columbia – Great Excitement," *Daily Alta California*, November 17, 1853.
88 "Arrest of Franklin Sanford," *Sacramento Daily Union*, July 1, 1851, 2.
89 Reid, "Governance of the Elephant."

90 McDowell, "Criminal Law beyond the State," 373–7.
91 Frederick Marryat, *Diary in America* (Philadelphia: Carey & Hart, 1839), 316.
92 R. E. Mather and F. E. Boswell, *Gold Camp Desperadoes: A Study of Violence, Crime, and Punishment on the Minnesota Frontier* (San Jose, Calif.: History West Pub., 1990), 147.
93 For a proslavery meeting, *see* Broadside, "At a meeting of a large number of the Farmers and Planters of the County of Fayette, at the Big Spring: The following resolutions were unanimously entered into and ordered to be published . . . April 28, 1798" (Fayette County, 1798). For minutes of a vigilance committee meeting, Enos Christman, *One Man's Gold; The Letters and Journal of a Forty-Niner* (New York: McGraw-Hill, 1930), 191.
94 McDowell, "Criminal Law beyond the State," 377–83.
95 Charles A. Murray, *Travels in North America during the Years 1834, 1835 & 1836* (London: Bentley, 1839), 2: 107.
96 "Lynching on the Cosumnes River – Two Men Hung!" *Sacramento Transcript*, March 10, 1851.
97 Christman, *One Man's Gold*, 174.
98 "Murder and Lynching at Curtis Creek," *Weekly Pacific News*, January 2, 1851, 2; see also Alfred Peabody, "The Early Days and Rapid Growth of California," in *Essex Institute Historical Collections* 12 (Salem, Mass.: Essex Institute, 1874), 108:

> He was taken by several persons to a tree near by, a rope put round his neck, and he was hoisted nearly from the ground, but his earnest protestations of innocence moved the hearts of his accusers, and they felt that they had made a mistake in the person and let him go.

99 David Goodman, *Gold Seeking: Victoria and California in the 1850s* (Stanford, CA: Stanford University Press, 1994).
100 M.H.E. Hayne and H. West Taylor, *The Pioneers of the Klondyke* (London: Low, Marston & Co., 1897), 124.
101 Hubert H. Bancroft, *History of California* (San Francisco: Bancroft, 1888), 6: 404 n. 65.
102 Samuel C. Upham, *Notes of a Voyage . . . Together with Scenes in El Dorado, in the Years 1849–'50* (Philadelphia: by the author, 1878), 328–9.

16

A GATEKEEPING NATION

Asian invasion and the rise of xenophobic immigration law

Edlie Wong

We often view nineteenth-century America as the era of free immigration before twentieth-century legal regulations put into place racialized restrictions and national-origins quotas; however, public anxieties over the influx of foreigners and changing foreign policies, especially in regard to China, transformed the country into what historian Erika Lee calls a "gatekeeping nation" well before the century's end.[1] In Ambrose Bierce's satirical anti-Chinese weekly, the San Francisco *Wasp*, illustrator Solly H. Walter visualized this new America in a lurid cover image titled "Now Shut the Back Gate" (1888). A lanky Uncle Sam stands before a fortified Chinese Exclusion wall and wields the crude bat of "frontier vigilance" against Chinese immigrants snaking across the United States border with British Columbia (see Figure 16.1). President Theodore Roosevelt lent additional force to this redefinition of America as a gatekeeping nation when he directed Congress in his 1903 annual address "to devise some system by which undesirable immigrants shall be kept out entirely, while desirable immigrants are properly distributed throughout the country."[2] In the following year, Congress indefinitely extended Chinese Exclusion in the United States and its recently acquired Pacific territories of Hawai'i and the Philippines, completing a system of racialized immigration restriction that had begun over a quarter of a century earlier. First forged in relation to nineteenth-century debates over the "Chinese Question," Roosevelt's call for selective and restricted immigration would come to define American immigration law over the course of the twentieth century.[3]

The passage and administration of the Page Act (1875) and the subsequent Chinese Exclusion Acts provided the "legal architecture" for America's modern immigration system.[4] This chapter reads a variety of cultural materials, including case law, fiction, political cartoons, journalism, and nativist propaganda to explore how American perceptions and attitudes toward the racialized foreignness of new immigrants informed, influenced, and refracted these radical changes in immigration law. Immigration policies shape American understandings of national membership through the dialectical interplay of legal inclusion and exclusion. With the Page Act, Congress ushered in a period of restrictive federal immigration control, banning from entry certain "undesirable" immigrants – namely, so-called immoral Chinese women. The nation's first racialized immigration ban, the 1882 Chinese Exclusion Act, soon followed. It barred the entry of Chinese labor immigrants and prohibited their naturalization. Racial exclusion tempered the liberal ideology of American citizenship founded on Lockean notions of universal natural rights, birthright citizenship, and membership through voluntary political allegiance. The Reconstruction Amendments

Figure 16.1 Solly H. Walter, "Now Shut the Back Gate" (*San Francisco Wasp* 21, October 27, 1888)

Source: Courtesy of Bancroft Library, University of California Berkeley

and the extension of nominal citizenship to black freedmen (which revised the longstanding 1790 Naturalization Act restricting citizenship to "any alien, being a free white person") did not break the constitutive link between whiteness and citizenship. Subsequently, in *Plessy v. Ferguson* (1896), the Supreme Court upheld the constitutionality of *de jure* racial segregation, affirming whiteness as the condition of *full* citizenship. Black Americans were included into abstract or formal citizenship yet stripped of substantive rights even as the ongoing exclusion of Chinese (expanded by the 1917 Immigration Act to cover all those originating from the so-called Asiatic Barred Zone) from naturalization expanded the meaning of whiteness (and Americanization) to include new European immigrants.[5] More groups came under restriction as additional pieces of legislation placed Chinese workers along with contract laborers, paupers, convicts, anarchists, and the mentally infirm beyond the bounds of acceptable immigration. At the dawn of the new era, Roosevelt's urgent call for the end of America's historically open immigration policy serves as the culmination of a paradigm shift that had begun during Reconstruction.

The end of slavery and expanding post–Civil War industrialization made the United States increasingly dependent upon foreigners both as imported "cheap" labor and overseas consumers of American goods.[6] In turn, the rising tide of foreign immigration created greater class divisions and conflicts in the American consumer economy. This was particularly true in the case of American relations with China. Brokered by Anson Burlingame, the United States–China Treaty or the Burlingame Treaty (1868), first encouraged Chinese immigration to the United States by granting China most-favored-nation status in recognition of "the mutual advantages of the free migration and emigration of their citizens and subjects . . . for purposes of curiosity, of trade, or as permanent residents."[7] However, in the final decades of the century, American relations with China underwent a significant shift as deterritorialized forms of economic neocolonialism in the Asia-Pacific region began replacing demands for Chinese "cheap" labor, especially once the transcontinental railroad was completed. Secretary of State John Hay's so-called Open Door Notes (1899, 1900) asked that the imperial powers already established in China (Britain, France, Portugal, the Netherlands, Germany, Russia, and Japan) respect the autonomy of China and the right of equal access to its trade.[8] The United States touted the virtues of this policy of nonterritorial appropriation, fashioning itself as China's protector and "greatest friend" even as it enforced increasingly restrictive legislation against Chinese immigrants in the United States, from the Chinese Exclusion Acts of 1882, modified in 1884, 1886, and 1888 (known as the Scott Act), to their extensions in 1892 (known as the Geary Act), 1902, and again in 1904 with no terminal date. Chinese Exclusion laws were not repealed until the 1943 Magnuson Act, a wartime measure passed in the year China became an allied nation to the United States in World War II.

Popular discourses, ranging from ghetto sketches, invasion narratives, and antilabor novels to urban exposés like early Progressive-era reformer Jacob Riis's oft cited work of investigative photojournalism, *How the Other Half Lives: Studies among the Tenements of New York* (1890), helped disseminate a growing spirit of antialienism by figuring unrestricted immigration as menace to the public health, moral order, social stability, and free labor of the young nation. Riis best captured the complex mix of pity, aversion, and fear that often greeted new immigrants to America's overcrowded urban cities. A Danish immigrant himself, Riis vacillated between sympathy for and repulsion from these new immigrants, especially the southern and eastern Europeans who "do not understand 'Engliska' " crowding New York's infamous Lower East Side (108).[9] Fusing sentimentalism with journalistic realism, Riis figuratively guides his readers on a titillating and terrifying journey through the various foreign colonies and ghettos taken root in the iconic American metropolis, from "Jewtown," the Bohemian quarter, and Chinatown, to old "Africa."[10] Depicted as vectors of infectious disease and criminality, this "queer conglomerate mass of heterogeneous elements," in Riis's words, had begun to supplant the original "American stock . . . dying out for want of children" (21, 26):

> One may find for the asking an Italian, a German, a French, African, Spanish, Bohemian, Russian, Scandinavian, Jewish, and Chinese colony. Even the Arab, who peddles "holy earth" from the Battery as a direct importation from Jerusalem, has his exclusive preserves at the lower end of Washington Street. The one thing you shall vainly ask for in the chief city of America is a distinctively American community. There is none; certainly not among the tenements. Where have they gone to, the old inhabitants?
>
> *(21)*

Fears of so-called Anglo-Saxon "race suicide" threatened in the precipitous decline in white marriage and reproduction augmented anxieties of foreign-born immigrants laying siege to industrial America.[11] Riis couches his social surveillance through the metaphor of warfare, likening himself to a "war correspondent" in his documentary forays into the tenement district, "the hot-beds of the epidemics that carry death to rich and poor alike; the nurseries of pauperism and crime that fill our jails and police courts; that throw off a scum of forty thousand human wrecks to the island asylums and workhouses year by year" (58, 6). At the end of the century, Riis's literary crusade shaped American perceptions of new immigrants and the potential dangers they posed to the nation, exerting a powerful influence on a reform-minded Roosevelt as he began his political ascent from the New York City Police Board to the White House.[12]

The Chinese, of all the various immigrants documented in *How the Other Half Lives*, managed to evade Riis's attempts at social surveillance and control.[13] "Perhaps the attitude of American civilization toward the stranger . . . has taught" the Chinese immigrant to adopt a defensive posture of "[s]tealth and secretiveness," Riis concedes (75). However, the Chinese "are in no sense a desirable element of the population" and "serve no useful purpose" (81). Unlike European immigrants, Riis entertains no hope for Chinese assimilation. They remain "a constant and terrible menace to society," particularly given fears of racial miscegenation (80). Riis's attitude toward Chinese immigrants was not usual for his era. By the time he published *How the Other Half Lives*, Chinese exclusion had become an established feature of his adopted country, although he remained ambivalent about "the law that shuts out the . . . Chinaman" (81). "Rather than banish the Chinamen," he admonishes, "I would have the door opened wider – for his wife; and make it a condition of his coming or staying that he bring his wife with him" (81). By controlling women's immigration and reproduction, the Page Act restricted Chinese family formation and strengthened perceptions of Chinese men as unnatural bachelors and sexual deviants. It also ensured an exploitable class of temporary male laborers. Race-making *and* gender control were constitutive of Chinese immigration regulation, as Catherine Lee points out.[14] Anti-Chinese agitators commonly presented Chinese alienation in the United States as the cause rather than the product of these restrictive immigration policies, but early Progressive-era reformers like Riis attributed their failed assimilation to the vast gender imbalance among Chinese immigrants, long imagined in American law and culture as sojourners and differentiated from more desirable European immigrants on this basis.

Urban exposés and reform tracts were not alone in depicting foreign-born immigrants as racialized others, carriers of moral contagion and disease, and political incendiaries invading and corrupting America from within and without. Popular new subgenres, like the antilabor novel, which includes Francis Hopkinson Smith's *Tom Grogan* (1896), Edward Fuller's *The Complaining of Millions of Men* (1893), and statesman John Hay's popular yet understudied *The Bread-Winners: A Social Study* (first serialized in *The Century Magazine* in 1883), likewise racialized (usually Irish) foreigners as unsavory vectors of labor radicalism, as in Hay's villainous Andy Offitt, the murderous "dark-skinned" "apostle of labor" who espouses a "war on capital."[15] The trope of foreign invasion also found a ready home in the social commentaries of religious reformers such as Josiah Strong, a leader in the Social Gospel movement, who envisioned an immigrant "invasion" of America in his influential *Our Country* (1886). "America, as the land of promise to all the world," he writes, "is the destination of the most remarkable migration of which we have any record. During the last ten years we have suffered a peaceful invasion by an army more than four times as vast as the estimated number of Goths and Vandals that swept over Southern Europe and overwhelmed Rome."[16] Invasion narratives, according to David Seed, are part of a "long tradition in American writing in which the underside of manifest destiny is explored – the fear of failure, defeat, and subversion."[17] They gave imaginative form to cultural anxieties, testing national ideology at moments of perceived crisis and change.[18] At the end of the nineteenth century, a proliferation of invasion narratives fixated on Chinese immigrants as the most "undesirable" of all foreigners to the United States, lending impetus to immigration regulations over the following decades.

During a prolonged economic crisis in the 1870s, Pacific Coast anti-Chinese interests began to coalesce into a coherent political movement, bringing "Sand Lot" agitator Denis Kearney and his Workingmen's Party to power in California. By constructing Asiatic difference as fundamentally " 'foreign'. . . [and] . . . antipathetic to . . . modern American society," the Chinese Exclusion movement united disparate interest groups behind a constructed idea of a homogeneous white Christian nation.[19] It also created a popular market for the varied cultural materials that would form the now familiar tradition of the American Yellow Peril. The figurative threat of Asiatic conquest has a long discursive history stretching back from Genghis Khan's Mongol invasion of the European continent to British novelist Sax Rohmer's wildly popular criminal mastermind Fu Manchu. In vicious populist campaigns against Chinese immigrants, Pacific Coast propagandists began investing this powerful trope of Asiatic invasion with a distinct literary form. Sensational futuristic plots of Chinese invasion first began appearing in American print and visual culture in the 1880s. The counterfactual forms and complex temporal schemas of Chinese invasion fiction made the subgenre especially conducive to political propaganda. As cautionary tales, these fictions promoted the virtues of Chinese Exclusion and white supremacy, paradoxically, through their antithesis. Set in a future in which the Chinese Empire has subjugated white America, invasion fiction tested the possibility of unity within the nation as wide-scale immigration, spurred on by industrial capitalism, began to dissolve "the fabric of all cohesive social groups."[20]

In these popular fictions, Chinese Exclusion serves as a pivotal turning point in American history, providing the historical premise for a range of conjectural speculations. From legal discourse, most infamously in the Supreme Court cases of *Chae Chan Ping v. United States* or the Chinese Exclusion Case (1889) and *Fong Yue Ting v. United States* (1893), to the once popular but largely forgotten novels of Pierton W. Dooner, Robert Woltor, and Arthur Dudley Vinton, the invasion trope came to dominate United States–China relations and public discussions of and federal policies on the so-called Chinese Question.[21] Chinese invasion fiction combated negative portrayals of white lawlessness and anti-immigrant violence by projecting the anxiety of white displacement from labor markets to displacement from the country. In linking industrial modernization to national dissolution, these invasion fictions offered a nonteleological vision of American history as they imagined China as the horizon of capitalist markets. Early stories like "The Battle of the Wabash" (1880), published in the *Californian* magazine (later revived as the *Overland Monthly*), tied American industrialism to Chinese infiltration as it imagined the United States in the year 2078, in which "villages had become cities . . . threaded by a net-work of railroad lines," yet densely populated by "pig-tails" and filled with "Asiatic architecture, with the queer gables and pagoda-shaped tops."[22] As aesthetic vehicles for political propaganda, Chinese invasion fictions transformed America into an unbounded Chinatown to frighten readers with the devastating consequence of the country's shortcomings on the Chinese Question. These fictions imagined Chinese immigration to the United States as covert espionage and prelude to military colonization, with San Francisco's Chinatown as the epicenter of China's new "American kingdom," in the words of one anti-Chinese polemic.[23] Hence, invasion fiction heightened the affective impact of anti-Chinese political ideologies and provided mass cultural instruction by negative example. By stimulating and exploiting racial fears, the subgenre also sought to reestablish white political hegemony as industrial capitalism, wide-scale immigration, and class antagonisms restructured Gilded Age America.

The earliest of the Chinese invasion novels published in the United States, Pierton W. Dooner's *Last Days of the Republic* (1880) sheathed its anti-Chinese ideology in the garb of a historiography that sets out to "trace the causes" – in the language of economic and health security – of "the poison that is slowly corroding the vital principle of our national life" and to "arrest the disease, before the power so to do shall have passed, forever, beyond the reach of political regeneration" (9).[24] Dooner published *Last Days* by subscription, and he collaborated with prominent illustrator George Frederick Keller to produce original illustrations for the novel – Keller's only known bookwork.[25] Keller was acclaimed for his political cartoons in *The Wasp*, and his illustrations for Dooner were an extension of this magazine work. A Prussian immigrant, Keller shared Dooner's anxieties about unregulated Chinese immigration and expressed them in the many illustrations he inked for *The Wasp*. In one representative illustration titled "Immigration East and West" (1881), Keller depicts a huge phalanx of European immigrants disembarking from steamboats in the East while a monstrous Asian serpent rises from the Pacific Ocean, bearing upon its elongated torso the threatening captions, "ruin to white labor," "beneficial to corporation and monopoly," "small pox," "immorality," and "selfishness" (see Figure 16.2). Keller's graphic vision

Figure 16.2 George Frederick Keller, "Immigration, East and West" (*San Francisco Wasp* 7, August 26, 1881)

Source: Courtesy of Bancroft Library, University of California Berkeley

of the promise and peril of foreign immigration anticipates the anxiety and ambivalence later found in Riis's *How the Other Half Lives*. Even as Uncle Sam and Columbia greet the orderly stream of European immigrants carrying placards announcing their contributions to the nation – "Agriculture," "Labor," "Capital", "Industry," and "Art," an ominous detail juts out from the frame of the image – a headstone engraved "In Memory of Puritanism" – signaling the end of America's so-called original Anglo-Saxon stock.

Unlike Keller's imagination of a menacing Asiatic force attacking Columbia from without, Dooner structures *Last Days* around the device of a "fifth column" – an internal foreign enemy erupting from within the nation. This fear lent persuasive force to the deportation clauses built into the Chinese Exclusion Acts as well as the Immigration Acts of 1903 and 1918. Dooner's novel begins in 1848, with the California gold strike catalyzing Chinese labor immigration to the West. It then moves forward in time to offer an apocalyptic vision "at the dawn of the Twentieth Century" (258). The novel incorporates verbatim text from the Burlingame Treaty but reinterprets it through the prism of a fictional Chinese conspiracy. "In justice to Mr. Burlingame," the narrator concedes, "it must be admitted that he never suspected the treachery . . . it had never flashed upon his mind that he had been betrayed into a foreign conspiracy against the independence of his country" (27). China's political ambition was to gain "control of the Western Hemisphere," and "the introductory act" in this stratagem involved the "transport [of] her surplus population to America and to have them learn to maintain themselves there" as immigrants (24). To this end, the "cunning statesmen of China" manipulated Burlingame to secure a new treaty with more lenient immigration provisions, thus ensuring the success of China's "scheme of invasion" (27). So began, according to Dooner, the "Coolie" invasion of the Pacific Coast.

Last Days envisions Chinese immigration and political assimilation as the first stages of military aggression against United States sovereignty. In this alternate future, the Chinese successfully overturn American naturalization law limiting citizenship to "free white persons" and "aliens of African nativity and to persons of African descent" to secure "for the Coolie the exercise of the elective franchise" (100).[26] According to assimilationist ideology, immigrants become American by participating in the political, economic, and social life of the United States. For the Chinese, assimilation is merely superficial. Despite intimidation by white militias, including the Ku Klux Klan, the Chinese, once enfranchised, "availed themselves of their great numbers and the high privilege of American citizenship; and at the general election voted themselves into power" (175). In the New South, racial antipathy explodes into armed conflict when white incumbents refuse to cede their positions to the newly elected Chinese, and the Southern states rise up in white rebellion under the banner of "State Sovereignty and white supremacy" (192). As the democratic expression of the "will of the majority," the election of Chinese officers forces the president to abide by the rule of law and declare the Southern states in a state of rebellion against the Union.

In considering the possibility that Chinese immigrants might have the capacity for democratic rule, Dooner toys with an idea that he must disavow. Chinese citizenship sets the stage for a catastrophic repetition crisis, plunging the nation into a second Civil War. Unable to bear the slaughter of their white countrymen, the federal regiment dispatched to assist in subduing the Southern rebellion turns on the Chinese, realigning the conflict between state sovereignty and federal authority into a "war of races." Dooner's *Last Days* thus gave figurative shape to the continued racialization of citizenship after Reconstruction in its construction of the Chinese as immutably foreign even after political assimilation and the need for them to be preemptively ostracized on this basis.[27] Even after naturalization, the Chinese immigrant remains an "internal enemy" who mimes the appearance of national loyalty while plotting to destroy it. In the landmark Supreme Court case of *United States v. Wong Kim Ark* (1898), the federal government later attempted to denationalize birthright citizens of Chinese descent, alleging that Wong's birth on

American soil did not make him a citizen (according to the doctrine of *jus soli* or "right of soil") for his parents remained "subjects of the Emperor of China" whose affinities to the Chinese Empire were severed by neither migration nor political assimilation. Dooner first limned the political contours of this argument in a novel that portrays Chinese political assimilation and citizenship as ineffectual in dissolving their "essential" (or racialized) allegiance to China. Two years after the publication of Dooner's *Last Days*, the federal government would write these same anxieties into law with the passage of the first Chinese Exclusion Act, banning both the entry of Chinese labor migrants *and* prohibiting Chinese immigrants from naturalization to citizenship.

Initially honed in such nativist propaganda and fiction, the trope of invasion began to shape the legal imaginary and rhetoric of Chinese immigration in critical ways. Specifically, jurists began invoking the subgenre's tropes and narrative structures in rulings that helped establish the plenary power doctrine of American immigration law. First developed in the context of Chinese Exclusion, the plenary power doctrine holds congressional and executive branch decisions on immigration and naturalization as largely exempt from normal constitutional constraints and judicial review.[28] Plenary power is based on the idea that immigration involved the question of sovereignty, relating to a nation's right to define and police its borders. The complex temporal schemas and tropes of Chinese invasion fiction began to find their way into the Chinese immigration case law of this period, especially in the failed 1889 Chinese test case, *Chae Chan Ping v. United States*, challenging the Scott Act (1888). Unlike previous modifications to the Chinese Exclusion Act, the Scott Act explicitly violated the terms of the United States–China Treaty: it retroactively canceled the reentry certificates of roughly twenty thousand Chinese resident noncitizens who were then traveling outside the United States without granting them the means to recover the personal property they left in the country. Earlier revisions to the 1880 United States–China Treaty had restricted but not ended Chinese immigration to the United States for teachers, students, merchants, tourists, and returning laborers with proof of residence numbered among those exempted from exclusion. *Chae Chan Ping* was followed by another Chinese test case, *Fong Yue Ting v. United States*, contesting the additional anti-Chinese restrictions enacted under the subsequent Geary Act. In these Chinese cases, the Supreme Court upheld discrimination against immigrants based on race and granted federal immigration law an unusual immunity from judicial review. At the end of the twentieth century, as legal scholar Gabriel Chin argues, *Chae Chan Ping* and *Fong Yue Ting* "continue[d] to be cited in modern decisions of the Supreme Court; because all constitutional immigration law flows from these cases, even decisions that do not cite them must rely on cases that do."[29]

Chae Chan Ping arrived in the United States in 1875. On June 2, 1887, he departed on the steamship *Gaelic* for a voyage to China. Before embarking, he secured a reentry certificate as required by the 1882 Chinese Exclusion Act and the 1884 statute amending it in order to facilitate his immigration processing upon return. After a yearlong sojourn abroad, Chae Chan Ping boarded a California-bound vessel on September 7, 1888, before the Scott Act was introduced into Congress. However, during his month-long Pacific passage, the Scott Act became law. The new statute had dire implications for him. When he attempted to land, immigration officials voided his reentry certificate, revoking his "right of return." After the federal circuit court rejected his habeas corpus petition, Chae Chan Ping, with the assistance of the San Francisco Chinese Six Companies, appealed his case to the Supreme Court. The Six Companies was an executive council for the various family and district associations that served as an "instrument of social and labor control within the community as well as its representative to mainstream society and voice of protest to the government," according to historian Mae Ngai.[30] Thomas Riordan served as council for the Six Companies. He represented Chae Chan Ping before the Supreme Court and Wong Kim Ark before the circuit court and arranged the test case of *Fong Yue Ting*.[31]

Chae Chan Ping's case was among the most significant of the numerous test cases that Chinese litigants and their American allies orchestrated to challenge the various Chinese Exclusion Acts.

Justice Stephen Field authored the opinion in the unanimous ruling against Chae Chan Ping. Field upheld the Scott Act, claiming that the nation held the sovereign power to maintain "absolute independence and security throughout the entire territory."[32] His opinion focused on the scope of federal power over immigration, concluding, "That the government of the United States, through the action of the legislative department, can exclude aliens from its territory is a proposition which we do not think open to controversy."[33] It responded to the contention that the Constitution did not mention immigration among the enumerated powers granted to Congress; it recognized this authority as inherent in absolute sovereignty: "the United States, in their relation to foreign countries and their subjects or citizens, are one nation, invested with powers which belong to independent nations, the exercise of which can be involved for the maintenance of absolute independence and security throughout its entire territory."[34] Moreover, Field, like Dooner's *Last Days*, invoked the politically charged rhetoric of "an Oriental menace" to portray Chinese immigration as a threat to the nation:

> To preserve its independence, and give security against foreign aggression and encroachment, is the highest duty of every nation, and to attain these ends nearly all other considerations are to be subordinated. It matters not in what form such aggression and encroachment come, whether from the foreign nation acting in its national character or from vast hordes of its people crowding in upon us. . . . If, therefore, the government of the United States, through its legislative department, considers the presence of foreigners of a different race in this country, who will not assimilate with us, to be dangerous to its peace and security, their exclusion is not to be stayed because at the time there are no actual hostilities with the nation of which the foreigners are subjects. The existence of war would render the necessity of the proceeding only more obvious and pressing. The same necessity, in a less pressing degree, may arise when war does not exist, and the same authority which adjudges the necessity in one case must also determine it in the other.[35]

Field utilizes Yellow Peril imagery to establish Congressional authority to limit and exclude the entrance of "foreigners of a different race," especially if they endanger the "peace and security" of the nation. He regards Chinese Exclusion as a kind of "war measure" as he counterfactually postulates race war as the inevitable consequence of Chinese labor immigration, revealing the figurative forms and counterhistorical causation involved in legal meaning-making. His opinion construed Chinese immigration as a national security threat; hence, the United States held the same rights and duties to curb this foreign menace as it did to protect citizens in a time of war.

By portraying "vast hordes" of Chinese "crowding in upon us" as a constitutive act of "foreign aggression and encroachment," Field's opinion assigns counterhistorical causation in an elaborate counterfactual mode. Counterfactuals are conditional statements that pertain to or express "what has not in fact happened, but might, could, or would, in different conditions."[36] As Stephen Best explains, a counterfactual supposition in legal analysis allows one "to make inferences regarding causation, to infer not merely what happened or will happen, but, in addition, 'what *would* have been the case if some actual event, which in fact happened, had not happened.' "[37] Before his appointment as an associate justice in 1863, Field served six years on the California Supreme Court (1857–1863), and the regional politics of Chinese immigration shaped his judicial career. His *Chae Chan Ping* ruling marks the success of anti-Chinese interests in transforming the largely Pacific Coast issue of Chinese immigration into a national concern. Advocates of Chinese immigration had warned against such attempts "to frighten a nation of well-nigh fifty millions of people into a proceeding unprecedented in its history."[38] However, by 1889, Chinese Exclusion had become a "necessary" measure to the federal judiciary even when "war does not exist." Field wrested the language of sovereignty – "the natural law of self-preservation" – from states' rights discourse and applied it to the national government. He departed from past holdings to root immigration regulation in "a doctrine of inherent sovereign powers," which delegated to the legislative and executive branches plenary power or absolute authority over immigration.[39]

In *Chae Chan Ping*, the federal judiciary legitimized the trope of Chinese invasion, transforming it into the legal rationale for the continued abrogation of the United States–China Treaty and the termination of the few remaining privileges it secured to Chinese immigrants in the United States.[40] After Chae Chan Ping was returned to China in 1889, Justice Horace Gray's controversial majority (6–3) opinion in the subsequent case of *Fong Yue Ting*, contesting the Geary Act, further strengthened the idea of unlimited Congressional discretion in legislating all aspects of the nation's immigration policy, including the rules and procedures for alien registration and deportation. The most restrictive of all modifications to the original Exclusion Act, the Geary Act renewed existing Chinese Exclusion laws for ten years and required all Chinese labor migrants to secure certificates of residence (tantamount to an internal passport system), making noncompliance punishable by a maximum one-year term of imprisonment at hard labor followed by deportation.[41] In *Fong Yue Ting*, a divided Supreme Court upheld the Geary Act, concluding that Chinese aliens acquired no "vested rights" in the Constitution by virtue of residence. Hence their privileges could be suspended or revoked at the will of the state and its police power to defend the nation.[42]

Chae Chan Ping established the federal plenary power to exclude as inherent in absolute sovereignty, and it laid the groundwork for the summary deportation of lawful resident noncitizens upheld in *Fong Yue Ting*.[43] In order to make Chinese Exclusion consistent with "republican principles," Field, like the anti-Chinese writers who preceded and followed him, invokes what political theorist Giorgio Agamben, building on Carl Schmitt, describes as the "state of exception": no system of law is fully complete unto itself but relies on an "exception" – a suspension of the norm – that exists both within and outside the juridical order it helps constitute.[44] By the end of the decade, exclusionists had succeeded in advancing the idea that Chinese immigration posed a great danger to the nation. In both literature and law, the imagined threat of Chinese invasion facilitated a claim to the natural right of national self-preservation that existed outside or above the existing legal order.

Chinese invasion fictions had long disseminated such elaborate counterfactual histories of the racialized state of exception by figuring Chinese labor migrants as national security threats. Published in San Francisco just as the first Chinese Exclusion Act became federal law, Robert Woltor's *Short and Truthful History of the Taking of California and Oregon by the Chinese in the Year A.D. 1899 by Robert Woltor, A Survivor* (1882) took the form of a historiography by a self-described "survivor" of Chinese invasion. Five months after the capture of California and Oregon by Chinese forces, the narrator sets out to chronicle "a brief, unprejudiced, and connected history of the Mongolian invasion of California" (10).[45] In tracing the causes for the present calamity, the novel admonishes past governments for their too liberal policies on Chinese immigration. Like Dooner's *Last Days*, Woltor's dystopia reimagines Chinese immigration as a military strategy to seed the Pacific Coast states with advance military agents. Speaking from the vantage of the future, the narrator warns:

> It should have been granted that the national and unwritten law of nations demands, when circumstances unexpectedly arise which oblige a nation to diverge from its general course for its own lawful advantage and future safety, that any necessary steps taken

> on such occasions should be, as in the only instance in which the United States could ever be called upon to act against their fundamental law of "equity to all," not only excusable, but warranted in the opinion of the world.
>
> (37)

Appealing to the higher law of "self-preservation," Woltor marshals Chinese invasion as a legitimate "excuse" for the United States to act against its "fundamental law 'of equity to all,' " anticipating the charged legal rhetoric of subsequent Chinese Exclusion cases.

One year after the *Chae Chan Ping* ruling fortified the legal architecture of Chinese Exclusion, lawyer-novelist Arthur Dudley Vinton crafted perhaps the most elaborate of Chinese invasion fictions, illuminating the role of literary discourse in the political project of destabilizing Chinese legal claims. *Looking Further Backward* (1890) draws its plot of Chinese invasion from the characters and fictional settings popularized by Edward Bellamy's influential utopian novel, *Looking Backward 2000–1887* (1888). In the original, Bellamy's protagonist, Julian West, falls into a deep hypnotic trance and reawakens one hundred and thirteen years later to discover a modern utopia regulated by a collective form of government referred to as Nationalism. Vinton's sequel envisions the end of Bellamy's future America in a Chinese invasion. Set after the Chinese capture of the United States in 2023, *Looking Further Backward* takes the form of a series of historical lectures delivered by Chinese Professor Won Lung Li, who succeeds Julian West as chair of the Historical Section at Boston's Shawmut College. Speaking at the end of the war, Vinton's Professor Won explains to his audience of American college students the causes for China's successful colonization of North America and the deportation of white Americans to Europe where they are sold as chattel slaves.[46]

Like Woltor's *Short and Truthful History*, Vinton's novel powerfully dramatizes the catastrophic scenarios that legislators and jurists conjured in their defense of the controversial Geary Act and the subsequent ruling in *Fong Yue Ting*. It portrays a future government so limited by its constitution (indeed one divested of military and police powers) that when faced "with an invader not only at [its] gates but on [its] soil," it cannot act to protect its own citizens against violent expropriation (129).[47] Vinton's incredulous Julian West challenges the president:

> You tell me that your powers are limited, and that it would be treasonous to assume such vast authority, But what limits your authority? – the Constitution. But what is the object of the Constitution? Is not its sole purpose to secure the lives, liberties and happiness of the people? How then in fulfilling the plain purpose of the Constitution do you override it?
>
> (129–130)

In appealing to the higher or natural law of self-preservation against a Chinese enemy, West urges the president to exceed Constitutional mandates in the name of the Constitution (and to preserve the Constitution itself), limning the duality central to the "state of exception." The suspension of law coincides with and depends on its invocation and enactment.

By the turn of the century, the dystopian imaginaries of Chinese invasion fiction had laid the foundation for an enduring American tradition of Yellow Peril and, in giving form to the legal and literary struggles over Chinese immigration, helped forge the idea of absolute sovereignty. This doctrine of inherent sovereign powers, according to legal scholar Lucy Salyer, "expanded . . . to bolster the absolute power of the federal government to control immigration and to diminish the rights of aliens and the participation of courts in immigration decisions," both limiting judicial review of immigration decisions and leading to the growth of immigration administration and the rise of the modern bureaucratic state. The popular association of Chinese immigrants with invasion and race war in American culture also provided the legal groundwork for the antiradical, antialien cast of twentieth-century federal immigration law. However, these new regulations and popular perceptions did not go unchallenged by the new immigrants who sought to make America their home.

In response to formal and informal modes of anti-immigrant violence and stigmatization, immigrants began to assert their own narrative accounts of diaspora, migration, and racial and ethnic difference. Characterized by "stories of economic uplift, self-making, immigrant displacement, [and] cultural and religious assimilation," the immigrant novel would become a familiar genre to twentieth-century readers.[48] Wong Chin Foo, Yan Phou Lee, and Edith Maude Eaton (better known by her pseudonym Sui Sin Far) number among the few writers of Chinese descent in this flood of English-language immigrant writers. Wong composed more than one hundred forty different short-form writings demystifying Chinese cultural practices – specifically Confucianism – for American audiences in a period of heightened violence against Chinese immigrants.[49] Wong's contemporary Lee documented his early life in *When I Was a Boy in China* (1887) while Eaton published numerous sketches about the North American Chinese, unlike her sister Winnifred Eaton, who wrote under the Japanese pen name Onoto Watanna to avoid the stigmatization of Chinese identity prevalent at the time. These varied immigrant novels, autoethnographies, and journalism, documenting the trials and tribulations of "greenhorns" adjusting to American life, offered powerful counterpoints to nativist fears of foreign invasion and corruption of the United States. Many of these writers, including Norwegian American novelist Hjalmar Hjorth Boyesen and the Russian-born Jewish American Abraham Cahan, author of what many call the quintessential immigrant story, *Yekl: A Tale of the New York Ghetto* (1896), carried the influential imprimatur of William Dean Howells, the so-called Dean of American Letters.[50]

Another lesser known archive of immigrant resistance can be found in legal records. In vast numbers, immigrants took to the courts to contest legislative efforts to remake America into a gatekeeping nation. Chinese immigrants and their American allies orchestrated numerous legal test cases to challenge the newly established Immigration Bureau and its abusive administration of the federal exclusion laws.[51] Over a twenty-five-year span, Chinese petitioners like Chae Chan Ping and Fong Yue Ting deluged circuit courts with habeas corpus suits challenging the admission and deportation decisions of federal immigration inspectors. In 1888, the year that Chae Chan Ping began his legal battle to return to the United States, the anti-Chinese San Francisco *Evening Bulletin* offered a "brief history of the operation of the [Chinese Exclusion] Acts of 1882 and 1884," opining that the

> future historian will find one of the most interesting chapters on the jurisprudence of the American Republic to consist in a description and analysis of the writ of habeas corpus as applied to landing Chinamen in violation . . . of the Restriction Acts in the United States Courts of California.[52]

Walter again offered satirical commentary in a *Wasp* illustration titled "There's Millions in It" (1888), lampooning the San Francisco–based United States Circuit Court for abetting the Chinese inundation of the West. The illustration depicts circuit judge Lorenzo Sawyer dumping out a barrel of miniaturized Chinese immigrants against the protests of the Roman goddess Minerva, the figure depicted on the Great Seal of the State of California (see Figure 16.3). Other Chinese immigrants resisted by circumventing exclusion laws through surreptitious or illegal entry through the "back gates" of Mexico and Canada and posing as "paper sons" (fraudulently claiming to be either the son of a citizen of Chinese descent or a minor son of a Chinese

Figure 16.3 Solly H. Walter, "There's Millions in It" (*San Francisco Wasp* 21, July 21, 1888)

Source: Courtesy of Bancroft Library, University of California Berkeley

merchant).[53] Economic incentives, combined with a conviction that American law was morally and socially illegitimate (and thus not worthy of obedience), motivated these early illegal Chinese border crossings.[54]

These longstanding Chinese struggles against the Exclusion Acts generated a vast body of case law, legislation, and writings that helped establish the basic contours of future immigration debates, American policies, and patterns of enforcement, as historian Patrick Ettinger argues.[55] They also paved the way for other ethnic groups to contest the racialization of American immigration and naturalization law. In theorizing these twentieth-century prerequisite cases, legal scholar Ian Haney Lopez charts the shifting ways in which whiteness functioned as a normative identity for citizenship, revealing the racialized terms of naturalization jurisprudence through which people became white (and American) by law.[56] Beginning with the Page Act, the United States reversed its long-standing policy of open immigration as it instituted over the next half century a series of exclusionary policies that limited entry by ethnicity, national origin, occupational status, likelihood to "become a public charge," literacy, political association, moral turpitude, and health.[57] By exploring the legal transformation of the United States into a gatekeeping nation, this chapter joins other work in demythologizing the often celebratory image of America as a "nation of immigrants."

Notes

1 For a detailed outline of this shift away from the assimilation and black/white paradigms favored by older immigration literature to the new immigration history, see Mae M. Ngai, "Immigration and Ethnic History," in *American History Now*, ed. Eric Foner and Lisa McGirr (Philadelphia: Temple University Press, 2011), 358–75.

2 Hans P. Vought, *The Bully Pulpit and the Melting Pot: American Presidents and the Immigrant* (Macon, Ga.: Mercer University Press, 2004), 42.

3 The 1921 Emergency Quota Act established the first quota system and numerical limits to immigration, limiting the annual number of admitted immigrants to three percent of the total number of people of each nationality in the United States at the time of the 1890 census. The Immigration Act of 1924 (or the Johnson-Reed Act) further reduced the overall number to two percent from each country and excluded all immigrants from Asia.

4 Erika Lee, *At America's Gate: Chinese Immigration during the Exclusion Era, 1882–1943* (Chapel Hill: University of North Carolina Press, 2003), 24.

5 Lisa Lowe, *Immigrant Acts: On Asian American Cultural Politics* (Durham, N.C.: Duke University Press, 1996), 2.

6 Matthew F. Jacobson, *Barbarian Virtues: The United States Encounters Foreign Peoples at Home and Abroad, 1876–1917* (New York: Hill & Wang, 2000), 63–9.

7 Burlingame Treaty, U.S.–China, art. V, July 28, 1868, 16 Stat. 739.

8 Michael L. Krenn, *The Color of Empire: Race and American Foreign Relations* (Washington, D.C.: Potomac Books, 2006), 56–7.

9 Jacob A. Riis, *How the Other Half Lives: Studies among the Tenements of New York* (1890; New York: Penguin, 1997). Hereafter cited parenthetically in the text.

10 Stephanie Foote, *Regional Fictions: Culture and Identity in Nineteenth-Century American Literature* (Madison: University of Wisconsin Press, 2001), 132, 134.

11 Colleen Lye, *America's Asia: Racial Form and American Literature, 1893–1945* (Princeton, N.J.: Princeton University Press, 2004), 51, 52.

12 Aviva Taubenfeld, *Rough Writing: Ethnic Authorship in Theodore Roosevelt's America* (New York: New York University Press, 2008), 45–6.

13 Foote, *Regional Fictions*, 144.

14 Catherine Lee, "'Where the Danger Lies': Race, Gender, and Chinese and Japanese Exclusion in the United States, 1870–1924," *Sociological Forum* 25 (2010): 248–71, 250.

15 John Hay, *The Bread-Winners: A Social Study* (New York: Harper, 1884), 78, 86; Scott Dalrymple, "John Hay's Revenge: Anti-Labor Novels, 1880–1905," *Business and Economic Weekly* 28 (1999): 133–42, 140.

16 Josiah Strong, *Our Country* (Cambridge, Mass.: Harvard University Press, 1963), 42.
17 David Seed, "Constructing America's Enemies: The Invasion of the USA," *Yearbook of English Studies* 37 (2007): 64–84, 64.
18 Ibid., 77.
19 Lowe, *Immigrant Acts*, 5.
20 Frederic Jameson, "Reification and Utopia in Mass Culture," *Social Text* 1 (1979): 130–48, 140.
21 Science fiction author William Wu's pioneering *Yellow Peril: Chinese Americans in American Fiction, 1850–1940* (Hamden: Archon, 1982) remains the only extended literary study of these early narratives. John K.W. Tchen and Dylan Yeats' *Yellow Peril! An Archive of Anti-Asian Fear* (London: Verso, 2014) provides a useful compendium of these cultural materials.
22 "Lorelle" (pseud.), "The Battle of the Wabash: A Letter from the Invisible Police," *Californian* 2, no. 10 (October 1880): 364–76, 365.
23 G. B. Densmore, *The Chinese in San Francisco: Description of Chinese Life in San Francisco* (San Francisco: Pettit & Russ, 1880), 21.
24 P.W. Dooner, *Last Days of The Republic* (San Francisco: Alta California Publishing House, 1880). Hereafter cited parenthetically in the text.
25 Richard S. West, *The San Francisco Wasp: An Illustrated History* (Northampton, Mass.: Periodyssey Press, 2004), 18.
26 Naturalization Act of 1870 (16 Stat. 254).
27 Claire J. Kim, "The Racial Triangulation of Asian Americans," *Politics & Society* 27 (1999): 105–38, 112.
28 Meredith K. Olafson, "The Concept of Limited Sovereignty and the Immigration Law Plenary Power Doctrine," *Georgetown Immigration Law Journal* 13 (1999): 433–53, 433.
29 Gabriel J. Chin, "Segregation's Last Stronghold: Race Discrimination and the Constitutional Law of Immigration," *UCLA Law Review* 46 (1998): 1–74, 15.
30 Mae M. Ngai, *Impossible Subjects: Illegal Aliens and the Making of Modern America* (Princeton, N.J.: Princeton University Press, 2004), 213.
31 Gabriel J. Chin, "*Chae Chan Ping* and *Fong Yue Ting*: The Origins of Plenary Power," in *Immigration Stories*, ed. David A. Martin and Peter H. Schuck (New York: Foundation, 2005), 7–29.
32 *Chae Chan Ping v. United States*, 130 U.S. 581 (1889).
33 Chin, "*Chae*," 13.
34 Ibid., 14.
35 *Chae Chan Ping*, 130 U.S. at 606.
36 *Oxford English Dictionary*, 2nd ed., 1989; online version, November 2010.
37 Stephen M. Best, *The Fugitive's Properties: Law and the Poetics of Possession* (Chicago: University of Chicago Press, 2004), 211 (quoting Herbert L. A. Hart and Tony Honoré, *Causation in the Law*, 2nd ed. [Oxford: Oxford University Press, 1985], 15).
38 Elliott C. Cowdin, *Chinese Immigration. Maintain the National Faith. Speech of Mr. Elliot C. Cowdin before the Chamber of Commerce of the State of New York* (New York: n.p., c. 1879), 2.
39 Ngai, *Impossible Subjects*, 11, 12.
40 *Facts upon the Other Side of the Chinese Question: With a Memorial to the President of the U.S. from Representative Chinamen in America* (San Francisco: n.p., 1876), 7. Field later dissented from the majority opinion in *Fong Yue Ting*, arguing that while the power to exclude was plenary, government "power to deport from the country persons lawfully domiciled therein by its consent . . . has never been asserted . . . except for crime, or as an act of war." *Fong Yue Ting v. United States*, 149 U.S. 698, 746 (1893) (Field, J., dissenting).
41 Lucy E. Salyer, *Law Harsh as Tigers: Chinese Immigrants and the Shaping of Modern Immigration Law* (Chapel Hill: University of North Carolina Press, 1995), 46.
42 Ibid., 51, 182.
43 Chin, "*Chae*," 19.
44 Giorgio Agamben, *State of Exception*, trans. Kevin Attell (Chicago: University of Chicago Press, 2005), 1–2.
45 Robert Woltor, *A Short and Truthful History of the Taking of California and Oregon by the Chinese in the Year A.D. 1899 by Robert Woltor, a Survivor* (San Francisco: Bancroft, 1882). Hereafter cited parenthetically in the text.
46 See Eric Hayot, *The Hypothetical Mandarin: Sympathy, Modernity, and Chinese Pain* (Oxford: Oxford University Press, 2009), for a detailed discussion of Vinton's novel in terms of Enlightenment philosophical discourses of Chinese otherness.
47 Arthur D. Vinton, *Looking Further Backward: Being a Series of Lectures Delivered to the Freshman Class at Shawmut College, By Professor Won Lung Li* (New York: Albany Book Co., 1890). Hereafter cited parenthetically in the text.

48 Joshua L. Miller, "The Immigrant Novel," in *The American Novel: 1870–1940*, Oxford History of the Novel in English, vol. 6, ed. Priscilla Wald and Michael A. Elliott (Oxford: Oxford University Press, 2014), 200–17, 200.
49 Scott D. Seligman, *The First Chinese American: The Remarkable Life of Wong Chin Foo* (Hong Kong: Hong Kong University Press, 2013), xi.
50 Miller, "The Immigrant Novel," 203, 210.
51 The 1891 Immigration Act established the Office of the Superintendent of Immigrants within the Treasury Department. In 1903, the Immigration Bureau was reorganized under the Department of Commerce and Labor, under the Department of Labor after 1913, and again under the Department of Justice after 1940.
52 "Chinese Restriction," *Evening Bulletin* (San Francisco), January 24, 1888, 1.
53 Emily Ryo, "Through the Back Door: Applying Theories of Legal Compliance to Illegal Immigration during the Chinese Exclusion Era," *Law & Social Inquiry* 31 (2006): 109–46, 110–11.
54 Ibid., 112.
55 Patrick Ettinger, *Imaginary Lines: Border Enforcement and the Origins of Undocumented Immigrations, 1882–1930* (Austin: University of Texas Press, 2009), 20.
56 See Ian H. Lopez, *White by Law* (New York: New York University Press, 1997) for a discussion of these racial prerequisite cases, especially *Takao Ozawa v. United States*, 260 U.S. 178 (1922) and *United States v. Bhagat Singh Thind*, 261 U.S. 204 (1923), which applied the racially excluded category of the "Asiatic" to Japanese and East Indians, making them ineligible for naturalization according to precedents set in the earlier Chinese cases.
57 Lee, "Where the Danger Lies," 266.

17

FICTIONS OF RACE AND PERSONALITY

Nineteenth-century law and Mark Twain's *Pudd'nhead Wilson*

Trinyan Mariano

> Oh what a transition it was to be changed from the state of a slave to that of a free man! Really when [I think] of my former condition and [my] present [I] am puzzled to know whether Frederick Douglass then, was the same Frederick Douglass now.[1]

Frederick Douglass's words, delivered to a crowd in Limerick, Ireland, in 1845, express the strangeness of the change in status that accompanied his travel from the United States, where he was a black (escaped) slave, to Ireland, where he was a free man. The shift, one he claims was accomplished "in the language of the law,"[2] is represented as an existential rupture that disorients his sense of a continuous self bridging both statuses. He later described the experience in mystical terms: "I breathe, and lo! the chattel becomes a man."[3] Douglass's description articulates the law's power to convert property to person and encapsulates the impossible dichotomy between race law and lived experience in the nineteenth century. The nineteenth century in the United States is sometimes described as an era that began in slavery and ended in freedom. The reality is, of course, more complicated. Slavery and race were never coextensive, and, as slavery formally disappeared, new methods of legal discrimination emerged, ensuring that black citizenship fell far short of free and full. Yet the historical arc of the nineteenth century turns on a set of potent legal constructs – race, property, and personality. Together, they comprise the extraordinary legal alchemy by which property became persons and by which race supplanted slavery as the relevant status for defining access to rights. As Douglass's disorientation underscores, these transitions had consequences for the human beings tasked with locating themselves within what were unstable systems of legal meaning and significance.

These high stakes, combined with the hopelessly inadequate strategies by which the law attempted to define race in the nineteenth century, gave rise to the anxiety-marked narratives of racial belonging, exclusion, and alienation that dominated the literary period and provide the focus of this chapter. Mark Twain's *The Tragedy of Pudd'nhead Wilson*, written in post-emancipation 1894 but set in pre-emancipation 1830s, stages the volatile junction of race, slavery, and legal personhood. In it, Twain addresses the nineteenth century's unsettled configurations of race and rights by narrating his characters' never clean transition back and forth between being white and black, free and slave, chattel and person. The novel is both comedy and tragedy – comic in its caricature of the law's fictions, tragic in its depiction of the law's power over those subject to its fictions.

In *Pudd'nhead Wilson*, Twain interrogates the seams joining race, property, and personhood by narrating the transition of characters across slave and color lines. Set in the sleepy small town of Dawson's Creek, Missouri, the plot is driven by a murder mystery that captivates the novel's eponymous character, David "Pudd'nhead" Wilson, whose search for the killer threatens to uncover the hidden identity of Tom, a black man living – unbeknownst to the townsfolk and himself – as a white man in their midst. Twenty-three years earlier, Tom's mother, a slave named Roxy, frightened by the possibility of her baby being sold "down the river," switched him for the child of her master. Nobody noticed. The character we know as Thomas a Becket Driscoll was born Valet de Chambre, a free white man who, also unbeknownst to the townsfolk and himself, has been held as a slave all of these years in Tom's stead. At the end, the two mysteries collide as Tom is simultaneously revealed as the killer and outed as black through a trial that restores the town's tranquility by returning everyone to their proper racial places.

In this chapter, I use Twain's novel to analyze the matrix formed from the competing legal and cultural articulations and disarticulations of race, slavery, and personhood. The term "matrix" commonly refers to a table used to organize elements and simplify complex equations. The table allows one element to be posited as fixed in order to measure the outcome for the others. "Matrix," from the Latin word for mother, also refers to "the medium in which something is originated, produced, or developed," for example, the rock substance in which a fossil is embedded or the material that surrounds the structural elements of a cell. The term is used to describe things produced inside of interconnecting networks that comprise complex social structures and political and economic systems.[4] Thus, a matrix is at once a classification tool and a figure for comprehending how the tool produces the things it classifies. The plural sense of milieu embodied in the term "matrix" helps us comprehend Twain's engagement with race, slavery, and personhood as conditions that are both given and created, physical and formal.

I have called race, chattel slavery, and personhood "legal fictions." By this term I mean the knowing assumption of a thing as fact, which is not literally true.[5] A fiction is a deliberate untruth, pragmatically posited in order to enable a judge to avoid or stretch the strict application of the law without changing its primary structure. The rule that a corporation is a person is the most well known example. As corporations became increasingly common, courts were called upon to help govern corporate behavior, but they lacked adequate guiding legislation and were inherently unable to construct wholesale a new system of applicable common-law rules. The workaround they devised involved "simply" designating corporations "persons" and so grafting them piecemeal into the preexisting structures of the common law that defined the rights attending personhood.

William Blackstone saw fictions as a "troublesome, but not dangerous" part of the common law, the means by which the "interior apartments" of a "magnificent and venerable, but useless" "old Gothic castle" are "fitted up for a modern inhabitant."[6] Henry Sumner Maine similarly believed fictions were historically necessary "for overcoming the rigidity of law." His concern focused on the veiled nature of change accomplished by fictions, which he defined as "any assumption which conceals, or affects to conceal, the fact that a rule of law has undergone alteration, its letter remaining unchanged, its operation being modified." In Maine's view, particular legal fictions rely on a generalized one – "[t]he fact is. . . that the law has been wholly changed; the fiction is that it remains what it always was."[7]

These and other apologists argue that fictions are narrowly contained rhetorical or logical devices that provide judges with the scaffolding necessary to advance the law without losing internal consistency. For these, the literal falsehood of fictions is irrelevant since nobody is actually deceived (no one believes a corporation to be literally a person). Lon Fuller, for example, whose mid-twentieth-century work on fictions remains the standard, believed that fictions evidence the law's basic pathology, rooted in its linguistic nature. When the conceptual and linguistic tools that the judge possesses are inadequate to resolve the dispute, fictions enable the judge to "feel the way" toward a solution. As such, they express inevitable "growing pains of the language of the law,"[8] and are not problematic so long as they are used "with a complete consciousness of [their] falsity."[9] A fiction becomes "dangerous," Fuller warned, when its constitutive force is forgotten and the fiction is believed.[10]

However, the doctrine of precedent guarantees that, with repeated use, the fiction will take on a life of its own. With each iteration, the fiat power of law produces the very reality once posited as consciously false.[11] The legal fiction remains false in one sense while becoming true in another. Words have no *a priori* meaning. The "literalness" of their signification changes with usage and custom. Thus, the meaning of "person" has been and continues to be altered by the legal history of corporate personhood such that, for many intents and purposes, a corporation is now, in point of fact, "literally" a person.

In *Pudd'nhead Wilson*, Twain depicts the process of forgetting that enables fictions to become facts. Far from functioning as narrowly contained rhetorical or logical devices, the fictions of law that Twain addresses mark the site of the most fractious political and social disagreements of the last two hundred years. They express conflicted "normative assumptions about social status"[12] and obscure deep contradictions in the operation of the law in society. Beginning with the fiction of race, my reading of *Pudd'nhead Wilson* first illustrates the tension between formal statutory blood-fraction laws and informal cultural notions of race and then analyzes the legal fiction that transformed persons into chattel and chattel into persons in order to give weight to the embodied beings behind the fictions configured in the matrix.

Justice Roger B. Taney's holding in the *Dred Scott* case (1857) that Negroes were not American citizens targeted not only enslaved persons but all people of African descent living in the United States.[13] This decision helped to consolidate a shift then under way that configured citizenship as a function of one's racial status. Although there has always been a dominant racial component to American slavery, prior to the nineteenth century, the most important dividing line in the United States for the formal legal definition of rights was not one's racial category but one's status as free or slave.[14] Free blacks could be found at every social stratum, propertied free men of color enjoyed at least some rights of citizenship in most regions of the United States, and the history of U.S. slavery included persons of African, Asian, and European descent (not to mention the prominently white European class of indentured servants).[15] Racial intermixing was commonplace, and many persons, free and slave, could claim both African and European ancestry.[16]

Laws strengthening the connection between race and slavery accrued gradually with regional differences depending on local economic, demographic, and political challenges. Before the nineteenth century, for example, South Carolina, lacking an adequate free nonslaveholding class critical to their society, gave a broad body of rights to free blacks. Blacks could vote and could serve in militias and on juries. Though many imposed property qualifications, only three colonies formally restricted the vote to white men. National law followed a similar pattern. The Articles of Confederation gave free black men the same privileges and immunities as citizens of the various states.[17] While Americans had deeply seated racial prejudices, until the later nineteenth century, for legal purposes, race did not matter in the all-consuming way announced by the *Dred Scott* decision. Some historians attribute this to an "eighteenth-century equality thesis";[18] others point to the fact that it was only in the nineteenth century that free blacks existed in numbers that began to pose a threat to the economic and political dominance of whites;[19] still others view the shift as a jurisdictional issue as the seat of power was transferred from the system of indwelling plantation law that gave slave owners far-reaching discretionary power over slaves toward more centralized state and federal laws.[20] As the nation attempted to dismantle slavery and then to define the rights of former slaves, the legal color line in the South did not dissipate but intensified until, as Ariela Gross writes, "the color line replaced the boundary between free and slave, race replaced slave status, and a regime of whiteness replaced the regime of slavery as the weapon of oppression."[21]

The consolidation of race as the dividing line for rights surfaced problems in the law. Slave status was a function of matrilineal descent and was easier to establish than racial identity.[22] One was a slave if one's mother was a slave, regardless of racial ancestry or physical appearance.[23] Race, by contrast, relied on a multifaceted and contradictory set of legal, social, and scientific criteria that judges, lawmakers, and others unsuccessfully attempted to crystallize throughout the nineteenth century and beyond. The familiar example of the slave family sired by Thomas Jefferson illustrates the complex articulation of race with slavery. Eston and Madison Hemings were among the six children of Jefferson and his slave, Sally Hemings.[24] According to Isaac Jefferson, another slave at Monticello, Sally Hemings was "mighty near white" with very light skin and straight hair.[25] Her mother was "a bright mulatto woman," and her father is believed to have been a white man.[26] At the time, Virginia used a blood-fraction rule to define race, deeming "white" any person with no more than one-eighth African ancestry. By this standard, the children of Sally Hemings and Thomas Jefferson were very likely legally white. Yet by the law of matrilineal descent, all were slaves.[27] Upon his death, Jefferson's will freed Eston and Madison. Despite having identical "blood proportion," Eston, a fair-skinned, reddish-headed, freckled man, assimilated into white society and was reported as "white" on the census. Madison, a darker-skinned man, joined the black community and was reported as "black."

The example illustrates the difficulty of defining race in the shadow of slavery, as well as the antagonism between legal rules, social dimensions of racial belonging, and individual identity. After *Dred Scott*, legislators and courts attempted to stabilize the vast range of racial admixture in the American population by fashioning laws that increasingly assigned persons to one of only two racial statuses – white or black.[28] Emancipation only heightened the perceived need to define and contain a racial underclass, a need that statutory law met by moving toward ever smaller "blood fraction" rules to assign racial categories. The *Dred Scott* decision announced the legal significance of these racial determinations in absolute terms: whites were entitled to all rights; blacks to none, at least none that could be enforced against whites.[29]

The complexity of Twain's narrative in *Pudd'nhead Wilson* is a function of the instability inherent to race and slave statuses in the nineteenth century. Twain constructs a matrix with the categories of black and white, slave and free, and then populates it with characters who shift back and forth among the categories. To follow the plot, readers must stabilize one category – race or slave – in order to test outcomes for the other and assess the logical relationship between them. Twain's matrix sets up some of the conflicting rules and expectations about the racial identity of slaves and calls into question which status is to be posited first. Does racial status attend slave status or vice versa? Roxy, for example, is both black and white and neither. She has white skin and is of largely white European ancestry, but she codes as black through her speech, her clothing, and her status and reputation as a slave.[30] David Wilson, a.k.a. "Pudd'nhead," as a newcomer to town, figures out Roxy's racial identity from such clues. Before he sees her, he hears her speak. He is stunned, then, to later discover that she is visually white. "From Roxy's manner of speech," the narrator comments, "a stranger would have expected her to be black, but she was not. Only one-sixteenth of her was black, and that sixteenth did not show."[31] The narrator's elaboration on the ways in which the black didn't show make it clear that the social assumptions around white appearance are favorable, while those surrounding black appearance are not. Roxy has a "very fair" complexion, "brown" eyes, a "heavy suit of fine soft hair." Roxy is "majestic," "statuesque," "noble," and "grace[ful]." Her face is "shapely, intelligent, and comely – even beautiful" (8).

Despite the conclusion that would seem to follow from all of this evidence, we learn Roxy is not white after all: "To all intents and purposes Roxy was as white as anybody, but the one-sixteenth of her which was black outvoted the other fifteen parts and made her a negro."[32] The narrator's characterization of Roxy as white for "all intents and purposes" is belied by the fact that the part of her that is black renders her "a slave, and salable as such."[33] The same paragraphs that figure Roxy's physical and legal whiteness also give clues to her social blackness, including her speech patterns, the checkered handkerchief she wears on her head, and her mannerisms (she is "high and 'sassy' " with "her own caste" but "meek and humble" with white people).[34]

Judged by either blood-fraction rules or by appearance, whether in 1830 when the novel was set or in 1894 when the novel was written, Roxy would have been legally white in every state in the United States. The first statute to define racial categories was enacted in Virginia in 1705 and defined as black anyone having one or more black great-grandparents and as white anyone having less than one-eighth black blood.[35] Among the states that had such statutes, the one-eighth rule was the most common and was the law in Missouri throughout the nineteenth century.[36] The legal "whiteness" of Roxy's son is indisputable. His father, Colonel Cecil Burleigh Essex, is an "F.F.V. [First Families of Virginia] of formidable caliber," one of the best families in town.[37] Roxy's son has blond hair, blue eyes, and, to the white community, is indistinguishable from his master's son. He is "thirty-one parts white," and yet, "he, too, was a slave, and by a fiction of law and custom a negro."[38]

Literary critics often connect Twain's reference to Tom and Roxy's proportion of "black" blood to the so-called one-drop rule that came to define whiteness as a category of racial purity, but one-drop rules were not formally adopted until the twentieth century.[39] Roxy and Tom would both meet the statutory qualifications for whiteness in Missouri. However, statute was not the whole picture. Judged from legal practice, racial classifications were much more "unstable and impermanent."[40] Writing at the close of the nineteenth century, before the one-drop rule had been codified in statutes across the nation, Booker T. Washington named what he believed was a customary one-drop rule:

> [I]f a person is known to have one per cent of African blood in his veins, he ceases to be a white man. The ninety-nine percent of Caucasian blood does not weigh by the side of the one per cent of African blood. The white blood counts for nothing. The person is a Negro every time.[41]

Historians have since confirmed that Washington's impressions were correct. As Frank Sweet puts it, while states paid "lip service to the old blood-fraction laws in theory," by 1865, they had "become comfortable with a one-drop rule in practice."[42] Of course, despite how clear-cut (or not) the law was, there was a vast gulf between being legally white and being accepted as white by the community where appearance, reputation, and other markers of blackness continued to matter.[43] Laws declaring persons of African appearance to be socially white would not have been followed. Even the rumor of black ancestry was enough to deem someone socially black, despite appearance, regardless of blood fraction.

Through the operation of the law, Roxy and Tom gain and lose racial definition with a complexity that is perhaps appreciated only by lawyers. Thomas Reed Powell famously characterized the legal mind: "if you think that you can think about a thing inextricably attached to something else without thinking of the thing it is attached to, then you have a legal mind."[44] It is by such a process of analytic detachment and abstraction that the lawyer Wilson is introduced to the town. On his unfortunate first day in Dawson's Landing, he hears "an invisible dog" barking and declares, "I wish I owned half of that dog."[45] When asked to explain, Wilson answers, "Because

I would kill my half."[46] Puzzled, the townsmen withdraw to discuss their assessment of him in light of his comment:

> "Said he wished he owned *half* of the dog, the idiot. . . What did he reckon would become of the other half if he killed his half? Do you reckon he thought it would live?"
>
> "Why, he must have thought it, unless he *is* the downrightest fool in the world; because if he hadn't thought it, he would have wanted to own the whole dog, knowing that if he killed his half and the other half died, he would be responsible for that half just the same as if he had killed that half instead of his own. Don't it look that way to you, gents?"
>
> "Yes, it does. If he owned one half of the general dog, it would be so; if he owned one end of the dog and another person owned the other end, it would be so, just the same; particular in the first case, because if you kill one half of a general dog, there ain't any man that can tell whose half it was, but if he owned one end of the dog, maybe he could kill his end of it and –"[47]

Aside from furnishing an instance of Twain's unmatched wit, the discourse in this scene is oddly legal in tone. We hear legal echoes in the topics of ownership and responsibility, in the fictional abstractions of half dogs and "general dogs" and in the attempt to isolate legally significant consequences from hypothetical situations.

Here, the rhetorical practice mirrors the racial matrix as the law defines abstract qualities, like blood fraction or matrilineal descent, and accords them legal relevance. And, as with many fictions, the abstractions fabricated by law create "the [racial] categories they claim[ ] only to elucidate."[48] At the same time, the shifting status of race and slave in *Pudd'nhead Wilson* demonstrates the broader social and cultural meanings of race that in some ways competed with and in other ways informed legal definitions. Although it is possible for scholars to construct the meaning of race without thinking about the "things" attached to them, Twain's novel reunites the abstractions with the persons said to embody them, demonstrating both the power and the absurdity of the abstractions. The final and greatest mystery of Twain's novel, then, is not solved by but is dramatized in the narrative – that is, the simultaneous reality and unreality of race created by the contradictions, inconsistencies, and absurdities of nineteenth-century race law.

The unstable status of Twain's characters within the narrative resonates with the legal trajectory for blacks in the nineteenth century, many of whom began the century as slaves and then were freed and granted rights of personhood, all the while finding themselves subject to a dizzying set of legal and cultural practices that undercut their status as legal persons and established one version after another of second-class citizenship. Roxy begins as a slave, is freed, is sold back into slavery, and then buys her freedom again. Her second time as a slave is especially vexed. Since her resale into slavery was illegal, Roxy was technically already free when she buys back her freedom. Tom begins as a slave, becomes free, and then is eventually reclaimed as a slave. Chambers begins as free, becomes a slave, and then is reassigned as free. By mapping race onto slave status, all three characters occupy, at some point in the novel, every possible combination in the matrix of black/white, free/slave, person/property. Twain points to race's double existence as a purely formal legal status and as a cultural fact fixed by custom. The lived meanings of race exceed, produce, and countermand its legal definitions, just as the legal definitions produce the conditions within which the cultural meanings of race are generated and experienced. Twain's farcical dramatization of the circularity between formal law and social reality describes the crux of legal fictions and is explained by sociologist Pierre Bourdieu: "It would not be excessive to say that [law] *creates* the social world, but only if we remember that it is this world which first creates the law."[49]

The period between the 1830s and the end of the century was marked by great transition: the Civil War was fought, emancipation was announced, Reconstruction was undertaken and abandoned, the Civil Rights amendments were ratified, the *Dred Scott* case was decided, and the tyranny of Jim Crow was firmly ensconced. In the midst of this unsettled period, legal historians tend nonetheless to point to consistent patterns in the way race was defined, as states in the South and the North were "being persuaded by a new way"[50] of seeing the color line that defined race as an "internal function based on biology."[51] Seen as a way of simplifying (albeit only theoretically), the law tried to eradicate the nuances of racial mixture. Whiteness increasingly came to mean a state of racial purity, the absence of black blood, while blackness was defined as an adulterated state, colored by any presence of visible or invisible black blood.[52]

There is something suspicious about historical constructions that posit a steady, logical progression of law in the face of such conflict and upheaval. The narrative characterizing the nineteenth century as moving linearly from a paradigm that defined race according to appearance to one that defined race according to biology relies on the assumption that statute serves as a stable location from which legal meaning can be reliably and comprehensively extracted. The law's discursive practices, including the interpretive primacy of statute over common law and the doctrine of precedent, underscore this assumption and engender inherently linear and conservative frameworks for understanding legal developments. However, recently, scholars like Daniel Sharfstein and Ariela Gross have provided a more complex vision of nineteenth-century race law by shifting our gaze from statutes and appellate practice to trials where racial identity was at issue. Contrary to the converging uniformity of statutory law, Gross's groundbreaking study of nineteenth-century trials found a "complex interplay between legal and cultural meanings of race" wherein biology, or "blood," was only one of a mixed stew of factors that claimed legal relevance.[53]

Gross's work dismantles the traditional view of nineteenth-century race law as coalescing around biological definitions of race based on blood fractions. Instead, she shows how trials that tasked courts with determining a party's racial identity relied on understandings of race drawn from social and cultural practices.[54] Trial courts faced with applying the legal fiction of race were given an impossible task. They were directed by statute to determine racial identity based on blood fraction but lacked the scientific ability to do so. Thus, they had no option but to devise other methods of identification. As Gross explains:

> Trials required a confrontation between everyday ways of understanding race and definitions that fit into the "official," well-articulated racial ideology that supported the maintenance of slavery and postwar racial hierarchy. That is, legal rules based on "blood" had to be translated into practical action "on the ground," where people were more likely to describe someone's race in terms of how they looked and behaved than in terms of their fractional ancestry.[55]

Trials embedded cultural practices and assumptions into juridical determinations of race, including "folk law" concerning the appearance of black blood, "kinky" and "wooly" hair, the shape of noses and lips, the nuances of skin color, and, in one case, the "peculiar formation of the *negro foot*."[56] The trials evidenced cultural assumptions about black and white manners, dialect, and behaviors and used those assumptions to make legal determinations about who was white and who was black. Thus, while biological definitions of race were made the explicit standard in nineteenth-century statutes, when trial courts attempted to apply those statutes, biological notions were supplanted by customary white Southern beliefs about race.

Perhaps the most salient fact distilled by Gross's work is that many Southern judges and lawyers believed that formal guidelines for racial identification were unnecessary. Race was finally a matter of "common sense" for Southerners who simply "know a negro when they see one."[57] Gross writes:

> [J]udges in the nineteenth-century South repeatedly held that the determination of an individual's race was 'a question very proper for a jury,' because the jury represented the sense of the community; race was something commonsensical – something we *know when we see it*. Witnesses in the courtroom reinforced the notion of race as common sense by invoking the idea that there was an ineffable quality making someone white that any Southerner could discern – and, likewise, that a drop of African blood would make itself known, and a Southerner could sense it "as the alligator . . . knows three days in advance that a storm is brewing." It was not unusual for witnesses to explain that they did not need to know the finer points of physiology or craniology to know "the distinction between the caucasian and african races" – they just *knew*. [*sic*] [citations omitted]

Cultural and social considerations were most important for resolving the race of persons whose racial identity fell into a "middle ground" that could not be resolved easily by the social and physical "facts" known about the person.[58] This range of considerations can be gathered under the umbrella of "performance." In practice, how a person behaved was more important than a person's blood fraction, and, as race grew in legal importance, the "performance" of whiteness (or blackness) carried greater legal significance in determining someone's racial status.[59] As Gross explains, the "definition of race as performance operated in a law-like fashion, prescribing certain rules of behavior for people of different races." These performances included not only speech, clothing, manners, and behaviors, but also, paradoxically, the "exercise of legal rights," so that whiteness could be proved by evidence of performing "acts of citizenship" ("voting, mustering for the militia, sitting on a jury," etc.).[60]

Aviam Soifer writes that legal fictions "allow the lawyer to plunge to the bottom line without ever revealing what is left up in the air."[61] What is left up in the air, obscured by these competing social, cultural, and legal understandings of race, is the individual whose very personhood is at stake in the outcome. The legal significance of race as performance signals an imperative to act white or to act black, based on one's self-identification. In *Pudd'nhead Wilson*, Twain stages the questions of whether individuals can be said to act out their true nature and whether those true natures can be said to include race. For Tom, whose racial status is shifting and unstable, there is a corresponding dilemma for his understanding of his self as a racial being and the behavior that such an understanding entails. Mikhail Bakhtin's explanation of the contest between externally authoritative discourse and internally persuasive discourse helps explain the struggle that Tom undergoes as he attempts to reconcile his own identity with his understanding of what blackness means legally and culturally. Authoritative discourse, Bakhtin claims, "demands that we acknowledge it, that we make it our own; it binds us, quite independent of any power it might have to persuade us internally; we encounter it with its authority already fused to it."[62] Discursive authority emanates from many sites of power and can represent the authority of the law, of tradition, of culture. The individual, situated at the intersection, must locate or dislocate him- or herself within the preexisting networks of authoritative meaning. As Bakhtin writes, for the individual, language "lies on the borderline between oneself and the other."[63] Words "[do] not exist in a neutral and impersonal language" but "in other people's mouths, in other people's contexts, serving other people's intentions."[64] Every word already "tastes of the context and contexts in which it has lived its socially charged life."[65]

"Black," "nigger," "Negro," and "slave" are terms that signify complex and internally contradictory sets of political, social, legal, and cultural meanings and regimes of power. In *Pudd'nhead*

Wilson, Tom's reaction to learning that he is Roxy's son dramatizes the battle between the authoritative meaning of race and its subjective lack of persuasiveness. In the midst of his first fitful night of sleep after learning this great secret, Tom groans, "A nigger! I am a nigger! Oh, I wish I was dead!"[66] He does not muster evidence of his blood fraction to challenge his racial designation, nor does he look to mobilize rules of appearance, reputation, or any other standard that could be used to legally assign his race as "white." Instead, he bows to the cultural meanings surrounding blackness and racial difference as he questions, "Why were niggers *and* whites made? What crime did the uncreated first nigger commit that the curse of birth was decreed for him? And why is this awful difference made between white and black?"[67] His existence on both sides of the color line positions him to see the constructed enormity and inherent emptiness of racial difference.

The difference that race makes is momentous and fabricated, life-altering and meaningless. This paradox is emphasized by the narrator's melodramatic depiction of the revelation that Tom is black. The revelation is "a tremendous catastrophe," "a gigantic eruption, like that of Krakatoa . . . with the accompanying earthquakes, tidal waves, and clouds of volcanic dust," a shift that "changes the face of the surrounding landscape beyond recognition, bringing down the high lands, elevating the low, making fair lakes where deserts had been, and deserts where green prairies had smiled before."[68] Just one page after the hyperbolized depiction of land-altering change, we learn that "with the subsidence of the storm," his character and habits "began to settle toward their former places." In the space of about "a week," Tom has returned to his previous state of being. "[T]he main structure of his character was not changed."[69] He returns to his life as a secret black man among whites, and no one but Roxy knows any better. The narrator comments that "no familiar of his could have detected anything in him that differentiated him" from the Tom they knew before.[70]

During Tom's week of Krakatoa, the difference that race makes happens at the level of performance as he "mysterious[ly]" and "involuntarily" adopts the mannerisms and behaviors that he believes are "black" in an effort to "get his bearings":

> If he met a friend, he found that the habit of a lifetime had in some mysterious way vanished – his arm hung limp, instead of involuntarily extending the hand for a shake. It was the "nigger" in him asserting its humility, and he blushed and was abashed. And the "nigger" in him was surprised when the white friend put out his hand for a shake with him. He found the "nigger" in him involuntarily giving the road, on the sidewalk, to the white rowdy and loafer. When Rowena, the dearest thing his heart knew, the idol of his secret worship, invited him in, the "nigger" in him made an embarrassed excuse and was afraid to enter and sit with the dread white folks on equal terms. The "nigger" in him went shrinking and skulking here and there and yonder, and fancying it saw suspicion and maybe detection in all faces, tones, and gestures.

Tom encounters the term "nigger" with a complex set of authoritative expectations "already fused to it."[71] The term comes already "populated – overpopulated" with the intentions of others. In this scene, however, the word is not half someone else's; it is all someone else's. The authoritative worldview embodied in "nigger" is that of Tom's literal and figurative fathers – the First Families of Virginia, whose code of honor and whiteness dictate the expectations for blacks and whites alike. The pendulating significance of racial identity speaks to the doubleness of race as constituted by authoritative discourse and as experienced by the individual. For Tom, this difference is everything and nothing. Well, not quite "everything." Tom's racial identity is a secret. It is only when his private encounter with his race becomes public, when he is outed as being a black man that the ultimate difference that race makes is realized and Tom is "sold down the river."[72]

For Southerners in the nineteenth century, behavior could determine race. The meaning of blackness as a set of subservient behaviors is evidenced by Tom's unconscious performance of them upon learning he is black, while the short-lived nature of that performance suggests their lack of internal persuasiveness. In the novel's closing scenes, deviance is conflated with blackness as Tom's murder conviction coincides with the community's recognition of him as black. The actions accorded legal relevance in determinations of race included the performance of virtue and honor, or their lack. Internal racial character was equated to its outward manifestation, and the "more strongly virtue and honor were identified with whiteness, the more it became a requirement to perform virtue and honor to prove one's whiteness."[73]

Tom's race has been suspect throughout. Like Chambers, he is a "mis'able imitation nigger"[74] who also falls far short of living up to the standards of aristocratic whiteness proven by unfailing adherence to a set of "unwritten laws," "as clearly defined and as strict as any that could be found among the printed statutes of the land."[75] For the white male aristocrat in Dawson's Landing, "those laws were his chart. . . if he swerved from it by so much as half a point of the compass it meant shipwreck to his honor; that is to say, degradation from his rank as a gentleman."[76] Tom's behavior includes grave code violations, most seriously, filing a criminal complaint against a man who kicks him in public when he should have challenged him to a duel.

Twain's depiction of race as performance explains the racial anxiety of the white townspeople. If race is performance, then a black man can pass as white by adopting white manners and behaviors. The fact that Tom was able to perform whiteness without detection for twenty-three years threatens the entire apparatus of white supremacy and undercuts the claim that race was "commonsense," something that white Southerners could know when they saw. Further, the ability to distinguish race was part of the behavior that defined one as white. The "greatest blow to a white man's honor would be to be deceived into bestowing the honors of whiteness on a 'negro.' "[77] The final joke in the novel, then, is on the white folk of Dawson's Landing who have, for two decades, bestowed on Tom the honor of whiteness, despite the behavioral clues he left to the contrary – a mistake that calls their own whiteness into question. When the townspeople recognize that Tom has fooled them, his bad acts are retroactively constructed as evidence of his blackness, reinforcing the association of whiteness with virtue and allowing the town to nurse their wounds by casting out any who are not virtuous, using a circular logic that renders them black.

For Roxy, unlike for Tom, the authoritative language of race is persuasive. She claims the ancestry of "Ole Virginny Stock" as a badge of honor for her son and expects him to abide by those rules. She appeals to white precedent to justify her usurping of the Driscoll heir, remembering the story of Moses: "It ain't no sin, glory to goodness it ain't no sin! . . . *Dey* [white folks] done it – yes, *dey* done it; en not on'y jis' common white folks nuther, but de biggest quality dey is in de whole bilin.' "[78] Roxy has internalized the code of the F.F.V. and so views Tom's behavior as a "blemish" or "taint" on his honor. Her assumption of white codes of behavior is complete when she condemns Tom for refusing to duel with a man who has insulted him: "You has disgraced yo' birth. What would yo' pa think o' you?"[79] Roxy connects his shortcomings to his hidden blackness: "It makes me sick! It's de nigger in you, dat's what it is. 31 parts o' you is white, en on'y one part nigger, en dat po' little one part is yo' soul."[80]

Roxy embraces the cultural assumptions about race as an invisible taint, evidenced by behavior. Tom, on the other hand, acknowledges the structural legal signification of his just acquired blackness and the new relationship that it creates between himself and his "uncle": "He is white; and I am his chattel, his property, his goods, and he can sell me, just as he could his dog."[81] Ultimately, the complex interstices between cultural, social, personal, and legal discourses of racial meaning are dissolved in the face of the power of the state as Tom is reclaimed and sold as a slave. The novel ends in the tension-filled ambiguity about race with which it began. Cultural and social fictions produce the very notions of racial inferiority justifying the systems of legal oppression that, in turn, concretize racial inferiority and perpetuate social fictions about race. The fictions become racial reality, in all of its paradoxical glory.

In the end, all complexity of racial meaning collapses into the naked force of the law that operates by virtue of its forgotten fictions. Finally, the law simply *is*. The law's force is not created by legal and social ambiguity but works in spite of it. The law's force is created through another fiction, legal personhood, that accompanies the legal determination of racial status and accomplishes the conversion of Tom from man to chattel. If the opening swipe in Twain's novel is at the legal fiction of race, the closing swipe is at the legal fiction of personality. The formal law restores Chambers to his rightful position where social and cultural laws dislocate him. He is unable to "endure the terrors of the white man's parlor." His speech, "gestures," "bearing," "laugh" all mark him as black and a slave, while his new status as rich, free, and white prevent him from taking "refuge" with other blacks.[82] For Tom, though, speech, education, and mannerisms are irrelevant. The final bow in the novel is to the power of the law to convert Tom from a man capable of being held responsible for his own actions to an item on an inventory, a piece of chattel without agency and so without any rights of personhood.

Tom has been sentenced to life in prison for the murder of Judge Driscoll. But eight years later, creditors with claims on the Percy Driscoll estate (Tom and Roxy were Percy's slaves) come forward to complain that Tom should have been "inventoried" with the rest of the property. As the creditors make their argument, and we hear again the strange and strained voice of the law that once weighed in on the legal significance of half and general dogs:

> [I]f [Tom] had been delivered up to them in the first place, they would have sold him and he could not have murdered Judge Driscoll; therefore it was not he that had really committed the murder, the guilt lay with the erroneous inventory. Everybody saw that there was reason in this. Everybody granted that if "Tom" were white and free, it would be unquestionably right to punish him – it would be no loss to anybody; but to shut up a valuable slave for life – that was quite another matter.

In this passage, the narrator absurdly attributes personality to the "inventory" in such a way as to deny it to Tom. Pecuniary interests behind the conflation of race and slavery are laid bare here, as social, legal, economic, and political forces in the novel combine to speak in a single voice – "everybody saw," "everybody granted," including the Governor who, "as soon as [he] understood," "pardoned Tom at once" so that the creditors could sell him "down the river."[83]

The term "person" is as overdetermined as "race," and the two terms collide to define the transition into and out of slavery. This transition confronts the far-reaching legal fiction that rendered human beings as chattel. The anxiety represented in that fiction permeates the law, even as the law struggled to define personality in such a way as to incorporate the slave. The law distinguishes between "natural" and "legal" persons. A natural person represents a human being that is embodied, has mental powers, is aware of the world, can think, feel, and act.[84] To eliminate confusion, I use the terms "being" and "human being" to denote "natural person." To such a being, the wholly formal status of legal personhood is *added*, along with a varying set of rights and responsibilities that attend its designation. In this way, legal personality creates an inherent disjunction between the natural person, the subject who experiences, and the legal person, the subject artificially created from a conglomeration of attributed rights and responsibilities.

Legal personality was both given and denied to slaves and blacks. On the one hand, slaves were explicitly defined as "chattel" by statutory and common law in many states, and historians often characterize the system of racially discriminatory laws that followed the Civil War as treating blacks as nonpersons.[85] On the other hand, depending on the political and economic interests at stake, a slave was a person, or at least part of one.[86] A slave was quantified in the U.S. Constitution as being exactly three-fifths of a free person, for purposes of congressional representation.[87] In some contexts, states took the humanity of slaves seriously. Some, including Alabama, Mississippi, Florida, and Georgia, granted slaves procedural rights, and slaves in nearly every jurisdiction could be held liable for crimes and torts.[88] The Black Codes and their progeny, Jim Crow laws, passed in the North and the South following the Civil War, explicitly relied on the recognition of blacks as "human beings and free persons."[89] As Kermit Hall argues, under the laws, "Blacks could buy, sell, own, and bequeath real and personal property. They could make contracts . . . , sue and be sued, and testify in courts in cases in which blacks were a party."[90] Post-emancipation, laws recognized the humanity and personality of blacks and imposed quasi slavery nonetheless. Pre-emancipation, as race and slavery became increasingly aligned, the freed slave had an especially vexed status as the existence of such persons underscored the moral contradictions of slavery by pointing to the fact that the same abiding human body could be once chattel and now person.

Analyzing the legal fiction of the slave as chattel reveals the deep-seated ambivalence in the United States about the slave as property and as a person. The sociologist Wilbert Ellis Moore voiced the contradiction at the heart of the law when he wrote, "[T]he chief value of the slave as property lay in his being a person, but his chief value as a person lay in his being held as property."[91] Just as judges, lawyers, and scholars tried unsuccessfully to wrestle the uncooperative notion of race into compliance, legal theorists struggled to come up with definitions of personhood that would resolve the absurdities of laws that defined human beings as not legally persons. John Austin, in his postbellum 1875 landmark *Lectures on Jurisprudence*, notes the incompatibility between the classical definition of "natural person" as "a human being invested with, or capable of rights" and the common use of the term "person" to include slaves, though they are divested of rights. Austin's response is to redefine "personality." Drawing on theater for the metaphor (a metaphor borrowed from ancient Roman law), Austin contends that legal "personhood" is like a dramatic character; it is a "status or condition" that is worn, as a player wears a mask.[92] Like actors, every human being, then, "bears a *number* of persons," for example, "citizen," "son," "husband," "father."[93] In the case of slaves, the relevant status or condition to be worn is a negative status. Austin reasoned that since "person" can be used to refer to a foreigner by virtue of *not* being a member of a society, by analogy, a slave can be a person by virtue of the slave's incapacity.[94]

The notion of personality as a role that can be put on or taken off dissolves the human person behind the mask. While a natural person comes into being at birth, legal persons may have many lives that start and stop during their physical lifetime. For the layman, the rights of persons are thought of as intrinsic to or derived from one's natural personhood. However, when the term "legal person" is used by a lawyer, "it reflects the conclusion, not a premise,"[95] as Austin's definition erodes any essential relationship between the person in law and the human person. Since legal personality is wholly formal, "anyone or anything can be a legal person."[96] From the human, the law creates a slave, a person whose personhood consists in the absence of the rights of personality – an abstraction worthy of Twain's farcical treatment. Twain's novel helps us see that, by defining the absence of rights as a form of personhood, the law calls forth a wholly formal legal person untethered in its abstract design from any embodied being but bound tightly in its concrete consequences for the bodies of black human beings. Thus, the human being haunts the abstraction of personhood as a materialization of dispossession.[97]

Austin's rendering of legal personality as a status that confers negative capability provides a clear example of what Colin Dayan calls "negative personhood."[98] Dayan writes that it is "through law that persons . . . gain or lose definition."[99] Through the operation of law, the embodied person is both effaced by the legal fiction of personhood and brought into being as an empty mask – one that signals only negative capacity. In this way, the fiction of personality inverts the relationship between natural and legal persons by making the unreal the real. This is the law's inherent power – the ability to conjure object-like categories from words. Pierre Bourdieu declares that the law's power is the power to "name," and by so doing, to "create the thing named," conferring "upon the reality which arises from [its] operations the maximum permanence that any social entity has the power to confer upon another, the permanence we attribute to objects."[100] In the case of the slave, this grotesque metamorphosis, the very "art" of the law, proves the absoluteness of its power.

Dayan connects this power and art of law to Jeremy Bentham's vitriolic condemnation of legal fictions. Like the ghosts that famously haunted Bentham's nightmares, legal fictions were "acknowledged to be false" and yet were "argued from, and acted upon, as if true." Describing such fictions, Bentham wrote, "words – words without a meaning – or with a meaning too flatly false to be maintained by anybody . . . you look to the letter, you find nonsense: – you look beyond the letters, you find nothing."[101] Yet the movement of characters in Twain's matrix renders the power of the law visible. Thus the terrible force of legal fictions is the reality of their unreality. Embodied persons in *Pudd'nhead* bear the real and measureable consequences of legal fictions as dispossession comes to life in the raced bodies of the slaves.

White personality too is an abstraction, a wholly formal status fabricated to define the freedom of the self-possessed, the realm of the universal detached from any physical reality, but in the black body, the legal abstraction of absent rights takes monstrous physical form. Saidiya Hartman explains the insistent embodiment of the abstraction of personality in black people, made most visible at the moment of transformation, when "chattel becomes man through the ascension to the hallowed realm of the self-possessed."[102] Under the "harsh light of scrutiny," we see that lurking behind the "disembodied and self-possessed" person fabricated as "free" is "the fleshy substance of the embodied and encumbered – that is, the castigated particularity of the universal."[103]

Notes

1 "Anti-Slavery Soiree," *The Liberator* (Boston, December 26, 1845), 206 (reprinted from *Limerick Reporter*, November 25, 1845).

2 Frederick Douglass, *My Bondage and My Freedom*, Autobiographies (1855; New York: Penguin, 1996), 373.

3 Ibid., 374.

4 "Matrix," *Oxford English Dictionary*, 2nd ed., 1989; online version, November 2010.

5 The term has been given many definitions. For example, Henry S. Maine wrote that "legal fiction" signified "any assumption which conceals, or affects to conceal, the fact that a rule of law has undergone alteration, its letter remaining unchanged, its operation being modified." Henry S. Maine, *Ancient Law* (New York: Holt, 1873), 25. Roscoe Pound defined legal fictions as "creative devices of far-reaching effect which did not evolve spontaneously but were deliberately made by known men to meet definite needs in concrete cases." Roscoe Pound, *Interpretations of Legal History* (1923; Cambridge, UK: Cambridge University Press, 2013), 131. Lon Fuller's account, the most comprehensive and also the best known, defines a legal fiction as "either (1) a statement propounded with a complete or partial consciousness of its falsity, or (2) a false statement recognized as having utility." Lon Fuller, *Legal Fictions* (Stanford, CA: Stanford University Press, 1967), 9. For a discussion of this definition and its implications, see Simon Stern, "Legal and Literary Fictions," in *New Directions in Law and Literature*, ed. Elizabeth Anker and Bernadette Meyler (New York: Oxford University Press, 2017), 313–26.

6 William Blackstone, *Commentaries on the Laws of England*, 4 vols., ed. Wilfrid Prest (1765–69; Oxford: Oxford University Press, 2016), 3: 178.

7 Maine, *Ancient Law*, 25.

8 Fuller, "Legal Fictions," 21–2.

9 Ibid., 9–10.

10 Ibid.

11 For further explanation of this phenomenon, see Thomas Ross, "Metaphor and Paradox," *Georgia Law Review* 23 (1989): 1053–84, 1072, 1073.
12 "What We Talk about When We Talk about Persons: The Language of a Legal Fiction," *Harvard Law Review* 114 (2001): 1760–1.
13 *Dred Scott v. Sandford*, 60 U.S. 393 (1857).
14 Robert Cottrol, *The Long, Lingering Shadow: Slavery, Race, and Law in the American Hemisphere* (Athens: University of Georgia Press, 2013).
15 Ibid., 86–8. For an overview of slave demographics in the Americas, see http://www.gilderlehrman.org/history-by-era/slavery-and-anti-slavery/resources/facts-about-slave-trade-and-slavery.
16 Cottrol, *Long, Lingering Shadow*, 87.
17 Ibid., 87–8. Forms of unfree labor such as indentured servitude could look at lot like slavery, and, conversely, slavery could look a lot like indentured servitude. The first Africans were sold in Virginia before there was a formal slave status. They were treated as indentured servants who worked a number of years and then were set free. Association between black and white servants and slaves was widespread, and in the seventeenth and eighteenth centuries, few legal or social distinctions were made between them. They worked together, had sexual relations together, and hatched plots to escape together. Ibid., 87.
18 Ibid., 96.
19 Ibid., 98–9.
20 Kermit Hall, *The Magic Mirror: Law in American History* (New York: Oxford University Press, 1989), 132.
21 Ariela Gross, "Litigating Whiteness: Trials of Racial Determination in the Nineteenth-Century South," *Yale Law Journal* 108 (1998): 109–88, 177.
22 This approach differed from most other slaveholding societies in the Americas. The rule of matrilineal descent perpetuated a slave class and provided economic incentive for the rape of slave women by white masters.
23 In practice, the circularity between race and slavery muddied the formal rules. At least some courts considered evidence of the race of one's maternal ancestors in order to determine whether that ancestor had been a slave or not.
24 Although some scholars continue to dispute the claim that Jefferson fathered Sally Heming's children, the Thomas Jefferson Foundation accepts the claim on the basis of extensive evidence, http://www.monticello.org/site/plantation-and-slavery/appendix-h-sally-hemings-and-her-children. However, given that DNA evidence indisputably proves that *a* Jefferson man was the father of Heming's children, my foundational argument, namely that slave and race status were not necessarily correlated, remains unchanged, regardless of which of the white Jefferson men (Thomas's brother, Randolph, is sometimes put forward as an alternate candidate) fathered Hemings' children.
25 James A. Bear Jr., *Jefferson at Monticello* (Charlottesville: University of Virginia Press, 1967), 4.
26 Ibid. Sally's father, John Wayles, was also the father of Thomas Jefferson's wife, Martha Wayles Skelton, making Martha and Sally half-sisters.
27 Virginia's law of racial proportion, which remained unchanged from 1705 until 1910, stated that persons possessing no more than one-eighth black ancestry were deemed to be legally white. Ian Haney-Lopez, *White by Law: The Legal Construction of Race* (New York: New York University Press, 2000), 83.
28 The creation of strict though counterfactual categories was not the only possible path. Spain and France, by contrast, both recognized one hundred twenty-eight different categories of color, ranging from "absolute white" to "absolute black." At one time, "mulatto," "quadroon," "octoroon," and the like were recognized racial categories in the United States, particularly in Louisiana, whose civil code closely resembled France's; however, these classes increasingly dropped out of view, and the term "mulatto" began to lose its more precise definition as a person with one black and one white parent and was increasingly used to reference anyone of mixed race in any proportion. Jennifer L. Hochschild, "Policies of Racial Classification and the Politics of Racial Inequality," in *Remaking America: Democracy and Public Policy in an Age of Inequality*, ed. Joe Soss, Jacob Hacker, and Suzanne Mettler (New York: Russell Sage Foundation, 2007), 159–82, 162.
29 Taney's claim that the Negro had "no rights" was hyperbole. The law accorded some rights to both slaves and free blacks, though these rights varied widely by place and were inconsistently enforced. Cottrol writes:

> At times, the law's protection of slavery was clear; at other times, less so. . . . At certain times and in certain places, the law protected manumission; at other times not. The law at times treated free people of color as citizens with rights and duties similar to those of other

> citizens. At other times the law limited the privileges of free Afro-Americans, although rarely with the rigidity that would occur in the nineteenth century.

Cottrol, *Long, Lingering Shadow*, 82.

30 For further analysis of the racial cues signaled by Roxy's clothing, see Garrett Nichols, "'Clo'es could do de like o' dat': Race, Place, and Power in Mark Twain's *The Tragedy of Pudd'nhead Wilson*," *Southern Literary Journal* 46 (2013): 110–26.

31 Mark Twain, *Pudd'nhead Wilson* (1894; New York: Bantam, 1981), 8.

32 Ibid., 8–9.

33 Ibid.

34 Ibid., 8–9.

35 Virginia changed the definition to a one-fourth rule in 1785. Haney-Lopez, *White by Law*, 83.

36 Frank Sweet, *Legal History of the Color Line: The Rise and Triumph of the One Drop Rule* (Palm Coast, Fla.: Bakintyme, 2005), 174.

> By 1910, Florida, Georgia, Indiana, Missouri, South Carolina, Kentucky, Maryland, Mississippi, North Carolina, Tennessee, and Texas defined anyone with 1/8 or more negro blood to be black, as in 1705 Virginia. Nebraska, Oregon, Virginia, and Michigan used a 1/8 rule. Alabama used a 1/32 rule. . . . [T]he most popular blood-fraction rule before Jim Crow was the 1/8 rule.

Ibid.

In 1853, the one-drop rule was argued in an attempted rape case in a Missouri court and rejected. *State v. Anderson*, 19 Mo. 241 (1853). The jury convicted an African-looking man of attempting to rape a European-looking victim. Racial status was vital since the laws provided stricter sentences for black-on-white attempted rape. The defendant appealed because no testimony had been offered at trial that he was black or that the victim was white. The jury had apparently reached such a conclusion merely by observing the defendant and the victim in the courtroom. The defendant's lawyers argued that a one-drop rule should have been applied to the victim, that proof of her whiteness was necessary for the conviction. The Missouri State Supreme Court upheld the conviction, concluding that since color and race were synonymous, the jury did not need testimony to determine what they could see with their own eyes – that the victim was white.

37 Twain, *Pudd'nhead*, 3.

38 Ibid., 9.

39 Daniel J. Sharfstein, "The Secret History of Race in the United States," *Yale Law Journal* 112 (2003): 1473–509. Frank Sweet identifies Tennessee as ground zero for the formal one-drop rule: Tennessee led the way, and by 1919, a dozen states had adopted racial group membership rules based on one-drop. Another dozen states "retained blood fraction statutes de jure but amended them to such tiny fractions that they were often one-drop de facto." Sweet, *Legal History*, 405.

Ian Haney-Lopez also provides a useful overview of the blood fraction laws as constituted in the early twentieth century.

> Alabama and Arkansas defined anyone with one drop of "Negro" blood as Black; Florida had a one-eighth rule; Georgia referred to "ascertainable" non-White blood; Indiana used a one-eighth rule; Kentucky relied on a combination of any "appreciable admixture" of Black ancestry and a one-sixteenth rule; Louisiana did not statutorily define Blackness but did adopt via its Supreme Court an "appreciable admixture of negro blood" standard; Maryland used a "person of negro descent to the third generation" test; Mississippi combined an "appreciable amount of Negro blood" and a one-eight rule; Missouri used a one-eighth test, as did Nebraska, North Carolina, and North Dakota; Oklahoma referred to "all persons of African descent," adding that the "term 'white race' shall include all other persons"; Oregon promulgated a one-fourth rule; South Carolina had a one-eight standard; Tennessee defined Blacks in terms of "mulattoes, mestizos, and their descendants, having any blood of the African race in their veins"; Texas used an "all persons of mixed blood descended from negro ancestry" standard; Utah law referred to mulattos, quadroons, or octoroons; and Virginia defined Blacks as those in whom there was "ascertainable any Negro blood" with not more than one-sixteenth Native American ancestry.

Haney, *White by Law*, 83.

40 Hochschild, "Policies of Racial Classification," 159.

41 Booker T. Washington, *The Future of the American Negro* (Boston: Small, Maynard & Co., 1900), 158.

42 Sweet, *Legal History*, 350.

43 Ibid.
44 Colin Dayan, *The Law Is a White Dog* (Princeton, N.J.: Princeton University Press, 2011), 12.
45 Twain, *Pudd'nhead*, 4.
46 Ibid.
47 Ibid., 4–5.
48 Haney-Lopez, *White by Law*, 83 (emphasis in original).
49 Pierre Bourdieu, "The Force of Law," *Hastings Law Journal* 38 (1987): 814–53, 839.
50 Hochschild, "Policies of Racial Classification," 166. Virginia serves as a representative example. In Virginia, prior to 1910, a person with one-eighth black ancestry was, by statute, white. After 1910, Virginia concentrated the category of "white" by reserving its designation to persons who were at least fifteenth-sixteenths white. In 1924, in the Act to Preserve Racial Integrity, the Virginia legislature configured whiteness as a racially pure category, with "white" meaning having "no trace" of any but Caucasian ancestry. "Its sister category was formally articulated a few years later, in 1930, when Virginia lawmakers defined blacks as people with 'any blood.'" Ibid.
51 Nichols, "Clo'es Could Do," 111.
52 Ibid.
53 Gross, "Litigating Whiteness," 118.
54 Ibid., 114.
55 Ibid., 118.
56 Ibid., 138.
57 Ibid., 126.
58 Ibid., 118.
59 Ibid., 112.
60 Ibid., 113.
61 Aviam Soifer, "Reviewing Legal Fictions," *Georgia Law Review* 20 (1986): 871–915, 874.
62 Mikhail M. Bakhtin, "Discourse in the Novel," in *The Dialogic Imagination*, trans. Caryl Emerson and Michael Holquist (1934–35; Austin: University of Texas Press, 1982), 342.
63 Ibid., 292.
64 Ibid., 294.
65 Ibid., 292.
66 Twain, *Pudd'nhead*, 53.
67 Ibid.
68 Ibid., 54, 53.
69 Ibid., 55.
70 Ibid.
71 Bakhtin, "Discourse in the Novel," 342.
72 Twain, *Pudd'nhead*, 143.
73 Gross, "Litigating Whiteness," 156.
74 Ibid., 42.
75 Twain, *Pudd'nhead*, 71.
76 Ibid., 71.
77 Gross, "Litigating Whiteness," 129.
78 Twain, *Pudd'nhead*, 16.
79 Ibid., 86.
80 Ibid. Often, this passage is read as Twain's conflation of race and criminality, making race the answering factor in Tom's bad behavior. Yet Roxy also reveals the incoherence of this conflation. Reciting Tom's lofty ancestry, she lists not only the "Essex blood" but his "great-great-great-great-gran'father" "Cap'n John Smith," the "highest blood dat Ole Virginny ever turned out," and John Smith's parents, "Pocahontas de Injun queen" and her husband, "a nigger king outen Africa." Ibid., 87.
81 Ibid., 55.
82 Ibid., 143.
83 Ibid., 143.
84 Rom Harre, "Persons and Selves," in *Persons and Personality*, ed. Arthur Peacocke and Grant Gillett (New York: Blackwell, 1987), 99.
85 See, for example, Hollis Lynch:

> The black codes had their roots in the slave codes that had formerly been in effect. The general philosophy supporting the institution of chattel slavery in America was based on the

> concept that slaves were property, not persons, and that the law must protect not only the property but also the property owner from the danger of violence.

http://history-world.org/black_codes.htm (accessed October 25, 2014).

86 The word "slave" never appears in the Constitution, and "free persons" ironically includes indentured servants. The clause avoids using the term "slave" and the term "indentured servant," instead opting for the less clear work-around:

> Representatives and direct Taxes shall be apportioned among the several States which may be included within this Union, according to their respective Numbers, which shall be determined by adding to the whole Number of free Persons, including those bound to Service for a Term of Years, and excluding Indians not taxed, three fifths of all other Persons.

U.S. Constitution, Article 1, section 2, paragraph 3.

87 On the significance of this provision, see Jeannine Marie DeLombard's chapter 2 in this volume.

88 Hall, *Magic Mirror*, 133, 135.

89 The Black Codes varied by place but often included laws that criminalized vagrancy, created long "apprentice" conditions for blacks convicted of crimes, excluded blacks from practicing certain kinds of trades, restricted blacks' ability to carry firearms, testify in court, serve on a jury, etc. For a basic historical introduction, see http://www.history.com/topics/black-history/black-codes. For a sample of four Black Codes enacted in Mississippi, see https://chnm.gmu.edu/courses/122/recon/code.html. For analysis of the Codes, see Hall, *Magic Mirror*, 143–6.

90 Hall, *Magic Mirror*, 144.

91 Moore, "Slave Law and the Social Structure" (1941), in *The Law of American Slavery*, ed. Kermit Hall (New York: Garland, 1987), 325.

92 John Austin, *Lectures on Jurisprudence: The Philosophy of Positive Law* (New York: Holt, 1875), 163–4. Personality as a dramatic character harks back to Roman law where the "person in law" was represented by various statuses – the *status libertatis* (all men are either free or slave), the *status civitatis* (all men are either citizens or aliens), and the *status familia* (all men are either *pater* or *filins*, either the head of the house or under its control). These legal personas were interlocking and changeable. Thus, a slave could gain freedom and become subject to the rights and responsibilities attending that status. Richard Tur, "The 'Person' in Law," in *Persons and Personality*, 16–17.

93 Austin, *Lectures on Jurisprudence*, 163.

94 Ibid., 164.

95 Tur. "The 'Person' in Law," 127–8.

96 Ibid. Tur cites historical instances where nonhuman and inanimate objects were given status as legal persons, including animals, rivers, the wind, and, in one case, an Indian idol. The most familiar example is, of course, the corporation.

97 Dayan, *The Law Is a White Dog*, 40.

98 Ibid., xii.

99 Ibid., vi.

100 Bourdieu, "Force of the Law," 838.

101 Quoted in Dayan, *The Law Is a White Dog*, 15.

102 Saidiya V. Hartman, *Scenes of Subjection: Terror, Slavery, and Self-Making in Nineteenth-Century America* (New York: Oxford University Press, 1997), 123.

103 Ibid.

PART IV

Affective relations

INTRODUCTION

Nan Goodman and Simon Stern

Under the direction of Christopher Columbus Langdell, dean of Harvard Law School from 1870 to 1895, law in nineteenth-century America took a "scientific" turn. The law, Langdell believed, operated according to a set of principles that could in theory be applied logically and objectively to any given set of facts. In practice, however, the law operated quite differently. Judges, lawyers, plaintiffs, and defendants throughout the nineteenth century were attentive to the ways in which the law reflected and directed all aspects of human experience, including the affective relations that lay far outside the traditional understanding of "science." Nineteenth-century judges, Peter Karsten demonstrates, were just as likely to cite matters of "the heart" as they were matters of "the head" in laying out the rationales for their decisions. Many, for example, were mindful of making law that would advance of the goals of "neighborly relations," while others were explicitly attuned to the needs of the oppressed.[1] Indeed, as more recent scholars remind us, emotions are "everywhere in the law" and far from interfering in the application of the law are central to it.[2]

To the primacy of emotions in the law in general we might add that the nineteenth century was an especially emotional century in which, as Shirley Samuels writes, "sentimentality was a national project."[3] The large number of lawsuits for what was known as "alienation of affection" in a marital context gives us some idea of how important emotions were within the law, as does the law's response to the most pressing social issues of the day, such as slavery, temperance, and immigration, in which emotions understandably ran high. In the chapters in this section, emotions are front and center in accounts of how nineteenth-century American law responded to these and other issues, including the rise of religious pluralism (Whitehead), a highly emotional topic with roots in the heart rather than the head; advances in the understanding of human cognition (Pitts), including an individual's capacity to understand right from wrong; and the role of passion in creating legal communities (Gewirtzman). Laura Appleman's chapter addresses the range of emotions that characterized the criminal mind within the law and the wildly popular gothic fiction of the period.

Among other things, reinserting "affect" into our consideration of nineteenth-century American law allows us to see how the law not only shaped emotions like those underlying community coherence, but also laid the groundwork for the twentieth century's more explicit engagement with the law and emotions in its move from legal formalism to legal realism. These chapters not only uncover a range of emotions – from anger to joy to horror – that accompanied legal decision-making in the nineteenth century, but also reveal the law's role in shaping emotions in turn, integrating affect into the law's role as a normative force in society.

Notes

1 Peter Karsten, *Heart Versus Head: Judge-Made Law in Nineteenth-Century America* (Chapel Hill: University of North Carolina Press, 1997), 10–13.

2 Kathryn Abrams and Hile Keren, "Who's Afraid of Law and the Emotions," *Minnesota Law Review* 94 (2010): 1997–2074. See also, for example, Susan Bandes, ed., *The Passions of Law* (New York: New York University Press, 1999).

3 Shirley Samuels, *The Culture of Sentiment: Race, Gender, and Sentimentality in Nineteenth–Century America* (New York: Oxford University Press, 1992), 3.

18

CIVIC CAPACITY AND PARTICIPATORY CITIZENSHIP IN NINETEENTH-CENTURY UNITED STATES

Yvonne Pitts

In January 2005, when Harvard University President Lawrence Summers commented that men might have a higher aptitude for math and science than women, indignant outrage ensued. Academics, bloggers, feminists, and scientists condemned his comments, arguing that differences were rooted in social practices and not in mental capacity determined by biological sex. His observations reinvigorated calls to use law to change inequalities. Senator Ron Wyden (D-Oregon) called for broader enforcement of Title IX of the Education Amendments of 1972 to address "the entrenched attitudes of the math and science establishment that women are somehow second-class scholars."[1] Wyden's comment about "second class scholars," was not a new articulation of inequality. In *The History of Woman Suffrage*, authors Elizabeth Cady Stanton and Matilda Joslyn Gage argued that a woman's social "training," rather than her innate ability had "dwarfed her capacity [and] . . . made her a retarding force in civilization." A century before the suffrage debates, John Adams contended that, "there are inequalities which God and nature have planted [in humans], and which no human legislator ever can eradicate." Summers, nineteenth-century suffragists, and Adams revealed the same contradiction; in a nation whose most soaring, inspiring rhetoric trumpets the equality of its citizens, law and social practices have been used to exclude citizens from full participation based on perceptions of their lack of capacity.[2]

I. Epistemological foundations of capacity

"Capacity" and its relationship to citizenship offer a rich site for interrogation through an interdisciplinary, humanities-based approach. "Capacity," seemingly drawn from natural, immutable, sometimes biological hierarchies, emerges instead from historically situated political and epistemological contexts. The methods of historical and discursive analysis and the insights of disability and feminist theory illuminate how capacity and citizenship, separate yet often overlapping concepts, were used implicitly as metonyms for full civic participation.[3] For this chapter, the rights and obligations of citizenship included suffrage, jury service, and the ability to participate in what legal theorist Wesley Hohfeld calls "fundamental legal relations."[4] Citizenship and its attendant rights and obligations first required recognition that its bearer was a member of the political community, the imagined space that Supreme Court Chief Justice Roger B. Taney identified when he excluded Dred Scott and all African Americans from citizenship in 1857. As Taney held, "When the Constitution was adopted, they [African Americans] were not regarded in any of the States as members of the community which constituted the State, and were not numbered among its 'people or citizens'" because they were "beings of an inferior order."[5] Taney made explicit what other jurists, judges, lawmakers, and ordinary people held to be true: those lacking capacity should be denied access to the rights and protections of full citizenship. This chapter draws on local trial proceedings, case law and treatises, and medical and political texts to examine how the language of capacity and its deficit, variously labelled as incapacity, incompetency, unfitness, or insanity, sustained deeply entrenched inequalities.

Capacity traditionally slips beneath our historical radar because it relied on and created distance from other markers of exclusion and inferiority: namely race, disability, immigrant status, and sexual and gender identity. At the same time, these other markers were powerful because many of their defining characteristics were premised on lack of capacity when compared to the fully constituted, universalized citizen groups or individuals who articulated their difference from unfit groups but rarely questioned the category of capacity itself. Capacity was a fluid, multivariate category that resisted wholesale analysis by the groups and individuals arguing against their exclusion from it. Thus, African American men, white women, immigrants, physically disabled persons, and individuals labeled mentally deviant could claim their unjust exclusion without destabilizing or interrogating its antecedent exclusionary power. Whereas American notions of equality increasingly promoted an initial sameness of status in jural and civil participation, its implementation depended on making antecedent distinctions according to deficits of capacity.

Figure 18.1 reveals the discursive power of capacity. The viewer must recognize first that the universal citizen, not shown but imaginatively present, was a white, physically and mentally competent man, most likely of Northern or Western European ancestry. The woman in the center is Frances Willard, suffragist and temperance advocate. Except for her sex, she embodied traits similar to the idealized white male citizen; she wore glasses, signaling her intelligence and literacy, had a determined, sober stare, and was modestly dressed in respectable, middle-class clothing. Indeed, throughout the nineteenth century, jurists and medical experts believed that some forms of incapacity could be identified through visual inspection.[6] In a hugely influential medico-legal treatise on insanity, Francis Wharton and Moreton Stille assured doctors and lawyers that mental unsoundness could be readily identified through the subject's eyes, observing,

> What most distinctly characterizes a mental disease . . . is the physiognomy of such a patient. He lacks the calm unobstructed gaze peculiar to the sane . . . [as compared to] the cunning leer of a lunatic, the savage glare of a maniac, the lack-lustre eyes of a splenetic, or the meaningless stare of an imbecile; such things cannot be counterfeited.[7]

Wharton and Stille used as foils two of the four categories of incapacity with which Willard was compared: the "lunatic" and the "imbecile." The other two categories in "American Woman" lacked capacity because of racial categorization (the Native American "savage") and moral deviance (the convict). Willard was the translation into feminine form of the rationality and sobriety associated with the judicious use of free will, illustrated through the contrast to the irrationality, immorality, and unfitness displayed by the men surrounding her.

"American Woman and Her Political Peers" makes visual the concept of civic capacity that was the ability to participate in the activities of citizenship through the exercise of reason, sound moral judgment, and free will. Those possessing civic capacity had the intellectual and moral ability to exercise the rights of citizenship and assume its obligations. Even as the proof that certain groups lacked civic capacity had shifted by mid-century from evidences rooted in divine

Figure 18.1 W. A. Ford, "American Woman and Her Political Peers" (1893): a postcard depicting suffragist and temperance advocate Frances Willard among other disfranchised groups – an "idiot," a convict, a "savage," and a "lunatic"

Source: Chronicling Illinois, accessed February 3, 2017, http://alplm-cdi.com/chroniclingillinois/items/show/13575

ordinance to ones based in science and explained through taxonomies, the exclusionary power of incapacity remained constant.[8] The nineteenth century witnessed the legal consolidation of the category of "capacity" and sophisticated articulations of the boundaries between those who had capacity and those who did not.

Incapacity, particularly "mental unsoundness," was an unstable category. It could be congenital, lost through life events or physical or psychic trauma, and was feared and reviled. Medical experts referred to it in terms such as "the most afflictive of all the diseases to which human nature is liable" or the "most appalling of all human maladies."[9] Nineteenth-century doctors cited causes of mental incompetency as various as "disappointed ambition," afflictions peculiar to females," "grief," "loss of kindred or property," "coup de soleil" (sunburn), worms, masturbation, and "powerful excitement of the *female* mind" among others.[10] Capacity was an unstable category that one could lose through the caprices of life.

Sorting groups and individuals into categories of possessing or not possessing capacity was made through political, medical, and social practices, mobilized through legal exclusions, and preceded most civil participation. By the early decades of the nineteenth century, juridical categories, judicial opinions, medical experts, and the cultural values infusing ideas about race, gender, disability, and morality formed a grammar of civic capacity with its own syntax, vocabulary, and structure that was shot through society. It was encoded in law, politics, and medicine, used colloquially, implemented in everyday practices, simultaneously flexible in its definitions and rigid in its exclusions. For example, during the New York state constitutional convention in 1821, former New York State Supreme Court Justice Jonas Platt argued that "most free negros [*sic*] are unfit to be entrusted with the right of suffrage" because they lacked "sufficient intelligence." He continued, expanding capacity exclusions beyond race to "ignorant and depraved white men, who are as unfit to exercise the power of voting as men of colour."[11] These groups, all free black men and "depraved" white men, lacked the requisite control to exercise reason, moral judgment, and legal responsibility and were instead enslaved by uncontrolled passions, delusions, or immoral instincts.[12] The vocabulary of civic capacity was flexible enough to add moral deviance as "depraved white men" to the excluded racial category of those "unfit to be entrusted with the right of suffrage." Platt had echoed Thomas Jefferson, who postulated that blacks were "inferior to the whites in the endowments both of body and mind" when he contemplated the benefits of gradual emancipation.[13] Jefferson and Platt structured their assessment of black capacity through a syntactic relation (equal/not equal) inherent in the grammar of civic capacity.[14] Defining capacity and mobilizing exclusions based on capacity was an ongoing project of containment, through which Americans claimed to secure the survival and progress of nation premised on equality.

II. History of a concept

Capacity is an ancient concept, although its ontological framework has changed across time. Legal categories identifying those who lacked capacity and their attendant loss of legal rights go back at least to the fourteenth century. According to oft cited nineteenth-century treatise writers Pollock and Edward Maitland, Edward II's 1324 *Prerogativa Regis* declared, "The King shall have custody of the lands of natural fools, taking the profits of them without waste or destruction, and shall find them their necessaries of life."[15] Capacity, in this case the distinction between "natural fools" and all others, was a principle encoded in law that protected "natural fools" and their families from imprudent decisions made in a state of mental unsoundness and excluded the "fool" from control over his property. Parliament required that property holders meet a juridical standard of sanity in their first testation statutes passed during the reign of Henry VIII. The 1540 Statute of Wills prohibited "idiots," married women, and persons "*de non sane*" from writing wills and was designed to prevent incapacitated property holders from squandering their estates to the detriment of their heirs.[16] The exclusionary clause grouped married women with insane people and "idiots" because wives lost their independent legal identity, becoming one with their husbands and subject to their decisions about property.[17] The Statute of Wills reveals the enduring relationship between women and other groups considered incapacitated, as illustrated three hundred fifty years later in "American Woman and Her Political Peers" (1893) (Figure 18.1).

European and American Enlightenment thinkers made capacity an organizing concept for civic participation. John Locke argued in his *Second Treatise of Government* (1689) that "[t]he freedom then of man, and liberty of acting according to his own will, is grounded on his having reason, which is able to instruct him in that law he is to govern himself by."[18] Civic capacity – the precondition to legitimate consent – displaced the right to exercise political power due to birthright, a transition that was nearly complete in the United States in 1787.[19] Rather than eliminate exclusions, this shift transformed them. Categories of people including women, racial groups, and mentally deviant individuals remained excluded, but the justifications changed. Nineteenth-century historian Francis Parkman recounted the transformation when he claimed in 1878 that the American Revolution remedied "a factitious inequality and a real and intrinsic one. Rank, titles, privileges, and wealth make up the first; and character, *ability* and culture the second."[20] Parkman goes on to refute the "illusion that one man is essentially about as good as another" in terms of "quality." The embrace of the grammar of civic capacity to mediate civic participation was an essential part of excluding the unfit from a nation premised on Jefferson's "self-evident truth" that "all men are created equal."

The widely circulated revolutionary era writings of Thomas Paine illustrate the turn toward reason and the rejection of received knowledge, religion, and birthright as a basis for knowledge. While philosophers including Francis Bacon, René Descartes, Thomas Hobbes, and John Locke had been advocating for rationality and empiricism as routes to truth since the sixteenth century, Paine's writings illustrate the maturation and political diffusion of those principles in colonial America and then in the United States. Paine is best known for his tract "Common Sense," in which he eviscerated hereditary monarchy as a "degradation and lessening of ourselves" because hereditary rulers lacked the ability and intelligence (civic capacity) to rule. Hereditary rulers, Paine claimed, "opens a door to the FOOLISH, the WICKED, and the IMPROPER, it hath in it the nature of oppression [emphasis his]." A "foolish" monarch devoid of the capacity to rule would inevitably occupy the throne, leading to misery and the eventual destruction of the kingdom. Paine based his critiques of monarchism and embrace of republicanism on the notion that elective politics provided the best hope of selecting leaders with civic capacity.

Paine's later writings further develop his arguments that civic capacity rather than bloodline were the only legitimate, moral basis for authority. In the "Rights of Man" (1791), Paine rooted his condemnation of hereditary rank in the external, inevitable processes of nature, arguing that "nature acts as if she disowned and sported with the hereditary system; that the mental character of successors, in all countries, is below the average of human understanding; that one is a tyrant, another an idiot, a third insane, and some all three together." Paine's description of incompetent rulers foreshadowed the categories depicted in "American Woman and Her Political Peers" (1893) (Figure 18.1). Paine assumed that political rulers were men. Paine's definition of political incapacity and those depicted in "American Woman and Her Political Peers" reveals the persistent power of civic exclusions based on incapacity. Paine had briefly addressed women's capacity in 1775, alluding to them as equals in reason but never elaborating on the idea. He asserted that how men treated women was a gauge of their fitness for enlightened rule, observing that in half the world, men had "none of those moral ideas which only can soften the empire of force . . . subjecting to his despotism those whom *reason had made his equal, but whose imbecility betrayed them to his strength*."[21] A few of Paine's contemporaries, such as women's rights advocate Judith Sargeant Murray argued for women's civic equality based in women's equal capacity, a position that would not be realized until the destruction of coverture and ratification of the Nineteenth Amendment granting female suffrage.[22]

Paine clarified his distinctions between incapacity and reason in his pamphlet, "Age of Reason," arguing, "Were I, or any other man, to write in such a disordered manner, nobody would read what is written; and everybody would suppose that the writer was in a state of insanity." He presented a morally situated definition of "reason" in the essay's last paragraph, writing that his motives in all his political tracts were to free men from "superstitious absurdity of monarchy and hereditary government . . . to bring man to a right use of the reason that God have given him; to impress on him the great principles of divine morality, justice, mercy." Paine did not see reason as incompatible with religious belief, positing that God had created humans according to a divine plan. For Paine, reason enabled moral and civic capacity and undergirded civic virtue, a necessary prerequisite for the survival of the Republic.

III. Citizenship, law, and civic capacity in the nineteenth century

Civic capacity had eclipsed property requirements almost entirely as a requisite for exercising full citizenship rights by the end of the 1830s.[23] Most states imported and then adapted capacity standards from English common law, most visible in the surviving records in capacity challenges in contracts and wills.[24] Zephaniah Swift's treatise on the law of evidence revealed the disciplinary power of civic capacity for determining who was qualified to testify in court. Swift held that "witness testimony could be excluded from Idiots and lunatics, who have not sufficient memory to retain facts, or understanding to relate them, or any sense of right and wrong, may not be witnesses."[25] This prohibition also included persons suffering from "ignorance merely." Swift's definition of lunacy incorporated culturally situated moral judgments ("any sense of right and wrong") with prohibitions against those without reason – "idiots" and "lunatics." Civic capacity also structured private relations. In a treatise on divorce in Ohio, Indiana, and Michigan, jurist Henry Folsom Page explained that "consent is absolutely requisite to matrimony, and neither idiots nor lunatics are capable of consenting to anything." Page quoted an English jurist in 1745 who stated, "A defect in capacity . . . invalidates the marriage contract as well as any other contract," a maxim well established in American law.[26] Early in the nineteenth century English treatise writer John Haslam articulated a basic level of capacity for criminal culpability, propounding that to mitigate criminal culpability, the offender had to be "bereft of the reason of an ordinary man," a general standard accepted and later elaborated upon by American jurists.[27] Local communities also debated the threshold of capacity in lunatic inquests and civil commitment procedures. Whereas challenges to contractual or testamentary capacity were moments when judicial officials and community members had to make capacity's contours explicit, most legal participation was preceded by an explicit or implicit capacity requirement.

The early nineteenth-century investment in the concept of civic capacity as undergirding legal and political participation also emerged from how citizens expressed their private relationships to others through contracts. In the first years of the republic, historians and political scientists have argued that Americans came to understand their relationships in terms of liberal individualism.[28] Legal contracts became the basis for enforcing responsibilities and obligations to one another.[29] Contracts, fairly negotiated, became a mode of communicating one's will and a means of national progress through creating legal certainty, all the while retaining much older moral valences steeped in the religious obligations of covenant theology.[30] Contracts were vehicles through which one exercised legal and economic power; the loss of contractual capacity marked individuals as weak willed, unworthy of civic, economic, and political participation.

Conversations about civic capacity transpired in many contexts as American jurists, medical experts, and ordinary citizens discussed civic capacity and its inverse in discussions over suffrage expansion, racial and sex differences, and the meanings of good civic participation in a democracy. At the same time, capacity determinations became increasingly grounded in physiognomy, inherited traits, and the seeming objectivity of empirical science. A robust dialogue continued among medical jurists about juridical tests for the determination of legal capacity. As the century progressed, older ideas about the moral component of capacity persisted, insinuated into law and discussions about civic capacity. The New York State Commissioner on Lunacy in the late nineteenth century, John Ordronaux, connected rationality, morality, and civil participation when he argued in 1875 that "the fundamental proposition from which all government starts, viz., that men are rational beings, and their personal accountability to God or their legal responsibility to society rests upon this cornerstone, no civil part can logically be assigned [to those lacking this standard]."[31]

For all the emphasis on capacity as grounded in reason and objective empiricism, its determinations were deeply rooted in discursive constructions of race, gender, and ableism, as illustrated by the rising – if short-lived – popularity of phrenology. Leading German phrenologist Johann Spurzheim believed that the "faculties of the mind" could be found through precisely measuring the skull, a theory rooted in observable, empirical science that allowed phrenologists to make sweeping generalizations about the capacities of different races.[32] During 1866 debates over extending suffrage to African American men in Washington, D.C., Kentucky Senator Garrett Davis pointed to Spurzheim and fellow phrenologist Franz Gall to argue that the "brain of the negro is smaller," which "denot[ed] less capacity for reasoning. No well-informed and candid person can doubt the mental inferiority of the negro race."[33] Although mainstream medical experts had discredited phrenology by mid-century, its central tenets about innate racial inferiority had infused and hardened scientific beliefs about race, physiognomy, and capacity.

Exclusions based in civic incapacity ranged from jury service and suffrage to outright denial of citizenship. An 1859 Texas statute designated that a ground for a challenge for cause against a juror may be made if the juror "has such defect in the organs of seeing, feeling or hearing, or such bodily or mental defect or disease as renders him unfit for jury service."[34] New York City's law mixed the moral with the rational, requiring jurors to be "an intelligent man, of sound mind, and good character."[35] The debate over jury service, which many Americans saw as part of a civic obligation and as a cornerstone of a fair judicial system, turned on which people had the capacity to assess evidence and make reasoned, impartial decisions.

Civic capacity as an arbiter of citizenship derived its power and longevity from its fluidity; it resisted a static definition, and individuals and groups could move into and out of its boundaries. If some groups could join the ranks of those possessing civic capacity, all groups and individuals risked possible regression. Many medical experts believed that insanity increased as societies progressed, a view widely shared by the end of the nineteenth century. Social progress, for all its benefits, could trigger dangerous reversals in civic capacity. As medical jurist John Cowles Prichard observed "from the rare occurrence of insanity in rude nations, and its comparative frequency in those which are civilized . . . the most influential causes of the disease are circumstances connected with the improved state of human society."[36] In 1858, Detroit physician John Ellis worried about the physical and mental degeneration of American citizens. He worried that "the citizens of this great republic are physically in their decline, and that nothing but a speedy reformation of bad habits . . . can open to us, as a nation, a glorious and 'eventful future.' "[37] Edward Jarvis, a national expert on insanity, connected progress, atavism, and capacity to race, arguing that among Native Americans and African Americans, insanity rarely existed because these groups lacked the capacity for progress. After reviewing asylum records, he concluded that insanity "is seldom found in the savage state, while it is well known to be frequent in the civilized state."[38]

While medico-legal jurists and treatise writers wrote thousands of pages on defining civic capacity and the characteristics of those who lacked it, their pronouncements had few legal ramifications until judges, juries, and lawmakers implemented the grammar of civic capacity to exclude persons from the rights and protections of citizenship. Civic capacity took its most immediate definitions in local courtrooms, most often in cases involving contractual or testamentary capacity. In one instance in 1846, Louisville, Kentucky, Chancery Judge S. S. Nicholas sought to clarify the testamentary capacity requirement for the jury. The case involved a challenge to testator Polly Bullitt's will on the ground that she lacked the mental capacity required to write a valid will. Nicholas began with establishing the lowest level of capacity required to manage property. He told the jury, "[T]he general aptitude of the sex [female] for the management of property is so small that it would not do to make that the criterion of capacity for making a will."[39] Nicholas then offered an "illustration" which drew upon racial and gendered ideas about innate capacity. Referring to "the best house servant I ever knew," he acknowledged that this man "had the mental capacity to dispose of it [property] by will – though no one could pretend that he was capable of trafficking with or judiciously managing it." He then turned to women's ability to control property, informing the jury,

> The whole female part of our society . . . you must in candor admit that the capacity of most of our females for trafficking with & managing property, consists pretty much in the capacity to select an agent or friend to do it for them.[40]

Nicholas used women and African Americans as examples of groups inherently lacking the capacity of white men and whose citizenship right (negotiating contracts, under the power/liability binary of Hohfeld's matrix) was circumscribed by their incapacity. These trials in which basic civic participation was tied to capacity served as sites in the ongoing process of creating racial and gender subordination through preserving white male legal authority.

Two lunatic inquest hearings in Kentucky illustrate how civic capacity structured property rights. In 1860, in a Scott County, Kentucky, courtroom, twelve jurors heard evidence that Narcissa Bradford was "of imbecile and unsound mind and has been so since her infancy." This routine hearing, thousands of which occurred throughout the United States in the nineteenth century, divested Bradford of the ability to participate in jural relations. The jury found that Bradford had property in a portion (four-sixths) of fourteen "negroes" and that "she herself is capable of attending to some business but incompetent to manage . . . or control her person or estate." The judge then declared her a lunatic and ordered that a committee be established to manage her estate.[41] An 1858 Scott County case reveals a more complete denial of capacity and its attendant legal rights. In the case of Harriet West, inquest records indicate that she had been married and divorced, had a "common English education," and had resided quietly on a farm. In about 1853, she began to exhibit episodic signs of "derangement," which were attributed to "general bad health and a derangement of the uterine organs." While she had "no disposition to do mischief," she continued to live in the community. Only when local officials believed she set fire to her brother's barn did the proceedings begin to designate her as legally incapacitated. After hearing her case, the jury declared her a lunatic, and the judge committed her to the Eastern State Lunatic Asylum in Lexington, Kentucky.[42]

In many of these cases, the individual had managed his or her property for years until some triggering event led to initiating an inquest. As other studies have indicated, these triggering events were sometimes based in considerations other than the capacity of the property holder. In Illinois, Elizabeth Packard's 1864 challenge to her asylum commitment reveals how property interests, community pressure, and marital discord were among many conflicts that could underlie commitment proceedings.[43] Packard and her supporters contended that her husband, a Calvinist minister, initiated commitment proceedings because she challenged his theological positions. Packard's case and others involving the dangers of bogus commitments led to campaigns for state "Personal Liberty" laws designed to protect individuals from designing relatives seeking to acquire property. In these commitment cases, local county courts trammeled individuals' property, liberty, and contractual rights through a legal process in which they were found incapacitated. Local witnesses, through their testimony, and finally county judges continually manufactured the meanings of civic capacity through determinations situated in community conflicts, knowledge, and medical and moral evaluations.

IV. Conclusion

The grammar of civic capacity was imbricated throughout nineteenth-century law. Law was (and is) a cultural narrative and a system of rule, however incomplete, a meta-language encoding values and articulating a system of inclusions and exclusions. Law validated or repudiated behavior. Capacity was not just encoded in law through elite jurists and medical experts; it was a juridical concept negotiated through countless interactions among ordinary people. Groups designated as barbaric, primitive, or savage, categories often associated with racialized minorities, lacked the capacity necessary to fulfill the obligations of citizenship. Assigning incapacity to an individual or group differed in terms of its civic restrictions from a total loss of legal personhood (Dred Scott and African Americans after 1857) to a partial loss of rights or privileges in specific circumstances (voting, jury service, contractual capacity, testamentary capacity).[44] Capacity did not determine rights; rather, affirming or assuming an individual possessed capacity preceded access to "fundamental legal relations."[45] In its most complete designation, incapacity erased access to civil participation or decision making, reducing individuals or groups to legal dependency. Juridical conceptions of capacity sustained inequalities when women, African Americans, or those designated mentally or physically incapacitated were refused ballots, were denied seats on juries, or were excluded from exercising other markers of the fully constituted citizen, emphasizing and reinforcing their deficiencies and their alterity.

Lack of civic capacity, be it framed as insanity, idiocy, or racial or gender unfitness, served as a powerful justification for exclusion. It was a flexible concept, adaptable to changing epistemological frameworks. Throughout the nineteenth century, the civic capacity requirement was defined and refined through a latticework of legal, social, medical, and cultural modalities. Conflict over the legal and social meanings of capacity drew upon and brought into courtrooms social cultural narratives that shot through society. The grammar of civic capacity possessed insidious characteristics not present in other languages of rights claims. Groups made claims to specific rights that they understood to be part and parcel of American equality, liberty, and citizenship; African Americans and women argued for suffrage, inclusion on jury rolls, and the ability to make contracts. Groups identified as lacking capacity argued that they were misrepresented and did possess the requisite capacity to enjoy the rights of citizenship. They rarely questioned the framework of the category of capacity itself or that incapacity justified exclusion.

Capacity's power and definition relied on deeply imbricated, manifest values; excluding those from it appeared obvious and just. When Lawrence Summers made his imprudent comments in 2005, his words drew on the centuries-old, persistent, discursive power of capacity. Undoubtedly, Summers had no intention of excluding women from access to science education or opportunities. At the same time, Senator Ron Wyden and those who vehemently protested Summers' remarks recognized that linking one group to lesser capacity could have devastating consequences because of its remarkable versatility in organizing taxonomies of inclusion and exclusion. In a republic that rejected hereditary advantage and embraced "merit," its embrace of John Adams' "natural aristocracy among mankind" recreated the conditions for establishing hierarchies among ostensibly equal citizens.

Notes

1 Marcella Bombardieri, "Summers' Remarks on Women Draw Fire," *Boston Globe*, January 17, 2005, A1; "Title IX and Science: Hearing before the Subcommittee on Science, Technology and Space of the Committee on Commerce, Science, and Transportation," October 3, 2002 (Washington, D.C.: U.S. Printing Office, 2005).

2 Elizabeth Cady Stanton, Susan B. Anthony, and Matilda Joslyn Gage, eds., *History of Woman Suffrage, Volume One: 1848–1861* (New York: Fowler and Wells, 1889), 27; John Adams, "Defence of the Constitution of Government of the United State of America," in *The Works of John Adams, Second President of the United States*, vol. 4, ed. Charles F. Adams (Boston: Little, Brown, 1851), 392.

3 For discussions of groups excluded from the rights of citizenship, see Linda K. Kerber, *No Constitutional Right to Be Ladies: Women and the Obligations of Citizenship* (New York: Hill & Wang, 1998); Nancy Isenberg, *Sex and Citizenship in Antebellum America* (Chapel Hill: University of North Carolina Press, 1998); Margot Canaday, *The Straight State: Sexuality and Citizenship in Twentieth Century America* (Princeton, N.J.: Princeton University Press, 2011); Christian G. Samito, *Becoming American under Fire: Irish Americans, African Americans, and the Politics of Citizenship during the Civil War Era* (Ithaca, N.Y.: Cornell University Press, 2009). For an analysis of political inclusion and exclusion based in disability history and theory, see Douglas Baynton, "Disability: A Useful Category of Historical Analysis," *Disability Studies Quarterly* 17 (Spring 1997): 82–96.

4 Wesley Hohfeld described jural relations as four binary sets creating a conceptual space in which the clusters of legal performance not explicitly associated with citizenship are integrated. They are right/duty, liberty/no right, power/liability, immunity/disability. Civil identity is more completely translated into its legal meaning through Hohfeld's jural relations. Wesley Hohfeld, "Some Fundamental Legal Conceptions as Applied in Judicial Reasoning," *Yale Law Journal* 23 (1913): 16–59. Kerber, *No Constitutional Right*, defines citizenship through a series of rights and obligations, including jury service, taxation, and military service.

5 *Scott v. Sandford*, 60 U.S. 393 (1857).

6 The most obvious indicators of civic incapacity were racial categorizations. For an early and influential discussion of the visible signs of mental incapacity, see Isaac Ray, *A Treatise on the Medical Jurisprudence of Insanity* (Boston: Little, Brown, 1838).

7 Francis Wharton and Moreton Stille, *Medical Jurisprudence*, 3rd ed. (Philadelphia: Kay, 1873), 337. Most legal treatises on insanity had lengthy descriptions of the physical deviations of insane, unfit, and idiotic persons. Each category was identifiable through unique characteristics.

8 On the shift from divine ordinance to scientific authority, see Yvonne Pitts, "Disability, Scientific Authority, and Women's Political Participation in the Turn of the Twentieth Century United States," *Journal of Women's History* 22 (2012): 37–61; Cynthia Eagle Russett, *Sexual Science: The Victorian Construction of Womanhood* (Cambridge, Mass.: Harvard University Press, 1989); Stephen Gould, *The Mismeasure of Man* (New York: Norton, 1981).

9 *Louisiana Advertiser* (December 6, 1826); "Hereditary Insanity," *Boston Medical and Surgical Journal* 22 (1840): 335.

10 James C. Prichard, *A Treatise on Insanity and Other Disorders Affecting the Mind* (Philadelphia: Carey & Hart, 1837), 135–40; "Insanity Produced by Masturbation," *Boston Medical and Surgical Journal* 12 (1835): 109; Amariah Brigham, "Causes of Insanity," *American Ladies' Magazine* 7 (February 1834), 79.

11 Nathaniel Carter and William Stone, eds., *Reports of the Proceedings and Debates of the Convention of 1821 Assembled for the Purpose of Amending the Constitution of the State of New-York* (New York: Hosford, 1821), 374.

12 Susanna Blumenthal approaches capacity and closely related issues of free will through the "problem of responsibility." Susanna L. Blumenthal, "The Mind of a Moral Agent: Scottish Common Sense and the Problem of Responsibility in Nineteenth Century American Law," *Law and History Review* 26 (2008): 99–159.

13 Thomas Jefferson, *Notes on the State of Virginia* (London: Stockdale, 1787), 239.

14 On Jefferson and capacity as civic virtue, see Jean Yarbrough, *American Virtues: Thomas Jefferson on the Character of a Free People* (Lawrence: University of Kansas Press, 1998).

15 Frederick Pollock and Frederic Maitland, *The History of English Law Before the Time of Edward I: Volume I* (Boston: Little, Brown, 1895), 464. For terminology and a description of early legal categories see Homer D. Crotty, "History of Insanity as a Defence to Crime in English Criminal Law," *California Law Review* 12 (1924): 105–23.

16 "Explanation of the 1540 Statute of Wills," 34 & 35 Henry VIII c. 5 (1542) in John Baker, *Sources in English Legal History: Private Law to 1750*, 2nd ed. (Oxford: Oxford University Press, 2010), 140.

17 On the nineteenth-century application of the Statute of Wills in English law, see William Cruise, *A Digest of the Laws of England Respecting Real Property* (London: Strahan, 1806), 15–17.

18 John Locke, *Second Treatise of Government*, ed. Crawford B. McPherson (1690; Indianapolis: Hackett, 1980).

19 On the transition in authority from birthright to consent see James H. Kettner, *Development of American Citizenship, 1608–1870* (Chapel Hill: University of North Carolina Press, reprint 1978); Holly Brewer, *By Birth or Consent: Children, Law, and the Anglo-American Revolution in Authority* (Chapel Hill: University of North Carolina Press, 2005). For a treatment of the different strains of European thought that influenced the American Enlightenment thinkers, see Henry May, *The Enlightenment in America* (New York: Oxford University Press, 1976). This transition is delineated in the philosophy of Robert Filmer, who argued for divine right rule based in hereditary transmission from fathers to sons. John Locke responded with the *First Treatise of Government* in which he rejected Filmer's absolutism and propounded a belief in reason and consent as the basis for political community, on which he elaborated in the *Second Treatise of Government*.

20 Francis Parkman, "The Failure of Universal Suffrage," *North American Review* 127 (1878): 263.

21 Thomas Paine (attrib.), "An Occasional Letter on the Female Sex," *Pennsylvania Magazine* 1 (1775): 362 (emphasis added).

22 For arguments about women's equal capacity to men, see Judith S. Murray, "On the Equality of the Sexes," in *Selected Writings of Judith Sargeant Murray*, ed. Sharon M. Harris (1790; New York: Oxford University Press, 1995) or Mary Wollstonecraft, *A Vindication of the Rights of Woman*, ed., Deidre Shauna Lynch (1792; New York: Norton, 2009).

23 Legal scholar Jacob Katz Cogan describes this shift through suffrage requirements in Jacob K. Cogan, "The Look Within: Property, Capacity, and Suffrage in Nineteenth Century America," *Yale Law Journal* 107 (1997): 473–98.

24 On the importation of common law to America, see William Nelson, *The Americanization of the Common Law: The Impact of Legal Change on Massachusetts Society, 1760–1830* (Cambridge, Mass.: Harvard University Press, 1975); Mary S. Bilder, *The Transatlantic Constitution: Colonial Legal Culture and Empire* (Cambridge, Mass.: Harvard University Press, 2009), esp. 91–115; Peter C. Hoffer, *Law and People in Colonial America*, rev. ed. (Baltimore: Johns Hopkins University Press, 1998); on the capacity requirement specifically, see Yvonne Pitts, *Family, Law, and Inheritance in America: A Nineteenth Century History of Kentucky* (New York: Cambridge University Press, 2013).

25 Zephaniah Swift, *A Digest of the Law of Evidence, in Civil and Criminal Cases* (Hartford, Conn.: Cooke, 1810), 44.

26 Henry F. Page, *A View of the Law Relative to the Subject of Divorce, in Ohio, Indiana and Michigan* (Columbus, Ohio: Riley, 1850), 184.

27 John Haslam, *Medical Jurisprudence, As It Relates to Insanity, According to the Law of England* (London: Hunter, 1817), 50; Ray, *Medical Jurisprudence*. On the development of the standard, see John S. Hughes, *Into the Law's Darkness: Isaac Ray and the Medical Jurisprudence of Insanity in Nineteenth Century America* (New York: Oceana, 1986). On common law, capacity, and criminal culpability, see Simon Stern, "Blackstone's Criminal Law: Common-Law Harmonization and Legislative Reform," in *Foundational Texts in Modern Criminal Law*, ed. Markus Dubber (New York: Oxford, 2014), 61–78.

28 Mark McGarvie, *One Nation under Law: America's Early National Struggles to Separate Church and State* (DeKalb: Northern Illinois University Press, 2004). See also Willard Hurst, *Law and the Conditions of Freedom in the Nineteenth Century United States* (Madison: University of Wisconsin Press, 1956), esp. chaps. 1 and 2. Hurst notes the "overwhelming predominance of the law of contract" (10) in the early nineteenth century.

29 On the transformation from status to contract in the nineteenth century, see Brewer, *By Birth or*; Christopher L. Tomlins, *Law, Labor, and Ideology in the Early American Republic* (New York: Cambridge University Press, 1993). For an analysis of the post–Civil War critique of the free will basis of contracts, see Amy Dru Stanley, *From Bondage to Contract: Wage Labor, Marriage, and the Market in the Era of Slave Emancipation* (New York: Cambridge University Press, 1998).

30 On the pivotal importance of contracts being fairly negotiated, see *Fletcher v. Peck* 10 U.S. 87 (1810) and *Dartmouth College v. Woodward*, 17 U.S. 518 (1819). On contracts as a legal expression of free will, see Tomlins, *Law, Labor, and Ideology*. On the older tradition of covenanting with God and its influence on

colonial religious and political thinkers, see Robin W. Lovin, "Equality and Covenant Theology," *Journal of Law and Religion* 2 (1984): 241–62 and Glenn Moots, *Politics Reformed: The Anglo American Legacy of Covenant Theology* (Columbia: University of Missouri Press, 2010). On exploring the paradox of free will and divine ordinance, see Jon Pahl, *Paradox Lost: Free Will and Political Liberty in American Culture, 1630–1760* (Baltimore: Johns Hopkins Press, 1992).

31 John Ordronaux, "The Proper Status of the Insane and Feebleminded," in *Papers Read before the Medico-Legal Society of New York*, third series, 1875–78, rev. ed. (New York: Medico-Legal Journal Association, 1886), 51.

32 Johann Spurzheim, *Phrenology, Or the Doctrine of the Mind* (London: Knight, 1825).

33 *Congressional Globe*, 39th Cong., 1st Sess. 246 (1866).

34 William S. Oldham and George W. White, *A Digest of the General Statute Laws of the State of Texas* (Austin, TX: Marshal, 1859), 632.

35 *Digest of the Laws of New York* (New York: Cockcroft, 1875), 2: 390 ("Division V – Jury Law as to New York City, §26").

36 Prichard, *A Treatise on Insanity*, 133.

37 John Ellis, *The Avoidable Causes of Disease, Insanity, and Deformity* (New York: Boericke & Tafel, 1870), xvi.

38 Edward Jarvis, "On the Supposed Increase of Insanity," *American Journal of Insanity* 8 (1852): 362.

39 Judge S. S. Nicholas, "Charge to the Jury, May 2, 1846," Box 28, FL 255, *Howard v. Churchill*, Bullitt Family Papers, Filson Historical Society. For a fuller examination of the case, see Pitts, *Family, Law, and Inheritance*, chap. 3.

40 Ibid.

41 *Inquest of Lunacy in the Case of Narcissa v. Bradford*, September 12, 1860, Box 32, Folio 335 (1860) Scott County, Kentucky Circuit Court Records (SCKCCR), Kentucky Department for Libraries and Archives (KDLA), Frankfort, Kentucky.

42 *Commonwealth v. Harriet West as Lunatic*, May 22, 1858, Box 28 Folio 318 Case 14, SCKCCR, KDLA.

43 Elizabeth Packard, *Marital Power Exemplified in Mrs. Packard's Trial, and Self Defence from the Charge of Insanity* (Chicago: Clarke, 1879); Hendrik Hartog, "Mrs. Packard on Dependency," *Yale Journal of Law & the Humanities* 1 (1988): 79–103; Greg Andrews, *Insane Sisters, Or, the Price Paid for Challenging a Company Town* (Columbia: University of Missouri Press, 1999).

44 Individuals and groups could lose rights for numerous reasons (domicile, for example) not related to a capacity determination. This chapter focuses on how capacity could determine the access to or denial of rights.

45 Hohfeld, "Fundamental Legal Conceptions," 30.

19

"VITAL TISSUES OF THE SPIRIT"

Constitutional emotions in the antebellum United States

Doni Gewirtzman[*]

In 1837, Theodore Weld, a revivalist minister and abolitionist, wrote a letter to his wife and sister describing his methods for changing hearts and minds on the issue of slavery: "[I]f it is not felt in the very vital tissues of the spirit, all the reasoning in the world is a feather thrown against the wind."[1]

Weld's comment reflects a prolonged nineteenth-century struggle over the relationship between law and emotion in constitutional culture.[2] Throughout the antebellum era, Americans wrestled with the way feelings affected constitutional interpretation, the emotional worth of the Constitution as a symbol worth fighting for, and the need for law and legal institutions to cultivate certain emotions while constraining others in order to maintain a sustainable constitutional order. The debates pushed at the boundaries between law and politics, passion and reason, morality and formalism, elites and laypeople. The capacity of feelings to both revitalize and degrade constitutional culture became a recurring theme in attempts to resolve the role of "We the People" in constitutional interpretation, the institutional competition for interpretive supremacy, moral reform, and competing visions of union and disunion.

Two dynamics – ambivalence and reciprocity – lie at the heart of the relationship between the United States Constitution and emotion. Ambivalence about emotion is hardwired into the 1787 Constitution through its simultaneous embrace of popular sovereignty and written constitutionalism.[3] Popular sovereignty recognizes "the People" as the ultimate authority within the constitutional regime, situating collective emotions as a vital part of the system's founding myth and integral to its status as supreme law.[4] Constitutional commitments are imagined, legitimated, perpetuated, and renewed through collective social practices motivated by emotion and systems of belief that rely upon emotional cues to sustain their power. Constitutional law is deeply dependent on feelings to produce certain social outcomes, facilitate constitutional change, and generate the loyalty and allegiance necessary to preserve constitutional institutions and structures. At the same time, written constitutionalism, with its embrace of positivism and "Ulysses tied to the mast" precommitments,[5] instills into American constitutional law's DNA a preference for rational decision making and a healthy suspicion about the potentially destructive effects of collective emotions. Written constitutional commitments operate as constraints on emotional performance and expression in the political arena by channeling popular input into decision-making processes and institutions that introduce deliberation, delay, rationality, and reflection into the process of forming legal norms, the resolution of disputes, and the construction of legal meaning.

The dynamic between constitutional law and emotion is also reciprocal: just as constitutional law works to construct emotions, emotions work to construct constitutional law.[6] Constitutions establish institutional structures that construct, influence, and guide collective emotions in the public arena. For example, Article I's requirement that legislation pass through two separate legislative bodies rests in part on assumptions about how certain emotions affect decision making and a belief that extended deliberation will help manage the deleterious effects of passion.[7] At the same time, the feelings constructed by those institutions are fed back into the system, altering the evolution of constitutional meaning through public opinion, social movements, and other forms of democratic popular expression.[8]

This chapter provides a framework for examining the ambivalent and reciprocal connection between constitutional law and emotion in the antebellum era[9] through three distinct lenses that correspond to three interrelated constitutional functions: text, instrument, and symbol.

Text. First, how did beliefs about emotion affect the process and methodology of constitutional interpretation? Early nineteenth-century Americans recognized feelings as an essential part of how individuals made sense of the world around them.[10] Consequently, emotion's role in the interpretation of a newly created legal text filled with ambiguous language became an inevitable source of contention. During the 1830s and 1840s, the divide between reason and emotion became a commonly used weapon in the struggle for supremacy between a judicial elite that used reason and rationality to legitimize their use of interpretive power and popular social movements that used emotions to spur alternative visions of constitutional meaning. A closer examination of the period also highlights the rich historical lineage of debates about the reason–emotion divide[11] and the way those debates helped to shape contemporary American legal culture, as well as providing essential context for a range of related questions that continue to occupy scholars well into the twenty-first century: the extent to which reason and emotion are mutually dependent,[12] their respective effects on decision making,[13] the malleability of each category's definition,[14] and the ability of each to exacerbate or correct for deficiencies in the other.[15]

Instrument. Second, how did constitutional law construct and manage popular emotion? The Constitution was designed to serve a core instrumental function: to control, channel, and dilute the harmful effects of "passion" on public life. One of the antebellum era's lingering puzzles is why the framers' assumptions about the Constitution's capacity to constrain popular emotion failed so dramatically. In the years leading up to the Civil War, the political world became infused with anger, indignation, and jealousy, all of which the Constitution was supposed to manage and transform into an enlightened reasoning process through the machinations of constitutional institutions. Yet by the mid-nineteenth century, Thomas Jefferson's inaugural vision of a "rising nation . . . united with one heart and one mind" by "harmony and affection" was in tatters.[16]

Symbol. Third, how did different American subcultures feel about the Constitution itself? The document, then and now, maintains a unique status at the intersection of law and feeling. It is not simply a legal text and source of supreme law but a contested cultural symbol imbued with emotion that connects political principles to particular affective responses. The Constitution's evolution as a national symbol during the antebellum period was slow and uneven, as other symbols – like the Declaration of Independence and "Union" – were far more established and emotionally resonant, raising questions about the reasons behind the Constitution's relative lack of semiotic power.

Within the realms of text, instrument, and symbol, antebellum American writers and artists responded and contributed to developments in the political and legal arena. They offered portrayals of judges who struggled with constraints upon their use of feeling and moral sentiments when interpreting legal texts, mobilized and channeled emotions into constitutional culture, and sought to create alternative emblems of national unity. The evolving relationship between constitutional law and emotion was constructed through legal and nonlegal texts and through interactions that occurred both within and outside law's domain.

I. Constitution as text

Legal and literary historian Perry Miller called "the never-ending case of Heart versus Head" the "great issue" of nineteenth-century America,[17] reflecting the dichotomous division within moral philosophy that characterized the era.[18] During the period leading up to the Civil War, the tension between Heart and Head played itself out through conflicting approaches to constitutional interpretation that were deeply intertwined with class divisions.[19] One, anchored in populism, frontier culture, and evangelical reform, used theatricality, sentiment, and feeling to assert popular sovereignty over the interpretive process. Political parties and social movements helped create an antebellum political climate bathed in emotion, using feelings to generate moral outrage and spur collective action in order to redefine the terms of core constitutional commitments. The other theory centered around an increasingly professionalized and elite group of legal practitioners who saw law as a rational science.[20] This approach positioned judges, guided by reason, as critical to maintaining the positivist limits imposed by a written constitution and barriers against the corrosive effects of popular emotion on constitutional meaning.[21]

Each side claimed legitimacy from Founding era commitments to popular sovereignty and written constitutionalism as they became embroiled in a power struggle for interpretive supremacy over the constitutional text, using the divide between emotion and reason to negotiate the often permeable boundaries between the worlds of law and politics. In turn, interpretive power ebbed and flowed between a judiciary with limited capacity to recognize and engage with the highly emotional culture of antebellum American politics and social institutions that were capable of cultivating and valuing emotional expression.

A. Popular constitutionalism

Popular sovereignty emerged as a powerful animating force in American constitutionalism in the years immediately after the Founding,[22] taking hold during a sentimental era where emotions were a major preoccupation in political and social life. Early-nineteenth century Americans openly celebrated their capacity for feeling and viewed their emotional sensitivity as a defining characteristic that separated them from Great Britain.[23] As Andrew Burstein describes it, the Declaration of Independence "played up the distinction between the feeling and the unfeeling."[24] In Jefferson's words, it was the betrayal of America's "agonizing affection" that forced Americans to "renounce forever these unfeeling brethren."[25] This type of political rhetoric survived into in the post-revolutionary era, where political elites embraced sentiment to "sustain the enterprise of nation building. . . . used by a people who routinely called themselves peace-loving" as a "defense against inner and outer turmoil."[26]

During the early antebellum period, the performance of emotions like sympathy and affection was culturally valued[27] and feelings were treated as essential drivers of moral action.[28] Many recognized that emotions were socially constructed: they could be shaped by public opinion and transmitted from generation to generation.[29] It is therefore not surprising that politics were often framed in emotional terms, even beyond the so-called Era of Good Feelings. The successful "pursuit of happiness" was seen as an essential goal of politics,[30] and analogies to affective familial bonds were often used to describe the foundation of the new political union.[31] James Madison used *The Federalist* to attack skeptics who believed that "the people of America, knit together as they are by so many chords of affection, cannot live together as members of the same family."[32]

In his 1826 eulogy for John Adams and Thomas Jefferson, Daniel Webster placed the heart of the union in the collective emotions generated by mourning, reminding his audience that "the tears which flow, and the hours that are paid, when the founders of the republic die, give hope that the republic itself may be immortal."[33] Many Whig constitutionalists, including Joseph Story, used cemetery dedication addresses and college speeches to lend emotional content to their constitutional vision, invoking a language of sentiment to promote allegiance to a constitutional republic grounded in moral progress and economic development.[34]

Within this post-Founding era emotional context, there was widespread support for the idea that popular will, even with its vulnerability to volatile and unpredictable emotional forces, had a role to play in constitutional interpretation. For many, the Constitution represented the embodiment of popular sovereignty,[35] and constitutional law emerged as a special form of "popular law" where judges, elected officials, and the people shared interpretive power.[36] This populist vision of constitutional interpretation invited members of the public to engage as active participants in a wider cultural dialogue over constitutional meaning, welcoming collective emotions into the interpretive process. Larry Kramer's account of "popular constitutionalism" in the Founding era describes mechanisms for asserting popular input over legal meaning outside of the formal political system, including juries, petitions, parades, and "mobbing."[37] Civic associations often adopted their own constitutions, giving ordinary citizens a firsthand experience with a scaled-down version of constitutional self-governance.[38]

This populist lens also informed early narratives about the legitimacy of judicial interpretation. When early American jurists exercised the power of judicial review, they operated not as countermajoritarian and undemocratic elites but as representatives of "the People" that provided an institutional check against the power of self-interested and corrupt elected officials.[39]

Gradually, this link between popular sovereignty and judicial review began to deteriorate, as deep suspicions about the political and elitist motives of federalist judges drove efforts to constrain the exercise of judicial power and limit the influence of common law.[40] Gerry Leonard describes a historical transition from a moderate form of populism embodied by Jefferson, who sought to balance a commitment to reason and the rule of law with popular sovereignty, to the more unabashed party-centered populism of Andrew Jackson and Martin Van Buren.[41]

By the late 1820s and 1830s, the political party had evolved into a primary institutional mechanism for introducing popular emotion into constitutional interpretation. Under Van Buren's guidance, mass political parties began to position themselves as prominent competitors to judges in the battle for interpretive supremacy, despite conscious efforts by the founding generation to limit their existence and influence.[42] Jacksonians saw political parties, not the courts, as the true antiaristocratic embodiment of popular sovereignty and the primary vehicles for ensuring that the ultimate definition of constitutional meaning remained firmly in the hands of "the People."[43] By the 1840s, they had used the party system to effectively implement a constitutional agenda that revolved around strict construction and state sovereignty[44] and had begun to bring greater democratization to the judicial branch through the popular election of state judges.[45] Within a cultural environment that celebrated oratory and theatricality,[46] political party rituals injected emotional rhetoric into constitutional culture through personal appeals, long speeches, and parades.[47] Political parties also "domesticated" and managed popular interpretive input by filtering collective emotion through organizational frameworks and channeling populist energy into the winning of elections.[48]

Reform movements operated alongside the party system, using emotions as tools to motivate social action and inject strongly held moral beliefs into conversations about constitutional meaning. Perry Miller's classic account of antebellum intellectual thought describes a dichotomous battle between reason and emotion conducted through legal and nonlegal texts, with the evangelical Protestant Revival embodying the forces of the Heart.[49] By the 1840s, religious evangelism was "the largest, and most formidable, subculture in American society."[50] Revivalist efforts at moral reformation embraced a rhetorical style that was both emotional and imaginative,[51] where feelings operated "like electricity moving through the telegraph line to God, who would respond to the sender upon receiving the message."[52] This evangelical style had a widespread influence on American culture beyond the pulpit as lurid literary descriptions of vice became more common,[53] facilitating a national conversation about moral reform with constitutional implications. Temperance literature became more and more dramatic and sensational in describing the social and familial effects of alcohol use, a rhetorical tactic embraced by antislavery novels from the period as well.[54]

Evangelical movements influenced antebellum constitutional culture in a range of ways, reacting against the idea that constitutional interpretation was the exclusive terrain of judges and reason.[55] John Compton describes the Revivalists' use of law as a tool for moral reform through zealous efforts to abolish slavery, alcohol, and lotteries, driven by the belief that "the will of democratic majorities should be accorded greater weight in constitutional adjudication."[56] In turn, "the judiciary came to be viewed as among the most serious obstacles blocking moral regeneration," as reform efforts came into conflict with constitutional rules that protected property rights, the movement of goods through interstate markets, and the rights of slaveholders.[57] Judges repeatedly invoked the Contracts Clause to strike down efforts to interfere with existing state lottery grants, upheld the constitutional property rights of liquor licensees whose livelihoods were threatened by temperance legislation, and relied upon the Fugitive Slave Clause to strike down state laws that protected escaped slaves.[58] In response, evangelicals "reacted against the elevation of law into an intricate system of reason by insinuating that lawyers . . . separated substance from form, spirit from letter, and sacrificed justice to technicality."[59]

Abolitionists, many with deep roots in evangelical religion and transcendentalism,[60] used emotional rhetoric to accompany their legal attacks on slavery.[61] On the legal front, antislavery activists relied on arguments based in natural law and moral principle to address a constitutional text that offered few legal remedies for addressing human bondage.[62] Outside the courtroom, they relied on a language of feeling to create "moral shocks" and motivate popular support for the abolitionist cause.[63] Abolitionist narratives about the institution of slavery often evoked sympathy and mourning for its victims, while portraying the South as immune to the emotional impact of human suffering. Through "indignation rallies" throughout the North, they sought to mobilize opposition to the slave power and facilitate "a sense of moral superiority and unity of purpose by defining slavery's champions as the objects of righteous outrage."[64] Antislavery narratives of the 1830s and 1840s often contained gruesome accounts of human pain and suffering designed to create strong feelings of sympathy, laying the popular groundwork for a rights discourse and a shift in moral reasoning that culminated in the legal reforms of the Reconstruction era.[65]

B. Judicial interpretation

It is difficult to characterize the early nineteenth-century relationship between judicial interpretation and emotion in a monolithic way. Most, though certainly not all, legal historians describe early nineteenth-century judicial interpretation as heavily influenced by instrumentalism,[66] a theory of reasoning that emerged from the common-law tradition and treated judge-made law as mutable and changeable in the service of certain larger social goals, like economic prosperity and the preservation of the national Union.[67] While still maintaining a deep commitment to the use of reason, precedent, and logical inference in judging, the instrumentalist approach also allowed some space for judges to experience emotion in the interpretive process.[68] During this period, the effective administration of law was often linked to feelings, with the ideal jurist maintaining a strong, love-like, affective bond with justice, uniformity, or prosperity.[69] Peter Karsten describes a "Jurisprudence of the Heart" that was embraced by some antebellum jurists (particularly outside the Northeastern judicial elite), whose religious convictions influenced the application of common-law rules to aid the victims of economic growth and entrepreneurship.[70]

At the same time, early American judges also demonstrated a strong respect for reason, *stare decisis*, and English common law. Karsten identifies a distinct "Jurisprudence of the Head," where judges routinely invoked precedent and tools of logical inference to position law as a rational inductive process rather a creative tool to facilitate a larger set of normative values.[71] In contrast to private law, where instrumentalism remained dominant, formalism dominated the public law arena, often as a tool for judges to constrain legislative efforts to redistribute wealth.[72]

To the extent that reason and emotion were able to coexist within the judicial sphere, the status quo became increasingly untenable as the judicial branch, and common law came under political attack during the Jeffersonian and Jacksonian eras. As codification began to supplant common law in the 1820s and the political environment became increasingly skeptical of judicial power, influential Supreme Court judges fought back by claiming interpretive legitimacy and supremacy based on their ability to subordinate themselves to the will of the people as expressed in written codes and the Constitution itself. Narratives of judicial power increasingly treated law as a science best practiced by experts in the art of deduction and reason that would remain unaffected by the temporary erratic sway of popular passions that surrounded them.[73]

Joseph Story, a Supreme Court justice, law professor, author of a highly influential 1833 constitutional law treatise, and published poet, led the battle to insulate constitutional law from the effects of collective emotions and their potential effects on judicial independence and subjectivity.[74] In his *Commentaries on the Constitution*, Story lamented that

> the rules of interpretation have often been shifted to suit the emergency; and the passions and prejudices of the day, or the favour or odium of a particular measure, have not infrequently furnished a mode of argument, which would, on the one hand, leave the constitution crippled and inanimate, or, on the other hand, give it an extent and elasticity, subversive of all boundaries.[75]

In line with the growing treatise tradition, he saw his task as articulating "true rules of interpretation . . . so that we may have some fixed standard by which to measure [the Constitution's] powers and limit its provisions"[76] and worried about "how easily men satisfy themselves that the Constitution is entirely what they want it to be."[77] In 1835, lawyer and orator Horace Binney described Chief Justice John Marshall's judicial methodology, placing constitutional law solidly within the exclusive domain of judges and rationality. In Binney's depiction of Marshall, "[r]eason is the great authority upon constitutional questions, and the faculty of reasoning is the only instrument by which it should be exercised."[78]

Reason became a tool to establish judicial supremacy over constitutional interpretation, as Story's solution to interpretive malleability was to identify the Supreme Court as the "final and common arbiter" of constitutional meaning.[79] Elite jurists began to see law as a specialized science that should be governed by trained professionals – individuals whose powers of observation and experience gave them the unique ability to discern general principles that would lead to a "rational understanding of the universe"[80] that existed apart from their personal subjective values. Constitutional law, from this perspective, began to look less like a special form of "popular law" and more like "ordinary law," subject to interpretive rules designed and implemented by judges.[81]

The dichotomous relationship between passion and reason not only reflected Enlightenment thinking but also served the interests of the increasingly elite and professionalized federal judiciary. In a competition with political parties for interpretive power, Story and others began to reinforce the idea that the judiciary's institutional competence was based on its ability to bring rationality to the legal system and remain independent from politics and popular will. In this context, it is not surprising that the divide between reason and emotion became one way for antebellum judges to dismiss abolitionist efforts in the 1840s and 1850s to read constitutional texts through an explicitly moral lens. Many jurists saw the antislavery movement's move toward legal arguments based in natural law and morality as an attack on the positivism that came with the invention of a written Constitution,[82] inviting too much subjectivity into the process of defining constitutional meaning[83] for a founding document that was supposed to embody core principles that remained consistent across generations.[84] In rejecting an antislavery reading of the New Jersey Constitution in 1845, the New Jersey Supreme Court dismissed the natural law arguments made by abolitionists as "addressed to the feelings" rather than to "the legal intelligence of the court."[85] Judges responded to abolitionist arguments with an increasingly formalist, rationality-driven conception of their own role, as antislavery judges professed helplessness when confronted with legal attacks on slavery.[86] Story, the author of the Supreme Court's decision in *Prigg v. Pennsylvania* declaring a state kidnapping law unconstitutional under the Constitution's Fugitive Slave Clause, wrote to a friend after the decision: "you know full well that I have ever been opposed to slavery. But I take my standard of duty as a judge from the Constitution."[87] Even Justice Benjamin Curtis's blistering dissent in *Dred Scott* reinforced this conception of the judicial role: "General considerations concerning the social and moral evils of slavery" were "reasons purely political" that made "judicial interpretation impossible – because judicial tribunals cannot decide upon political considerations."[88]

Popular American authors noticed this move toward the sublimation of judicial emotion, attacking judges whose embrace of rationality and formalism immunized them from the feelings necessary to generate moral outrage and appreciate the human suffering caused by slavery. In a pair of texts, *A Key to Uncle Tom's Cabin* and *Dred: A Tale of a Great Dismal Swamp*, Harriet Beecher Stowe condemned "the severe, unflinching accuracy of logic"[89] in American legal decisions, as judges with "unflinching calmness . . . walk . . . through the most extreme and terrible results and conclusions, in obedience to the laws of legal truth."[90] A judge in Stowe's novel *Dred* reveals that he "can only perceive and declare. What I see, I must speak, though it go against all my feelings and all my sense of right."[91] Whitman's idealized vision of law in "Great Are the Myths" situates "Justice" not in "legislators or laws" but in the "Soul," with "perfect judges" ruling "on the highest grounds."[92] And in James Fenimore Cooper's *The Pioneers*, Judge Marmaduke Temple finds his commitment to reason and law in direct conflict with the unbounded spirit of frontier culture embodied by Natty Bumppo.[93]

The pre–Civil War battles over interpretive power and methodology would culminate after the War in the triumph of legal formalism, with judges purporting to administer law as a science governed by logic and inference from precedent. Melville's Captain Vere in *Billy Budd* would come to embody the spirit of the moral–formal divide, agonizingly rejecting any appeal to "private conscience" in sentencing Billy to death.[94] Years of emotional struggle (among a multitude of other factors) left many Americans eager to turn their attention away from politics and matters of constitutional interpretation, leaving the federal judiciary ample room to chart the course of the Reconstruction Amendments in the war's aftermath.

II. Constitution as instrument

Judicial efforts to emphasize the importance of reason in constitutional interpretation aligned with one of the Constitution's critical instrumental functions: to serve as an elaborate system of emotion management, channeling popular passions into institutional structures designed to bring deliberation, contemplation, and rationality into democratic decision making.[95] The document was written by a group of elite statesmen who saw collective emotions as volatile and chaotic, threatening to constitutional commitments, connected to divisive factionalism, and a potentially destructive force in public life.[96] The belief that "the passions of men will not conform to the dictates of reason and justice without constraint"[97] led to the design of constitutional institutions – like a bicameral legislature, large legislative districts, and an onerous and time-consuming amendment process – that would slow public decision making and allow reason to take hold.[98] In his 1826 *Commentaries on American Law*, James Kent complemented the Senate's ability "to destroy the evil effects of sudden and strong excitement, and of precipitate measures springing from passion, caprice, prejudice, personal influence, and party intrigue."[99]

Early nineteenth-century legal and political elites echoed Founding era beliefs about "passion's" detrimental impact on public decision making, seeing a clear division between law and politics as vital to creating the stability necessary for a commercial economy to thrive.[100] Reason held an exalted status over emotion, and the effective exercise of popular sovereignty required a balance of both.[101] Jefferson noted that "although the will of the people is in all cases to prevail, that will to be rightful must be reasonable."[102] As mob violence became a greater threat in the 1830s and started to affect the national debate over slavery, collective emotions began to seem more dangerous and destructive to the rule of law.[103] In his 1838 Lyceum speech, Abraham Lincoln reinforced a sharp hierarchy between reason and emotion: "passion has helped us; but can do so no more. It will in future be our enemy. Reason, cold, calculating, unimpassioned reason, must furnish all the materials for our future support and defence."[104] Antebellum judges often echoed these themes, warning about the threat that popular emotions and passion presented to the constitutional regime and the rule of law.[105]

Among many other forces contributing to the fragmentation of the Union,[106] growing sectionalism in the 1840s and 1850s placed extreme pressure on the ability of constitutional institutions to use political compromise as a mechanism to manage emotions in the absence of a social or political consensus about how to deal with slavery and western expansion. In both North and South, feelings that were inextricably linked to moral judgment[107] helped create a polarized and sectarian political environment, resulting in a nation with two very different emotional subcultures that constitutional structures seemed unable to deal with effectively.[108] Jealousy, an emotion viewed with sharp disdain by many Northerners, became a source of sectional unity in the South, where it became closely linked to the proslavery cause and generated a moral obligation for Southern whites to defend their rights and honor against Northern infringements. In the North, feelings of indignation about slavery, the beating of Senator Charles Sumner on the floor of United States Senate, and other affronts "nurtured a sense of moral superiority and unity of purpose"[109] against the slave power. Many antebellum constitutional movements increasingly relied upon a "paranoid style" that saw conspiracies at the heart of America's problems,[110] triggering strong feelings and sharp in-group/out-group distinctions that contributed to sectional division. These culturally validated emotions generated a strong sense of regional allegiance, making efforts by constitutional institutions to generate political or legal compromises about slavery nearly impossible.

As these tensions became more acute, the constitutional system's inability to manage the effects of passion became a major preoccupation among political elites. Throughout the lead-up to the

Civil War, many began to frame the conflict in explicitly emotional terms. Daniel Webster lamented that slavery had brought up "grievances, real or supposed, [that] alienate the minds of one portion of the country from the other, exasperate the feelings, subdue the sense of fraternal connect, and patriotic love, and mutual regard,"[111] while Jefferson warned that antislavery activism would "kindle such mutual and mortal hatred, as to render separation preferable to eternal discord."[112]

An emotional disease required an emotional cure.[113] Emotions that brought divergent perspectives together were seen as critical to ensuring that the Constitution made good on its promise of perpetuity and political union, just as divisive emotions were seen as pivotal to tearing that union apart. As Michael Woods demonstrates, an "affective theory of the Union" pervaded antebellum American political culture, embracing the idea that "the power of feeling, not force, made the United States uniquely harmonious and free."[114] Politicians from across the ideological spectrum thought the key to resolving sectional conflict lay in cultivating "brotherly feelings and harmony" and "a better feeling and more fraternal sentiments between the South and the North."[115] In his farewell address, Andrew Jackson recognized this critical role for emotions, asserting that the "foundations" of the constitutional regime lay "in the affections of the people."[116] Similarly, James Buchanan cautioned "that if the Union 'can not live in the affections of the people, it must one day perish.' "[117] John Quincy Adams' description was typical of many who saw the Union as a tie based in feelings, intuition, and spirit:[118] "the indissoluble link of Union between the people . . . is, after all, not in the right, but in the heart."[119] In his First Inaugural Address, Lincoln reinforced this same theme, where he imagined an America where the "mystic chords of memory" would "swell the chorus of the Union" and maintain "our bonds of affection."[120]

As sectional tensions increased, evangelicals used a discursive method that "addresse[d] itself to the heart" and "lay[ ] the foundations of union in . . . affections, sympathies, and hopes."[121] They saw a shared religious vision driven by emotion as the solution for a problem the symbolic Constitution seemed unable to solve: national unity. In Perry Miller's words, "the explosive Revival became a gallant effort, by insisting upon the purification of American hearts, to conserve the Republic."[122]

Antebellum literature fed into efforts on all sides, using feelings both to overcome increasingly rigid and irreconcilable social divisions and to stoke political passions. Whitman's *Leaves of Grass* is a massive literary effort to "hold America together" through emotional ties forged by a vision of common humanity, history, and democratic spirit.[123] Whitman prophesized that "affection shall solve the problems of freedom yet, Those who love each other shall become invincible, They shall make Columbia victorious."[124] In *Uncle Tom's Cabin*, Harriet Beecher Stowe used grief and other collective emotions to generate empathy and to facilitate interracial bonds between both characters and activists, while also generating emotional responses that would help galvanize the abolitionist movement.[125] Frederick Douglass said the book "rekindled the slumbering embers of anti-slavery zeal into an active flame. Its recitals have baptized with holy fire myriads who before cared nothing for the bleeding slave."[126] William Lloyd Garrison had a similar response: "We confess to the frequent moistening of our eyes, and the making of our heart grow liquid as water, and trembling every nerve within us, in the perusal of incidents and scenes so vividly depicted in her pages."[127]

III. Constitution as symbol

While reason was deemed essential to effective decision making within a constitutional system, the cultivation of certain emotions was also essential to constitutionalism's legitimacy and survival. Constitutional regimes sustain themselves through symbol, using myth, foundational text, iconography, and ritual to create emotional ties that legitimize the use of power over extended periods of time.[128] The creation of constitutional systems is "ideological and social in nature," a process that requires a culture to "shift allegiances, realign sources of authority, and cultivate new identities, mind-sets, and habits consistent with good citizenship."[129] Constitutions are a legal instrument for making and preserving long-term social commitments,[130] and symbols facilitate the affective attachments necessary for those commitments to sustain and legitimate themselves over time.[131] The determination of how individuals "felt" about the constitution requires attention to the use of cultural symbols as much as it requires attention to law.

Within this context, the most striking thing about the Constitution as a national cultural symbol in the antebellum era is its absence. When compared with the reverence and emotional rhetoric generated by the Declaration of Independence, the Founding generation (and George Washington in particular), the Revolutionary War, and the concept of Union, the Constitution itself seems, at times, to enjoy an almost second-class status within the world of antebellum American semiotics, emerging as a major national symbol only "slowly and inconclusively."[132] The Constitution's Golden Jubilee in 1837–1839 appears to have generated little enthusiasm (particularly when compared with the pomp and circumstances that accompanied the fiftieth anniversary of the Declaration of Independence in 1826),[133] the physical document itself spent much of its pre–Civil War life hidden from public display in the North Wing of the Treasury Department,[134] artistic images of the document and the Convention were relatively rare,[135] and many lamented the pervasive public ignorance about the document and its provisions.[136]

Indeed, the Declaration of Independence was a far more common and emotionally resonant symbol in antebellum political life. Abraham Lincoln referred to the Constitution as a mere "frame of silver" around the Declaration's "apple of gold," and both the Gettysburg Address and the Emancipation Proclamation reference the Declaration and 1776 rather than the Constitution and 1787 as the most important moment in the American cultural mythos.[137] Just prior to his inauguration, Lincoln observed that he had "never had a feeling politically that did not spring from sentiments embodied in the Declaration of Independence."[138] When compared with the Constitution, which was increasingly seen as a "compromise document," the Declaration offered a set of core principles that could form the basis for a coherent and unified national identity.[139] In Lincoln's words, it was the Declaration that provided the "electric cord . . . that links the hearts of patriotic and liberty loving men together."[140]

In the lead-up to the Civil War, the symbol of "Union" did far more work to generate emotional ties "of regard and reverence . . . [of] attachment and pride" to the Founding constitutional regime than the Constitution itself.[141] Union imagery was common in antebellum iconography, often portrayed by artists as a chain to provide comfort and reassurance during difficult times.[142] Many political leaders believed that the Union preceded and transcended the Constitution, which confirmed the Constitution's status as a secondary symbol within the antebellum political order.

The Constitution's failures and omissions, including the lack of any commitment to racial or sex equality, also made it an easy target for symbolic attack. Radical abolitionists like Wendell Phillips called it "a piece of parchment," while William Lloyd Garrison famously called it "a covenant with death, an agreement with hell."[143] This forced many to seek out and develop other texts capable of providing symbolic value that would generate a shared vision of equality and a common sense of humanity. Abolitionists sought out the Bible,[144] first-wave feminists created the 1848 Seneca Falls Declaration of Sentiments, Whitman called upon the power of epic poetry, while Lincoln relied heavily on the Declaration of Independence.

If the strength of symbols is tied to a strong foundational myth, the Constitution's semiotic weakness as a unifying symbol can be partially attributed to a lack of consensus around a unifying narrative about the Founding.[145] Secessionist Southern leaders subscribed to a contractual theory about the Constitution's formation in which states rather than the People were the agents that constituted the Republic through a legalistic compact that could be repudiated by the parties. By contrast, Unionists saw a Constitution that obtained its legitimacy from the People, created by a set of transcendent bonds that linked individuals together as part of a collective polity. The inability to reconcile these two founding stories – one transactional and impersonal, the other metaphysical and affective – made it challenging for the Constitution to cohere as a national symbol.

In the crowded world of post-revolutionary symbolism, the Constitution did maintain some cultural relevance. Whitman called the Constitution "a perfect and entire thing . . . the grandest piece of moral machinery ever constructed" whose "architects were some mighty prophets and gods."[146] John Calhoun situated the Constitution at the root of the nation's shared emotional connection, the instrument that made "the Union a union in truth – a bond of mutual affect and brotherhood, and not a mere connection."[147] Lincoln himself referenced emotions to describe his bond with the document when debating its meaning with David Dudley Field: "He loves [the Constitution] in his way; I in mine."[148] And there are numerous examples of the Constitution serving as a framing device for public discourse on all sides of the sectional conflict in the years right before the Civil War.[149]

Even if the Constitution never achieved true primacy as an emotionally resonant unifying symbol, constitutionalism nevertheless became embedded in the practices of more radical antebellum social movements that sought to reconstitute America's founding commitments. As a symbol of popular sovereignty, written constitutions based on the founding document retained value as a tool for "public acts of defiance" by groups who sought to renegotiate the terms of the 1787 text.[150] Several groups engaged in acts of constitution writing, using this new form of law to enhance the legal status of their moral principles and form a bridge between the emotional world of politics and a world of law that operated by inference from universal principles. John Brown's 1856 provisional constitution was an integral part of his moral war against slavery, while the 1861 Confederate constitution – despite substantial overlap with the content of the 1787 Constitution – became a vehicle for expressing "cultural sovereignty" and "regional distinctiveness."[151] Both documents are efforts to imagine and implement efforts to reconstitute the nation in ways that address slavery far more directly than the 1787 document ever did.

One remarkable outcome of the antebellum era is that the Constitution emerged without shouldering much of the blame for a conflict that left two percent of the American population dead on the battlefield. If the Constitution's primary symbolic mission was to create an affective environment of loyalty and allegiance that would allow the new nation to resolve disputes about deep-seated cultural questions without imploding, it is hard to see the 1787 document as anything short of an utter failure. Yet despite the paranoia provoked by the Reconstruction Amendments throughout large swaths of the South,[152] the late nineteenth century witnessed a period of cultural "constitution worship," where the narrative of the Union surviving the Civil War meant the Constitution emerged intact as well.[153] The document's substantive and symbolic failings were largely glossed over, causing *The Nation*'s E. L. Godkin to note during the Constitution's 1887 Centennial that "so little mention has been made of the failure of the instrument to overcome the main difficulties in the way of its original framers."[154]

IV. Future work

While it has attracted increased scholarly attention in recent years, the field of law and emotions remains relatively new, and there are many opportunities for major interdisciplinary contributions that use nineteenth-century legal and nonlegal sources to develop richer historical and cultural accounts of constitutional law from textual, instrumental, and symbolic perspectives.

Within the realm of text, there is no comprehensive account of the evolving and historically contingent relationship between constitutional interpretation and emotion or of the ways that the relationship developed differently from other areas of legal doctrine. From this starting point, there are a number of underexplored areas: in a system that maintains simultaneous normative commitments to judicial supremacy and various forms of popular constitutionalism, how did shifting beliefs about the effect of different emotions on legal and political decision making influence institutional power struggles over constitutional meaning? How have nonlegal texts described the relationship between feelings and legal decision making over time, and to what extent do literary and artistic portrayals of that relationship influence or accurately reflect the actual lived experiences of practitioners, judges, and other actors within the legal system? How do major constitutional disputes, like the tension between nationalism and state sovereignty, adopt narratives with a particular emotional valence within and outside law's domain? How did discourse about emotion help to define and alter interpretive struggles over class, sex, and race? What subcategories of persons were seen as capable of having emotions (or only capable of displaying particular emotions), and how did legal practitioners use narratives about emotional capacity to reinforce constitutional categories or spur constitutional change? How did feelings arise as a dynamic in the interpretation of state constitutions? How have changing cultural perceptions about collective emotions affected the dynamic relationship between public opinion and constitutional law?

As an instrument for emotion management, there is need for further work on exactly how the framers' assumptions about emotion and emotion management were embedded into constitutional design, the extent to which those assumptions were dependent on particular political realities, where those assumptions failed in the lead-up to the Civil War, and the degree to which contemporary understandings about the relationship between emotion and reason might help to explain that failure. There are larger questions as well: how, if at all, should constitutional design and institutions address the presence of multiple emotional subcultures within a heterogeneous society? How do interpretive systems perform in the absence of strong collective emotions, during periods of high public disengagement, inattention, and apathy? How did the framers of the Reconstruction Amendments think about the Constitution's emotion management function in the aftermath of the Civil War, and how did their assumptions affect legal and political developments in the Reconstruction and post-Reconstruction eras?

Finally, how did different subcultures, reform efforts, and social movements respond affectively to the Constitution as a symbol, and to what extent did narratives about those responses play a role in efforts to mobilize constitutional change? How did different power centers within American culture work to reinforce the Constitution's symbolic resonance, and to what extent did those efforts emphasize particular aspects of the constitutional regime and deemphasize others? How did feelings about the Constitution as a symbol evolve in response to the Reconstruction Amendments?

Notes

* Professor of law, New York Law School. Thanks to Ed Purcell and Rebecca Roiphe for their thoughts and comments, Michael Roffer for his incredible research assistance, and Daniel Ellis-Ferris for his support.

1 Michael P. Young, "A Revolution on the Soul: Transformative Experiences and Immediate Abolition," in *Passionate Politics and Social Movements*, ed. Jeff Goodwin, J. Jasper, and F. Polletta (Chicago: University of Chicago Press, 2001), 103; Robert H. Abzug, *Passionate Liberator: Theodore Dwight Weld and the Dilemma of Reform* (New York: Oxford University Press, 1980), 129.

2 There is an extensive body of multidisciplinary literature dedicated to exploring the widespread disagreement about how to define the term "emotion" and the way it intersects with concepts like "reason," "rationality," and "interests." Susan A. Bandes and Jeremy A. Blumenthal, "Emotion and the Law," *Annual*

Review of Law and Social Science 8 (2012): 161–81, 163–4. While the core "definitional" question is beyond the scope of this piece, for the purposes of this article, I use Bandes and Blumenthal's definition:

> Emotions are a set of evaluative and motivational processes, distributed throughout the brain, that assist us in appraising and reacting to stimuli and that are formed, interpreted, and communicated in social and cultural context. They help us screen, categorize, and interpret information; influence our evaluations of the intentions of others; and help us decide what is important or valuable. Perhaps most important, they drive us to care about the outcome of our decision making and motivate us to take action, or refrain from taking action, on the situations we evaluate.

Ibid. Reva Siegel defines "constitutional culture" as a "network of understandings and practices that structure our constitutional tradition, including those that shape law but would not be recognized as 'lawmaking' according to the legal system's own formative criteria." Reva B. Siegel, "Text in Contest: Gender and the Constitution from a Social Movement Perspective," *University of Pennsylvania Law Review* 150 (2001): 297–351, 303.

3 Robert L. Tsai, *America's Forgotten Constitutions: Defiant Visions of Power and Community* (Cambridge, Mass.: Harvard University Press, 2014), 2. Throughout the antebellum era, this ambivalence was often framed as a tension between "liberty" and "order." Michael Kammen, *Spheres of Liberty: Changing Perceptions of Liberty in American Culture* (Jackson: University Press of Mississippi, 2001), 69–75.

4 Paul W. Kahn, *The Cultural Study of Law: Restructuring Legal Scholarship* (Chicago: University of Chicago Press, 1999), 120–1.

5 Jon Elster, *Ulysses and the Sirens: Studies in Rationality and Irrationality* (New York: Cambridge University Press, 1984).

6 András Sajó, *Constitutional Sentiments* (New Haven, Conn.: Yale University Press, 2011), 4; Peggy A. Thoits, "The Sociology of Emotions," *Annual Review of Sociology* 15 (1989): 317–42, 336.

7 Jon Elster, *Ulysses Unbound: Studies in Rationality, Precommitment, and Constraints* (New York: Cambridge University Press, 2000), 130–1.

8 Barry Friedman, *The Will of the People: How Public Opinion Has Influenced the Supreme Court and Shaped the Meaning of the Constitution* (New York: Farrar, Straus and Giroux, 2009).

9 The primary focus of this chapter is the United States Constitution. But the historical narrative of nineteenth-century American constitutional law also includes state constitutions, which underwent dramatic transformations during the antebellum era. Laura Scalia, *America's Jeffersonian Experiment: Remaking State Constitutions, 1820–1850* (DeKalb: Northern Illinois University Press, 1999).

10 John Corrigan, *Business of the Heart: Religion and Emotion in the Nineteenth Century* (Berkeley: University of California Press, 2002), 4.

11 Shelly Chaiken and Yaakov Trope, eds., *Dual-Process Theories in Social Psychology* (New York: Guilford Press, 1999); David Hume, *A Treatise of Human Nature*, ed. David F. Norton and Mary J. Norton (1738; Oxford: Oxford University Press, 2007).

12 Antonio R. Damasio, *Descartes' Error: Emotion, Reason, and the Human Brain* (New York: Penguin Books, 2005); Joseph E. LeDoux, *The Emotional Brain: The Mysterious Underpinnings of Emotional Life* (New York: Simon & Schuster, 1996).

13 Drew Westen, *The Political Brain: The Role of Emotion in Deciding the Fate of the Nation* (New York: PublicAffairs, 2007); Robert H. Frank, *Passions within Reason: The Strategic Role of the Emotions* (New York: Norton, 1988).

14 Keith Oatley, Dacher Keltner, and Jennifer M. Jenkins, *Understanding Emotions* (Malden, Mass.: Blackwell, 2006).

15 Doni Gewirtzman, "Our Founding Feelings: Emotion, Commitment, and Imagination in Constitutional Culture," *University of Richmond Law Review* 43 (2009): 623–83, 668–9.

16 Merrill D. Peterson, ed., *The Portable Thomas Jefferson* (New York: Penguin, 1975), 290–2.

17 Perry Miller, *The Life of the Mind in America: From the Revolution to the Civil War* (New York: Harcourt, Brace & World, 1965), 100.

18 Alfred L. Brophy, "Reason and Sentiment: The Moral Worlds and Modes of Reasoning of Antebellum Jurists" (book review), *Boston University Law Review* 79 (1999): 1161–214, 1169–76.

19 For more on the relationship between class tensions and interpretive method, see Richard D. Parker, *Here, the People Rule: A Constitutional Populist Manifesto* (Cambridge, Mass.: Harvard University Press, 1998).

20 Larry D. Kramer, *The People Themselves: Popular Constitutionalism and Judicial Review* (New York: Oxford University Press, 2004), 164.

21 G. Edward White, *The Marshall Court and Cultural Change 1815–1835* (New York: Oxford University Press, 1991), 755.
22 Kramer, *The People Themselves*, 45.
23 Andrew Burstein, *Sentimental Democracy: The Evolution of America's Romantic Self-Image* (New York: Hill & Wang, 1999), 4–6.
24 Ibid., 4.
25 Ibid., 5; Sarah Knott, *Sensibility and the American Revolution* (Chapel Hill: University of North Carolina Press, 2009), 22.
26 Burstein, *Sentimental Democracy*, 6–7.
27 Jan Lewis, "'Those Scenes for Which Alone My Heart Was Made': Affection and Politics in the Age of Jefferson and Hamilton," in *An Emotional History of the United States*, ed. Peter N. Stearns and Jan Lewis (New York: New York University Press, 1998), 54.
28 Nicole Eustace, *1812: War and the Passions of Patriotism* (Philadelphia: University of Pennsylvania Press, 2012), xi–xii.
29 Eustace, *1812*, xii–xiv.
30 Michael E. Woods, *Emotional and Sectional Conflict in the Antebellum United States* (New York: Cambridge University Press, 2014), 37.
31 Lewis, "Those Scenes," 57.
32 *The Federalist* No. 14; Lewis, "Those Scenes," 57.
33 Burstein, *Sentimental Democracy*, 270.
34 Alfred L. Brophy, "The Road to the Gettysburg Address," *Florida State University Law Review* 43 (forthcoming 2016); Alfred L. Brophy, "The Republics of Liberty and Letters: Progress, Union, and Constitutionalism in the Graduation Addresses at the University of North Carolina," *North Carolina Law Review* 89 (2011): 1879–964, 1940–9.
35 Michael Kammen, *A Machine That Would Go of Itself: The Constitution in American Culture* (New York: Knopf, 1986), 13.
36 Kramer, *The People Themselves*, 45–9.
37 Ibid., 108–13.
38 Jason Mazzone, "The Creation of a Constitutional Culture," *Tulsa Law Review* 40 (2005): 671–98, 673–4.
39 Stephen M. Engel, *American Politicians Confront the Court: Opposition Politics and Changing Responses to Judicial Power* (New York: Cambridge University Press, 2011), 74, 129; Daniel J. Hulsebosch, *Constituting Empire: New York and the Transformation of Constitutionalism in the Atlantic World 1664–1830* (Chapel Hill: University of North Carolina Press, 2005), 256.
40 Kramer, *The People Themselves*, 200; Jed H. Shugarman, *The People's Courts: Pursuing Judicial Independence in America* (Cambridge, Mass.: Harvard University Press, 2012), 49–56.
41 Gerald Leonard, "Jefferson's Constitutions," in *Constitutions and the Classics: Patterns of Constitutional Thought from John Fortescue to Jeremy Bentham*, ed. Denis Galligan (New York: Oxford University Press, 2014).
42 Gerald Leonard, *The Invention of Party Politics: Federalism, Popular Sovereignty, and Constitutional Development in Jacksonian Illinois* (Chapel Hill: University of North Carolina Press, 2002), 1.
43 Ibid., 14; Engel, *American Politicians*, 144.
44 Leonard, *Invention of Party Politics*, 251; Gerard N. Magliocca, *Andrew Jackson and the Constitution: The Rise and Fall of Generational Regimes* (Lawrence: University Press of Kansas, 2007), 61–73.
45 Shugarman, *The People's Courts*, 105–6.
46 David S. Reynolds, *Walt Whitman's America: A Cultural Biography* (New York: Alfred A. Knopf, 1995), 166–75.
47 Thomas Hunter, "The Institutionalization of Legal Education in North Carolina, 1790–1920," in *The History of Legal Education in the United States: Commentaries and Primary Sources, Volume I*, ed. Steve Sheppard (Pasadena, Calif.: Salem Press, 1999), 420.
48 Kramer, *The People Themselves*, 168. Alexis De Tocqueville described presidential elections as intense, emotional departures from a "calmer season," where the "ardor of action is redoubled . . . all the artificial passions which the imagination can create in the bosom of a happy and peaceful land are agitated and bright to light . . . [and] the whole nation glows with feverish excitement."
49 Miller, *Life of the Mind*, 65.
50 John W. Compton, *The Evangelical Origins of the Living Constitution* (Cambridge, Mass.: Harvard University Press, 2014), 29.

51 Reynolds, *Walt Whitman's America*, 155.
52 Corrigan, *Business of the Heart*, 10.
53 David S. Reynolds, *Beneath the American Renaissance: The Subversive Imagination in the Age of Emerson and Melville* (New York: Knopf, 1988), 64.
54 Ibid., 62–76.
55 Peter Karsten, *Heart versus Head: Judge-Made Law in Nineteenth-Century America* (Chapel Hill: University of North Carolina Press, 1997), 293.
56 Compton, *Evangelical Origins*, 15; Sarah Barringer Gordon, *The Spirit of the Law: Religious Voices and the Constitution in Modern America* (Cambridge, Mass.: Harvard University Press, 2010), 7–9.
57 Compton, *Evangelical Origins*, 8.
58 Ibid., 16–17.
59 Miller, *Life of the Mind*, 188.
60 William E. Nelson, "The Impact of the Antislavery Movement upon Styles of Judicial Reasoning in the Nineteenth Century," *Harvard Law Review* 87 (1974): 513–66, 525–7.
61 András Sajó, "Emotions in Constitutional Institutions," *Emotion Review* 8 (2016): 44–9.
62 Nelson, "Impact of the Antislavery Movement," 534–5. This is not to suggest that antislavery advocates saw moral or natural law readings of the Constitution as driven by emotion and feeling. To the contrary, many abolitionists saw themselves as employing conventional legal reasoning techniques, using deduction and inference to apply universal principles to specific circumstances.
63 Young, "Revolution on the Soul," 106, 112.
64 Woods, *Emotional and Sectional Conflict*, 150.
65 Elizabeth B. Clark, "'The Sacred Rights of the Weak': Pain, Suffering, and the Culture of Individual Rights in Antebellum America," *Journal of American History* 82 (1995): 463–93.
66 Morton J. Horwitz, *The Transformation of American Law, 1780–1860* (Cambridge, Mass.: Harvard University Press, 1977), 1–30.
67 Nelson, "Impact of the Antislavery Movement," 520–1.
68 Bruce A. Green and Rebecca Roiphe, "Regulating Discourtesy on the Bench: A Study in the Evolution of Judicial Independence," *New York University Annual Survey of American Law* 64 (2008): 497–557, 508.
69 Ibid.; Simon Stern, "Blackstone's Legal Actors: The Passions of a Rational Jurist," in *Impassioned Jurisprudence: Law, Literature and Emotion, 1660–1800*, ed. Nancy Johnson (Lewisburg, Pa.: Bucknell University Press, 2014), 1–19.
70 Karsten, *Heart versus Head*, 4–8.
71 Ibid., 25–46; Polly J. Price, "Precedent and Judicial Power after the Founding," *Boston College Law Review* 42 (2000): 81–121, 102.
72 Horwitz, *Transformation of American Law*, 255–6.
73 Ibid., 256–9.
74 William P. LaPiana, *Logic and Experience: The Origin of Modern American Legal Education* (New York: Oxford University Press, 1994), 29, 35.
75 Joseph Story, *Commentaries on the Constitution* (Boston: Hilliard Gray & Co., 1833), 383; Robert M. Cover, *Justice Accused: Antislavery and the Judicial Process* (New Haven, Conn.: Yale University Press, 1975), 136.
76 Ibid.
77 Kammen, *Machine*, xxii.
78 Miller, *Life of the Mind*, 119.
79 Daniel W. Howe, *What Hath God Wrought: The Transformation of America, 1815–1848* (New York: Oxford University Press, 2007), 123; Kramer, *The People Themselves*, 184–5.
80 LaPiana, *Logic and Experience*, 29.
81 Kramer, *The People Themselves*, 164.
82 White, *The Marshall Court*, 740.
83 Cover, *Justice Accused*, 29.
84 White, *The Marshall Court*, 374.
85 *State v. Post*, 20 N.J.L. 386, 369 (1845); Cover, *Justice Accused*, 56–7.
86 Cover, *Justice Accused*, 121.
87 Ibid., 119.
88 *Scott v. Sandford*, 60 U.S. 393, 620 (1856) (Curtis, J., dissenting); Mark A. Graber, *Dred Scott and the Problem of Constitutional Evil* (New York: Cambridge University Press, 2006), 77.

89 Harriet Beecher Stowe, *A Key to Uncle Tom's Cabin* (Boston: Jewett, 1853), 82; Alfred L. Brophy, "Humanity, Utility, and Logic in Southern Legal Thought: Harriet Beecher Stowe's Vision in Dred: A Tale of the Great Dismal Swamp," *Boston University Law Review* 78 (1998): 1113–61, 1136–7.
90 Stowe, *Key*, 77; Brophy, "Humanity," 1136.
91 Harriet Beecher Stowe, *Dred: A Tale of the Great Dismal Swamp* (Cambridge, Mass.: Riverside Press, 1856), 438; Brophy, "Humanity," 1138.
92 Reynolds, *Walt Whitman's America*, 337.
93 Brophy, "Humanity," 1116–17.
94 Cover, *Justice Accused*, 1–6.
95 Gewirtzman, "Our Founding Feelings," 645; *Federalist* no. 49, in *The Federalist*, ed. Jacob E. Cooke (Middletown, Conn.: Wesleyan University Press, 1961), 343 (James Madison) ("[I]t is the reason, alone, of the public, that ought to control and regulate the government. The passions ought to be controlled and regulated by the government."); White, *The Marshall Court*, 54.
96 Richard K. Matthews, *If Men Were Angels: James Madison and the Heartless Empire of Reason* (Lawrence: University Press of Kansas, 1995), 81; Cheryl Hall, *The Trouble with Passion: Political Theory Beyond the Reign of Reason* (New York: Routledge, 2005), 23–4 (2005); Kammen, *Spheres of Liberty*, 72–9.
97 *Federalist* no. 15, in *The Federalist*, ed. Cooke, 96 (Alexander Hamilton).
98 Gewirtzman, "Founding Feelings," 647.
99 Miller, *Life of the Mind*, 216.
100 Saul Cornell, "The People's Constitution vs. the Lawyer's Constitution: Popular Constitutionalism and the Original Debate over Originalism," *Yale Journal of Law & the Humanities* 23 (2011): 295–337, 307–8.
101 Kramer, *The People Themselves*, 111–12; Terry A. Maroney, "The Persistent Cultural Script of Judicial Dispassion," *California Law Review* 99 (2011): 629–81, 634–6.
102 Thomas Jefferson, First Inaugural Address (March 4, 1801), in *A Compilation of the Messages and Papers of the Presidents*, ed. James D. Richardson (Washington, D.C.: Government Printing Office, 1897), 1: 321, 322–3; Kramer, *The People Themselves*, 112.
103 David Grimsted, *American Mobbing, 1828–1861: Toward Civil War* (New York: Oxford University Press, 1998).
104 Abraham Lincoln, "Address Before the Young Men's Lyceum of Springfield, Illinois (January 27, 1838)," in *The Collected Works of Abraham Lincoln*, ed. Roy P. Basler (New Brunswick, N.J.: Rutgers University Press), 1: 108, 115.
105 Brophy, "Reason and Sentiment," 1180–1.
106 Michael E. Woods, "What Twenty-First Century Historians Have Said about the Causes of Disunion: A Civil War Sesquicentennial Review of the Recent Literature," *Journal of American History* 99 (2012): 415–39.
107 For more on emotions and moral judgment, see Jonathan Haidt, "The Emotional Dog and Its Rational Tail: A Social Intuitionist Approach to Moral Judgment," *Psychology Review* 108 (2001): 813–34, 823.
108 Woods, *Emotional and Sectional Conflict*, 2.
109 Ibid., 150.
110 Ronald G. Waters, *American Reformers 1815–1860* (New York: Hill & Wang, 1997), 10–11; James H. Huston, "The Origins of 'The Paranoid Style in American Politics': Public Jealousy from the Age of Walpole to the Age of Jackson," in *Saints and Revolutionaries*, ed. David D. Hall (New York: Norton, 1984), 332–72.
111 Woods, *Emotional and Sectional Conflict*, 26–7.
112 Ibid., 28.
113 Ibid., 26.
114 Ibid., 22.
115 Ibid., 27.
116 Ibid., 22.
117 Ibid., 23.
118 Paul C. Nagel, *One Nation Indivisible: The Union in American Thought 1776–1861* (New York: Oxford University Press, 1964), 69.
119 Woods, *Emotional and Sectional Conflict*, 24.
120 Abraham Lincoln, "First Inaugural Address (March 4, 1861)," in *Abraham Lincoln: Complete Works*, ed. John G. Nicolay and John Hay (1894; New York: Century, 1902), 2: 7.
121 Miller, *Life of the Mind*, 65.

122 Ibid., 72.
123 Reynolds, *Walt Whitman's America*, 307.
124 Walt Whitman, "Over the Carnage Rose Prophetic a Voice," *Leaves of Grass*.
125 David S. Reynolds, *Mightier Than the Sword: Uncle Tom's Cabin and the Battle for America* (New York: Norton, 2011), 88–9.
126 Ibid., 129–30.
127 Ibid., 130.
128 David I. Kertzer, *Ritual, Politics, and Power* (New Haven, Conn.: Yale University Press, 1989), 60–5, 133; Martha C. Nussbaum, *Political Emotions: Why Love Matters for Justice* (Cambridge, Mass.: Harvard University Press, 2013), 134.
129 Tsai, *Forgotten Constitutions*, 4.
130 Jed Rubenfeld, *Freedom and Time: A Theory of Constitutional Self-Government* (New Haven, Conn.: Yale University Press, 2001); Elster, *Ulysses Unbound*.
131 Gewirtzman, "Founding Feelings," 630.
132 Kammen, *Machine*, 90.
133 Ibid., 89–90.
134 Ibid., 72–3.
135 Ibid., 91–2.
136 Ibid., 3–4.
137 George P. Fletcher, *Our Secret Constitution: How Lincoln Redefined American Democracy* (New York: Oxford University Press, 2001), 36–7.
138 Priscilla Wald, *Constituting Americans: Cultural Anxiety and Narrative Form* (Durham, N.C.: Duke University Press, 1995), 48.
139 Ibid., 49.
140 Ibid., 59.
141 Nagel, *One Nation Indivisible*, 21.
142 Ibid., 211.
143 G. Edward White, *Law in American History* (New York: Oxford University Press, 2012), 1: 342–3.
144 Howe, *What Hath God Wrought*, 475.
145 Mark E. Brandon, *Free in the World: American Slavery and Constitutional Failure* (Princeton, N.J.: Princeton University Press, 1998), 63.
146 Reynolds, *Walt Whitman's America*, 144.
147 Nagel, *One Nation Indivisible*, 21.
148 Brian McGinty, *Lincoln's Greatest Case: The River, the Bridge, and the Making of America* (New York: Norton, 2015), 21.
149 Laura F. Edwards, *A Legal History of the Civil War and Reconstruction: A Nation of Rights* (New York: Cambridge University Press, 2015), 1–2.
150 Tsai, *Forgotten Constitutions*, 16.
151 Ibid., 118–51.
152 Mark W. Summers, *A Dangerous Stir: Fear, Paranoia, and the Making of Reconstruction* (Chapel Hill: University of North Carolina Press, 2009).
153 Kammen, *Machine*, 22, 153.
154 Ibid., 141.

20
BEYOND BELIEF
Religion, law, and popular culture in the "forgotten century"

Deborah Whitehead

In his landmark 1835 survey of American political and social life, *Democracy in America*, Alexis de Tocqueville famously remarked, "In the United States religion exercises but little influence upon the laws and upon the details of public opinion; but it directs the customs of the community, and by regulating domestic life, it regulates the state." By "religion," he meant Christianity, which, he said, "reigns without obstacle, by universal consent." He continued:

> Religion in America takes no direct part in the government of society, but it must be regarded as the first of their political institutions; for if it does not impart a taste for freedom, it facilitates the use of it. Indeed, it is in this same point of view that the inhabitants of the United States themselves look upon religious belief. I do not know whether all Americans have a sincere faith in their religion – for who can search the human heart? – but I am certain that they hold it to be indispensable to the maintenance of republican institutions.[1]

Tocqueville's travels through the United States convinced him that while religion played "no direct part" in law and government, it exerted tremendous power to regulate these spheres *indirectly* via religion's strong influence on domestic and community life. His observations highlight the intricate relationship between religion and politics in early nineteenth-century America and emphasize the importance ascribed to individual religious *belief* – even if not sincerely held – as a social good with the power to shape public life. Tocqueville argued that the heritage of Anglo-American Protestantism indelibly shaped the emergence and maintenance of a popular democratic sensibility in the United States, one that was widely shared by Americans of diverse religious persuasions and that undergirded the young republic's fragile federalism. But Tocqueville's optimism about the inclusive nature of a generically Christian democratic populism is belied by the many religious, legal, and political contestations over American identity that loomed large over the course of the century. The same Anglo-American heritage Tocqueville praised also functioned to control and in some cases coerce and punish non-Protestant religious practice. These attempts to regulate the practices of minority religious groups under the law disturb our familiar clichés about the progressive and untroubled increase of religious freedom from the founding of the United States in the late eighteenth century to the present. This chapter explores two particular instances of contestation over the meaning and scope of "religion" that found expression in the law and popular culture in nineteenth-century America. Surveying a range of materials from legal cases to fiction to editorial cartoons, I show how the language of "belief" became a primary way of framing the relationship between religion and the law and how this formulation intersected with Protestant anxieties about increasing religious diversity, rhetoric of the United States as a Christian nation, and debates about "true" versus "false" religion in ways that continue to impact the present.

The First Amendment, ratified in 1791 as part of the Bill of Rights, states that "Congress shall make no law respecting an establishment of religion, or prohibiting the free exercise thereof." These words constitute the two so-called religion clauses among the First Amendment's protections of civil liberties. The Establishment Clause accomplished religious disestablishment at the federal level and helped to inaugurate the decades-long process of state disestablishment, a process sometimes referred to as "the second disestablishment," although its process was far from uniform or smooth.[2] This process of severing formal church–state ties extended from the passage of the Virginia Statute of Religious Freedom in 1786, authored by Thomas Jefferson, to well into the nineteenth century, when Massachusetts finally relinquished its town-centered system of church support, becoming the last state to disestablish in 1833. Because the familiar narrative of religious liberty in American history often jumps from the First Amendment to the flurry of religious freedom cases beginning in the mid-twentieth century, the nineteenth century is often overlooked in surveys of religion and law. Legal scholar Steven Green notes that "for years, the nineteenth century was the 'forgotten century' for traditional views of church–state relations," whereas it should more properly be understood as "the crucible for a religious identity that left an indelible imprint on the culture and its institutions."[3] For Green, religion in nineteenth-century America represents a "rich paradox": discourses of the United States as a "Christian nation" embodied in evangelical Protestant "revivals and reform associations, blasphemy and Sabbath laws, religious oath requirements, and state maintenance of a Protestant-oriented public school system" coexisted with a dramatic national increase in religious diversity as the result of mass immigration.[4] Untangling these seemingly contradictory strands reveals a much more complicated picture of the development of religious liberty.

In the early 1800s, the U.S. Constitution anchored a weak federalist model of government in which the protections of the Bill of Rights limited the power of the federal government but did not apply to states. The establishment clause prevented the federal government from establishing a national church, yet at the same time it "protected the established religions in six of the original thirteen states from federal interference," precisely because the clause was held to apply at the national level only and not to states.[5] The passage of the Fourteenth Amendment after the Civil War extended the federal guarantee of civil rights to states, but the Supreme Court would not directly apply First Amendment protections to state infringements of individuals' rights to free exercise until 1940, when *Cantwell v. Connecticut* upheld the ability of Jehovah's Witnesses to canvas neighborhoods to proselytize. This meant that in the nineteenth century, religious minorities who looked to the federal government to uphold what they believed were their constitutionally guaranteed rights to religious freedom over and against oppressive and discriminatory state and local actions found no such safe haven. Mormon citizens, for example, who regarded themselves as faithful Americans and the Constitution as divinely ordained, were unsuccessful in their attempts to secure federal protection from local and state harassment, including an 1838 extermination order by the governor of Missouri, since, under the federalist system, "the protection of the religious freedom of individual citizens was a local rather than a national affair."[6]

Conceptions of church–state relations in the nineteenth century also "dovetailed comfortably with Protestantism" and reflected what Sarah Barringer Gordon calls "a fundamentally Protestant conception of religious liberty," characterized by democratic principles of "local decision-making, majority rule, and a minister's accountability to his congregation."[7] Such a conception of religious liberty as meshing with Protestant sensibilities as opposed to distant hierarchical authorities reflected widespread nativism and anti-Catholic bias and meant that any attempts to claim First Amendment protection for non-Protestant religions were immediately coded as antidemocratic and "sectarian." At the same time, a peculiarly Protestant conception of religion itself, primarily understood in terms of "belief" or individual assent to propositions, undergirded the developing notion of religious liberty. Talal Asad has shown how this modern Western conception of religion derives from a particular set of historical and political conditions such as the rise of the modern nation-state, the decoupling of religion from authorizing discourses of state power and knowledge, and the subsequent marginalization and abstract universalization of religion as a discourse of belief. This dramatically narrowed formulation, whereby religion comes to occupy a separate sphere from the domains of law, politics and science, "is a product of the only legitimate space allowed to Christianity by post-Enlightenment society, the right to individual *belief*."[8] Winnifred Sullivan argues that the legal consequences of such a conceptual shift have been far-reaching: it has only been the "modern protestant kind" of religion, she argues, that has been "free" in the course of U.S. history because legal protections for religion have depended upon a particular conception of religion as that which is "private, voluntary, individual, textual, and believed." This is juxtaposed with a notion of religion as "public, coercive, communal, oral, and enacted," which has been "closely regulated by law," historically associated most strongly with Roman Catholicism, and far more common globally.[9] The processes by which these developments of particular understandings of "religion" took shape in law and popular culture in the nineteenth century are historically instructive, for they show us how "specific forms of Protestant belief and practice come enduringly to be subsumed under the heading of 'Christian' – to the exclusion of non-Protestant and differently Protestant ways of being Christian – and how, in many cases, . . . the 'Christian' comes to stand in for the 'religious' to the exclusion of non-Christian ways of being religious."[10] According to Tracy Fessenden, this specifically Protestant formulation of religion exerted tremendous power to define and regulate *both* the domains of "the religious" and its purported opposite, "the secular."

But federal disestablishment also fostered a climate of religious voluntarism that found expression in the Second Great Awakening, a period of intense religious revivalism and growth in the early republic. From this fertile soil grew many new religious movements, including Methodism, the Baptists, the Church of Jesus Christ of Latter-Day Saints (Mormonism), independent African American churches, and the Disciples of Christ/Christians.[11] Between 1776 and 1850, the American religious landscape shifted dramatically from one dominated by state-supported churches like Episcopalianism and Congregationalism to one dominated by evangelical Protestantism. With their emphases on individual conversion and social reform, evangelical Protestant denominations like Baptists and Methodists grew rapidly in the early nineteenth century without any formal church–state ties, based on grassroots organizing, transatlantic communication networks, new forms of religious publishing, itinerant preachers (circuit riders), outdoor revivals, and "new methods" drawn from popular entertainment.

Evangelical Protestantism's numbers were strongest on the frontier, but the frontier was also the locus of many challenges to their aspirations for individual and national conversion. Facing stiff competition for national dominance from Catholics, Mormons, and Spiritualists, among other contenders in the highly competitive U.S. religious landscape, evangelical Protestants doubled down on their "Christian nation" rhetoric and attempted to forge new kinds of church–state ties in the spaces opened up by state disestablishment. The exercise of Protestant influence at the local, state, and national levels, particularly courts and schools, became an attempt to shore up this power while also regulating other, non-Protestant forms of religious expression in public life. At the same time, evangelicals sought to shape the new nation's destiny as a distinctively Protestant one through participating in missionary efforts at home and abroad, promoting assimilationist policies, and supporting the doctrine of manifest destiny.

Derek Chang has coined the term "evangelical nationalism" to describe the "overlapping civic and religious belief in the exceptional, providential destiny of America as a Christian nation" among evangelical Protestants, a belief that was both "fueled by the mandate to convert more souls and supported by geographic and demographic expansion."[12] In the aftermath of the emancipation of millions of African Americans in the South after the Civil War, assimilationist government policies toward Native Americans, the arrival of millions of Catholics and Jews on the East Coast, and the arrival of tens of thousands of Chinese on the West Coast, nineteenth-century Anglo-American Protestant anxieties about racial difference and assimilation found expression in the visionary hope of transforming all of these diverse elements into a unified Christian nation and Protestant empire. The doctrine of manifest destiny, articulated by Harvard professor John Fiske in an 1885 lecture, provided political-religious justification for U.S. westward expansion, as it claimed the continent by divine right and promised to bring Anglo-Saxon civilization and Protestant Christianity to the "uncivilized" western territories, by then home not just to Native Americans but also to a large community of Latter-Day Saints in Utah and Roman Catholics of Hispanic descent in the Southwest and California.[13] Congregationalist minister Josiah Strong's popular tract *Our Country* (1885) argued that "the final competition of the races" was at hand, and the apocalyptic battleground for America's destiny would be the West. Though civilization was endangered by the threats of Roman Catholicism, Mormonism, urbanism, parochial schools, alcohol, immigration, socialism, and the love of wealth, Strong argued that disaster could be averted if the "mighty Anglo-Saxon race" would claim its messianic role to establish a Protestant empire at home and abroad.[14] *Our Country* sold more than 175,000 copies during its first thirty years, and remains the most famous example of nineteenth-century evangelical Protestant nativism.

Strong's concern for the establishment of Protestant empire at home, specifically in the West, is also an important example of nineteenth-century anti-Mormon rhetoric. The Church of Jesus Christ of Latter-Day Saints was founded in 1830 in upstate New York by Joseph Smith and grew rapidly as the nascent movement, led by Smith as its Prophet and President, spread its controversial new revelation of Jesus Christ, contained in scripture called the *Book of Mormon*. The community fled religious persecution from New York to Missouri to Ohio to Illinois and found no constitutional protections from state-sanctioned violence, and in 1844 Smith was assassinated by an angry mob while in jail in Carthage, Illinois. Mormons moved westward during the great migration of 1846–47, in which Brigham Young led thousands of the faithful across the Mississippi and the Plains to establish a new settlement in Utah territory, where they claimed the right to self-govern. Yet once the long-rumored Mormon practice of polygamy was officially confirmed by Young in 1852 in his capacity as Church President and Prophet, an intense constitutional conflict over religion and law began to take shape in nineteenth-century America.

Nativist critiques of Catholicism and Mormonism accused them of

> (1) deliberately subverting American values; (2) posing a threat to the constitutional separation of church and state; (3) submitting to autocratic control from Rome and Salt Lake City . . .; (4) sponsoring secret ceremonies of dubious repute; and (5) encouraging the licentious or economic exploitation of women.[15]

The last concern was specifically directed at the practice of polygamy, which in the mid-nineteenth century "became the preoccupation of novelists, journalists, political cartoonists, and newspaper editors, clerics, lecturers, lobbyists, women's rights activists, political theorists, missionaries, state and local politicians, criminal defendants and their families, constitutional and criminal defense lawyers, federal and territorial officials, presidents, and Supreme Court justices."[16] The Republican Party's platform in 1856 included the express provisions of combatting what it termed "the twin relics of barbarism – Polygamy and Slavery" in the U.S. territories.[17] As Gordon argues, "the identification of slavery with Mormon polygamy allowed opponents of both to claim that the patriarchs of Utah and those of the slaveholding states and territories violated Christian mandates" and hence rhetorically situated the Republican party as the protector of Christianity and civilization.[18] The platform also represented an opening salvo in the push for federal legislation to counter states' rights, and in particular, the right of the federal government to intervene in "domestic relations," a category encompassing both marriage and slavery. The so-called Mormon Question, then, was central not just to the issue of states' rights but also to the matter of religion and law in the nineteenth century more generally, as I will discuss.

An editorial cartoon by Thomas Nast exemplifies the political, legal, and religious dimensions of nativism during this time period, as American Catholics and Mormons both attempted to contest Protestant dominance in the public sphere by claiming the religious protections of the Constitution (see Figure 20.1). For Catholics, the issue was Protestant bias in public schools; for Mormons, the issue was the right to practice polygamy in accordance with their religious convictions. Nast's cartoon illustrates how such claims on the part of religious minorities were *not*, contra Tocqueville, seen as participating in and extending a national shared understanding of religious liberty. Instead, the Protestant majority interpreted such claims unsympathetically, as hostile, "sectarian," and "foreign." Captioned "Religious liberty is guaranteed: but can we allow foreign reptiles to crawl all over us?," the cartoon depicts two menacing reptiles, a crocodile labeled "Roman Church" and a turtle labeled "Mormon Church," atop the U.S. Capitol.

Figure 20.1 Thomas Nast, drawing, "Religious liberty is guaranteed: but can we allow foreign reptiles to crawl all over us?" (1880)

Source: Library of Congress

For Nast, the issue was clear: religious liberty as the "law of the land" had its limits, and First Amendment protections did not extend to these heretical, "foreign" entities.

A series of anti-Mormon and anti-Catholic novels printed during the nineteenth century reflected a similar set of anxieties about threats to a Protestant Christian nation. With titles like *Master-Key to Popery*, *Mysteries of Popery Unveiled*, *Priestcraft Exposed*, *Danger in the Dark: A Tale of Intrigue and Priestcraft*, *The Female Jesuit, Or a Spy in the Family*; *The Nun*, and *Six Months in a Convent*, these sensational anti-Catholic novels, circulating from the 1830s through the end of the century, claimed to expose the dark secrets of convents and of the Roman Catholic Church more generally and fueled mob attacks such as the burning of the Ursuline convent in Charlestown, Massachusetts, in 1834.[19] *The Awful Disclosures of Maria Monk*, with all of the intrigue of a Gothic horror novel, outsold them all. First published in 1836 and popularized by the nativist newspaper *American Protestant Vindicator*, it purported to be an account of the abuses suffered by a young nun who had escaped from the Hotel Dieu convent in Montreal after witnessing horrors like murder and infanticide. Monk's narrative went on to sell three hundred thousand copies by the start of the Civil War and continued to be reprinted well into the twentieth century, despite serious questions about her credibility and mental stability. Even the *Vindicator* came to believe that the book was largely fiction and written not by Monk herself but rather by her sometime companion, an opportunistic anti-Catholic activist named William Hoyte.

Terryl Givens notes that anti-Mormon literature appeared mid-century against a historical backdrop in which "the question of American identity was moved from the realm of abstract Tocquevillian conjecture to explicit political debate."[20] A genre of some eighty anti-Mormon novels appearing from the 1850s forward, such as Orvilla Belisle's *The Prophets; Or, Mormonism Unveiled*, similarly drew on a seemingly vast Protestant imagination of Mormonism's secrets and abuses, often from a common ground of nativist sentiment; Belisle, for example, had also authored an anti-Catholic novel. According to Timothy Marr, anti-Mormon novels were one means by which "Protestant Christians rendered Mormonism into a domestic Islam," figuring the West as a "domestic orient," Joseph Smith as the "American Mahomet," the *Book of Mormon* as a new Qur'an, and the migration to Utah as a "hegira" (from the Arabic *hijrah*) on the model of Muhammad's flight from Mecca to Medina in 622.[21] The effect of these associations, which reflected Protestant perceptions of Islam as a Christian heresy as well as anxieties about national expansionism, represented the western part of the continent as an untamed, "barbarous" territory threatening the orthodox Christian nation and served to associate Mormonism in a broader discourse of Islam in the modern Western imagination. Just as Islam had threatened Christian Europe, so too was Mormonism threatening Christian civilization in America.

But it was the issue of polygamy and the protection of monogamous marriage as a bulwark of national virtue that occupied most of the energies of anti-Mormon novelists. The antipolygamy campaign, according to Gordon, attracted so much popular support because it evidenced a "profound concern with the imposition and maintenance of monogamy as an essential component of democracy, liberty, and stability"; polygamy therefore threatened the nation by threatening the home, "our national hearthstone," and "corrupting the very fount of virtue and purity."[22] Polygamy struck at the heart of the home, family, and domestic sphere, the site of shared religious sentiment and national unity. Fears about the protection of the domestic sphere and the preservation of national honor from the corrupting influence of polygamy were often figured in foreign terms, particularly in rhetoric and imagery drawn from constructions of Islam in the modern Western imagination. Anti-Mormon novels often contained orientalist literary allusions to the "barbarism" of polygamy and its association with the Ottoman empire. Two of the most famous examples of the genre were *Female Life among the Mormons*, which was the best-selling anti-Mormon novel at mid-century, selling forty thousand copies in the space of a few weeks in 1855; and

Figure 20.2 Frontispiece to Alfreda Eva Bell, *Baodicea, the Mormon Wife: Life-Scenes in Utah* (New York: Arthur Orton, 1855)

Baodicea, the Mormon Wife: Life-Scenes in Utah, also published in 1855 (see Figure 20.2). *Baodicea* depicts a couple descending into polygamy and decadence among the Mormons, a horrifying transition represented visually by the book's illustrations. The images depict the couple's gradual transition from a landscape of Western scenery and Western dress to one characterized by Turkish slippers and Ottoman architecture. "Through Mormonism," Marr argues, "the corruptions associated with islamicism – superstition, tyranny, and sensuality – were made manifest within the territory of the United States" and represented as a grave threat that must be halted and destroyed.[23]

Spurred by the "twin relics of barbarism" rhetoric and broad-based popular antipolygamy sentiment, Congress took action by passing legislation targeting the Church of Jesus Christ of Latter-Day Saints. The Morrill Anti-Bigamy Act of 1862 was specifically designed to outlaw Mormon plural marriages in the territories, although it was largely unenforced due to the

Lincoln administration's preoccupation with the Civil War. It was followed by the Edmunds Act of 1882, which declared polygamy a felony, and the Edmunds-Tucker Act of 1887, which dissolved the Church as a corporation, authorized the seizure of Church property, and reinforced a number of antipolygamy provisions including fines and imprisonment. The Edmunds-Tucker Act also disenfranchised women in Utah territory, who had been given the right to vote in 1870. Church leaders set out to test the First Amendment's protection of Mormons' religious liberties in *Reynolds v. United States*, a case in which George Reynolds, secretary to Brigham Young, appealed his bigamy conviction on the grounds that polygamy was his religious practice.[24] *Reynolds* challenged federal antibigamy laws on the grounds of the First Amendment's free exercise clause, or, as the Court framed it, "the question is raised whether religious belief can be accepted as a justification of an overt act made criminal by the law of the land."[25] While Reynolds did prove that polygamy was an accepted doctrine of the Church of which he was a member, the Court upheld Reynolds' conviction and sentenced him to two years' hard labor and a $500 fine, the first successful conviction under the Morrill Act.

The Constitutional question posed by *Reynolds* was whether federal antibigamy laws could be properly applied to a citizen who claimed the right to polygamy as a religious duty and hence a matter of "free exercise." In ruling that it could, the Court asserted that while "religious freedom is guaranteed everywhere throughout the United States . . . [t]he question to be determined is, whether the law now under consideration comes within this prohibition." Yet since the Court acknowledged that "the word 'religion' is not defined in the Constitution," it turned to history, particularly the writings of Jefferson and Madison, to ascertain its meaning. In particular, Jefferson's 1801 letter to the Danbury, Connecticut, Baptists, containing the phrase "wall of separation," was used in the Opinion as an "authoritative declaration of the scope and effect of the amendment thus secured." Quoting Jefferson's statement in the letter, "Believing with you that religion is a matter which lies solely between man and his God; that he owes account to none other for his faith or his worship; that the legislative powers of the government reach actions only, and not opinions," the Court concluded that this was sufficient to draw a distinction between Constitutional protection for religious "opinions" versus "actions." Thus, stated the Court, "Congress was deprived of all legislative power over mere opinion, but was left free to reach actions which were in violation of social duties or subversive of good order." Polygamy clearly fell into this category, as the Court's opinion, laced with racist and nativist overtones, makes clear: "Polygamy has always been odious among the northern and western nations of Europe, and, until the establishment of the Mormon Church, was almost exclusively a feature of the life of Asiatic and of African people"; in the tradition of English common law, it "has been treated as an offence against society."[26]

In distinguishing between what it termed religious "opinion" or belief on the one hand and "actions" or practice on the other, *Reynolds* provided a key test case for legal protections of religious liberty in U.S. history. The Court's interpretation of the First Amendment significantly narrowed its reach by enacting a definition of religion as a matter of private conscience or belief. This was a definition that dovetailed well with Protestant understandings of religion. This distinction between religious "belief" as inviolable versus religious "action" that could and should be regulated by the federal government when it was seen to pose a threat to social order meant that Mormons lost their claim to the constitutional protection of polygamy as religious practice. In 1890, Church President Wilford Woodruff issued a Manifesto suspending the practice of plural marriage; Utah's long-fought admission to statehood followed six years later.

Reynolds and the broader context of popular anti-Mormonism revealed national contestations over how religion was defined and legitimated in relation to perceived threats to a properly Christian nation at home, on the frontier, and abroad. It also demonstrates how First Amendment interpretation, shaped by a Protestant conception of religion, marked the discourse of religious liberty in the nineteenth century and beyond, regulating and excluding other forms of religion, particularly those emphasizing religious practice, from its protections. In classifying polygamy as an "offence against society," the Court claimed the right to restrict religious practice when individual interests in pursuing a particular practice were seen to be in conflict with compelling societal interests or customs in restricting or preventing it. The lingering effects of the decision extended into the twentieth century and beyond, heavily influencing First Amendment jurisprudence. According to Ray Davis, "[T]he *Reynolds* rationale transforms the crucial issue [in First Amendment cases] to the classification of an interest as either a religious belief or an act based on religion . . . [and] in case after case the protection of beliefs . . . has been more often re-affirmed" than the protection of practice.[27]

Reynolds demonstrates how the law provided one strategy of containment of religious minorities by virtue of its power to define and delimit religious liberty. Another strategy resided in the power of classification. Spiritualist fraud trials in the mid-1800s reveal how the authority to classify particular types of practices and experts as religious or nonreligious *regardless of how they are self-defined*, a power that in earlier times had belonged to the church, now belonged to the law, which became the arbiter of "true" and "false" religion. Because Spiritualism claimed to be a religion that produced concrete evidence for the existence of life after death, it raised issues of classification: was it indeed a religion, or a science, or a form of paid popular entertainment?

Founded in 1848 in upstate New York, the Spiritualist movement believed in personal survival after death and claimed to offer scientific proof for it. The proof came in the form of communications from beyond the physical world, delivered by and through mediums, who were predominantly female. Spiritualism was appealing to many Americans raised on a diet of Protestant belief understood as "the evidence of things unseen" because it promised a religion that did not depend on blind faith but was compatible with science and the evidence of the senses.[28] Spiritualists also claimed to provide physical "manifestations," or demonstrations, of the existence of spirits via rappings, table tipping, automatic writing, answers to unseen questions, ghostly apparitions, messages from deceased loved ones, and a number of other materializations. Its demonstrations were embodied or mediated by religious professionals known as mediums.[29] As conduits for spiritual energies and communications, mediums and their bodies became central sites of religious belief and practice, as well as central objects of scientific investigation. The National Spiritualist Association of Churches (NSAC), founded in 1893 and one of the oldest and largest denominations in the tradition, defines Spiritualism not simply as a religion but also as a philosophy and a science "because it investigates, analyzes and classifies facts and manifestations demonstrated from the spirit side of life."[30]

Spiritualism frequently used the language of "laws" both to distinguish itself from other religious traditions and to describe the eternal natural and supernatural mechanisms that determine the course of life and knowledge: "all flows according to Natural Law. Where the ancients believed in the supernatural, miracles and magic, punishment and rewards, we believe in the natural, God's Laws, growth and love. We are a truth seeking religion that incorporates science and testing as a part of our philosophy," the NSAC website states.[31] The reference to natural law becomes another way to signal the tradition's compatibility with modern, secular forms of knowledge and governance. The presence of these laws and their accessibility to all have meant that, for Spiritualists, "individuals could serve as vehicles of truth because each embodied the laws of nature in his or her being," lending a fierce democratic individualism and antiauthoritarian sensibility to the tradition.[32] Yet though Spiritualism espouses the discovery of laws as the path to morality, truth, and knowledge, its own relationship to the law has always seemed uncertain, giving rise to many curious legal questions ranging from allegations and admissions of fraud to the Comstock Act and obscenity laws to ghostwriting and copyright.[33]

Science, testing, and the discovery of laws were part of Spiritualist self-understanding from its beginnings, placing those who viewed its demonstrations in the roles of, variously, curious onlookers, faithful believers, scientific investigators, and jurors, a mixed public looking for evidence and conviction. Underlying the question of classification was the issue of truth or deception and how to distinguish it from trickery or fraud, even as the legal definition of "fraud" remained vague throughout the nineteenth century so that courts would not be overly bound to it.[34] As several historians have argued, in the nineteenth century the urban American middle class was preoccupied with "questions of fraud in almost every facet of its historical development" as it struggled with anxieties over respectability, class, and masculinity in an era of rapid social and economic transformation.[35] These anxieties were embodied in the figure of the "confidence man," the era's paradigmatic criminal, and corresponding concerns about how to distinguish such con men from respectable citizens.[36] The concern with fraud extended also to how to distinguish "deception in the spirit world" and led to numerous "public investigations to differentiate between authentic mediums and a distressingly large assortment of parlor charlatans."[37] In this sense, as Jeremy Stolow has written:

> [T]he séance chamber was transformed into a sort of laboratory: a stage for investigating the spirit world, for obtaining its secrets, and also for surveilling the body of the spirit medium as a source of certain knowledge or, as the case may be, a site of misinterpreted evidence, indeterminacy, or even duplicity, imposture, and fraud.[38]

From the séance chamber as laboratory, it was not such a leap to another key site for the sifting of evidence: the courtroom.

An 1865 spiritualism trial in Buffalo, New York, concerned a Mr. Charles J. Colchester, who had been working as a medium in Rochester. According to the *New York Times* coverage of the trial, Colchester had been conducting séances that "resembled other exhibitions of the kind, including rapping out answers to inquiries, answering questions which are claimed not to have been seen, [and] . . . writing on the arm."[39] But because, the *Times* continued, the "officials in that district [did not have] that reverence for 'the spirits' as made known by Mr. Colchester," they classified him as a juggler and ordered him to pay the requisite $20 license fee. A contemporary dictionary defined "juggler" as "one who practices or exhibits tricks by sleight of hand," and the IRS provision likewise stated that "every person who performs by sleight of hand shall be regarded as a juggler." Though on the surface this case was a simple matter of commercial licensing, from the perspective of Spiritualists, the designation and the government's power to make such designations struck at the heart of the question of the truth and legitimacy of their religion. Knowing full well the stakes, Colchester refused to accept the appellation and the license and was brought to trial under the Internal Revenue Act's provision regarding "jugglers." Outlining the facts of the case, the opinion states:

> The defendant denies that he is a juggler. It appears that he offered to take out a license as a 'spiritual medium,' but the government officials refused to give him a license unless he would take out such license as a juggler, in other words consider himself a juggler. This the defendant absolutely refused to do.[40]

At issue in the case was whether Mr. Colchester's mediumistic "performances" were acts of skill and trickery performed by himself or whether they actually evidenced "facts and manifestations demonstrated from the spirit side of life," as Colchester and other mediums claimed. If the former, the statute would apply to him; if the latter, Colchester was a true medium, a religious expert, and not a (mere) performer.

The trial became a sensation and was heavily covered by the media. The district attorney, in his opening remarks to the jury, protested the media sensationalism and asserted that the import of the trial was restricted to the simple matter of whether Colchester was a true medium or a sleight of hand artist. "The case seems to be one simple of solution, and involving no great public concern," he said, but the press

> has been made the instrument of magnifying this case into undue proportions, and to cause the public to believe that it is a contest between the United States and a large body of citizens calling themselves spiritualists, and an endeavor, on the part of the former, to crush out a religious sect and to expose its heresies if it has any, and that the result of this trial will establish the fact whether spiritualism is true or false. Nothing can be further from the truth.[41]

For the district attorney, the trial would settle the matter of whether Colchester was a juggler according to the proof of performance. He told the jury:

> If to show you that the performances of the prisoner, and which he claims to be the result of spiritual control, can be performed and have been performed by men who can show you how it is done, and who disclaim any such influences, I trust that will be enough to establish the fact that he is a juggler.[42]

Accordingly, he produced several witnesses claiming to have learned Colchester's methods directly from him and to be able to reproduce them. The defense's response was to call other witnesses who could not successfully replicate Colchester's performances. But, as the *Times* reporter observed, the defense did not call "other spiritual mediums to testify that such things were done by supernatural power."[43]

Given the testimony, the jury concluded that at least some of the performances were "done by Colchester himself by sleight-of-hand."[44] He was found guilty of operating as a juggler without a license and ordered to pay a fine. The implications of the Colchester trial for Spiritualism were clear: so long as mediums demonstrated their powers privately and for free, the revenue laws did not apply, but receiving remuneration as religious professionals would require that they either take out a juggler's license and hence, under the statute, admit themselves to be practicing sleight of hand – admit that their powers came not from supernatural sources but from themselves – or forego the license in favor of claiming supernatural power with the attendant risk of prosecution and fines. The Buffalo case shows quite clearly, as do British laws during the same time period and even extending to the 1951 Fraudulent Mediums Act, that Spiritualism's legal status as a religion depended on its classification; not being recognized as a religion under the law meant that it was not afforded the protections of the First Amendment, but instead was regulated under revenue, commerce, and even vagrancy laws.[45]

The popular association of mediumship with popular entertainment extended beyond the law in several directions. First, lecture tours of Spiritualist mediums and speakers provided forums for women to speak to public audiences on a large scale for the first time in American history, and led directly to the rise of the women's movement.[46] Elements of performance were also present in the séance room, with female mediums serving as master of ceremonies on the stage of the séance table, often both performing Victorian gender roles and subverting them.[47] The medium

Eva Carrière often conducted séances partially concealed by curtains and in various stages of undress, as depicted in a series of photos taken in 1912–1913 by German psychic researcher Baron von Schrenck-Notzing, seen in Figure 20.3.[48] Performance was a central element of Carrière's mediumship; in fact, she was on her second career as a medium after being exposed as a fraud while first working as a medium under her given name, Marthe Béraud, in 1905. Finally, popular authors and entertainers like Harry Houdini, perhaps viewing mediums as unwelcome competition for their paying audiences, set out to expose them as frauds by learning to mimic and perform their demonstrations for large crowds of curious onlookers. Historian Leigh Eric

Figure 20.3 The medium Eva C. with a materialization on her head and a luminous apparition between her hands (May 17, 1912)

Source: Institut für Grenzgebiete der Psychologie und Psychohygiene, Freiburg im Breisgau

Schmidt notes that nineteenth-century Spiritualists "became the greatest commodity in this ongoing commercial exchange between religion and stage magic," as "hardly a showman missed the opportunity to exploit the fascination with Spiritualism through counter-demonstrations of how all this otherworldly contact was accomplished through various sleights."[49]

In the context of such doubts about the (un)trustworthiness of the senses for distinguishing truth from fraud in matters of both performance and religion, spirit photography emerged as a new technology for ascertaining truth. The exhibition catalog *The Perfect Medium: Photography and the Occult*, a collection of spirit photography extending from the 1860s to the 1960s, illustrates how the new technology of photography coincided with increasing interest in occult phenomena in the nineteenth century, producing hundreds of experimental photographic images. The collection illustrates how for many Spiritualists, the medium of photography provided the hope that "the camera would prove more efficient than the human eye in capturing the unseen."[50] In the photograph of Carrière shown in Figure 20.3, two substances materialize from the medium's body: a filmy substance called ectoplasm, a substance believed to be excreted from mediums' bodies during contact with spirits, emerges from the crown of her head, while a thin ribbon of light, resembling an electrical current, forms between her outstretched hands. Both of these material phenomena served as manifestations of the medium's abilities and of the genuineness of her powers. But the light materialization had not been visible to those in the séance audience; it was revealed only through the developed image. Spirit photography thereby "exposed" real presence and could serve as a medium of truth, as a revelatory text. The darkroom revealed what those in the darkened séance room did not see.

Nineteenth-century American literature also exhibited a preoccupation with deception that was in many ways continuous with the general climate of the time. But in the examples just discussed, there is a shared belief that the truth can be found out eventually, whether through investigating mediums scientifically or legally, unmasking tricks through performance or testimony, or affirming unseen manifestations through the new technology of photography. In contrast, Cohen states that the central issue for literature of the time period was "the more elusive condition of *fraudulence*":

> "[F]raud" is something of a misnomer, implying as it does a deliberate deception regarding what legal scholars call a "matter of fact." . . . Frauds are specific crimes perpetrated by particular agents with intent to deceive. They are actionable because they cause discernible injury to identifiable victims. Fraudulence, by contrast, can be neither decisively located nor contained, and its effects, while palpable, are not necessarily measurable. Fraud is actual, or at least aspires to be so; fraudulence is perceptual, a matter of determination.[51]

According to Cohen, fraudulence was about the "hopelessness of distinguishing impostures, forgeries, plagiarisms, and hoaxes from literature proper," a problem that stemmed from both the fact that literature is not science and does not have as its primary goal the determination of truth, as well as the problem of representation as "Americans increasingly called upon literature to represent formations such as nationhood, democracy, and race that were not themselves 'matters of fact.' "[52] In the writings of (or ascribed to) women, people of color, and frontiersmen, literary cultural productions "from the margins" of society were seen as more "natural" and "authentic," yet also highly suspicious. In antebellum literature, "the expanding literary marketplace transformed fraudulence from a national dilemma into a sorting mechanism that helped define racial, regional, and gender identities" and also, at times, subvert them.[53]

But while literature and sometimes mediums themselves might play with fraudulence, the law was deployed to determine fraud. As in *Reynolds*, the Colchester trial demonstrates how nineteenth-century legal attempts to contain, define and manage the protected category of "religion" not only intersected with a set of social and cultural anxieties about national identity, truth and fraud, but also were determinative for a particular conception of religious liberty that extended only to certain authorized forms of private belief, a legacy that continues into the present. A 2008 attempt to introduce a new set of Consumer Protection Regulations in the UK governing psychics and mediums shows how the power of the state to regulate and classify continues to directly contravene spiritualist beliefs. In response to the requirement that mediums would need to issue disclaimers to their clients such as "this is a scientific experiment, the results of which cannot be guaranteed," a spiritualist healer in Essex said that doing so would force her to "lie and deny our beliefs. No other religion has to do that."[54] The forgotten century continues to cast a long shadow.

Notes

1 Alexis de Tocqueville, *Democracy in America* (New York: Vintage Books, 1990), 1: 304, 305–6.
2 See Sarah Barringer Gordon, "The First Disestablishment: Limits on Church Power and Property before the Civil War," *University of Pennsylvania Law Review* 162 (2014): 307–72.
3 Steven K. Green, *The Second Disestablishment: Church and State in Nineteenth-Century America* (Oxford: Oxford University Press, 2010), 8.
4 Ibid., 9. For more on blasphemy laws, see Phillip I. Blumberg, *Repressive Jurisprudence in the Early American Republic: The First Amendment and the Legacy of English Law* (Cambridge, UK: Cambridge University Press, 2010).
5 Sarah Barringer Gordon, *The Mormon Question: Polygamy and Constitutional Conflict in Nineteenth-Century America* (Chapel Hill: University of North Carolina Press, 2002), 7.
6 Ibid., 107–8.
7 Ibid. 8.
8 Talal Asad, *Genealogies of Religion: Discipline and Reasons of Power in Christianity and Islam* (Baltimore: Johns Hopkins University Press, 1993), 46.
9 Winnifred Fallers Sullivan, *The Impossibility of Religious Freedom* (Princeton, N.J.: Princeton University Press, 2005), 8.
10 Tracy Fessenden, *Culture and Redemption: Religion, the Secular, and American Literature* (Princeton, N.J.: Princeton University Press, 2007), 4.
11 Nathan Hatch has argued that this period in U.S. history gave rise to the "democratization" of American Christianity, a spirit of religious populism that characterized Christian practice across race, class, and gender lines. Nathan O. Hatch, *The Democratization of American Christianity* (New Haven, Conn.: Yale University Press, 1989).
12 Derek Chang, *Citizens of a Christian Nation: Evangelical Missions and the Problem of Race in the Nineteenth Century* (Philadelphia: University of Pennsylvania Press, 2010), 7.
13 Fiske, a Harvard professor, first coined the term in his famous lecture, published in *Harper's* in 1885, but the ideas were certainly in circulation much earlier. Thomas Hietala makes the argument that manifest destiny's roots lie in Jacksonian policy making; see *Manifest Design: American Exceptionalism and Empire*, rev. ed. (Ithaca, N.Y.: Cornell University Press, 2003).
14 Anders Stephanson, *Manifest Destiny: American Expansion and the Empire of Right* (New York: Hill & Wang, 1995), 79–80; Josiah Strong, *Our Country: Its Possible Future and Its Present Crisis*, ed. Jurgen Herbst (1891; Cambridge, Mass.: Harvard University Press, 1963).
15 Terryl Givens, *The Viper on the Hearth: Mormons, Myths, and the Construction of Heresy*, rev. ed. (Oxford: Oxford University Press, 2013), 49.
16 Gordon, *The Mormon Question*, 1.
17 Ibid., 55.
18 Ibid., 57.
19 See Susan Griffin, *Anti-Catholicism and Nineteenth-Century Fiction* (Cambridge, UK: Cambridge University Press, 2009).
20 Givens, *The Viper on the Hearth*, 50.

21 Timothy Marr, *The Cultural Roots of American Islamicism* (Cambridge, UK: Cambridge University Press, 2006), 186. See also Leonard Arrington and Jon Haupt, "Intolerable Zion: The Image of Mormonism in Nineteenth Century American Literature," *Western Humanities Review* 22 (1968): 243–60, 247–8.
22 Sarah Barringer Gordon, "'Our National Hearthstone': Anti-Polygamy Fiction and the Sentimental Campaign against Moral Diversity in Antebellum America," *Yale Journal of Law & the Humanities* 8 (1996): 295–350, 298, quoting Metta Victor, *Mormon Wives: A Narrative of Facts Stranger Than Fiction* (New York: Derby & Jackson, 1856), vii–viii.
23 Marr, *Cultural Roots*, 212.
24 *Reynolds v. United States*, 98 U.S. 145 (1879).
25 Id. at 162.
26 Id. at 164.
27 Ray J. Davis, "Plural Marriage and Religious Freedom: The Impact of *Reynolds v. United States*," *Arizona Law Review* 15 (1973): 287–306, 296.
28 Hebrews 11:1, KJV.
29 Ibid. The National Spiritualist Association of Churches defines a medium as "one whose organism is sensitive to vibrations from the spirit world and through whose instrumentality, intelligences in that world are able to convey messages and produce the phenomena of Spiritualism."
30 "Definitions," National Spiritualist Association of Churches, https://www.nsac.org/definitions.php (accessed 15 March 2015).
31 Ibid.
32 Ann Braude, *Radical Spirits: Spiritualism and Women's Rights in Nineteenth-Century America* (Boston: Beacon, 1989), 6. See also John L. Modern, *Secularism in Antebellum America* (Chicago: University of Chicago Press, 2011), 246–50.
33 See Molly McGarry, "Spectral Sexualities, Nineteenth-Century Spiritualism, Moral Panics, and the Making of U.S. Obscenity Law," *Journal of Women's History* 12 (2000): 8–29, and Christine A. Corcos, "'Ghostwriters': Spiritualists, Copyright Infringement, and Rights of Publicity," in *Law and Magic: A Collection of Essays*, ed. Christine A. Corcos (Durham, NC: Carolina Academic Press, 2009), 79–100.
34 See Erika White Dyson, "Gentleman Mountebanks and Spiritualists: Legal, Stage and Media Contest between Magicians and Spirit Mediums in the United States and England," in *Ashgate Research Companion to Nineteenth-Century Spiritualism and the Occult*, ed. Tatiana Kontou and Sarah Wilburn (Burlington, Vt.: Ashgate, 2012), 231–66, and Kembrew McLeod, *Pranksters: Making Mischief in the Modern World* (New York: New York University Press, 2014), 73–93. See also "Fraud," in Bryan A. Garner, *A Dictionary of Modern Legal Usage* (Oxford: Oxford University Press, 2001), 374.
35 James W. Cook, *The Arts of Deception: Playing with Fraud in the Age of Barnum* (Cambridge, Mass.: Harvard University Press, 2001), 26.
36 See Karen Halttunen, *Confidence Men and Painted Women: A Study of Middle-Class Culture in America, 1830–1870* (New Haven, Conn.: Yale University Press, 1982), and Lara Langer Cohen, *The Fabrication of American Literature: Fraudulence and Antebellum Print Culture* (Philadelphia: University of Pennsylvania Press, 2012).
37 Cook, *The Arts of Deception*, 26.
38 Jeremy Stolow, "Salvation by Electricity," in *Religion: Beyond a Concept*, ed. Hent de Vries (New York: Fordham University Press, 2008), 681.
39 "Some Legal Points in the Buffalo Spiritualist Trial," *New York Times*, August 28, 1865.
40 *United States v. Colchester*, 25 Fed. Cas. 492 (S.D.N.Y 1865) (headnote).
41 Id. (DA's address to jury).
42 Id.
43 "Some Legal Points in the Buffalo Spiritualist Trial," *New York Times*, August 28, 1865.
44 Ibid.
45 For a more recent attempt to regulate mediumship and protection from fraud in the U.K., see Caroline Davies, "Psychic Crackdown on the Cards," *The Guardian*, April 5, 2008.
46 Ann Braude, *Radical Spirits: Spiritualism and Women's Rights in Nineteenth-Century America* (Boston: Beacon, 1989).
47 See Alex Owen, *The Darkened Room: Women, Power, and Spiritualism in Late Victorian England* (Chicago: University of Chicago Press, 2004).
48 Baron von Schrenck-Notzing, *Phenomena of Materialisation: A Contribution to the Investigation of Mediumistic Teleplastics*, trans. Edmund E. Fournier d'Albe (New York: Dutton, 1923).
49 Leigh E. Schmidt, *Hearing Things: Religion, Illusion, and the American Enlightenment* (Cambridge, Mass.: Harvard University Press, 2000), 158–9.

50 Clément Chéroux *et al.*, *The Perfect Medium: Photography and the Occult* (New Haven, Conn.: Yale University Press, 2005), 18.
51 Cohen, *Fabrication*, 2.
52 Ibid.
53 Ibid., 19.
54 Davies, "Psychic Crackdown on the Cards."

21

GOTHIC STORIES, *MENS REA*, AND AMERICAN CRIMINAL LAW

Laura I Appleman

The early to mid-nineteenth century was a turbulent period for the cities of an expanding America. The 1830s were a time of "epic homicidal riots,"[1] which prompted the creation of the first urban police force. The explosion of real-life crime[2] was accompanied by a new enthusiasm for gothic storytelling, focusing largely on the wily criminal and the internal dialogues of the guilty. How did these tremendously popular stories influence the development of nineteenth-century criminal law, in particular the parallel development and explication of criminal *mens rea* in both literature and the law?

The most emblematic example of this fascination with American criminality was the writing of Edgar Allan Poe, whose *Tales of the Grotesque and Arabesque* was published in 1840. Equally influential was the gothic fiction of writers like Nathaniel Hawthorne and Washington Irving. All of these authors' works focused on the psychological motivations of the criminal offender beguiling a developing nation. These highly popular stories, strongly focused on the process of criminal justice,[3] were steeped in mystery, internal psychology, and vaguely evil protagonists and had some influence in the shaping of nineteenth-century criminal law. More generally, nineteenth-century crime was a crucible where American culture's assumptions and values often split apart and reformed,[4] and there was no better place to explore such a reformation than in the era's popular American gothic fiction.

How did nineteenth-century fiction, gothic and otherwise, affect the development of contemporaneous criminal law? In an era largely devoid of institutions for formal legal training, law treatises and advocacy manuals were essential for the future lawyer "reading law." These legal treatises and advocacy manuals often relied heavily on literature to flesh out points of doctrine.[5] Additionally, many treatises, particularly those on advocacy, presented literary examples as tools for lawyers to use in the courtroom.[6]

Subtler forms of linkage exist, however, between nineteenth-century crime-focused fiction and the intellectual development of nineteenth-century American criminal law. One example involves the rise of new narrative techniques in developing character studies, including third-person narrative forms and the simultaneous development of *mens rea* analysis,[7] which required liability for wrongdoing to be based not on sheer "wickedness," but on actual intent to commit a specific crime. As literary fiction explored a new, more complex understanding of criminal defendants' actions, this exploration matched – and possibly even influenced – the way the legal understanding of *mens rea* became more refined, shifting from a simple finding of general wrongdoing to a more sophisticated, elemental approach.[8]

Moreover, the development of an objective standard for criminal wrongdoing in nineteenth-century American law was mirrored in the popular American literature at the time, including Gothic fiction. Both demanded a more detailed inquiry into the actions and reactions of the criminal suspect/protagonist, examining the causes, qualities, and results of a particular mental state on both mind and body. Nineteenth-century jurists focused on the ideal of the independently willed individual and felt compelled to promulgate this image far and wide.[9] Both the American Gothic and American criminal law shared a similar focus on the details of the distressing event to make sense of the narrative, and both were likewise "concerned with the acquisition and internalizing of kinds of knowledge."[10] This chapter explores the similarities and cross-pollination between the two.

I. The expansion of *mens rea* in the nineteenth century

Motive has always been a requirement for a criminal conviction in the Anglo-American criminal justice system. For hundreds of years, however, what was meant by this motive, or *mens rea*, was vague and indeterminate. This broadness was neatly summed up by the nineteenth-century scholar Joel Prentiss Bishop, who noted in his seminal criminal law treatise that "there can be no crime, large or small, without an evil Mind. . . . It is therefore a principle of our legal system, as probably it is of every other, that the essence of an offence is the wrongful intent, without which it cannot exist."[11] In fact, there is some argument that even today, *mens rea* is a vague and ill defined concept, in part due to the concept's "history of imprecise and ambiguous exposition at the hands of common-law courts, legislators, and commentators alike."[12] Nonetheless, lawyers, courts, and legislatures continue to use the term despite its ambiguity, and thus it is best if we examine the concept briefly, if only to understand better the fluidity of the term over the past few centuries and what that means today.[13]

Prior to the twelfth century, proving intent was not a crucial part of conviction,[14] since early legal systems paid little attention to any specific mental element as a requirement for criminal liability.[15] No regular *mens rea* requirements existed until at least the early thirteenth century.[16] This began to change during the seventeenth century when the early requirement of a "bad motive" for homicide was eventually replaced by mere intent to kill, to cause "grievous bodily harm," to commit "any felony," or to resist an officer known to be making a lawful arrest.[17] A similar process happened with the *mens rea* of most other crimes.

Before the nineteenth century, both in America and in England, a defendant could not be found guilty of an offense unless she manifested an "evil mind."[18] The American Revolution, however, coupled with a strong suspicion of judicial lawmaking on the part of the voting public, encouraged a movement to codify and clarify the criminal law.[19] Many lawyers and reformers in the beginning of the nineteenth century were very skeptical of the old English common law.[20]

In part, this was because many reformers viewed the English criminal law, with its focus on capital crimes, as bloody and outdated.[21] Indeed, Anglo-American common law continued to lack an intelligible conception of *mens rea* even by the time of Blackstone's collection at the very end of eighteenth century.[22] About half of the most serious crimes discussed in Blackstone's tome were not defined by reference to any culpability.[23] Where culpability was required, it was broadly defined; some crimes required a type of knowledge, and some required a sort of intent while committing the offense, together with the three more general requirements of willfulness, malice, or felonious intent.[24]

Additionally, Blackstone's broad understanding of *mens rea* included circumstances in which the offender "did not foresee or intend" harm.[25] Only complete lack of "will" removed culpability from the offender.[26] Even the doctrine of mistake did not save a wrongdoer from criminal liability.[27] Put more broadly, under Blackstone's understanding, an offender's will did not need to evince any *particular* crime or risk any *particular* harm.[28]

During the nineteenth century, criminal law finally rejected this limited understanding and began to impose liability based on objective criteria. In part, this change reflected a growing movement away from courts defining offenses and toward legislative control of delineating the *mens rea* of various crimes.[29] As courts attempted to clarify the *mens rea* elements of these new legislatively created criminal offenses, the "evil motive" approach was often rejected in favor of describing particular states of mind as essential for criminal liability.[30] Thus most American states reformed their homicide laws, relying less on old English versions with a general *mens rea* and adopting more detailed statutes that began to differentiate murder into various degrees.[31]

Put another way, the old *mens rea* requirement of possessing an underlying evil motive, based on a theory of moral guilt, was eventually supplanted by the requirement of specific forms of intent, evolving separately for each particular felony.[32] This clarification of *mens rea* and movement toward objectivity was ultimately crystallized by Oliver Wendell Holmes in *The Common Law* (1881).[33] By the early twentieth century, criminal law was less concerned with a general *mens rea* than with a more constrained question of whether a defendant's conduct reflected the specific mental state required by the statute.[34]

What happened in the nineteenth century to change this centuries-long understanding of *mens rea* from a concept of general wickedness to a specific, objective mental state? Various partial explanations have been offered, from the rise of a utilitarian philosophy of punishment, to legal positivism, to the growing popularity of negligence theory,[35] but none of these rationales completely explains the change. To understand the change, we must place criminal law and its history within the context of the modern meaning of *mens rea* and its history.[36]

One possible, underexplored rationale for this change involves the influence of American literature on nineteenth-century lawyers, legislators, and judges. To understand the influence this writing had, it is helpful to look at two unexpected sources of nineteenth-century American legal influence: legal treatises and gothic fiction.

II. Treatises, literature, and criminal statutes

Nineteenth-century legal treatises were not the straightforward hornbooks with which we are familiar today. Because many lawyers of the era did not go to law school but relied on apprenticeships or self-study, treatises and law books played a critical role in both educating and training the average lawyer. This was particularly true for lawyers educating themselves through self-study, since they relied almost entirely on legal treatises.[37] Formal legal training only gradually shifted from apprenticeship to law schools starting in the 1870s, and the transformation did not fully take place until at least 1920.[38]

Of course, legal treatises don't give the entire picture of how law was interpreted and practiced at the time.[39] These compilations can still be useful, however, in establishing some sense of the warp and woof of the law.[40] Examining why treatise writers chose to develop certain arguments can provide a reliable historical snapshot of the time.[41] At the very least, legal treatises help illustrate what normative effect the books had in their wider social and political worlds.[42]

The standard writings for American lawyers in the nineteenth century included Edward Coke, Matthew Hale, William Hawkins, and Michael Foster, as well as the *Commentaries* of Joseph Story, Chancellor Kent, and William Blackstone.[43] This use of English legal texts, whether imported or produced in special editions, continued throughout the early nineteenth century.[44] Often English versions of the law were prepared or edited for an American audience, including J. F. Archbold's *Pleading and Evidence in Criminal Cases*[45] and J. C. Perkins's 1841 edition of J. Chitty's *A Practical Treatise on the Criminal Law.*[46]

Contemporaneous American treatises were far from the dry, technical instruction manuals that we currently encounter. These treatises were much more colorful and accessible, routinely relying on literature to explain doctrinal points.[47] In addition, the law of evidence, which also became more sophisticated during the nineteenth century, began to posit increasingly more complex distinctions that were important for an advocate to explain to a jury.[48] As a result, nineteenth-century legal treatises and manuals routinely recommended using memorable examples from literature to better explain these fine points.[49]

James Ram's *A Treatise on Facts as Subjects of Inquiry by a Jury*, first published in 1861, provides an excellent example. Ram's text cited more examples from poetry, drama, and fiction than from legal cases.[50] Specifically, the third edition included "more than a hundred literary examples and, in addition to a table of cases, featured separate tables of the authors and of the works quoted in the text,"[51] including such writings as James Thompson's "The Castle of Indolence,"[52] Jonathan Swift's *Gulliver's Travels*, Sir Walter Scott's "Lady of the Lake," and Anthony Trollope's *Vicar of Wakefield.*[53]

Indeed, legal treatises of the late eighteenth and early to mid-nineteenth centuries were rich with literary and intellectual meaning. The celebrated Joseph Story's *Commentaries on Conflicts of Law* (1832) cited and included quotations from such contemporary writers as Louis Boullenois, Achille Rodemburg, Paul Voet, John Voet, Charles D'Argentré, and Ulricus Huberus.[54] In addition, John Taylor's *Elements of the Civil Law*,[55] which was popular on both sides of the Atlantic and continued to be updated and published well into the 1830s, was originally conceived as much as a training manual for gentlemen as a legal treatise.[56] This literary and intellectual richness of the nineteenth-century legal treatise is important because these compendia, like all law books, operated "in the shadow of legal practice";[57] an effective legal treatise had to take account of both practice and precedent to be successful.[58]

One example of this combination of practice and precedent was Joel Prentiss Bishop, a criminal law scholar who, along with his specific compilations of the criminal law, wrote a more general treatise, *First Book of the Law: Explaining the Nature, Sources, Books, and Practical Applications of Legal Science, and Methods of Study and Practice*, in 1858.[59] All of Bishop's work, from this general treatise to his well-known commentaries on criminal law and procedure, were "highly original and thorough works that significantly influenced their fields."[60] The courts adopted his views, and practitioners followed his advice.[61] Accordingly, Bishop's understanding of *mens rea* can be assumed to be a popular one for the nineteenth century. By his eighth edition of his *Commentaries on Criminal Law*, published in 1892, Bishop spent an entire section differentiating between first- and second-degree murder and the various levels of manslaughter, thus reflecting the changed meaning of *mens rea.*[62] Along with treatises, advocacy books were also extremely popular with mid- to late nineteenth-century lawyers. These advocacy manuals relied directly on literary fiction as a tool for better forensic performance.[63] For example, Edward Cox's *The Advocate: His Training, Practice, Rights and Duties* (1852)[64] devotes a significant amount of space to advice on what to read and how to read it.[65] "Polite Literature should not be neglected"[66] because "[a] good novel . . . exhibits man in spheres of action beyond the immediate circle of your own observation, and therefore, next to society itself, it is most instructional."[67] Indeed, even though Cox was an English barrister writing for English advocates, he recommended reading the works of the American novelist James Fenimore Cooper.[68] Reading literature not only allowed an aspiring advocate to learn how to speak and proclaim most effectively; it also offered insight into others' mental habits, which was critical for developing a more complex understanding of *mens rea* and intent.

During the remainder of the nineteenth century, a plethora of trial advocacy manuals by legal professionals appeared in both England and America.[69] Most of these manuals viewed Cox as an important underpinning, particularly in regard to trial strategy and tactics.[70] Thus literature played a significant role in influencing both the shape and practice of law in the nineteenth century, whether through advocacy manuals or legal treatises. Quantifying the influence of a specific type of fiction – American Gothic fiction – on a specific requirement in the criminal law – the clarification of *mens rea* – is a more complicated matter, however. Although Gothic fiction, which is fascinated as it is with murder, intrigue, betrayal, and the presentation of diabolical deeds, seems to celebrate criminal behavior, the horror associated with such criminal transgressions becomes a meaningful way to assert standard societal values,[71] serving "to reinforce or underline their value and necessity."[72]

III. Gothic fiction

Writers of American gothic fiction such as Poe, Hawthorne, and Charles Brockden Brown explored the knotty problem of criminal intent from a psychological point of view, which neatly paralleled increasingly complex thinking about the architecture of *mens rea*. As Simon Stern argues, "[T]he growing interest, among criminal lawyers, in formalizing the concept of *mens rea* is itself part and parcel of the culture that sponsored these intricate fictional investigations of agency, motive, and intent,"[73] particularly in early to mid-century American Gothic fiction. Before the nineteenth century, the more ad hoc proceedings of criminal justice allowed judges and juries wide discretion in adjudicating criminal cases.[74] As the nineteenth century proceeded, however, various reforms removed discretion from the triers of fact and law,[75] including the clarification and further specification of the meaning of *mens rea*. This restructuring of *mens rea* offered an "increasingly precise individuation," designed to produce an accurate knowledge of the subject.[76] Put another way, nineteenth-century criminal responsibility came to encompass internal intent in addition to overt criminal acts in both law and fiction.

American literature itself reflected and influenced this great intellectual change in criminal law. As we have seen, nineteenth-century law went from an idea of crime handed down from religious courts and structured by a broad religious theory of a guilty, generally wicked mind, to a more definable idea of the "genetically inherent, atavistic quality found in the natural, born criminal."[77] This concept of the natural-born criminal, with complicated inner thoughts that helped create the differentiated states of criminal *mens rea*, began to appear in a variety of American writing as the nineteenth century wore on, including in the stories of the American Gothic.

Indeed, Gothic fiction gave us precisely what the judge and jury can never know for sure: the thoughts of the offender at the time of the crime.[78] By delving into the mind of the evildoer, Gothic fiction, like other American genres of the time, may very well have prompted its readers to think about what it means to have the *bad intent* to commit the crime. Victorian literature on both sides of the Atlantic was worked alongside the law to expose the relationship of hidden motives to acts.[79] Thus the drive to classify and codify the different states of *mens rea* for each crime, along with the psychological motivations driving the offender, might have been stimulated in part by the complex unpacking of mental state in popular American Gothic literature.

The changes in criminal procedure and penal reform in the early to mid-nineteenth-century United States helped create a "juridical self-fashioning" that was reflected in American writers such as Hawthorne and Poe, among others.[80] During the first half of the century especially, these popular writers appealed to the heightened legal awareness of their fellow citizens, who began to form a "national community governed by law."[81] These influences played an important role in a country where legal standards of responsibility were in flux, particularly in criminal law, which was refashioning its entire understanding of criminal liability around the offender's intent.[82] This was likewise true with the American Gothic writers, literary fantasists who reached "an unofficial yet undeniable"[83] authority with their confident, if not entirely official understanding of criminal intent in legal discourse.[84] To illustrate how these gothic storytellers focused on *mens rea* in their fiction, I trace the path of intent and self-knowledge in the works of three exemplary Gothic authors: Edgar Allan Poe, Nathaniel Hawthorne, and Washington Irving.

A. Edgar Allan Poe

He is that *monstrum horrendum*, an unprincipled man of genius.

Edgar Allan Poe, "The Purloined Letter" (1845)

Edgar Allan Poe's fiction explored subjects such as self-destruction, madness, psychological motivation, and human will. For example, "The Murders in the Rue Morgue" (published in *Graham's Lady's and Gentleman's Magazine*, April 1841) begins with a discussion of intellectual methods of analysis and carefully examines criminal purpose and psychological motivation to determine the *why* of the crime, a trend paralleled in American criminal law's ordering and division of various states of *mens rea*. What Poe humorously described as "the hair-splitting of my French friend, Dupin"[85] (his famous detective) was, of course, another way of verbalizing the new requirements of determining criminal motive for a particular crime. No longer was it enough to find "bad intent" or general wickedness of purpose; now, as Poe demonstrated in his short stories, the reconstruction and analysis of an offender's acts needed to be scrutinized to ensure he or she actually performed the alleged crime.

The "Murders in the Rue Morgue" begins not with the facts of the case but with a meditation on the nature of analysis: "[S]o glories the analyst in that moral activity which *disentangles*. . . . His results, brought about by the very soul and essence of method, have, in truth, the whole air of intuition."[86] Poe then explains the importance of analysis and careful identification in the work of uncovering information, a practice that could just as easily be associated with the task of uncovering an offender's criminal motive: the analyst makes "a host of observations and inferences."[87] Our player "confines himself not at all; nor, because the game is the object, does he reject deductions from things external." Although Poe is talking about the analysis that goes into playing a game of chess, he could just as easily be discussing the lawyer's work in proving a certain mental state for a crime, often from circumstantial evidence. That Poe is not really talking about chess but instead about the work of the investigator/lawyer/judge in a criminal case is apparent from the story that follows, in which Dupin discovers the identity of a murderer by deducing the actor's state of mind when the crime was committed.

Dupin thinks about the details of the crime scene and tries to imagine who – or what – might have done such a crime and why. By putting himself in the place of the scared "Ourang Outang," Dupin determines the animal's "criminal motive." He thus demonstrates the importance of separating bad acts from the specific mental state required to convict an offender of a crime. Indeed, throughout the story, Poe notes the importance of being able to determine a person's particular mental state or psychological motivation in every capacity, not merely in solving crimes. Dupin constantly demonstrates his ability to break down a person's actions into parts in order to show what he has been thinking; in part by "retracing the steps by which particular conclusions of their own minds have been attained."[88] In describing Dupin's analytical abilities, Poe might be describing the role of the prosecutor in a criminal trial: identifying what the accused has done and tying his or her actions to a specific mental state.

Dupin's process of solving the murder mystery highlights both the superiority of the analytic method and the dangers of relying on old-fashioned ways to determine *mens rea*. After giving us the newspaper's account of the facts, Poe mentions that the police had imprisoned a suspect, "although nothing appeared to criminate him."[89] More damningly, Dupin observes that the Paris police do not approach the problem in an orderly or logical fashion: "There is no method in their proceedings, beyond the method of the moment."[90] Poe underscores the question of *mens rea* even more emphatically when Dupin notes that "[t]he police are confounded by the seeming absence of motive – not for the murder itself – but for the atrocity of the murder."[91] Poe thus directs attention to the importance of properly determining criminal motive.

In "The Purloined Letter,"[92] (published in *The Gift* in 1845),[93] Poe uses the inner workings of the offender's mental state to solve the crime, focusing on criminal motive for the plot of the story. Dupin, again the star of the show, explains why he was the only person who could find the stolen letter hiding in plain sight. Poe, through Dupin, takes great care in explaining this method of investigation, which involves the ability to think like one's opponent in order to understand what he may have done, a technique Poe calls "identification." Specifically, Poe recommends solving crimes by matching the *mens rea* of the criminal – "identif[ying] . . . the reasoner's intellect with that of his opponent."[94]

Poe's most direct interest and involvement in the way American crimes were being solved came with his story "The Murder of Marie Roget"[95] (published in *Snowden's Lady's Companion*, November 2, 1842), the first detective story that attempted to solve a real crime. Indeed, Poe's cover note to the publisher explains the true reason for writing the short story: to illustrate how to deduce criminal motive, or *mens rea*:

> [U]nder pretence of showing how Dupin unravelled the mystery of Marie's assassination, I, in reality, enter into a very long and rigorous analysis of the New-York tragedy. . . . I believe not only that I have demonstrated the fallacy of the general idea – that the girl was the victim of a gang of ruffians – but have *indicated the assassin* in a manner which will give renewed impetus to investigation.[96]

Although a later confession from a witness meant that Poe's original story did not solve the mystery, this is less important for our purposes than his belief and desire that his means of reconstructing the offender's *mens rea* in a crime would work not only in the world of fiction but in the world of criminal justice.

Throughout the story, Poe focuses on the need to understand the suspect's motive to understand the crime. As he notes, once again in Dupin's voice, "[N]ot the least usual error, in investigations such as this, is the limiting of inquiry to the immediate, with total disregard of the collateral or circumstantial events."[97] This observation is particularly important because in determining criminal *mens rea*, particularly in intentional homicide, the specific intent of the wrongdoer must be assessed from circumstantial evidence – a very modern view. Poe then criticizes the standard judicial application of evidentiary rules, bemoaning the rigidity that would exclude circumstantial evidence as unimportant.[98] In all three of Poe's Dupin stories, the actual answer to the mystery is far less important than the detective's method: the rational, logical method of determining criminal motive and identifying the potential *mens rea* of an offender.

B. Nathaniel Hawthorne

Hawthorne's short stories were masterpieces of subtlety, insinuation, and deliberation. His *Twice-Told Tales*, a compendium of gothic stories, was recommended and praised by none other than Edgar Allan Poe, who noted approvingly that in Hawthorne's work, "[t]ruth is often, and in very great degree, the aim of the tale. . . . Some of the finest tales are tales of ratiocination." Much of

Hawthorne's work was threaded through with an analysis of motive, a task that he assigned the reader to help explain the confusing, disturbing, and often deadly acts of his main characters. Like Poe, Hawthorne helped "transform[ ] the American short story into a form capable of psychological investigation."[99] This focus on interior thoughts as manifested in outward acts was reflected both in the law and in the literature of the era.

Two of Hawthorne's short stories illustrate this theme. "The Minister's Black Veil" and "The Birth-mark" both underscore Hawthorne's point that what mattered were not the physical manifestations the accused showed on the outside but rather the mysterious criminal motives on the inside and the difficulty of fully proving such knowledge. Each of these gothic tales focuses on the mysteries of what lies underneath and the frustration that this continual lack of knowledge provokes in the stories' protagonists. More importantly, for our purpose, both stories evince the era's deep fascination with determining the truth about motive: why certain characters acted the way they did, and how those characters' actions could be used to deduce their motivations and the truth.

In these two stories Hawthorne's writing requires the reader to reject "the obvious meaning in favour of some hidden true import and constructing an alternative version of the story."[100] Hawthorne repeatedly demonstrated his concern and obsession with rooting out a protagonist's true motive – whether it be guilt, evil, scientific inquiry, or the like – by focusing his tales on what lies beneath or behind a person's actions.

In "The Birth-mark," the thrust of the story is twofold: as the obsessed scientist Aylmer focuses on finding the origins of his wife's heart-shaped birthmark, the reader is equally focused on the motivation of Aylmer's obsession – finding the disturbing *mens rea* that drove him to perform the experiment to remove the birthmark that ended in his wife's death. Likewise, in "The Minister's Black Veil," the townspeople of the story and the reader are consumed in attempting to find out why the village's minister has suddenly donned a black veil; what are the minister's motivations, thoughts, potential criminal acts?

In both stories, all the reader has to go on is the circumstantial evidence; Hawthorne never offers a definitive answer to the mystery of why the protagonists did what they did. This reader-led exploration neatly parallels the real-life work of the criminal jury, whose job became much more complex in the nineteenth century, requiring close and careful analysis of the criminal offender's motives to determine what *mens rea* he or she possessed at the time of the crime.

Hawthorne's stories, which repeatedly return to the question of *motive*, reflected the rising contemporary interest in specifying how and why wrongdoers did what they did. His desire to ponder these questions by "engag[ing] the multiple dimensions – both ontological and epistemological – of his fictional realms in all of their implications" also describes the job the criminal jury was now supposed to do in the nonfictional realms of crime.

C. Washington Irving

Like Poe and Hawthorne, Washington Irving was also deeply interested in his characters' intentions and psychological motivations. Widely credited as having "invented" America's first short stories, Irving's tales were avidly read on both sides of the Atlantic.[101] His two best known stories, "The Legend of Sleepy Hollow" and "Rip Van Winkle," both published in 1820, are American classics and were part of the work that helped Irving achieve an international reputation.[102]

"The Legend of Sleepy Hollow"[103] explores the ambiguities that surround any exploration of potential criminal motive. In the well-known tale, schoolmaster Ichabod Crane competes with a local farmer, Brom van Brunt, for the attentions of the wealthy Katrina Van Tassel.[104] The story culminates in Crane's mysterious encounter with a headless horseman, sporting a pumpkin in lieu of a head, and the schoolmaster's subsequent disappearance.[105]

The ambiguity of the tale lies at the end of the narrative. Irving provides the reader with two possible endings. One ending states "Ichabod Crane was still alive; . . . he had left the neighborhood, partly through fear of the goblin . . . partly in mortification at having been suddenly dismissed by the heiress."[106] Crane, according to an old farmer, becomes a lawyer, a politician, an electioneer, a newspaperman, and then a judge. It is the alternate ending, however, which provides both the moral ambiguity and debate over intent and *mens rea*. In the last paragraph, the narrator of the tale tells us that "the best judges of these matters – "the old country wives" – continue to argue that Crane was "spirited away by supernatural means." According to this ending, the appearance of the Headless Horseman – clearly engineered by romantic rival Brom van Brunt – may very well have resulted in the murder of Crane. As Irving tells us,

> [Crane] saw the goblin . . . in the very act of hurling his head at him [and] endeavored to dodge the horrible missile, but too late. It encountered his cranium with a tremendous crash – he was tumbled headlong into the dust, and Gunpowder, the black steed, and the goblin rider, passed by like a whirlwind.[107]

The next morning Crane's hat, lying next to the pulped pumpkin, is found, but there is no trace of the schoolteacher.

As with a real crime, there is little but circumstantial proof of the potential murder, found in both Brom's previous hazing of Crane and the farmer's reaction to Crane's disappearance. Initially, irritated by Ichabod's "obstinately pacific system," Brom "draws upon . . . funds of rustic waggery" and collects his "gang of rough riders" to make Ichabod "the object of whimsical persecution."[108] Afterwards, Brom's actions were equally vague but suspicious:

> Brom Bones . . . was observed to look exceptionally knowing whenever the story of Ichabod was related, and always burst into a hearty laughter at the mention of the pumpkin, which led some to suspect that he knew more about the matter than he chose to tell.[109]

By leaving us with this unsolved mystery, Irving highlights the complicated question of criminal intent, ambiguous motive, and circumstantial evidence. As with the criminal law, it was not enough to simply suspect someone of wicked motivations. Instead, there must be specific intent to commit the particular crime. Because nothing could be proved, Brom Bones could marry the girl he had and Crane had wooed with impunity and leave Ichabod Crane to his uneasy and indeterminate fate.

IV. Conclusion

Law, like literature, is deeply intertwined with the narratives a culture tells itself.[110] This was particularly true in the post-revolutionary and early national periods of American culture, where there was "a striking coincidence of legal and literary minds."[111] It is no surprise, then, that at a time when there was tremendous debate within the criminal justice community about how to delineate various mental states to prove criminal intent, there would also be a concomitant interest in Gothic fiction, which focused on the place of evil in human nature.[112] The movement in American criminal law from an idea of general "wickedness" to a specific *mens rea* was both foreshadowed and paralleled in American Gothic fiction, which treated the wrongdoer as a psychological puzzle for the reader to analyze, an exercise in inferring why and how the protagonist committed these evil acts.

Ultimately, both law and literature in nineteenth-century America were focused on how to determine and isolate moral blameworthiness. These anxieties were displayed on the pages of American gothic fiction, as well as transformed into judicial and procedural reform.[113] In a society where the realms of law and literature had not yet been sundered, the influence of popular fiction on the developing realm of *mens rea*, specific intent, and burden of proof was very significant. The tide of jurisprudential and philosophical thought that washed over the first half of the nineteenth century reached both literary and legal shores.

Notes

1 These riots were primarily over religion, race, and politics. Roger Lane, "Murder in America: A Historian's Perspective," *Crime and Justice* 25 (1999): 191–224, 199–200.

2 Paul Dolan, "The Rise of Crime in the Period 1830–1860," *Journal of Criminal Law and Criminology* 30 (1940): 1857–64. See also *Skillman's New York Police Reports* (New York: Ludwig and Tollfree, 1830) (seeking to educate the public about "art and devices which are resorted to by the idle and iniquitous"), a contemporary collection of various crimes and magistrate/offender interactions in and around Manhattan, in a humorous and educational vein.

3 Bridget M. Marshall, *The Transatlantic Gothic Novel and the Law, 1790–1860* (Burlington, Vt.: Ashgate, 2013), 18.

4 Rosemary Mundhenk, "Crime, Literature and Culture," in *Villany Detected! Crime and Consequences in Britain and America in the Eighteenth and Nineteenth Centuries*, http://digital.lib.lehigh.edu/crime/literature/litessay/more/.

5 See, e.g., James Ram, *A Treatise on Facts as Subjects of Inquiry by a Jury* (New York: Baker, Voorhuis & Co, 1861).

6 One notable (albeit early twentieth-century) list, compiled by well-known treatise writer John Henry Wigmore, primarily extolled novels concerning criminal law issues.

7 Simon Stern, "Law and Literature," in *The Oxford Handbook of Criminal Law*, ed. Markus D. Dubber and Tatjana Hörnle (Oxford: Oxford University Press, 2014), 111–30, 126. Prior to the nineteenth century, American criminal law held that a defendant could not be found guilty of an offense unless he had truly acted in a malicious and malevolent way – that he had not only "the" mental state for the crime but that, more generally, he manifested a full-blown *mens rea*: an "evil mind." During the nineteenth century, however, the criminal law began to jettison this focus, edging toward imposing liability based upon objective criteria. Richard Singer, "The Resurgence of Mens Rea I: Provocation, Emotional Disturbance, and the Model Penal Code," *Boston College Law Review* 27 (1986): 243–322.

8 Stern, "Law and Literature," 127.

9 Peter J. Hutchings, *The Criminal Spectre in Law, Literature and Aesthetics: Incriminating Subjects* (New York: Routledge, 2014), 166.

10 Louis Gross, *Redefining the American Gothic from* Wieland *to* Day of the Dead (Ann Arbor: UMI Research, 1989), 1.

11 Joel P. Bishop, *Commentaries on Criminal Law* (Boston: Little, Brown, 1856–58), 1: §287, cited in Francis Sayre, "Mens Rea," *Harvard Law Review* 45 (1932): 974–1026, 974.

12 Martin Gardener, "The Mens Rea Enigma: Notes on the Role of Motive in Criminal Law Past and Present," *Utah Law Review* (1993): 635–750, 637–8.

13 As Gardener has correctly noted, "Given that a sharpened awareness of words . . . sharpens our perception of . . . phenomena, any steps towards understanding the slippery notion of *mens rea* can only lead to greater understanding of criminal law." Ibid., 638 (internal quotations omitted).

14 Sayre, "Mens Rea," 975.

15 Gardener, "The Mens Rea Enigma," 642.

16 Ibid., 642.

17 Ibid., 671.

18 Richard Singer, "The Resurgence of Mens Rea I." See also John Langbein, "The Criminal Trial before the Lawyers," *University of Chicago Law Review* 45 (1978): 263–316.

19 Guyora Binder, "The Origins of American Felony Murder Rules," *Stanford Law Review* 57 (2004): 59–208, 122.

20 Ibid., 115.

21 Ibid.

22 Guyora Binder, "The Rhetoric of Motive and Intent," *Buffalo Criminal Law Review* 6 (2002): 1–96, 15.

23 Ibid., 16. These undefined crimes included rape, robbery, piracy, poaching in disguise, destroying tollhouses and similar structures, exporting wool, fraudulent bankruptcy, plague victims violating

quarantine, bigamy, soldiers wandering without leave, jailers coercing prisoners to testify, obstructing justice, escape, convicts or Catholic recusants returning from exile, demanding a reward for the return of property, serving a foreign prince, desertion, and harboring a Catholic priest. Ibid.

24 Ibid., 17.

25 William Blackstone, *Commentaries on the Laws of England*, 4 vols., ed. Wilfrid Prest (1765–69; Oxford: Oxford University Press, 2016), 4: 17.

26 Ibid., 20–1.

27 Gerald Leonard, "Towards a Legal History of American Criminal Theory: Culture and Doctrine from Blackstone to the Model Penal Code," *Buffalo Criminal Law Review* 6 (2003): 691–832, 715.

28 Ibid., 714. Binder, "Rhetoric," 16–20.

29 Gardener, "The Mens Rea Enigma," 671.

30 Ibid., 673.

31 Binder, "Origins," 118.

32 Sayre, "Mens Rea," 1019.

33 Singer, "The Resurgence of Mens Rea I," 244.

34 Ibid., 244.

35 Gardener, "The Mens Rea Enigma," 677.

36 Marcus D. Dubber, "The Historical Analysis of Criminal Codes," *Law and History Review* 18 (2000): 433–40.

37 Patricia Mell, "Not the Primrose Path: Educating Lawyers at the Turn of the Last Century," *Michigan Bar Journal* 79 (2000): 846–9.

38 Laura I Appleman, "The Rise of the Modern American Law School: How Professionalization, German Scholarship, and Legal Reform Shaped Our System of Legal Education," *New England Law Review* 39 (2005): 251–306, 252.

39 Angela Fernandez and Marcus D. Dubber, "Putting the Legal Treatise in Its Place," in *Law Books in Action: Essays on the Anglo-American Legal Treatise* (Oxford: Hart, 2012), 3.

40 Robert W. Gordon, "Critical Legal Histories," *Stanford Law Review* 36 (1984): 57–126, 120–3 (discussing usefulness of "mandarin" legal materials, i.e., case law and treatise literature).

41 Dubber and Fernandez, "Putting the Legal Treatise in Its Place," 4.

42 Ibid., 5.

43 Singer, "The Resurgence of Mens Rea I," 258.

44 Alfred W.B. Simpson, "The Rise and Fall of the Legal Treatise: Legal Principles and the Forms of Legal Literature," *University of Chicago Law Review* 48 (1981): 632–79, 668.

45 John F. Archbold, *A Summary of the Law Relative to Pleading and Evidence in Criminal Cases* (New York: Shaw & Sons, 1843). Simpson, "Rise and Fall," 669.

46 Joseph Chitty, *A Practical Treatise on the Criminal Law*, 4th Amer. ed. (Boston: Bradford & Reed, 1843) (1st ed. London, 1816).

47 Stern, "Law and Literature," 120–1.

48 Ibid.

49 Ibid.

50 Ibid.

51 Ibid.

52 James Thompson, *The Castle of Indolence* (1748). More importantly for our purposes, Washington Irving used the first four stanzas of the poem to set the tone for one of his most famous stories, *The Legend of Sleepy Hollow*. Moreover, Canto I, XXX of the poem is found at the beginning of Chapter XIII of Ann Radcliffe's *The Mysteries of Udolpho* (1794), an archetypical Gothic novel.

53 James Ram, *A Treatise on Facts as Subjects of Inquiry by a Jury*, 3rd ed. (New York: Baker, Voorhis & Co.: 1861), 13–15.

54 Dubber and Fernandez, "Putting the Legal Treatise in Its Place," 13.

55 John Taylor, *Elements of the Civil Law* (Cambridge: Bentham, 1755).

56 Simpson, "Rise and Fall," 657. Taylor's treatise had a broadly humanist bent and was originally written

> to lay out the Rudiments of Civil Life, and of Social Duties; to enquire into the Foundations of Justice and Equity; and to examine the principal Obligations, which arise from these several Connections, into which Providence has thought proper to distribute the Human Species.

Ibid.

57 Dubber and Fernandez, "Putting the Legal Treatise in Its Place," 11.

58 Ibid.
59 Joel Bishop, *First Book of the Law* (Boston: Little, Brown, 1868).
60 Stephen A. Seigel, "Joel Bishop's Orthodoxy," *Law and History Review* 13 (1995): 215–59, 219.
61 Ibid., 220.
62 Joel P. Bishop, *New Commentaries of the Criminal Law*, 8th ed. (Chicago: Flood, 1892), 723–31.
63 See, e.g., ibid., 88, 122–3; Stern, "Law and Literature," 120 n. 29, and sources cited there.
64 Edward W. Cox, *The Advocate: His Training, Practice, Rights and Duties* (London: John Crockford, 1852); Stern, "Law and Literature," 120 n. 29.
65 Ibid., 88–9, 92–4.
66 Ibid., 122.
67 Ibid., 127.
68 Ibid., 128.
69 Philip Gaines, "Writing the Discursive Proto-Culture of Modern Anglo-American Trial Advocacy: Edward William Cox's *The Advocate*," *American Journal of Legal History* 51 (2011): 333–58.
70 Ibid.
71 John Scaggs, *Crime Fiction* (Oxford: Routledge, 2005), 16.
72 Fred Botting, *Gothic* (Oxford: Routledge, 2001), 7.
73 Stern, "Law and Literature," 113.
74 Lisa Rodensky, *The Crime in Mind: Criminal Responsibility and the Victorian Novel* (New York: Oxford University Press, 2003), 46.
75 Ibid., 46.
76 Hutchings, *Criminal Spectre*, 72.
77 Ibid., 150.
78 Rodensky makes a similar argument regarding the narrator in the Victorian novel. Rodensky, *The Crime in Mind*, 63.
79 Jeannine M. DeLombard, *In the Shadow of the Gallows: Race, Crime, and American Civic Identity* (Philadelphia: University of Pennsylvania Press, 2012), 186.
80 Ibid., 183.
81 Ibid., 184.
82 Ibid.
83 Rodensky, *The Crime in Mind*, 4.
84 DeLombard, *In the Shadow of the Gallows*, 184.
85 Letter from Poe to Philip P. Cooke, August 9, 1846, in Preface, Edgar Allan Poe, "The Murders in the Rue Morgue," in *The Collected Works of Edgar Allan Poe*, ed. Thomas Ollive Mabbott (Cambridge, Mass.: Belknap Press, 1978), 2: 521.
86 Ibid., 527–8.
87 Ibid., 529.
88 Ibid., 528.
89 Ibid., 544.
90 Ibid., 545.
91 Ibid., 547.
92 Edgar A. Poe, "The Purloined Letter," in *Collected Works*, 3: 972.
93 Rosemary Herbert, Catherine Aird, John M. Reilly, and Susan Oleksiw, *The Oxford Companion to Crime and Mystery Writing* (Oxford: Oxford University Press, 1999), 126.
94 Ibid., 984.
95 Edgar Allan Poe, "The Mystery of Marie Roget," in *Collected Works*, 3: 715.
96 Ibid., 717.
97 Ibid., 751–2.
98 Ibid., 752.
99 Alfred Bendixen, "Towards History and Beyond: Hawthorne and the American Short Story," in *The American Companion to the Short Story*, ed. Alfred Bendixen and James Nagel (Malden: Wiley-Blackwell, 2010), 58.
100 Peter K. Garrett, "The Force of a Frame: Poe and the Control of Reading," in *Yearbook of English Studies*, vol. 26, Strategies of Reading: Dickens and after Special Number (Cambridge, UK: Modern Humanities Research Association, 1996), 54–64, 59.
101 Joyce C. Oates, "Introduction," in *The Oxford Book of American Short Stories*, ed. Joyce C. Oates (Oxford: Oxford University Press, 2013), 15.
102 Ibid.

103 Washington Irving, "The Legend of Sleepy Hollow," in *The Sketch Book of Geoffrey Crayon* (Paris: Baudry's European Library, 1846), 304.
104 Ibid.
105 Ibid.
106 Ibid., 333.
107 Ibid., 331.
108 Ibid., 318.
109 Ibid., 333.
110 Brook Thomas, *Cross-Examinations of Law and Literature* (Cambridge, UK: Cambridge University Press, 1987), 6.
111 Carl Smith, "Law as Form and Theme in American Letters," in *Law and American Literature*, ed. Carl Smith, John P. McWilliams, and Maxwell H. Bloomfield (New York: Knopf, 1983), 21.
112 Karen Halttunen, *Murder Most Foul* (Cambridge, Mass.: Harvard University Press, 1998), 47.
113 Marshall, *The Transatlantic Gothic Novel*, 17.

INDEX

abolitionism 8, 12, 13, 20, 25–6, 29–31, 60–3, 66, 108, 152–5, 172, 198–202, 219–21, 243, 327, 329, 331
African Americans xviii, 5, 8, 12, 20–32, 104, 108, 132, 144–6, 220–2, 230, 237, 312, 317–19, 342
Alcott, Louisa May 14
Alcott, William A 7
alienation of affection 309
alien registration 283
American Revolution 38–9, 99, 104, 144, 315, 357
Ames, James Barr 126, 127
Anthony, Susan B. 11, 64
anthropometry 226, 231–4
anti-Catholic novels 345
anti-Mormon novels 345
archive xvii–xviii, 117–18, 167, 222, 285
Asiatic Barred Zone 276
assimilation 75, 85, 159, 277, 280–1, 285, 343
Auburn System 243, 252
Austin, John 301
Avery, Ephraim 139–40

Beard, Dan 48–9
Beaumont, Gustave de 248–9, 251
Beccaria, Cesare 245
Beecher, Catharine 10
Beever, Thinas 242
Belisle, Orvilla 345
Bell, Alfreda Eva 346
Bellamy, Edward 284
Bellew, Frank 178–80, 182
benevolent societies 257
Bertillon, Alphonse 231–3, 235
Bill of Rights 155, 211, 213, 341
Binney, Horace 328
biometrics 226, 231
birthright 30, 274, 280, 315
Bishop, Joel Prentiss 357, 359
Black Codes 30, 301
blackmail 215
Blackstone, William 5, 21, 22, 98, 100, 101, 125, 158, 291, 357–8
blood-fraction rule 292–8
Borthwick, John D. 263–4, 265
Bouvier, John 21, 24
Bradford, Andrew 119
Bradley, Joseph P. 8, 66
Bradwell v. Illinois 8, 65–6
Brandeis, Louis 127, 211, 222
Brickey, William Josiah xiv
Brown, Charles Brockden 248, 360
Brown, Henry Billings 30, 156
Brown, John 62, 153, 199, 333
Bryan, William Jennings 158
Bryant, Edwin 262
Buntline, Ned 248
Burlingame Treaty 276, 280
Burr, Aaron 172–5
Burroughs, Stephen 138
Burton, Maria Amparo Ruis de 16
Bushnell, Horace 8, 197–8

capital punishment xix, 131–2, 135, 166, 169, 242–8, 253
Carrière, Eva 351–2
case method 126
Catholicism 140, 342–5
Chae Chan Ping v. United States 278, 281–3, 285
chattel slavery 291
Cherokee Nation v. Georgia 74, 76, 77–80, 85
Child, Lydia Maria 12, 135, 248, 253
Chinese Exclusion Acts 274, 276, 280–5
Chinese invasion, plot of 278–9, 281–4
Christian nation 278, 341–7

Civil Rights Act (1875) 30, 67
Civil Rights Cases (1883) 30–1, 67
Civil War xi, 7, 9–10, 29–30, 47, 62, 104, 120, 124–8, 144, 155–9, 163, 174–6, 182, 243, 276, 280, 296, 300–1, 324–5, 329, 331–4, 341–53
claim clubs 260–3, 268–9
codification movement xv, 144, 166
Cohen, Felix S. 76
Coke, Sir Edward 358
Cole v. Van Riper 65
color line 222, 291, 293–6, 298
Common Sense School 100
Commonwealth v. Blanding 215–16
Commonwealth v. Clap 215
Comstock Act 349
Confederate theory of law 155
contracts xviii, 5, 30, 36, 56, 59–61, 66, 107, 126, 151–2, 261, 276, 301, 316–19, 327, 332
Cooke, George xiv
Cooper, James Fenimore 143–4, 193, 201, 329, 359
Cornell, Sarah Maria 139
courthouses, design of xviii, 132, 140–4, 166
court martial 188–9, 192, 194–6, 202
courtroom fiction 132, 138
Cox, Edward W 359–60
crime literature 132, 138–9
criminal behavior xxi, 209, 360
criminal law xvii, xxi, 3, 60, 117, 175–6, 356–65
Crofutt, George A. 73–4
Crow, Jim 67, 170, 296, 301
Cummins, Maria S 219
Curtis, Benjamin R. 28, 329
Cushing, Luther Stearns 258–9, 261

Dana, Richard Henry, Jr. 199–201
Dartmouth College v. Woodward 40–1
Davis, Rebecca Harding 15
Dawes General Allotment Act (1887) 74
Declaration of Independence 21, 28, 29, 98, 153, 158, 244, 324, 325, 332,
defamation 167, 176, 215–16
Delany, Martin 8
De May v. Roberts 221
democracy xiii, 35, 37, 102–3, 118, 151, 158, 262, 316, 340, 345, 352,
deportation 280, 283–5
Deptford Murder Trial 236
De Pue, F. H. 232
Dewey, John 96
Dickens, Charles 16, 253–4
Dickinson, Charles 174
Dix, Dorothea 243
Dixon, Thomas A., Jr. 20, 31
domesticity 29, 43, 197, 211–13, 219, 222
Dooner, Pierton W 278–83
Douglass, Frederick 9, 20, 22–9, 62, 221, 290, 331
Dred Scott v. Sandford 20, 27, 29, 154, 292, 293, 296, 312, 319, 329
dueling xviii, 107, 118, 121, 163, 165–7, 169, 171–7, 183, 299
Due process 30, 42, 154–5, 167–70, 177
Dwight, Louis 243, 250–1

Eastman, Mary Henderson 12
Eaton, Edith Maude (Sui Sin Far) 285
Eaton, Winnifred (Onoto Watanna) 285
Edmunds Act (1882) 347
Edmunds-Tucker Act (1887) 347
Eisenstadt v. Baird 211
Elk v. Wilkins 75, 84–5, 86
Emancipation Proclamation 154, 332
Emerson, Ralph Waldo 7, 14, 56, 58–9, 214
emigration companies 260–1
emotions 105, 309, 323–6, 330–4
Enlightenment xvii, 97, 99–100, 106, 109–10, 242, 245, 315, 329, 342
execution xvii, 25–6, 132–5, 138, 140, 144, 168, 170, 176, 188–92, 195–8, 200, 242–5, 257, 266
execution broadsides 133

Faurot, Joseph 238
Federalist, The 24, 25, 75, 325
federalists xiv, xvii, 24–5, 46, 75, 99, 158, 166, 326, 341
Fern, Fanny 10, 14–15, 17
Field, David Dudley 333
Fifteenth Amendment 12, 29, 30, 81, 84
fingerprints xx, 156, 226–38
First Amendment 66, 213, 341–2, 345, 347–8, 350
Fletcher v. Peck 85
Fong Yue Ting v. United States 278, 281, 283–4, 285
Foo, Wong Chin 285
Ford, W.A. 312–13, 314–15
Foster, George 215
Fourteenth Amendment 29, 30, 42, 66, 67, 82, 84, 155, 341
Franklin, Benjamin 119, 135, 212, 214–15, 245, 250
Free Negro 29, 237, 314
Fugitive Slave Act 12, 56, 57, 62, 63
Fugitive Slave Clause 327, 329
Fuller, Horace W. 127
Fuller, Lon 291–2
Fuller, Margaret 13–14

Gage, Matilda Joslyn 11, 311
Galton, Francis 226, 231–2, 233
Garrison, William Lloyd 331, 332
Gast, John 73
Geary Act (1892) 276, 281, 283, 284
General Allotment Act (1887) 74
Gilded Age 109, 157, 176, 183, 279
Gilman, Charlotte Perkins 11, 221
gothic fiction xxi, 63, 309, 356–60, 364

Gould, Jay 48
Greeley, Horace 135
Green, Anna Katherine 143
Grimké sisters 8, 13
Guiteau, Charles 109

Hamilton, Alexander 24, 172–6
Hanno, Joseph 25–6
Harlan, John Marshall 30–1, 156
Harper, Frances 12
Harris, George E. 225
Harrison, William Henry 196
Hause, Luther 230
Hawthorne, Nathaniel 57–9, 164, 214, 216, 219, 242, 253–4, 356, 360, 362–3
Hay, John 276, 277–8
Hayes, Rutherford B. 16, 178
Hemings, Sally 293
Hillmon case 231
Hoag-Parker case 229–30
Hoffman, David 100–1
Holmes, Oliver Wendell, Jr. 109, 358
Hone, Philip 198
Hopkins, Sarah Winnemucca 16
Hopkinson, Francis 119
Houdini, Harry 351
Howells, William Dean 47, 285,
human identification 209
Hurst, James Willard 41

immigration acts 276, 280
imposture xix, 229, 349, 352
indentured servant 23, 28, 230, 292
insanity xxi, 11, 97, 99, 103–10, 251, 312, 316–17, 319
Irving, Washington 193, 356, 361, 363–4
Islam 345–6, 353

Jackson, Andrew 39, 170, 173–4, 183, 326, 331
Jacobs, Harriet 12–13, 26, 62–3, 221
James, Henry 64
Jay, John 24, 244
Jefferson, Thomas 21, 45, 125, 163, 258, 260, 293, 314–15, 324–6, 330–1, 341, 347
Jewett, Helen 139
Johnson v. M'Intosh 76
joint-stock companies 257, 260–5, 269
jury service 311, 317, 319

Keller, George Frederick 279–80
Kent, James 7, 196, 330, 358
Kernan, Thomas J 169–70, 183

Langdell, Christopher Columbus 126, 309
Latina/Latino 144
legal fictions 25, 291–2, 295–7, 300–1
legal formalism 309, 329
legal realism 309
Legare, Hugh Swinton 119, 125
libel 167, 176, 215–16, 220
Liberalism xix, 104, 212–21
Lieber, Francis 243, 249
Lincoln, Abraham 154–5, 330–3
Livingston, Edward 243, 244
Livingston, John 122
Locke, John 99, 104, 315
lynching xviii, 30–1, 67, 118, 132, 144–6, 163, 165–71, 177, 182–3, 257, 266–8

McKay v. Campbell 81–2
Maine, Henry Sumner 291
Maitland, Frederic 314
Manifest Destiny 278, 343
Marshall, John 41, 74, 76, 77, 79, 80, 328
Martineau, Harriet 10
Mather, Cotton 20, 25–6
medical jurisprudence 97, 104–5, 108, 227
Melville, Herman 8, 43, 59–61, 188–205, 253–4, 329
mens rea xxi, 356–64
Methodism 342
mining codes 258, 263, 266, 269
Minor v. Happersett 64
Missouri Compromise 199
monomania 105, 107
Moriarty, Aubrey 225, 228
Mormons xxi, 14, 341–6
Morrill Anti-Bigamy Act 346–7
Murat, Achille 38
mutiny xviii–xix, 118, 133, 188–201

Nast, Thomas 344–5
national security 118, 188, 200–1, 282–3
Native Americans xvi, 3, 16. 104, 144, 317, 343
newspapers xviii, xix, 13–14, 32, 86, 107, 117–18, 120, 132, 135, 139, 143–6, 150–5, 168, 172, 215, 258, 264, 266, 343, 345, 362, 364
Norris, Frank 35, 48

Okmulgee Constitution 159
Ottoman Empire 345
overland companies 262

Packard, Elizabeth 106–7, 318
Page Act 274, 277
Paine, Thomas 315–16
Parkman, Francis 315
parliamentary procedure 257–69
passing 156, 215, 222
passports 227, 283
pedagogy 75–6, 85, 117
penny press xvii, 138–9
personhood xvi–xi, 3, 21–32, 35–6, 40–9, 96–7, 103, 107–10, 212–13, 290–309, 319
Phelps, Elizabeth Stuart 15–16, 43

phenotype 236
phrenology 317
plenary power 281, 283
Plessy v. Ferguson 30, 67, 156, 222, 276
Poe, Edgar Allan 124, 139, 356, 360-3
polygamy 66–7, 343–53
populism 158, 325–6, 340, 353
presidential discourse 154
Prigg v. Pennsylvania 329
Prince Albert v. Strange 217–18
print capitalism 150
privacy xix, 209–22
Protestantism 340–2

Ram, James 359
Rantoul, Robert 244–5
Ray, Isaac 105
reasonable man xvii, 109, 111
Reconstruction 12, 29–30, 42, 60, 64, 66, 85, 132, 144, 155, 182–3, 274, 276, 280, 296, 327, 329, 333–4
Reid, Thomas 99–100, 104
Reynolds v. United States 66–7, 347–8, 353
Richardson, Henry Hobson 141–2
Robert's Rules of Order 257, 259–60
Rogers, W.A. 181
romance 124, 216–17, 219, 247–8
Rush, Benjamin 99, 103, 135, 242, 244–8, 250

Santa Clara v. Southern Pacific Railway 40, 42
Scott Act 281–2
Second Great Awakening 182, 342
Sedgwick, Catharine Maria 199
Sedgwick, Theodore 39–40, 193, 199
seduction 65, 220–1, 249
Seneca Falls Declaration 11, 13, 158, 332
sentimental novel 216, 219–20
settler sovereignty 151
Sevier, John 173–4, 176
Shaw, Lemuel 30, 57–8
Sims, Thomas 57
Slaughterhouse Cases 155
slave narratives 62, 221
slavery xv–xvi, 3, 8–9, 10–16, 20–3, 25–31, 38–50, 56–67, 101–2, 108, 152–6, 159, 163, 172, 189, 196, 199–200, 219, 243, 248, 268, 276, 290–6, 300–2, 309, 323, 327, 329–31, 344
Smith, Adam 37, 131
Social Gospel movement 278
solitary confinement 242, 246–51
Southworth, E.D.E.N. 13, 14
Spear, Charles 135–7, 253
spiritualism 348–52
Spurzheim, Johann 317
Stanton, Elizabeth Cady 11–12, 64, 158, 311
Story, Joseph 119, 196, 326, 328, 358, 359
Stowe, Harriet Beecher 12–13, 15, 20, 27, 153, 219–20, 329, 331
strikes 15, 26, 48, 118, 163, 165, 167, 169–71, 176–82, 201, 280, 327
Strong, Josiah 278, 343
suffrage xvi, 11–17, 29, 64, 311, 314–19
Sumner, Charles 199, 200, 251, 330
Swift, Zephaniah 316

Taney, Roger B. 27–9, 154, 292, 311–12
tax reforms 157–8
Taylor, Frederick Winslow 46
temperance 12, 219, 243, 258, 261, 309, 312–13, 327
Thirteenth Amendment 29, 154
Thoreau, Henry David 213–17, 221
Tichborne case 229–30
Tocqueville, Alexis de 22, 102–3, 151, 227, 248–9, 251, 258, 261, 340, 344, 345
Tourgee, Albion 222
Tucker, St George 101
Twain, Mark 47–8, 156, 227, 230, 233–8, 290–306

Udderzook v. Commonwealth 231
United States ex rel Standing Bear v. Crook 82–3
United States v. Clapox 88
United States v. Elm 82
United States v. Osborn 83–4
United States v. Wong Kim Ark 280–1
U.S. Constitution 20, 21–5, 28–30, 38, 40–1, 56, 64, 75–6, 78, 98, 102, 153–5, 178, 182, 281–4, 301, 323–9, 341, 344, 347

Van Buren, Martin 326
Vernacular xviii, 118, 151–2, 159
Victor, Metta Fuller 143
Victorian literature 360
vigilantes xviii, 170, 268
Vinton, Arthur Dudley 278, 284
Virginia Statute of Religious Freedom 341

Walker, David 153
Walker, Timothy 101, 120
Walter, Solly H. 274–6
Warner, Susan 14, 219
Webster, Daniel 57, 326, 331
Webster, Noah 83, 119
Wells, Ida B. 31, 146
white slaves 230
Whitman, Walt 9, 35, 44, 151, 329, 331–3
Wigmore, John Henry 229
Willard, Emma 10, 312–13
Williams, Catherine 139
Wilson, Harriet 221
Woltor, Robert 283–4
woman, virtuous 220
Woodhull, Victoria C 64

Yellow Peril 278, 282, 284
Young, Brigham 343, 347

For Product Safety Concerns and Information please contact our EU representative GPSR@taylorandfrancis.com
Taylor & Francis Verlag GmbH, Kaufingerstraße 24, 80331 München, Germany

www.ingramcontent.com/pod-product-compliance
Ingram Content Group UK Ltd.
Pitfield, Milton Keynes, MK11 3LW, UK
UKHW050753180926
475701UK00007B/1015

* 9 7 8 1 0 3 2 0 9 6 9 0 2 *